PRINCIPLES OF
Operating
Systems

Naresh Chauhan

Professor
Department of Computer Engineering
YMCA University of Science and Technology, Faridabad

OXFORD
UNIVERSITY PRESS

OXFORD
UNIVERSITY PRESS

Oxford University Press is a department of the University of Oxford.
It furthers the University's objective of excellence in research, scholarship,
and education by publishing worldwide. Oxford is a registered trade mark of
Oxford University Press in the UK and in certain other countries.

Published in India by
Oxford University Press
YMCA Library Building, 1 Jai Singh Road, New Delhi 110001, India

© Oxford University Press 2014

The moral rights of the author/s have been asserted.

First published in 2014

All rights reserved. No part of this publication may be reproduced, stored in
a retrieval system, or transmitted, in any form or by any means, without the
prior permission in writing of Oxford University Press, or as expressly permitted
by law, by licence, or under terms agreed with the appropriate reprographics
rights organization. Enquiries concerning reproduction outside the scope of the
above should be sent to the Rights Department, Oxford University Press, at the
address above.

You must not circulate this work in any other form
and you must impose this same condition on any acquirer.

ISBN-13: 978-0-19-808287-3
ISBN-10: 0-19-808287-8

Typeset in Times New Roman
by Mukesh Technologies Pvt. Ltd, Puducherry 605005
Printed in India by India Binding House, Noida 201301

Third-party website addresses mentioned in this book are provided
by Oxford University Press in good faith and for information only.
Oxford University Press disclaims any responsibility for the material contained therein.

Dedicated to
my wife, *Anushree Chauhan*
and my loving children, *Smiti* and *Atharv*

Features of the Book

Case Studies

The first six parts of the book include case studies on operating systems, such as UNIX, Solaris, Linux, and Windows.

The chapter on real-time OSs contains two case studies on VxWorks and QNX.

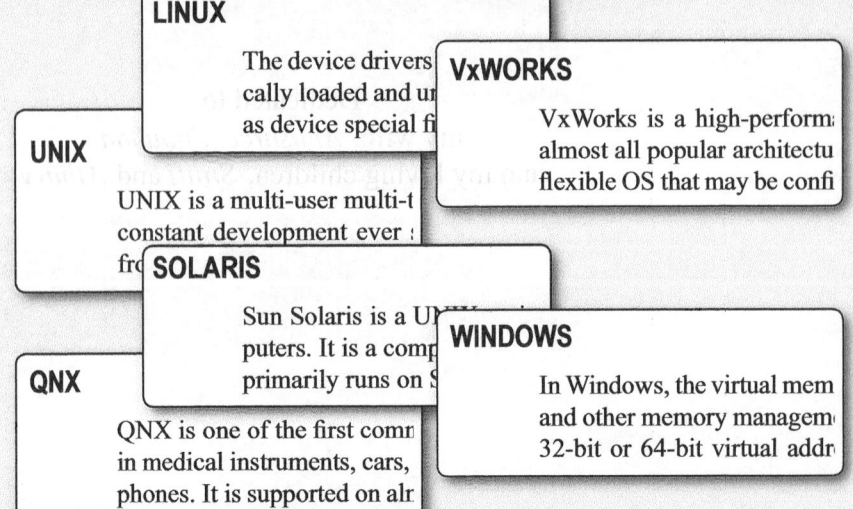

LINUX
The device drivers cally loaded and ur as device special fi

UNIX
UNIX is a multi-user multi-t constant development ever fr

VxWORKS
VxWorks is a high-performa almost all popular architectu flexible OS that may be confi

SOLARIS
Sun Solaris is a U puters. It is a comp primarily runs on S

QNX
QNX is one of the first comr in medical instruments, cars, phones. It is supported on alr

WINDOWS
In Windows, the virtual mem and other memory managem 32-bit or 64-bit virtual addr

---

Example 10.2

A process is to be swapped-in at the location 20100 in memory. If logical addresses generated by the process are 200, 345, 440, and 550, what are the corresponding physical addresses?

Solution

The relocation register will be loaded with the address 20100. So adding the logical addresses to the relocation register, the corresponding physical addresses are:
20100 + 200 = 20300
20100 + 345 = 20445
20100 + 440 = 20540

Solved Examples

Numerous solved examples interspersed within the book facilitate the understanding of the concepts discussed.

Multiple Choice Questions and Review Questions

Also provided at the chapter end, they help students to prepare for their examination.

MULTIPLE CHOICE QUESTIONS

1. The modern OSs are _____.
   a) programmed-I/O driven   c) software-driven
   b) interrupt-driven   d) hardware-driven

2. Interrupt is a signal to the _____ generated by hardware or software.
   a) memory   c) processor
   b)

3. I
   a
   b

4. The number of hardware interrupts is limited by the number of _____.
   a) processes   c) IRQ lines
   b) processors   d) none

5. _____ is also known as an *adapter*.
   a) memory   c) device

REVIEW QUESTIONS

1. What is an interrupt? What are its types?
2. What are the tasks to be executed when an interrupt arrives on the processor?
3. What is IVT?
4. What is ISR?
5. What is a trap?
6. Provide some examples when software interrupt is generated.

12. What is a device driver? Explain its functioning with device controller and operating system.
13. What were the basic problems in multi-programming-based modern operating systems?
14. What is the need of a dual mode protection?
15. What is the need of memory protection?
16. What is the need of processor protection?
17. What is the need of I/O protection?

BRAIN TEASERS

1. Can you work without operating system in your computer system?
2. The major drawback of multiprogrammed batch systems was the lack of user/programmer interaction with their jobs. How can you overcome this?

Brain Teasers

Provided at the chapter end, test the conceptual understanding of students.

Mobile Operating Systems

The chapter on mobile OSs delves into the characteristics of various mobile devices and issues related to mobile OSs. It also discusses the Android OS.

21 Mobile Operating Systems

21.1 INTRODUCTION

We are living in a world of mobile devices such as smartphones, laptops, and tablets. These mobile devices are different as compared to general desktop systems. These are designed and run in very restricted environment/resources. Therefore, the OSs for these devices cannot be the same as those for desktop systems. The mobile OSs have been designed for each category of mobile devices. This chapter explores the types and characteristics of mobile devices and then discusses the mobile OSs.

21.4 ANDROID OPERATING SYSTEM

Android is a software stack including mobile OS that has been primarily designed for touch-screen-based mobile devices. It was originally developed by Android Inc. and was later sold to Google in 2005. Android consists of the following components (see Fig. 21.1):

23 Shell Programming and UNIX Shells

Shell Programming

The last part of the book discusses shell programming, which will aid students in performing the practicals for this course. The chapter consists of numerous programming examples and exercises.

23.1 INTRODUCTION

This chapter gives an overview of the UNIX shells and how to perform shell-programming exercises. The shell programming is as simple as we do in any high-level language. The only difference is the syntax of the commands used in the shell. Therefore, the prerequisite for this chapter is that the reader should be well aware of any high-level language constructs. This chapter introduces various UNIX shells and the related programming constructs with the help of programming examples.

Preface

An operating system is an interface through which we are able to access and operate the computer hardware. Thanks to the operating system, the user need not worry about hardware or interact with different devices. The operating system, therefore, works in the background without letting us know who is doing the job. It is the software through which all the hardware devices are managed and utilized. However, an operating system is much more than just that and encompasses a vast domain. One reason is that an operating system and computer architecture affect each other and co-evolve. Sometimes, the computer architecture has forced the operating systems to evolve, and sometimes the operating system demanded the architecture to change. This has given rise to the operating system concepts in the light of computer architecture. Another reason is that the technology has shifted from single-processor to multi-processor technology. This has given birth to so many operating systems, such as multi-processor, distributed, networked operating systems, and so on. Another development that we have seen in the last 15 years is the mobile technology. Today, we are living in the world of mobile devices. The mobile technology has bred various developments in mobile operating systems. Besides this, there is the world of embedded and real-time systems, which produced yet another category of operating systems—embedded and real-time operating systems. The list is endless! All these advances have made operating systems a subject of rich concepts and frequent changes in user applications and technology.

About the Book

This book has been written after reviewing the syllabi of various Indian universities and, therefore, provides a wide coverage of the subject—operating systems. The target readers of this book are undergraduate students of computer engineering and IT. The book will also be useful to postgraduate students of MCA and M.Tech. as it includes many chapters on specialized operating systems as well as several other advanced topics.

Each chapter begins with the learning objectives and ends with a summary containing a quick review of important concepts discussed in the chapter. Each chapter provides plenty of solved examples in-between the text for a practical understanding of the method or technique. Multiple choice questions, review questions, and brain teasers provided at the end of each chapter will assist the teaching faculty to prepare their students for the examinations.

The book covers every aspect of the subject. It describes the development of modern operating systems, explaining the evolution starting from the mainframe systems. Since operating system is considered to be a concept-rich subject, this book has focused on each and every concept in depth and explained the same in a lucid manner. The book also covers the practical aspect of the subject, emphasizing shell programming. It has a complete chapter on shell programming, which will help the students in the operating system laboratory. Case studies of four operating systems, namely, UNIX, Solaris, Linux, and Windows are presented at the end of Parts I-VI. The different features of various versions of each operating system are explained. In UNIX, version SVR4; in SOLARIS, version 10; in Linux, version 2.6; and in Windows, Windows XP are emphasized in the case studies.

Key Features

This book is packed with the following features:

- Explains how the modern operating system has been developed and discusses different types of OSs and OS architectures

- Highlights the hardware issues necessary to understand operating system concepts
- Contains dedicated chapters on specialized OSs such as distributed OSs, multi-processor OSs, real-time OSs, mobile OSs (including Android OS), and multimedia OSs
- Covers every concept in depth and provides numerous solved examples interspersed within the text
- Provides specially designed brain teasers at the end of each chapter for the students to develop an analytical approach to problem solving
- Includes case studies of four OSs, namely, UNIX, Solaris, Linux, and Windows and two real-time OSs, VxWorks and QNX
- Contains a separate chapter on shell programming that will be helpful for operating system laboratory

Online Resources

The following resources are available to help the faculty and the students using this text:
For Faculty
- Chapter-wise PowerPoint Slides

For Students
- Solved questions for competitive examinations
- Practical exercises for OS laboratory

Content and Coverage

The book consists of 23 chapters divided into eight parts. A brief outline of each chapter is as follows:

PART I Introduction

Chapter 1 introduces operating systems and explains their goals and functions along with their types.

Chapter 2 discusses the need of hardware support for OSs and explains the hardware components such as I/O devices, device controllers, magnetic disk, etc. It explains the interrupt-driven nature of OSs along with the hardware protection mechanisms to implement multi-programming or multi-tasking OSs.

Chapter 3 explains how an operating system functions as a resource manager. Various resource types, along with the components of resource manager, are also discussed.

Chapter 4 explains the general working of an operating system along with the coverage of various structures of an operating system.

PART II Process Management

Chapter 5 introduces the basic concepts related to process management along with discussion on process life cycle. Further, it explains the implementation of process with various data structures and modules and various process operations.

Chapter 6 discusses every detail of process scheduling. Types of schedulers and scheduling algorithms are dealt with in detail.

Chapter 7 introduces the concept of synchronization of processes with the help of various methods. Solutions to some classical synchronization problems are also discussed.

Chapter 8 introduces the problem of deadlock in multi-programming environment, explaining how to represent deadlock and various conditions responsible for it. It also explains how to deal with deadlocks.

Chapter 9 introduces the concept of multi-threading and various thread types and its operations.

PART III   Memory Management

Chapter 10 introduces the concepts related to basic memory management and explains various concepts like memory allocation, paging, and segmentation.

Chapter 11 explains the importance of virtual memory and its implementation using various methods.

PART IV   File Management

Chapter 12 introduces the concept of files, and their types, attributes, and operations along with details of directories.

Chapter 13 elucidates file system structure and its implementation, data structures, along with the details of various file operations, file allocation methods, and implementation of directories.

PART V   Input–Output Management

Chapter 14 introduces types of I/O, explains various issues related to I/O management, and kernel I/O subsystem along with the life cycle of an I/O request.

Chapter 15 introduces the need for disk scheduling and various concepts related to disk management.

PART VI   Security and Protection

Chapter 16 mainly deals with security issues in operating systems and various types of attacks and threats.

Chapter 17 explains the protection mechanisms in operating systems to tackle threats and attacks.

PART VII   Advanced Operating Systems

Chapter 18 introduces distributed operating systems and its features.

Chapter 19 introduces multi-processor operating systems and various related issues.

Chapter 20 introduces real-time operating systems and explains various issues therein. The chapter contains case studies on VxWorks and QNX.

Chapter 21 discusses mobile devices and mobile operating systems and explains various issues therein. A popular operating system, Android OS, is discussed in detail.

Chapter 22 discusses the various concepts in multimedia operating systems.

PART VIII   Shell Programming

Chapter 23 introduces various types of shells of UNIX operating systems and explains various structures used in shell programming along with some programming examples.

The readers are requested to send their valuable suggestions, comments, and constructive criticism for further improvement of the book at nareshchauhan19@gmail.com.

Naresh Chauhan

Acknowledgements

Big projects are not realized without the cooperation of great personalities and the society. I would like to thank all who have directly or indirectly helped me in completing this project. My interest in the subject started in the days when I was working in the industry, especially on real-time operating systems. I am thankful to Dr A.K. Sharma (Dean, PG Studies, BSAITM, Faridabad) for the real technical approach to the subject. He has been my guide in research work as well as in other areas of life. I am extremely grateful to all my colleagues with whom I discussed many issues relating to the subject. I thank my colleagues Ms Rashmi and Ms Preeti for their invaluable support in preparing case studies. I thank Ms Anita who helped me in writing some portions of the manuscript. My special thanks to Harsh Bhasin (Assistant Professor, Jamia Hamdard, Delhi) who helped me with material on web resources. Many thanks to my students whose questions always helped me to refine my understanding of these topics.

I am indebted to my family for their love, encouragement, and support throughout my career. I owe a lot to my dear wife, Anushree Chauhan. I am thankful for her never-ending patience and unconditional moral support. I thank my children Smiti and Atharv who let me complete this book with love and encouragement.

My acknowledgement would be incomplete if I do not thank the editorial team at Oxford University Press, India, who gave an effective transformation to the raw manuscript. I also thank all the reviewers who, with their constructive comments and suggested changes, helped to improve the book.

Naresh Chauhan

Brief Contents

Detailed Contents

PART II Process Management 101

PART III Memory Management

Part IV   File Management   395

PART V Input–Output Management **451**

PART VII Advanced Operating Systems **551**

PART I
Introduction

1

Introduction to Operating Systems

1.1 INTRODUCTION

The power of computing has changed the lives of common people in the last two decades. Computer systems have also been through a lot of change. In this information age, everybody is concerned with the computer and its speed; whether you are surfing the web, booking tickets through the Internet, or accessing online banking. Mobile phones have also doubled up as mini computers known as *smartphones*. Everyone needs a computer system that will meet their requirements at a great speed. Whether you are working on a stand-alone system or transferring your files on the network, the job is done with not much effort. Have you ever thought how all this works? How does a machine know whether you are working on a stand-alone system or on the network or a distributed system? Is the machine capable of knowing all your needs? Do you think that the hardware performs all these functionalities for you? The fact is that the hardware cannot perform on its own.

There was a time in the history of computer systems when every work was done manually. At that time we were very close to the machine. But it had a lot of problems and there was no efficiency in working as we get today. Therefore, a software was designed, which worked on the hardware to relieve a general user from the machine view of the system. This software did all the functionalities that need to be performed on the hardware on behalf of the user. This software that operates the computer system is known as *operating system* (OS). It acts as a layer between the user and the hardware. It provides a friendly environment for a user. In the absence of an OS, a user would have had to be aware of every configuration of the hardware and how to interact with the devices. Thanks to the OS, the user does not need to worry about hardware or interact with the different devices. The OS, therefore, works in the background without letting us know who is doing the job.

The operating system has also been through a lot of changes in the past. In fact, with the advancement and technological changes in the computer architecture, OSs have also been evolved in parallel. The improvements in computer system have always impacted the structure of the OS. Sometimes, there is a need to modify the hardware as there is demand from the OS's designers. The design motivation of the OS has also been changed from time to time. There was a time when CPU was a costly resource and innovations in OSs were developed to utilize the CPU efficiently. As the CPU speed was increased with technological

Learning Objectives

After reading this chapter, the reader should be able to understand:

- The need for an Operating System (OS)
- The evolution of OSs
- Batch processing systems
- Multi-programming systems
- Multi-user systems
- Multi-tasking systems
- Multi-processor systems
- Distributed systems
- Real-time systems
- Embedded systems
- Goals of an OS
- Functions of OSs
- Generic components of OSs

advancements, it is not a major design issue. Today, the major issue is user convenience and response time for the user's multiple tasks. This is the reason Apple's Macintosh and Windows OSs were developed and today we are using their much improved versions.

The aim of this book is to have a basic understanding of the OS and know its components in detail. This book presents a detailed and systematic discussion of OSs.

1.2 THE NEED FOR OPERATING SYSTEMS

Before discussing or defining OSs, it would be better to first understand why we need OSs. Let us look at some questions that will help to understand the basic need of OSs as well as its functionalities:

- By the time we are ready to learn this subject, we must be conversant in at least one programming language. So let us find an answer to the question—while saving and running a program in file, what is the part of the computer system that allocates memory to this file?
- How are the files as a logical concept mapped to the physical disk?
- Today, we are able to open many windows at a time; who is managing all these windows despite a single processor?
- Who ensures that the CPU is not sitting idle or busy forever?
- Sometimes we see some messages like memory error or power failure, connection failure in network, paper jam in printer, etc. Who is detecting these errors and displaying error messages?
- Who manages the limited memory despite the large size of user programs?
- Our processes can also communicate and cooperate via some synchronization mechanisms. Who provides the communication and synchronization mechanisms?
- Who schedules tasks to the CPU for execution?
- What happens to a task when the CPU is already busy in processing some other task?
- Despite a single processor, it seems that many jobs are being executed in parallel. How does this happen?
- Suppose, some users are working in a LAN (local area network) with a single printer and more than one user gives a print command. How are the requests of multiple users on a single printer managed?
- Who protects one user's area from unauthorized access by another user's task?
- Why is it that sometimes our system hangs?

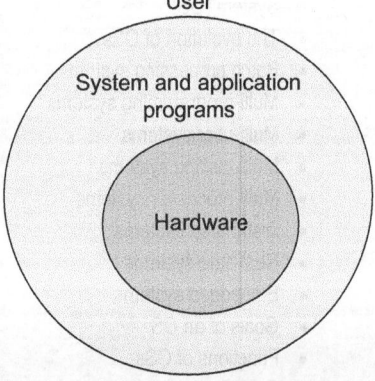

Fig. 1.1 Computer system

We always think that a computer system is a hardware and through the use of programs and other utilities, we are utilizing the system as shown in Fig. 1.1.

We work on the computer system in different ways: we write, compile, run the programs in the files or make a word file, etc. Whatever we do, we need not worry how the file is created physically, how much memory the file will take or whether the program is larger than the present RAM. So, coming back to the question, who manages and controls all the resources of the computer system?

There is a software layer between the programs and the hardware of the computer that is performing all these functions

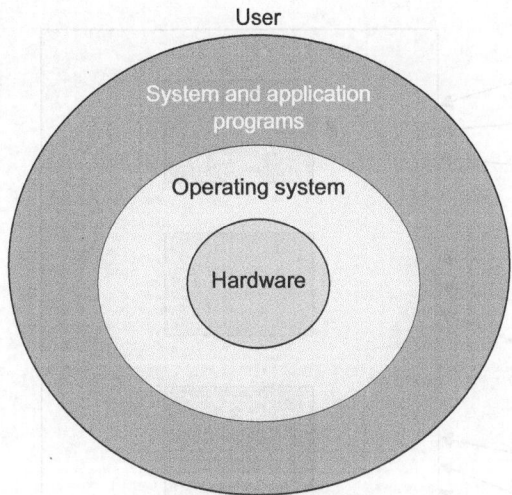

User

System and application programs

Operating system

Hardware

Fig. 1.2 Computer system with OS

(see Fig. 1.2). This software is known as *operating system* (OS) and is the answer to all the questions asked earlier. The OS starts functioning right from the moment we switch on the computer system and continues till we shut down the system.

From the earlier discussion, it is obvious that the OS performs the following functions:

- Presents an environment for the user so that he or she can easily work without worrying about the hardware resources, i.e., the user is not directly interacting with the resources
- Manages all the resources in an efficient manner

After understanding the role of an OS, there is still a question: Can we work without the OS? Yes, but subject to the conditions if all the functions listed earlier can be performed manually. However, this condition is not valid due to technological development in computer systems, software, and information technology. We cannot manually perform the functions of loading, saving, running, debugging, allocating memory, etc., for large-sized programs. One cannot interact with the hardware devices manually every time you need to access them. Moreover, we are living in the world of multi-tasking where users open many windows simultaneously and have a perception that they are working on all the windows in parallel. So there is no question of having just a single process for execution. The present scenario on computer systems is of multiple users with multiple processes to be executed on limited resources (see Fig. 1.3). Suppose, multiple tasks are open on a system with single CPU. The CPU time needs to be shared among all these tasks. It seems very difficult to manage CPU time among all the tasks manually. In this environment, we in fact need a software that manages all this multiplicity and controls it. This is the reason that we need OS—a software that takes care of any peripheral of the system. A software that is preparing the environment for the users such that they need not worry about the hardware details of the system. A software that is managing conflicting requests from multiple users to be executed on limited resources. A software that is protecting one user from another so that they do not interfere with one another.

It is clear now that there are certain tasks (from initialization of hardware to management and control of all the resources) that need to be performed while working on the computer system. All these tasks are put together in a single software known as the operating system. The OS can be defined in the following ways:

- A software that acts as an interface between the users and hardware of the computer system
- A software that provides a working environment for the users' applications
- A resource manager that manages the resources needed for all the applications in the background
- A software in which all common functions required to work on the computer system have been put together

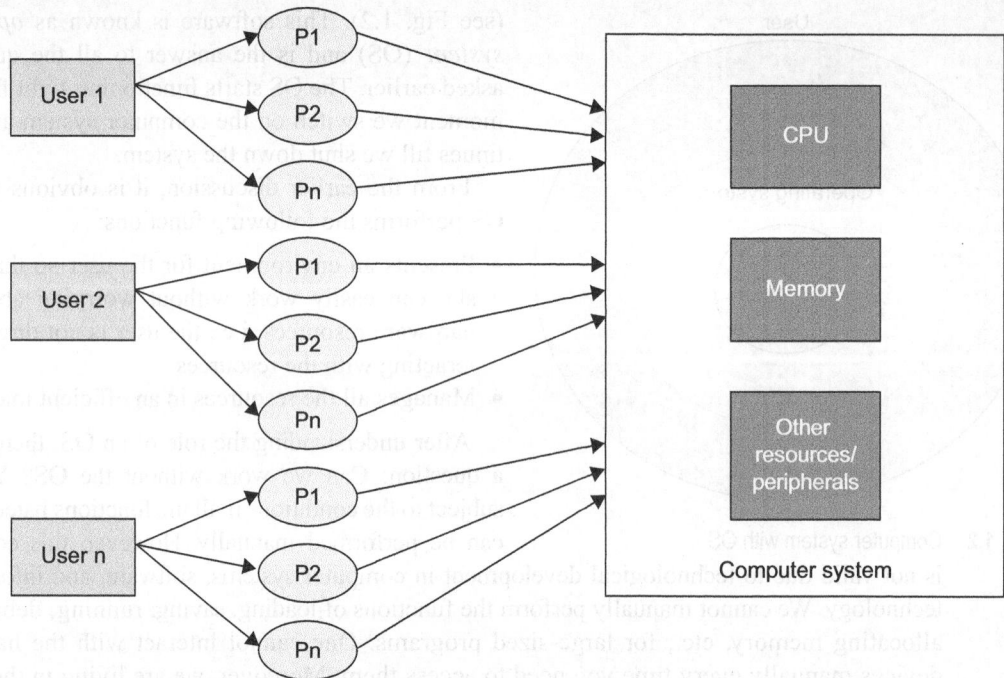

Fig. 1.3 Multiple users with multiple processes accessing the limited resources

1.3 EVOLUTION OF OPERATING SYSTEMS

It is necessary to understand the evolution of OSs. Understanding how they were developed will help us in understanding the functions of OSs we use today. There was a time when a programmer working on the computer needed to do all the activities from writing the program to loading the program into the memory, execution, debugging, and printing the output. Every activity was needed to be performed manually consuming a lot of time and resources. But today, a programmer is relieved of all other tasks of programming such as loading and linking and he or she does not care about the actual hardware details also. The programmer is only concerned with writing the program in a flexible and friendly editor and debugging it. So once we understand this, we are able to understand what the OSs mean to us today and get closer to their real requirements and objectives.

The important point in the evolution of OSs is that their development means parallel development in computer systems. As there is advancement in computer system hardware, the OSs also get updated. Sometimes, there is a demand from the OSs developers to modify the hardware. So there is influence of one on the other.

Let us have a look at how the OSs have been developed.

1.3.1 First Generation

The first generation of computer systems was the era of vacuum tubes, plug boards, and punched cards. The programmer used to interact with the machine directly through punched cards and used to write the programs in machine language. All the tasks for executing a program would be performed by the programmer only. There was no help like programming language, linker, loader, etc. Obviously, there was no operating system as we use today.

1.3.2 Second Generation

In the first generation, the programmers used to perform every task manually. There were no tools or aids for them. Therefore, in the second generation, many new softwares and hardwares were developed along with the programming languages, e.g., line printers, magnetic tapes, assemblers, linkers, loaders, and compilers for the convenience of programmers. Now the programmer would first write the program in any high-level language. To compile it, the required compiler would be loaded into the computer by mounting the compiler tape on a tape drive. Students should note that in this generation there was no hard disk to store compiler in it as we do today. The only secondary storage available was magnetic tape. But it needed to be mounted on tape drive first. After this, the program would be read through the card reader. As an output, the compiler would produce the assembly language output. This assembly language would then be assembled through an assembler. But for this purpose, it would need to mount another tape consisting of the assembler. Finally, the assembler would produce the binary object output to be loaded in the memory for execution. However, this operation of computer systems suffered from the following drawbacks:

- Since each programmer or user was allotted a fixed amount of time to execute the program on the computer system, it meant that the user would need to start all over again if there was an error at any step. This resulted in wastage of time and further delaying other users.
- Set-up time for various tasks wasted a significant amount of time of the computer system. As seen earlier, for execution of a program, there may be the following steps:

    i) Loading the compiler tape of the required compiler
    ii) Reading from card reader
    iii) Running the compiler
    iv) Unloading the compiler
    v) Loading the assembler tape
    vi) Running the assembler
    vii) Unloading the assembler tape
    viii) Loading the object program
    ix) Running the object program

For a single program execution, the loading and unloading of tapes for various purposes wasted a lot of time and delays other users.

The set-up time delay was not desirable not only for the reason that it delayed the job of users but also for the impact it had on the utilization of the CPU. In this era, the computer systems were so expensive that everyone wanted to use the system resulting in high utilization of the system. However, owing to time taken to set up, the CPU was idle most of the time. This prompted efforts towards reducing this idle time.

The solution adopted to reduce the set-up delay was that one operator was hired for loading/unloading and other tasks as listed earlier. The operator trained in loading and unloading the tapes reduced the time taken in set-up as compared to an untrained user. But, this solution was not able to reduce the actual set-up time taken by loading/unloading the tapes. Besides this, another problem was that the waiting time for the users was still high. One user had to wait while the other user executed programs on the system.

The delay in set-up time would increase further if some jobs in queue were of different requirements. For example, one job is written in FORTRAN, second in COBOL and the third is again in FORTRAN. This sequential processing of jobs would require more set-up delay as loading and unloading the tapes again and again for different jobs would be needed. If the jobs are known in advance, then we could combine these two FORTRAN jobs and send them for execution together. This would save time for loading and unloading tapes for the third job in the queue. As a solution, to reduce the waiting time of users, the jobs of users prepared with same programming language were batched together. With this solution, it was possible to execute multiple jobs instead of one and thereby saving set-up time for an individual job. For example, if there are three FORTRAN written jobs placed at different places in the queue, then a batch of these three jobs could be prepared and executed with a single set-up time as compared to three.

But in this process, the operator/user would need to check when one job would get finished and prepare the set-up for next job. So during this manual intervention, again CPU was idle. This idle time could be reduced if the switching to another job was automated instead of manual process. But this automation further required the recognition of the tasks like executing the compiler, executing the assembler, etc.

We can say that this was the turning point in the history of computer systems, when the automation for the job sequencing was conceived and thus the first operating system was born. It was thought that there would be a software called *monitor program* that would perform the automatic job sequencing. For identifying the tasks to be done for a job, the concept of *control cards* was introduced. Control cards contained the directives to tell the software which tasks to perform for a job. In this way, the software with automatic job sequencing was written that switched from one job to another. Since all the events were being controlled by the monitor now, it had to be in the memory forever. Therefore, it was called *resident monitor* and given space in the memory (see Fig. 1.4).

Resident monitor would read the control card, and load the appropriate program into the memory and run it. This process was repeated until all the cards got interpreted. Thus, the first OS in the form of resident monitor improved the execution on the computer systems. It reduced the manual intervention needed for set-up and job sequencing.

The monitor read in jobs one at a time from the card reader or tape. The job was then placed into memory in the user area and control was passed to this job. When the job was complete, the control was passed to the monitor. But the monitor needed to do several other tasks for a job. Let us look (see Fig. 1.5) at the structure of a job in the form of *job control language* (JCL), a special type of language developed to provide instructions to the monitor. The meanings of these control instructions prefixed with '$' are given in Table 1.1. At the time of executing control instructions, the control was transferred to the monitor. Otherwise, the control was transferred to the user program.

The batch systems mentioned earlier also faced one problem. In this generation, input/output (I/O) devices were mostly electro-mechanical. On the other hand, the CPU was an electronic device. While reading the input or printing the output, there was a clear mismatch between the speed of CPU and I/O devices. It was not possible to cope up with the speed of even a slower CPU that performed thousands of instructions per second. Moreover, in batch systems, it was required to execute multiple jobs with multiple control cards quickly. As a solution, it was thought that all the inputs from the card readers would be read and copied to a magnetic tape. The input would be processed in one go using this input magnetic tape. Similarly, the output, instead of being sent to the

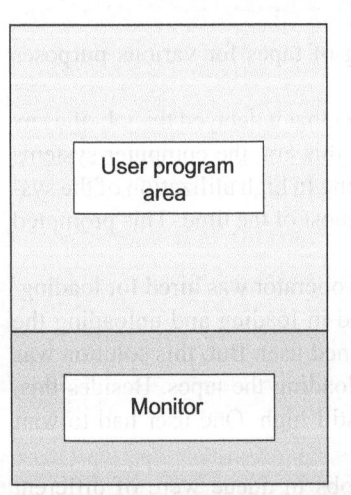

Fig. 1.4 Memory structure consisting of resident monitor

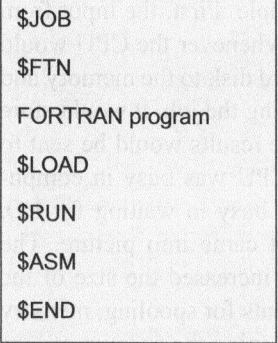

```
$JOB

$FTN

FORTRAN program

$LOAD

$RUN

$ASM

$END
```

Fig. 1.5 Format of a job in JCL

Table 1.1 Control instructions

$JOB	Start of a job
$END	End of a job
$ASM	Execute the assembler
$FTN	Execute the FORTRAN compiler
$LOAD	Load the object code from tape to memory
$RUN	Execute the user program

printer directly, was copied to the magnetic tape to be printed later on (see Fig. 1.6). This reduced the time taken in online processing, i.e., processing the inputs or outputs directly through the CPU. Students should note that magnetic tapes were of faster speed as compared to card readers or printers. This concept gave birth to *offline* operation. The CPU was now not constrained with the speed of slow I/O devices and was busy in processing with the I/O on tapes. The offline concept eliminated the need of processing the I/O operations through the CPU directly.

1.3.3 Third Generation

Batch systems with offline operation continued for a long time in second generation. But, still there were problems due to the nature of magnetic tapes. First, the tapes were sequential access devices. The tape needed to be rewound again and again if there was a need to write and read in between. Second, we needed to carry separate tapes for input and output as their storage capacity was low. There was no other option until the disks came into existence. The disks solved the problem faced with the tapes as disks were random access devices and of higher storage capacity as compared to tapes. Now it was possible to read or write quickly from/to any area on the disk. The cards were written directly onto the disk and read and executed the jobs from the disk. Similarly, the outputs were written directly to the same disk instead of another disk. The output was printed actually after the job is executed completely.

In this era, due to technological improvements in hardware, the speed of CPU became faster than the second generation. The result of this technological improvement was that CPU was more idle. The batch systems with disks improved the performance of the system, but CPU was still idle. When a job executed, it might need to have input or output, which means it needed to access devices. And the access to the devices was slow at that time as compared to the speed of CPU. So while performing I/O operation for a job, there was sufficient time for CPU to sit idle. If there had been another job, CPU would switch to it. As a solution, it was thought that instead of one job, there would now be multiple jobs in memory. Consequently, it required the memory to be partitioned for multiple jobs because till now only single job was in the memory for execution (see Fig. 1.7). This gave birth to *multiprogrammed batch systems*. It was now possible to overlap the I/O of one job with computation of another job. It means when one job was waiting for its I/O, CPU switched to another job. This was possible only with the disk systems and the method is called as *simultaneous peripheral operation online* (SPOOL). Later on, the process was famous with the name *spooling*.

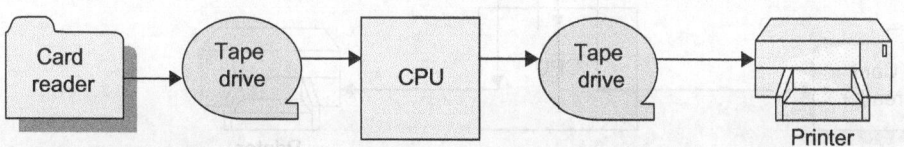

Fig. 1.6 Offline operation

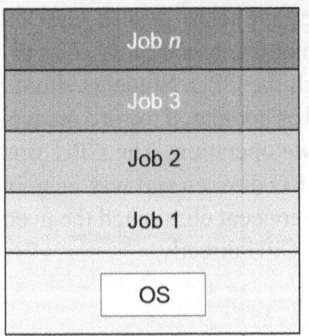

| Job n |
| Job 3 |
| Job 2 |
| Job 1 |
| OS |

Fig. 1.7   Memory structure consisting of multiple jobs

The process for spooling was very simple. First, the input from input device would be read to the disk. Whenever the CPU would be free, the OS loaded the job from the hard disk to the memory and CPU would execute the job. After executing the job, it would store the results again to the disk. Later on, the results would be sent to the output device (see Fig. 1.8). Thus, CPU was busy in computation of another job while first job was busy in waiting for I/O. In this way, *multi-programming* concept came into picture. The requirements for the multi-programming increased the size of the OS because now the OS had the components for spooling, memory management (memory partitioning and keeping the account of jobs in the memory slots), managing multiple jobs, scheduling of tasks to CPU, and many more. In fact, this was the point where all other components of the OS were added. In other words, multi-programming was the basic concept around which all concepts of modern OS have been developed.

Although multi-programmed systems were able to improve the performance in terms of CPU time and throughput, still the jobs were batched and, therefore, there was no interaction of the job and the programmer. In fact, batch systems were not suitable for every type of job. There are certain jobs that need attention of user, i.e., interactive jobs. Due to batch of jobs, there was a long gap before the programmer would get the result back. Moreover, if there was a single error somewhere, the whole cycle of batch processing would get repeated causing further delays in getting the output. As a result, the debugging process became a time-consuming and irritating process. It was felt that even first-generation computers were better as they at least had the machines for a fixed time slot. Thus, the major drawback of multi-programmed batch systems was lack of user--programmer interaction with their jobs.

The solution found for the interaction between the job and the user was to have the dedicated dumb terminals for each user connected to the main system having CPU whose time would be shared among the multiple users. (Students should note that at that time, we did not have personal computers.) The idea was that user should have a feeling that he/she is using the system alone. Instead of submitting the job in a batch, the user would directly submit the job to the system. In this way, the user would be able to interact with his job. But the basic concept, i.e., multi-programming was still there. The jobs being submitted to the system would be stored in the partitioned memory. As the CPU time on the main system was shared among multiple users, these types of systems were known as *time-sharing multi-user systems*.

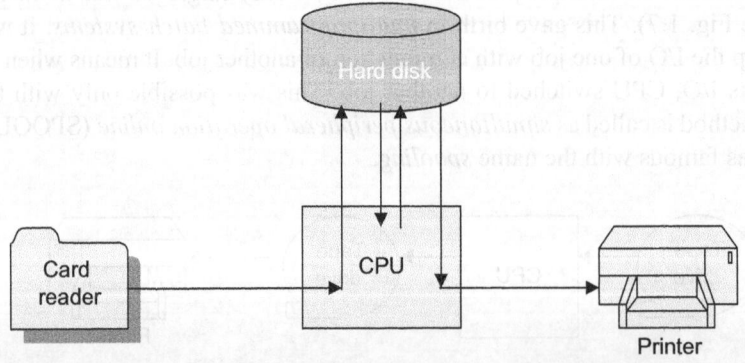

Fig. 1.8   Spooling

One of the earlier time-sharing systems was *compatible time-sharing system* (CTSS) developed at MIT. This system got popular as it supported many interactive users as compared to the batch systems. With the success of CTSS, it was thought that there should be a power-ful machine which would support thousands of users at a time. For this type of project, MIT, Bell Labs, and General Electric came together with a system called *MULTiplexed Informa-tion and Computing Service* (MULTICS). But the idea of supporting thousands of users on Mainframe computers of that time did not work. Due to many reasons, the project could not be a success. Bell Labs dropped the project. Later on, General Electric also withdrew from the project and even left the computer business. But the story of time-sharing systems does not end here. MULTICS, despite the commercial failure, had a great impact on the future development of operating systems.

One of the scientists, Ken Thompson of Bell Labs, working on MULTICS thought of the idea of running the single-user version of MULTICS on PDP-7, a discarded minicomputer that time. With great surprise, Thompson's idea worked and it started supporting multiple users. Encouraged with his success, Brian Kernighan, Dennis Ritchie, and his other colleagues joined the project. Brian Kernighan started calling this project as UNICS (*UNiplexed Information and Computing Service*); however, later it was renamed as UNIX. After this, UNIX was ported to PDP-11/70, PDP-11/45, and PDP-11/70, the other modern computers of that time. These computers also had the mechanism of memory protection hardware. But the major problem realized at that time was that porting UNIX on different machines was becoming a tough job because UNIX was written in assembly language, and new hardware required rewriting of the code. It was surveyed and found that no language was suitable for making UNIX as a portable operating system. So it was realized that a new language should be designed for this purpose. Ritchie developed a language called 'C' for rewriting the UNIX. Finally, with the efforts of Thompson and Ritchie, UNIX was rewritten in 'C' high-level language and its portable version was prepared. In this way, the path of a time-sharing multi-user operating system was paved that dominated the world for a long time after that.

1.3.4 Fourth Generation

Undoubtedly, UNIX was a major achievement as a time-sharing multi-user OS in the third gen-eration. Now the users do not need to wait for the response of their jobs for long hours. If there was an error in the user program, the user could debug it at that time only instead of waiting for a long time as in the batch systems. Thus, there was an interactive session between the user and the job. But, still this was a multi-user system which was sharing the processing time of a single system. It was desired that there should be a single system for a single user, which is not shared with others, i.e., the demand for personalization of processing time. However, this was not possible on the minicomputers of third generation.

With a leap of time, hardware technology further advanced and now it was possible to have thousands of transistors on a very small area of silicon chip due to LSI (Large Scale Integra-tion) and VLSI (Very Large Scale Integration) technology. With the result of this success, the size of computers reduced beyond imagination. Due to this architecture, the processing speed of CPU further increased. This was the sunrise of microcomputers, later on called as *personal computers* (PCs). It was possible now to have a personal computer as compared to Mainframe or mini computers system shared by many users. Now the question was to design the OS for personal computers as the others present were not compatible with them. As Intel 8080 was the first microprocessor for personal computer, there was a need to design an OS for it. Gary Kildall in Intel designed an OS called '*CP/M*' (control program for microcomputers). With the success of CP/M, Kildall formed his own company Digital Research to support this OS for other microcomputers like Zilog Z80.

After some years, IBM came into the market with IBM PCs. IBM with Bill Gates hired Tim Paterson who had written one OS known as *disk operating system* (DOS). Tim modified DOS according to the modifications desired by IBM and came up with Microsoft DOS (MS-DOS). This OS with PCs revolutionized computing and became very popular among general users. On one hand, Intel was coming out with many new advancements in microprocessors like 8086, 80286, 80386, and 80486, and on the other, Microsoft modified MS-DOS and released many versions as per the microprocessors released. A number of utilities like dBASE, LOTUS, Wordstar and languages like BASIC, COBOL, C under DOS were also developed. This made programming and other jobs on the personal computer a very convenient task for a general user, which was not possible till third generation.

Despite the success of MS-DOS on PC, UNIX was also being modified with many versions to cater to many features of operating systems. The major and unique success point of UNIX was still multi-user time-sharing system which no other operating system of that time provided. Even DOS versions were also being updated as an impression of UNIX, e.g., the hierarchical file system incorporated in DOS was based on UNIX file system only. Microsoft was aware of the success of UNIX due to multi-user capability. Intel 80286 and other 80x86 family microprocessors were very fast in speed and were able to execute the jobs of multiple users. But MS-DOS on PC was designed only to handle a single-user job. So having the impression of multi-user feature of UNIX on mind, Microsoft came up with XENIX. After this, IBM also joined Microsoft for developing an OS known as *OS/2* for multi-user feature to be installed on 80286- and 80386-based systems.

The CP/M and MS-DOS operating systems were based on the commands to be typed by the user. It means whatever the task we wanted to do on these systems, we need to remember or refer the appropriate commands first, type them, and then perform the operation. This was becoming cumbersome to have so many commands to work with. Moreover, we needed to understand the hierarchical file system to work with the files, which was not user friendly. Thus, there was now another goal for OS developers—user friendliness and convenience. The research for this goal was being performed at Stanford Research Institute by Doung Engelbart who invented GUI (graphical user interface). This GUI concept was adopted by Steve Jobs who was working with Apple Computer at that time. Jobs's first attempt as *Lisa* system failed as it was too costly. His second attempt as *Apple Macintosh* was commercially successful not only due to its cheaper cost but also because of its user friendliness. The convenience and user friendliness concept relieved the users from command system and was very easy to learn.

Later on, Microsoft also realized the need to have an OS with GUI as impressed with the success of Apple Macintosh. By this time, Intel came up with 80386- and 80486-based systems which were faster as compared to the previous ones. This speed factor invented the graphic displays. Later on, Microsoft designed GUI-based operating system called *Windows*. But, Windows was just a graphical interface running on top of MS-DOS. It was in 1995 only that Windows 95 was released as a true operating system. After this, Windows has continued to rule over the world with many evolving versions: Windows 98, Windows NT, Windows NT 4.0, Windows 2000 (Windows NT 5.0), Windows Millennium, Windows XP, Windows Vista, and Windows 2007. The latest version is Windows 2008.

Intel continued to release the faster microprocessors (80486 and Pentium family), and applications of the users were becoming complex. At the same time, users demanded to execute multiple windows at a time in Windows OS. Every user wanted to open many tasks at a time on the system. This motivated to have an OS which would handle many tasks of a single user. This was termed as *multi-tasking* and implemented in many versions of Windows mentioned earlier.

The success of Windows as a user-friendly OS influenced the UNIX developers as it was lacking GUI. This motivated them to incorporate GUI features and come up with *X Windows*. X Windows included only basic window management. Another version having complete GUI features was released, known as *Motif*.

Another advancement in the hardware technology was the network system. In a network system, there were some basic functionalities like file transferring, remote login, etc. To provide these functionalities to a general user, network interface controller and a low-level software were required. Therefore, another type of OS was designed, known as *network operating system*. Similarly, distributed systems were developed, and thus *distributed operating systems*. The distributed systems were also network systems but there was a difference that in network systems the users were aware of the network and computer in that network. For example, if a user is copying a file to another computer through network, then user must have the address of that destination computer. It means the user has the knowledge of the task and is aware of the location in the network where the task will be performed. On the other hand, in a distributed system, the user submits the complex task and gets the result back. He does not know how the task has been divided among multiple tasks; at which nodes in the network these tasks have been sent for processing. All these functionalities are performed by a distributed operating system without the knowledge of the user. Moreover, a distributed system requires a different operation compared to a centralized system such as distributed scheduling, i.e., scheduling of various tasks on various processors, distributed synchronization among tasks, distributed file systems, etc.

The evolution of all major OSs is given in Table 1.2.

Table 1.2   Evolution of different operating systems

Generation	Period	Computer architecture	Problems and development of OSs
First	1940s–1950s	Vacuum tubes based technology, plug boards and punched cards, magnetic core memories	No operating system
Second	1950s–1960s	Transistors based technology, Mainframe computers, line printers, magnetic tapes, assemblers, linkers, loaders, compilers, FORTRAN, COBOL	Set-up delay problem due to loading and unloading of tapes in earlier computer systems.
			CPU was idle.
			Jobs of users prepared with same programming language were batched together.
			Automated job sequencing
			Resident monitor
			Batch systems
			Mismatch between the speed of CPU and I/O devices
			Offline operation with magnetic tapes
			Tapes were sequential access devices

(Contd)

(*Table 1.2 Contd*)

Third	1960s–1980s	IC-based technology, Minicomputer Magnetic disk	Hard disks came into existence Spooling Multi-programming Multi-programmed batch systems Lack of user–programmer interaction with their jobs in multi-programmed batch systems Time-sharing multi-user systems CTSS MULTICS UNICS UNIX UNIX written in C
Fourth	1980s–Present	LSI- and VLSI-based technology, Microcomputer	CP/M for PCs MS-DOS Multi user facilities were not there in DOS XENIX OS/2 No user friendliness and convenience due to command driven and complex file systems Apple Macintosh Windows Multi-tasking Multi-threading X Windows Motif Network operating systems Distributed operating systems

1.4 TYPES OF OPERATING SYSTEMS

We have traced the history of OSs and seen how they have been developed. Today, a variety of OSs exist according to the project environment and requirements of the user. For daily use, we use Windows OS as it has become a general-purpose OS today. On the other hand, if the project is embedded with a real-time system, then Windows will not suffice. Instead, a real-time OS (RTOS) will be required to meet the requirements of real-time system project. If we are working on a multiprocessing distributed system, then the OS should be able to distribute the processes on various processors, coordinate between distributed processes, etc. Thus, OSs are there to meet our needs. We should identify the requirements and project types and then select an appropriate operating system. Here we describe various types of OSs.

1.4.1 Batch Processing Systems

The batch processing system was developed as a result of more set-up time for execution of different types of user programs. But today, we do not have the problems of set-up time. However, batch processing can be used for the user jobs which do not want user attention. These jobs can be combined in a batch and sent for execution without the intervention of the user. Thus, batch processing systems take a sequence of jobs in a batch and executes them one by one without any intervention of the user. The main advantage of batch processing is to increase the CPU utilization. The batch processing, obviously, is not meant for a quick response to the users, but it is still used to quantify the user service turnaround time. The turnaround time of a user job is the time since the job was submitted to the system to the time when the user gets the result back.

1.4.2 Multi-programming Systems

Multi-programming is a very basic concept today. In evolution of operating systems, it was described that multi-programming means to place several programs or jobs in the main memory instead of a single program. It means that now several jobs are ready to be executed, but CPU can execute only one job at a time. Then how do we execute all the jobs in the main memory? The idea is switching between the jobs.

There can be two types of instructions in a program: CPU bound and I/O bound. CPU bound instruction means when CPU has an instruction for processing or computation. I/O bound instruction means there is a request to an input or output device to read or write. It means during the I/O bound instructions, CPU is not doing work and is idle, i.e., the job which CPU was executing is now waiting for an I/O service. It has been observed that most of the time in a job is wasted in waiting for I/O. When there is a single program in memory or in monoprogramming concept, the CPU sits idle and waits for I/O to complete and then moves to next CPU bound instruction. Since, due to multi-programming concept there are many jobs ready in the main memory, the CPU can switch to its second job while the first is waiting for an I/O. If the second job also reaches an I/O bound instruction, then CPU switches to another job and so on. The CPU comes back to its previous jobs and executes them in the same fashion. With this concept, the CPU always has a job to execute and remains busy. For example, see Fig. 1.9; there are two programs

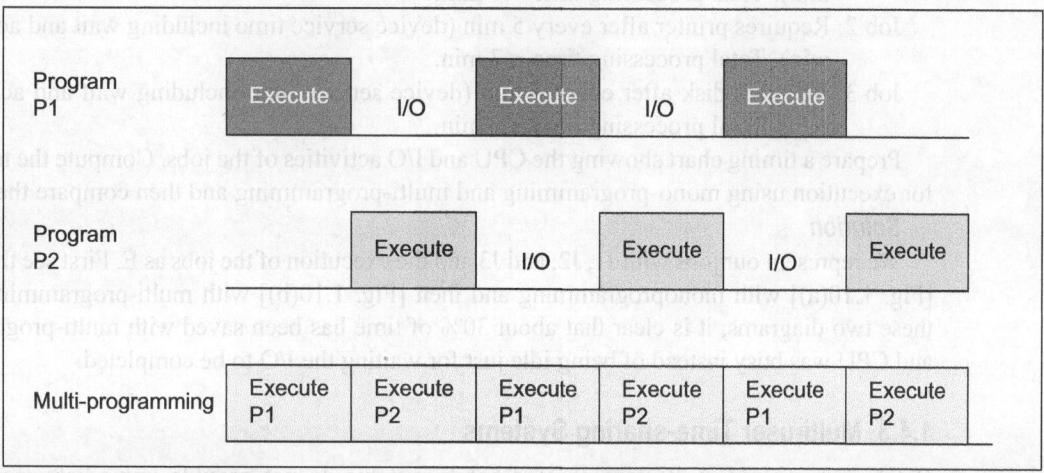

Fig. 1.9 Multi-programming

P1 and P2. With monoprogramming, there would be only P1 in the main memory and P2 will arrive in the memory and be executed only after the execution of P1. But with multi-programming, both programs will be stored in the memory. Suppose if P1 is first sent to CPU for execution, then after some time if P1 waits for some I/O, then in monoprogramming, CPU will sit idle. But in case of multi-programming, it will switch to P2 and start executing it. With this arrangement, the CPU does not sit idle; and in this example, both P1 and P2 will be executed in the same time as required to execute P1 in monoprogramming. Obviously, there is higher CPU utilization (ideally in this example, it is 100%) and throughput is doubled. Although this is an example of an ideal case, there is high CPU utilization and throughput in multi-programming systems.

The major benefits of multi-programming systems are as follows:

- *Less execution time* As compared to batch systems, the overall execution time for users' job is less because of spooling and switching between the jobs frequently by CPU.
- *Increased utilization of memory* Instead of storing a single program in the memory as done before, now more than one program is stored, thereby utilizing the main memory.
- *Increased throughput* Since in multi-programming, CPU does not sit idle and switches between all the jobs, the number of jobs executed in time *t* is more as compared to batch systems, thereby increasing the throughput. Throughput may be given as follows.

Throughput = Number of jobs completed per unit time

Throughput is increased if *degree of multi-programming* is increased. Degree of multi-programming is the number of programs in main memory. As we increase the number of programs in memory, i.e., increase the degree of multi-programming, throughput also increases. However, this increase in throughput depends on two factors. First, how much memory for storing programs is available and second, the type of program. If the programs under multiprogrammed execution are either CPU bound or I/O bound, the throughput will be low. If there is a proper mix of these two types of programs, only then the throughput will be improved.

Example 1.1

There are three jobs running in a multi-programming system with the following requirements:
Job 1: Requires disk after every 2 min (device service time including wait and access = 2 min). Total processing time = 6 min.
Job 2: Requires printer after every 5 min (device service time including wait and access = 2 min). Total processing time = 7 min.
Job 3: Requires disk after every 3 min (device service time including wait and access = 2 min). Total processing time = 5 min.

Prepare a timing chart showing the CPU and I/O activities of the jobs. Compute the total time for execution using mono-programming and multi-programming and then compare the results.

Solution

We represent our jobs with J1, J2, and J3 and the execution of the jobs as E. First see the timing [Fig. 1.10(a)] with monoprogramming and then [Fig. 1.10(b)] with multi-programming. From these two diagrams, it is clear that about 30% of time has been saved with multi-programming and CPU was busy instead of being idle just for waiting the I/O to be completed.

1.4.3 Multi-user Time-sharing Systems

Batch systems and multi-programmed batch systems do not provide immediate response to the user. If one user submits his/her job, he/she has to wait for the execution of all the jobs in that batch and then get the output. In this way, waiting time of a user is more and he/she is not

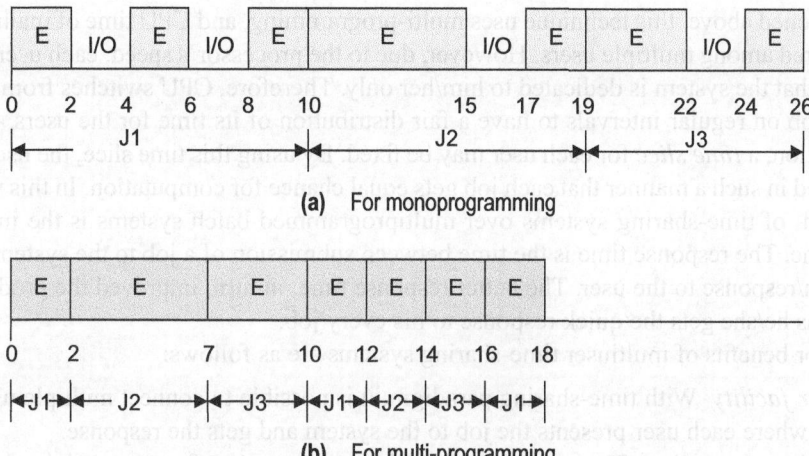

(a) For monoprogramming

(b) For multi-programming

Fig. 1.10 Timing diagram

in direct touch with his/her job. If something goes wrong in the job, the user needs to correct it, submit it in another batch, and again wait for a long time to execute the full batch. This behaviour of batch systems and multiprogrammed batch systems were due to non-interactive input and output devices. With the invention of interactive devices like keyboard and video terminals, another paradigm was designed wherein multiple users with their terminals (having no processors) were connected to a computer system (with processor) to perform their jobs. In this arrangement, the jobs of multiple interactive users were placed in the main memory instead of batched jobs. It means that multi-programming was still used here. This system was called *multiuser* as it supported multiple interactive users. It was also known as *time sharing* as CPU time of main computer system was shared among multiple users to execute their jobs. Thus, multiuser time-sharing systems are the systems where multiple interactive users connected through their dumb terminals (for interface only) access the main computer system (with CPU) to perform their jobs (see Fig. 1.11).

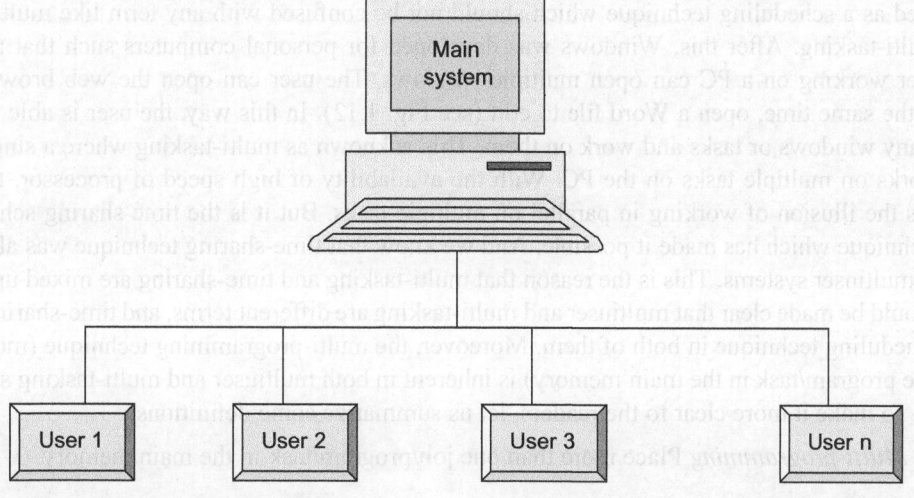

Fig. 1.11 Multi-user time-sharing system

As mentioned above, this technique uses multi-programming, and CPU time of main system is being shared among multiple users. However, due to the processor's speed, each user has the impression that the system is dedicated to him/her only. Therefore, CPU switches from one job to another job on regular intervals to have a fair distribution of its time for the users. For this fair distribution, a *time slice* for each user may be fixed. By using this time slice, the users' jobs are scheduled in such a manner that each job gets equal chance for computation. In this way, the major benefit of time-sharing systems over multiprogrammed batch systems is the improved response time. The response time is the time between submission of a job to the system and its first reaction/response to the user. The better response time, in turn, improved the productivity of the user as he/she gets the quick response to his every job.

The major benefits of multiuser time-sharing systems are as follows:

- *Multiuser facility* With time-sharing paradigm, it is possible to connect multiple users to a system where each user presents the job to the system and gets the response.
- *Improved response time* The major benefit is the *response time* for a user's job which was not possible in batch systems. The user now is in direct touch of his job and due to easy interface, he views everything regarding his job.
- *Improved debugging and productivity* From the programmer's point of view, debugging of the programs is now easy because the user can easily view his mistakes. In this way, he quickly modifies the program and runs again, thereby increasing the productivity also.

1.4.4 Multi-tasking Systems

In most of the literature, multi-programming and multi-tasking have been used interchangeably. In the literary sense of both these terms, they seem to mean the same thing and one may get confused with these two terms. Similarly, time-sharing and multi-tasking are also used interchangeably. Let us understand these terms first.

As mentioned above, multi-programming was the basic concept wherein more than one program were stored in the main memory and first batch systems were developed around this concept of multi-programming. Due to no interaction of users with their jobs in batch multi-programming, multiuser time-sharing systems were developed. So it should be noted here that in history, the term time-sharing was used for multiuser systems. Today time-sharing has been used as a scheduling technique which should not be confused with any term like multiuser or multi-tasking. After this, Windows was developed for personal computers such that a single user working on a PC can open multiple windows. The user can open the web browser and at the same time, open a Word file to edit (see Fig. 1.12). In this way, the user is able to open many windows or tasks and work on them. This is known as multi-tasking where a single user works on multiple tasks on the PC. With the availability of high speed of processor, the user has the illusion of working in parallel on multiple tasks. But it is the time-sharing scheduling technique which has made it possible. And we know that time-sharing technique was also used in multiuser systems. This is the reason that multi-tasking and time-sharing are mixed up. But it should be made clear that multiuser and multi-tasking are different terms, and time-sharing is the scheduling technique in both of them. Moreover, the multi-programming technique (more than one program/task in the main memory) is inherent in both multiuser and multi-tasking systems.

To make it more clear to the readers, let us summarize some definitions:

- *Multi-programming* Place more than one job/program/task in the main memory.

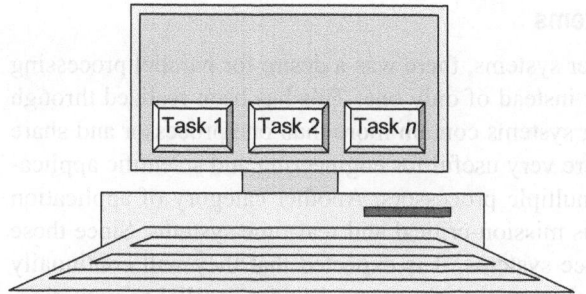

Fig. 1.12 Multi-tasking System

- *Multiprogrammed batch systems* Place more than one job/program/task in the main memory of a batch prepared for same type of jobs, and execute them by switching between them.
- *Multiuser systems* Place more than one job/program/task in the main memory of the main computer system. Here jobs come from the different users who are connected through terminals to the main computer. The jobs are scheduled by time-sharing technique.
- *Multi-tasking systems* Place more than one job/program/task in the main memory of the system. The jobs here are of a single user working on the system. The jobs are scheduled by time-sharing technique.

1.4.5 Network Operating Systems

The network operating system is the earliest form of operating system that coordinates the activities on a network system. Network operating system may be considered as loosely coupled operating system software on a loosely coupled hardware that allows nodes and users of a distributed system to be quite independent of one another but interacts in a limited degree. In a network, each node has its own local operating system. A user sitting on a node may work as on the local machine through its local operating system. However, on the network system, there may be some control operations that may be performed by the user sitting on his/her machine. In other words, the user working on a node is also able to perform non-local functions. For example, the user may remotely log on to some other node. Similarly, the user may transfer the files to another node also. For the functioning of these non-local operations, the operating system software is required to coordinate the activities. Here the role of network operating system starts. The network operating system may be considered as another layer of software on the operating system on a local machine. This layer works between the user computations and the kernel on the local machine. The processes of user first contact the network operating system. If the operation to be performed is local on the node, the network operating system passes the request to the local operating system on the node. But if the operation to be performed is non-local, the network operating system contacts the network operating system on the node.

A network operating system also targets the resource sharing across multiple nodes of the network where each node has its own local operating system and a layer of network operating system. Each node on the network is able to perform some control operations that are run locally as well as on some other node on the network. However, to work on a network system using network operating system, the user must be aware of the network nodes and their access rights to perform the control functions. For instance, if a user wants to log on to some other node on the network, i.e., remote login, he must know the address of the node and must have permission to log on the system. Similarly, while transferring the files, the user must explicitly transfer the file from his machine to another one, i.e., he must be aware of where all files are located and where they will be copied. Thus, in network operating system based system, a user must know where a resource is located in order to use it leading to poor transparency of system resources and services.

1.4.6 Multi-processor Operating Systems

In the technological evolution of computer systems, there was a desire for parallel processing with the help of more than one processor instead of only one. This has been realized through multi-processor systems. Multiprocessing systems contain more than one processor and share other resources. These types of systems are very useful for engineering and scientific applications by processing data in parallel on multiple processors. Another category of application suitable in multiprocessing environment is mission-critical and real-time systems. Since these systems are specially designed for defence systems, it is expected that they will continually work in warfare conditions. Therefore, in these types of systems, besides parallel computation, there is a high demand of fault tolerance and graceful degradation of services when any of the processor fails. Thus, multiprocessing systems are most suitable for these applications. Multiprocessing systems offer the advantage of increased throughput due to multiple processors, are economical to work on, and have increased reliability due to fault tolerance.

It is obvious that for multiprocessing systems, different operating systems are required to cater to the special requirements. These are called multiprocessing operating systems. These operating systems have more challenges as compared to single-processor systems. Since in this environment there are multiple processors, all of them should be busy. The processes should be distributed on various processors for parallel computation. The process scheduling is another challenge as it is needed to schedule multiple processes on multiple processors. Moreover, the coordination of various processes should also be taken care of. Different inter-process communication and synchronization techniques are required. In multiprocessing systems, all processors share a memory; therefore, there is a need to check that all processors operate on consistent copies of data stored in shared memory.

1.4.7 Distributed Operating Systems

Distributed systems are also multi-processor systems but with the following differences:
- Distributed system works in a wide area network.
- Each node in a distributed system is a complete computer having full set of peripherals including operating system.
- The users of a distributed system have an impression that they are working on a single machine.

Resource sharing is the main motive behind distributed systems. If we want to take advantage of hundreds of processors, it may not be possible to have all of them on a single board. But the multiple processors are realized as a single powerful machine in a network system and this machine is known as a distributed system. In this way, a number of users can share the resources of all the machines on the distributed system.

Besides the resource sharing, the distributed systems also provide computational speed up by partitioning a computation into some subcomputations which are distributed and run concurrently on various nodes on the system. A distributed system also provides the enhanced availability of the resources through redundancy and communication paths thereby increasing the reliability of the system. For example, a distributed file system places files on separate machines and allows many users to access the same set of files reliably providing the view of a single file system.

Distributed operating systems have been designed for this special type of system. These operating systems providing distributed computing facility employ almost same communication methods and protocols as in network operating systems. But the communication is transparent to the users such that they are unaware of the separate computers that are providing the service. The following are some important tasks to be met by distributed operating system:

- Since distributed systems need to access any resource or transfer any task on any node, there are three types of migration provided by the operating systems:

    Data migration Transferring the data from one site to another site

    Computation migration Transferring the computation on a particular node

    Process migration The process or its subprocesses may also need to be transferred to some other nodes due to some reasons like load balancing, computation speed, etc.

- Distributed OS must provide the means for inter-process communication. Some of the methods are as follows:

    Remote Procedure Call A process on one node may invoke a function or procedure in a process executing on another node.

    Remote Method Invocation Allows a Java process to invoke a method of an object on a remote machine.

    CORBA (*Common Object Request Broker Architecture*) It is a standardized language that supports different programming languages and different operating systems for distributed communication.

    DCOM (*Distributed Component Object Model*) Another standard developed by Microsoft included in Windows operating system.

- Due to multiple processes, synchronization methods should be supported by the operating system.

- There may be deadlock when processes distributed over several nodes in a network wait for the resources not released by other processes. Therefore, deadlock should also be handled by OS.

1.4.8 Real-time Operating Systems

In time-sharing systems, there was a drawback, i.e., if there was more load on the system, the response time was more and further increased with the increase in load. But there are some computations in a system which cannot bear the delay. Therefore, after the development of time-sharing systems, new kinds of computer systems were developed in 1980s. In these systems, response to a user request has to be immediate or within a fixed time frame, otherwise the application will fail. This is known as *real-time processing*. This type of processing is largely useful in defence applications which are mission specific, i.e., if there is no timely response, there might be loss of equipment and even life. Therefore in these systems, there are deadlines of time which should be met to prevent failures, otherwise the purpose of the system is lost. For example, suppose there is an electric motor being controlled through a computer system. The motor running at a speed, if crosses a threshold speed, will burn. The system is controlling the motor in such a way that if motor crosses the threshold, it will lower the speed of the motor. Now, when motor is crossing the threshold speed, and system does not respond in that time period, the motor will burn. So, this is an example of real-time system which in case of failure results in loss of equipment. Similarly, there are many defence applications like guided missile systems, air traffic control systems, etc. which in case of failure may result in loss of life.

Real-time systems are of two types: *hard real-time* systems and *soft real-time* systems. The systems that have hard deadlines and must be met are called hard real-time systems. All defence applications are of this type. There is another type known as soft real-time system where missing of some deadline is acceptable. For example, in a video conferencing system, if some audio or video data are somehow delayed for a fraction of time, then it may be acceptable and there is no harm. Thus, digital audio, multimedia systems, virtual reality are all examples of soft real-time systems. However, missing the deadlines does not mean that they are not real-time systems. The delay of soft real-time systems must be bounded and predictable and should not be infinite.

Real-time operating systems (RTOS) are there to meet special needs of a real-time system. They have the major characteristic of providing timely response to the applications besides other facilities. The major challenge for an RTOS is to schedule the real time tasks. In a real-time system design, all deadlines requirements are gathered and analyzed. The RTOS schedules all tasks according to the deadline information and ensures that all deadlines are met. Another feature of a real time system is to have fault tolerance. Since a real time system must work continuously in every condition, therefore in case of any hardware or software failure, the system should not stop working. To achieve this target, fault tolerance is provided by means of redundancy both in hardware and software. For example if one processor fails, another processor in the standby will take over the charge and the system continues to work. The RTOS must use some special techniques such that the system can tolerate the faults and continue its operations. Obviously, with the fault tolerant feature, there is degradation in the performance of the system. But OS should take care that this degradation is graceful, i.e., no critical functioning should be stopped or delayed.

1.4.9 Embedded Operating Systems

Embedded systems are specialized systems that tend to have very specific tasks. The last decade has filled our daily life with embedded systems. From the household systems to defence systems, the embedded systems are seen everywhere. Either you purchase the toys for your children or the smartphone for yourself, these systems have dominated every walk of life. Washing machines, televisions, and cars are other examples where these systems are being used.

Embedded systems have also operating systems but they are not generalized ones. The user uses these devices without any awareness of operating systems. Embedded operating systems are there to perform all the basic functionalities in these systems like initialization, task management, memory management, etc. but with little or no user interface. Thus, in the embedded systems, there are operating systems but not in the same structure as found in general purpose computer systems.

A large number of devices categorized as consumer electronics are mobile. They are better known as mobile devices or hand-held devices. One of the category of mobile devices is personal digital assistants (PDAs), such as palm top computer, are hand-held devices that combine elements of computing, telephone/fax, Internet, and networking in a single device. A typical PDA can function as a cellular phone, fax sender, web browser, and personal organizer. Thus, these devices allow us to access the email, messaging, web browsing, work on documents, and much more. The examples for PDAs are Palm Pilot, Toshiba Pocket PC. PalmOS is a well-known OS for them. The second category is mobile phones and smartphones. Smartphones combine both mobile phone and hand-held computers into a single device. They allow users to store information (e.g., e-mail), install programs, along with using a mobile phone in one device. The examples of operating systems for smartphones are: Symbian OS, iPhone OS, BlackBerry, Windows Phone, Linux, Palm WebOS, Android, and Materno.

Another category of mobile devices is smart cards. Smart cards have the capacity to retain and protect critical information stored in electronic form. The smart card has a microprocessor or memory chip embedded in it. The chip stores electronic data and programs that are protected by advanced security features. When coupled with a reader, the smart card has the processing power to serve many different applications. Smart cards provide data portability, security, and convenience. Smart cards are being used in various sectors, such as telephone, transportation, banking, healthcare transactions, etc. There are two basic types of smart cards: contact and contact-less smart cards. Contact cards have a 1-cm-diameter gold-plated pad that has eight contacts on it. These contacts are in turn wired to a microchip underneath the pad. The microchip can be a memory-only chip or a microprocessor chip containing memory and a CPU. Memory cards are used mostly as telephone cards, whereas microprocessor cards can be used for multiple applications on the same card. Although both cards can have stored value and stored data areas, the microprocessor card can in addition process the data since it contains a CPU, RAM, and an operating system in read only memory (ROM). Contact-less cards not only have an embedded microprocessor chip, but also contain a miniature radio transceiver and antenna. They only operate within close proximity to the reader. Instead of inserting the card, we simply pass the card close to the reader. Contact-less cards tend to be more costly than contact cards and are best suited for transportation and building access applications

The smart card's chip operating system (COS) is a sequence of instructions permanently embedded in the ROM of the smart card. The baseline functions of the COS which are common across all smart card products include

- management of interchanges between the card and the outside world, primarily in terms of the interchange protocol
- management of the files and data held in the memory
- access control to information and functions (select file, read, write, and update data)
- management of card security and the cryptographic algorithm procedures
- maintaining reliability, particularly in terms of data consistency, and recovering from an error

There are some challenges for the designers of the operating systems for mobile devices. Some of them are as follows:

- All the mobile devices have a very small memory. So the memory must be managed efficiently.
- All the devices have a slow power CPU as faster CPU will require more power and thereby a larger battery. And larger battery cannot be there in a small mobile device. Therefore, the operating system should not load the processor with heavy computations.
- Devices like mobile phones and smartphones have a small screen area. So the contents should be mapped to the available size of the display screen.

The features of major types of operating systems discussed above are given in Table 1.3.

Table 1.3 Types of operating system

Type of operating system	Features/benefits	Example	Applicable to which type of application
Batch systems	More than one job can be stored in main memory	FMS (FORTRAN monitor system), IBM's operating system for 7094	Background jobs in which the user interaction is not necessary

(Contd)

(*Table 1.3 Contd*)

	Batches of same type of jobs can be executed quickly		
Multiuser systems	Jobs of different users who are connected to a main computer are executed through the multi-programming	CTSS by MIT, TSS by IBM, MULTICS, UNIX	When multiple users need to share a single system
	Interaction of jobs with the user is possible		
	Debugging is easy		
Multi-tasking systems	Multiple tasks of a single user can be opened on the system through multi-programming	Windows	When a user wants to open and work simultaneously on many windows on the system
Network systems	The user is able to connect to another machine and perform many operations	Novell Netware, Windows NT, Windows 2000, Windows XP, Sun	When a user wants to remote log on to a system, wants to transfer a file, etc. on a network system
	The user is aware of the location of the network node where he/she wants to connect	Solaris	
Distributed systems	When multiple nodes of a wide network realized as a powerful machine sharing the resources on the network. The users are not aware where their processes are being sent and executed.	Amoeba, V system, Chorus	When computational speed and resource sharing is required and implemented through various full computer systems in a network
Real-time systems	Used to handle time-bound responses to the applications	pSOS, VxWorks, RTLinux, etc.	Applicable to systems which require time-bound response, i.e., for the real-time processing systems
Embedded systems	Specialized systems with size, memory and power restrictions	Palm Pilot, Toshiba Pocket PC, Palm OS, Symbian OS, iPhone OS, RIM's BlackBerry, Windows Phone, Linux, Palm WebOS, Android and Maemo.	Used in consumer electronics items, mobile phones, smart cards, etc.

1.5   GOALS OF AN OPERATING SYSTEM

We have seen how operating systems have been developed in the past. It can be noticed that as soon as the concept of multi-programming came into picture, a number of problems started to occur. The solution of these problems in fact contributed for further development of operating systems. All these operating systems have been developed keeping in view the convenience of the user of the system. As discussed, there was a time when all the tasks related to programming had to be done by the user only, whether it is loading the program in memory or debugging the program. The journey from multi-programming through multiuser is still continuing with multi-tasking and multi-threading. The central theme is the user's convenience. Either it is the throughput, i.e. the number of tasks being performed, or the response time of a user's job, or the user wants to execute more than one tasks at a time or the environment wherein the user can perform the tasks conveniently without worrying about the CPU time, memory partitions, memory size, etc. All these developments signify that an operating system provides an environment to a user such that he concentrates on his job instead of being concerned about the hardware.

Another point that we have observed through the development of operating systems is that operating systems have been designed to utilize the hardware and other resources. For instance, CPU time had always been the target for its utilization. From the batched multi-programming systems to multi-tasking systems, CPU time had been the central resource to be utilized. The goal of CPU usage also changed as the generation of computer systems changed. In initial operating systems, the goal was the throughput and that CPU should be made busy in executing more number of jobs. But in the recent operating systems, the goal has changed to response time, i.e., CPU executes the jobs to provide a user the minimum response time for his jobs in multi-tasking environment. Another important resource is memory. With the invention of multi-programming, many jobs started residing in the memory. Therefore, it was necessary to keep maximum jobs in the main memory and utilize it as much as possible. Even the concept of virtual memory was given with the help of which the user does not need to worry about the size of the memory to write a program. In fact, it is possible to have a program larger than the actual size of memory. There is another concern of utilization—devices utilization. All devices should be shared and utilized fairly among the tasks. As we will go through the chapters in this book, we will realize the need of utilization of all the resources being used in the computer system. Therefore, to meet the needs of resources utilization, an operating system is required. Thus, the operating system provides an abstraction to the user of a system that he is best utilizing the resources of the system even without his knowledge.

As a result of resource utilization, another goal for operating system has been added, i.e., resource allocation. In multi-programming environment, there is need to allocate resources to various tasks. For instance, when there are many tasks in the memory, it is required that one of them will go to the CPU for execution. Someone has to take this decision for process allocation. The operating system has been designated to perform this function. It uses various scheduling algorithms according to the need and chooses one of the tasks in memory and sends it to CPU for execution. For memory utilization, there is a problem of memory allocation to a task, i.e., which vacant space should be allocated to a task? Similarly, devices are very limited as compared to the tasks. Therefore, again the operating system allocates the devices to the tasks in best possible manner. Thus, another goal in designing the operating system is to allocate resources to various tasks. Therefore, it is also known as *resource allocator*.

It should be noted that there is a side effect of multi-programming and multi-tasking. We know that more than one job resides in the memory in these concepts. Moreover, operating system is also loaded in the memory in a separate partition. However, it may be possible that one user accesses the memory region of another user or even the operating system. Till the development of DOS, there was no protection among users' jobs and operating systems. Therefore, the next goal for an operating system is to have protection in this form such that no user is able to access others memory regions and of operating system.

Let us summarize these goals as follows:

Convenience

The convenience of a user, who performs a job using the computer system, is the prime goal of an operating system. Let us understand the user requirements. Some of them are as follows:

Hardware abstraction/virtual machine

The user does not want to care for hardware resources and to access the devices because the details of all the hardware are too complex to work. The details of hardware also hinder the thinking process of a programmer. Therefore, operating system provides an abstraction layer between the user and the hardware so that the user can work on the hardware without actually knowing it.

Convenient programming environment

The process of program execution includes several steps. We should have a good editor to write a program, debugger to debug the program, linker, loader, etc. The operating system provides all these facilities to a programmer so that a convenient environment is present and the user can concentrate on the programming and nothing else.

Response time

As we know through the evolution of operating systems that there was a time when there was a gap of hours or even a day between the user's job submission and its first response of execution. With the invention of high-speed processors, the user desired to have immediate response from the job. This desire has resulted in the development of multiuser and multi-tasking operating systems.

Easy-to-use interface

The users' convenience has taken another shape when the use of GUI became popular. This was another goal for an operating system which resulted in Mac OS and Windows OS. The use of an operating system in the form of GUI makes a user understand the operation he wants to perform. Moreover, the user is relieved from remembering the commands which needed to be typed in older UNIX and DOS systems.

Resource Utilization/Management

We know that multi-programming introduced many new challenges for an operating system. Due to multi-programming, there was a need to partition the memory and allocate memory to various tasks. So memory partitioning and memory allocation jobs added to the operating system. As the number of users and tasks increased, there was need to utilize the memory efficiently. Thus, memory management techniques were devised.

Another concern that arose due to multi-programming was CPU utilization. When there was a single program to execute, there was no issue of memory management and CPU utilization. But when there are multiple tasks in memory, all compete for execution. Since CPU can execute a single task at a time, others need to wait. So the issue is to schedule the tasks such that CPU does not sit idle and all the tasks get the CPU time fairly.

Device utilization is another important issue for operating system. As the devices are less in number as compared to the number of users and tasks, there is need of controlled allocation to them. For example, if we allow all the users to access a shared printer, then there will be a chaos. It means we must have some mechanisms to share the devices. This device management is also supported by the operating system.

Likewise, there are many resources today in the computer system which need to be allocated and managed in a controlled manner. In this way, operating system's jobs to manage and utilize the resources are as follows:

    i) grants access to resource requests from different users
    ii) keeps track of which task is using which resource
    iii) keeps account of usage of the resources
    iv) resolves the conflicting requests from users
    v) utilizes the hardware and other resources in best possible manner

Thus, it can be said that operating system acts as a resource allocator and resource manager in order to provide an efficient operation on computer system to the user. The efficiency is the major goal for an operating system which takes care of the best utilization and allocation of resources on the computer system.

Protection

Due to multi-programming and multi-tasking, there was a challenge that one user should not be able to access other user area in memory. Similarly, one user should not be able to access the operating system area in memory. For this purpose, hardware was first modified and then protection feature was added in the operating system (we will discuss this issue later in detail). Thus, an operating system should be able to protect the task of one user from another and operating system from any user.

1.6 FUNCTIONS OF OPERATING SYSTEM

We have understood what an operating system is and broadly what it does. Now it is time to discuss the various functions being performed by an operating system. The functions can be categorized as per two viewpoints: user view and system view. The user view is a top-down view of functions performed by an operating system, whereas system view is bottom-up view of functions performed by an operating system.

1.6.1 User View

The user view is to execute the user's task on the computer system. But a user does not want to be overwhelmed with the complex hardware details of the system. He simply wants an interface between his application and the hardware. There are many system programs or utilities to help him in developing his application. The operating system is also a system program developed to act as an interface between the application and the hardware. He is not concerned how the application will get resources from the system and get executed. All these jobs will be done by the operating system. Thus, an operating system does hardware abstraction for the user by hiding the complex details of the hardware, thereby providing a flexible user-friendly interface to the user for developing his application. In other words, operating system acts as a mediator between the application and the computer system that makes easy use of hardware and other resources without even knowing. From the user's point of view, the following are some functions performed by an operating system:

User Interface

The operating system provides the interface to use the computer system. There are two types of interfaces: command-driven interface and graphical user interface (GUI). As discussed earlier, in older systems, there was only command-driven interface. But with the invention of Windows, now almost every operating system provides GUI.

Program Development and Execution

For executing a program, there are certain tasks like loading the program in main memory, initializing and accessing I/O devices and files, scheduling various resources, etc. All these program executions are performed by the operating system without the knowledge of the user. Moreover, operating system provides some utilities such as editors, debuggers, etc., which although are not part of the operating system but are packed with the operating system for the convenience of the programmer.

Accessing I/O Operations

If you have written some programs in high-level language, then you write some standard input-output instructions according to the language being used. For example, in 'C' language, for reading the input the instruction is *scanf* and for output the instruction is *printf*. You do not care for the type of input/output devices and use only standard instructions for any type of devices. The operating system relieves the user from details of input/output devices and accesses them on behalf of the user.

Accessing File Systems

A file is a logical concept to store the user's data or program. A user creates the file using some editor and saves and retrieves the files conveniently through the operating system's interface. But the file as a logical entity is mapped to some physical memory. Operating system in background keeps track of memory provided to the files and performs all the operations related to file management.

Error Detection

While working on a computer system, one may encounter different types of errors. Either it is a hardware error or error in some user program. There may be a memory access failure or a device failure. A user may give a command for printing a file but there may be no paper in printer or there is a paper jam. Or the errors may be in user programs such as arithmetic overflow, divide by zero error, or accessing an illegal memory location. All these errors must be identified by the operating system and an appropriate action must be taken and the user should be notified through a message on the screen.

1.6.2 System View

Beyond the user's convenience, most of the functionalities are performed in background by the operating system. These activities are to manage or utilize the hardware and other resources of the computer system. Therefore, from the computer system's point of view, the operating system is a program that controls the allocation/execution of all the resources in the system. There are three major functionalities done by the operating system:

Resource Manager

The operating system is a program that controls the allocation/execution of all the resources in the system. In this way, operating system schedules and manages the allocation of all resources in the computer system. It is best called as a resource allocator and resource manager. If there are multiple processes, then their creation, deletion, and other operations are handled by the operating system only. Memory is to be provided to all these processes. It is the job of operating system to look for the available memory and allocate to the process. When multiple processes are simultaneously running there may be problems such as how to communicate with other processes and how to access the shared objects. Therefore, an operating system needs to also handle inter-process communication and synchronization. It utilizes the resources in the best possible manner. Users work on the computer using various files. The user sees these files as only a logical concept. The operating system implements the file systems in the physical memory. Similarly, I/O devices, which are not directly accessible to the user, are given access by the operating system. Thus, from the system's viewpoint, process management, file management, I/O management, memory management, etc., are all the functions performed by the operating system.

Control Program

The operating system acts as a control program in the sense that it protects one user's program from another. It is necessary in multi-programming because a user may try to enter other user's memory and even in operating systems' region. Also, it does not allow the users to access any I/O devices directly as the user may misuse them. It detects any exception in the system if it happens and informs the user. Thus, operating system acts as a control program that controls the user activities, I/O access, and all other activities performed by the system.

Virtual Machine Manager

A very different view to see the operating system is as a virtual machine manager. As we know that operating system acts as an abstraction which hides the complex details of the hardware from the user and presents a user-friendly environment to him. Even a programmer does not want to interact directly with the I/O devices. Interacting with I/O devices, memory, and hard disk is too clumsy and no one can easily work on these hardware details. Due to this fact, operating system provides a layer on the actual hardware on which it performs the tasks of the user. And to the user, it seems that all the work done is by the hardware. In other words, there is an illusion created by the operating system that there is a virtual machine that is performing all the work. Let us see how a virtual computer is created:

   i) The operating system creates virtual processors by creating multiple processes.
  ii) The operating system creates multiple address spaces out of the physical memory and allocates to various processes.
 iii) The operating system implements a file system out of the hard disk, i.e., virtualization of disk space.
  iv) The operating system implements virtual devices out of the physical devices because it is cumbersome to work with physical devices and virtual devices prepare a simple interface instead.

In this way, virtual machine or extended machine (in the form of virtual processors, virtual memory, and virtual devices) is created from the physical computer. On a single physical machine, multiple virtual computers are created in the form of multiple processes (see Fig. 1.13). Each user has an illusion that he is using a single machine. Therefore, operating system is also viewed as a manager of the virtual machine or extended machine.

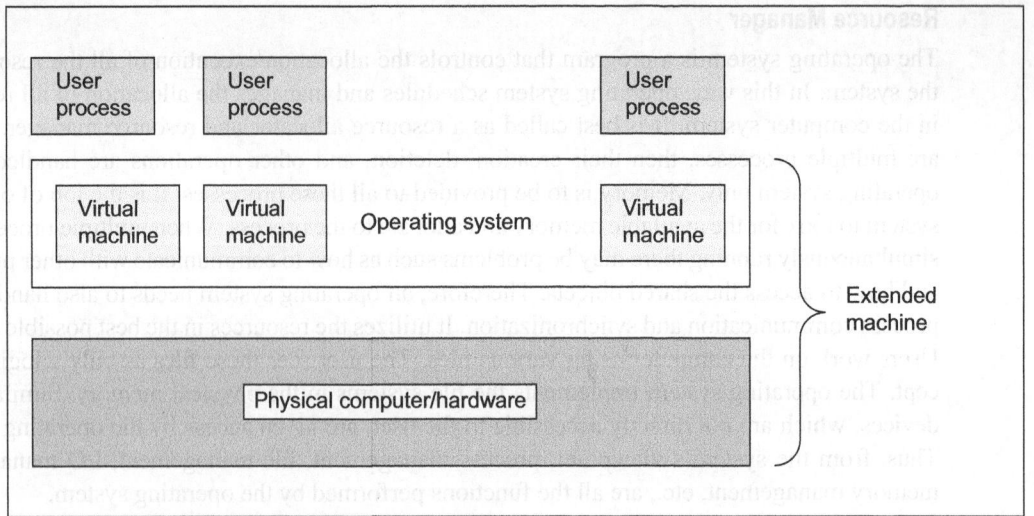

Fig. 1.13   Operating system as a virtual machine manager

1.7   OPERATING SYSTEM'S GENERIC COMPONENTS

In this section, a generic structure of operating system is discussed. The detailed structure and various types will be discussed later. The emphasis here is to know how the interfaces between user, operating system, and hardware are in place. The reader should be aware that the user or programmer cannot access hardware resources directly. Even, in the subsequent chapters a concept will be established that no user is allowed to perform any I/O operations. Therefore, it becomes necessary to know the generic structure of an operating system.

In Fig. 1.2, we have seen the computer system where operating system fits therein. We have seen there that operating system is the interface between user's applications and hardware. It means that whatever job a user wants to perform through the hardware of the computer system will be performed by operating system on behalf of the user. But there is a question of how to tell the operating system the functions we want to perform. It means there should be an interface by means of which user tells the operating system to perform operations on the hardware. This interface is the place where the users give the commands through control statements. There is a program which reads and interprets these control statements and passes the signals to operating system. This program is known as *command-interpreter* or *shell*. Thus, there is a clear separation between the user application, OS, and hardware as shown in Fig. 1.14. The shells may be in the graphical form wherein commands are in the form of mouse-based window and menu system as used in Windows OSs or commands form wherein commands are typed in by the user as used in MS_DOS or UNIX operating systems.

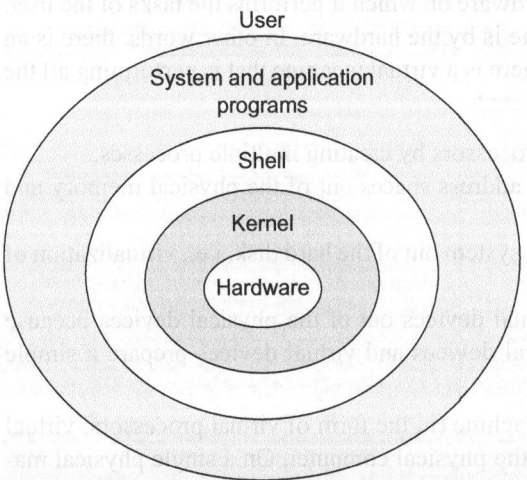

Fig. 1.14   Operating system structure with shell and kernel

As the requirements have grown, the size of the operating systems has also increased. But we know that it needs to be loaded into the main memory which is already packed with user programs. Therefore, the operating system to be loaded into the memory should be of smaller size otherwise most of the memory will be taken by the operating system only. Therefore, essential modules of the operating system such as task management, memory management, etc. are only loaded into the memory known as *kernel*. The kernel is the innermost layer close to the hardware to get things done. Other modules of operating system are stored in the secondary storage like hard disks and get loaded as and when required. For example, virtual memory module is not part of kernel but will be loaded if required. In this way, the operating system part is also divided into two parts: essential part (kernel) and secondary part.

SUMMARY

There was a time when a user on the computer system used to get the program executed in days because everything for program execution was manual and in fact the user was close to the machine. But with the advancement in the technology, a software layer between the user programs and hardware was added so that the user is relived from the details of the hardware and all the work related to machine was done via this software layer. This software layer is known as operating system. The OSs evolved with the increase in demands of the user and inventions in computer hardware and I/O devices. The advancements in computer architecture have always impacted the development of OSs. But sometimes, the researchers of OSs also demanded to have modifications in the architecture. Thus, OSs and architecture both have affected each other and developed in parallel.

Multi-programming is a central concept in operating systems. The multi-programming, i.e., placing more than one program in the main memory, has given birth to other modules of operating system. In fact, the multi-programming originated many problems. As a solution to these problems, other modules of operating system were developed. For example, multi-programming demanded that memory should be partitioned and allocated to the required processes. All the processes must be protected. Multiple processes will compete for limited I/O devices. Multiple processes must communicate and synchronize with each other. Therefore, memory management, process management, process scheduling, device management, process communication, process synchronization, protection, etc., have been developed in response to the problems of multi-programming. All these concepts are relevant to a designer. For a system designer, the operating system is a resource allocator, extended machine manager, and control program. As a resource manager it allocates and manages the resources in the system. As an extended machine manager, it acts as an extended machine in support of the actual hardware and seems to a general user that all the facilities have

been provided by the machine hardware only. As a control program, the operating system protects all the programs and itself from any malicious job.

However, all these concepts are not related to the user. A general user's view is different from the system's view. The user wants the convenience while working on the system. There are many facets of the user convenience. The user does not want to indulge into the hardware details. The user wants the interaction with his job so that he can debug it. The user does not want to work with the commands. He wants the GUI based flexibility and convenience. And all these have been incorporated in the operating systems. Thus, the prime goal of an operating system is to have the user convenience so that there is a friendly environment on the system for the user. The other goal of the operating system is the utilization of the hardware and all other resources in the system.

Let us have a quick review of important concepts in this chapter:

- An OS is a software that acts as an interface between the users and hardware of the computer system.
- An OS is a software that provides a working environment for the users' applications.
- An OS is a resource manager that in background manages the resources needed for all the applications.
- Multi-programming is the central concept in operating system that originates all other concepts of operating system.
- Multi-programming places more than one job/program/task in the main memory.
- Multi-programmed batch systems place more than one jobs/programs/tasks in the main memory of a batch prepared for same type of jobs and execute them by switching between them.
- Multi-user systems place more than one job/program/task in the main memory of the main computer system. The jobs are of different users who are connected through terminals to the main computer. The jobs are scheduled by time-sharing technique.

- Multi-tasking systems place more than one job/program/ task in the main memory of the system. The jobs here are of a single user working on the system. The jobs are scheduled by time-sharing technique.
- The primary goals of operating system are convenience of the user and best utilization of the hardware.
- There are two views to look at the functioning of the operating systems: user view and system view.
- From the user's viewpoint, the operating system acts as an easy interface between the user and computer system and presents a friendly environment wherein the user can work efficiently without worrying about any configuration or details of the hardware.
- From the system's viewpoint, the operating system acts as a resource manager, control program, and virtual machine manager.
- As a resource manager, operating system schedules and manages the allocation of all resources in the computer system.
- As a control program, operating system controls the user activities, I/O access, and all other activities performed by the system.
- As a virtual machine manager, operating system provides a layer on the actual hardware on which it performs the tasks of the user. And to the user, it seems that all the work done is by the hardware. In other words, there is an illusion created by the operating system that there is a virtual machine which is performing all the work.
- There are two generic components of operating system: shell and kernel.
- Shell is a program which reads and interprets the control statements entered by the user to perform a task. It is also known as command interpreter.
- Kernel is the part wherein only essential modules of the operating system are placed.

MULTIPLE CHOICE QUESTIONS

1. Automatic job sequencing is performed by _____.
   (a) operating system   (c) job pool
   (b) resident monitor   (d) none

2. Disks were invented in _____ generation.
   (a) first   (c) third
   (b) second   (d) none

3. SPOOL is _____.
   (a) simultaneous printer operation offline
   (b) simple peripheral operation offline
   (c) simultaneous peripheral operation offline
   (d) simultaneous peripheral operation online

4. MULTICS is
   (a) multiplexed information control system
   (b) multiple input control system
   (c) multiplexed information and computing service
   (d) none

5. PDP-7 was a ___.
   (a) mini computer   (c) PC
   (b) Mainframe   (d) none

6. IBM with Bill Gates hired Tim Paterson who had written one OS known as
   (a) UNIX   (c) Windows
   (b) DOS   (d) none

7. Batch systems were developed in ____ generation.
   (a) first   (c) third
   (b) second   (d) none

8. Spooling was developed in ____ generation.
   (a) first   (c) third
   (b) second   (d) none

9. Time-sharing was developed in ____ generation.
   (a) first   (c) third
   (b) second   (d) fourth

10. Multi-tasking/Multi-threading was developed in ____ generation.
    (a) first   (c) third
    (b) second   (d) fourth

11. _____ processing is largely useful in defence applications.
    (a) Batch   (c) Parallel
    (b) Real-time (d) None

12. Symbian OS is used in ____.
    (a) smartphones   (c) Palm pilot
    (b) smart cards   (d) none

13. When a user wants to open and work simultaneously on many windows on his system, what OS should be chosen?
    (a) Multi-user OS   (c) Batch OS
    (b) Multi-tasking OS   (d) Networked OS

14. When a user wants to remotely log on to a system, wants to transfer a file, etc., on a network system, what OS should be chosen?
    (a) Multi-user OS   (c) Batch OS
    (b) Multi-tasking OS   (d) Networked OS

15. When computational speed and resource sharing is required and implemented through various full computer systems in a network, what OS should be chosen?
    (a) Real-time OS   (c) Embedded OS
    (b) Distributed OS   (d) Networked OS

16. What OS should be chosen which is applicable to systems that require time-bound response?
    (a) Real-time OS   (c) Embedded OS
    (b) Distributed OS   (d) Networked OS

17. What OS should be chosen which will be used in consumer electronics items, mobile phones, smart cards, etc.?
    (a) Real-time OS   (c) Embedded OS
    (b) Distributed OS   (d) Networked OS

18. Program which reads and interprets these control statements and passes the signals to operating system is known as
    (a) system programs   (c) shell
    (b) system call   (d) kernel

19. _____is the innermost layer close to the hardware to get things done.
    (a) System programs   (c) Shell
    (b) System call   (d) Kernel

20. *Apple Macintosh* was commercially successful not only due to its cheaper cost but also because it was_____.
    (a) taking less memory (c) accessing I/O faster
    (b) user friendly   (d) none

REVIEW QUESTIONS

1. What is the need for an operating system?

2. What are the functions of an OS from user's viewpoint?

3. What are the functions of an OS from system's viewpoint?

4. What were the difficulties in second generation from OS viewpoint?

5. What is a resident monitor?

6. What is JCL?

7. What is offline operation?

8. What is the difference between online and offline operation on a computer system?

9. How did the disks solve the problem faced with the magnetic tapes?

10. What is SPOOL? What is the benefit of spooling?

11. Give a brief overview of development of UNIX?

12. Explain the difference between DOS, UNIX, Apple Macintosh, and Windows?

13. Explain the differences between multi-programming, multi-user, and multi-tasking OSs.

14. Explain the characteristics of multi-processor and distributed systems.

15. What is the differences between network and distributed OSs?

16. What is the difference between real-time and embedded operating systems?

17. How does operating system function as resource manager?

18. How does operating system provide protection?

19. What is a virtual machine? How does operating system function as a virtual machine manager?

20. Discuss the role of shell and kernel in operating system.

21. What are the challenges in designing a multiprocessing/distributed operating systems?

22. What is the difference between a smart card and smartphone?

BRAIN TEASERS

1. Can you work without operating system in your computer system?

2. The major drawback of multiprogrammed batch systems was the lack of user/programmer interaction with their jobs. How can you overcome this?

3. The response time is the major requirement of a multiuser time-sharing OS. What are the things that need to be improved for this requirement from a system designer's viewpoint?

4. Is time-sharing OS suitable for real-time systems?

5. Examine the following conditions and find appropriate operating system for them:

(a) In a LAN, users want to share some costly resources like laser printers.

(b) Multiple users on a system want quick response on their terminals.

(c) Railway reservation system

(d) A user wants to work with multiple jobs on his system.

(e) In a network system you want to transfer file and log on to some node.

(f) There are some jobs in the system which does not want user interaction.

(g) Washing machine

6. Explore the features of operating system being used in recent design of smartphones.

7. Do all operating systems contain shell?

8. Multi-programming is inherent in multiuser and multi-tasking systems. Explain how.

9. There are four jobs running in a multi-programming system with the following requirements:

   job 1: requires disk after every 1 min, device service time including wait and access = 3 min, total processing time = 4 min.

   job 2: does not require any I/O, total processing time = 7 min.

   job 3: requires printer after every 3 min, device service time including wait and access = 2 min, total processing time = 9 min.

   Prepare a timing chart showing the CPU and I/O activities of the jobs. Compute the total time for execution using monoprogramming and multiprogramming and then compare the results.

2

Hardware Support for Operating Systems

2.1 INTRODUCTION

The first chapter introduced the basic concepts of an OS. Before we delve into the details of an OS, the knowledge of computer system architecture is a prerequisite to understand the concepts of an OS. Since there was a parallel development in computer architecture and the OSs as we have seen in Chapter 1, it is necessary to understand the relation of architecture with OS. Therefore, some basic concepts that are related to OS have been discussed in this chapter. Since the modern OSs are interrupt driven, the interrupt mechanism has been explained. The protection among the user jobs and the OS is a major issue to implement the multi-programming-based concepts in OSs. Therefore, it is necessary to understand how the protection has been achieved in the hardware. The management of I/O devices is a major area where the OS plays a great role. All the fundamental issues related to I/O devices such as type of devices, device controllers, and the device drivers have also been discussed. The magnetic disk is a widely used secondary storage device and used in many concepts of OS such as scheduling, virtual memory, and so on. Therefore, the structure of the disk and its related issues have also been discussed.

2.2 INTERRUPT-DRIVEN OPERATION FOR OPERATING SYSTEM

The modern OSs that support the multi-programming/multi-user/multi-tasking environment perform interrupt-driven operation, i.e., everything an OS does is interrupt driven. If there is no event and no processes to execute, the OS does nothing. It simply waits for an event. The OS is activated when there are processes to execute or an event causing the interrupt. Therefore, it is important to understand what an interrupt is and what happens to the processor when an interrupt arrives. So, let us discuss the concept of interrupt.

Interrupt is a signal sent by hardware or software to notify the processor about the occurrence of an event that needs immediate attention. On the processor hardware, there is an interrupt request (IRQ) line that the processor senses for any interrupt after execution of each instruction of the process. If there is no interrupt, it moves to next instruction to execute. But if there is an interrupt, the state of the process being executed is saved so that the processor can resume its execution from the place where it left off (see Fig. 2.1).

Learning Objectives

After reading this chapter, you should be able to understand:

- Interrupts, their types, and interrupt-driven operation of an OS
- Types of I/O devices
- Introduction to timers
- Role of device controllers and device drivers
- Multiple mode of protection
- Input-output protection
- Memory protection
- CPU protection
- Input-output communication techniques
- Structure of a magnetic disk
- Disk partitioning
- Disk formatting

```
while (fetch next instruction)
{
    Execute the instruction;
    If (there is an interrupt)
    {
        Save the state;
        Find address of ISR;
        Execute ISR;
        Return from ISR and restore the state;
    }
}
```

Fig. 2.1 Interrupt view of processor

After saving the state of the old process, a program known as an *interrupt handler* or *interrupt service routine* (ISR) is executed, which is a part of microcontroller firmware (such as ROM-BIOS that provides a small library of basic input/output functions used to operate and control the peripherals such as the keyboard, display, disk, etc.), OS or a device driver. There is an ISR corresponding to each interrupt generated. After executing the ISR, the control is returned to the interrupted program and its execution is resumed by loading its saved state.

But we do not know the address of an ISR to be executed. The addresses of all ISRs are placed in a list known as *interrupt vector table* (IVT). The IVT is generally placed in low memory. Each interrupt has a unique number and therefore in IVT, corresponding to an interrupt number, the address of the ISR is stored. Whenever an interrupt is sensed by the processor, it finds out its number and the address of the ISR in IVT. After finding the address of the ISR, the control is transferred to the ISR and it is executed. In the x86 architecture, each address in the IVT is 4 bytes long and supports 256 total interrupts (0-255). To access the location of an interrupt in IVT, the interrupt number is multiplied by 4 as each address is 4 bytes long. For example, hitting a keyboard generates a hardware interrupt whose number is 9. It means the address of ISR corresponding to this interrupt will be found on locations 36, 37, 38, and 39.

The steps of the interrupt processing are summarized as follows (see Fig. 2.2):

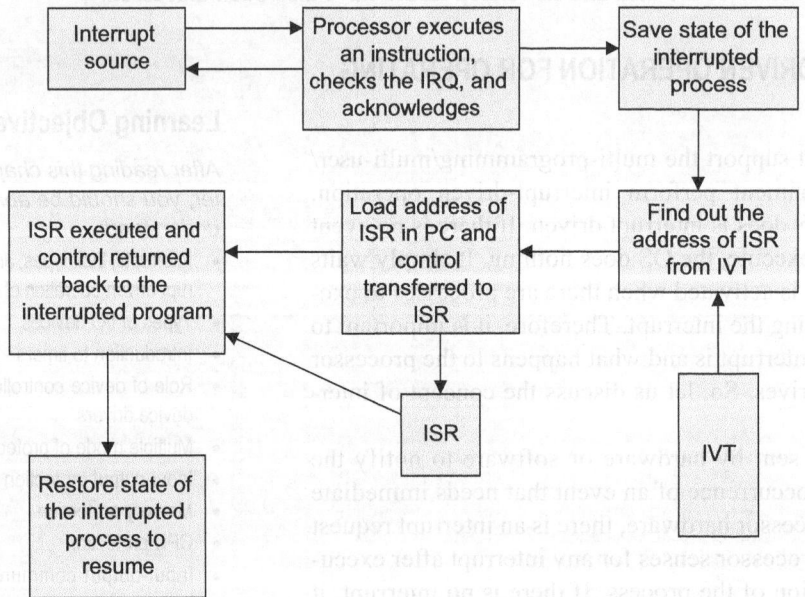

Fig. 2.2 Steps of interrupt processing

1. The interrupt is generated from its source (hardware or software).
2. The interrupt signal generated is pending on the interrupt request (IRQ) line of the processor hardware.
3. The processor finishes its current instruction execution and then checks for the interrupt.
4. The processor determines that there is a pending interrupt request and sends an acknowledgement signal to the source that generated the interrupt.
5. After the acknowledgement, the source of the interrupt removes the interrupt request signal.
6. The processor saves the current state of the process that was interrupted such as program status word (PSW), program counter (PC), processor registers, and other data structures that will be discussed later in the book. These can be pushed onto a control stack.
7. The processor finds out the type and number of the interrupt generated and finds the address of the corresponding ISR in IVT.
8. The processor loads the address of the ISR in PC and executes it.
9. After executing the ISR, the control is returned back to the interrupted program and saved state is loaded again so that the program can be resumed.

2.2.1 Types of Interrupts

There may be various sources of interrupts. In general, there may be two types of interrupts as follows:

Hardware Interrupts

A hardware interrupt is generated from an external device, which could be either a part of the computer itself such as a keyboard, disk, or an external peripheral. For example, when we press a key on the keyboard or move the mouse, the hardware interrupts are triggered, which in turn causes the processor to read the keystroke or mouse position.

Software Interrupts

A software interrupt may be generated due to the following:

• There may be conditions caused within the processor that require OS attention. For example, if there is an arithmetic exception like divide-by–zero during the execution of a process.

• There are some instructions in the user process which are treated as a request to the OS. These instructions, known as privileged instructions, are the medium through which a user process can indirectly interact with hardware through the OS. For example, if the user process wishes to read input data from the keyboard, then the user process will use a privileged instruction that will be passed to the OS and treated as a software interrupt.

Thus, the software interrupts are the result of an exceptional condition in the process or may be caused due to a special instruction in the instruction set that triggers the interrupt when executed. The exceptional condition is sometimes known as a *trap*. In general, it is used for errors or events occurring during the program. The maximum number of hardware interrupts that can be handled depends on the number of IRQ lines to the processor. However, the software interrupts are not limited to the number of IRQ lines and therefore can be hundreds in number.

2.2.2 Multiple Interrupts Handling

It is not so that only one interrupt may arrive at a time. We will see later in the exploration of multi-programming concept that multiple interrupts may also arrive and require the processor's attention. For example, in a multi-programming environment, a printer is printing the output, the keyboard is receiving the input, and the data is read from the disk. All these events cause interrupts. However, the processor is able to execute one interrupt at a time. There are two approaches to solve this problem. One is to disable the other interrupts while the ISR corresponding to one interrupt is being executed. The interrupts arrived during the execution of the ISR are treated as pending and may be stored in FIFO queue. Once the ISR execution is over, the other interrupts in the queue are processed. But the disadvantage of this approach is that some interrupts which need immediate attention and not get serviced may do some loss. For example, if an ISR is being executed and the keyboard interrupt arrives that is reading some data. If keyboard interrupt is not processed immediately, the input data may be lost. Therefore, the second approach—a priority mechanism—is taken that decides the priority of the interrupts arriving. On the basis of the priority decided, the interrupts are serviced. If a lower priority ISR is being executed and a higher priority interrupt arrives, the ISR is interrupted and the control is passed to the high priority ISR. After the execution of this high priority ISR, the control is returned to the older ISR. Even if no ISR is being executed and two interrupts arrive at the same time, the interrupt with higher priority is executed first. In this way, the priority based interrupt mechanism is used to handle multiple interrupts.

2.3 INPUT–OUTPUT DEVICES

Since the OS provides a generic, consistent, convenient, and reliable way to access I/O devices, a brief introduction of I/O devices is provided in this section. There are various types of devices available today. They may vary depending on their operation, speed, data transfer, etc. Some devices may be categorized based on these characteristics. Even within a category the devices may vary. This is the reason that device management is necessary as part of operating system function. The devices may be categorized as human readable and machine readable. The human readable devices are mouse, keyboard, monitor, etc. The machine readable devices are sensors, controllers, disks, tapes, etc.

The devices may transfer the data as a stream of bytes or in the form of a block. If the device accepts and delivers the data as a stream of characters/bytes, it is known as character device. *Character-oriented devices* are suitable where linear stream of bytes are required. For example, while accepting input data from the keyboard, a block of characters cannot be expected in one instance. Therefore, input devices like keyboard, mouse, modems, etc., are all examples of character devices. Even the output devices of this nature, like printers, are also character devices. On the other hand, if the device accepts and delivers the data as a fixed sized block, it is known as *block-oriented device*. Disk is the example of a block device. Another criterion is how a device accesses the data. On the basis of accessing data sequentially or randomly, the devices are called as *sequential device* such as a tape drive and *random access device* such as a disk.

A different type of I/O device is the *network device*. The network devices differ from conventional devices like disk in the sense that they need special I/O interfaces to send or receive data on a network. For example, socket is the major I/O interface used for network devices.

There may be two types of I/O devices: blocking and non-blocking. In blocking devices, the program is blocked with an I/O action and is not allowed to execute the program until the I/O action completed. For example, the word processor program waits for a key press or a mouse click (I/O) done by the user and then starts processing. In non-blocking devices, the device is checked periodically for an I/O. If there is a process that processes the data and displays it on the screen but needs to check the I/O on keyboard and mouse as well. In this case, the process periodically checks the keyboard and mouse for I/O while processing and displaying the data. In another example, the video application reads data from a file and simultaneously decompressing and displaying the data on the screen.

Other criteria to define the types of devices may be based on complexity of control, data representation, error conditions, etc.

2.3.1 Timers or Clocks

The timer is an important device that is used in the operating system to implement multi-tasking and other jobs. It is used to have the current time and elapsed time and to trigger some operation at a particular time instant. The timers are used for the following purposes:

- The periodic interrupts may be generated.
- It may be used by a scheduler to generate an interrupt when there is need to preempt a process when its time slice expires.
- It may be used by a disk subsystem when there is need to flush the modified cache buffers to the disk.
- It may be used to cancel the operations in a network that are causing congestion and therefore taking a long time to process.
- It may be used to cancel the operation of a process that is not releasing the processor and holds it for a long time. It helps in sharing the processor time among multiple tasks and every task gets fair time and no task holds the processor.

A timer is implemented with a hardware known as up-counter that counts incoming pulses. A counter acts as a timer when the incoming pulses are at a fixed known frequency. For example, the programmable interval timer (PIT) hardware is used for the function of a timer.

A timer consists of the following components:

- Pre-scaler
- N-bit timer/counter register
- N-bit capture register

The pre-scaler component allows the timer to be clocked at the rate we wish. It takes the basic timer clock frequency (may be the CPU clock frequency or some higher or lower value may also be taken), divides it by some value, and then feeds it to the timer. The timer register (an up-counter) reads and writes the current count value and may stop or reset the counter. The regular pulses which drive the timer are called *ticks*. Thus, a tick is a basic unit to express the timer value. When there is some event, the current count value is loaded in the capture register. Besides these components, a compare register is also used that holds a value against which the current timer value is continuously compared. When the value in timer register and the value in compare register matches, an appropriate event is triggered.

2.4 DEVICE CONTROLLERS

A device controller, also known as an *adapter*, is an electronic device in the form of chip or circuit that controls the communication between the system and the I/O device. It is inserted into an expansion slot of the mother board. It functions as a bridge between the device and the operating system, i.e., the operating system deals with the device controller of the device to which it wishes to communicate. It takes care of low level operations such as error checking, data transfer, and location of data on the device. Each device controller is designed specifically to handle a particular type of device but a single controller may handle multiple devices also.

To perform an I/O operation on a device, the processor sends signals to its device controller. For example, it may be the case that the data needs to be read from a serial device. So the processor sends a command to the device controller of that serial device first to read the desired bytes of data. In turn, the controller collects the serial bit stream from the device and converts it into a block of bytes. It may also perform some necessary error corrections if required. There is a buffer inside the controller that stores the block of bytes thus obtained. After this, the block of bytes from the buffer of controller is copied to the memory. Now if these data need to be displayed, the device controller for the display reads the data from the memory and sends the signal to the CRT to display the data. In this case, the operating system initializes the device controller with required information such as address of the bytes to be read, number of characters per line, and the number of lines on the screen to be displayed.

For the purpose of communication with the processor, each device controller has a set of following device registers (see Fig. 2.3):

Control Register

These are used by the processor to configure and control the device. This register is meant to write the data, i.e., the processor can alter but not read them back.

Status Register

These registers provide the status information about an I/O device to the processor. This register is meant to be read-only, i.e., the processor can only read the data and is not allowed to alter.

Data Register

This register is used to read and write data from/to the I/O device.

The operating system performs I/O operations with the use of these registers only by sending commands to an appropriate register. The parameters of the commands are loaded first into the

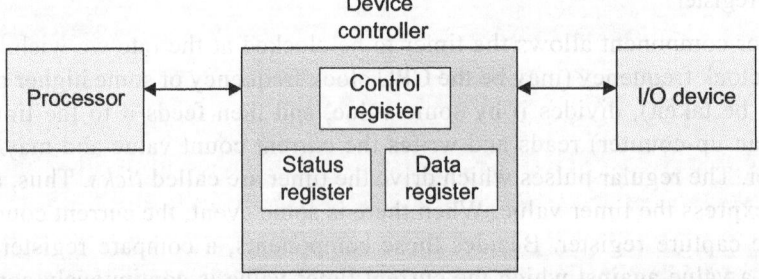

Fig. 2.3 Device controller registers

controller's registers. When the command is accepted, the control is passed to the controller by the processor. When the control is passed to the controller, the processor is free to do other job during this time. When a command has been completed, the controller triggers an interrupt to inform the operating system that the desired operation has been completed. The operating system after gaining the control again gets the result of the operation and checks device status by reading information from the controller's registers.

2.5 DEVICE DRIVER

The most challenging task for an operating system is to manage the I/O devices in a computer system. It acts as an interface between devices and computer system. This interface should be simple, easy to use for a user, and preferably same for any type of device. However, today there are a myriad of input and output devices. Each I/O device has its own detail and complexity. In this case, operating system needs to be changed to incorporate every newly introduced device. Therefore, the I/O functionalities should be treated separately in the operating system so that the other parts of the operating system are not affected. The software which deals with the I/O is known as *I/O software*. In I/O software, there are two types of modules. First module deals with the general functionalities when interfacing with any type of device, i.e., these functions are common while interfacing with any I/O device and are known as device-independent I/O software. For example, there should be a general interface for any type of device. The second module provides device-specific code for controlling it and is known as device driver. The second module in fact takes care of the peculiarity and details of a particular device, i.e., how to read or write data to the device. In this way, operating system does not need to change its code again and again to incorporate any new device. Its I/O software takes care of all the I/O devices to be interfaced with the system without changing the OS code.

Each device needs a device-specific code in the form of device driver for controlling it. As discussed earlier, each device has a device controller that has some device registers for performing I/O operations on the device. But the number of device registers and the nature of commands for performing I/O operations vary from device to device. Therefore, to communicate with each type of device controller, a specific code in the form of a device driver is written, which takes care of the specific device controller registers and the commands. Thus, the device drivers act as a layer that hides the differences among the device controllers.

The device drivers are part of the operating system, but not necessarily part of the OS kernel. These are software modules that help the operating system such that there is easy access to the hardware. They need to be installed on the system for each device we need to use. In general, the manufacturer of the device supplies the device drivers. However, the device drivers may differ according to the operating system type and its version.

The device driver communicates with the device controllers and thereby with the device with the help of interrupt-handling mechanism. When the device controller interacts with the actual device, the data are transferred between the actual device and the controller according to the I/O operation, i.e., the data from the device are written to the controller's register in case of input operation or the data from the controller's register are sent to the device in case of output operation. After completion of I/O operation at the level of device and device controller, the device controller generates an interrupt to the device driver

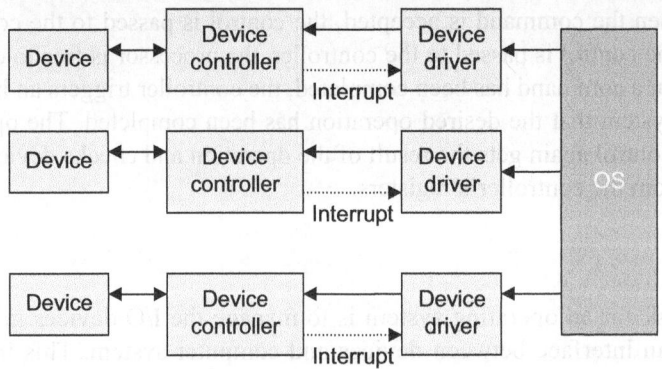

Fig. 2.4 Functioning of device driver

(see Fig. 2.4). The interrupt service routine is executed in order to handle a specific interrupt for an I/O operation. This routine extracts the required information from the device controller's register and performs the necessary actions. After the completion of an ISR, the blocked device driver is unblocked and may run again.

2.6 PROBLEMS IN THE DESIGN OF MODERN OSs

When the multi-programming concept was introduced, a new generation of OSs was evolved. The modern OSs have multi-programming as an inherent concept. But when the multi-user time-sharing and multi-tasking concepts were developed, many problems arose for their implementation. To implement them, there was no architectural support. For example, the Intel microprocessor series till 80186 was not able to support the multi-user and multi-tasking concepts. Let us first discuss the problems occurred:

- Since the multi-programming concept allows the switching between the processes, there was a need to preserve the state of the process that was stopped temporarily so that it can be resumed when the processor switches back to it. Similarly, the state of the process where the processor switches currently needs to be loaded. In this way, a mechanism is needed to save and load the state of a process.
- Since the resources are limited as compared to the number of processes in a system, the processes need to share them. There are several problems due to this environment. One of them is that the processes may try to access the devices at the same time. There should be a mechanism so that the processes have an orderly access to the devices.
- The multiple processes sometimes may be trapped in a deadlock situation while accessing the resources. Suppose there are two processes P1 and P2 and two resources R1 and R2 in a system. P1 is using R1 and needs to have R2 to continue its execution. But R2 is used by P2 which needs to have R1 to continue its execution. In this situation, both the processes are waiting for each other to release the resource to continue thereby causing a deadlock situation.
- Another problem in multi-programming environment is that all the processes may try to update the contents of a memory location at the same time.
- Since all the processes and operating system reside in the main memory, a process may try to access the memory locations of another process or even access the operating system area in the memory. It may corrupt the operating system or some process.

- A process may engage the processor for an infinite time by having such instructions in it and does not release it. In this case, the other processes will be in wait for that process to release the processor.
- A process while accessing any I/O device may do any illegal operation on it thereby damaging the devices. For instance, in disk operating system (DOS), there is no protection of devices from the user programs. A user may write some virus programs and do some mischievous operation on the devices, e.g., infecting the boot disk by loading the virus program in boot sector, jamming the printer, etc.

All the problems discussed earlier were faced in the design of the multi-programming-based operating systems. The single-user operating systems like DOS were not able to provide the solutions to these problems.

2.7   NEED FOR PROTECTION

Some of the problems discussed earlier may be solved with the help of software support from the operating system. For example, the solution to deadlock or accessing the same memory location is provided by the operating system through deadlock avoidance or detection algorithm and semaphore, respectively. But there are some issues which may not be implemented without the architectural support. Since the problems discussed earlier largely address one problem, i.e., the protection, the processor architecture of that time (e.g., Intel 8086, 8088, 80186) was not able to provide any kind of protection. Any user was able to write a program that might access the memory area of operating system and corrupt it. Any user was able to enter in the memory area of any other user area. These problems initiated the demand for a mechanism that the processes and even the operating system were not protected as there was no provision to prohibit the user from illegal accessing of memory area or I/O device. Further, memory areas divided among various processes and the operating system were not protected.

After this demand for protection, various architectures were developed to incorporate the protection mechanisms such that the multi-programming-based operating system could be implemented. Thus, this protection demand emerged from the operating system implementation need and the result was the new processor architecture. The Motorola MC68000 family of microprocessors, AT&T UNIX operating system, and Intel 80286 and its other derivatives are examples of the modified processors that considered the protection need in multi-programming operating systems.

2.8   HARDWARE PROTECTION FOR MULTI-PROGRAMMING/ MULTI-TASKING

To address all the problems described, various architectural support/modifications taken are discussed as follows.

2.8.1   Multiple Modes of Operation

The basic idea in implementing the protection feature is to separate the regions of operating system and users in order to protect the operating system and hardware devices from damage by any malicious user/program. The modern operating systems separate code and data of the operating system from the code and data of the user processes. This separation was termed as dual mode operation. This dual mode operation has two modes: the kernel mode and the user mode. The processor now can execute in one of the mode at a time, either in the kernel mode or in the user mode. The contemporary processors implement this by having a mode bit in the *program status word*

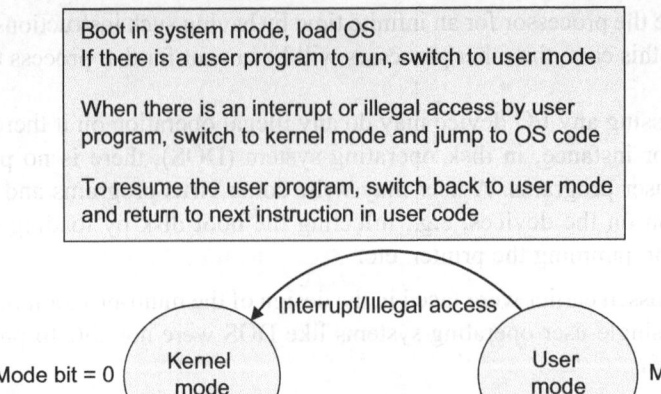

> Boot in system mode, load OS
> If there is a user program to run, switch to user mode
>
> When there is an interrupt or illegal access by user program, switch to kernel mode and jump to OS code
>
> To resume the user program, switch back to user mode and return to next instruction in user code

Interrupt/Illegal access

Mode bit = 0   Kernel mode   User mode   Mode bit = 1

Set user mode

User program

Fig. 2.5 Mode switching

(PSW) to specify whether the processor is executing in kernel-mode code or user-mode code. The PSW is a collection of control registers in the processor. The control registers control the operation of the processor itself. Initially, the mode bit is set to 0, thereby meaning that the control is with the operating system when the computer system is started. When a user process wants to gain the control, the mode bit is set to 1 and the user is able to execute in his own area but prevented all access to the kernel memory space. However, if a user attempts to access any illegal memory area or instruction, the processor generates an illegal access exception and the mode is switched to the kernel mode. Similarly, if a user wants to access any hardware, the mode is switched from the user to kernel mode. The mode switching is shown in Fig. 2.5.

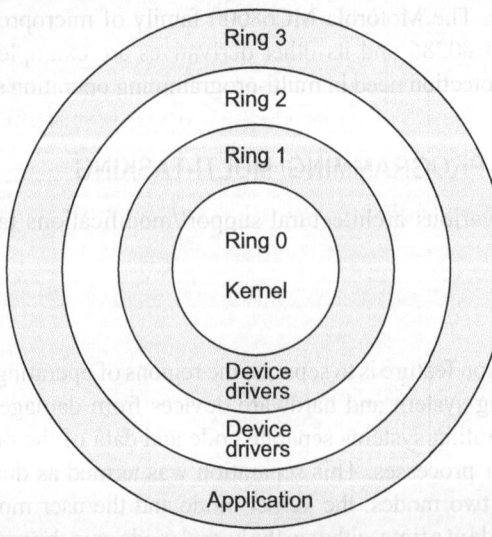

Ring 3

Ring 2

Ring 1

Ring 0

Kernel

Device drivers

Device drivers

Application

Fig. 2.6 Intel privilege rings

Since the operating system has more privilege over user processes, the kernel mode has high privilege as compared to user mode. This is why the kernel mode is also called *privileged mode*. The kernel mode is also known as *system mode, monitor mode,* or *supervisor mode*. Thus, the system is booted first with the kernel mode and the operating system has all the access to the hardware, thereby initializing a protected environment.

There are multiple levels of protection known as *privilege rings* or *levels*. For example, the MC68000 processor was designed to have two privilege rings as dual mode. The AT&T UNIX was designed with three levels: kernel, shell, and the application. The kernel here is the innermost level and the application is on the outermost level.

The Intel modern processors come with four privilege rings (0–3) as shown in Fig. 2.6. In this architecture, the operating system is in the innermost level (most trusted) having the highest level of privilege and protected. The outermost level (least trusted) is application level having the least privilege. The other two levels are for device drivers having the high privilege as compared to the application but less privileged than the OS.

2.8.2 Input–Output Protection

The multiple mode operation of the system enhances the security between the user processes and operating system. But, the users should also be prohibited to access the I/O devices directly. Therefore, all I/O instructions are privileged and the privilege to access the devices is with operating system only. It means no user process can access the I/O device directly. To access any I/O device, the process may request the operating system through a *system call*. The system call is a user request to the operating system which is interpreted and executed on the hardware by the operating system on the behalf of the user. In this way, all I/O instructions are privileged thereby providing another level of security. In this sense, the instructions are divided into two parts: *privileged instructions* and *unprivileged instructions*. The illegal instructions mentioned in previous section are unprivileged instructions only. The user process cannot execute privileged instructions. In fact, whenever there is a system call in the user process, the control switches from the user mode to the kernel mode thereby transferring the control to the operating system. After servicing the system call, the mode is again switched back to the user mode and control is with the user process again (see Fig. 2.7). This privilege mechanism with mode switching ensures that the user never gains control to access the devices directly, thereby protecting the I/O devices.

The system call being used in a user process is basically a software interrupt. As a result of this software interrupt, the control is passed to an appropriate interrupt handler and the mode is switched to the kernel mode. The operating system determines and verifies the details of the interrupt occurred, executes the interrupt handler, and then returns the control back to the user by switching mode to user mode.

2.8.3 Memory Protection

Besides the earlier-mentioned protection, a user program can still access the memory region of some other user process. It means the user processes are not protected from any illegal access by some process or any malicious process. Moreover, a user process may access the IVT in memory and may change the address of any interrupt handler and do some illegal operations on the devices. There should be some mechanism to protect the memory regions of each process as well as the operating system. For this kind of protection, each process must know its boundary of execution, i.e., there should be a start address and a limit address that defines the boundary of each process. This was supported by the architecture in the form of *base register* and *limit register*. Each process has defined limits to its memory space. The start address of a process is stored in the base register and the maximum size of the process is stored in the limit register. Whenever a process starts executing and references some memory location (say, *m*), it is checked against the base register. If the memory location being referenced is greater than or equal to the base register and less than the addition of base address and limit, then only it proceeds for execution; otherwise it is considered as illegal memory access. In case of illegal access, the control is transferred to the operating system by switching the mode back to the kernel mode as shown in Fig. 2.8. This check for memory protection is done by the hardware for each process. The base

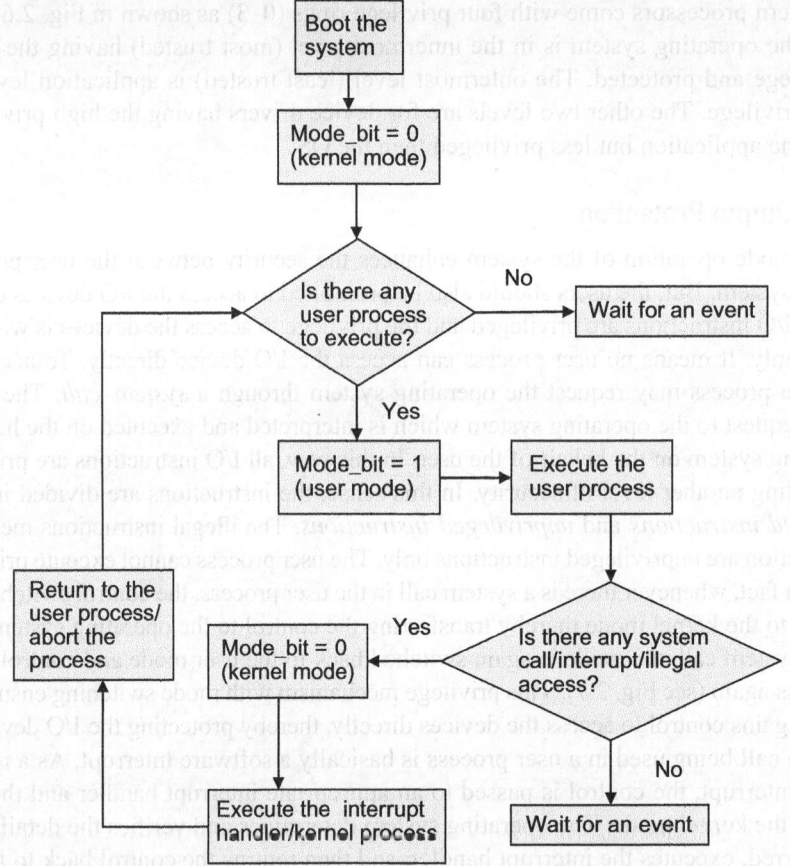

Fig. 2.7   I/O protection flow

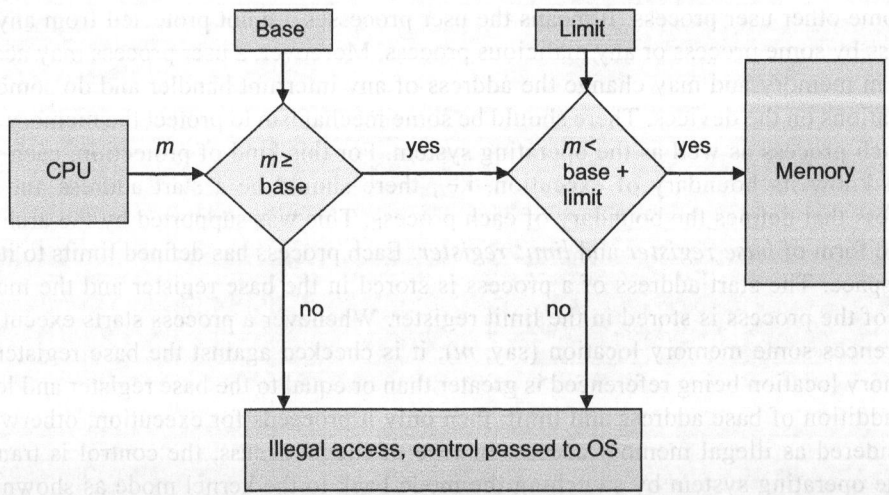

Fig. 2.8   Memory protection

and limit registers are updated for every process (which is to be executed) in the kernel mode by the operating system. This mechanism thus prevents any user process to access or modify another user process or operating system area.

Example 2.1

Figure 2.9 shows the memory structure of some processes and operating system with their legal memory addresses. The base and limit registers are loaded with the addresses 1050 and 1000, respectively. Suppose P1 and P2 reference the memory locations 2040 and 3052, respectively. Check if the processes will be allowed to execute.

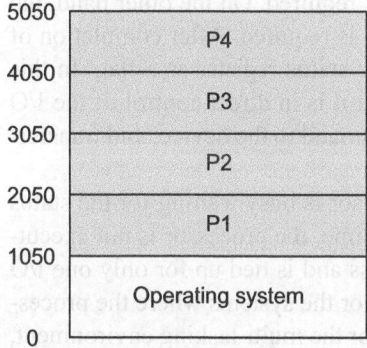

Fig. 2.9 Memory protection

Solution

P1 is first checked against the base register 1050. In this case, the reference memory location of P1, i.e., 2040, is greater than base register. Now, P1 is checked against the sum of base and limit registers, i.e., $1050 + 1000 = 2050$. Since it is less than 2050, it will be allowed to execute.

On the other hand, if P2 references a memory location 3052, it is not allowed to execute because it violates the second criterion, i.e., $m < \text{limit} + \text{base}$. So the control is passed to the operating system as it attempts to access the memory location of P3.

2.8.4 CPU Protection

There may be some situation that a user process gains the control of the processor and has a set of instructions that are being executed for an infinite time and thereby not relinquishing the control of the processor. Thus, it leads to the situation when the processor is also not safe and must be protected from the user processes. There should be a mechanism such that the processor does not get trapped infinitely in a user process and returns the control back to the operating system. To achieve this, again the hardware support is required. A timer is used that interrupts the processor after a specified period of time. The timer is implemented with the clock and a counter. All the operations related to the timer modification are executed by the operating system as these are treated as privileged operations. The operating system sets the counter for a time period. Every time the clock ticks, the counter is decremented and an interrupt is generated when the counter reaches to 0. On the generation of interrupt, the control is switched to the operating system. In this way, no user process can hold the processor beyond a limit and has to relinquish it after a specified period of time, thereby protecting the processor. The timers are also helpful in implementation of multiuser time-sharing systems. In these systems each user gets a uniform time to execute his process. This is achieved by setting the timer for a fixed period of time and interrupt is sent when the time of a user process expires.

2.9 INPUT–OUTPUT COMMUNICATION TECHNIQUES

There are three techniques by which I/O operation can be performed on a device. These are known as I/O communication techniques. These techniques are used to have a mode of communication between the user request and the device, taking device characteristics into account.

2.9.1 Programmed I/O

Whenever a process is being executed and the processor finds an I/O instruction, it issues the commands to the appropriate device controller. The device controller performs the operation by interfacing to the physical device and then sets the status of the operation in a status register. But this is the job of the processor to check whether the operation has been executed or not. For this purpose, it continually checks the status of the operation until it finds the operation is complete. Therefore, the process is busy waiting until the I/O operation has not been performed.

The I/O operation is performed using a processor register and a status register. The device puts the data in the processor register when input operation is required. On the other hand, the device reads the data from the register when output operation is required. After completion of the I/O operation, the status of the operation is written in the status register as a flag. In this way, the processor executes the instruction in such a way that it is in direct control of the I/O operation, i.e., sensing a device status, sending read/write command to the device, and transferring the data.

There is one disadvantage of this technique that the processor is busy waiting for the status of the operation while the I/O module is performing. At this time, the processor is not executing other instructions of the same process or any other process and is tied up for only one I/O operation. For the I/O operations that consume very less time or the systems where the processor has no other job to do, the programmed I/O is better. But for the multi-tasking environment, programmed I/O is not a better choice where several processes are in queue waiting for the processor.

2.9.2 Interrupt-driven I/O

In programmed I/O technique, the processor time is wasted as it continually interrogates the status of I/O operation. It would be better if the I/O operation is started and the processor switches to another process to be executed instead of waiting. Therefore, the processor issues I/O command to the device controller for performing I/O operation and switches to another processor by calling the scheduler that schedules the process to it. The question is how the processor knows when the I/O is complete. This is done through the interrupt mechanism. When the operation is complete, the device controller generates an interrupt to the processor. In fact, the processor checks for the interrupt after every instruction cycle. After detecting an interrupt, the processor will stop what it was doing by saving the state of the current process and resumes the previous process (where I/O occurred) by executing appropriate interrupt service routine. The processor then performs the data transfer for the I/O operation.

For example, when a user requests a read operation from an input device, the processor issues the read command to the device controller. The device controller after receiving this command starts reading from the input device. The input data from the device needs to be stored on the controller's registers. But it may take some time and this time is sufficient to serve any other process. Therefore, the processor is scheduled to execute any other process in the queue. As soon as the data become available in the controller's register, the controller signals an interrupt to the processor. The appropriate interrupt handler is run so that the processor is able to get the data from the controller's register and save them in the memory.

Since the modern operating systems are interrupt driven, they service the I/O requests using the interrupt mechanism only.

2.9.3 Input/output Using DMA

When a user wants to input some data through the keyboard or some data are printed on the screen after every character to be input or output, the processor intervention is needed to transfer the data between the device controller and the memory. Suppose a user inputs a string of 50 characters length and for every character to input there is 10 millisecond time required. It means between two inputs there is a 10-ms time duration, thereby having an interrupt. It causes to have a number of interrupts just to enter 50 characters long string. Thus, when the data are large, interrupt-driven I/O is not efficient. In this case, instead of reading one character at a time through the processor, the block of characters is read. This operation is known as *direct memory access* (DMA), i.e., without the processor intervention. In DMA, the interrupt will not be generated after every character input. Rather a block of characters is maintained and this block is read or written. So when a user wishes to read or write this block, the processor sends the command to the DMA controller and rest of the responsibility to do I/O operation for one block is given to this DMA controller. The processor passes the following information to the DMA controller:

- The type of request (read or write)
- The address of the I/O device to which I/O operation is to be carried out
- The start address of the memory where the data need to be written or read from alongwith the total number of words to be written or read. This address and the word count are then copied by the DMA controller in its registers.

Let us suppose, we need to perform a read operation from the disk. The CPU first sends the information mentioned above to the DMA controller. The information is stored in the disk controller registers. There are three registers as follows:

- *Memory address register* states the address where the read/write operation is to be performed.
- *Byte count register* stores the number of bytes to be read or written
- *Control register* specifies the I/O port to be used, type of operation, the data transfer unit, etc.

The DMA controller initiates the operation by requesting the disk controller to read data from the specified address and store in its buffer. The buffer data are then transferred to the specified memory location. When this write is complete, the disk controller sends an acknowledgement signal to the DMA controller. The DMA controller increments the memory location for the next byte and decrements the byte count. The disk controller again copies the next byte in the buffer and transfers the byte to the memory. This process goes on until the byte count becomes zero. When the full I/O operation is complete, the DMA controller sends an interrupt to the processor to let it know that the I/O operation has been completed.

Thus, in DMA-based I/O, instead of generating multiple interrupts after every character, a single interrupt is generated for a block, thereby reducing the involvement of the processor. The processor just starts the operation and then finishes the operation by transferring the data between the device controller and memory.

2.10 MAGNETIC DISKS

A magnetic disk is a widely used secondary storage device in the computer system. It consists of a set of circular shaped metal or plastic platters coated with magnetic material. Both the surfaces of each platter are used to store the information on the disk by recording data

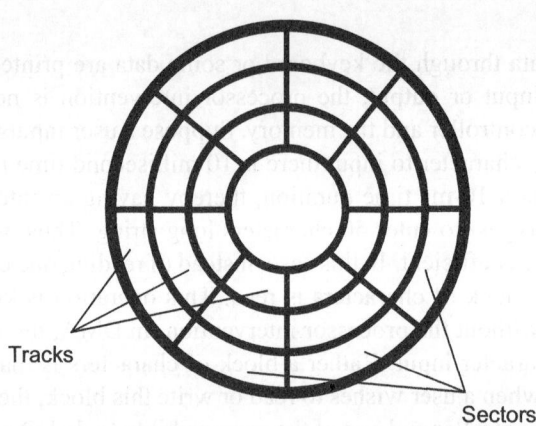

Tracks

Sectors

Fig. 2.10 Track and sectors on a disk platter surface

magnetically. To organize the data on the disk, each platter is logically divided in a concentric set of rings called *tracks*. There may be thousands of tracks per surface of each platter depending on the storage capacity of the disk. Each track is further divided into *sectors* (see Fig. 2.10). A sector is the smallest unit where the actual data are stored on the disk. Each track may consist of hundreds of a sectors. The size of sector may be variable or fixed. But in contemporary systems, sector size is fixed. The fixed sector size is 512 bytes. Thus, the data are transferred to and from the disk in sectors only.

The older disks store the same number of sectors per track as shown in Fig. 2.10. But, as we move outward, the number of sectors per track may be increased as there is more space on the outer tracks as compared to the inner tracks. The modern disks exploit this feature and store more number of tracks as we move from the innermost track to the outermost track. There can be various zones of tracks storing different capacities of sectors. For example Zone 1 has three tracks and each track in this zone stores 90 sectors. Similarly, Zone 2 has four tracks and each track in this zone stores 120 sectors.

The magnetic disk is mounted on a *disk drive* consisting of the following components:

Spindle
The part where the disk spins around, i.e., the spindle is a mechanism through which it rotates the disk.

Read/write head
A device that is able to read from or write to the sectors of a track on one platter surface, i.e., to transfer the information it just moves above the surface of a platter. The head may be either movable or fixed. In fixed-head disk, there is one head per track whereas in movable-head disk, there is only one head for all the tracks. The movable head moves to all the tracks. In movable-head, however, the head is separate for both surfaces of a platter, i.e., each platter has two heads.

Disk arm
The head is mounted on an arm that can be extended or retracted for positioning the head on any track. In case of a movable-head disk, there are multiple arms depending on the number of platters.

A disk in common use comes with multiple platters and movable read-write head mechanism as shown in Fig. 2.11. The tracks that appear at the same location on each platter form a *cylinder*. Whenever we need to store sequentially related information, it should be stored in a cylinder. This is done by first storing the information on a track of a platter and continuing the information on the same track of others platters.

There may be some error due to misalignment of the head or interference of magnetic fields. Due to this reason, some gap (see Fig. 2.12) is required between any two tracks (inter-track gap) and similarly between any two sectors (inter-sector gap). This gap avoids any error due to misalignment or the effect of magnetic field on adjacent tracks or sectors.

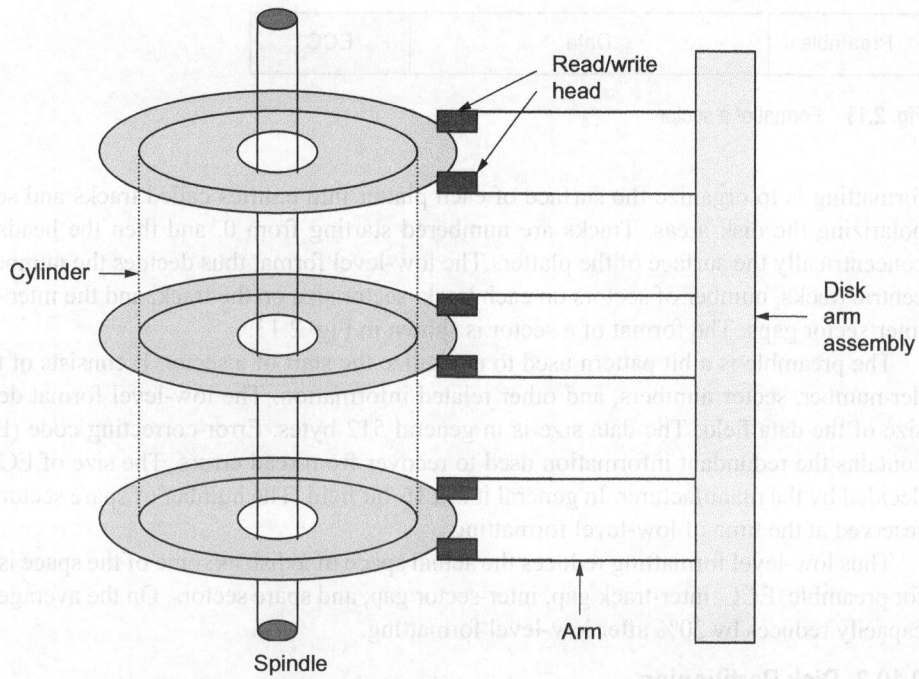

Fig. 2.11   Physical structure of a disk

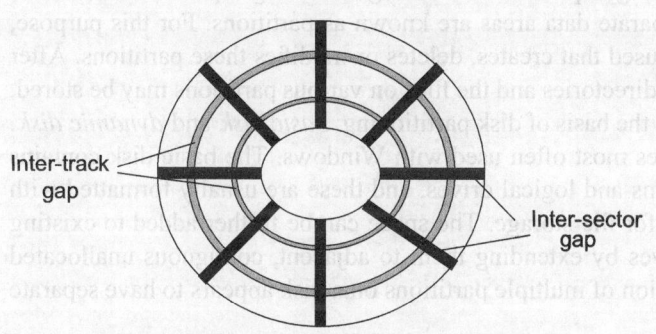

Fig. 2.12   Inter-track and inter-sector gap on the disk surface

The disk starts functioning with the help of a motor. The drive motor spins the disk at a high speed and the head performs read/write on a portion of the surface of the platter rotating beneath it. The processor initiates a disk read operation by first writing a command, then the logical block number from where the data are to be read, and finally the destination memory address to a port, which is associated with the disk controller. To find the location on the disk, the head first locates the desired track by moving on it and then the platter under the head rotates such that the desired sector comes under the head. Disk controller reads the sector and performs a DMA transfer into the memory. On completion of the DMA transfer, the controller sends the interrupt to processor for notifying it the completion of the operation.

2.10.1 Disk Formatting

The disk formatting prepares the raw disk to be used. There are three steps in disk formatting: low-level formatting, disk partitioning, and logical formatting. The *low-level formatting* is performed by the manufacturer and the other two steps are performed by the operating system and therefore are linked to it. The manufacturer of the disk performs the low-level formatting and is able to test the disk and later on use the disk for storage. The purpose of low-level

Fig. 2.13 Format of a sector

formatting is to organize the surface of each platter into entities called tracks and sectors, by polarizing the disk areas. Tracks are numbered starting from 0, and then the heads polarize concentrically the surface of the platters. The low-level format thus decides the number of concentric tracks, number of sectors on each track, sector size on the track, and the inter-track and inter-sector gaps. The format of a sector is shown in Fig. 2.13.

The preamble is a bit pattern used to recognize the start of a sector. It consists of the cylinder number, sector numbers, and other related information. The low-level format decides the size of the data field. The data size is in general 512 bytes. Error-correcting code (ECC) that contains the redundant information used to recover from read errors. The size of ECC field is decided by the manufacturer. In general it is a 16-bit field. The number of spare sectors are also reserved at the time of low-level formatting.

Thus low-level formatting reduces the actual space of a disk as some of the space is reserved for preamble, ECC, inter-track gap, inter-sector gap, and spare sectors. On the average, the disk capacity reduces by 20% after low-level formatting.

2.10.2 Disk Partitioning

On a disk, separate areas need to be created as per the convenience of the user to keep his work separate. Thus, disk partitioning is process of dividing the storage space of a hard disk into separate data areas. These separate data areas are known as partitions. For this purpose, a partition editor program may be used that creates, deletes or-modifies these partitions. After creation of different partitions, the directories and the files on various partitions may be stored. There may be two types of disks on the basis of disk partitioning: *basic disk* and *dynamic disk*.

Basic disks are the storage types most often used with Windows. The basic disk contains partitions, such as primary partitions and logical drives, and these are usually formatted with a file system to become a volume for file storage. The space can be further added to existing primary partitions and logical drives by extending them to adjacent, contiguous unallocated space on the same disk. The provision of multiple partitions on a disk appears to have separate hard disk drives to the user.

The following operations can be performed only on basic disks:

- Primary and extended partitions can be created and deleted.
- Logical drives within an extended partition can be created and deleted.
- A partition can be formated and marked as active.

The first physical sector on a basic disk contains a data structure known as the *master boot record* (MBR). The MBR contains the following:

- A boot program (up to 442 bytes in size)
- A disk signature (a unique 4-byte number)
- A partition table (up to four entries)
- An end-of-MBR marker (always 0x55AA)

Thus, there may be two types of partitions based on the above discussion: *primary* and *extended*. There may be multiple primary partitions but one of the primary partitions is used to store and boot an operating system. The primary partition that is used to boot the system is set active to indicate that this is the *boot partition*. If more than one or no primary partition is set active, the system will not boot. The extended partition is divided into logical drives and is viewed as a container for logical drives where data are located. This partition is formattable and is assigned a drive letter.

Another data structure known as the *partition table* stores the information about each partition such as its starting sector, size of each partition, etc. The partition table is also stored at sector 0 as shown in Fig. 2.14.

Dynamic disks, on the othe hand, have the ability to create volumes that span multiple disks. The volumes thus

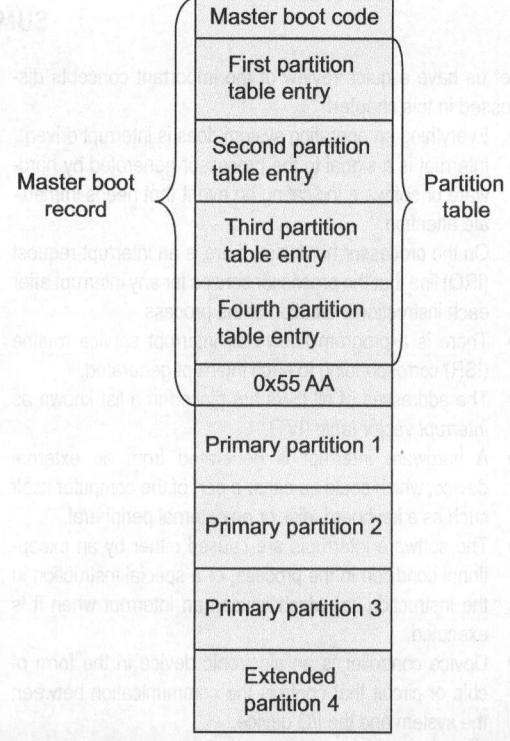

Fig. 2.14   MBR partition

created are known as dynamic volumes. The volume management is very flexible in case of dynamic disks as they use a database to track information about dynamic volumes on the disk and about other dynamic disks in the system. The following operations can be performed only on dynamic disks:

- Create and delete simple, striped, mirrored, and RAID-5 volumes (striped, mirrored, and RAID will be discussed in detail in Chapter 15).
- Remove a mirror from a mirrored volume or break the mirrored volume into two volumes.
- Repair mirrored or RAID-5 volumes.

Another step in disk formatting is logical formatting concerned with the operating system. This is also known as high-level format. This operation is performed for each partition. The logical formatting operation lays down a boot block in the partition and creates a file system. The initial file system data structures such as free and allocated lists or bitmaps, root directory, and empty file system are also stored. Since different file systems may be there in different partitions, the partition table entries will indicate which partition contains which file system.

SUMMARY

Let us have a quick review of the important concepts discussed in this chapter:

- Everything an operating system does is interrupt driven.
- Interrupt is a signal to the processor generated by hardware or software indicating an event that needs immediate attention.
- On the processor hardware, there is an interrupt-request (IRQ) line that the processor senses for any interrupt after each instruction execution of the process.
- There is a program known as interrupt service routine (ISR) corresponding to each interrupt generated.
- The addresses of all ISRs are placed in a list known as *interrupt vector table* (IVT).
- A hardware interrupt is generated from an external device, which could be either a part of the computer itself such as a keyboard, disk or an external peripheral.
- The software interrupts are caused either by an exceptional condition in the process, or a special instruction in the instruction set which causes an interrupt when it is executed.
- Device controller is an electronic device in the form of chip or circuit that controls the communication between the system and the I/O device.
- To communicate with each type of device controller a specific code in the form of a device driver is written that takes care of the specific device controller registers and the commands. Thus, the device drivers act as a layer that hides the differences among the device controllers.
- The modern OSs separate code and data of the OS from the code and data of the user processes. This separation is termed as *dual mode operation*. The dual mode operation has two modes: the kernel mode and the user mode.

- Initially, the mode bit is set to 0, which means the control is with the OS when the computer system is started. When a user process wants to gain the control, the mode bit is set to 1 and the user is able to execute in his own area but is prevented all access to the kernel memory space.
- The Intel modern processors come with four privilege rings (0-3).
- All I/O instructions are privileged. To access any I/O device, the process may request to the OS in the form of a system call.
- The system call is a user request to the operating system which is interpreted and executed on the hardware by the operating system on the behalf of the user.
- In programmed I/O technique, the processor time is wasted as it continually interrogates the status of I/O operation.
- In DMA-based I/O, instead of generating multiple interrupts after every character, a single interrupt is generated for a block, thereby reducing the involvement of the processor.
- There are three following steps in disk formatting: low level formatting, disk partitioning, and logical formatting. The *low-level formatting* is performed by the manufacturer and the other two steps are performed by the OS and, therefore, they are linked to it.
- The purpose of low-level disk formatting is to organize the surface of each platter into entities called tracks and sectors, by polarizing the disk areas.
- Disk partitioning is a process of dividing the storage space of a hard disk into separate data areas. These separate data areas are known as partitions.
- *Primary partition* is a partition that is required to store and boot an operating system.

MULTIPLE CHOICE QUESTIONS

1. The modern OSs are _____.
   - (a) programmed-I/O driven
   - (b) interrupt-driven
   - (c) software-driven
   - (d) hardware-driven

2. Interrupt is a signal to the _____ generated by hardware or software.
   - (a) memory
   - (b) device controller
   - (c) processor
   - (d) none

3. IVT is generally placed in _____ memory.
   - (a) low
   - (b) high
   - (c) disk
   - (d) none

4. The number of hardware interrupts is limited by the number of _____.
   - (a) processes
   - (b) processors
   - (c) IRQ lines
   - (d) none

5. _____ is also known as an *adapter*.
   - (a) memory
   - (b) processor
   - (c) device
   - (d) device controller

6. Which of the device controller register is read-only?
   - (a) control
   - (b) status
   - (c) data
   - (d) none

7. Which of the device controller register is write-only?
   (a) control
   (b) status
   (c) data
   (d) none

8. Initially, the mode bit is set to _____.
   (a) 1
   (b) 0
   (c) 2
   (d) none

9. The base and limit registers are updated for every process in _____ mode.

   (a) user
   (b) kernel
   (c) both user and kernel
   (d) none

10. The first physical sector on a basic disk contains a data structure known as the _____.
    (a) partition sector
    (b) basic sector
    (c) boot record
    (d) master boot record

REVIEW QUESTIONS

1. What is an interrupt? What are its types?

2. What are the tasks to be executed when an interrupt arrives on the processor?

3. What is IVT?

4. What is ISR?

5. What is a trap?

6. Provide some examples when software interrupt is generated.

7. Provide some examples when hardware interrupt is generated.

8. How are multiple interrupts handled?

9. Differentiate between blocking and non-blocking I/O devices.

10. What is a timer? Explain its role in operating system.

11. What is a device controller? How does it work?

12. What is a device driver? Explain its functioning with device controller and operating system.

13. What were the basic problems in multi-programming-based modern operating systems?

14. What is the need of a dual mode protection?

15. What is the need of memory protection?

16. What is the need of processor protection?

17. What is the need of I/O protection?

18. Explain the physical structure of a magnetic disk.

19. What is a cylinder on a disk?

20. What is disk partitioning?

21. Differentiate between primary and extended partitions.

22. What is MBR?

BRAIN TEASERS

1. The interrupt number of an hardware interrupt is 8. At what location in the IVT, its ISR address will be found?

2. Is nested interrupt possible? If yes, how are they handled?

3. All I/O instructions are privileged. Then, how does a user access the devices?

4. Which of the following instructions should be privileged?
   (a) Switch from user mode to kernel mode
   (b) Updating base and limit register
   (c) Clear memory location
   (d) Set value of timer
   (e) Read a clock
   (f) Interrupts are disabled

   (g) Executing a loop to enter user data
   (h) Load a value in processor register
   (i) Abort a process
   (j) Read input from keyboard
   (k) Send a file to printer to print
   (l) A global variable in the user process reinitialized

5. Inter-sector and inter-track gaps are used on the disk to avoid errors. How do these gaps affect storage utilization on the disk?

6. Study the DOS and Windows operating systems with reference to dual mode protection and find out which operating system provides a better protection in terms of multi-tasking.

3 Resource Management

3.1 INTRODUCTION

The hardware resources are not easy to interface. There is a lot of complexity in using them. Moreover, there are very limited resources in the system and multiple processes. Owing to this, there should be some schedule and management for accessing and using the resources. The OS performs all these functionalities. It schedules the limited resources among multiple tasks and gives an easy interface to I/O devices. The hardware resources are abstracted or transformed into virtual devices. The virtual devices are easy to work from the user's viewpoint. The resources are of three types: hardware, virtual, and software. In this chapter, responsibilities of the OS as a resource manager are discussed, along with the types of resources and the goals of resource management. The functions and the components of the resource manager and all the components of resource management are also discussed. Since all these components are part of the operating system, all of them, along with other parts, will be discussed in different chapters of this book.

3.2 FUNCTIONS OF A RESOURCE MANAGER

The OS as a resource manager performs the following functions:

3.2.1 Resource Abstraction/Transformation

As discussed in Chapter 1, it is really difficult to work with hardware devices. To perform read or write function from I/O devices, we need to know the structure of every device in the form of registers: data registers, control registers, and so on. A user or programmer cannot work efficiently if he or she works so close to the hardware, since there are numerous details that need to be taken care of; thus, hardware resources are complex interfaces to work with. To ease the job of the user, the OS hides the complex details of the hardware and presents I/O devices to them in such a form that it is easy to interface with these devices. In fact, actual hardware devices are simulated in the form of a program known as virtual device. The user program interfaces with the virtual device, which, in turn, interfaces with the actual device. In this way, actual device has been abstracted or transformed into a virtual device and presents the user with an easy interface.

Learning Objectives

After reading this chapter, you should be able to understand:

- Operating system as a resource manager
- Transformation of hardware devices into virtual devices
- Time division multiplexing
- Space division multiplexing
- Resource scheduling
- Hardware resources
- Virtual resources
- Software resources
- Nature of resources
- Goals of resource management
- Working of resource manager
- Components of resource management

Virtual processor P1	Virtual processor P2	Virtual processor P3	Virtual processor P1	Virtual processor P2

CPU time slices

Fig. 3.1 Time division multiplexing

Besides providing an easy interface to the devices, another benefit of abstraction is that the concept of virtual devices provides the best utilization of the devices. For example, if multiple users have requested for printing, a single printer cannot handle all of them simultaneously. Moreover, it may mix up the output of many users. Therefore, multiple virtual printers can be created to give the impression to the users that they are using printers exclusively. In this way, actual single device is converted into multiple virtual devices. Another problem is that while executing the program, a fast CPU cannot cope up with the slow speed of I/O devices. It cannot wait to read from a card reader or keyboard or to print on the printer because all I/O devices are much slower as compared to the speed of a CPU. The third advantage of having virtual devices is that with the use of these devices, the program can be executed without any speed limit of I/O devices.

3.2.2 Resource Sharing/Multiplexing

As discussed in Section 3.2.1, since virtual devices will be more as compared to actual devices, there is a need to share the actual devices among the virtual devices. This is known as resource sharing or multiplexing. The resource sharing is done by following two methods:

Time Division Multiplexing

In this type of resource sharing, a device is shared by programs at different times. As seen in time-sharing systems, CPU time is shared by multiple programs. There is a single-processor, but with the help of virtual processors, single-processor time is shared. Every virtual processor is given time on the actual CPU. In this way, all virtual processes share the processor at different times. This is known as time division multiplexing or time-sharing (see Fig. 3.1).

Space Division Multiplexing

In this type of sharing, the actual device or resource is divided into smaller versions, and each virtual device is allocated a part of the resource. For example, main memory is divided into several partitions to accommodate several programs. It means that for every virtual processor, a virtual memory (VM) is needed, which is provided by dividing the actual memory (see Fig. 3.2). Similarly, hard-disk space is also divided to accommodate several programs to have the impression of separate secondary storage of their own. This is known as space-division multiplexing.

Virtual memory N
Virtual memory 3
Virtual memory 2
Virtual memory 1

Fig. 3.2 Space division multiplexing

3.2.3 Resource Scheduling

It is a well-known fact that all the resources are limited as compared to the number of processes. That is why there is a need to schedule the processes to the limited resources. There are many instances in the lifetime of a process when scheduling is needed. Whenever a job is submitted in a batch system, it is first stored in a job pool in the hard disk. A job pool is maintained in the hard disk for all incoming jobs entering the system first time. When there is a space in the main memory, a job is brought from job queue to the ready queue in the main memory. Ready queue is the place where jobs are fetched from job pool and the jobs wait there for their turn to be executed. The process of bringing a job from job pool to the ready queue is called *job scheduling*. However, there is no need of job scheduling in a time-sharing system because jobs directly enter the ready queue instead of a job queue. Now, in the ready queue, there are multiple processes that are ready and that need to be executed on a single CPU. There is a need to schedule the processes on CPU as it can execute only one process at a time. This is known as *process scheduling*. There may be many process scheduling algorithms depending on the situation and type of the system. Similarly, limited I/O devices are needed by a number of processes. There must be a scheduling mechanism for allocation of these devices to the processes. Likewise, there are memory, virtual memory, hard disk, and files that need to be scheduled for multiple processes. As students will study more components of the OS in the book, they will come across some more scheduling concepts.

There are many schedulers needed to perform scheduling. For example, for job scheduling, there is a scheduler called long-term scheduler. Similarly, for process scheduling, short-term scheduler is used. The scheduler is the software that selects the job to be scheduled according to a particular algorithm. We will study in detail all the schedulers and their functioning.

3.3 RESOURCE TYPES

In this section, all the resources available to the OS are described. The OS needs to manage all these resources, and hence to understand the functioning of an operating system, it is imperative to learn about these resources in detail. There are three types of resources (see Fig. 3.3): hardware, virtual, and software.

Hardware resources do not require any description. The major hardware resources are processors, memory, I/O devices, and hard disk. The hardware resources that have been abstracted or transformed into other resources are known as virtual resources. The processes, virtual memory, logical devices, and files are examples of virtual resources.

The next type of resources includes virtual resources. Since the hardware resources are very complex in nature for direct usage, there is a need to hide their details such that there is some abstraction in their use that makes it easy to use and interface them. For example, when there are multiple users to share a single CPU, they cannot use it. However, if separate processes are made for each user, then these processes act as virtual processors such that the computational power of a single CPU is shared among multiple users. Similarly, the physical memory available cannot accommodate the user programs that are larger than the size of the available memory. However, with the use of VM concept using hard disk, it is possible to accommodate

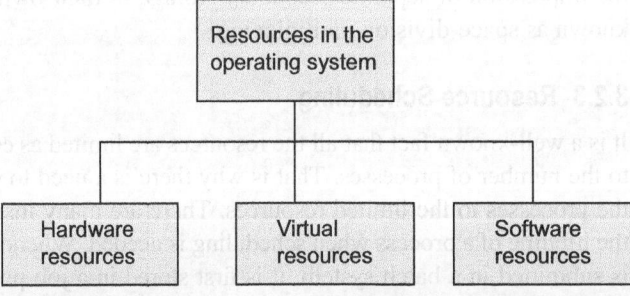

Fig. 3.3 Resource types

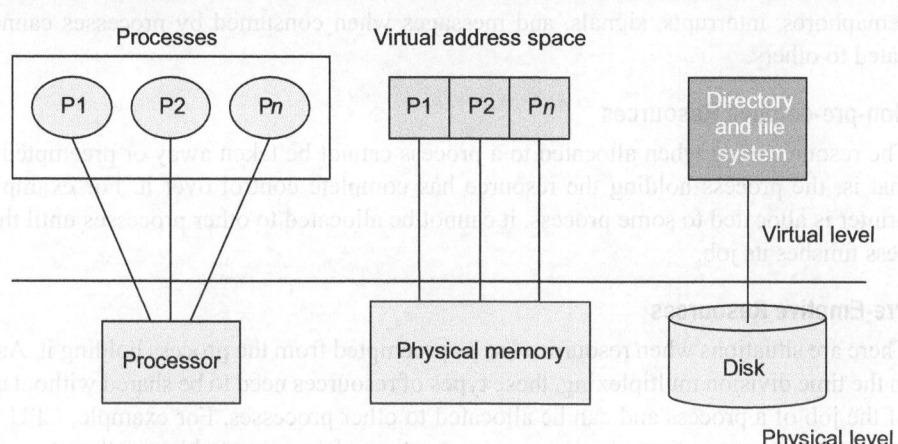

Fig. 3.4   Mapping of virtual resources to hardware Resources

the larger size programs in main memory in spite of less memory available. Similarly, hard disks are very complex if used directly. Therefore, to use them conveniently without taking care of its internal structure, the concept of files and directories are there. Files and directories are easily understandable concepts through which a user stores, updates, and retrieves his or her work on the hard disk. In this way, all hardware devices that are very complex in nature have been abstracted into virtual devices in such a manner that they do not present complex details to the user, but instead are very flexible, easy, and understandable (see Fig, 3.4).

Software resources have no direct relation with the hardware resources, that is, they are independent of hardware and virtual resources but may be used in managing them. For example, the starting address of a page (it is a logical entity used to represent the divisions of a process and is discussed in Chapter 10, Memory Management) will be stored in a page table. So the pages of a process need to obtain the slots in a page table. Therefore, page-table slot is a software resource. Similarly, for inter-process communication, messages in a message queue or mailbox are software resources. There is a resource used for synchronization between the processes known as semaphore. Semaphore is also a software resource. Other examples of software resources may be segment-table slot, file allocation table slots, local descriptor table (LDT) slots, global descriptor table (GDT) slots, and so on. The students become familiar with these resources as they progress through the chapters.

3.3.1 Nature of Resources

The resources can also be categorized according to their nature. The resources are consumable or non-consumable. Resources are also categorized based on the fact that when one resource is in use, whether it can be taken by a process or not. Based on these characteristics, the resources have been categorized as follows:

Non-consumable Resources

The resources that cannot be consumed but can be used, that is, when one process has used the resource, another can use it. For example, memory, CPU, and I/O devices are shared by the processes. All physical resources are non-consumable resources.

Consumable Resources

The resources when used by a process are consumed and cannot be used by others. For example, semaphores, interrupts, signals, and messages when consumed by processes cannot be allocated to others.

Non-pre-emptive Resources

The resources that when allocated to a process cannot be taken away or preempted by others, that is, the process holding the resource has complete control over it. For example, when a printer is allocated to some process, it cannot be allocated to other processes until the first process finishes its job.

Pre-Emptive Resources

There are situations when resources can be preempted from the process holding it. As explained in the time division multiplexing, these types of resources need to be shared without completion of the job of a process and can be allocated to other processes. For example, CPU when allocated to a process in time-sharing environment may be preempted by another process when its time slice expires. It may be possible that within the time slice, the process holding the resource has not completed its execution but will be preempted by other processes on the expiry of its time slice. However, the process will get CPU time again when its turn comes. However, this is not easy to do. When one process is interrupted, we know that it has to be resumed when its turn comes. Therefore, the state of one process is required to be saved. Therefore, pre-emption is achieved with overhead. This will be discussed in detail in process management.

3.4   GOALS OF RESOURCE MANAGEMENT

We discussed various types of resources in Section 3.3. These resources need to be shared among the multiple processes. While allocating the resources to processes, the resource manager in the OS should take care of the following goals:

Resource Utilization

As described in the Chapter 1, all the resources must be utilized as there is always a scarcity of resources in the operating system. For example, CPU should not be idle and must be utilized. There are many concepts in the OS that originated only from this goal. As we have already discussed, multi-programming, multi-tasking, and multi-threading (discussed in detail in Chapter 9) are the concepts in response to keep the CPU busy. Similarly, VM is the concept to utilize the available physical memory.

Protection

In multi-programming and Multi-tasking environment, processes should not be allowed to access other processes' area or operating-system area, as user processes and the OS both are in the main memory.

Synchronization

Resource manager should not allow the multiple processes to access a resource that is mutually exclusive. Otherwise, there may be a chaos and the results will be disastrous. For example, if multiple processes access a shared memory location to read and write simultaneously, then there will be wrong results. It means that synchronization must be provided among processes by the resource manager.

Deadlock

When multiple processes share the resources, it may be possible that one process P1 is holding a resource R1 and waiting for another resource R2. However, R2 is held by another process P2 and P2 is waiting for R1 held by P1. In this situation, both processes are waiting for one another to release the resource. This situation is called a *deadlock*, and the processes are in a deadlocked state. It is the responsibility of the resource manager to check that deadlock condition never occurs in a system.

Fair Distribution

In some systems, such as in multiuser systems, all processes should get equal time of the CPU. Therefore, in this case, resources should be allocated to all the processes such that the processes get a fair distribution.

3.5 HOW RESOURCE MANAGER WORKS?

When a process requests for some resource, there are chances that it does not get it immediately because some other process has already acquired it. Therefore, there are queues where the process waits for its turn. There may be a scheduling criterion for processes in the queue implemented by the resource manager. The resource manager, therefore, according to the scheduling criterion, selects the process in the queue and assigns the resource as seen in Fig. 3.5. However, before assigning the resource to the process, it performs the following tasks:

Accounting of Resources

The resource manager keeps the account of number of instances of a resource to check which instance is free and which already allocated. If there are no free resources, then the process is asked to wait.

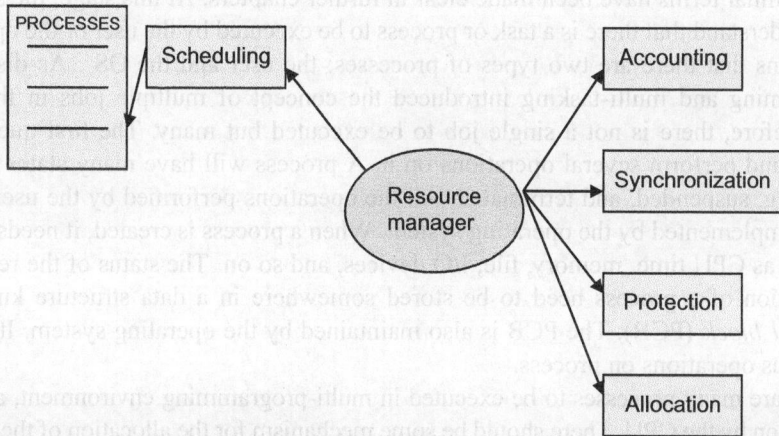

Fig. 3.5   Resource manager functions

Synchronization

If a process requests a resource, the resource manager first checks whether the resource is mutually and exclusively accessible or not. If it is not, then it cannot allocate the resource to the process and waits until it becomes free.

Protection

The resource manager should check the authorization access on a resource. If a resource is only readable, then a process should not be able to write on that resource. Moreover, if a process requests to access the memory location of the OS or other users, it should not be allowed to do so.

Scheduling

In a waiting queue, the way the processes are to be retrieved is decided by the resource manager. This process is known as scheduling.

Allocation

After passing through synchronization and protection checks, and if there is availability of resource, then the resource is finally allocated to the process.

After allocation of resources, the process uses and returns them to the resource manager so that other processes can use them.

3.6 COMPONENTS OF RESOURCE MANAGEMENT

In this section, all the components of resource manager are discussed. In other words, the way all the resources in the OS are managed and utilized is described. Largely, these components form the operating system. A brief overview of them is given here and will be discussed in detail in separate chapters throughout the book.

3.6.1 Process/task Management

The terms *job*, *process*, or *task* have been used interchangeably till now, but the meanings of all these and similar terms have been made clear in further chapters. At this stage, the students should only understand that there is a task or process to be executed by the user or the operating system. It means that there are two types of processes: the user and the OS . As discussed, multi-programming and multi-tasking introduced the concept of multiple jobs in the main memory. Therefore, there is not a single job to be executed but many. The first question is how to create and perform several operations on it. A process will have many states such as ready, executing, suspended, and terminated. All the operations performed by the user on the processes are implemented by the operating system. When a process is created, it needs certain resources such as CPU time, memory, file, I/O devices, and so on. The status of the resources and the execution of a process need to be stored somewhere in a data structure known as *process control block* (PCB). The PCB is also maintained by the operating system. It is very useful in various operations on process.

Since there are many processes to be executed in multi-programming environment, all compete for execution by the CPU. There should be some mechanism for the allocation of the CPU to one process. This is known as *process scheduling*. Process scheduling should be fair enough to all processes. The process scheduling job is performed by the operating system.

As discussed, the multiple processes have increased the problems and challenges for the operating system. When there are some shared resources, there is a need to control the access of resources by the processes such that at a time, only one process should have the control of that resource, otherwise, there may be inconsistencies. The mechanism to manage the accesses is called *process synchronization*. Process synchronization demands that the processes co-operate. For example, if two processes are sharing a data structure and if both try to access it simultaneously, there will be a data inconsistency; thus, process synchronization is a complex feature performed by the operating system. Similarly, co-operating processes need to communicate with each other. The OS provides an *inter-process communication* (IPC) mechanism by which the processes communicate. The importance of inter-process communication facility increases in a distributed environment where processes reside in geographically separate locations. The message passing system is a convenient method for this purpose.

Another problem in process management is deadlock as described in Section 3.5. The OS resolves the deadlock such that the system should be in the safe state and the normal execution of the system resumes.

To summarize, the OS performs the following process-management functions:

i) Process creation, deletion, and other operations on process
ii) Process scheduling
iii) Inter-process communication
iv) Process synchronization
v) Deadlock management

3.6.2 Memory Management

Memory management consists of two parts: main memory and virtual memory. The main memory is central to any operation done by the system. Whenever we want to execute on the system, we need to first store it in the main memory. It means that the user process should also be stored in the main memory first. The multi-programming and multi-tasking concepts require more than one process to be in the main memory. Therefore, memory must be partitioned first and allocated to the processes. The OS partitions and allocates the memory to the processes using some mechanisms. The size of memory partitions can be fixed or varied. The processes in these partitions can be allocated as contiguous or non-contiguous. The contiguous allocation means that the space allocated to a process should be contiguous in the memory. If small chunks of memory are scattered in the memory, then they cannot be allocated to a process due to their non-contiguous locations. On the other hand, non-contiguous allocation allocates the scattered memory chunks to the process in the memory. Non-contiguous allocation is implemented as *paging*. The OS keeps account of available memory partitions and occupies portions of memory. It also has an account of memory requirements of each process. In this way, keeping in view the available memory, the OS allocates the space to the process in the memory. All these concepts will be discussed in detail in the individual chapters. Based on these criteria, we have contiguous allocation and non-contiguous allocation methods. It should be noted that all memory-management mechanisms provided by the OS are supported by the hardware.

There is another concept in the memory management. When a user writes a program larger than the size of the memory, in normal memory management scheme, this program cannot be stored in the memory and executed. However, a VM concept has been invented that allows the programmers to write the programs of very large size, which, in spite of their size, can be stored and executed. The OS supports VM mechanism at some cost of secondary memory and speed. This will also be discussed further in detail.

To summarize, the OS performs the following memory management functions:

i) Keeps account of the allocated space to the processes and the available space
ii) Partitions the memory as per fixed partition or variable partition methods
iii) Allocates the memory to the processes as per contiguous or non-contiguous methods
iv) Manages VM

3.6.3 Secondary Storage Management

Since the main memory cannot accommodate every program or data, some other mechanism is required to store them. For this purpose, hard disk as a secondary storage is a widely used device for storing every program or data. We have already discussed that whenever a job enters the system, it is first entered in the job queue, which is maintained on the hard disk only. The system programs like compilers, debuggers, editors, and so on, including a large part of the operating system, are stored in the hard disk. In VM concept, we need to swap out some pages of the process from the main memory for some time. These swapped-out pages are also stored in the hard disk; thus, secondary storage provides the backup for the main memory to store programs and data. However, to utilize the hard disk for several purposes, there efficient management of space on it is required. There should be mechanisms for managing the free space on the hard disk, as it is necessary to know which part of the disk is free to be allocated to some program. Then, it must be decided how to utilize the available space in the best manner, that is, storage allocation methods should be devised. Swap space for VM should be allocated and reserved only for this purpose. Disk as a device may have queue of the processes to be accessed. Therefore, disk-scheduling techniques should be there for a better utilization of the hard disk.

To summarize, the OS performs the following secondary storage-management functions:

i) Free space management of secondary storage
ii) Allocation on secondary storage
iii) Disk scheduling
iv) Swap space management on secondary storage

3.6.4 File Management

Whenever we work on the computer system, the files are the entities where we store our work. Either we write a Word file or a C program, files are there to store the work. Basically, files are logical concepts similar to the physical files where we store or place our related work at one place. Logically, we understand files very well. We save a file after writing program into it, compile it, run it, debug it, and, later on, retrieve it. However, have you thought how these files have been implemented in the system? The operating system presents a very convenient way of representing the files to a user but implements the *file system* with the help of some physical medium such as magnetic tapes or disks. The files containing the data are stored on the physical media through the related physical devices. For example, for magnetic tapes, there are tape drives, and for disks, there are disk drives. A logical file is mapped to physical memory by the operating system, and a table is maintained for the location of each file in the storage known as *file allocation table*. There are many allocation methods to allocate space to a file on the physical medium such as hard disk. These methods are known as *file-allocation* methods. The

OS implements the allocation method that will take less space, and a file can be retrieved quickly. Before allocating space to a file on the disk, the OS must be in a position to have the account for free space on it. Therefore, the OS manages a free space list that records all free disk blocks.

When a user requests for a file operation, the OS retrieves the required file from its physical medium location and presents it to the user. The OS also provides a directory system under which related files can be arranged and stored for the convenience of the user. The directory contains information about the files, for example, its name, location, size, access rights, and so on.

A file is considered a resource of the system. Therefore, multiple processes may share the files or access the same file at the same time. It means that the protection of files is also necessary as a controlled access to the users. The OS also defines the access rights to the users for a file such as read, write, execute, and so on.

To summarize, the OS performs the following memory-management functions:

  i) File operations such as creation, deletion, and so on.
 ii) Directory creation and deletion
iii) File-allocation methods
 iv) File-retrieval methods
  v) Free-space management
 vi) File protection

File management will be discussed in detail in Chapter 13.

3.6.5 Input–Output Management

The most challenging task for an OS is to manage the I/O devices in a computer system. It acts as an interface between devices and other computer systems. This interface should be simple, easy to use for a user, and preferably same for any type of device. However, today, there are myriad I/O devices. Each I/O device has its own detail and complexity. In this case, the OS needs to be changed to incorporate every newly introduced device. Therefore, the I/O function-alities should be treated separately in the OS so that the other parts of the OS are not affected. The software that deals with the I/O is known as *I/O software* or *I/O subsystem*. In I/O soft-ware, there are two types of modules. First module deals with the general functionalities when interfacing with any type of device, that is, these functions are common while interfacing with any I/O device and are known as *device-independent I/O software*. For example, there should be a general interface for any type of device. The second module provides device-specific code for controlling it and is known as *device driver*. The second module in fact takes care of the peculiarity and details of a particular device, that is, how to read or write data to the device. In this way, the OS needs not to change its code again and again to incorporate any new device. Its I/O software takes care of all the I/O devices to be interfaced with the system without changing the code of it. I/O management will be discussed in detail in Chapter 14.

3.6.6 Security and Protection

In this age, various types of confidential information are being stored either on computer systems or transmitted over the Internet. However, the information/data are not safe from the security breaches. The OS must be able to secure the computer system from outside attacks. In general, it is done by providing passwords. Moreover, as a resource manager, the OS should also protect the resources either from the inside users or outside hackers if they are successful in entering the system. Therefore, the OS must prohibit the processes or users from accessing the resources if they are not authorized for them. Each object, either hardware (CPU, memory, disk, printers, etc.) or software (processes, files, databases, etc.), has a set of operations that can be performed on it. These set of permitted operations corresponding to an object are known as *rights*. These rights can be viewed as a kind of permission to access an object. When a process or user tries to access an object, its rights must be checked first. If the user tries to access the resources he or she has been authorized, then only the access will be granted, otherwise, it is denied. The pair of object and its rights is known as a *domain*. The OS provides the protection in the form of these domains. Security and management will be discussed in detail in Chapters 16 and 17.

SUMMARY

Operating systems primarily are resource managers. The hardware resources such as the CPU, memory, I/O devices, secondary storage devices, and so on are managed only by the OS, and this management includes not only using the resources but also utilizing them properly. As a resource manager, the OS also hides the unnecessary details of the hardware resources from the user and abstracts the resources in such a manner that the user does not worry about the configuration of the hardware resources. For example, the user only knows the process but not the CPU. Of course, the process will be executed on the CPU, but the user is not aware of the execution details of its process, that is, when the process will be sent to the CPU, how the process has been scheduled for how much time. These issues are not concerned with the user. Therefore, the OS abstracts the hardware resources into virtual resources. Besides the hardware and virtual resources, there are also some software resources that again need to be managed by the operating system. A message in message queue to be consumed by a process is a software resource; thus, the OS manages three types of resources: hardware, virtual, and software. Moreover, the resources can be classified based on their nature. Some resources can be consumed and preempted. Based on this, the resources can be non-consumable, consumable, preemptive, and non-preemptive.

The management of these resources is not an easy job. In a multi-programming and multi-tasking environment, the resources need to be shared by the processes, and in case of non-consumable resources, there is a need to keep account of which resource is free and which resource has been allocated. Further, in case of pre-emptive resources, when the process is preempted its state, it must be saved so that it can be resumed again. There are many issues regarding the resource management. In this chapter, all the resource types, resource-management goals, working of resource manager, including the components of resource manager, have been discussed.

Let us have a quick review of the important concepts in this chapter:
- There are three types of resources: hardware, virtual, and software.

- The hardware resources that have been abstracted or transformed into other resources are known as virtual resources. The processes, virtual memory, logical devices, and files are examples of virtual resources.
- Software resources are the resources that have no direct relation with the hardware resources. It means that they are independent of hardware and virtual resources but may be used in managing them. For example, messages in a message queue or mailbox are software resources.
- The OS abstracts the hardware devices into virtual devices.
- The OS allows the resource sharing by two methods: time division multiplexing and space division multiplexing.
- Time division multiplexing means to share the mutual exclusive resource at different times by the processes, for example, the CPU.
- Space division multiplexing means to share the resource at the same time. For example, memory can be partitioned and allocated to different processes at the same time.
- The OS schedules the resources according to a scheduling algorithm, that is, a criterion by which the resource is shared. For example, the CPU is scheduled among different processes according to first come first served criterion.
- The main goals of resource management are resource utilization, protection, synchronization, deadlock prevention, and fair distribution.
- The resource manager is responsible for accounting of resources, synchronization among processes, protection of processes, scheduling of processes, and allocation of resources.
- The resources can be classified based on their nature. Some resources can be consumed and preempted. Based on this, the resources can be non-consumable, consumable, pre-emptive, and non-pre-emptive.
- Main components of resource management are process/task management, memory management, secondary storage management, file management, I/O management, and security and protection.

MULTIPLE CHOICE QUESTIONS

1. The processes, VM, logical devices, and files are examples of
   (a) hardware resources
   (c) software resources
   (b) virtual resources
   (d) none

2. ____are the resources that have no direct relation with the hardware resources.
   (a) hardware resources
   (c) software resources
   (b) virtual resources
   (d) none

3. All physical resources are _____ resources.
   (a) non-consumable
   (c) pre-emptive
   (b) consumable
   (d) none

4. Printer is a _____resource.
   (a) non-pre-emptive
   (c) pre-emptive
   (b) consumable
   (d) none

5. The CPU is a _____resource.
   (a) non-pre-emptive
   (c) pre-emptive
   (b) consumable
   (d) none

6. The status of the resources and the execution of a process need to be stored somewhere in a data structure known as
   (a) status block
   (c) PCB
   (b) resource block
   (d) none

7. Non-contiguous memory allocation is called
   (a) memory partitions
   (c) demand paging
   (b) paging
   (d) none

8. Which of the following is a memory-management function performed by the operating system:
   i) Keeps account of allocated space to the processes and available space
   ii) Partitions the memory as per fixed partition or variable partition methods
   iii) Allocates the memory to the processes as per contiguous or non-contiguous methods
   (a) i and ii
   (c) i and iii only
   (b) i only
   (d) all

9. Swap space for VM should be allocated and reserved in _____.
   (a) main memory
   (c) ROM
   (b) logical memory
   (d) disk

10. The OS provides a _____ system under which related files can be arranged and stored for the convenience of the user.
   (a) file
   (c) directory
   (b) disk
   (d) none

REVIEW QUESTIONS

1. What is resource abstraction? Explain with an example.
2. What are the benefits of resource abstraction?
3. What is the difference between time division multiplexing and space division multiplexing?
4. Give examples of hardware, software, and virtual resources.
5. How are hardware resources mapped into their virtual resources?
6. Explain various resource-management functions.
7. What is the difference between (a) consumable and non-consumable resources and (b) pre-emptive and nonpre-emptive resources
8. Give examples of the resources asked in Question 7.
9. Name the resource type of the following: process, semaphore, memory, VM, file, and page table

10. What is a deadlock?
11. What is process synchronization?
12. What are the methods to allocate a process in memory?
13. What is VM?
14. What is free-space management?
15. What is disk scheduling?
16. What is swap space management?
17. What is a file system?
18. What is the purpose of file allocation table?
19. What is I/O subsystem?
20. What is a device driver?

BRAIN TEASERS

1. Is it true that the role of IPC mechanisms will increase in real-time systems?
2. What is the cost incurred in resource abstraction?

3. Is it possible to implement time division multiplexing on a system with multiple processors?
4. If VM is not there, what will be the effect on performance of the system?

4 Operating System Architectures

4.1 INTRODUCTION

In this chapter, the basic working of an OS and related terminologies is presented. Booting is the start process of an OS through which it sets up its environment and starts working. After booting, the OS begins its initial process and hands over the control to the user process. Since a user is not allowed to perform any I/O operation, all these are performed by the OS. However, a user needs to request the OS for all I/O operations. System call is the medium through which a user sends the request. The OS works on the hardware on behalf of the user and provides the results back to the user. Thus, system call execution and its types are fundamental for understanding the working of the OS. After a discussion of the details of the working, various architectures developed have been discussed in this chapter. The architectures have been evolved over time, catering to the needs of various requirements and keeping pace with technological advancement in computer hardware.

4.2 GENERAL WORKING OF AN OPERATING SYSTEM

The role of an OS starts as soon as the computer system is switched on and lasts till it is shut down. But where is the OS in the computer system? How does the OS get loaded in the system? How does it start? These are some questions addressed here in this section. Before delving into the working of an OS, there are some basic definitions/concepts that need to be understood.

4.2.1 BIOS

Basic Input-output System (BIOS) is a software that basically consists of input-output functions. These functions are low-level routines that the OS uses to interface with different I/O devices, such as keyboard, mouse, monitor, ports, and so on. This is the reason that this software is named as such (BIOS). However, the meaning of BIOS was extended beyond this functioning. Since the OS is on the hard disk, it needs to be loaded onto the main memory to start the functioning of the system. So the problem is to find a way to tell the microprocessor to load the OS. It needs some instructions that, when executed, load the OS. These instructions are provided by the BIOS. In this way, along with providing the basic input-output low-level routines, it also provides the

Learning Objectives

After reading this chapter, you should be able to understand:

- General working of an OS
- Booting of the OS
- System calls, their execution, and types
- System programs
- System generation programs
- General structure of OS
- Monolithic architecture
- Layered architecture
- Virtual machine OS
- Microkernel architecture
- Exokernel architecture
- Hybrid architecture
- System generation

initialization function. This is the reason that the BIOS is embedded in the ROM or flash-RAM so that whenever the system is switched on, the initial instructions get executed automatically and the process of loading the OS initiates. However, it was found that BIOS was inefficient for OSs such as Linux and Windows written for 32-bit CPUs. Therefore, with the advent of new CPU architecture and development in OSs, BIOS is getting replaced. For example, since 2008 in x86 Windows systems, Extensible Firmware Interface (EFI) booting is being supported. The EFI is more flexible in accessing devices. In this way, today, BIOS is primarily used for loading the OS and initialization purposes and otherwise not used, as during the general operation of the system. Instead of calling BIOS, OSs use device drivers for accessing the hardware.

4.2.2 Booting/Bootstrapping

When a system is switched on the first time, it does not have an OS. We need to get the OS ready from the hard disk or other secondary storage onto the memory. A set of sequence of operations is needed to load the OS. This process of placing the OS in memory is known as *booting* or *bootstrapping*.

4.2.3 Boot Software/Boot Loader/Bootstrap Loader

The set of instructions needed for booting, that is, to load the OS in RAM is known as *boot software/boot loader/bootstrap loader*.

4.2.4 Boot Device

The OS is originally stored in a non-volatile secondary storage such as hard disk, CD, and the like. In the process of booting, there is a need to search this storage device, where an OS is stored, to load it onto the RAM. The device that stores the OS is called *boot device*.

4.2.5 Privileged Instructions

There are some operations, provided in the form of instructions, that need to interact with hardware devices. But a user is not allowed to access the devices directly. The instructions are first passed on to the OS, and the OS then interacts with devices on behalf of the user. Thus, the instructions, which are not directly executed by the user but need to be passed to the OS, are known as *privileged instructions*.

4.2.6 System Call

All privileged instructions, that is, instructions, which need to interact with hardware and other resources, and therefore passed on to the OS for execution, are known as *system calls*. For example, when the user needs to write something on the screen, he/she writes the output instruction in the appropriate format. This instruction in the program is system call.

The general working of an OS is discussed in the following steps:

Initialization

It was discussed that the OS acts as a resource manager, so it must have the initialized set of devices in the system. Therefore, whenever the computer is switched on, the control is transferred to the BIOS in the ROM by the hardware. The first job for the BIOS is to initialize and identify system devices such as the video display card, keyboard and mouse, hard disk, CD/DVD drive, and other hardware. This initialization job is known as *power on self test* (POST). It is a built-in diagnostic program that initializes and configures a processor and then checks the hardware to ensure that every connected device is present and functioning properly. In other words, it tests the computer to make sure it meets the necessary system requirements and that all the hardware is working properly before starting of the system. There may be some errors while the execution of POST. These errors are stored or reported through auditory or visual means, for example, through a series of beeps, flashing LEDs, or text on a display.

Booting

(a) After the execution of POST, the BIOS determines the boot device, for example, floppy, CD, or hard disk.

(b) BIOS contains a program that loads the first sector of the boot device called *boot sector*.

(c) The boot sector contains a program. The program in boot sector, when loaded onto the memory and executed, first examines the partition table at the end of the boot sector to determine which partition is active.

(d) In the partition, there is a boot loader/bootstrap loader, which is now loaded onto the memory by the boot sector program (see Fig. 4.1). The area where the boot program/loader is stored is called *boot block* of the boot device.

(e) Boot loader contains the instructions that, when executed, load the OS onto the main memory (bootstrapping) and the control is passed on to the OS by setting bits, corresponding to the privileged mode. It means that whenever the system boots, the control is with the OS, that is, the CPU is in privileged mode.

Start the Operation

(a) After being loaded and executed, the OS first queries the BIOS to get the configuration information.

(b) For each device, it checks the corresponding device driver. After confirming all the device drivers, it loads them into the kernel.

(c) The OS initializes its tables, creates needed background processes, and kicks off the start-up of the first process, such as the login program.

(d) The user programs are loaded onto the memory as the users log in. The control is transferred to the scheduler that selects a user program from the memory and transfers control to the selected program by setting bits corresponding to the user mode, that is, the CPU is now in user mode.

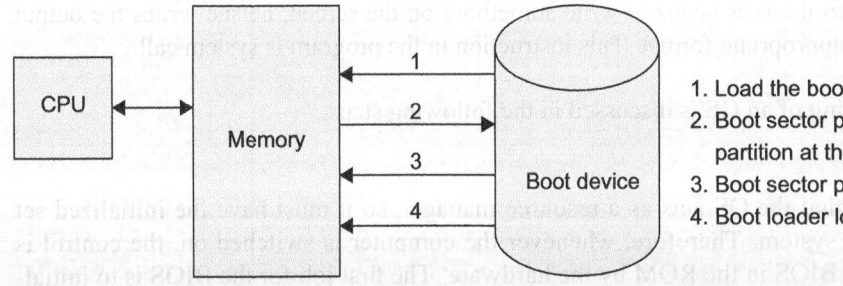

1. Load the boot sector
2. Boot sector program examines the active partition at the end of the boot sector
3. Boot sector program loads the boot loader
4. Boot loader loads the OS

Fig. 4.1 Booting sequence

(e) Given the interrupt-driven nature of the OS, it waits for an event. When there is an event signalled by the interrupt from the hardware or software, it starts responding. The hardware interrupts are triggered by sending a signal to the CPU on the system bus. Software interrupts are triggered by executing a special operation or control instruction called a *system call*. For instance, when a user wants to access an I/O device, he/she will send a request to the OS in the form of a system call, which, in turn, executes a software interrupt and transfers the control to the OS.

(f) These system calls are handled by the system call handler that identifies the cause of interrupt by analyzing the interrupt code and transfers control to the corresponding interrupt-handling routine/event handler in the OS. For example, if there is an I/O interrupt, then control is passed on to the I/O interrupt handler. Thus, the OS has many event handlers that are invoked through the system calls.

4.3 SYSTEM CALLS

The role of system calls is important for understanding the operation of the OS. It is clear now that there are two modes in the operation of the system, that is, user mode and system mode. In the user mode, all user processes are executed and in system mode, all privileged operations are executed. The user programs and kernel functions are being executed in their respective spaces allotted in the main memory partitions. But it is obvious that user mode programs need to execute some privileged operations, which are not permitted in the user mode but allowed in the system mode. Since the processor prevents direct access to kernel-mode functions, user-mode programs must use an interface, which forms the only permitted interface between user mode and kernel mode. This interface is called system call. It means that the system call is an interface between the user programs and the OS. System calls expose all kernel functionalities that user-mode programs require. In other words, system call is an instruction that requests the OS to perform the desired operation that needs hardware access or other privileged operations. Whenever the user uses privileged instructions in the program, he/she uses system calls. For instance, when the user wants access to some hardware operations or resources like files and directories or communication with other processes, he/she uses system calls.

But it should be clear here that a system call does not perform the operations itself. System call, in fact, generates an interrupt that causes the OS to gain control of the CPU. The OS then finds out the type of the system call and the corresponding interrupt-handler routine is executed to perform the operations desired by the user through the system call. Therefore, system call is just a bridge between user programs and the OS for executing the privileged operations as shown in Fig. 4.2.

System calls are inherently used for security reasons. Due to the use of system calls, a user program is not able to enter into the OS or any other user's region. Similarly, I/O devices are also safe from any misuse by the user. Thus, through the use of system

Fig. 4.2   System call interface

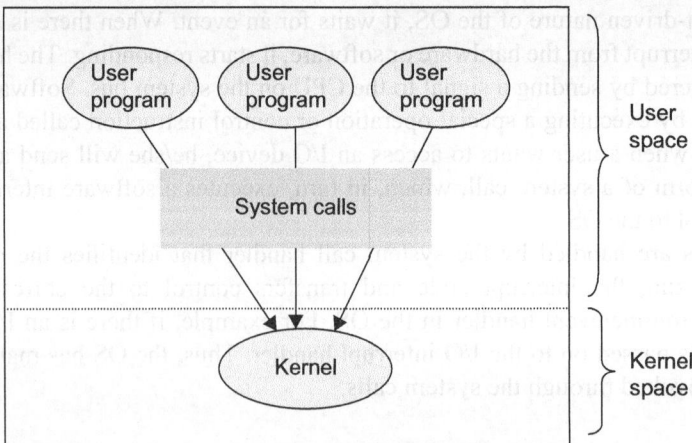

Fig. 4.3 Kernel space and user space in main memory

calls, kernel, other user programs, and I/O devices are safe and secure from malicious user programs (see Fig. 4.3).

4.3.1 Making a System Call

It is obvious that system calls for executing privileged operations or system operations, are used in a process while writing its code. System calls are generally available in the form of assembly language instructions. But with the introduction of system programming in high level languages like C or C++, system calls are directly available and used in high level languages. Therefore, it has become easy to use system calls in a program. For a programmer, system calls are same as calling a procedure or function. System calls demand nothing extra and the format is similar to that of a normal function call. The only issue is that these system calls should be available in the form of a library. The difference between a system call and a normal function call is that a system call enters the kernel but a normal function call does not. Another difference is that a system call itself does not execute anything but generates an interrupt that changes the mode to system mode and passes control on to the OS.

4.3.2 Executing the System Call

As discussed earlier, a system call is not a general function call. There is a sequence of steps to execute a system call. For execution of system call, there is the need to pass various parameters of system call to the OS. For passing these parameters to the OS, three methods are used, as follows:

1. Register method, wherein the parameters are stored in registers of the CPU.
2. If parameters are more in number, compared to the size of registers, a block of memory is used and the address of that block is stored in the register.
3. Stack method, wherein parameters are pushed onto the stack and popped off by the OS.

Another parameter to be passed on to the OS is the code of the system call being used in the user process. There is a code or system call number that is to be placed in the processor register. This is, in fact, performed by the mechanism of a system call table. A table consisting of system calls and their numbers are maintained. The numbers may differ according to different processors and OSs. When a user uses a system call in his/her program, the number of that system call is retrieved from the system call table and placed in the processor register. However, the user or programmer who writes the program does not need to worry about all these system call numbers. The library function being called in response to the system call retrieves the system call number and places the same in the processor register. The set of library functions are included with the compiler of the high-level language that makes a run-time support package.

The kernel retrieves the system call number of the system call and needs to execute the corresponding system call handler. For this purpose, it uses the system call dispatch table that stores the system call number and the location of its system call handler. After finding the address, it dispatches to execute the handler.

The following is the sequence in which a system call is executed (Fig. 4.4):

1. In the user program when the system call is executed, first of all, its parameters are pushed onto the stack and later on saved in the processor registers.
2. The corresponding library procedure for the system call is executed.
3. There is a particular code for every system call by which the kernel identifies which system call function or handler needs to be executed. Therefore, library procedure places the system call number in the processor register.
4. Then the library procedure traps to the kernel by executing interrupt instruction. With this interrupt execution, the user mode switches to kernel mode by loading Program Status Word (PSW) register to 0.

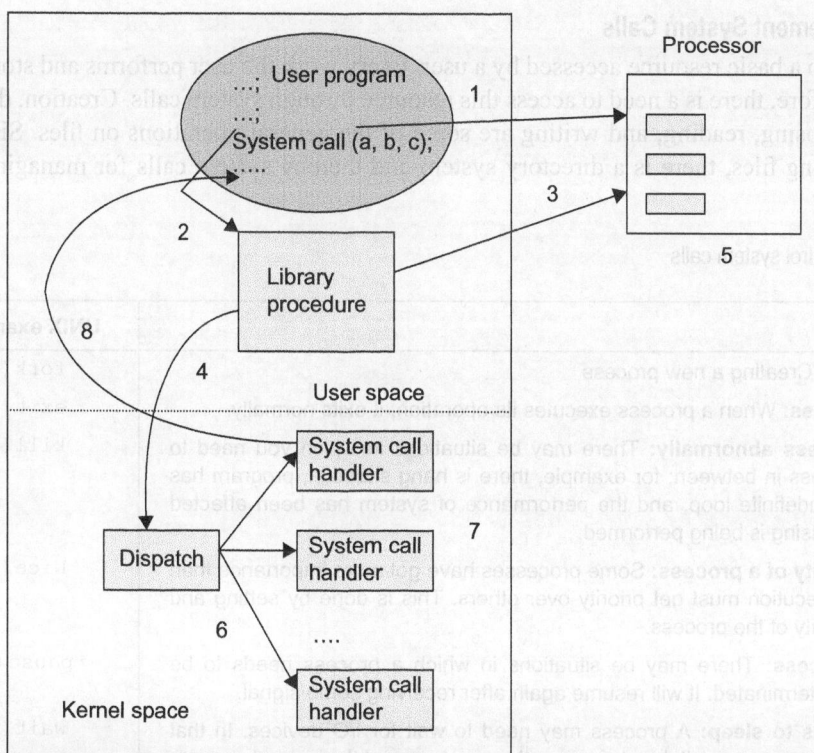

Fig. 4.4   Steps to execute a system call

5. The hardware saves the current contents of CPU registers, so that after executing the system call, the execution of the rest of the program can be resumed.
6. The kernel identifies the system call by examining its number and dispatches the control to the corresponding system call handler.
7. The system call handler executes.
8. On completion of system call handler, the control is returned to the user program and it resumes its execution.

4.3.3 Types of System Calls

Since a user needs to access many resources, the type of system calls depends on the use of these resources. For example, the user needs to have system calls related to process control and management, such as creating a process, putting a process in wait, exiting a process. Similarly, for file management, we must have system calls such as creating a file, deleting a file, opening and closing a file, reading a file, writing to a file, and so on. In this section, let us have a look at some important system calls. Basically, there are five broad categories of system calls.

Process Control System Calls

As discussed in Chapter 3, a process is a basic entity in the system. The processes in the system need to be created, deleted, and aborted. Besides these, many operations are required on the processes for their management. All these operations are performed by system calls (see Table 4.1).

File Management System Calls

A file is also a basic resource accessed by a user. Every work the user performs and stores is as files. Therefore, there is a need to access this resource through system calls. Creation, deletion, opening, closing, reading, and writing are some of the general operations on files. Similarly, for organizing files, there is a directory system and thereby system calls for managing them (Table 4.2).

Table 4.1 Process control system calls

System call	UNIX example
Create a process: Creating a new process	`fork()`
Terminate a process: When a process executes its operation, it exits normally.	`exit()`
Terminate a process abnormally: There may be situations in which you need to terminate the process in between; for example, there is hang situation, program has been stuck in an indefinite loop, and the performance of system has been affected such that no processing is being performed.	`kill()`
Increase the priority of a process: Some processes have got more importance than others. So their execution must get priority over others. This is done by setting and increasing the priority of the process.	`Nice()`
Suspend the process: There may be situations in which a process needs to be suspended but not terminated. It will resume again after receiving some signal.	`pause()`
Cause the process to sleep: A process may need to wait for I/O devices. In that period of time, the processor switches to some other process and the current process is blocked to wait or sleep for some time.	`wait()`

Table 4.2   File management system calls

System call	UNIX example
Create a file: Creating a new file.	Creat()
Open a file: Opening a file that is already created.	Open()
Close a file: Closing a file that has been opened earlier.	Close()
Read a file: Reading a file that has been opened earlier.	Read()
Write a file: Writing into a file that has already been opened.	Write()
Change the position of the read-write pointer: There is a need to access any part of a file randomly. File pointer indicates the current position in the file. This call changes its position as desired.	Lseek()
Give another name to a file: This call allows a file to appear in different directories with different names. But the copy of the file is single. It means that if there is change in the file, it is visible in all the directories wherever it appears. This is done through the unique ID of the file (known as i-number), which is an index into a table of entries known as *i-nodes*. These entries in the table store the information of a file, such as who owns the file, its disk blocks, etc. So, the i-number is same for all entries of the file in different directories. However, there is a single file; only the name is different under different directories. The file is accessible through either name.	Link()
Delete a file in a directory: This call removes the entry of a file in one directory.	Unlink()
Make a directory: Create a new directory.	Mkdir()
Remove a directory: Delete an existing directory.	Rmdir()
Change the directory: When you are working in a directory, you can move to some other directory by using this call.	Chdir()
Change the mode: There are various modes and groups of users who will use the files. For a particular group, there may be different access permissions (modes) such as read, write, or execute. This call changes the access permissions of a file to the specified mode.	Chmod()
Change ownership of file: Changes the owner and group of the indicated file.	Chown()

Device Management System Calls

The user cannot work without accessing the I/O devices. However, accessing them directly is not possible. Therefore, system calls are there for accessing the devices. The general commands related to this category are request of the device, release of the device, read and write operations, and so on. Since files are treated as virtual devices, most of the system calls related to file systems are used for device access also.

Information Maintenance System Calls

Some of the system calls are for accounting and providing information to the user. This information can be about a process, memory, device, computer system, OS, disk space, and so on (Table 4.3).

Communications System Calls

There is a need for communication among the processes in the system. All communication operations are also performed through system calls. The general operations in this category are opening and closing the connection, sending and receiving messages, reading and

Table 4.3   Information maintenance system calls

System call	UNIX example
Get process identification number: Every process has a unique identification number. If the user wants to see the same, this call is used.	`Getpid()`
Get status information of a file: The information regarding a file such as the file type and its permissions, size, time of last access, and so on.	`Stat()`
Set the system date and time	`Stime()`
Get statistics about a file system: Gets the statistics about a file system such as number of free blocks, file system name, and so on.	`Ustat()`

Table 4.4   Communications system calls

System call	UNIX example
Sending a message	`Msgsnd()`
Receiving a message	`Msgrcv()`

writing messages, and so on. These system calls may be related to the communication between processes either on the same machine or between processes on different nodes of a network. Thus, inter-process communication is provided by the OS through these communication-related system calls (Table 4.4).

4.4   SYSTEM PROGRAMS

These are some utilities programs above the layer of the OS, that is, programs that help a user in developing and executing his/her applications. System programs should not be confused with system calls. System programs are utilities programs that help the user and may call further system calls. For example, creating a file is a system program, which helps in creating a file, and this system program calls the system call for doing this. Thus, system call and system programs are not the same. Some examples of system programs are: file management programs (create, delete, copy, print, and so on), compilers, assemblers, debuggers, interpreters, loaders, editors, communication programs (establishing connections, sending email, browsing web pages, and so on), and status information programs (date, time, disk space, memory, and so on).

4.5   SYSTEM GENERATION PROGRAMS

Although the general architectures of a computer system and OS are the same for all machines, there may be some differences of configuration. For example, machines may differ in processor speed, memory size, disk size, I/O devices available in the system, and so on. Therefore, the OS must be configured according to the specifications available on the system on which it has to run. For this purpose, the detailed description of the configuration of the machine is stored on a file, or the hardware is directly probed at the time of booting. The description of the configuration may be in terms of the following:

- The processor type and its options selected
- Disk formatting information, its partitions
- Size of memory
- CPU scheduling algorithm

- Disk scheduling algorithm
- I/O device type and model, its interrupt number

The system generation program takes the input from the file of description about the configuration details and generates the OS accordingly. In system generation, it basically selects some code modules from the system generation library as per the hardware details and compiles and links these modules to form the OS.

4.6   GENERAL STRUCTURE OF OS

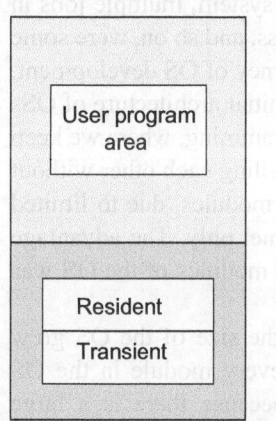

It is clear now that the OS resides in the main memory. However, as the size of the OS increased, there was the problem of keeping it in the limited memory. Therefore, the OS was structured into two parts: *Resident part* or *kernel* and *Transient part* (see Fig. 4.5). The resident part contains programs that are crucial and needed always. Therefore, they must reside in the memory forever. Thus, this makes up the resident part. The transient part is based on programs that are not always needed and, therefore, need not be in the memory forever. Therefore, this part is loaded only when needed, thereby reducing the memory requirement. In this way, the resident- and transient-part programs structure the OS.

The decision to put programs or data structures in resident or transient part depends on its frequency of use in the OS. If the function is inherent and used every time in the operation of the OS, it must be included in the resident part. Otherwise, it should be in the transient part.

Fig. 4.5   Resident and transient parts of an OS in the memory

The resident part may contain the following programs or data structures:

Resource Allocation Data Structures

The data structures related to the allocation of various resources must be in the resident part. A device, if allocated to some process, needs to be checked before being allocated to some other process. Therefore, this data structure is important for smooth allocation of resources.

Information Regarding Processes and their States

Every process contains some information such as its ID, priority, state, and so on. This information is useful while switching from one process to another. The switching operation is quite frequent in multi-programming OSs. Thus, this data structure should also be in the resident part.

System Call Handler

Since the user uses system calls frequently in his/her programs, there is a need to handle these system calls by the OS. Therefore, system call handler must be in the resident part.

Event Handlers

Some event handlers are also necessary for the working of the OS, that is, they are in frequent use. For example, the memory handler or disk I/O handler is required for almost every operation.

Scheduler

This is a frequently used program in the OS whose job is to select the jobs in the queue and send it for dispatching. As we know, in a multi-programming system, there always are jobs to be executed in the queue. Therefore, there is a need to schedule them as well. So, this program should also be in the resident part.

4.7 MONOLITHIC ARCHITECTURE

In the evolution of the OS, it was demonstrated that it was developed in response to the various requirements realized. Keeping the CPU busy, multiple jobs in batch system, multiple jobs in multi-user environment expecting immediate response, user friendliness, and so on, were some of the motivation points against which OSs were designed. In this journey of OS development, one can easily realize that the development was not planned and the initial architecture of OSs was not efficient. The OSs were developed in the same way as in programming, where we keep on developing the program in one file or adding some functions and calling each other without any boundary between them. Initially, the OS consisted of very few modules, due to limited functionality. Therefore, all the functionalities were added in the kernel only. The advantage of this type of architecture was that intercommunication between the modules of the OS was efficient, as all the modules were in the kernel together (Fig. 4.6).

Later on, due to multi-programming and its extended concepts, the size of the OS grew beyond limit. This resulted in a complex structure of OS because every module in the OS accessed hardware directly. Thus, programming effort was high because there is a large gap between the meaning of operations required by the user and the meaning of operations performed by the hardware. This gap is known as *semantic gap* between the user application and bare hardware. When a user creates a process, one process or task is being created for the user. For the OS, it is a collection of some algorithms like allocating the memory for the process, scheduling the process, and so on. But at the hardware level, these operations are performed at the level of machine instructions. Therefore, there is a large gap in understanding the operations at OS level and machine level as shown in Fig. 4.7.

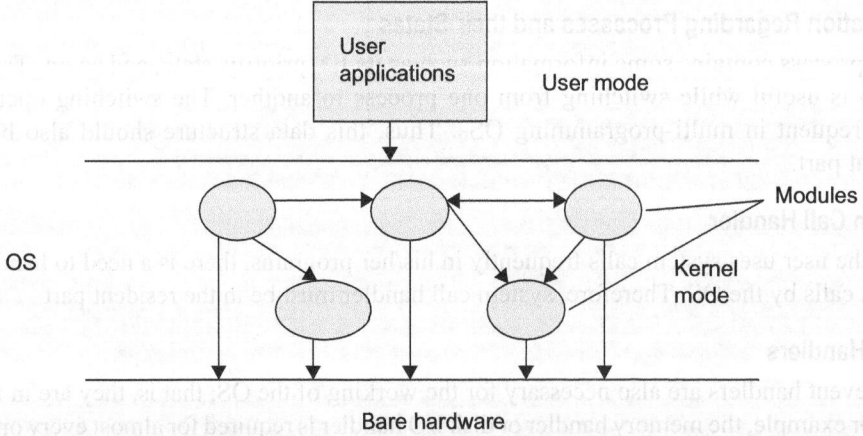

Fig. 4.6   Monolithic architecture

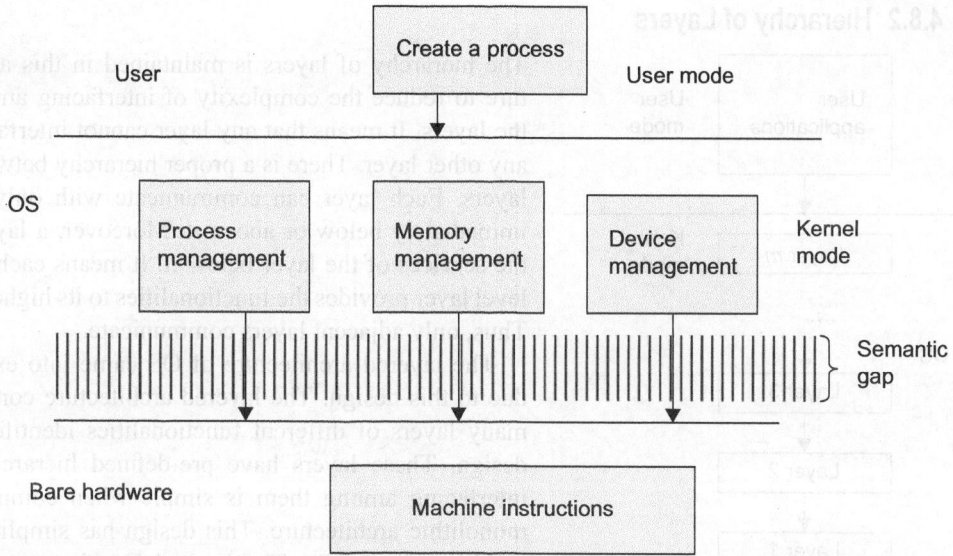

Fig. 4.7   Semantic gap between the OS and hardware

Due to all functionalities merged in a single layer, it was difficult to do modifications in a module. This is because, as a result of a lot of interfacing among modules, it is hard to imagine which module may be affected due to a single change in a module. Consequently, debugging in the modules of the OS became a difficult job. Another disadvantage of this architecture was that there was no protection. Since in this structure, there is unrestricted access of any module to the system and among them, therefore, there was the danger of malicious code. A user job can enter into the area of another job or even of the OS.

Monolithic systems were not suitable for multi-programming/multi-tasking environments due to unprotected behaviour of the system. Any user's job can corrupt any other user's job and even OS. For example, in DOS, any user job has direct access to BIOS device drivers. Therefore, there it is possible to change the functionality of any device driver. The DOS, initial architecture of UNIX, and Linux are some examples of monolithic structures.

4.8   LAYERED ARCHITECTURE

With the advancement in OSs, monolithic structures became complex and then obsolete after some time. There was the need to design the OS such that there is no single layer consisting of all the functionalities. This resulted in layered architectures (see Fig. 4.8). This architecture is based on the following two points of design:

4.8.1   Grouping of Functions in a Layer

The functions related to a category are grouped together and made into a layer of that category. For example, process creation, deletion, saving the context of a process, and so on, may be grouped together and named as process management layer. The topmost layer provides the interface to applications of the users. The lowest layer interacts with the underlying hardware.

4.8.2 Hierarchy of Layers

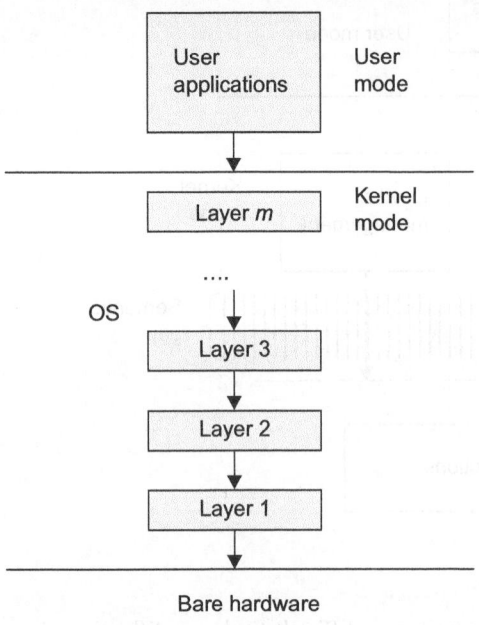

Fig. 4.8 Layered architecture

The hierarchy of layers is maintained in this architecture to reduce the complexity of interfacing among all the layers. It means that any layer cannot interface with any other layer. There is a proper hierarchy between the layers. Each layer can communicate with only layers immediately below or above it. Moreover, a layer uses the services of the layer below it. It means each lower-level layer provides the functionalities to its higher level. Thus, only adjacent layers communicate.

The layered architecture of OS came into existence due to this design. The layered architecture consists of many layers of different functionalities identified in a design. These layers have pre-defined hierarchy, and interfacing among them is simple when compared to monolithic architecture. This design has simplified the architecture of OSs. The limited interface among the layers has resulted in a simple architecture. The layered architecture provides the modularity wherein there is a defined layer for each group of functionality. Therefore, if there is a need to change a module or debug an error, it becomes easy because changes or debugging an error are localized to only one layer. It means changes made in one layer do not affect the other layers. Similarly, if we want to find some error in one layer, we are concerned with only that layer. Debugging is easy due to this localization of errors.

Another advantage in this architecture is that there is protection among different modules of different layers. Due to limited interface among layers and a proper hierarchy, no module can enter into others' area, thereby giving protection among layers and their modules. For instance, the upper layer can invoke a module only of the lower layer and does not know the addresses of data and instructions of that module. It means implementation and interfaces of a module have been separated. The upper layer needs to know how to interface with the lower module or what modules of the lower layer is to be called but need not know how those modules have been implemented. Thus, this design prevents a malicious code and corruption of data from one layer to another.

There are also some disadvantages in layered architecture. In this design when a system call appears, it needs to pass through all the layers for getting the functionality of the requested resource. Since there is hierarchy of layers and limited interaction between them, it will take some time to execute a system call due to time taken in getting the system call request from the topmost layer to the lower layer and then to the actual resource. Thus, this design may suffer from efficiency problems if there is a large number of layers. The increasing number of layers may again lead to a complex architecture. Another problem in the layered architecture is to group the modules in a layer such that the upper layer is able to invoke the modules of the lower layer. It may be difficult sometimes to isolate functionalities from one another. Then in this case, the decision of placing the modules in a fixed layer or defining the roles of each layer may be difficult.

4.9   VIRTUAL MACHINE OS

A user may have different types of requirements to execute jobs. Some jobs are batch oriented, that is, these jobs do not need attention or any interaction of the user. Some jobs require immediate attention and quick response. However, the OS structure is either batch oriented or time-sharing. It means that the same structure of the OS cannot be used for different types of requirements for executing jobs. The same happened to OS/360, which was a batch system. But users also demanded to have a time-sharing environment in the system. IBM then developed Time-Sharing System/360 (TSS/360), which was big and slow and, in turn, abandoned. It means the same structure of OS would not be suitable for providing different requirements. Later on, the system was redesigned and called Control program/Conversational monitor system (CP/CMS). Later this was renamed as Virtual Machine Facility/370 (VM/370).

The solution adopted in VM/370 to support different types of requirements of the user was to have different types of OSs. These different types of OSs would support the different functionalities desired by the user. The different OSs were realized through virtual machine concept (see Fig. 4.9). It means these OSs will run on virtual machines. If there are three virtual machines, then it means three different OSs can be supported. But these virtual machines are not extended machines as discussed in Chapter 1 but are exact copies of the bare hardware machine. Each virtual machine has the same architecture as the actual hardware. A virtual machine will have a virtual processor, memory, and I/O devices. The OSs on these virtual machines have facilities as of normal OSs on actual machines such as user/system mode, interrupt processing, and the like. However, the configuration of the virtual machine may not be the same as that of actual hardware. For instance, the size of memory will be smaller in the virtual machine. To implement the virtual machine, in fact, they are mapped on to the bare hardware machine. The services of various OSs, running on their virtual machines, are also required. This is done by the *host OS*, which is running on the bare hardware. The host OS multiplexes the virtual processors onto the actual CPU of the host computer. The host OS decides which OS to run next. This is just like how the normal OS performs scheduling of jobs on the CPU. The host OS switches

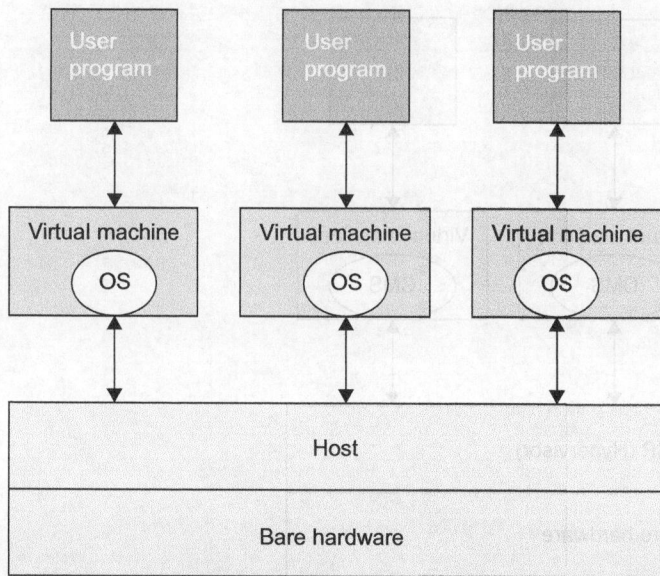

Fig. 4.9   Virtual machine architecture

the control between various OSs running on virtual machines in the same fashion as done for different jobs. In this way, the host OS maps the virtual machine onto the bare hardware and the functionality of the OS running on that virtual machine is achieved. Thus, different virtual machines may run different OSs as required. This architecture of the OS is known as *virtual machine OS*. The obvious advantage of virtual machine OS is that the same hardware is being shared to run different execution environments, that is, multi-programming, time-sharing can be on a single machine. Another advantage of these OSs is that all virtual machines are isolated and, thus, protected. Similarly, host OSs running on bare hardware are protected from virtual machines. For example, a virus in the host OS may corrupt it but cannot corrupt guest OSs.

The virtual machine concept in OSs can be seen in various systems. Some of them are discussed here. As discussed earlier, VM/370 was a virtual machine-based OS. Other versions of this system are VM/SP and z/VM. The host OS in this system (see Fig. 4.10) is a control program known as hypervisor or, generally, VM-CP. It runs on the bare hardware and creates the virtual machine environment by coordinating among various virtual machines. The VM-CP implements the virtualization of the actual hardware, including all I/O and other privileged operations. It performs the system's resource sharing, including device management, dispatching, virtual storage management, and other traditional OS tasks. Each user views the system as having a separate machine, the virtual machine. All virtual machines have their own address spaces, I/O, interrupts, and so on, just like the real machine has. Thus, virtual machines are not extended machines but limited versions of exact hardware.

The OS running on the virtual machines, sometimes called guest OSs, is known as Conversational Monitor System (CMS), which is a single-user interactive system. But any other mainstream OS can also run on virtual machine. These guest OSs are prevented from using privileged instruction by the hypervisor. However, the hypervisor simulates privileged instruction on their behalf.

Another use of virtual machines has been made in Pentium machine. On this machine, along with Windows, MS-DOS programs can be run. Intel provided a virtual 8086 mode on this Pentium architecture and in this mode, DOS programs are started up.

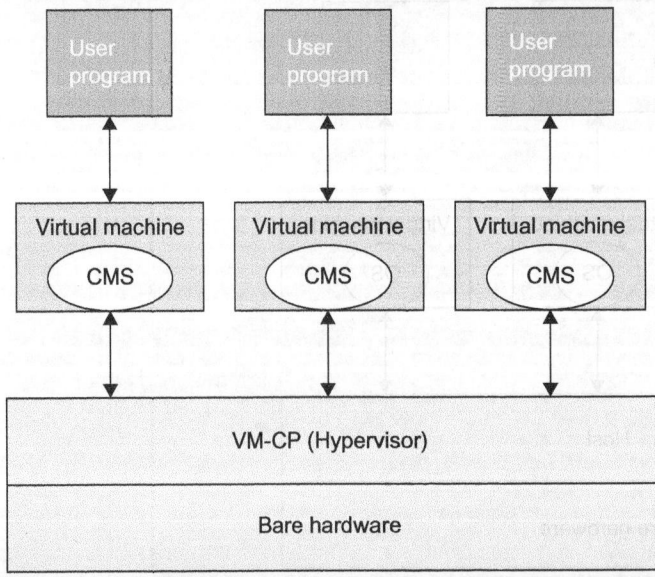

Fig. 4.10   *VM/370 architecture*

4.10 CLIENT–SERVER OR MICROKERNEL-BASED OS

As the computer architecture improved over time and demands from an OS increased, the size of kernel expanded beyond limit. Larger-sized kernels were more prone to errors and difficult to maintain. Whatever the architecture; the large kernel size became unmanageable and suffered from the difficulty of extensibility, efficiency, and reliability. A number of new devices have appeared and many of them have already disappeared. There is a need to add or delete their support in the OS. But due to the monolithic or layered structure of kernel, it was not easy to add or delete the modules, because there was dependency among modules or layers. In layered architecture, as the number of layers increased with more demands in the functionality of the kernel, the OS started to perform badly as compared to previous architectures. Due to this reason, Windows NT with layered architecture gave bad performance as compared to Windows95. Due to the more integrated nature of layers or modules, if one component fails, then the whole OS goes down. It decreases the reliability of the system.

To remove heavy functionalities from the kernel, it was thought that some essential functionality will remain inside the kernel known as *essential core* of the OS code. The kernel, consisting of essential core, is called *microkernel*. The components of the essential core may be process management, inter-process communication, low-level memory management, and so on. The other OS modules, which were considered as non-essential, were moved up in the user space. In this way, microkernel was designed to manage the large-size kernel by dividing it into two parts: kernel space code and user space code. The only difficulty in microkernel is to decide the essential core of the kernel. Developers have discussed features to be included inside the kernel and features to be incorporated in the user space.

The modules implemented outside the kernel in user space are called *server processes*. The application programs of the user (client programs) communicate with the server processes as shown in Fig. 4.11. The server processes provide various services like file system management, process scheduling, device management, networking, and so on. The communication between

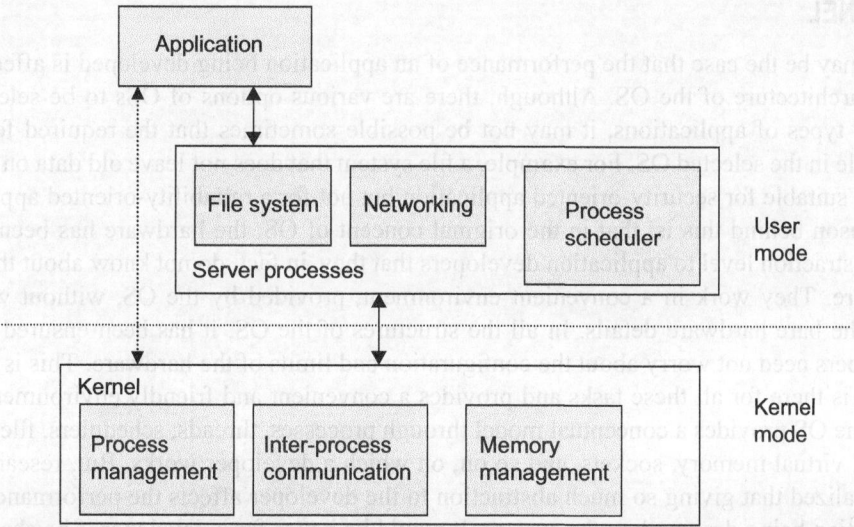

Fig. 4.11 Microkernel architecture

the client applications and server processes is through the message-passing communication method, called as Inter-process Communication (IPC). This is the reason this architecture is also known as client-server architecture of OSs. The microkernel facilitates this message-passing communication by validating the messages, passing them on to various modules and giving access to hardware. Thus, IPC is the basic mechanism in microkernel through which a service is provided. Any service is obtained by sending an IPC message to a server, and obtaining the result in another IPC message from the server. The server processes are like any other program that allows the OS to be modified simply by starting and stopping these server programs. For example, in a machine, if networking support is not required, then the server module supporting networking is not started without any further change in the OS. But if this is the case in other architectures of OSs, then the kernel needs to be recompiled after removing the networking module. Therefore, the microkernel structure is more adaptable as compared to others. Similarly, if a server module fails, it can be stopped, rather than crashing the kernel itself. In this way, microkernel is more robust and reliable.

The extensibility feature of microkernel architecture can be used for developing various types of OSs, using the same microkernel. For example, Mach microkernel has been used to develop several OSs like True64 UNIX and SPIN.

Microkernel architecture has been used in many systems. Mach was the first OS designed with this approach. Mach, developed in the 1980s, was the most successful microkernel and has been used in various commercial systems. For example, True64 UNIX and SPIN were built on Mach microkernel. The microkernel has been evolved over several generations. The first-generation microkernels (Mach, L3, and so on) were slower in nature due to IPC used for communication between kernel and servers. This inefficiency was removed in later generations of microkernel. Some examples of the latest generation, which are now faster than the first-generation microkernels, are L4, SPIN, and QNX. 'PARAS' developed by Centre for Development of Advance Computing (C-DAC), India, is another example of microkernel architecture.

4.11 EXOKERNEL

There may be the case that the performance of an application being developed is affected due to the architecture of the OS. Although, there are various options of OSs to be selected for various types of applications, it may not be possible sometimes that the required feature is available in the selected OS. For example, a file system that does not leave old data on the disk may be suitable for security-oriented application but not for a reliability-oriented application. The reason behind this is, that in the original concept of OS, the hardware has been at such high abstraction level to application developers that they, in fact, do not know about the actual hardware. They work in a convenient environment, provided by the OS, without worrying about the bare hardware details. In all the structures of the OS, it has been ensured that the developers need not worry about the configuration and limits of the hardware. This is because the OS is there for all these tasks and provides a convenient and friendly environment to the user. The OS provides a conceptual model through processes, threads, schedulers, file system, paging, virtual memory, sockets, and so on, on which a developer works. But, researchers at MIT realized that giving so much abstraction to the developer affects the performance of the application being designed on the system. It would be better for a developer if he/she decides on his/her own about what to do with resources instead of following the abstractions provided by the OS. In this way, performance of an application, not bounded by the abstractions and policies of the OS, may perform better.

To implement this idea, control of the resources need to be provided to the developers. One way is to program directly on the hardware and remove the kernel as we did in the past, without the OS. But this idea is to return to the past and we have seen how difficult life was without OSs. The compromising idea is to use a kernel with minimum functionality and providing access of resources to the developer as well. This kernel is called exokernel. The exokernel performs the job of allocation and synchronizing of resources with user jobs. But the way in which the application makes use of resources will be decided by the developer. In other words, the exokernel works as an executive for application programs such that it ensures the safe use of resources and allocates them to the applications. It means that the developer can implement the customized abstraction on the resources. The applications implemented in this way are known as *library OSs*. Library OSs (see Fig. 4.12) may request the exokernel to allocate resources like some disk blocks, memory addresses, CPU, and so on, and use these resources the way it suits the application best. In this way, the exokernel also provides the efficiency, because now there is no need to map the resources from the conceptual model provided by the conventional OS to the physical model. For example, in the MIT Exokernel Project, the Cheetah web server stores pre-formatted Internet Protocol packets on the disk, the kernel provides safe access to the disk by preventing unauthorized reading and writing, but the method in which the disk is abstracted is up to the application or the libraries the application uses.

Though the concept of exokernel has been in use since 1994, and MIT has developed two exokernels, namely Aegis and XOK, this concept has not been used in any commercial OS and research is still going on.

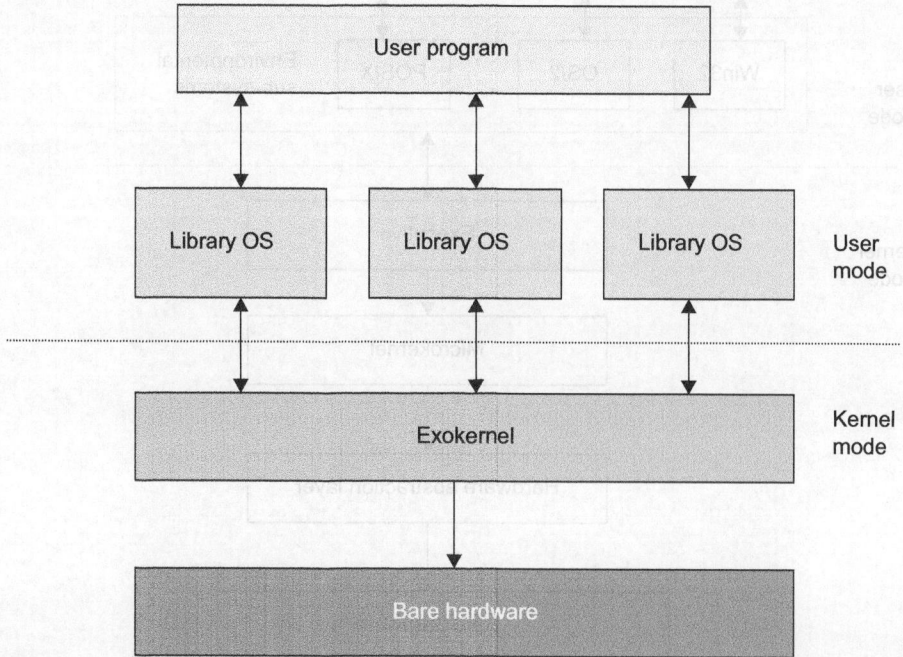

Fig. 4.12   Exokernel architecture

4.12 HYBRID KERNEL-BASED OS

In microkernel architecture, there was a cost involved in IPC for context switching from user mode to kernel mode and vice versa. Context switching will be elaborated in Chapter 5. In a component like networking, the overhead of context switching is too high. Therefore, some kernels were designed to bring back some of the components inside the kernel. Moreover, the advantages of a layered approach were also merged with microkernel architecture. This type of kernel, having the mixed approach of various structures, is known as *hybrid kernel*. Various OSs have been designed using hybrid kernels. For example, the architecture of Windows NT and Windows 2000 has been designed with the hybrid approach, taking advantage of layered as well as microkernel approaches. In order to reduce the cost of IPC in microkernel, the modules that were in the user space have been brought back inside the kernel. But these modules are still not inside the microkernel. It means the kernel's non-essential functionalities and core essential functionalities are still separate. This has been achieved by the layered concept. There are separate layers of kernel functionalities called as the executive layer and below this layer is the microkernel layer. There are basically three layers: executive layer, microkernel layer, and hardware abstraction layer. The executive layer includes high-level kernel functionalities like object management, IPC, virtual memory management, and so on. The microkernel layer provides minimal kernel functionality such as process synchronization, scheduling, and the like, as discussed in microkernel architecture. Hardware abstraction layer provides easy portability to a number of hardware architectures. In this way, a hierarchy of layers to separate the microkernel from other functionalities of kernel has been designed. But both microkernel and executive layers are in kernel mode, thereby reducing the context switch overheads.

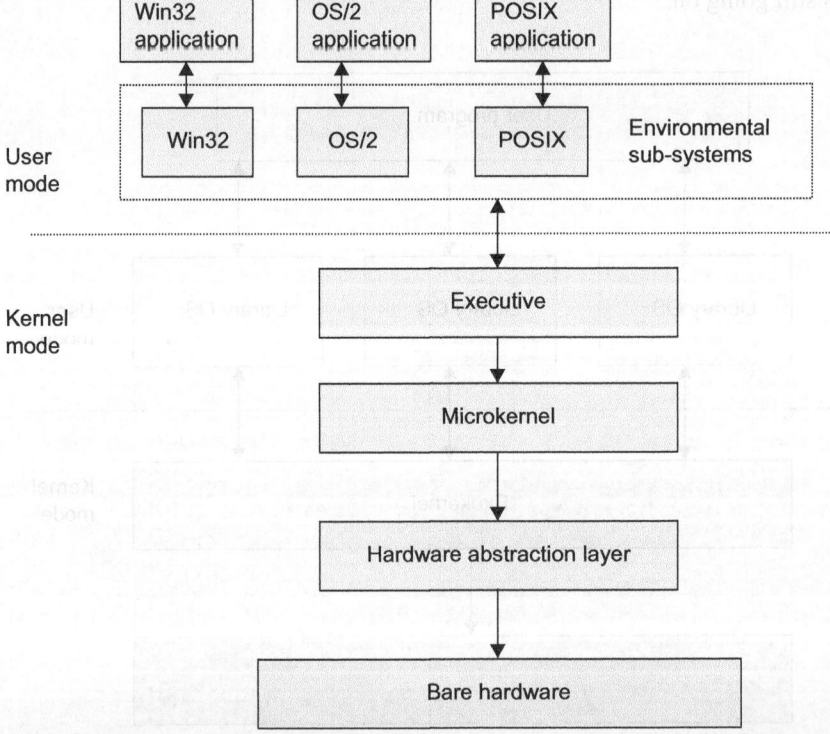

Fig. 4.13 Windows hybrid architecture

SUMMARY

The very first architecture of an OS was monolithic. With the introduction of multi-programming, it was evolved to layered architecture due to some constraints like security, debugging, and so on. The layered architecture provides the modularity wherein there is a defined layer for each group of functionality. Therefore, if there is a need to change a module or debug an error, it becomes easy to do so because changes or debugging an error are localized to one layer only. It means changes made in one layer do not affect the others. Another architecture known as virtual machine OS was designed to cater to the different needs of a user. As the computer architecture improved over time and demands from an OS increased, the size of the kernel expanded beyond limit. Larger-sized kernels were more prone to errors and difficult to maintain. Therefore, another architecture was designed, known as Microkernel-based OS. Since the OS abstracts the hardware to a user and hides the complex details of the hardware, it was realized that the performance of the application being developed may be affected somewhere, as all the decisions regarding the resources in the system are with the OS. In response to this, exokernel architecture was developed, giving some access of resources to the user. Finally, a hybrid architecture combining the merits of some OS architectures was designed.

Let us have a quick review of important concepts discussed in this chapter:

- BIOS is a software that consists of input-output functions. These functions are low-level routines that the OS uses to interface with different I/O devices like keyboard, screen, ports, and so on.
- The set of instructions needed for booting, that is, to load the OS in RAM is known as Boot software/Boot loader/Bootstrap loader.
- The instructions, which are not directly executed by the user but need to be passed to the OS, are known as privileged instructions.
- All the privileged instructions, that is, instructions that need to interact with hardware and resources, and therefore passed on to the OS for execution, are known as system calls.

- POST is a built-in diagnostic program that initializes and configures a processor and then checks the hardware to ensure that every connected device is present and is functioning properly.
- The difference between system call and a normal function call is that a system call enters the kernel but a normal function call does not. Another difference is that the system call itself does not execute anything but generates an interrupt, which changes the mode to system mode and passes the control over to the OS.
- System programs help a user in developing and executing his/her applications. System programs should not be confused with system calls. System programs are utilities programs, which help the user and may call for further system calls.
- System generation is the process of configuring the OS according to the hardware and other specifications on a particular machine.
- Monolithic systems were not suitable for multi-programming/multi-tasking environments due to the unprotected behaviour of the system. Any user job can corrupt another user's job and even the OS.
- Layered architecture provides the modularity wherein there is a defined layer for each group of functionality. Therefore, if there is a need to change a module or debug an error, it becomes easy because changes or debugging an error are localized to one layer only.
- The advantage of the virtual machine OS is that same hardware is being shared to run different execution environments, that is, multi-programming and time-sharing can be on a single machine. Another advantage of these systems is that all virtual machines are isolated and, thus, protected.
- Exokernel works as an executive for application programs such that it ensures the safe use of resources and allocates them to the applications. It means that the developer can now implement the customized abstraction on the resources.
- Hybrid architecture combines the features of microkernel and layered architectures.

MULTIPLE CHOICE QUESTIONS

1. All the privileged instructions, that is, the instructions, which need to interact with hardware and other resources, and, therefore, passed on to the OS for execution, are known as _____.
   - (a) OS procedures
   - (b) kernel functions
   - (c) system calls
   - (d) none

2. POST is a built-in _____ that initializes and configures a processor and then checks the hardware to ensure that every connected device is present and functioning properly.
   - (a) system program
   - (b) diagnostic program
   - (c) system call
   - (d) none

3. Boot loader contains the instructions, which, when executed, load the OS in the main memory called _____.
   - (a) bootstrapping
   - (b) POST
   - (c) system program
   - (d) none

4. The BIOS contains a program that loads the first sector of the boot device called _____.
   (a) boot loader   (c) boot program
   (b) boot sector   (d) none

5. System call is just a bridge between user programs and _____ for executing privileged operations.
   (a) system programs   (c) OS
   (b) users   (d) none

6. What is the UNIX command for terminating a process abnormally?
   (a) fork   (c) suspend
   (b) kill   (d) none

7. What is the UNIX command for increasing the priority of a process?
   (a) priority   (c) nice
   (b) lseek   (d) none

8. What is the UNIX command for suspending a process?
   (a) sleep   (c) pause
   (b) wait   (d) none

9. What is the UNIX command for causing a process to sleep?
   (a) sleep   (c) pause
   (b) wait   (d) none

10. What is the UNIX command for changing the position of read/write pointer?
    (a) sleep   (c) link
    (b) lseek   (d) none

11. _____ must reside in the memory forever.

(a) resident   (c) OS
(b) transient   (d) none

12. DOS is an example of _____.
    (a) layered architecture   (c) exokernel
    (b) monolithic architecture   (d) none

13. The OS running on virtual machines, sometimes called guest OSs, is known as
    (a) CMS   (c) VMS
    (b) TMS   (d) none

14. The modules implemented outside the kernel in user space in microkernel architecture are called
    (a) servers   (c) special modules
    (b) clients   (d) none

15. _____ architecture is also known as client-server architecture.
    (a) layered architecture   (c) microkernel
    (b) monolithic architecture   (d) none

16. TRUE64 UNIX is an example of _____.
    (a) layered architecture   (c) microkernel
    (b) monolithic architecture   (d) none

17. PARAS is an example of _____.
    (a) layered architecture   (c) microkernel
    (b) exokernel architecture   (d) none

18. Aegis and XOK are examples of _____.
    (a) layered architecture   (c) microkernel
    (b) exokernel architecture   (d) none

REVIEW QUESTIONS

1. Define the following terms:
   (a) BIOS   (b) Booting
   (c) Boot loader   (d) Boot device

2. Explain all the steps of the general working of an OS.

3. What is the need of a system call? With the help of example, explain how it is executed.

4. What is the difference between a system call and a function call?

5. Explain all types of system calls using some examples.

6. What is the difference between a system call and system program?

7. What is the need of a system generation program?

8. What are the two parts in the general structure of an OS?

9. What are the shortcomings of monolithic architecture?

10. What are the advantages and disadvantages of layered architecture?

11. Explain the architecture of VM/370.

12. Explain the architecture of microkernel-based OS.

13. What is the idea behind the development of exokernel?

14. What are the good features of a hybrid-based architecture?

BRAIN TEASERS

1. Would microkernel architecture work well for design of an object-oriented OS? Justify your answer.

2. Design a format of message in message-passing system of microkernel architecture.

3. How is reliability increased in microkernel architecture?

4. Explore some research issues in designing an exokernel.

5. What steps would you suggest while designing an OS in order to reduce the semantic gap between user application and bare hardware?

6. Explore how UNIX has been modified to support protection.

Case Study I: History and Architecture of Operating Systems

UNIX

UNIX is a multi-user multi-tasking OS. It was first developed in the 1960s and has been under constant development ever since. As discussed in Chapter 1, UNIX was developed initially from the MULTICS project that began in the mid 1960s as a joint effort by General Electric, Massachusetts Institute of Technology (MIT), and Bell Labs. Through continuous development, Ken Thompson in the University of California at Berkeley, along with his two graduate students, wrote the first Berkeley version of UNIX, which was distributed to students. This resulted in the source code being worked on and developed by many different people. The Berkeley version of UNIX is known as *Berkeley Software Distribution* (BSD). The BSD supported Vi editor, C shell, virtual memory (VM), and TCP/IP.

Table CS1.1 summarizes the decade wise growth of UNIX since its inception.

Table CS1.1 Decade-wise growth of UNIX

1969–1979	The first decade initially witnessed the origin of UNIX as a joint venture by Dennis Ritchie, Ken Thompson, and others at MIT. Later, the *First Edition* was developed, which was used for text processing of patent documents. Thereafter, UNIX was rewritten in C. It was termed as *Fourth Edition* and proved to be a major milestone for an OS's portability among different systems. *Version 6* was also developed in this decade, which was the first to be widely available outside Bell Labs. It became the basis of the first Berkeley version of UNIX developed at the University of California, Berkley. Finally, the *Seventh Edition* was developed, in which the kernel was more than 40 KB.
1980–1990	Xenix was introduced by Microsoft. Later, AT&T's UNIX System Group (USG) developed *System III*, the first public release outside Bell Labs. Henceforth, Computer Research Group (CRG), USG, and a third group together formed Unix System Laboratories. In the later years, the University of California at Berkeley released *4.2BSD*, which included TCP/IP, new signals, and much more. Thereafter, *System V Release 2* (SVR2) came in, which introduced demand paging, copy on write, and so on. Subsequently, *4.3BSD* released, which included Internet name server. It had separated machine-dependent and independent code and introduced the implementation of OSI network protocol stack and virtual memory system. The next year in succession witnessed the origin of *SVR3*. It had *file system switch* (FSS), virtual file system (VFS) mechanism, shared libraries, and *transport layer interface*. Towards the end of this decade, *SVR4* brought with itself TCP/IP, socket support, VFS, and *network file system* NFS. The last year marked the launch of *XPG3* Brand by X/Open System
1992–2001	The third decade began with the launch of *SVR4.2*. In the subsequent year, *4.4BSD* was released by Berkeley. It had TCP/IP, socket support, and so on. The *Single UNIX Specification* was introduced, which separates UNIX trademark from any other stream. Later on, *Version 2* of *Single UNIX Specification* was introduced. This version includes real-time support, threads, and 64-bit processor support. Furthermore, *Version 3* of *Single UNIX Specification* was released.

(Table CS1.1 Contd)

2002–2009	The core volumes of *Version 3* of the *Single UNIX Specification* were approved as an international standard.

Architecture of UNIX OS

UNIX was initially developed in monolithic structure. Many modules and interfaces were added over the years in this structure only. The classic architecture of UNIX is divided into layers with the hardware and application programs existing at the extreme ends. The structure of UNIX is shown in Fig. CS1.1. It consists of two parts: kernel and system programs. The kernel was evolved into a series of interfaces and device drivers. The kernel architecture supports the key requirements of UNIX that fall into two categories, namely, functions for *file management* (files include device files) and functions for *process management*. Process management entails allocation of resources including the CPU and memory, and offers services that processes may need. The file management in itself involves handling all the files required by the processes, communicating with device drivers, and regulating transmission of data to and from peripherals.

Later on, UNIX was modified as microkernel architecture. *True64* is the microkernel-based UNIX version. The latest versions of UNIX including SVR4 and Solaris are based on a modular and dynamic architecture. The modular architecture design is based on object-oriented programming techniques that help in creating a modular kernel. The kernel in this architecture has a core kernel that is always resident in memory along with the modules that can be linked to the core kernel either during boot time or run time without any kernel re-configuration or compilation. This is why these modules are also known as *dynamically loadable modules*. The object-oriented approach helps in loading the modules dynamically and links them to the core kernel, thereby running them in kernel mode. The advantage of this modular architecture is that any module can be replaced or added without affecting the rest of the structure. Due to this dynamic architecture, it may evolve to accommodate new modules (for new devices and services) without even rebooting. Since the modules are loaded on demand, the memory footprint is also reduced.

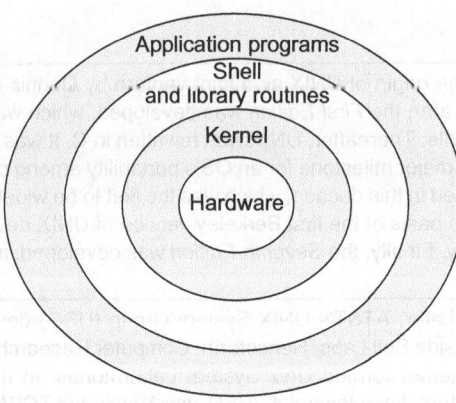

Fig. CS1.1   UNIX structure

SOLARIS

Sun Solaris is a UNIX variant OS that was originally installed on SPARC computers. It is a complete operating environment built on a modular and dynamic kernel. Solaris primarily runs on SPARC and Intel x86 processors.

The growth of this OS, since its inception, is summarized in Table CS1.2.

Table CS1.2   Growth of Solaris

Year	Release	Notes
1982	Sun Unix 0.7	First version of Sun's UNIX, based on 4.BSD from UniSoft
1983	SunOS 1.0	Sun-2 workstation, 68010 based
1985	SunOS 2.0	VFS and vnode framework allows multiple concurrent file system types
1988	SunOS 4.0	New virtual memory system and dynamic linking was added
1990	SunOS 4.1	OpenWindows graphics environment
1992	SunOS 4.1.3	Asymmetric multiprocessing (ASMP) for sun4m systems (SPARCstation-10 and -600 series MP (multi-processor servers)
1992	Solaris 2.0 and Solaris 2.1	Solaris 2.x is born, based on a port of SVR4.0. It was only a uni-processor system Later version supported 4-way SMP.
1993	Solaris 2.2 and Solaris 2.3	It had larger than 2GB support This version supported 8-way SMP
1994	Solaris 2.4	20-way SMP New kernel memory allocator (slab allocator) replaces SVR4 buddy allocator Caching file system (cachefs)
1995	Solaris 2.5	Large-page support for kernel and System V shared memory NFS Version 3
1996	Solaris 2.6	Supported file system larger than 2GB Dynamic processor sets Dynamic re-configuraton
1998	Solaris 7	64-bit kernel and process address space Priority paging memory algorithm
2000	Solaris 8	Supports IPv6 and DNS
2001	Solaris 9	Support for disks more than 1 TB
2005	Solaris 10	Supports Zettabyte file system (ZFS), Dynamic trace
2011	Solaris 11	Supports cloud computing, network virtualization

Architecture of Solaris and Its Key Features

The modular design of kernel in Solaris OS permits it to link into itself additional services either during boot time or run time. The Solaris kernel is composed of a core system that is always resident in memory. Some of the core kernel components include the following:

- System calls
- Scheduler

- Memory management
- Clocks and timers
- Interrupt management
- Boot and startup
- Trap management

There are several components in the kernel of the Solaris system that are loadable dynamically (Fig. CS1.2). Some of these are as follows:

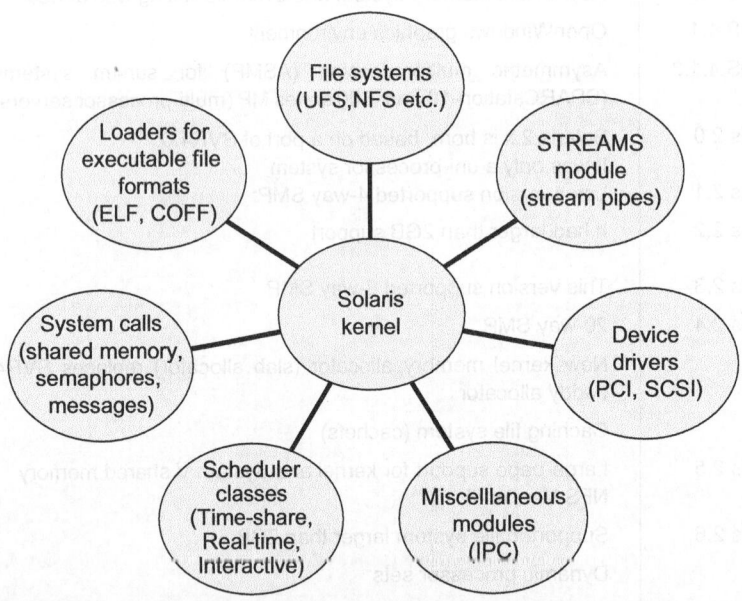

Fig. CS1.2   Solaris Kernel and its various loadable modules

- Scheduler classes
- File systems
- System calls
- Loaders for executable file formats
- STREAMS module

The detailed view of the architecture of Solaris 10 and its distinguishing components are described as follows (Fig. CS1.3).

Processor-specific and Platform-specific Code

As seen in the diagram, this layer is the closest to the hardware and enables Solaris software to easily support different processors and system architectures.

Device Drivers

Like any other OS, device drivers in Solaris too provide access to I/O devices such as disks, tapes, CD drives, serial ports, and networks. Above these device drivers, software is layered to support device-specific functions. The device drivers in Solaris, however, are written using stable interfaces that do not change from release to release.

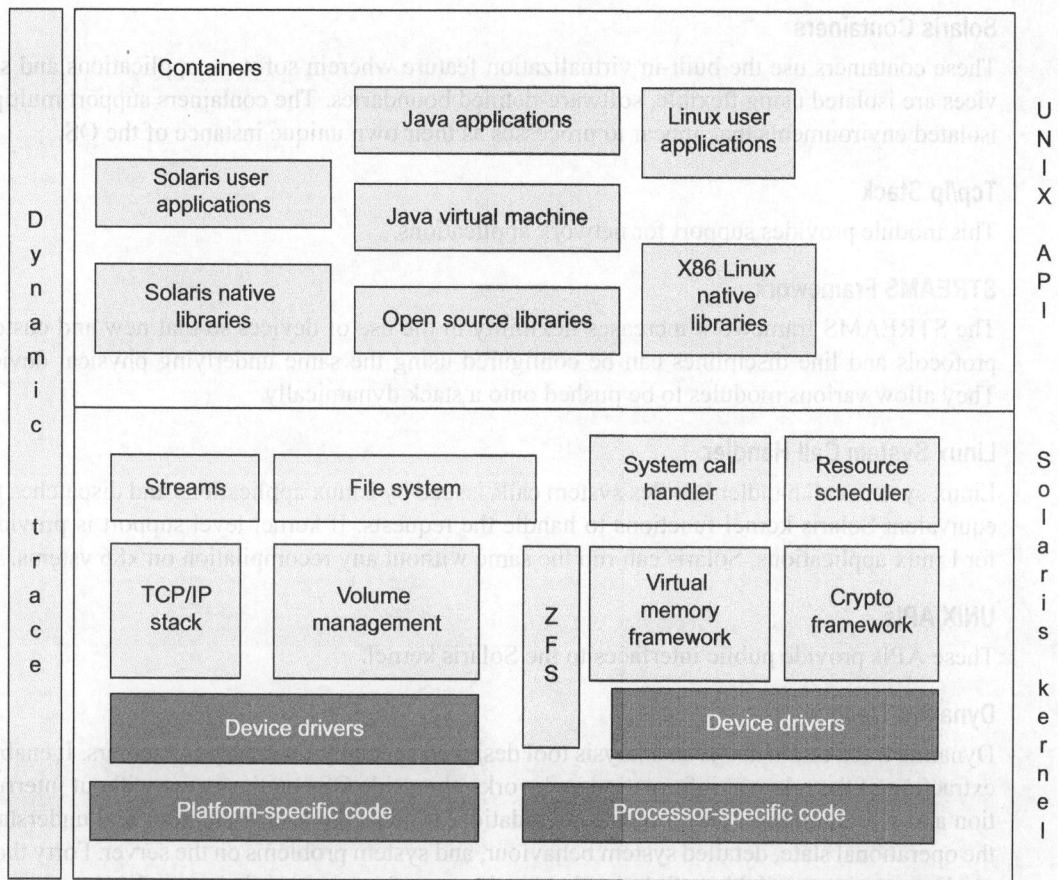

Fig. CS1.3   Architecture of Solaris 10

File Systems and Volume Management

This module helps to manage large number of disks as a single volume. It provides facilities for integration of various file systems such as NFS, Sun StorEdge™ SAM-FS file system, Sun StorEdge QFS file system, PC file system (PCFS), and VERITAS file system (VxFS).

ZFS Solaris also supports a dynamic file system known as ZFS. The major features of this file system are its almost unlimited data capacity and data-protection mechanisms. It also uses a storage pool that manages multiple disk devices and provides a virtual storage interface to file systems. Due to this, file systems can be extended while the system is operational.

Solaris Cryptographic Framework

This framework provides the API that has both kernel and user-based cryptographic functions.

Resource Scheduler

As the name suggests, this component provides supports for scheduling. Solaris 10 supports fair share scheduling.

Solaris Containers

These containers use the built-in virtualization feature wherein software applications and services are isolated using flexible, software-defined boundaries. The containers support multiple isolated environments that appear to processes as their own unique instance of the OS.

Tcp/Ip Stack

This module provides support for network applications.

STREAMS Framework

The STREAMS framework increases flexibility in the use of devices so that new and custom protocols and line disciplines can be configured using the same underlying physical device. They allow various modules to be pushed onto a stack dynamically.

Linux System Call Handler

Linux system call handler handles system calls issued by Linux applications and dispatches the equivalent Solaris kernel functions to handle the requests. If kernel-level support is provided for Linux applications, Solaris can run the same without any recompilation on x86 ystems.

UNIX APIs

These APIs provide public interfaces to the Solaris kernel.

Dynamic Trace

Dynamic trace or *Dtrace* is an analysis tool designed specially for enterprise servers. It enables extraction of the relevant information and works alongside OSs on the server without interruption and with minimum performance degradation. It helps the user to monitor and understand the operational state, detailed system behaviour, and system problems on the server. Forty thousand trace points available in Solaris 10 spare the users from writing their own debug programs. They also let the user obtain relevant records close to the fault site. This ensures faster detection of cause of faults and swift resolution of application and system bottlenecks. In addition, since the user can filter out irrelevant trace points, good system performance can be maintained.

LINUX

Linux originated as an attempt by a Finnish student, Linus Torvalds, to create a free OS kernel. Linux came into origin when Linus and his friends realized that there was a need of an OS that could take into account users' comments and suggestions for improvements. The first source code of Linux was released in 1991.

It is important to mention here that Linus developed only the kernel. It was later combined with another OS, *GNU,* which had developed most of the parts of the OS. This is the reason why Linux is most of the time called as *GNU/Linux.*

The growth of Linux along with its versions is briefly described in Table CS1.3.

Linux is originally a monolithic kernel but has been enhanced as a modular architecture of UNIX and Solaris (described earlier). Linux is also a collection of modules that can be loaded and unloaded dynamically. Since a kernel module contains an object code, it is dynamically linked to the kernel when loaded. For this purpose, there is a kernel sub-system known as *kmod.* When the kernel requires access to a module, it issues the request to kmod. The kmod first checks any dependencies to load the requested module. If there are, it first loads these modules and then the requested one.

Table CS1.3   Growth of Linux

Year	Development
1991	Linux kernel was introduced.
1992	Linux kernel was relicensed under the GNU general Public License (GPL).
1994	Linux Version 1.0 was released. It was published by the companies Red Hat and SUSE
1996	Version 2.0 of the Linux kernel was released. This kernel can now serve several processors at the same time.
1998	Work for developing the GUI for Linux began.
1999	Work on another graphical environment for Linux, i.e., GNOME started to make it a free replacement of KDE.
2001	Linux Version 2.4 was released by Linus. This new version had improved network support, improved performance for memory transactions and extended hardware support.
2004	Linux kernel 2.6.4 was released. This year also marked the release of Ubuntu.

Loadable kernel modules in Linux are loaded with the help of command *modprobe*. These modules are located in file, /lib/modules. Version 2.6 onwards, they have the extension as. *ko* (kernel object). The modules can also be listed out also with the command *lsmod*.

WINDOWS

Windows OS was developed in response to command-based OS like DOS to provide GUI to a user. The GUI was an interesting and convenient feature at that time that attracted a lot many users. This OS has also gone through various versions since its inception with more and more features in every version. The journey of Windows has been shown in Table CS1.4.

The structure of Windows has been evolved from layered to hybrid. At one time, Windows NT was designed with layered architecture. However, later on, Windows was first modified to microkernel and then to hybrid architecture. As a hybrid structure, it has all the advantages of layered, microkernel, and modular approach. Windows 2000 onwards, Windows has adopted hybrid structure. Let us discuss Windows XP architecture.

Table CS1.4   Growth of Windows

Version	Release year	Feature
Windows 1.0	November 1985	Windows Paint, Notepad, Windows Write, clock, calculator, etc.
Windows 2.0	December 1987	Excel, Word for Windows, Corel Draw, etc.
Windows 3.0	May 1990	Virtual memory, icon based program manager, sound card, Multimedia extension, etc.
Windows 3.1	April 1992	Microsoft Mail, network mail package, workgroup scheduler
Windows NT3.1	July 1993	First release of Microsoft Windows NT server and business desktop OSs.

(Contd)

(*Table CS1.4 Contd*)

Windows 95	August 1995	Built-in Internet support, dial-up networking, new *plug and play* capabilities to install software and hardware, integrated networking, etc.
Windows 98	June 1998	To support DVD discs and USB devices
Windows Me/2000	September 2000	System Restore, Windows Movie Maker tools to digitally edit, save, and share videos
Windows XP	October 2001	Active Directory Domain, Remote Desktop Server, Internet Information Services (IIS) Server, and advanced networking features
Windows Vista	November 2006	Windows Smart Security, Windows DVD Maker, IE 7, and Media Player 11, available in 35 languages
Windows Server	February 2008	Advanced in technological and security concerns
Windows 7	October 2009	Fast booting, device stage, Windows Power Shell, multi-touch
Windows Home Server 2011	April 2011	Web-based media functionality and 'add ins' feature with an app store
Windows Thin PC	February 2011	In-place installation available, cloud computing in a business network
Windows 8 (current version)	October 2012	Redesigned user interface for touchscreen users

Architecture of Windows XP

Windows XP comprises various layers such that lower layers provide functionalities to higher layers. Therefore, it may be called a layered structure. However, it is not pure layered as sometimes, non-adjacent layers communicate. It also incorporates microkernel features as it provides base services inside the kernel. However, again, it is not pure microkernel as some components like file system are in kernel mode instead of user mode. Windows XP has the features of modular architecture as the kernel has been designed with object-oriented approach and all the OS entities are in the form of objects. The modular architecture provides the flexibility to adopt or delete any module in the kernel. Thus, Windows XP is a hybrid structure incorporating other structures.

Windows XP has been divided into the following layers (Fig. CS1.4):

1. Hardware abstraction layer (HAL)
2. Kernel layer
3. Executive layer
4. Sub-system and service layer

Largely, the functionality of the OS has been divided into two modes: kernel and user modes. The first three layers work in kernel mode and the last layer operates in user mode.

Hardware Abstraction Layer

This layer abstracts the hardware-specific details and isolates the OS from them. In other words, it is a software module that interfaces between the hardware and the OS. The OS need not have the specific hardware details. This provides the convenience of portable OS. The OS accesses the hardware through HAL whenever it wants. The HAL interacts with device components directly and also with device drivers to support access to devices.

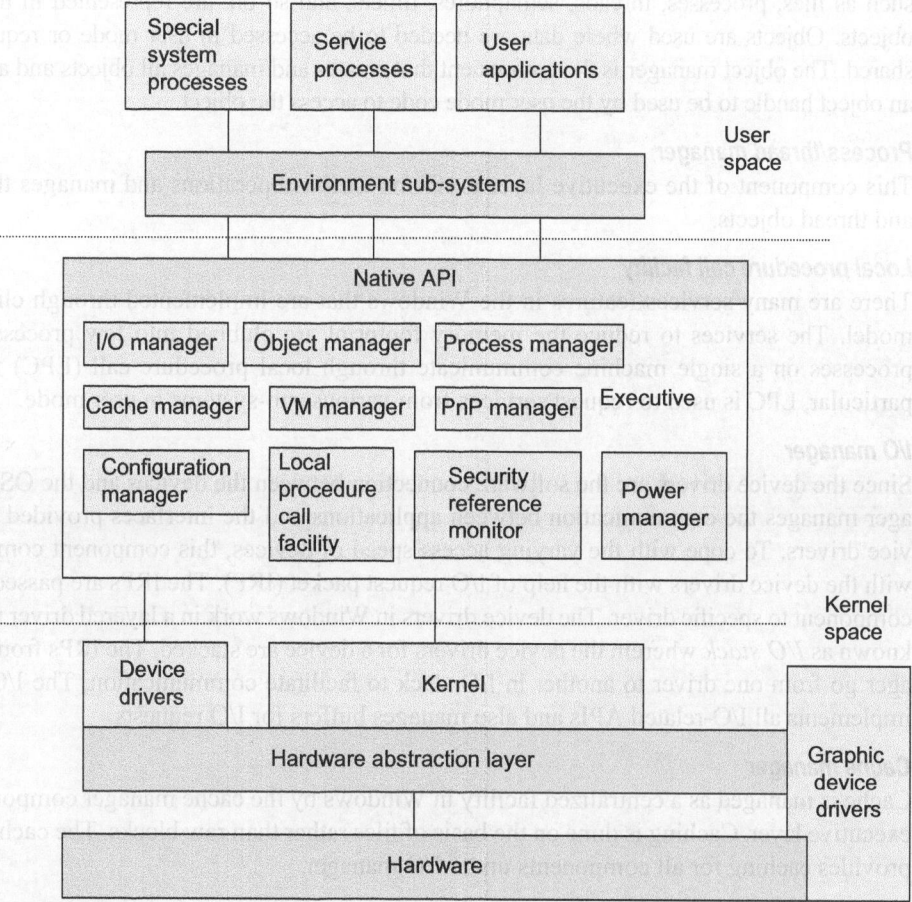

Fig. CS1.4   Windows XP architecture

Kernel Layer

This layer provides the basic kernel functionalities such as thread scheduling, process switching, exception and interrupt handling, and low-level processor synchronization, and therefore consumes very less space in the kernel space. This layer abstracts architecture specific differences between different systems. Thus, kernel layer and HAL together make Windows XP portable.

Executive Layer

This layer provides functions responsible to administer the OS sub-systems, such as process management and memory management. The executive layer provides a set of services in the form of APIs to be used by sub-systems in user mode. These APIs are known as *native APIs*. The functionalities in this layer are as follows:

Object manager

Since the kernel of Windows has been designed using object-oriented concept, various entities such as files, processes, threads, semaphores, timers, and so on. are represented in the form of objects. Objects are used where data are needed to be accessed in user mode or required to be shared. The object manager is the component that creates and manages all objects and also creates an object handle to be used by the user mode code to access the object.

Process/thread manager

This component of the executive layer performs various operations and manages the process and thread objects.

Local procedure call facility

There are many services/features in the Windows that are implemented through client-server model. The services to reduce the memory footprint are clubbed into few processes. These processes on a single machine communicate through local procedure call (LPC) facility. In particular, LPC is used to request services from various sub-systems in user mode.

I/O manager

Since the device drivers are the software connection between the devices and the OS, I/O manager manages the communication between applications and the interfaces provided by the device drivers. To cope with the varying access speed of devices, this component communicates with the device drivers with the help of I/O request packet (IRP). The IRPs are passed from this component to specific driver. The device drivers in Windows work in a layered driver model also known as *I/O stack* wherein the device drivers for a device are stacked. The IRPs from I/O manager go from one driver to another in I/O stack to facilitate communication. The I/O manager implements all I/O-related APIs and also manages buffers for I/O requests.

Cache manager

Cache is managed as a centralized facility in Windows by the cache manager component of the executive layer. Caching is done on the basis of files rather than raw blocks. The cache manager provides caching for all components under I/O manager.

Virtual memory manager

Windows uses a page-based virtual memory management scheme. Virtual memory manager manages the virtual addresses, physical memory allocation, and paging-related issues.

Power manager

The power management activities are performed by this component. It reduces power consumption by suspending idle processes, puts the processor to sleep, and so on. Windows XP power management schemes are user based only, that is, the power scheme changes as per the current user or the new user who logs on. The entire system has only one active power scheme and that is based on the power configuration of the user who last logged in.

Plug and play manager

Plug and play (PnP) manager recognizes any new hardware configuration and adapts accordingly. After recognizing the new installed devices, it determines which device drivers are required to support a particular device. Once the device drivers are identified, it loads them.

Security reference monitor

Windows OS uses a uniform security mechanism for every user-accessible entity in the system. Since the object-oriented design of the OS enforces the uniform security, the security reference monitor (SRM) uses the same routines for access validation and audit checks. To examine the access validation, it checks each process' security token and access control list of objects. Some users may require the permission to perform backup or debug the processes. For this, SRM provides special privileges in security tokens. It also logs the security audit events.

Configuration manager

The configuration information is stored in a database known as *registry database*. It is called a *hive*. Separate hives are there for various types of configuration information, such as system information and default user preferences. Since the system hive is required to boot the system, the configuration manager is implemented in the executive layer.

Sub-system and Service Layer

As discussed within executive layer topic, the native APIs are used by user processes. However, most user processes do not call native APIs directly but the APIs given by user-mode system components. These system components are called *environment sub-systems*. These are user-mode processes inserted between the executive and the user space. For example, Win32 and POSIX are environment sub-systems. It means the processes in Win32 or POSIX call functions are defined in Win32 or POSIX. The Win32 or POSIX then translates these function calls into system calls in the native APIs. Windows XP allows user mode processes to call native APIs directly. Besides environment sub-systems, there are some *special system processes*. These processes are required to manage the system, such as managing the sessions, authentication, and logon process. There are some *service processes* also in this layer to provide various services, for example, printer spooler, event logger, network services, and so on. To make use of the system, the users require some DLLs and EXEs known as *user applications*. These user applications are also present in this layer.

PART II
Process Management

5 Fundamentals of Process Management

5.1 INTRODUCTION

Process is a basic term to understand the operation of an operating system. Since there are a number of user and system processes, there is a need to manage them. A running process may be interrupted at any time. Due to this concept, the processes are not in the same state forever. They change state according to an event in the system. Moreover, the state of an interrupted process needs to be saved so that it can resume its work. If a process is interrupted, another process is scheduled to be dispatched to processor for execution. Besides this, processes also need to communicate and synchronize with each other. Therefore, it is critical to manage the processes in the system from the view point of their state change, scheduling, dispatching, process switching, communication, synchronization, and so on. In this chapter, we will study these basic concepts regarding the management of processes in the system.

5.2 TERMINOLOGY

To perform a computation on the computer system, we must have a unit of work or execution for the user computation. Basically, we need a term to call all CPU activities performed by the operating system. Various terms are in use interchangeably. First of all, we take two terms: *Program* and *Job*. These two terms were in use when the batch systems developed. The term 'Program' was very common at that time and also used frequently today. A program can be considered a set of instructions in the form of modules. Thus, program is a classic term used for user's computation. Since in a batch system, there was a requirement to load and unload the magnetic tapes for various activities such as compiling, linking, loading, and so on, the term 'job' was used for performing the execution of a program through the execution of those activities. These activities were termed as a sequence of job steps as shown in Fig. 5.1. For example, the job is to execute a C program and the execution of compiler, linker, and loader programs are job steps. These job steps are in sequence, that is, loading is meaningless without the execution of linking program. Thus, *job is a sequence of single programs*. However, the terms 'job' and 'program' were used interchangeably and are also popular today as generic terms for unit of execution.

Learning Objectives

After reading this chapter, you should be able to understand:

- Difference between job, program, task, and process
- Implicit and non-implicit processes
- Process environment
- Life cycle of a process with its states and state transitions
- Implementation of processes with process control block
- Context switching
- Process switching
- Process schedulers
- Various operations on processes

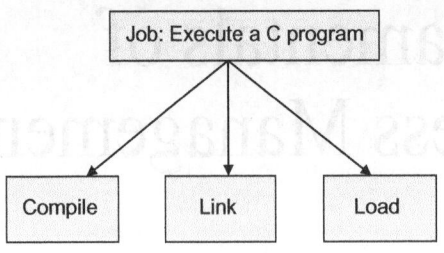

Fig. 5.1 Job as a sequence of programs

The term 'task' was used when there was a need to have concurrent execution on a single processor, that is, more than one program of a single user. For example, when a user works in Windows environment, he or she is able to open and work on multiple windows such as Word file, email, web browser, and so on. To distinguish it from the multi-programming and multiuser, the term 'task' was used and that is why it is called multi-tasking. Therefore, the term is used in the sense of multi-tasking.

The term 'process' is different from the terms 'job' or 'program.' We need to understand the nature of a program and process for this difference. A program is a set of instructions the user/programmer has written and stored somewhere. It means that a *program is a passive entity* and continues to exist at a place. On the other hand, when a program is ready for the execution, it becomes active and is known as a process. In other words, a *program in execution is called a process*. Thus, a process is an active entity with a limited span of time as compared to a program. The term 'task' is also sometimes used interchangeably with the term 'process'.

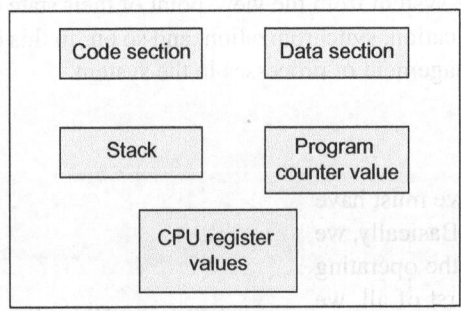

Fig. 5.2 Process environment

When a program is ready to execute or, in other words, when it becomes a process, it means that now it is able to compete for resources. Since there may be many processes ready at one time, the process needs to compete for the resources such as CPU time, memory, I/O devices, and so on. Thus, a process is eligible to compete for resources, whereas a program is not. When a process needs to execute, that is, when it gets the CPU time, it has a program counter (PC) value (initialized with process's address) also for moving to the next instruction while executing along with a code section or program code. Moreover, a data section and a stack are also allocated to a process along with other resources. When a process starts executing, the data may be stored in some CPU registers. Therefore, CPU register values are also attached to processes that are null (blank) before execution. In this way, all these together make a process's environment as shown in Fig. 5.2.

Consider an example for the difference between a program and a process (see Table 5.1). In multiuser environment, many users may open a Word program. When a user tries to open the Word file, the OS loads the Word program into memory, creating a process for the user. Now this process has separate set of resources as mentioned in Section 5.1 for execution. The process is then scheduled for execution. If another user opens the Word file, the OS again creates and schedules a separate process for the editor program. In this way, the same editor program can be invoked as separate processes. It means that there are multiple processes sharing the text editor

Table 5.1   Difference between program and process

Program	Process
Passive/Static	Active/Dynamic
Cannot compete for resources	Competes for resources
Has a code section	Has a code section, data section, stack, and program counter

code section, but the data section, stack, program counter, and resources of each process will be different. Thus, each process has its own *address space* consisting of code section, data section, and stack section. The code section stores the program code. The data section consists of global variables. The stack stores local variables, parameters in a module call, and return addresses.

5.3   IMPLICIT/SYSTEM AND NON-IMPLICIT/USER PROCESSES

While working on the computer system, processes must be defined to execute the jobs. These processes also need to be initialized. There are two types of processes depending on how they are defined and initialized. If the OS defines a process, it is called an implicit or system process. If the process is defined by the programmer, then it is an explicit or user process. Sometimes, there is a requirement that processes be defined by the OS itself. However, for the reasons of efficiency and control, some processes need to be defined by the programmer. Therefore, both types of processes exist in the system.

In general, implicit processes are created when multi-programming and multi-tasking environment are implemented. For example, when a user submits his or her program in multiuser time-sharing environment, the OS creates a process for each user program. In this case, the OS is responsible for initializing the process attributes. Similarly, the batch job submitted to the system may also be divided into several processes. For example, to execute a C program (job), the OS will create processes for compiling, linking, and loading programs. In this way, the implicit processes may be created for single programs as independent processes or a job may be divided into multiple processes by the operating system.

It is not necessary that the OS created processes, that is, implicit processes will provide the efficiency in executing the jobs on the computer system. Sometimes, the programmer needs to divide a job into processes according to his or her convenience and wants control of these processes with him or her, not the operating system. In this case, the programmer may divide the jobs into processes as per the need and create explicit processes. The explicit processes may also be initialized by the programmer during development or at runtime. Moreover, the control of some of the attributes of the processes is also with the programmer. For example, in Real-time systems, the division of processes is a critical work and is performed by the programmer. There are some processes with higher priority that must be executed even if a lower priority process is executing then. The higher priority process will preempt the lower priority process and gain the excess of processor. A process responsible for accepting the sensor data and updating the data accordingly will get the higher priority over other processes. It means that the control of process priority should be with the programmer. The programmer will initialize the priority of every process according to its priority, and the priority of the process is determined on the basis of its functionality. The critical real-time functionality process will get the higher priority. In real-time systems, there may be the case when the priority of the process needs to be changed to reduce the starvation of lower-priority processes. Therefore, the dynamic priority is provided to the process. Thus, explicit processes with dynamic priority are under control of the programmer. In this way, there may be other attributes of the processes that can be initialized and are under control of the programmer.

5.4 RELATIONSHIP BETWEEN PROCESSES

In Section 5.2, a process was discussed as a program in execution in the context when a program is executed sequentially. The program may consist of a set of procedures or functions, but each of them executes in a sequence. This program when executed becomes a single process consisting of all procedures inside the program. However, there may be some procedures or functions in a program that can be executed simultaneously, that is, there is no sequence of order of execution between them. In this case, the program when executed consists of many processes. This type of program is known as *concurrent program*. In general, there are some processes (created out of a program or concurrent program) whose executions overlap in time. These processes are known as *concurrent processes*.

In a multi-programming system, processes are interleaved to be executed efficiently on a single processor. These processes are concurrent processes. Concurrent processes may be independent of each other and are known as *independent processes*. However, they may also interact with each other. They may share a data, send a message to each other, or send signals to coordinate their activities. These are known as *interacting* or *cooperating processes*. Cooperating processes are very critical and important in the system. These processes are critical in the sense that if they will not cooperate with each other, a chaos may occur in the system. The problems related to concurrent processes will be discussed in Chapter 7.

Another relation between processes is the parent–child relationship. It means that when a process creates its sub-processes, the parent–child relation exists between the parent process and its sub-processes. A child process may further create another child process. In this way, the parent–child relationship between processes gives rise to a tree structure.

5.5 LIFE CYCLE OF A PROCESS

Since a process is an active entity as discussed in Section 5.4, it changes its state with time. A process from its creation to termination passes through various states. A process when created is in a new state as a program/job. Whenever a new job is entered into the system, it is stored in the *job pool/queue* maintained in the hard disk (see Fig. 5.3) in case of a batch system. In the job queue, a job waits for its turn to be moved to the main memory. When a job is selected to be brought into the main memory, it is called *job scheduling*. When a job is loaded into the memory, it becomes a process and is stored in a waiting queue where all processes wait for their turn to be sent to the CPU for execution. This waiting queue is called *ready queue*. A process in ready queue becomes ready for execution as it can compete for the CPU and resources.

A new job is stored in the ready queue in case of a time-sharing system. Therefore, there is no need of job scheduling in these systems. The processes in ready queue are then selected for the next execution called *process scheduling* or *CPU scheduling*. After this, the selected process is sent for execution called *process dispatching*. After getting the CPU time, the running

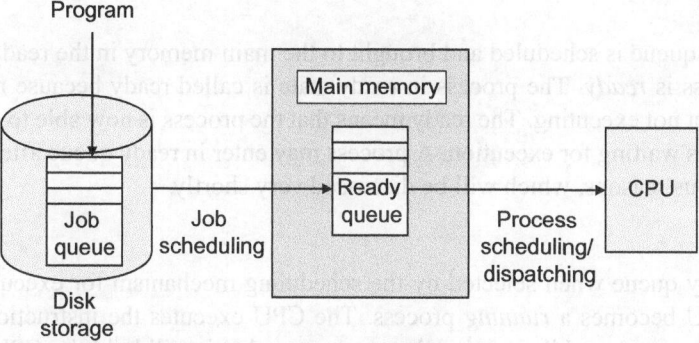

Program

Main memory

Job queue

Job scheduling

Ready queue

Disk storage

Process scheduling/ dispatching

CPU

Fig. 5.3   Job scheduling and process scheduling

process executes its full code and terminates. The scheduling and dispatching functions are performed by the *scheduler* and *dispatcher*, respectively. These are the modules of the operating system, which will be discussed later in this chapter.

This may not be the case always. A process may be interrupted while executing, or it may transition to wait state while trying to access an I/O device. Thus, a process as an active entity is not in a static state but changes its state with time. Let us now discuss the states a process can have and how it transitions from one state to another.

5.5.1 Process States and State Transitions

The state of a process is an effective way to manage the processes in a multi-programming environment. A process may be running and another process may be waiting for an I/O device at the same time. Therefore, through the states of the processes, the situation of every process at a given time is identified and every process is managed such that it gets a uniform execution. Various events happening in the system cause a process to change its state. Thus, a process moves through a series of discrete states. The states of a process are depicted as follows (see Fig. 5.4):

New State

Whenever a job/program enters the system, it is put into a job queue in case of a batch system. In the job queue, the process is in its *new* state. It means that the process is still in the secondary storage as a program and not admitted to the main memory. However, the control information regarding the new process is being updated and maintained in the memory.

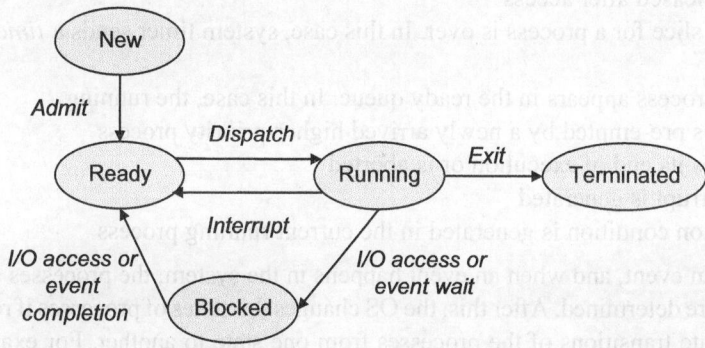

New

Admit

Ready

Dispatch

Running

Exit

Terminated

Interrupt

I/O access or event completion

I/O access or event wait

Blocked

Fig. 5.4   Process state diagram

Ready State

When program in job queue is scheduled and brought to the main memory in the ready queue, the state of the process is *ready*. The process in ready state is called ready because now it is ready for execution but not executing. The ready means that the process is now able to compete for the resources and is waiting for execution. A process may enter in ready queue after getting its execution for various reasons, which will be discussed very shortly.

Running State

A process in the ready queue when selected by the scheduling mechanism for execution and dispatched to the CPU becomes a *running* process. The CPU executes the instruction in the code of the process. A process while running does not mean that it will hold the CPU until it terminates. It can either be interrupted or its allotted time expires.

Blocked State

A process while executing may reach an instruction where it has to wait for some I/O devices or some other event. In this case, the processor will be taken away from the running process and may be given to another ready process. Therefore, the current running process becomes a *blocked* process. A blocked process will wait for the I/O device and its access or the other event to happen. The blocked process waits for the event only in the main memory but in a separate queue known as *blocked queue*. When the I/O access or the other event is over, the process is now again ready to execute further. However, now, it cannot be given the processor because some other process may be executing at that time. Therefore, the blocked process after its wait will move again to the ready queue for its turn to execute.

Terminated State

A process executed completely till its end and terminated becomes a *terminated* process. There may be some other reasons also for terminating a process, for example, when a process is not able to recover from an error or some other process aborts it in between for some reasons. The terminated process will release all the resources that have been allotted to it.

The process changes its state when there is an event causing a state transition. The events can be of the following types:

- A new process is created
- The process makes a resource request
- Resource is released
- The process requests an I/O device
- An I/O device is released after access
- The allocated time slice for a process is over. In this case, system timer sends a *timer interrupt*
- A higher-priority process appears in the ready queue. In this case, the running lower-priority job is pre-empted by a newly arrived higher-priority process
- The process reaches its end of execution or is aborted
- Any hardware interrupt is generated
- An error or exception condition is generated in the current running process

The OS looks for an event, and when an event happens in the system, the processes affected with the recent event are determined. After this, the OS changes the states of processes if required. Thus, events cause state transitions of the processes from one state to another. For example, if a running process reaches an instruction or system call where it needs to access an I/O device.

Table 5.2   Event handling in OS

Event	Current state	New state	OS actions
A new process is created.	--	NEW	Assigns an ID to the process and some other related information.
Process makes a resource or an I/O request.	RUNNING	BLOCKED	Schedules the next process from ready queue and dispatches it to the processor.
The resource or an I/O device is released.	BLOCKED	READY (If the resource or I/O device released is what the BLOCKED process requires)	Schedules the next process from ready queue and dispatches it to the processor.
An interrupt is generated by another process or due to any other reason.	RUNNING	READY	Schedules the next process (interrupting process if the interrupt has come from this process) from ready queue and dispatches it to the processor.
Process reaches its end of execution or is aborted.	RUNNING	TERMINATED	Schedules the next process from ready queue and dispatches it to the processor.

The state transitions occur due to various events, which are listed as follows:

If the device requested cannot be granted immediately, the process needs to wait on the device queue of the device requested. Now, there is a need to change the state of process because the processor will be taken away from this process and given to some other process in the ready queue. Thus, the state of this process will be changed from running to blocked or sleep. Similarly, when the event happens such that the requested device is released, this blocked process will be awakened and its state will be changed from blocked to ready. In this way, events become the source of state transitions of the processes and help in managing the processes (see Table 5.2).

Admit (New → Ready)

This event takes place when there is a need to increase the degree of multi-programming in the system. It means that a process can be accommodated in the memory. Therefore, admit event allows fetching one job from the job pool to the main memory and the process is admitted to ready queue. In this way, the state of the process changes from new to ready.

Dispatch (Ready → Running)

The dispatch event sends a process to the CPU for execution after selection. The state of the process changes from ready to running due to this event. How the process is selected for dispatching depends on a scheduling algorithm, which will be discussed later on.

Exit (Running → Terminated)

When a running process reaches its completion or aborts due to any reason, the exit event changes its state from running to terminated.

Interrupt (Running → Ready)

The running process may also be pre-empted from execution by some other process. It may happen due to several reasons. For example, in a time-sharing multi-user system, a fair distribution is done of the processor time to provide equal amount of processor's time to each process.

Therefore, in this case, a fixed time slot is given to each process for execution. On the expiry of this time slot, interrupt will stop the execution of this process for the time being and changes its state to ready again. In another case, in real-time systems, every process is provided a priority for execution. The highest-priority process has the privilege to execute first. Therefore, if a lower-priority process is executing and a higher-priority process arrives, it will send the interrupt and cause the running process to stop the execution, changing the state of the running process to ready. Whenever interrupt event changes the state of a running process to ready again, the process that has been interrupted will enter the ready queue once again and will compete for the processor.

I/O or Event Wait (Running → Blocked)

A running process reaches an instruction in the code that it needs to wait for some access. For example, the instruction may be to access an I/O device; in this case, the process must wait for the device on its device queue if the device is busy then. In this way, a process may need to wait for an event or request that cannot be granted immediately. Therefore, this wait event causes change of state from running to blocked. A blocked process will wait for the event to happen or the request to be granted.

I/O or Event Wait Completion (Blocked → Ready)

The blocked-process wait is over when the event-wait completion happens. It means that the process has accessed the device, or the request for which it was waiting has been serviced. The blocked process can then again resume its operation for which it needs the processor. However, it cannot be granted the processor immediately as some other process is executing then. Therefore, this process will move to the ready queue causing the state transition from blocked to ready. In the ready queue, the process will again wait for its turn to get the processor.

Example 5.1

Consider Example 1.1 of Chapter 1 illustrate the state transitions for all the processes in the system.

Solution

The state transitions for all the processes are as follows:

Time	J1	J2	J3	Event	State transitions	OS actions
0	RUNNING	--	--	--	--	--
2	BLOCKED	RUNNING	--	J1 requests I/O	J1: Running to Blocked	Puts J1 to Blocked queue.
						Schedules the process J2 from ready queue and dispatches it to the processor.
7	--	BLOCKED	RUNNING	J2 requests I/O	J2: Running to Blocked	Puts J2 to Blocked queue.
						Schedules the process J3 from ready queue and dispatches it to the processor.

(Contd)

(Table Contd)

10	RUNNING	--	BLOCKED	J3 requests I/O	J3: Running to Blocked	Puts J3 to Blocked queue. Schedules the process J1 from ready queue and dispatches it to the processor.
12	BLOCKED	RUNNING	--	J1 requests I/O	J1: Running to Blocked	Puts J1 to Blocked queue. Schedules the process J2 from ready queue and dispatches it to the processor.
14	--	TERMI-NATED	RUNNING	J2 Exits	J2: Running to Terminated	Schedules the process J3 from ready queue and dispatches it to the processor.
16	RUNNING	--	TERMI-NATED	J3 Exits	J3: Running to Terminated	Schedules the process J1 from ready queue and dispatches it to the processor.
18	TERMI-NATED	--	--	J1 Exits	J1: Running to Terminated	--

5.5.2 Suspended Processes and Their State Transitions

This is understood now that the processes change their states when there is an event. As per the knowledge of multi-programming, when a process waits for an I/O device, that is, when the process is blocked, another process from the ready queue is scheduled. However, there may be the case that all the processes need I/O devices, that is all the processes at a particular instant of time are blocked and are waiting for some event to happen and no process is under execution, that is, in the running state. In this case, no useful work is being done by the processor. Therefore, it is necessary to bring in some process that is ready for execution. However, there may be a situation that there is no space so that a new process may be swapped in. Therefore, we need to create the memory space for this purpose. Since blocked processes cannot be executed unless their I/O devices are released, some blocked process may be swapped out.

The swapped-out process is known as *suspended process* and the queue where it waits is called *suspended queue* in the secondary storage such as disk. The state of the process then changes from blocked to suspended. In this way, sometimes, there is a need to have this suspended state also in consideration to manage the processes in this situation. The question arises that when these suspended processes will come back to the ready queue. Since the suspended process was in blocked state, it was waiting for an I/O device before suspension. Therefore, when the wait for an I/O device is over, the suspended process can be brought back to the ready queue. In fact, whenever the suspended process is swapped out in the disk, there are two choices for bringing in a process that is ready for execution. First is a suspended process from the suspend queue whose waiting event is now over, that is, it is now ready for execution. Second, a new process from the job queue can be scheduled in the ready queue. However, the new job from the job queue will increase the load of the system. The second choice is only valid if we want to increase the degree of multi-programming of the system, otherwise the first choice is preferred.

Two more states for suspended processes can be added to the previous model of process behaviour. These are as follows (see Fig. 5.5):

Blocked–Suspended

The blocked process waiting in blocked queue in the memory is suspended and moved to suspended queue in disk. The state of the process is called blocked–suspended. The blocked–suspended process is still waiting for its desired event to happen but in the disk.

Ready–Suspended

When the event for which the blocked–suspended process was waiting has occurred, its state changes. The state is ready because now it is ready to be executed. However, yet, it cannot be executed as it is still in the disk. Therefore, its state is called ready-suspended.

The new transition states are as follows (see Fig. 5.5):

Suspend (Blocked→Blocked-Suspend)

This event takes place when a process is in blocked state and is waiting in blocked queue in the memory. After this event, the blocked process from the queue is taken away and placed in suspended queue in the disk. Now, the process will wait for its desired event in the disk instead of the memory. The state of the process changes from blocked to blocked–suspended.

I/O or Event Wait Completion (Blocked-Suspend→Ready-Suspend)

This event takes place when the I/O wait for a blocked–suspended process is over, changing the state of the process from blocked–suspended to ready–suspended. The new status is ready–suspended because the process is now ready to be executed, but it cannot get the processor because it is still in the suspended queue.

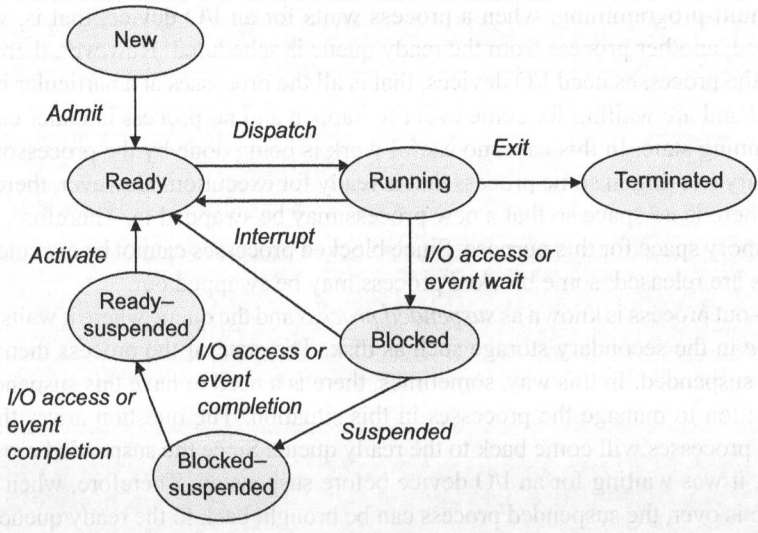

Fig. 5.5 Process state diagram with suspended states

Activate (Ready-Suspend→Ready)

This event takes place when there are no processes in the ready queue or the priority of the ready–suspended process is higher than the process in ready queue. Therefore, this event moves the ready–suspended process from the suspended queue to the ready queue, changing the state of the process from ready–suspended to ready. Now, the process that was originally blocked and then suspended is ready for execution in the ready queue.

The case of suspended processes has been discussed when there is a need to swap out some processes. There may be some other reasons also for suspending the processes. Some are discussed as follows:

- Imagine that there are processes in ready queue and some processes are blocked. However, it may be the case that we need to suspend some process to have a free memory block. Which process should be suspended? In general, blocked process is suspended because ready queue processes are ready to execute as compared to blocked processes that are still waiting for an I/O device. However, this is not the case always. A ready process may also become a candidate process for suspension. Some of the reasons may be

1. That the large memory space that we require may be available only when a ready process is suspended
2. The blocked process is of higher priority as compared to all ready processes
3. And that there are too many processes in the system causing performance degradation

In such cases, it would not be feasible to suspend a blocked process; rather, a ready process should be suspended.

To implement the suspension of a ready process, there is a need to have another transition state from ready state to ready–suspended as follows:

Suspended (Ready→Ready-Suspend)

This event takes place when a process is in ready state and is waiting in ready queue in the memory. After this event, the ready process from the queue is taken away and placed in suspended queue in the disk. Now, the process will be there until it is activated and called again in the ready queue. The state of the process changes from ready to ready–suspended (see Fig. 5.6).

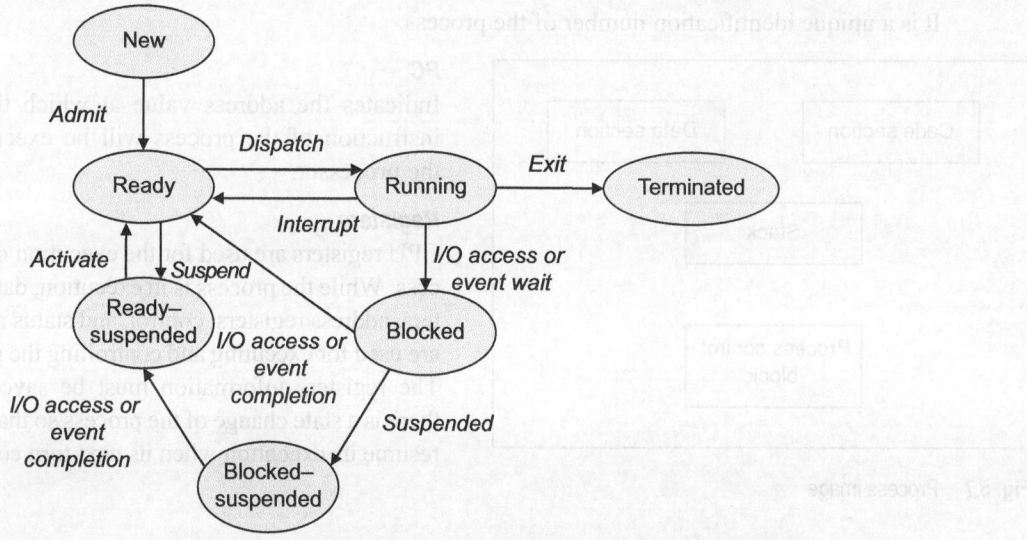

Fig. 5.6   Process state diagram with ready to ready–suspended transition

- There are many background processes that are of very low priority or utility processes that may be suspended in case there is no need or when memory space is required for other critical processes
- If the OS detects a deadlock, then the process causing the deadlock may be suspended for some time so that the deadlock situation is removed
- A parent process may also suspend its child process if there is an error in its execution

5.6 PROCESS CONTROL BLOCK

The process environment discussed in Section 5.5 consists of program (code), data section, and stack. However, this is not sufficient to control a process. The OS needs some attributes associated with the processes to implement and control them. The attributes are stored in the data structure known as *process control block* (PCB) or *process descriptor*. The collection of user program, data section, stack, and the associated attributes is called the *process image* as shown in Fig. 5.7.

The PCB is created for every process whenever a new process is created in the system. Similarly, it is also deleted as the process is terminated. The PCB contains all information about the process needed for its control. For example, for the identification of the process, there must be an ID for it. At a particular instant, the current state of the process and its PC value must be known. Whenever, there is process switching, the state of the process in PCB must be changed. At the same time, the processor register values for the current process must be saved so that it can resume the execution again. Some processes are more important than others. For this purpose, a priority of every process is maintained. Therefore, priority is also one field in the PCB. Since the process will be stored somewhere in the memory, the address information where the process image will be stored is also a part of the PCB. The information related to resources held by the process and accounting information such as CPU time used, disk used, and so on will also be stored in the PCB. Thus, there is a lot of information associated with a process stored in its PCB. The information stored in the PCB basically provides control over the execution of the process. The following are the fields associated with a PCB (see Fig. 5.8):

PID
It is a unique identification number of the process.

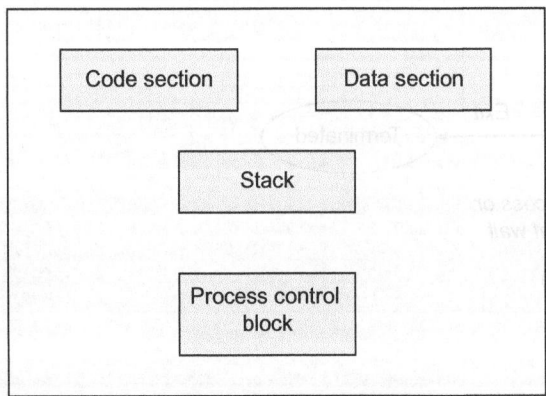

Fig. 5.7   Process image

PC
Indicates the address value at which the next instruction of the process will be executed by the processor.

Registers
CPU registers are used for the execution of a process. While the process is in execution, data registers, address registers, control, and status registers are used for executing and controlling the process. The registers information must be saved when there is a state change of the process so that it may resume its execution when its next turn comes.

PID
PC and CPU registers
Process state
Process priority
Event information
Memory-related information
Resource-related information
Scheduling-related information
Various pointers

Fig. 5.8   PCB

State

A process has a number of states in its life. For scheduling the processes, the current state of a process must be known.

Priority

The priority number can be assigned to a process to give preference to it over other. In general, the lowest number means the highest priority, for example, the process with Priority 1 will have the highest priority over all other processes. However, the priority scheme may be changed depending on the OS that we select.

Event information

This is the event for which a blocked process is waiting. If the awaited event is over, the information regarding this event must be stored in this field so that the status of the blocked process is changed to ready.

Memory-related information

Memory-management component of the OS uses many registers and tables. The information regarding all this memory-related information linked to a process is also mentioned in the PCB, for example, the values of the base and limit register of the process, page tables, segment tables, and so on. All these tables will be discussed in Memory Management chapter. The information is necessary while de-allocating the memory of the process.

Resource-related information

The resources allocated to a process are listed here. For example, all files opened by this process are listed in this field. The information is necessary to release the resources on the termination of the process. For example, all opened files must be closed on the termination of the process. Moreover, the information regarding the utilization of the resources may also be stored here. For example, the processor utilization may be required by the schedulers.

Scheduling-related information

A process will be executed according to a scheduling algorithm. The scheduling-related information of a process is also stored such as the time the process has waited, the amount of time the process executed the last time it was running.

Pointer to parent process

If a process is a child process, then the pointer to its parent process is stored here.

Pointer to child process

If a process has some child processes, then the pointer to its child processes is stored here.

Pointer to address space of the process

This is the pointer to the process's data and instructions in the memory.

5.7 IMPLEMENTATION OF PROCESSES

Now we can discuss the implementation of processes in the operating system. Using the knowledge of process states, process image, and the PCB, the implementation of processes can be explained. The OS manages and controls the resources by having a table. The tables are important data structures to store information about every process and resource. This is the reason the OS maintains memory tables, I/O tables, file tables, and process tables. The processes are implemented by the means of *process tables*. The process tables store the ID of every process and, corresponding to it, the pointer to its PCB as shown in Fig. 5.9.

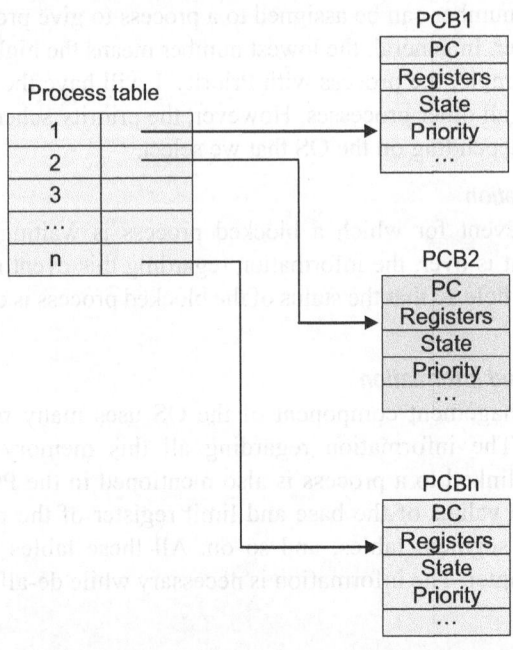

Fig. 5.9   Process table and the PCB

At the time of creation of a new process, the OS allocates a memory for it, loads a process code in the allocated memory, and sets up data space for it. In this way, process environment is created for a process. Further, the PCB for the process is created to have a control on it throughout its execution. The state of the process is stored as 'New' in its PCB. Whenever this process moves to the ready queue, its state is changed to 'Ready'. Similarly, when it is dispatched to the CPU, its state is changed to 'Running' in its PCB. When a running process needs to wait for an I/O device, its state is changed to 'Blocked'. The various queues used here are implemented as linked lists. There are mainly the following queues:

- *Ready queue* for storing the processes with state ready
- *Blocked queue* for storing the processes that needs to wait for an I/O device or a resource
- *Suspended queue* for storing the blocked processes that have been suspended
- *Free-process queue* for the information of empty space in the memory where a new PCB can be created

All these queues store a particular process's PCB only for the sake of search efficiency. If there is a process with the state ready, then its PCB is stored in the ready queue. Therefore, as soon as the state of a process is changed, its PCB is moved to its appropriate queue. All these queues are implemented as linked lists. Each PCB has a pointer that points to the next PCB. There is a header for each type of queue. The header stores the information about the first and the last PCBs in that queue. For example, there is a ready-queue header that provides the information about the first and the last PCBs in the queue (see Fig. 5.10). Similarly, there is a blocked-queue header. There is one more header giving the information about the running process information; however, there is no queue of running processes because there is only one

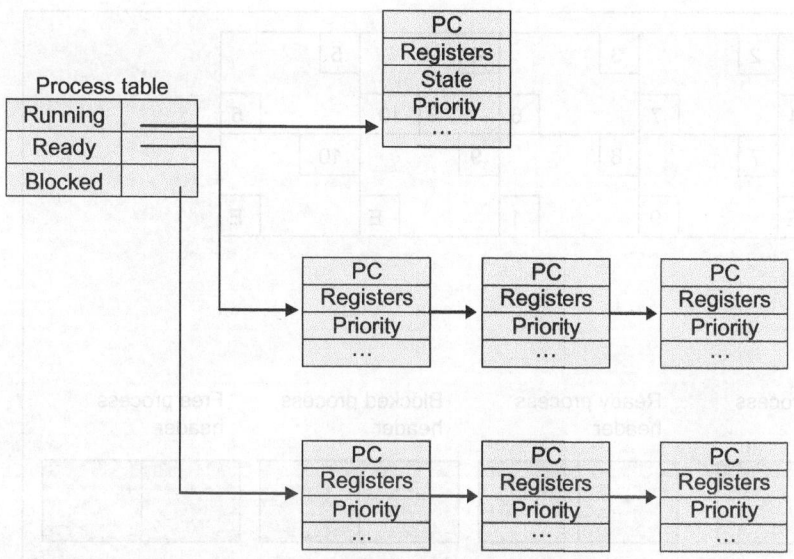

Fig. 5.10   Separate queues for different states of the processes

running process in the system. One more queue having the information of a process's area, which is free after the termination of a process, will release the memory after its termination. This memory area can be used for a new process. Therefore, the free process queue is a linked list of the free areas where the upcoming new processes can be stored. The free process queue also has a header. All the headers provide information about the address of the first and the last PCBs in that queue. Only running header gives the address of only one running process because there is a single running process in the system. Let us see one example (see Fig. 5.11) for the implementation of PCBs, queues, and their corresponding headers. As a notation, we are representing one PCB in the memory as one rectangle having two smaller rectangles inside it. The top rectangle represents the process ID, and the bottom rectangle represents the address of the next PCB in the queue. All the headers have been shown below the representation of all PCBs in the memory. In the bottom rectangle, symbol 'E' represents the end of the queue. The running process header shows in this example that Process 5 is running. The ready-process header shows that in this queue, Process 8 is the first and Process 10 is the last. Looking at the rectangle shaped PCB that starts with PCB Number 8, the next PCB is Number 1. When we move to the rectangle shaped PCB that starts with PCB Number 1, its next PCB number is 4. In this way, by observing the chain in the figure, we can say that Processes 8, 1, 4, and 10 are in the ready queue. Similarly, Processes 3 and 6 are in the blocked queue and 2, 7, and 9 are in the free-process queue.

Besides changing the state of a process, the PCB of this running process needs to be saved at this time so that the process can resume its execution from where it left off. Since all information of a running process is in its PCB, the PCB must be saved for this purpose. Initially, the process' program counter, program status word, registers, and other information are stored on the stack. After this, the stack information is stored in the corresponding PCB of the process. Once the current status of the process is saved in its PCB, the process can resume its execution when it will get the chance to be in the ready queue. This saving of the status of the running process in its PCB is called *context saving*.

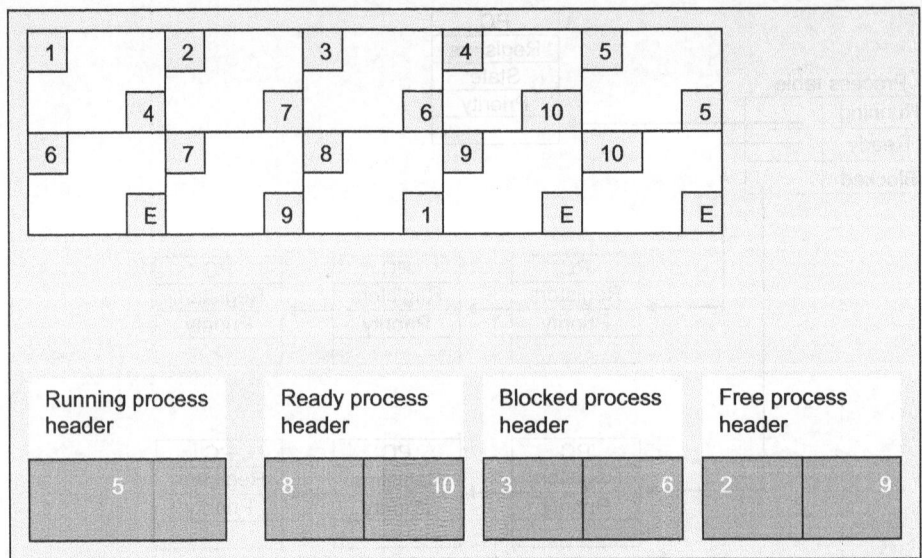

Fig. 5.11 PCB queues in memory

After saving the context of a process, the appropriate event-handling function is executed. For example, if the process needs to wait for an I/O device, then it is sent to the queue of the blocked processes. After this, there is requirement that another process be dispatched to the CPU because the current process has been interrupted. Therefore, scheduler is called to schedule a process from the ready queue. After selecting the process from the ready queue, its PCB is loaded and dispatched to the CPU for execution. In this way, the processes are implemented by saving their contexts in PCBs and making state change possible.

5.8 CONTEXT SWITCHING

The context saving as discussed in Section 5.7 is necessary whenever a running process is interrupted or waits for an I/O device. It means that the current context of a process always resides in its PCB. Therefore, whenever the running process stops, its context is saved in its PCB and the context of other scheduled process from its PCB is loaded. This is known as *context switching*. However, saving the context of the current process takes some time. It is obvious that saving the registers and other information will consume some time. Similarly, loading the context of other process also takes some time, which is known as *context switch time*. However, during this context switch time, what is the processor doing? Since the current process is not running and no new process has been scheduled for execution, the processor is idle during the context switch time. Therefore, the context switch time is a pure overhead for a multi-programming/multi-tasking environment because CPU is not doing any execution during this time. In the lifetime of a process, a process may either wait for an I/O device or be interrupted many times. Thus, the context switch time is proportional to the frequency of processes being stopped. For example, two processes in a multi-tasking environment will have the context switch time in saving the context of one process and in loading the context of another.

Example 5.2

Consider Example 1.1 of Chapter 1. In this example, we have seen the timing diagram of multi-programming without considering the context switch time. If we consider the context switch time of 1 unit time between two processes, then what will be the total execution time of three processes?

Solution

The timing diagram after considering the context switch time of 1 unit time between two processes is shown as follows:

The total execution time in this case is 24, whereas it was 18 without context switching (refer to Example 1.1). This example shows that the context switch time between the processes is pure overhead and no actual execution by the processor is being done.

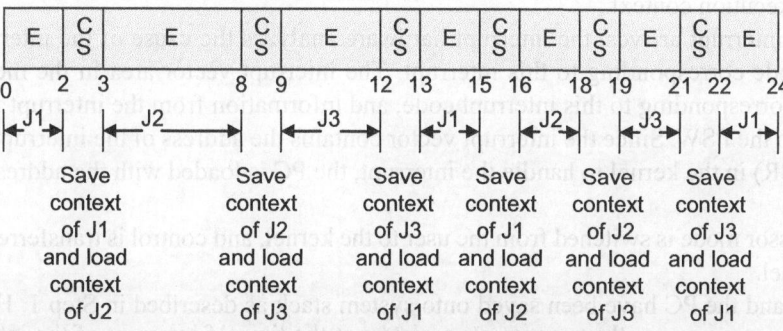

CS: Context switch time

5.9   PROCESS SWITCHING

When a running process is interrupted and the OS assigns another process to it and transfers control to it, it is known as process switching. Process switching occurs due to an event in the system. The events can be of any type as described in Section 5.4.1. However, only the events that interrupt the execution of the currently running process trigger the process switching. There are following broad categories of interrupts:

System Calls

The system calls used by a process always cause an interrupt. The system call requests the kernel to execute a request. For example, if a process has the system calls for reading or writing from/to a device, then it causes the interrupt.

Exceptional Conditions

There can be some instructions in the process that when executed cause some exceptions that need attention of the kernel. Arithmetic exceptions, reference to an illegal address, and so on are some examples that cause the interrupt.

I/O Completion

When an I/O device completes the read/write operation with a process, an interrupt is generated so that the process waiting for that device may use it.

External

Any external unit connected with the system may also generate an interrupt. For example, timer clock on completion of a time slice may send an interrupt.

As soon as an interrupt is generated due to events, the following actions are performed (see Fig. 5.12 and 5.13):

1. Since the current running process has been interrupted, its execution context must be saved. The execution context of a process includes PSW, processor's registers, and program counter (PC). Therefore, the processor pushes the PSW and the PC onto system control stack to save the execution context.

2. When the interrupt arrives, the interrupt hardware analyzes the cause of the interrupt and forms a code corresponding to this interrupt. The interrupt vector area in the memory is accessed corresponding to this interrupt code, and information from the interrupt vector is loaded into the PSW. Since the interrupt vector contains the address of the interrupt service routine (ISR) in the kernel to handle the interrupt, the PC is loaded with the address of this ISR.

3. The processor mode is switched from the user to the kernel, and control is transferred to ISR in the kernel.

4. The PSW and the PC have been saved onto system stack as described in Step 1. However, the processor's registers at the time of interrupt of the interrupted process have not been saved yet. The ISR does the remaining work of context saving of the interrupted process. The context-saved sub-function in the ISR locates the PCB of this process. After this, it saves the processor's registers, the PSW, and the PC from the stack in the PCB. It also changes the state of the process as the case may be. For example, if the interrupted process has been preempted by a higher priority, then the state of this process will be changed from 'running' to 'ready'. Besides this, there may be some other fields that need to be updated in the PCB such as accounting information related to interrupted information. For example, how much the processor time has been used by the process? Since the OS maintains the queue for various types of processes (ready, blocked, and suspended queues), the PCB of the interrupted process is moved to one of these queues according to its updated state.

5. After saving all information related to the interrupted process, the ISR proceeds to process the interrupt. The corresponding event-handling function is executed to service the generated interrupt.

6. After processing the interrupt, the next step in process switching is to schedule a process for execution as there is no process to execute. Therefore, a scheduler function is called that selects a process from the ready queue. However, if there is an event such that the running process has requested time or date or a resource such

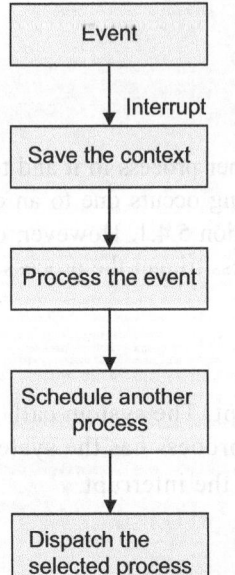

Fig. 5.12 Sequence of activities during process switching

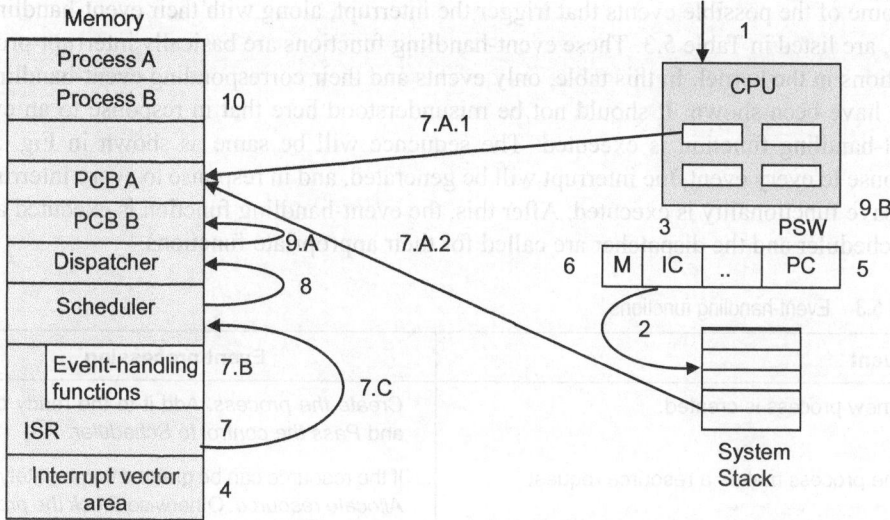

1. Initially process A is running and an Interrupt comes to the CPU.
2. PSW saved on system stack.
3. Interrupt hardware analyzes the type of interrupt and generates interrupt code in IC of PSW.
4. Corresponding to interrupt code, interrupt vector area is searched and information about the address of the ISR is retrieved.
5. Address of ISR is stored in PC field of PSW.
6. Mode is switched to kernel, i.e., mode bit M in PSW is set to 0 for kernel mode.
7. Processor starts executing ISR.
   - 7.A Calls context saving function.
   - 7.A.1 Save the processor's registers in the PCB A.
   - 7.A.2 Copy the PSW containing PC from the system stack in PCB A.
   - 7.A.3 Changes the state of the process from running to the blocked or appropriate state according to interrupt code.
   - 7.B Calls event handling function (or interrupt processing function).
   - 7.C Passes control to the scheduler.
8. Scheduler selects a process from the ready queue and control is passed to dispatcher.
9. Dispatcher
   - 9.A Finds the PCB of the process selected by scheduler, e.g. it is Process B.
   - 9.B Loads the PSW containing PC and other registers from its PCB to CPU.
   - 9.C Changes the state of the process to running in its PCB.
   - 9.D The mode bit M in PSW is changed to 1 for user mode.
10. As soon as the PC in PSW is loaded the process B starts executing by the processor.

Fig. 5.13 Detailed steps of process switching

as memory that can be granted immediately, then there is no state change. In this case, the scheduler function will select the same process for execution.

7. After this, a dispatcher function is called to prepare the process for the execution. It locates the PCB of the selected process and loads the saved PSW and CPU registers of the process onto the CPU registers from the PCB to resume the process from where it left off when last interrupted. The state of the selected process is also changed to running. These actions thereby set up the environment of the selected process for execution.

Some of the possible events that trigger the interrupt, along with their event-handling functions, are listed in Table 5.3. These event-handling functions are basically interrupt-processing functions in the kernel. In this table, only events and their corresponding event-handling functions have been shown. It should not be misunderstood here that in response to an event, an event-handling function is executed. The sequence will be same as shown in Fig. 5.12. In response to every event, the interrupt will be generated, and in response to every interrupt, context save functionality is executed. After this, the event-handling function is executed and then the scheduler and the dispatcher are called for their appropriate functions.

Table 5.3   Event-handling functions

Event	Event processing
A new process is created.	*Create the process*. Add it to the ready queue and *Pass the control to Scheduler*.
The process makes a resource request.	If the resource can be granted immediately, then *Allocate resource*. Otherwise *Block the process*. *Pass the control to Scheduler*.
A resource is released.	If there is any blocked process waiting for the resource (in the resource queue), which has been released recently, *Unblock the process and send it to ready queue*. If there is any blocked–suspended process waiting for the resource (in the hard disk), which has been released recently, *Unblock the process and send it to ready-suspend queue*. *Pass the control to Scheduler*.
The process requests an I/O device.	If the I/O device can be granted immediately, then *Allocate device*. Otherwise *Block the process*. *Pass the control to Scheduler*.
An I/O device is released after access.	If there is any blocked process waiting for the I/O (in the device queue) which has been released recently, *Unblock the process and send it to ready queue*. If there is any blocked–suspended process waiting for the I/O device (in the hard disk), which has been released recently, *Unblock the process and send it to ready-suspend queue*. *Pass the control to Scheduler*.
The allocated time slice for the process is over. In this case, system timer sends a *timer interrupt*.	Send the process to the ready queue. *Pass the control to Scheduler*.
A higher-priority process appears in the ready queue. In this case, the running lower-priority job is pre-empted by the newly arrived higher-priority process.	Send the process to the ready queue. *Pass the control to Scheduler*.

(Table 5.3 Contd)

The process reaches its end of execution or is aborted.	If the process is a parent having some child processes, then *terminate all child processes.* *Pass the control to Scheduler.*
Any hardware interrupt is generated.	Process the interrupt according to its type. *Pass the control to Scheduler.*
An error or exception condition is generated in the current running process. Some examples:	*Terminate the process.*
The process requires more memory than allowed.	*Pass the control to Scheduler.*
The process tries to access a resource or an I/O device or memory location that is not allowed to use.	
The process attempts an arithmetic operation that is not allowed, for example, divide by zero.	

5.10   SCHEDULERS

The process-scheduling procedure needs to be invoked as soon as a running process is interrupted after saving its context so that the CPU has one process to be executed. However, there are other instances also when scheduling is required. For this purpose, there are various types of scheduler modules in the OS that execute at their appropriate time. The classification of schedulers is based on the frequency of their use in the system. If the use is after a long time, then it is called a long-term scheduler. Similarly, when a scheduler is invoked very frequently, it is known as a short-term scheduler. The following are the types of schedulers used in an OS (see Fig. 5.14):

5.10.1 Long-term Scheduler

This scheduler is invoked when there is a need to perform job scheduling, that is, when a job from the job pool is selected to be sent to the ready queue. Since a job entering the system needs to be a process in the ready queue, this scheduler is invoked whenever there is a need to increase the degree of multi-programming in the system. However, this type of scheduling does not happen very frequently because a process needs some time in the system to be executed. If there are no slots in the ready queue for a new process to be accommodated, then there is no need to increase the degree of multi-programming and, hence, of the long-term scheduler. The long-term scheduler is needed only in case of a batch processing and is absent in multi-user time-sharing systems. In time-sharing systems, the jobs are directly entered into the ready queue as processes.

5.10.2 Short-term Scheduler

This scheduler is invoked when there is a need to perform process scheduling, that is, when a process from the ready queue is to be selected for dispatching to the CPU. There are various instances in the system when this type of scheduling is needed. We have studied in previous sections about various types of events that cause interrupt. Whenever there is an interrupt, the running process stops, and the short-term scheduler is invoked every time to select another process for execution. That is why this scheduler is called a short-term scheduler.

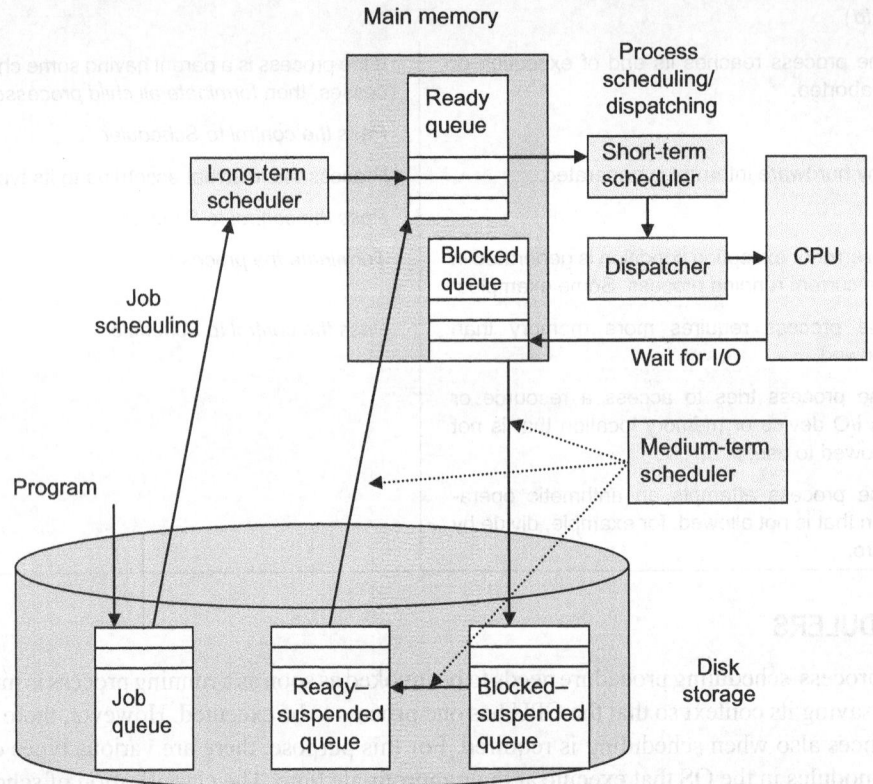

Fig. 5.14 Long-term, medium-term, and short-term schedulers

5.10.3 Medium-term Scheduler

This scheduler is invoked when there is a need to swap out some blocked processes. It can happen in the case when all processes are blocked for some I/O devices and there is no ready process to execute. Moreover, there is no space for any other process. In this case, some blocked processes need to be swapped out from the main memory to the hard disk. There is another queue called blocked–suspended queue for this purpose in the disk. The task of swapping the processes from the blocked queue to the blocked–suspended queue is performed by another type of scheduler known as medium-term scheduler. Further, when there is a signal of completion of an I/O device for which the process is blocked and presently in the blocked–suspended queue, the process changes its state to ready–suspended and moves to the ready–suspended queue. This task of moving a process from the blocked–suspended to the ready–suspended queue is also performed by this medium-term scheduler.

5.11 PROCESS OPERATIONS

As seen in the process state diagram, there are various operations performed on a process. The processes need to be created, deleted, suspended, blocked, and so on. The OS must have the mechanisms for all these operations. Let us see all these operations.

5.11.1 Creation

There may be various reasons for creation of a process in a system. It can be a part of a batch of jobs or whenever a user logs on the system or a process executes a process creation system call. The OS may also create a system process to provide a service. For example, when a user wishes to print a file, the operating system, on behalf of the user program, will create a process that will control the printing task. At the time of booting, there are several processes that run in the background known as *daemon processes*; for example, a process to accept an incoming request to host a web page on a web server machine.

On the creation of a process, the process identification (process ID) and its priority are assigned. The memory and other resources required by the process are allocated to it. After this, the code is copied in the code area, thereby setting the process environment. The OS looks for a free PCB space in the free-process queue for the newly created process and initializes all its fields.

The process creation is not limited to this only. An existing process may also create another process. This is known as *process spawning*. When a process spawns another, the process creating the other process is called parent process and the created process is known as a child process. A child process may also become a parent by further creating new processes, thereby forming a tree structure. In Fig. 5.15, P1, P3, and P6 are parent processes, whereas P3 and P6 are also child processes. There may be many child processes of a parent process. There is a hierarchy between these processes in the tree structure. All child processes at one level will have one parent process, and they work only under the control of this parent process. For example, in Fig. 5.15, Processes P2, P3, and P4 are child processes of Process P1, and all these processes work under the control of the parent P1. This tree structure has one parent root process and other processes at the other levels as child processes. In UNIX, there is one parent process called *init()*, and other system processes are created from this process. However, this process hierarchy is not necessary as seen in Windows operating system. This OS does not have any hierarchy of processes and treats all processes at same level. Though there is a provision of having parent and child processes, the parent of a child process can be changed, thereby violating the process-hierarchy concept.

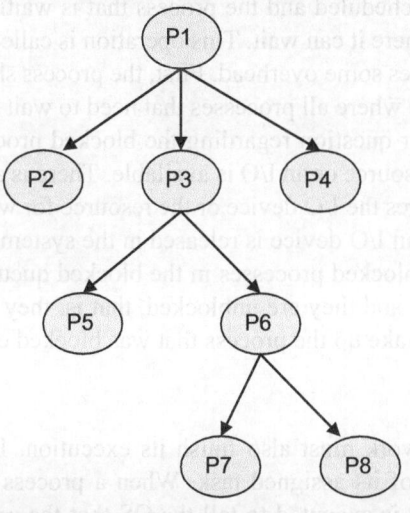

Fig. 5.15   Process hierarchy

One obvious question is that what functionality a child process will perform. Therefore, the creation of child processes should be logically justified, that is, the functionality of every child process should be defined and there should be communication and cooperation between them. The functionality of a child process depends on the application where a process has created it. For example, if a complex process creates its child process to divide its work, then the code of the child process will be different from the parent process. In another example, a web server needs to create a child process whenever there is a client connecting to it. In this case, the child functionality is same as the parent and therefore, the address space of the parent and the child processes is same. All these details related to a child-process creation differ in various operating systems. For example, in UNIX, after the *fork( )* command, a new child process is created having the same environment, resources, and so on as the parent process, that is, the new process has the copy of the address space of the parent process. Both parent and child processes continue to get execution. However, the copy of address space in the child process does not mean that there is sharing of the address space. Both address spaces are different and non-sharable except some shared resources such as files. If the child process wishes to have a separate code, then another system call *execlp( )* needs to be executed. This command loads the new program in the memory replacing the old parent's program. On the other hand, Windows and VMS OS does not have the provision of duplicating the address space while creating a child process. In these operating systems, at the time of the creation of a child process, a new program is loaded. Windows NT supports both types, that is, the parent process may duplicate the address space or a new program for the child process may be loaded.

The child process may get all or a subset of resources its parent has. It depends on the availability of resources and the number of child processes. A parent may allow sharing its resources among multiple child processes. The child process may also get some initialization data from its parent process.

5.11.2 Dispatching

This operation starts when there is a need to schedule a process from the ready queue. The scheduler according to scheduling policy of the system selects a process from this queue. Now this process will be sent to the processor for execution. For this purpose, the process environment must be set up, that is, its code must be loaded in the memory and data and stack must be initialized. After this, the PCB must be located and the saved fields (if the process has executed partially before) must be loaded in the processor's registers and initialized appropriately. The dispatcher performs all these functions resulting in start of the execution of this selected process.

5.11.3 Blocking/Wakeup

When a running process executes an instruction that requires a resource or an I/O device that cannot be fulfilled immediately, the process is not able to execute further as it needs to wait for that resource or I/O device. Since this process needs to wait, there will be no useful work by the processor; therefore, another process is scheduled and the process that is waiting for a resource or an I/O device is moved to a queue where it can wait. This operation is called blocking of the process. The blocking operation requires some overhead. First, the process should be maintained in a queue known as a blocked queue where all processes that need to wait for their resources or I/O devices reside. There is another question regarding the blocked process that how this process would come to know when a resource or an I/O is available. There is a field in the PCB known as *event information*, which stores the I/O device or the resource for which the blocked process is waiting. When a resource or an I/O device is released in the system, the OS must scan the event information field of all the blocked processes in the blocked queue. If the processes match, it means that their wait is over and they are unblocked, that is, they are sent to the ready queue. This operation is known to wake up the process that was blocked earlier.

5.11.4 Termination

The process that has started and executed its work must also finish its execution. It means that the process will terminate after execution of its assigned task. When a process reaches the execution of its last statement, a system call is executed to tell the OS that the process is terminating. For example, in UNIX, *exit( )*, system call is executed after the execution of the last statement in the process. In fact, this is necessary to tell the OS about a process's termination because the resources held by the process need to be released. Therefore, when a process terminates, the occupied memory, open files, and other resources are taken away from it.

However, this is not the only reason for the termination of a process. As a process is created when a new user logs on or a new window is opened, the same way when a user logs off or a window is closed, the corresponding process is terminated. Another reason for the termination of a process may be some error or exception generated in the execution of the process. It may be the case that the process may

- require more memory than allowed
- reference a memory location out of its limits
- try to access a resource or an I/O device that is not allowed to use
- attempt an arithmetic operation that is not allowed, for example, divide by zero
- find an error while accessing an I/O

The termination of a child process in the process-hierarchy tree structure may not be as simple as that of an independent process because it is dependent on its parent process. In case of child-process termination, there are different rules in various operating systems. The only requirement is that the parent process must have the knowledge of its child processes. When a child process is created, its ID is created and returned to its parent. This ID is used by the parent process while taking the decision to terminate the child processes. A parent process may terminate its child process at any time. The parent process looks after the state of its child process. If there is any error or exception, it may terminate the child. The problem occurs when a parent process is to be terminated while its children processes exist. In this case, the parent process needs to wait for the execution of its children. For example in Fig. 5.15, if Process P3 needs to be terminated, it cannot be because it has two children processes, P5 and P6. It needs to wait for the termination of P5 and P6 and then only it can be terminated.

SUMMARY

The first important component of the OS is process management. Process management is to handle various user and system processes. The basic terminology and concepts regarding process management have been discussed in the chapter. The process set up includes an environment consisting of code section, data section, stack, PC values, and other processor register values. The PCB is another data structure used to control the execution of processes in a multi-programming environment. Since in a multi-programming environment, there is a need to switch between processes, it becomes necessary to save the context of one process before switching to another process. The PCB helps in saving the context of a process. This arrangement of process switching works with the interrupt-driven nature of the operating system. With an event in the system, an interrupt is caused to the running process that stops the execution of

the current process. At this moment, the context of this interrupted process is saved in its PCB. The next step is process scheduling, that is, to select another process from the ready queue to send it to the CPU for execution. After this, dispatching function loads the context of the selected process from its PCB. In this way, process execution is managed through interrupt handling, process switching, scheduling, and dispatching.

Let us have a quick review of important concepts discussed in this chapter:

- A program in execution is called a process.
- Each process has its own *address space* consisting of code section, data section, and stack section.
- If the OS defines a process, then it is called an *implicit process*. If the process is defined by the programmer, then it is an *explicit process*.

- A process has seven states: new, ready, running, blocked, blocked–suspended, ready–suspended, and terminated.
- The process changes its state when there is an event causing a state transition.
- The state transitions are admit (new to ready), dispatch (ready to running), I/O wait (running to blocked), suspended (blocked to blocked–suspended), I/O complete (blocked to ready or blocked–suspended to ready–suspended), activate (ready–suspended to ready), and exit (running to terminated).
- There are many queues used for process management. These are as follows:

Queue	Purpose
Job queue	It is in the hard disk for storing the new jobs when first entered in the system.
Ready queue	It is in the main memory for storing processes. The jobs when brought from the job queue to the ready queue become processes.
Blocked queue	It is in the main memory for storing processes that need to wait for a resource or and I/O.
Suspended queue	It is in the hard disk for storing processes that have been suspended or kicked out of the main memory.

- When a job from the job queue is selected and moved to the ready queue, it is known as *job scheduling*.
- When a job arrives in the ready queue, it becomes a process.
- When a process in the ready queue is selected for execution, it is known as process scheduling.
- When a scheduled process is sent to the processor for execution, it is known as dispatching.
- The PCB is a data structure used to store various attributes related to it. The PCB is created for every process whenever a new process is created in the system. The PCB information is used for controlling and managing the processes in the system.
- Whenever there is an interrupt to the running process, the

process stops and its current status is saved in its PCB. This is known as context save operation.
- The process of saving the status of an interrupted process and loading the status of the scheduled process is known as context switching.
- Context switching is a pure overhead from viewpoint of processor time because during context switching no execution is being done.
- When a running process is interrupted and the OS assigns another process to the running process and transfers control to it, it is known as process switching.
- A scheduler is a component of the OS that performs the job of scheduling at various levels. There are three types of schedulers:

Type	Purpose
Long-term scheduler	Performs job scheduling.
Short-term scheduler	Performs process scheduling.
Medium-term scheduler.	Some processes need to swap out from the main memory and swap in at some appropriate time. These swap-in and swap-out functions are performed by this scheduler.

- Various types of schedulers are activated at different scenarios in the system as follows:

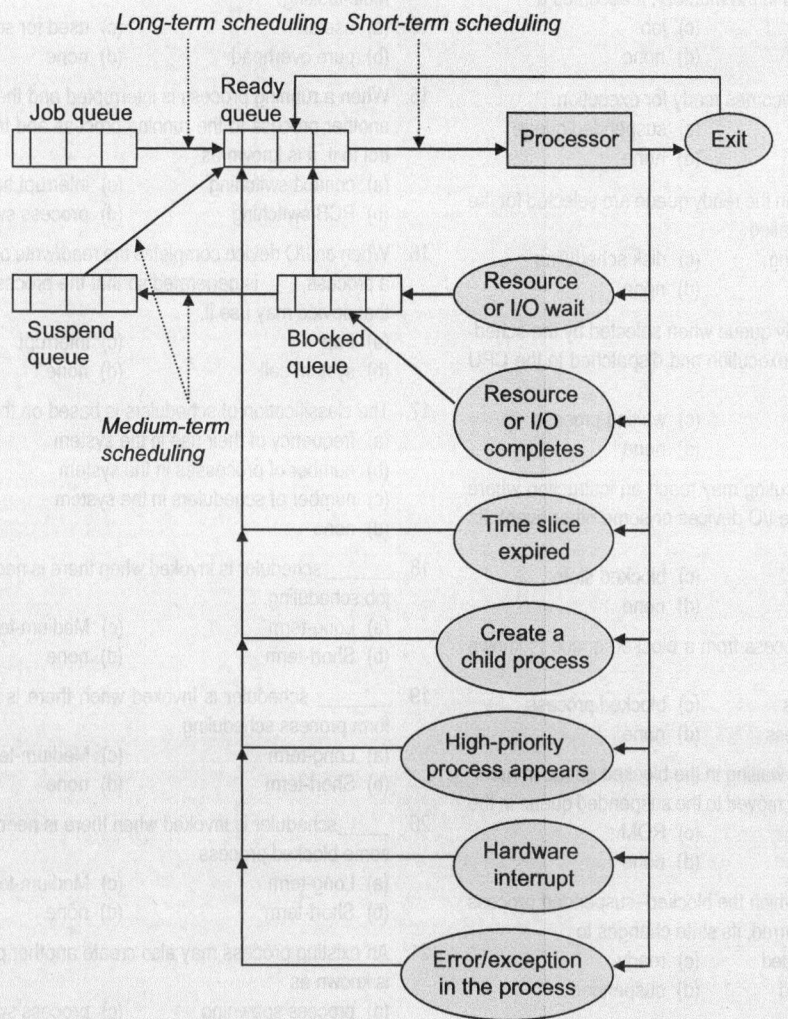

Long-term scheduling   Short-term scheduling

Job queue

Ready queue

Processor

Exit

Suspend queue

Blocked queue

Resource or I/O wait

Resource or I/O completes

Time slice expired

Create a child process

High-priority process appears

Hardware interrupt

Error/exception in the process

Medium-term scheduling

- A dispatcher is a component that locates the PCB of the process selected by a scheduler, loads its context, and passes the control to the processor for execution.

- At the time of booting, there are several processes that run in the background known as *daemon processes*.
- Process spawning is to create a child process by a parent process.

MULTIPLE CHOICE QUESTIONS

1. Program in execution is called
   (a) a process   (c) a job
   (b) a task   (d) none

2. Program is a _____ entity while process is ___.
   (a) passive, active   (c) both active
   (b) active, passive   (d) both passive

3. Whenever a new job is entered into the system, it is stored in the

   (a) ready queue   (c) suspended queue
   (b) job queue   (d) none

4. When a job is selected to be brought in the main memory, it is called

   (a) process scheduling (c) job scheduling
   (b) CPU scheduling   (d) none

5. When a job is fetched in the memory, it becomes a
   - (a) task
   - (b) process
   - (c) job
   - (d) none

6. A process in ____becomes ready for execution.
   - (a) ready queue
   - (b) job queue
   - (c) suspended queue
   - (d) none

7. When the processes in the ready queue are selected for the next execution, it is called
   - (a) process scheduling
   - (b) job scheduling
   - (c) disk scheduling
   - (d) none

8. A process in the ready queue when selected by the scheduling mechanism for execution and dispatched to the CPU becomes a
   - (a) ready process
   - (b) running process
   - (c) waiting process
   - (d) none

9. A process while executing may reach an instruction where it has to wait for some I/O devices or some other event. Its state becomes
   - (a) wait state
   - (b) running state
   - (c) blocked state
   - (d) none

10. The swapped out process from a blocked queue is known as
    - (a) swapped process
    - (b) suspended process
    - (c) blocked process
    - (d) none

11. The blocked process waiting in the blocked queue in memory is suspended and moved to the suspended queue in the
    - (a) disk
    - (b) memory
    - (c) ROM
    - (d) none

12. When the event for which the blocked–suspended process was waiting has occurred, its state changes to
    - (a) blocked–suspended
    - (b) ready–suspended
    - (c) ready
    - (d) suspended

13. The collection of user program, data section, stack, and the associated attributes is called the
    - (a) PCB
    - (b) process image
    - (c) process environment
    - (d) none

14. The context switch time is a ___for multi-programming/ multi-tasking.
    - (a) useful
    - (b) pure overhead
    - (c) used for scheduling
    - (d) none

15. When a running process is interrupted and the OS assigns another process to the running process and transfers control to it, it is known as
    - (a) context switching
    - (b) PCB switching
    - (c) interrupt handling
    - (d) process switching

16. When an I/O device completes the read/write operation with a process, ___ is generated so that the process waiting for that device may use it.
    - (a) trap
    - (b) system call
    - (c) interrupt
    - (d) none

17. The classification of schedulers is based on the
    - (a) frequency of their use in the system
    - (b) number of processes in the system
    - (c) number of schedulers in the system
    - (d) none

18. _____ scheduler is invoked when there is need to perform job scheduling.
    - (a) Long-term
    - (b) Short-term
    - (c) Medium-term
    - (d) none

19. _____ scheduler is invoked when there is need to perform process scheduling.
    - (a) Long-term
    - (b) Short-term
    - (c) Medium-term
    - (d) none

20. _____scheduler is invoked when there is need to swap out some blocked process.
    - (a) Long-term
    - (b) Short-term
    - (c) Medium-term
    - (d) none

21. An existing process may also create another process. This is known as
    - (a) process spawning
    - (b) process creation
    - (c) process switching
    - (d) none

22. There is a field in the PCB known as _____, which stores the I/O device or resource for which the blocked process is waiting
    - (a) resource information
    - (b) PCB information
    - (c) event information
    - (d) none

REVIEW QUESTIONS

1. Differentiate between job, program, and task.

2. What is the difference between a program and a process?

3. What is the difference between an implicit and a non-implicit process? Provide examples.

4. Define:
   - (a) PCB
   - (b) Process environment
   - (c) Process image

5. What is the difference between
   - (a) co-operating and independent processes?
   - (b) job scheduling and process scheduling?
   - (c) process scheduling and process dispatching?
   - (d) process scheduling and process switching?
   - (e) process switching and mode switching?

6. Explain the roles of different queues used in process management.

7. Explain the process state diagram considering the suspended processes.

8. What is the main cause that a process changes its state?

9. What are the steps to be followed for process management when an interrupt comes to a running process?

10. How is the context switching implemented?

11. What is context switch time? What is its disadvantage?

12. How is the process switching implemented?

13. How is the process scheduling implemented?

14. How is the process dispatching implemented?

15. What is process spawning?

16. What is the difference between a scheduler and a dispatcher?

17. Discuss various types of schedulers.

18. What is the need of swapping in and swapping out a process?

19. What are the situations when process scheduling is required?

20. What are the situations when a process needs to be terminated?

21. What are the situations when a process needs to be suspended?

22. What are the situations when a process needs to be spawned?

23. What are the steps performed by an OS to create, terminate, block, and suspend a process?

BRAIN TEASERS

1. In a large operating system, if there is a single queue for maintaining the blocked processes, it will be inefficient to search a required process that needs to be awakened on occurrence of an event. What can be the remedies for this inefficiency?

2. In a large operating system, if there is a single ready queue for maintaining the ready processes, it will be inefficient to search a required process for scheduling. What can be the remedies for this inefficiency?

3. Can a process switch from ready to terminated or blocked to terminated?

4. What can be the reasons for suspending a process other than mentioned in the chapter?

5. Is it necessary that every event causing interrupt will change the state of the running process?

6. The suspended queue is maintained on the hard disk and therefore, I/O operations are required with it. Does it have any impact on the performance of process management because all other queues are managed in the main memory?

7. How does a blocked or blocked–suspended process know about the completion of the I/O device or the resource for which it is waiting?

8. What event handler would be executed in the following cases:
   (a) The running process has finished its execution before completion of its time slice
   (b) The running process tries to access a memory location that it is not allowed to access
   (c) If there is failure in reading or writing an I/O device
   (d) A process is ready to execute but there is no space in the main memory

   (e) A periodic process is idle waiting for its next time slot to be executed
   (f) A background process has caused a problem

9. Multi-programming/Multi-tasking was developed so that there would be no processor idle time. However, there still may be some situation when the processor is idle. Explore these situations.

10. What will be the effect on performance of process management if there is a majority of CPU-bound or I/O-bound-processes in a system?

11. A parent process needs to be terminated but has two child processes: One child process is waiting for an I/O, and the other is executing. How will you terminate the parent process?

12. How will you design the device queues where processes are waiting to access them? Can the priority of a process be incorporated here?

13. Context switch time is a pure overhead. What can be the factors that can increase this overhead?

14. Consider Brain-Teaser Problem 9 in Chapter 1 and illustrate the state transitions for all the processes in the system.

15. Again consider Brain-Teaser Problem 9 in Chapter 1. Assume that there is context switch time of 2 minutes and then prepare a timing chart showing the CPU and I/O activities of the jobs in multi-programming with this context switch time. Compute the total time for execution.

16. In a system, Process A is running and Processes B and C are in a blocked state. An I/O-completion signal arrives for Process B. The priority of Process B is the

highest. Describe the sequence of actions in the operating system.

17. In a system, Process A is running and Processes B and C are in a blocked state. Process D is ready to execute but not in the ready queue as there is no space. What will you do to accommodate this ready process D? Describe the sequence of actions in the operating system.

18. In a system, Process 5 is running and Processes 2, 4, and 7 are in a blocked state. Processes 1, 3, and 6 are in a ready state. Show the PCBs and process headers of all these processes in the memory.

19. Can a process switch from a blocked–suspended to a blocked state?

6 Process Scheduling

6.1 INTRODUCTION

Process scheduling is an important component of process management. Its role starts in a multi-programming environment and expands to multi-user and multi-tasking environments. In fact, there is a difference in performance requirements of various environments. While some mainframes still demand batch processing of processes, a multi-user environment expects a minimum response time, so that every user feels that he/she is using a single system. Similarly, on multi-tasking systems, a user expects that he/she should be able to open many windows and every window should respond within a minimum period of time. On the other hand, in real-time systems, the processes are executed according to their defined priorities. A higher-priority process must always pre-empt the lower one. Moreover, in processing, there are deadlines which should be met, otherwise it may have adverse effects on the system. In this way, to meet the requirement of every type of system, scheduling mechanisms are needed to select the right process from the ready queue. Besides this, they have some general goals like processor utilization, throughput, context-switch time, and so on. Also discussed in this chapter are the various scheduling algorithms for different types of requirements and the keeping of various goals in consideration.

6.2 PROCESS BEHAVIOUR FOR SCHEDULING

When a process starts executing, the processor or CPU, starts working. However, in the execution of a process, apart from computations, some I/O operations may also be involved. A process may need to take input from an input device or send output to an output device. During an I/O operation, the CPU does not do anything and sits idle. When a process has long computations to be executed by the processor, it is then known as *CPU-burst*, and on the occurrence of I/O operation, it is known as *I/O burst*. If there is a process with intensive CPU-bursts, that is, longer CPU cycles and a low number of I/O bursts, then it is known as a *CPU-bound process*. If the process has a large number of frequent I/O bursts within the smaller CPU-bursts, then it is known as an *I/O-bound process* (see Fig. 6.1).

If there is a large number of CPU-bound processes, it may be difficult to achieve multi-programming. I/O wait slots are places where process switching occurs. If these are not there, then multi-programming will not give good performance. On the other hand,

Learning Objectives

After reading this chapter, you should be able to understand:

- CPU-bound and I/O-bound processes
- When to schedule a process
- Long-term scheduling
- Medium-term scheduling
- Short-term scheduling
- Non-pre-emptive scheduling
- Pre-emptive scheduling
- Scheduling goals
- Scheduling algorithms
- Multi-level scheduling algorithms
- Fair-share scheduling
- Lottery scheduling

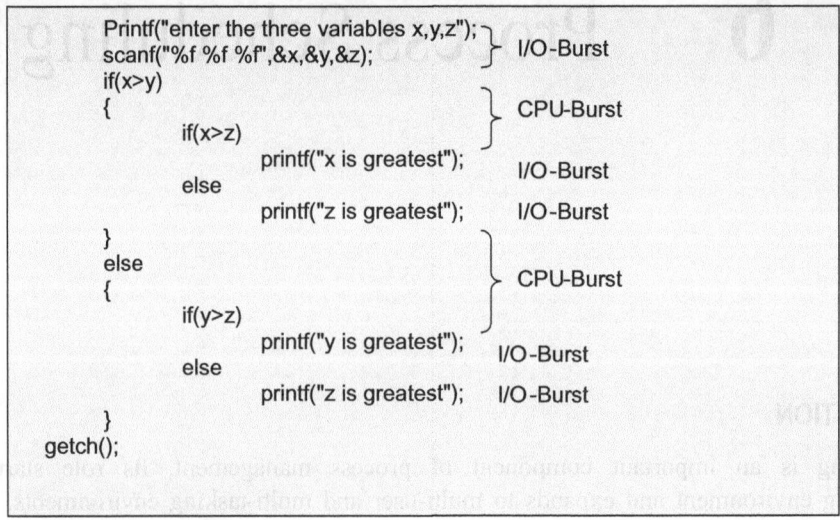

```
Printf("enter the three variables x,y,z");  ⎫
scanf("%f %f %f",&x,&y,&z);                  ⎬  I/O-Burst
if(x>y)
{                                            ⎫
        if(x>z)                              ⎬  CPU-Burst
                printf("x is greatest");        I/O-Burst
        else
                printf("z is greatest");        I/O-Burst
}
else
{                                            ⎫
        if(y>z)                              ⎬  CPU-Burst
                printf("y is greatest");        I/O-Burst
        else
                printf("z is greatest");        I/O-Burst
}
getch();
```

Fig. 6.1   CPU burst and I/O burst in a process

if there is a large number of I/O bound processes, then process execution will not happen in a multi-programming environment. Thus, for the scheduling of processes in a multi-programming environment, there should be a proper mix of CPU-bound and I/O bound processes. Otherwise, scheduling of processes will not be proper, thereby affecting the performance of the system.

6.3 SCHEDULING DECISION

It there is only a single process to be executed by the processor, then scheduling is not required. Since in multi-programming, there are multiple processes running at all times, scheduling is used. But scheduling does not happen when a process finishes. As process switching is another feature of multi-programming, it is not necessary that a process will execute completely for scheduling to take place. Due to process switching, when a process is interrupted, there is need to schedule another process from the ready queue. The following events can become the reason for scheduling:

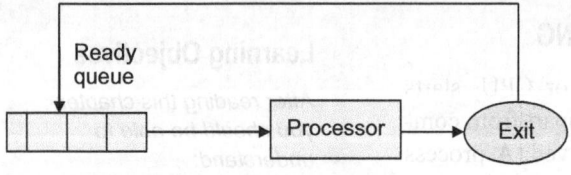

Fig. 6.2   Scheduling reason: Running process exits

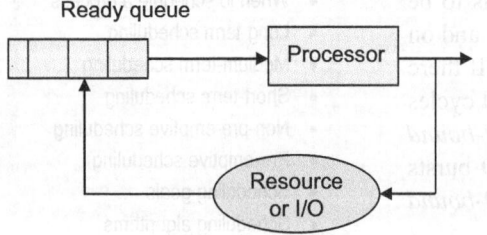

Fig. 6.3   Scheduling reason: Running process enters in a wait

1. When an executing process finishes its execution and exits, then another process is required for execution (Fig. 6.2).

   If there is no process in the ready queue, then scheduling is done on the job queue to select a job and send it to the ready queue.

2. When the executing process needs to wait for an I/O or resource, it is blocked. Therefore, there is need to select another process for execution (see Fig. 6.3). Therefore, the

scheduler is called for scheduling another process from the ready queue, which is further sent for execution.

3. When an I/O or resource being used by any process is released, then the blocked process, waiting for the I/O or resource, goes back to the ready queue (see Fig. 6.4). At this moment, there is need to perform scheduling, in order to give chance to the recently admitted process.

4. In a multi-user time-sharing environment, a fixed time period/time slice is allotted to every process, so that there is uniform response to every process. When a process finishes its allotted time slice, it moves back to the ready queue (see Fig. 6.5).

5. When an executing process creates its child process, then scheduling is performed to give the newly created process a chance for execution (see Fig. 6.6).

6. When a newly added process in the ready queue has higher priority compared to that of the running process, there is need to temporarily stop the execution of the running process and scheduling is performed, so that the higher priority process gets the chance to execute (see Fig. 6.7).

7. If there is an error or exception in the process or hardware, then the running process may need to be stopped and sent back to the ready queue. After this, scheduling is performed to select another process (see Fig. 6.8).

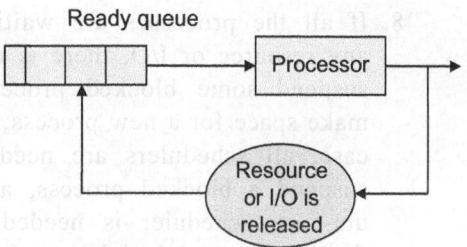

Fig. 6.4 Scheduling reason: I/O or resource is released

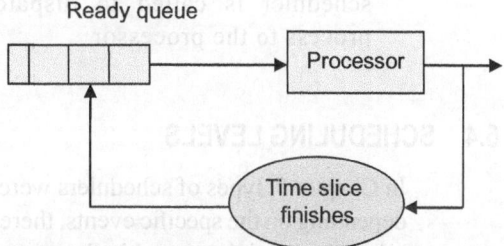

Fig. 6.5 Scheduling reason: Time slice of running process finishes

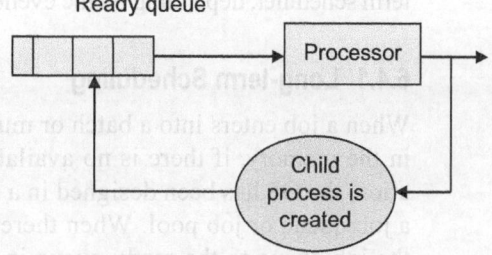

Fig. 6.6 Scheduling reason: Running process creates a child process

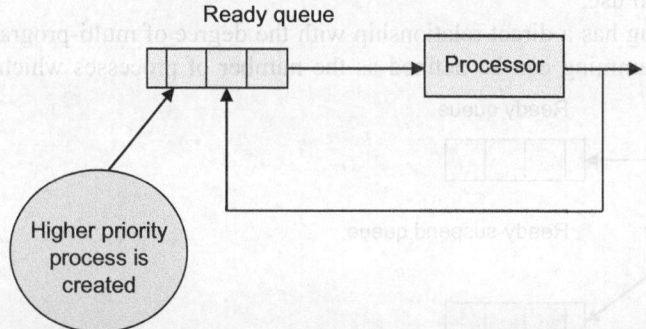

Fig. 6.7 Scheduling reason: Higher priority process arrives

8. If all the processes are waiting for any resource or I/O, there is need to suspend some blocked process and make space for a new process. In this case, all schedulers are needed. To suspend a blocked process, a medium-term scheduler is needed. Then the long-term scheduler is called to send a job from the job queue to the ready queue, and finally a short-term scheduler is called to dispatch this process to the processor.

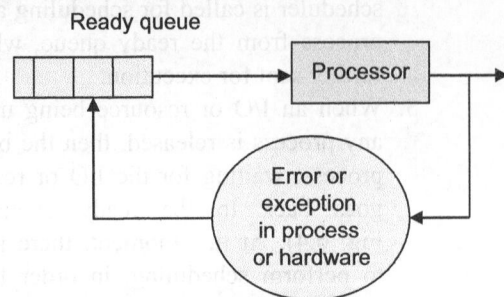

Fig. 6.8 Scheduling reason: Error or exception in process/hardware

6.4 SCHEDULING LEVELS

In Chapter 5, types of schedulers were discussed. There is no single scheduler in the system, but depending on the specific events, there are three levels of scheduling to be performed by different schedulers. A job entered in the system passes through various types of scheduling. First of all, a job needs to wait in a job queue. Then it is scheduled by a long-term scheduler and sent to the ready queue. After entering the ready queue, it may be scheduled either by a medium- or a short-term scheduler, depending on the event. The scheduling levels are discussed in the following list.

6.4.1 Long-term Scheduling

When a job enters into a batch or multi-programming system, it may need to wait for space in the memory, if there is no available slot. Therefore, keeping this situation in consideration, the OS has been designed in a way that a job entering the system first needs to wait in a job queue or job pool. When there is space in the memory, this job must be moved from the job queue to the ready queue in the memory. This is done by the long-term scheduler and is known as long-term scheduling. The job becomes a process in the ready queue and we say that a process is created. This is now able to compete for resources. The newly created jobs need to be moved to the ready-suspend queue in the swap space of the disk. The long-term scheduler sends these jobs from the job queue to the ready-suspend queue, as shown in Fig. 6.9. In this way, long-term scheduling can be performed in either way, depending on the system in use.

The long-term scheduling has a direct relationship with the degree of multi-programming. The degree of multi-programming can be defined as the number of processes which can be

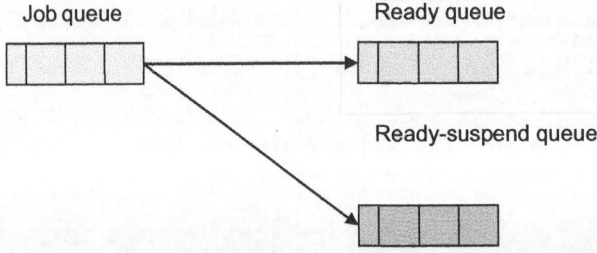

Fig. 6.9 Long-term scheduling

accommodated in the memory and is ready for execution. It means when a process finishes its execution, its memory space is released. This can be used by any other process. Thus, long-term scheduling is performed at this time and the scheduler brings another job from the job queue to the ready queue. The long-term scheduler is also requested when the CPU is idle for more than a threshold time. This idleness of the CPU may be due to unavailability of a process or other reason. At this time again, the long-term scheduler brings another process to be executed. In this way, the degree of multi-programming can be controlled through the use of long-term scheduling.

In a multi-user time-sharing environment, however, the users want quick response. Therefore, there is no provision for waiting in a queue for new users. Every user, when connected to the system, will get space in the memory. Thus, there is no role of long-term scheduler in these types of systems. But there will be a maximum limit, allowing the number of users to connect to the system, that is, the number of user processes that would be accommodated in the memory. When this limit is crossed, a new user is not allowed to connect.

Long-term scheduling is not frequent. After allowing a limited number of processes in the memory, there is no need to perform scheduling, because the admitted processes are busy in executing through the use of multi-programming concept. The criteria used to perform scheduling, such as to increase the degree of multi-programming and when a process finishes is not so frequent. Hence the name, long-term scheduling.

6.4.2 Medium-term Scheduling

In some systems, there is provision for medium-term scheduling. It is not necessary that a process in the ready queue will get the CPU. If its requirement of resources is known in advance, and if it cannot be fulfilled immediately, it would be better to send the process on the disk to optimize memory requirements. There may also be the case that at a particular instant of time in the system, all the processes need I/O, that is, all the processes are blocked and are waiting for some event to happen, and no process is under execution. In this case, it is necessary to bring in some process that is ready for execution. But if there is no space in the memory, space is to be freed, so that a new process can enter. The best way is to swap out a blocked process. The swapped-out processes are known as suspended processes. There is another queue called blocked-suspend queue, for this purpose in the disk. The task of swapping the process from blocked queue to blocked-suspend queue is performed by a medium-term scheduler (see Fig. 6.10). The memory manager takes the decision to swap-out a process from memory.

When there is a signal of completion of an I/O, for which the process is blocked and presently is in the suspend queue, the state of process is changed to ready-suspend and moved to the

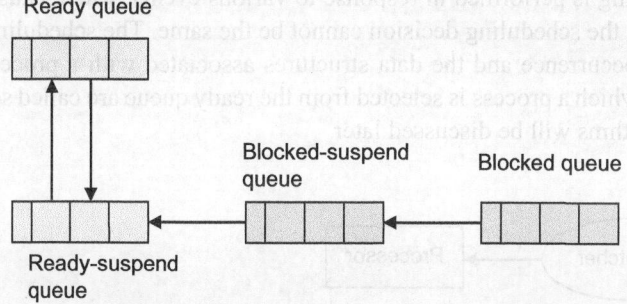

Fig. 6.10 Medium-term scheduling

ready-suspend queue. This task of moving a process from blocked-suspend queue to ready-suspend queue is also performed by the medium-term scheduler. Hence, the task of performing swap-out and swap-in is known as medium-term scheduling.

Whenever the suspended process is swapped out on the disk, there are two choices for bringing in a process, which is ready for execution. First is a suspended process from the suspend queue, which is now ready for execution. Second, a new process from the job queue can be scheduled and sent to the ready queue. However, the new job from the job queue will increase the load of the system. The second choice is only valid if we want to increase the degree of multi-programming of the system, otherwise, the first choice is preferred.

The frequency of this type of scheduling is not as low as that of long-term scheduling, and is not as frequent as that of short-term scheduling. A process may travel through phases of blocking, suspension, and execution very frequently. Therefore, in the multi-programming environment, if there is a single chance of a process being blocked and suspended, even then the frequency of this type of scheduling will be more as compared to long-term. This is the reason that this type of scheduling is known as medium-term scheduling.

6.4.3 Short-term Scheduling

This is the last level of scheduling. When the processor has no process to execute and there are several processes ready, waiting in the ready queue, then the type of scheduling performed to select a process and dispatch it to the processor is known as short-term scheduling (see Fig. 6.11). The scheduler, after selecting the process from the ready queue, passes the information about this process on to the dispatcher function. The dispatcher, after finding the location of PCB of the process, loads the PSW and other registers in the processor and execution of this process starts. Due to loading of these registers, the process may resume its work from the point where it was blocked, or suspended, or its time slice expired in the past and could not complete its execution.

Short-term scheduling is very frequent. A process goes through many events as discussed in Chapter 5. These events do not allow it to complete its execution in one go. Therefore, the process is stopped temporarily from execution and is sent to the ready queue again. So, it needs to compete for the processor again and wait for its execution. In this way, a process is interrupted many times and it goes back to the ready queue again and again. This is the reason behind the high frequency of short-term scheduling. Obviously, the frequency of this type of scheduling is very high as compared to the other two types of scheduling. This is why this type of scheduling is called short-term. There are many instances which lead to short-term scheduling. Some of them are shown in Fig. 6.12.

Since short-term scheduling is performed in response to various events, which cause interruption to a running process, the scheduling decision cannot be the same. The scheduling decision is based on the event occurrence and the data structures associated with a process. The scheduling mechanisms by which a process is selected from the ready queue are called scheduling algorithms. These algorithms will be discussed later.

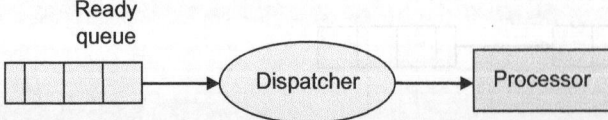

Fig. 6.11 Short-term scheduling

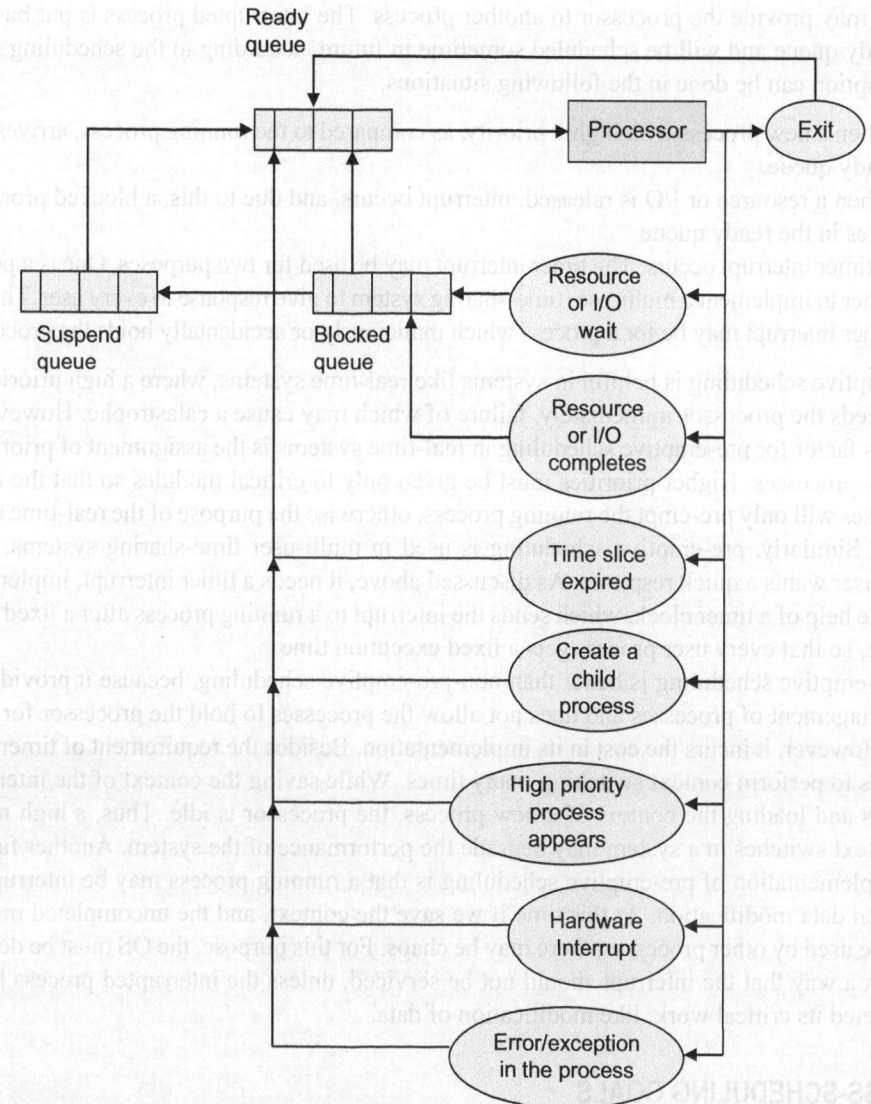

Fig. 6.12 Short-term scheduling decisions

6.5 SCHEDULING TYPES

The scheduling of processes is based on two broad categories. When a process is assigned to the processor, it is allowed to execute to its completion, that is, a system cannot take away the processor from the process until it exits. In that case, it is called *non-pre-emptive scheduling*. In this type of scheduling, the process may also voluntarily release the processor, for example, when the process needs to wait for an I/O. Thus, a new process will be allocated to the processor, only if the running process completes its execution or gets blocked due to a resource or I/O.

On the other hand, if a running process is interrupted in between, even if it has neither voluntarily released the processor nor exited, it is known as *pre-emptive scheduling*. In this type of scheduling, the system may stop the execution of the running process and after that, the context switch may provide the processor to another process. The interrupted process is put back into the ready queue and will be scheduled sometime in future, according to the scheduling policy. Pre-emption can be done in the following situations:

i) When a new process with higher priority, as compared to the running process, arrives in the ready queue.
ii) When a resource or I/O is released, interrupt occurs, and due to this, a blocked process arrives in the ready queue.
iii) A timer interrupt occurs. The timer interrupt may be used for two purposes. One is a periodic timer to implement a multi-user time-sharing system to give response to every user. The other timer interrupt may be for a process which maliciously or accidentally holds the processor.

Pre-emptive scheduling is helpful in systems like real-time systems, where a high priority process needs the processor immediately, failure of which may cause a catastrophe. However, the success factor for pre-emptive scheduling in real-time systems is the assignment of priorities to various processes. Higher priorities must be given only to critical modules so that the critical processes will only pre-empt the running process, otherwise the purpose of the real-time system is lost. Similarly, pre-emptive scheduling is used in multi-user time-sharing systems, where every user wants a quick response. As discussed above, it needs a timer interrupt, implemented with the help of a timer clock, which sends the interrupt to a running process after a fixed period of time, so that every user process gets a fixed execution time.

Pre-emptive scheduling is better than non-pre-emptive scheduling, because it provides better management of processes and does not allow the processes to hold the processor for a long time. However, it incurs the cost in its implementation. Besides the requirement of timer clock, it needs to perform context switching many times. While saving the context of the interrupted process and loading the context of a new process, the processor is idle. Thus, a high number of context switches in a system may degrade the performance of the system. Another factor in the implementation of pre-emptive scheduling is that a running process may be interrupted in between data modification. At this time if we save the context, and the uncompleted modified data are used by other processes, there may be chaos. For this purpose, the OS must be designed in such a way that the interrupt should not be serviced, unless the interrupted process has not completed its critical work, like modification of data.

6.6 PROCESS-SCHEDULING GOALS

After studying the basics of process-scheduling, now it is time to design various scheduling algorithms, according to which a process will be scheduled from its queue and dispatched to the processor. Here, the question that arises is the reason why we need to design an algorithm for the scheduling. The process could be selected on the basis of the order as they arrive in the queue. But that would not suffice, keeping in view the system's performance. In general, we want to optimize the behaviour of the system. And this behaviour may depend on various general factors such as throughput, response time, and so on. Some are also based on environmental factors such as real-time response in real-time environment. So, first we need to look at a set of criteria which decide the objectives or goals for design of scheduling algorithms. Once these criteria are fixed, these algorithms may be evaluated.

The goals of scheduling may be categorized as user-based scheduling goals and system-based scheduling goals. User-based goals are the criteria that benefit the user. A user has some expectation while working on a system. For example, a user in a multi-user environment expects the system to give quick response to the job. System-based goals are the criteria that benefit the system, that is, performance of the system. For example, how much the processor is being utilized in processing the processes. Let us discuss these two categories of scheduling goals.

6.6.1 User-based Scheduling Goals

Let us discuss some of the user-based scheduling goals in detail:

Turnaround Time

The time elapsed between the submission of a job and its termination is called the turnaround time. Turnaround time includes all time periods, such as time spent in waiting for getting entry in the ready queue, waiting time in the ready queue, execution time, waiting time for any resource or I/O, and so on. It is the sum of all these time periods. In other words, turnaround time of a process is

$t_r = wt + x$

where t_r is turnaround time of a process,

wt is waiting time of the process in the ready queue,

and x is the total service or execution time of the process

The scheduling algorithm should be designed such that the turnaround time is minimum, so that a process need not wait long in the system and performs its functions on time.

If turnaround time is divided by the execution time of the process, it becomes *weighted* or *normalized turnaround time*.

$Wt_r = t_r/x$

Where Wt_r is weighted or normalized turnaround time.

Wt_r is the indication of the service a process is getting. The minimum possible value of Wt_r is 1, which means that the process does not wait and gets the execution immediately. Increasing values indicate the delay in getting the processor or poor service. Thus, Wt_r should also be minimized while designing the scheduling algorithm.

Waiting Time

A process spends its time in the ready queue and gets execution as per the scheduling policy. Waiting time is the total time spent in the ready queue by a process. It includes all the time periods, starting from its arrival in the ready queue to its completion. The scheduling policy should be such that the waiting time is less, so that it does not wait too much in the ready queue and gets execution.

Response Time

In multi-user and multi-tasking systems, the user processes are of interactive nature, that is, they need attention immediately. Thus, response time is another important criterion from the user's viewpoint. It may be defined as the time period between the time of submission of a process and the first response given by the process to the user. The scheduling algorithm must be designed such that the response time is within an acceptable range.

Predictability

While working on the system, the human mind is able to predict the processing of some processes. But sometimes, a process takes a long time due to loading or some other reason. The scheduling algorithm should take care that a process does not take too long in processing as compared to the predictable behaviour of the processes.

Deadlines

Predictability is a feature based on which a user expects a process behaviour. But in real-time systems, there are fixed deadlines for completing the processing by a process. So a user knows very well, quantitatively, that a process would complete its work in a specific time period. If a process is not able to complete its work within the deadline, then the purpose of the real-time system is lost. For example, if a process in a system is handling RADAR data received from sensors and is not able to complete the processing of signals within its deadlines, then RADAR data will be lost. Consequently, the system which is supposed to work on this data will not work as a real-time system. So the scheduling algorithm must be designed such that real-time processes will execute within their deadlines.

6.6.2 System-based Scheduling Goals

Some system-based scheduling goals are discussed in detail in the following list:

Throughput

This is a general metric used to measure the performance of two systems or a single system over a time period. Throughput is the number of processes completed in a unit time. It indicates how much work has been finished and what is left. Though throughput may be affected due to the length of the processes, it is also affected by scheduling algorithms. So the process-scheduling should be designed in a way such that throughput in a system is maximized. For example, the performance of a system which completes four processes in one hour, is better than a system which completes two processes in the same time-period..

CPU Utilization

The fundamental goal of scheduling is that the processor should be busy all the time. Multi programming, multi-tasking, and other concepts of OSs have been developed for specific achievement of this objective. CPU utilization is the percentage of time that the CPU is busy in executing the processes. Due to architectural development today, the CPU is very fast. It may not be an important goal for some systems, but it may be important for a shared system, where a processor and other resources are shared.

Fairness

One system objective in process-scheduling is that all processes should be treated in the same way, unless there is some preference or priority for a specific process. Even if a priority scheme is implemented in the system, the processes with lower priority should not be ignored. Otherwise, the lower priority process may suffer from starvation. So the scheduling algorithm should not allow any process to starve.

Balance

As we discussed in CPU utilization, there should be utilization of every resource in the system. It should not be the case that some resources are underutilized and some resources are busy. At a particular instant of time, all resources should be used in balance. For this purpose, a good mix of CPU-bound and I/O-bound processes will help. If there are only CPU-bound processes, then all I/O-processes will be idle. If all I/O-bound processes are selected, then the processor will be idle. A proper mix of CPU-bound and I/O-bound processes ensures that if a process executes and needs to wait for I/O, the system will switch to another process, utilizing both processor and I/O devices. Some scheduling decisions can also be based on the utilization of resources. For example, if there is only one slot empty for a process in the memory, then the long-term scheduler will send one process to the memory, so that memory is not underutilized.

6.7   SCHEDULING ALGORITHMS

After discussion of scheduling objectives, we now know the desired properties of a scheduling algorithm. In general, a scheduling algorithm selects a process from the ready queue and the dispatcher sends this process to the CPU for execution. The various scheduling algorithms are discussed in the following sub sections. Gantt chart is used for showing the execution of all the processes in the system at a timeline. The timeline depicts the start time and end time of the execution of every process. Thus, it helps in judging the performance of every process in the system.

6.7.1 First Come First Served (FCFS)

There is always a simple approach to maintain a queue, that is, the item that comes first will be served first. It is in tune with this natural justice that people waiting in a queue will be served according to their position in the queue. The person in first position will be served first. The ready queue can also be maintained with this approach. The arriving process is added onto the tail of the queue and the process at the head of the queue is dispatched to the processor for execution. In this way, a ready queue is implemented as a linked list wherein the order of arrival of the processes is maintained with the simple logic of *first in, first out* (FIFO). A running process, if interrupted, is moved back to the ready queue and added onto the end/tail of the queue. It means a process that has been interrupted by any means does not maintain its previous order in the ready queue. Once it has been dispatched to the processor, it has no arrival order. If it comes back in the queue, it acquires the last position. This scheduling policy is non-pre-emptive because the process which has arrived first will be executed first to its completion. Obviously, this scheduling policy is useful in batch systems, where the jobs of users are ordered and executed as per their arrival time.

Let us take an example to understand how the processes are added and deleted from the queue. Suppose there are four processes in the ready queue and they have arrived in the order $P1$, $P2$, $P3$, and $P4$ (see Fig. 6.13). Now when the processor is free, the short-term scheduler will select the process $P1$ in the queue to dispatch it to the processor, because it is the first process at the head of the queue. So $P1$ will get the processor and start executing. Now there are three processes in the system $P2$, $P3$, and $P4$ (see Fig. 6.14). Now suppose the running process is interrupted and goes back to the ready queue. At this time, since $P1$ has been interrupted, there is no process to execute. Therefore, the scheduler will take another process $P2$ from the head of the queue (see Fig. 6.15). Since $P1$ has been placed in the ready queue again, so according to the rule of FIFO queue, the arriving process will be added onto the tail of the queue. Therefore, $P1$ will get the last place after $P4$, at the end of the queue.

Now let us illustrate the execution of this scheduling algorithm with the following example.

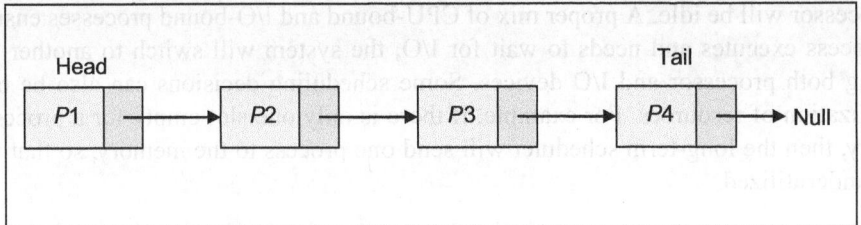

Fig. 6.13 Ready queue of processes

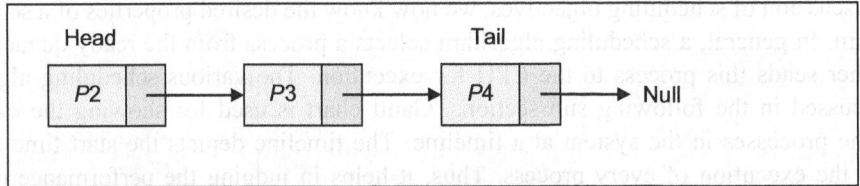

Fig. 6.14 Ready queue of processes: P1 gets execution

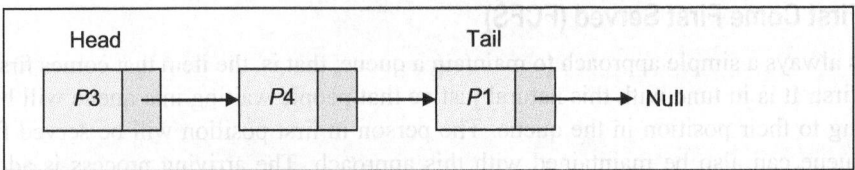

Fig. 6.15 Ready queue of processes: P1 interrupted, P2 gets execution and P1 moves back at the end of the queue

Example 6.1

Consider the following scenario of processes in a system:

Process	Arrival time	Execution time
P1	0	5
P2	2	4
P3	3	7
P4	5	6

Draw a Gantt chart for the execution of the processes, showing their start time and end time, using FCFS algorithm. Calculate turnaround time, normalized turnaround time, and waiting time for each process, and average turnaround time, average normalized turnaround time, and average waiting time for the system.

Solution

Let us illustrate the execution of these processes in the Gantt chart as given in the following space.

P1	P2	P3	P4
0	5	9	16	22

Table 6.1 Performance metrics for Example 6.1

Process	Arrival time	Execution time (x)	Turnaround time (t$_r$)	Normalized turn-around time (t$_r$/x)	Waiting time
P1	0	5	5	1	0
P2	2	4	7	1.75	3
P3	3	7	13	1.85	6
P4	5	6	17	2.84	11
			Average turnaround time = 10.5	Average normalized turnaround time = 1.86	Average waiting time = 5

The process P1 arrives at time 0 and completes at time 5. Therefore, its turnaround time is 5. Similarly, for the process P2, it arrives at time 2 and finishes at time 9, since it waits for the execution of P1 to complete. Hence, its turnaround time includes its wait time (3 units) and processing time (4 units), making its turnaround time 7. In this way, turnaround times for all processes and average turnaround time are shown in Table 6.1. Similarly the normalized turnaround time for all the processes is also shown.

Another performance metric for the system is waiting time. For process P1, waiting time is 0 as it arrives at time 0 and gets processor at the same time. Similarly, waiting time for process P2 is 3 unit time as it arrives at time 2 and gets processor at time 5. In this way, waiting time for all processes and average waiting time for the system are shown in Table 6.1. Though FCFS algorithm is simple to understand and implement, it may not be a good choice for multi-user or real-time systems, where quick response is expected. Example 6.1 shows that short processes also have high turnaround and high normalized turnaround times. Similarly, the waiting time for shorter processes is also high. It is obvious that short processes suffer due to long processes. It may also be the case that some important processes arriving late may suffer, as the processor is busy executing some unimportant process, which has arrived earlier. Thus, it can be said that FCFS algorithm may be better for longer processes as compared to shorter processes.

6.7.2 Priority Scheduling

In a computer system, all processes cannot be treated equally with FCFS policy. In some systems like real-time systems, each process is well defined with its functionality. It has a priority in the system, according to the importance of its functionality. It means the arrival of the processes does not matter. If a process with higher priority has arrived late or at its defined time, then it will be executed first according to its priority. For example, consider a process with low priority, whose job is to compute some data. At this time, a process which brings sensor data will pre-empt the first process, because if the sensor data are not processed at the right time, data are lost, and so will be the purpose of a real-time system.

The question is how to give priority to the processes. In real-time systems, the priorities are defined as a number associated with a process. This number scheme is also different in various OSs. Some systems follow lower numbers as higher priorities and others follow higher numbers as higher priorities. In general, lower numbers are considered as high priorities. For example, there are three processes as: P1 with priority 1, P2 with 6 and P3 with 8. In this case, P1 has the highest priority and P3 has the lowest priority.

There can be other methods to attach priorities to the processes. For example, processes can be prioritized based on their execution time. The drawback of FCFS scheduling can be mitigated using this priority scheme. The processes with shorter execution times will be executed first. Similarly, another priority scheme can be to give preference to those processes which have the shortest remaining execution time. All these priority schemes are discussed in the subsequent sections.

Priority Number-based Scheduling

In this type of scheduling, preference is given to the processes, based on a priority number assigned to it. This scheduling scheme is generally used in real-time systems and is of pre-emptive nature. It can be non-pre-emptive as well, but in real-time systems it makes no sense. We will follow the priority number scheme as low number means high priority and pre-emptive version of this type of scheduling. Let us understand this algorithm with an example.

Example 6.2

Consider the following scenario of processes with their priority:

Process	Arrival time	Execution time	Priority
P1	0	5	2
P2	2	4	1
P3	3	7	3
P4	5	6	4

Draw the Gantt chart for the execution of the processes, showing their start time and end time, using priority-number based scheduling. Calculate turnaround time, normalized turnaround time, waiting time for each process, and average turnaround time, average normalized turnaround time, and average waiting time for the system.

Solution

Let us illustrate the execution of these processes in the Gantt chart as shown in the following space.

P1	P2	P1	P3	P4
0 2		6	9	16 22

Table 6.2 Performance metrics for Example 6.2

Process	Arrival time	Execution time(x)	Priority number	Turnaround time (t_r)	Normalized turnaround time (t_r/x)	Waiting time
P1	0	5	2	9	1.8	4
P2	2	4	1	4	1	0
P3	3	7	3	13	1.85	6
P4	5	6	4	17	2.84	11
				Average turnaround time = 10.75	Average normalized turnaround time = 1.87	Average waiting time = 5.25

The process P1 arrives at zero and executes until P2 arrives at time 2. Since P2 has higher priority, P1 is interrupted and P2 gets execution. After the completion of P2 at time 6, execution of P1 is continued and it finishes at time 9 Hence, its turnaround time is 9. For P2, the turnaround time is 4. In this way, turnaround of all processes can be calculated as shown in Table 6.2. The waiting time for P1 is 4. For calculating this, consider the starting time of the last execution of the process. Now subtract the finishing time of the previous execution of the process, if any, and its arrival time. For P1, the starting time of last execution is 6, the previous execution is from 0 to 2 and its arrival is at 0. Therefore, its waiting time is $6 - 2 - 0 = 4$. Similarly for process P2, $wt = 2 - 0 - 2 = 0$. See Table 6.2 for all the calculated metrics.

Example 6.3

Consider the following scenario of processes with their priority:

Process	Arrival time	Execution time	Priority number
P1	0	3	3
P2	2	7	4
P3	3	5	1
P4	5	9	2

Draw the Gantt chart for the execution of the processes, showing their start time and end time, using priority-number based scheduling. Calculate turnaround time, normalized turnaround time, waiting time for each process and average turnaround time, average normalized turnaround time, and average waiting time for the system.

Solution

Let us illustrate the execution of these processes in the Gantt chart as shown in the following space.

P1	P3	P4	P2
0	3	8	17	24

In this example, process P1 appears first in the system and starts executing. During its execution, P2 arrives at time 2, but it does not get the processor because its priority is low compared to that of P1. After the full execution of P1, at time 3, P3, having the highest priority, arrived and therefore, gets the execution. By the time, P3 completes its execution, P4 has also arrived. Now all the processes except P1, compete for the processor. They get the execution according to their priority numbers.

All calculated performance metrics are shown in Table 6.3.

Shortest Process Next (SPN)

Another way to prioritize the processes is to run the processes with shorter execution times. This policy will overcome the drawback of FCFS that favoured long processes. In this algorithm, at an instant of time, the processes are compared based on their execution times. The process with the shortest execution time is executed first. This is a non-pre-emptive scheduling algorithm. This means that if a process with the shortest execution time appears, even then it cannot pre-empt a process with longer execution time. Since the preference is based on the execution time of processes, the shorter processes will be executed earlier,

Table 6.3   Performance metrics for Example 6.3

Process	Execution time (x)	Arrival time	Priority number	Turnaround time (t_r)	Normalized turnaround time (t_r/x)	Waiting time
P1	3	0	3	3	1	0
P2	7	2	4	22	3.14	15
P3	5	3	1	5	1	0
P4	9	5	2	12	1.34	3
				Average turnaround time = 10.5	Average normalized turnaround time = 1.62	Average waiting time = 4.5

thereby increasing the response time of processes. In comparison with FCFS, more number of processes will start responding and therefore, the performance of the system, in terms of response time, will increase.

One problem in the implementation of this algorithm is that we must know the execution time of every process in advance, so that comparison of processes can be done. But it is not possible practically. We will discuss this problem in the next scheduling algorithm.

Let us understand this algorithm with an example.

Example 6.4

Consider the following scenario of processes:

Process	Arrival time	Execution time
P1	0	5
P2	2	4
P3	3	7
P4	5	6

Draw the Gantt chart for the execution of the processes, showing their start time and end time, using SPN scheduling. Calculate turnaround time, normalized turnaround time, waiting time for each process and average turnaround time, average normalized turnaround time, and average waiting time for the system.

Solution

Let us illustrate the execution of these processes in the Gantt chart as shown in the following space.

P1	P2	P4	P3
0	5	9	15	22

P1 starts at 0 and P2, which appears at 2, is of shorter execution time. But it cannot start until P1 finishes, since SPN is a non-pre-emptive scheduling algorithm. During this period, P3 and P4 have also appeared. It means now there are three processes P2, P3, and P4 in the

Table 6.4 Performance metrics for Example 6.4

Process	Execution time (x)	Turnaround time (t$_r$)	Normalized turnaround time (t$_r$/x)	Waiting time
P1	5	5	1	0
P2	4	7	1.75	3
P3	7	19	2.7	12
P4	6	10	1.67	4
		Average turnaround time = 10.25	**Average normalized turnaround time = 1.78**	**Average waiting time = 4.75**

ready queue. But P2 will be executed first at time 5, as it has the shortest execution time among all the processes. After P2 finishes the execution at 9, P4 gets preference over P3, as shown in the Gantt chart. All calculated performance metrics are shown in Table 6.4.

Shortest Remaining Time Next (SRN)

This algorithm also considers the execution time of processes as in SPN. But it is a pre-emptive version of SPN. It means, here, we can pre-empt a process based on the execution time. The process with the shortest execution time will always pre-empt other processes. Since the processes may not be able to complete their execution as they may be pre-empted, the preference for pre-emption will be based on the remaining execution time of processes. Let us see one example of this scheduling.

Example 6.5

Consider the following scenario of processes:

Process	Arrival time	Execution time
P1	0	9
P2	1	5
P3	2	3
P4	3	4

Draw the Gantt chart for the execution of the processes, showing their start time and end time, using FCFS, SPN, and SRN scheduling. Calculate turnaround time, normalized turnaround time, waiting time for each process and average turnaround time, average normalized turnaround time, and average waiting time for the system.

Solution

FCFS

P1		P2	P3	P4
0	9	14	17	21

Table 6.5 Performance metrics for Example 6.5 (FCFS)

Process	Arrival time	Execution time (x)	Turnaround time (t_r)	Normalized turn-around time (t_r/x)	Waiting time
P1	0	9	9	1	0
P2	1	5	13	2.6	8
P3	2	3	15	5	12
P4	3	4	19	4.75	14
			Average turnaround time = 14	Average normalized turnaround time = 1.86	Average waiting time = 8.5

SPN

P1		P3	P4	P2	
0	9	12	16		21

SRN

Process P1 gets the execution as it arrives first. At time 1, P2 arrives, and its execution time is less than that of P1. Therefore, P2 pre-empts P1 and gets the execution. Similarly, P3 pre-empts P2 as the execution time of P3 is less than that of P2. P3 completes its execution as its execution time is less than others. At time 5, there are two processes P2 and P4 having execution time 4. In this case, we adopt FCFS scheduling. Therefore, P2 is given chance to execute. After completion of P2, P4, and then P1, get execution.

P1	P2	P3	P2	P4	P1
0	1 2	5	9	13	21

Table 6.6 Performance metrics for Example 6.5 (SPN)

Process	Arrival time	Execution time (x)	Turnaround time (t_r)	Normalized turn-around time (t_r/x)	Waiting time
P1	0	9	9	1	0
P2	1	5	20	4	15
P3	2	3	10	3.34	7
P4	3	4	13	3.25	9
			Average turnaround time = 13	Average normalized turnaround time = 2.89	Average waiting time = 7.75

Table 6.7 Performance metrics for Example 6.5 (SRN)

Process	Arrival time	Execution time (x)	Turnaround time (t_r)	Normalized turn-around time (t_r/x)	Waiting time
P1	0	9	21	2.34	12
P2	1	5	8	1.6	3
P3	2	3	3	1	0
P4	3	4	10	2.5	6
			Average turnaround time = 10.5	Average normalized turnaround time = 1.86	Average waiting time = 5.25

SRN is provably the best scheduling algorithm. In the above example, we can see that the average turnaround time and waiting time are reduced as compared to FCFS, thereby, increasing the performance of the system. But again, we need to know in advance, the execution time of every process as in SPN. Therefore, despite being the optimum scheduling algorithm, we cannot use it. The only solution to this problem is to estimate the execution time for a process from its past history of execution. Thus, this scheduling algorithm can be used if we have past data of execution time of the processes, so that the next CPU burst of a process can be estimated. While calculating, the recent past values must be given high weights as compared to older values, because recent values will reflect closer value of the actual burst time.

If recent observed burst time for a process is t_0, then its next estimated burst value will be

$$\alpha t_0 + (1-\alpha)\, t_1$$

where

α = weighting factor

t_1 = older burst value of the process.

If $\alpha = 0.4$, then successive estimates will be

$$t_0, 2t_0/5 + 3t_1/5, 4t_0/25 + 6t_1/25 + \ldots$$

So we can say that

$$S_{n+1} = \alpha t_n + (1-\alpha)\, \alpha t_{n-1} + \ldots.$$

Based on the past values on time series, the exponential average formula for predicting the next CPU burst value of process may be given as:

$$S_{n+1} = \alpha t_n + (1-\alpha)\, S_n$$

where

S_{n+1} = predicted value of next CPU burst

t_n = value of nth CPU burst, that is, recent information

S_n = past history information

α = constant weighting factor, and $0 \leq \alpha \leq 1$

In this equation, through the choice of α, we can quickly choose to forget the past data, or retain the same for a longer time. For example if $\alpha = 0$, then

$$S_{n+1} = S_n$$

It means that the recent information has no effect, and we are considering past data. Similarly if $\alpha = 1$, then

$$S_{n+1} = t_n$$

It means, only recent information is relevant and past data are ignored.
To have a balance between past data and recent data, we choose $\alpha = 1/2$.
That is, $S_{n+1} = (1/2)t_n + (1/2)S_n$

Example 6.6

What will be the exponential average for predicting the next CPU burst value of a process, if constant weighting factor is 0.2 and 0.7? Mention their significance as well.

Solution

Since $S_{n+1} = \alpha t_n + (1-\alpha) \alpha t_{n-1} + ...$
Putting $\alpha = 0.2$, we get
        $S_{n+1} = 0.2t_n + 0.16t_{n-1} + 0.128t_{n-2} + 0.1024t_{n-3}....$
This equation indicates that the exponential average is distributed over some past values, that is, past data are considered.
Putting $\alpha = 0.7$, we get
        $S_{n+1} = 0.7t_n + 0.21t_{n-1} + 0.063t_{n-2} + 0.0189t_{n-3}....$
This equation indicates that the exponential average considers two recent values, and other past data are given less weightage or are ignored.

6.7.3 Round Robin Scheduling

In multi-user time-sharing systems or multi-tasking systems, the requirement of scheduling is different. In these systems, response time is the most important objective. It is quite obvious that FCFS cannot be used for these systems, because it does not care about the response of processes, and they are processed according to their arrivals. It may be possible that a process arriving late may not get response for a long time, if processes arriving earlier are of long processing times. Shortest process next or shortest remaining time next algorithms can be beneficial sometimes, but not always, because they also suffer from starvation. Long processes may need to wait for a long period, again resulting in no response from the process. Thus, the above discussed algorithms cannot be applied for systems, where quick response time is a highly desirable feature.

Since the concept of multi-user and multi-tasking systems is to share the processor time among processes, we can design the algorithm such that each arriving process gets the same amount of time for execution. If each process gets same processor time, the response will be equally good for all the processes, and neither the short nor long process will suffer from starvation. But how will you design the ready queue then? The ready queue can be of the same pattern as that of FCFS, that is, FIFO queue. The only issue is that when one process is executing and its fixed allotted time finishes, it must be temporarily stopped, and the processor must be given to the next process in the queue. In this way, every process gets equal time for execution, and no process can hold the processor for a long time.

But what happens to a process which has been stopped, because its time period has expired but its execution has not been completed. There are some design issues which must be resolved. These are discussed with the functioning of the algorithm:

i) The ready queue is maintained as a FIFO queue.
ii) A fixed time period is allotted to every arriving process in the queue. This fixed time period is known as time slice or time quantum.

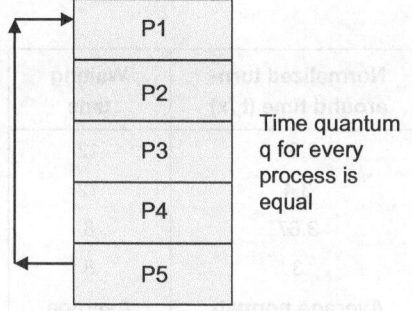

Time quantum q for every process is equal

Fig. 6.16   Round robin scheduling

iii) The first arriving process is selected and dispatched to the processor. But if it is not able to complete its execution within its time slice, then an interrupt is generated with the help of the timer.

iv) As soon as the timer interrupt arrives, the running process is stopped temporarily, and is placed back in the ready queue at the end of the queue (see Fig. 6.16). The context of the interrupted process is saved, so that it can resume when its turn comes in the future.

v) The scheduler selects another process from the queue and dispatches it to the processor. It is executed until the allotted time slice expires.

vi) In this way, scheduling is done in a round robin fashion, such that processes are executed for a fixed time slice again and again, unless all the processes are finished with their execution as shown in the figure.

Sometimes a process may finish its execution before the time slice expires. Will the timer complete its full time slice and then send the interrupt signal? No, it does not happen that way. There is time wastage in this design if a timer completes its time slice, even when a process has finished earlier than the time slice. Therefore, the design is such that whenever a process finishes before the time slice expires, the timer will stop and send the interrupt signal, so that the next process can be scheduled.

The RR scheduling is simple and the overhead in decision-making is very low. It is the best scheduling for achieving good and, relatively evenly, distributed terminal response time.

Let us understand this algorithm with some examples.

Example 6.7

Consider the following scenario of processes with time quantum = 2:

Process	Arrival time	Execution time
P1	0	9
P2	1	5
P3	2	3
P4	3	4

Draw the Gantt chart for the execution of the processes, showing their start time and end time, using round robin scheduling. Calculate turnaround time, normalized turnaround time, waiting time for each process and average turnaround time, average normalized turnaround time, and average waiting time for the system.

Solution

Let us illustrate the execution of these processes in the Gantt chart as shown in the following space.

P1	P2	P3	P4	P1	P2	P3	P4	P1	P2	P1	P1

```
0    2    4    6    8    10   12 13   15   17 18  20 21
```

Table 6.8 Performance metrics for Example 6.7

Process	Arrival time	Execution time (x)	Turnaround time (t_r)	Normalized turn-around time (t_r/x)	Waiting time
P1	0	9	21	2.34	12
P2	1	5	17	3.4	12
P3	2	3	11	3.67	8
P4	3	4	12	3	8
			Average turnaround time = 15.25	Average normalized turnaround time = 3.10	Average waiting time = 10

Every process gets time slice of 2 unit times and hence, every process gets pre-empted after 2 unit times. At time 12, P3 is left with only 1 unit time execution, so it completes its execution at time 13. Then, the timer sends the interrupt signal and P4 starts execution.

All calculated performance metrics are shown in Table 6.8.

Example 6.8

Consider the following scenario of processes with time quantum = 2:

Process	Arrival time	Execution time
P1	0	5
P2	2	3
P3	3	2
P4	5	7

Draw the Gantt chart for the execution of the processes, showing their start time and end time, using round robin scheduling. Calculate turnaround time, normalized turnaround time, waiting time for each process and average turnaround time, average normalized turnaround time, and average waiting time for the system.

Solution

Let us see the execution of these processes in the Gantt chart as shown in the following space.

P1	P2	P3	P4	P1	P2	P4	P1	P4	P4
0	2	4	6	8	10	11	13	14	16	17

The time quantum used in the round robin scheduling plays an important role in its performance. If the time quantum chosen is very large, it will be as good as the FCFS algorithm. The rule is that 80% of CPU bursts should be smaller than the time quantum. On the other hand,

Table 6.9 Performance metrics for Example 6.8

Process	Arrival time	Execution time (x)	Turnaround time (t_r)	Normalized turn-around time (t_r/x)	Waiting time
P1	0	5	14	2.8	9
P2	2	3	9	3	6
P3	3	2	3	1.5	1
P4	5	7	12	1.7	5
			Average turnaround time = 9.5	**Average normalized turnaround time = 2.25**	**Average waiting time = 5.25**

if it is too small, then there will be a large context switch time because after every time quantum, process switching will occur. The context switch time should not be more than the time quantum. Therefore, time quantum should be selected such that context switch time is a small fraction of time quantum. For example, if there are six processes of burst time of 1 unit time and time quantum is 1, then there will be five context switches. If time quantum is two, then there will be two context switches. In this way, the size of time quantum affects the performance of the system, if context switch time increases.

It can be concluded that we cannot choose time quantum as too large or too short, because in both cases the performance of the algorithm will be degraded. Thus, it should be selected in a balanced range, keeping in view the two rules:

Rule 1: 80% of the CPU bursts should be smaller than the time quantum.
Rule 2: Context switch time is nearly 10 % of time quantum.

If the time quantum is selected optimally, then besides the context switch time reduction, the processes need not wait long for their execution and get more service as compared to a bad choice of time quantum. Therefore, it results in reduction of turnaround time, normalized turnaround time, and waiting time. In Example 6.8, if we take time quantum as five instead of two, then it reduces context switches as well as turnaround time, normalized turnaround time, and waiting time. Let us again solve Example 6.7 with time quantum five.

Example 6.9

Consider the following scenario of processes with time quantum = 5:

Process	Arrival time	Execution time
P1	0	9
P2	1	5
P3	2	3
P4	3	4

Table 6.10 Performance metrics for Example 6.9

Process	Arrival time	Execution time (x)	Turnaround time (t$_r$)	Normalized turn-around time (t$_r$/x)	Waiting time
P1	0	9	21	2.34	12
P2	1	5	9	1.8	4
P3	2	3	11	3.67	8
P4	3	4	14	3.5	10
			Average turn-around time = 13.75	Average normalized turnaround time = 2.82	Average waiting time = 8.5

Draw the Gantt chart for the execution of the processes, showing their start time and end time, using round robin scheduling. Calculate turnaround time, normalized turnaround time, and waiting time for each process and average turnaround time, average normalized turnaround time, and average waiting time for the system.

Solution

Let us illustrate the execution of these processes in the Gantt chart as shown in the following space.

P1	P2	P3	P4	P1
0	5	10	13	17	21

Example 6.10

If there is n number of processes in a system and t is the time quantum, what is the maximum time a process needs to wait for its execution?

Solution

Suppose t = 2
n = 5

P1	P2	P3	P4	P5

Let us take P1. After first execution of P1, it needs to wait for all four processes to complete, that is, 8 time units. For P5, it needs to wait for 8 time units for its first execution. It means, in this example, waiting time of every process cannot be more than 8 time units.
We can generalize that the maximum waiting time of a process in round robin is
$$w = (n-1) * t$$

6.7.4 Improved Round Robin Scheduling

Round robin scheduling was developed to provide a uniformly-distributed execution time to every process, so that all of them respond equally. But in this scheduling, waiting time of processes, and thereby, average waiting time of the system increases. A long process needs to wait for more time. Moreover, a process with very short execution time, but more than the time quantum, may also wait for a complete cycle of execution. It means that both long and short processes may suffer from this type of scheduling. If we know the total estimated execution time for each process, we can calculate the ratio of actual CPU time consumed by the process to the total estimated time allowed to the process.

CPU consumption ratio = Actual CPU time consumed/total estimated execution time

This ratio will provide us the scenario about which long processes need attention, that is, their waiting time need to be reduced. So the process, which has minimum CPU consumption ratio, will be selected next for the scheduling. The scheduling interval will be the same as that of round robin, that is, after every time quantum. But what about the short processes? The CPU consumption ratio of short processes will be high very soon. So they will not be scheduled and need to wait for a long time. To accommodate short processes, we need to take another condition into consideration. If CPU consumption ratio of a process is greater than 0.6, it will be selected next. Thus, the combined rule for scheduling becomes:

Schedule a process if its CPU consumption ratio is greater than 0.60, else schedule a process whose CPU consumption ratio is minimum.

Let us see with an example how it has improved the response time and the waiting time of the process.

Example 6.11

Consider the following scenario of processes with time quantum = 2. Draw the Gantt chart for the execution of the processes, showing their start time and end time, using improved round robin scheduling. Calculate turn-around time, normalized turnaround

Process	Arrival time	Execution time
P1	0	9
P2	1	5
P3	2	3
P4	3	4

time, and waiting time for each process and average turnaround time, average normalized turnaround time, and average waiting time for the system. Compare all the metrics with round robin scheduling.

Solution

To draw Gantt chart of this example, we need to calculate the CPU consumption ratio and decide which process will be selected after every interval. Table 6.11 shows the CPU consumption ratio and the next process selected.

Table 6.11   CPU consumption ratio for Example 6.11

Time	Actual CPU time consumed/CPU time entitled				Process selected for next execution
	P1	**P2**	**P3**	**P4**	
0	–	–	–	–	P1
2	2/9 = 0.23	0	0	–	P2
4	2/9 = 0.23	2/5 = 0.4	0	0	P3
6	2/9 = 0.23	2/5 = 0.4	2/3 = 0.67	0	P4
8	2/9 = 0.23	2/5 = 0.4	2/3 = 0.67	2/4 = 0.5	P3
9	0.23	0.4	3/3 = 1	0.5	P1

(Contd)

(Table 6.11 Contd)

11	4/9 = 0.45	0.4	–	0.5	P2
13	0.45	4/5=0.8	–	0.5	P2
14	0.45	5/5 = 1	–	0.5	P1
16	6/9 = 0.67	–	–	0.5	P1
18	8/9 = 0.89	–	–	0.5	P1
19	9/9 = 1	–	–	0.5	P4
21	9/9 = 1	–	–	–	

Now we can draw the Gantt chart, using the information from Table 6.11.

P1		P2		P3		P4		P3	P1	P2	P2	P1		P1		P1	P4
0		2		4		6		8	9	11		13	14	16		18	19	21

The performance metrics calculated are shown in Table 6.12. This table shows the improvement in waiting time.

6.7.5 Highest Response Ratio Next (HRRN) Scheduling

This is another algorithm that can reduce the shortcomings of round robin scheduling. As discussed earlier, round robin may favour short or long processes. Since in multi-user and multi-tasking systems, each process must respond equally well, the idea is to consider the response time in the scheduling decision. Let,

Response ratio = Time elapsed in the system / CPU time consumed by the process

This response ratio will be able to indicate how much service a process has received. Higher the ratio, better will be the service received by the process. Therefore, scheduling decision will be: Schedule a process which has the highest response ratio.

For a newly arrived process, response ratio will be high and it will be able to get the attention of the processor. A process is allowed to execute until the response ratio of another process is the highest. When a process is executing, other processes are waiting. It means the time spent

Table 6.12 Performance metrics for Example 6.11

Process	Arrival time	Execution time (x)	Turnaround time (t_r)	Normalized turn-around time (t_r/x)	Waiting time
P1	0	9	19	2.12	10
P2	1	5	14	2.8	8
P3	2	3	9	3	4
P4	3	4	21	5.25	14
			Average turnaround time = 15.75	**Average normalized turnaround time = 3.10**	**Average waiting time = 9**

by them in the system is increasing, thereby increasing the response ratio. Therefore, they will also get the attention of the processor. In this way, this algorithm will be able to distribute the processor time more fairly as compared to simple round robin scheduling algorithm. Let us understand this algorithm with an example.

Example 6.12

Consider the following scenario of processes with time quantum = 1.

Draw the Gantt chart for the execution of the processes, showing their start time and end time, using RR and HRRN scheduling. Calculate turnaround time, normalized turnaround time, and waiting time for each process and average

Process	Arrival time	Execution time
P1	0	3
P2	2	3
P3	3	2
P4	5	4
P5	7	2

turnaround time, average normalized turnaround time, and average waiting time for the system. Compare all the metrics with round robin scheduling.

Solution

Round Robin

Let us illustrate the execution of these processes in the Gantt chart given in the following space:

P1	P1	P2	P3	P3	P4	P4	P5	P1	P2	P4	P5	P2	P4
0	1	2	3	4	5	6	7	8	9	10	11	12	13	14

HRRN

To draw Gantt chart of this example, we need to calculate response ratio and decide which process will be selected after every interval. Table 6.14 shows the response ratio and the next process selected.

Table 6.13   Performance metrics for Example 6.12 (RR)

Process	Arrival time	Execution time (x)	Turnaround time (t_r)	Normalized turnaround time (t_r/x)	Waiting time
P1	0	3	9	3	6
P2	2	3	11	3.67	8
P3	3	2	2	1	0
P4	5	4	9	2.25	5
P5	7	2	5	2.5	3
			Average turnaround time = 7.2	Average normalized turnaround time = 2.484	Average waiting time = 4.4

by them in the system is increasing, thereby increasing the response ratio. Therefore, they will also get the attention of the processor. In this way, this algorithm will be able to distribute the processor time more fairly as compared to simple round robin scheduling algorithm. Let us understand this algorithm with an example.

Table 6.14   Response ratio for Example 6.12 (HRRN)

Time	Response ratio = Time elapsed in the system/CPU time consumed by process					Process selected for next execution
	P1	P2	P3	P4	P5	
0	undef	–	–	–	–	P1
1	1/1=1	–	–	–	–	P1
2	2/2=1	undef	–	–	–	P2
3	3/2=1.5	1/1	undef	–	–	P3
4	4/2=2	2/1=2	1/1	–	–	P1
5	5/3=1.67 (completed)	3/1=3	2/1=2	undef	–	P4
6	–	4/1=4	3/1=3	1/1=1	undef	P2
7	–	5/2=2.5	4/1=4	2/1=2	1/1	P5
8	–	6/2=3	5/1=5	3/1=3	2/1=2	P3
9	–	7/2=3.5	6/2 (completed)	4/1=4	2/1=2	P4
10	–	8/2=4	–	5/2=2.5	3/1=3	P2
11	–	9/3=3 (completed)	–	6/2=3	4/1=4	P5
12	–	–	–	7/2=3.5	5/2=2.5 (completed)	P4
13	–	–	–	8/3=2.67	–	P4
14	–	–	–	9/4 (completed)	–	

Let us see the execution of these processes in the Gantt chart:

P1	P1	P2	P3	P1	P4	P2	P5	P3	P4	P2	P5	P4	P4
0	1	2	3	4	5	6	7	8	9	10	11	12	13	14

Table 6.15   Performance metrics for Example 6.12 (HRRN)

Process	Arrival time	Execution time (x)	Turnaround time (t_r)	Normalized turnaround time (t_r/x)	Waiting time
P1	0	3	5	1.67	2
P2	2	3	9	3	6
P3	3	2	6	3	4
P4	5	4	9	2.25	5
P5	7	2	5	2.5	3
			Average turnaround time = 6.8	Average normalized turnaround time = 2.484	Average waiting time = 4

Example 6.13

Consider the following scenario of processes with time quantum = 4:

Process	Arrival time	Execution time
P1	0	18
P2	1	3
P3	2	4
P4	3	5
P5	4	3

Draw the Gantt chart for the execution of the processes, showing their start time and end time, using FCFS, RR, improved RR, and HRRN scheduling. Calculate turnaround time, normalized turnaround time, and waiting time for each process and average turnaround time, average normalized turnaround time, and average waiting time for the system.

Solution

FCFS

P1			P2	P3	P4		P5	
0			18	21	25		30	33

Table 6.16   Performance metrics for Example 6.13 (FCFS)

Process	Arrival time	Execution time (x)	Turnaround time (t$_r$)	Normalized turn-around time (t$_r$/x)	Waiting time
P1	0	18	18	1	0
P2	1	3	20	6.67	17
P3	2	4	23	5.75	19
P4	3	5	27	5.4	22
P5	4	3	29	9.67	26
			Average turnaround time =23.4	Average normalized turnaround time = 5.689	Average waiting time = 16.8

RR

P1	P2	P3	P4	P5	P1	P4	P1
0 4	7	11	15	18	22	23	33

Table 6.17   Performance metrics for Example 6.13 (RR)

Process	Arrival time	Execution time (x)	Turnaround time (t$_r$)	Normalized turn-around time (t$_r$/x)	Waiting time
P1	0	18	33	1.84	15
P2	1	3	0	2	0
P3	2	4	9	2.25	5
P4	3	5	20	4	15
P5	4	3	14	4.67	11
			Average turnaround time =16.4	Average normalized turnaround time = 2.952	Average waiting time=9.8

Improved RR

Table 6.18   CPU Consumption ratio for Example 6.13 (Improved RR)

Time	Actual CPU time consumed/CPU time entitled					Process selected for next execution
	P1	P2	P3	P4	P5	
0	Undef	-	-	-	-	P1
4	4/18=0.23	Undef	undef	undef	-	P2

(Contd)

(Table 6.18 Contd)

7	0.23	3/3 (completed)	undef	undef	Undef	P3
11	0.23	–	4/4 (completed)	undef	undef	P4
15	0.23	–	–	4/5=0.8	undef	P5
18	0.23	–	–	0.8	3/3 (completed)	P4
19	0.23	–	–	5/5 (completed)	–	P1
23	8/18	–	–	–	–	P1
27	12/18	–	–	–	–	P1
31	16/18	–	–	–	–	P1
33	18/18	–	–	–	–	P1

6.7.6 Virtual Round Robin Scheduling

RR scheduling performs well and provides a uniformly distributed response time. However, this might not always be true. If all processes are CPU-bound, then RR performs well, but

Table 6.19   Performance metrics for Example 6.13 (Improved RR)

Process	Arrival time	Execution time (x)	Turnaround time (t_r)	Normalized turn-around time (t_r/x)	Waiting time
P1	0	18	33	5.5	15
P2	1	3	6	2	3
P3	2	4	9	2.25	5
P4	3	5	16	3.2	11
P5	4	3	14	4.67	11
			Average turnaround time =15.6	**Average normalized turnaround time = 3.524**	**Average waiting time =9**

HRRN

Table 6.20 Response ratio for Example 6.13 (HRRN)

Time	Response ratio = Time elapsed in the system/CPU time consumed by process					Process selected for next execution
	P1	**P2**	**P3**	**P4**	**P5**	
0	undef	–	–	–	–	P1
4	4/4=1	undef	Undef	undef	undef	P2
7	7/4= 1.75	6/3=2 (completed)	Undef	undef	undef	P3
11	11/4=2.75	–	9/4 (completed)	undef	undef	P4
15	15/4=3.75	–	–	12/4=3	undef	P5
18	18/4=4.5	–	–	15/4=3.75	completed	P1
22	22/8=2.75	–	–	19/4=4.75	–	P4
23	23/8=2.875	–	–	20/5 completed	–	P1
27	27/12	–	–	–	–	
31	31/16	–	–	–	–	
33	33/18	–	–	–	–	

P1	P2	P3	P4	P5	P1	P4	P1	
0	4	7	11	15	18	22	23	33

Table 6.21 Performance metrics for Example 6.13 (HRRN)

Process	Arrival time	Execution time (x)	Turnaround time (t_r)	Normalized turnaround time (t_r/x)	Waiting time
P1	0	18	33	4.125	15
P2	1	3	6	2	3
P3	2	4	9	2.25	5
P4	3	5	20	4	15
P5	4	3	14	4.67	11
			Average turnaround time = 16.4	Average normalized turnaround time = 3.409	Average waiting time = 9.8

this is not practical. We have a mix of CPU-bound and I/O-bound processes. Since I/O-bound processes have very small executions in between the long I/O accesses, these processes are not able to consume their time quantum in comparison with CPU-bound processes. I/O-bound processes, after executing for a very short period (less than the time quantum), are put into I/O waiting queues. After I/O operation, they get back to the ready queue, but at the end of it. Therefore, after every I/O, they need to compete with all other CPU-bound jobs. In this way, they are not able to consume their time quantum, while CPU-bound processes consume their full time quantum. It results in the starvation of I/O-bound processes over CPU-bound processes, because of the poor performance of I/O-bound processes. Moreover, no one can predict the response time of these processes, that is, the variance of response time is increased. Finally, due to this strategy, there is poor utilization of I/O devices.

To reduce this starvation of I/O-bound processes, a virtual round robin scheduling is adopted. In this scheduling, CPU-bound processes are executed in the same fashion as discussed in RR scheduling. Whenever this type of process reaches the head of the ready queue, it starts execution and consumes its time quantum. If it is not able to complete its execution within the time quantum, it releases the processor, and is put back at the end of the ready queue, where it waits for its next selection. But there is a difference in the working of I/O-bound processes. When an I/O-bound process gets execution, it uses its time quantum partially and initiates an I/O. It releases the processor and waits in an appropriate device queue for its I/O access. As soon as its I/O access is finished, it is put back at the end of the ready queue in RR scheduling. But here in virtual RR scheduling, the process is not put back at the end of the ready queue, but at the end of another queue called *auxiliary queue*. Auxiliary queue is the place where it will wait for its next selection of execution. It means, now there are two queues: ready queue and auxiliary queue. Auxiliary queue has been introduced so that I/O-bound processes, after completing their I/O, need not compete with other processes. They will get preference over other processes (see Fig. 6.17). It means, first of all, we need to provide priority-based scheduling among the queues. The priority of auxiliary queue is higher, such that a process in this queue will get priority over a process in the ready queue. In this way, I/O-bound processes are not starved, and there is fair distribution of processor time among all types of processes.

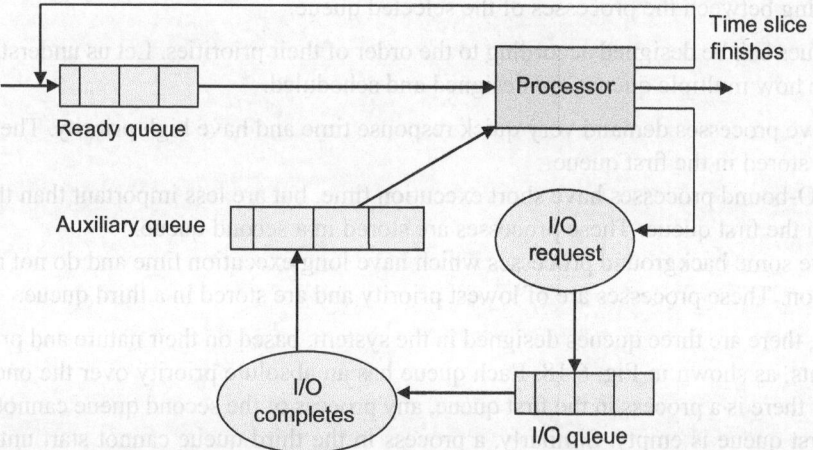

Fig. 6.17 Virtual round robin scheduling

The process at the head of the auxiliary queue gets the processor and runs till it finishes its remaining time quantum. For example, if in a system, the time quantum is t milliseconds and an I/O-bound process uses its n milliseconds of time quantum, it initiates an I/O and waits on the device queue. After getting a place in the auxiliary queue and consequently the processor, it executes for $t-n$ milliseconds.

6.7.7 Multi-level Queue Scheduling

Virtual RR scheduling can be generalized further as multi-level queue scheduling. The basic idea behind multiple queues is that all processes are not of the same nature. For example, we have seen in virtual RR that there are two types of processes, namely CPU-bound and I/O-bound. Also that I/O-bound processes will suffer, if we treat both type of processes in the same way and store them in a single ready queue. In this way, every process has a different nature and different requirement of execution. For example, an interactive process needs immediate attention and cannot wait. Therefore, this type of processes requires quick response time and should be at the highest priority. Some processes are less important than interactive, but are of short duration, so they must not wait for a long process. It means all processes have different requirements of processing as well. The various categories of processes can be:

- Interactive processes
- Non-interactive processes
- CPU-bound processes
- I/O-bound processes
- Foreground processes
- Background processes

Thus, it can be concluded that all processes are not of the same nature, and so, should not be stored in the same ready queue. Therefore, the idea of multi-level queue scheduling is to partition the original ready queue into various queues and store every process according to its category. Instead of designing a single ready queue storing all the processes, there is need to design multiple queues with different levels. The different levels mean that the priority of each queue is different. There are two types of scheduling in multi-level queue scheduling:

- Scheduling among the queues.
- Scheduling between the processes of the selected queue.

The queues can be designed according to the order of their priorities. Let us understand with an example how multiple queues are designed and scheduled.

- Interactive processes demand very quick response time and have high priority. Therefore, they are stored in the first queue.
- Some I/O-bound processes have short execution time, but are less important than the processes in the first queue. These processes are stored in a second queue.
- There are some background processes which have long execution time and do not need any interaction. These processes are of lowest priority and are stored in a third queue.

In this way, there are three queues designed in the system, based on their nature and processing requirements, as shown in Fig. 6.18. Each queue has an absolute priority over the one after it. It means, if there is a process in the first queue, any process of the second queue cannot execute until the first queue is empty. Similarly, a process in the third queue cannot start until all the

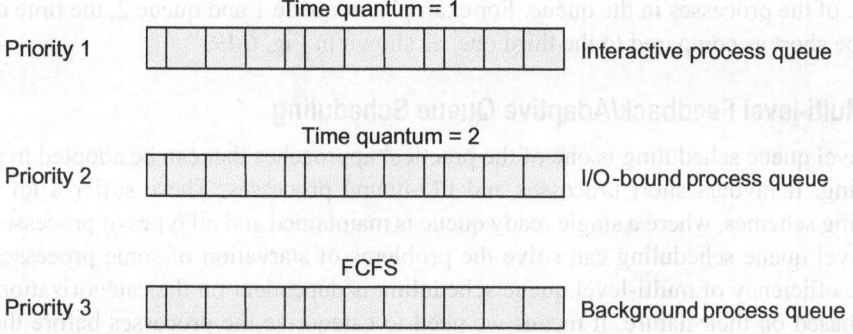

Fig. 6.18   Multi-level queue scheduling

processes in the second queue have finished their execution. If an interactive process appears in the system, when there is one background process running, then the new process will pre-empt the background process, as it belongs to the higher priority queue. This is how scheduling is performed among the queues.

Once a queue is selected, the second type of scheduling is done between the processes of this queue. Any type of scheduling can be taken for this purpose, depending on the type of queue. For example, round robin scheduling can be performed for first and second queues in our example, as they expect equal response time and service. Since background processes in the third queue have no such requirement of response time, they can be scheduled in FCFS order (see fig. 6.18).

The scheme given for the set of queues in our example is just as per the needs of the processes. Another scheme for the queue scheduling is to perform round robin scheduling in each queue. It means every queue will get a fixed time slice for its processes, so that lower priority processes do not starve. The time quantum for each queue may vary as per the requirement

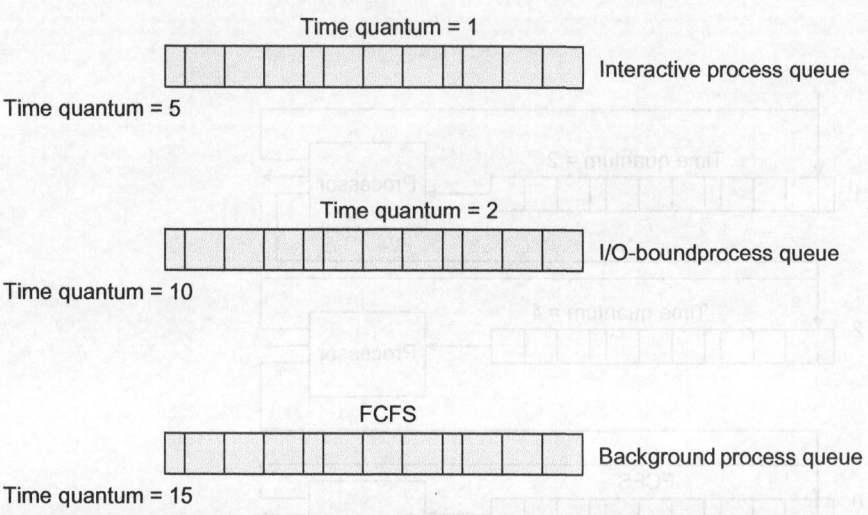

Fig. 6.19   Round robin scheduling among multi-level queues

and type of the processes in the queue. For example, in queue 1 and queue 2, the time quantum should be short as compared to the third one, as shown in Fig. 6.19.

6.7.8 Multi-level Feedback/Adaptive Queue Scheduling

Multi-level queue scheduling is one of the practical approaches that can be adopted in process-scheduling. It favours short processes and I/O-bound processes. These suffer a lot in other scheduling schemes, where a single ready queue is maintained and all types of processes reside. Multi-level queue scheduling can solve the problems of starvation of some processes. However, the efficiency of multi-level queue scheduling is dependent on the categorization of processes, based on their nature. It means we need to categorize the processes before they enter into the system. We cannot judge the behaviour of any process before its execution, therefore, we cannot categorize the processes in different queues.

In multi-level feedback queue scheduling, categorization is done on the basis of the feedback obtained from process behaviour. Here, the priority is decided based on the past execution time. Each queue will be given a time quantum. The higher priority queue will get the shortest time quantum, that is, the process entering the higher priority queue will get the shortest time quantum. If the process is able to complete its execution within the time quantum allotted, it is considered an interactive or I/O-bound or short process and resides in that queue only. Otherwise it means it is not a short process and requires more time to finish. In that case, it is moved to the next queue, where time quantum is more as compared to the first queue. If it is able to complete its execution, then it is considered a process of medium priority and resides in that queue only. But again if it is not able to complete its execution, it is moved to the next queue that is the third queue, where the time quantum is more as compared to the second queue. In this way, the process is demoted to the lower queue until it reaches the last queue designed in the system. The CPU-bound long processes get equal response time, because initially they get the processor in higher priority queues, and then get more time quantum in lower queues after the execution of short processes. In this mechanism, the following events may happen at every queue (see fig. 6.20):

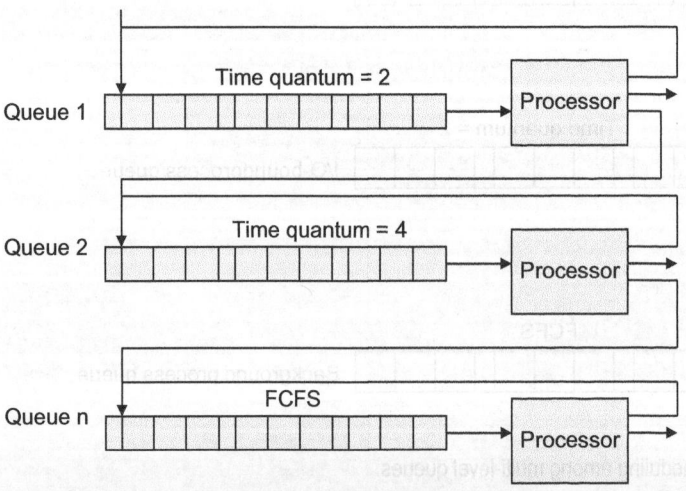

Fig. 6.20 Feedback/Adaptive queue scheduling

- A process consumes its time quantum and finishes its execution.
- A process releases the processor when it either initiates an I/O or is pre-empted by a higher priority process. In case of I/O, it is moved to the I/O queue and then to the end of its queue . And in case of pre-emption, it is moved back to the end of its queue.
- A process consumes its time quantum, but is not able to complete its execution within that time, and therefore, it is moved to the next lower queue.

As in multi-level queue scheduling, the scheduling of queues can be based on fixed priority or the time quantum. And the scheduling of processes in the queues may be based on the RR scheduling, providing time quantum to each process. The time quantum is inversely proportional to the priority of the queue: the lower the priority, the higher the time quantum.

One drawback in this mechanism is that if there are new processes arriving in the system which are of short execution time requirement, they will always pre-empt other processes, especially long processes which are residing in lower priority queues. Therefore, there are chances that these processes may starve for execution. Another problem here is that processes may change their behaviour. It is not necessary that a long CPU-bound process will always remain the same; it may become an I/O-bound process. A background process may also become a short process which requires priority over others. Therefore, another modification required in feedback queue scheduling is that a process can not only be demoted to lower priority queues, but can also be promoted to higher priority queues based on the change in their behaviour. If a process in a lower priority queue becomes I/O-bound, but still does not get the processor as it is in the lower priority queue, then it should be moved to the upper high priority queues where it can get the processor. Thus, instead of permanently assigning the queues to a process, the processes should be moved between the queues (either to lower or higher), so that they are in the appropriate queue according to their recent behaviour. But this incurs an overhead of maintaining the information about these processes. For example, we need to keep track of the waiting time of a process in the lower priority queue. Based on its waiting time, it will be promoted to the next higher queue. Similarly, there may be many parameters to be stored, based on which, a decision is taken about the promotion or demotion of a process. In this way, a feedback about the behaviour of a process is taken and the scheduling mechanism is adapted, according to its changing behaviour in the system.

6.7.9 Fair-share Scheduling

In our scheduling algorithms discussed so far, it has been assumed that corresponding to one user, there is a single process. Therefore, they consider one process for one user and divide the processor time considering this strategy. However, this is not true in practical situations. In a multi-user environment, there are multiple users (or groups of users) sharing a system, or a single user with multiple processes for running an application. But the process-scheduling algorithms designed so far are not capable of these situations. So we need to consider the issues of a user with multiple processes and groups of users.

Before we discuss what fair-share scheduling is, let us consider an example. Suppose there are two groups of users accessing a system. First group, having multiple users, is responsible for accessing only general information, which requires very short time. On the other hand, the second group, having one or two users, is responsible for accessing some critical data and performing some decisions, requiring longer time as compared to the first group. Algorithms like RR would give most of the processor time to the first group and the second group may starve for the execution. Therefore, previously discussed scheduling algorithms would not suffice for a user with multiple processes and group of users, which is quite a practical situation. Moreover, the large number of users in the first group may affect the performance of the second group. So we need to design algorithms which consider the needs of a user or group of users and distribute the processor time not among the individual processes, but among the users or group of users as the case may be. These algorithms are known as *fair-share* scheduling algorithms.

To implement fair-share scheduling, we need to know how much share of processor or resources a user or a group of users require in the system. Therefore, a share-weightage is necessary to be provided to the users or group of users. The fair-share scheduler will use this share-weightage to provide fair share of resources to every user or group of users. The users' share indicates the measure of their entitlement to work on the system. The more share a user has, the greater their entitlement. If a user x has 30% more shares than user y, then it means user x needs to work 30% more than y.

For example, in a system, there are two users U1 and U2. U1 has processes P11, P12, P13, and P14 and U2 has processes P21, P22, P23, and P24. Suppose U2 has to perform some critical computation-intensive job, which requires more time as compared to U1. Let the weightage fixed to U2 and U1 be 75% and 25 %, respectively. If conventional round robin scheduling is performed, then the execution sequence may be:

P11, P21, P12, P22, P13, P23, P14, P24.....

As we can see, U2 is not getting much time to complete its application, due to fixed time slice for every user. Now, if we apply fair-share scheduling, then the sequence of execution may be:

P11, P21, P22, P23, P12, P24, P21, P22, P13, P23, P24, P21, P14.....

Fair-share scheduling provides 75% time of the CPU to U2, thus providing the user time to perform its critical work in time and not starve due to a large number of processes in U1. Likewise, we can extend the scheduling for a group of users.

In the above example, we have already assumed that U1 consumes 25% and U2 consumes 75% processor time. But it may not be possible every time to predict the share of every user or group of users. Therefore, we need to generalize this concept of fair-share, such that every process of the user or every user in a group gets the required share of processor, depending on its need. We can calculate the priority of a process based on the following factors:

- Processor utilization by an individual process
- Processor utilization by a user or group of processes
- Weight assigned to a user or group of users
- Original base priority of the process

In this way, the priority of every process of a user or a group of users can be calculated, considering its past history of execution and the weight provided to it. The only overhead with this is that the priority needs to be calculated, say once per second.

A normalized share is calculated, considering processor utilization, which is a decayed measure of the work that the user has done and the weight assigned to the user. With the consumption of normalized share by the user, the response time from the system increases. This is in accordance to the philosophy of fair-share scheduling. The scheduler increases the response to users who have used their normalized share, so that other users can use their share. Thus, the response time to a user is directly proportional to the usage of their fair-share. The scheduler for this purpose decays each user's usage and updates the usage of all active users at a particular time periodically. Based on all the factors mentioned, the priority of a process is calculated and the process with the highest priority is scheduled next.

6.7.10 Lottery Scheduling

There are some drawbacks in fair-share scheduling. It is possible for a user to monopolize the processor by creating multiple processes so that he gets most of the share of the processor time. Another drawback is that for controlling execution rates, there is computation overhead for calculating the priority of a process, that is., there is no way to directly control relative execution rates, and therefore, we cannot directly conclude that one user should get this much proportion as compared to another.

Lottery scheduling is another mechanism through which these drawbacks can be mitigated. In lottery scheduling, the idea is based on lottery tickets. Every user is provided tickets based on their required share of processor execution. When there is need to perform scheduling, a lottery is held by executing a program for generating a random number from the set of tickets provided to all users. The user holding the winning ticket is allowed to execute. In this way, a user runs in proportion to the number of tickets it holds. Thus, lottery scheduling is a randomized resource allocation mechanism, wherein resource rights are represented by lottery tickets.

There are two good features possessed by this scheduling. They are:

Ticket transfers If a user who needs to wait for some resources like I/O or is blocked for any other reason and is not able to use his/her share, then he/she can temporarily transfer his tickets to a single user or multiple users who may be in need.

Ticket inflation A user can escalate resource rights by creating more lottery tickets. But ticket inflation should be rarely used, because any user can monopolize the processor by creating a large number of tickets.

SUMMARY

The processes in a multi-programming environment cannot be managed, if they are not scheduled in a proper manner as per the demands of various systems. If process-scheduling is not there, all processes will compete for the processor in a random order, which may result in chaos in the system and no process would be able to finish. Thus, process-scheduling is important to manage processes. There are various mechanisms for scheduling processes which have been discussed in this chapter. Every scheduling algorithm has an appropriate use in a particular system. FCFS scheduling is used in batch systems. Round robin is appropriate in a multi-user environment. However, these algorithms are very basic in nature and cannot be applied in practical OSs. This is because these algorithms consider the scheduling of a process as an individual, but processes in multi-user environment may belong to a user or group of users. Therefore, scheduling algorithms consider processes of users or of group of users. Multi-level queue scheduling and feedback queue scheduling are used for this purpose. Another problem in scheduling is that the requirement of a user and a group of users may be different. But every user or group of users must get the required share of processor execution.

Fair-share scheduling and lottery scheduling algorithms are used for distributing processor time to every user fairly.

Let us have a quick review of important concepts discussed in this chapter:

- The processes may be CPU-bound or I/O-bound, but there should be a good mix of both for good scheduling.
- There are three levels of process-scheduling: long-, medium-, and short-term scheduling.
- Long-term scheduling is the first level where a job from the job queue is selected to be sent to the ready queue.
- Medium-term scheduling is done to select a process from the ready queue to be sent to processor.
- Short-term scheduling is done to select a process from the ready queue, suspend it for some time by swapping it out from the memory and swap-in at an appropriate time. Long-term scheduling has a direct relationship with the degree of multi-programming. The degree of multi-programming can be defined as the number of processes which can be accommodated in the memory and made ready for execution.
- The short-term scheduler, after selecting the process from the ready queue, passes the information to the dispatcher function. The dispatcher, after finding the location

of PCB of the process, loads the PSW and other registers in the processor, and the execution of this process starts.

- The scheduling mechanisms, by which a process is selected from the ready queue, are called scheduling algorithms.
- When a process is assigned the processor, it is allowed to execute to its completion, that is, the system cannot take away the processor from the process until it exits. Then it is called *non-pre-emptive scheduling*.
- If a process is not allowed to execute to its completion, and is interrupted in between by another process, it is known as *pre-emptive scheduling*.
- Turnaround time is the total time spent by a process in the system.
- The turnaround time of a process is $t_r = wt + x$, where wt is waiting time of the process in the ready queue, x is the total service or execution time of the process.
- If turnaround time is divided by the execution time of the process, it becomes weighted or normalized turnaround time.
- The waiting time is the total time spent by a process in the ready queue.
- Response time is the time period between the time of submission of a process and the first response given by the process to the user.
- Predictability is the expected behaviour of a process.
- Throughput is the number of processes completed in a unit time.
- CPU utilization is the percentage of time that the CPU is busy executing the processes.
- A process should be scheduled such that there is minimum turnaround time, minimum weighted turnaround time, minimum waiting time, minimum response time, maximum predictability, maximum throughput, and maximum CPU utilization.
- FCFS works on FIFO queue and is suitable for batch systems.
- Priority scheduling is based on the idea of providing priority to the processes. Its types are:
  i) Priority number-based scheduling: where a priority number is provided to every process, according to its importance in the system
  ii) Shortest process next: where the shortest process in terms of its execution time is scheduled, but with non-pre-emption
  iii) Shortest remaining-time next: pre-emption version of

SPN, where the remaining time of a process, in terms of its execution, is the criterion for priority.

- Round robin scheduling algorithm provides equal chance to every process to run, by periodically providing a time quantum to every process.
- If the time quantum chosen is very large, RR algorithm will be as good as FCFS algorithm.
- If the time quantum chosen is too small, then there will be large context switch time, because after every time quantum process, switching will occur.
- Two rules must be followed while choosing the time quantum:
- *Rule 1*: 80% of the CPU bursts should be smaller than the time quantum.
- *Rule 2*: Context switch time is nearly 10% of the time quantum.
- The maximum waiting time of a process in round robin is
- $w = (n-1) * q$, where n is the number of processes and q is the time quantum.
- CPU consumption ratio = Actual CPU time consumed/ total estimated execution time.
- In improved round robin scheduling, the rule is to schedule a process, if its CPU consumption ratio is greater than 0.60, or else, schedule a process whose CPU consumption ratio is minimum.
- Response ratio = Time elapsed in the system / CPU time consumed by the process.
- Highest response ration next (HRRN) scheduling also improves the round robin in terms of response time, and schedules a process which has the highest response ratio.
- Various scheduling algorithms, according to their natures, can be distinguished as follows:

Scheduling algorithm	Nature
FCFS	Non-pre-emptive Favours longer processes
Priority number-based	Both pre-emptive and non-pre-emptive Favours highest priority processes
Shortest process next	Non-pre-emptive Favours short processes Good response time

(Contd)

(Table Contd)

SRN	Pre-emptive Favours short processes Good response time Reduced turnaround time and response time
Round robin	Pre-emptive Good response time

- Multi-level queue scheduling divides the ready queue into multiple queues, according to various categories of processes, and favours short-term and I/O-bound processes.

- The behaviour of processes cannot be judged before executing the processes. Therefore, a feedback is taken from every process after executing it for some time, and is then put to the appropriate queue. This is known as multi-level feedback queue scheduling.
- Fair-share scheduling considers the needs of a user or group of users, and distributes the processor time among users or group of users.
- Lottery scheduling is a randomized resource allocation mechanism, wherein resource rights are represented by lottery tickets.

MULTIPLE CHOICE QUESTIONS

1. If there is a large number of _____, then it may be difficult to achieve multi-programming.
   - (a) I/O devices
   - (b) CPU-bound processes
   - (c) I/O-bound processes
   - (d) none

2. Long-term scheduling has a direct relationship with the degree of _____.
   - (a) processes
   - (b) devices
   - (c) multi-programming
   - (d) none

3. When a process is assigned the processor, it is allowed to execute to its completion. This is called
   - (a) Dispatching
   - (b) Scheduling
   - (c) Non-pre-emptive scheduling
   - (d) Pre-emptive scheduling

4. If a process is not allowed to execute to its completion and is interrupted in between, such that it has neither voluntarily released the processor nor has it exited, it is known as:
   - (a) Dispatching
   - (b) Scheduling
   - (c) Non-pre-emptive scheduling
   - (d) Pre-emptive scheduling

5. The higher number of _____ in a system may degrade the performance of the system.
   - (a) context switches
   - (b) processes
   - (c) devices
   - (d) none

6. The minimum possible value of normalized turnaround time is
   - (a) 0
   - (b) 1
   - (c) 2
   - (d) 3

7. The total time spent by a process in the system is called
   - (a) turnaround time
   - (b) waiting time
   - (c) response time
   - (d) none

8. The total time spent by a process in the ready queue is called
   - (a) turnaround time
   - (b) waiting time
   - (c) response time
   - (d) none

9. FCFS is _____ scheduling algorithm.
   - (a) Pre-emptive
   - (b) Non-pre-emptive
   - (c) Both
   - (d) none

10. Priority is _____ scheduling algorithm.
    - (a) Pre-emptive
    - (b) Non-pre-emptive
    - (c) Both
    - (d) none

11. SPN is _____ scheduling algorithm.
    - (a) Pre-emptive
    - (b) Non-pre-emptive
    - (c) Both
    - (d) none

12. SRN is _____ scheduling algorithm.
    - (a) Pre-emptive
    - (b) Non-pre-emptive
    - (c) Both
    - (d) none

13. Round robin is _____ scheduling algorithm.
    - (a) Pre-emptive
    - (b) Non-pre-emptive
    - (c) Both
    - (d) none

14. HRRN is _____ scheduling algorithm.
    - (a) Pre-emptive
    - (b) Non-pre-emptive
    - (c) Both
    - (d) none

15. FCFS favours _____ processes.
    - (a) short
    - (b) long
    - (c) both
    - (d) none

16. SRN favours _____ processes.
    - (a) short
    - (b) long
    - (c) both
    - (d) none

17. Which algorithm is best suited to real-time systems?
    - (a) FCFS
    - (b) SPN
    - (c) Round robin
    - (d) Priority

18. Which algorithm is best suited to multi-user systems?
    (a) FCFS
    (b) SPN
    (c) Round robin
    (d) none

19. Which algorithm is best suited to batch systems?
    (a) FCFS
    (b) SRN
    (c) Round robin
    (d) none

20. Which algorithm is best suited to I/O-bound processes?
    (a) FCFS
    (b) SRN
    (c) Round robin
    (d) none

21. If time quantum is too short in RR scheduling, then it suffers from
    (a) high waiting time
    (b) high turnaround time
    (c) high context switch time
    (d) none

22. If time quantum is too large in RR scheduling, it becomes
    (a) FCFS
    (b) SRN
    (c) SPN
    (d) HRRN

23. Which is true regarding selection of time quantum in RR scheduling?
    (a) 50% of the CPU bursts should be smaller than the time quantum.
    (b) 70% of the CPU bursts should be greater than the time quantum.
    (c) 80% of the CPU bursts should be smaller than the time quantum.
    (d) nono

24. Which is true regarding selection of time quantum in RR scheduling?
    (a) Context switch time is a large fraction of time quantum, nearly 60 %.
    (b) Context switch time is a small fraction of time quantum, nearly 10 %.

25. Which one is true regarding response time?
    (a) CPU time consumed by the process/ Time elapsed in the system
    (b) Time elapsed in the system / CPU time consumed by the process
    (c) Time elapsed in the ready queue / CPU time consumed by the process
    (d) none

26. Auxillary queue is used in _____ scheduling.
    (a) FCFS
    (b) RR
    (c) Improved RR
    (d) Virtual RR

27. In _____ scheduling, the needs of a user or group of users are considered, and the processor time is distributed, not among the individual processes, but the users or group of users, as the case may be.
    (a) Improved RR
    (b) Multi-level queue
    (c) Feedback queue
    (d) Fair-share

28. If a user x has 50% more shares than user y, user x needs to work _____ than user y.
    (a) 50% more
    (b) 50% less
    (c) 100% more
    (d) none

29. _____ scheduling is a randomized resource allocation mechanism, wherein resource rights are represented by tickets.
    (a) FCFS
    (b) RR
    (c) Lottery
    (d) HRRN

30. The provision that a user can escalate his resource rights by creating more lottery tickets, is called
    (a) ticket transfer
    (b) ticket inflation
    (c) ticket deflation
    (d) none

REVIEW QUESTIONS

1. What is the meaning of CPU-burst and I/O-burst? How do they affect the performance of multi-programming?

2. Explain the situation when scheduling needs to be performed.

3. Differentiate between long-, medium-, and short-term process-scheduling.

4. Differentiate between non-pre-emptive and pre-emptive types of scheduling.

5. Define: turnaround time, waiting time, response time, weighted turnaround time, predictability, deadlines, throughput, CPU utilization, fairness, and balance.

6. How do you implement FCFS scheduling algorithm?

7. What is priority scheduling? What are the methods for giving priority to a process?

8. Explain the mechanism of priority number-based scheduling.

9. Explain the mechanism of shortest process next scheduling.

10. Explain the mechanism of shortest remaining-time next scheduling.

11. Explain the mechanism of round robin scheduling.

12. What are benefits and drawbacks of round robin scheduling?

13. What are the rules for selecting a time quantum?

14. What is the need of virtual round robin?

15. What is the need of improved round robin scheduling?

16. What is the need of highest response ratio next scheduling?

17. Explain the mechanism of virtual round robin scheduling.

18. How do you implement improved round robin scheduling?

19. How do you implement HRRN?

20. What is the need of multi-level queue scheduling?

21. What is the drawback in implementing multi-level queue scheduling?

22. How do you implement feedback queue scheduling?

23. What is the benefit of fair-share scheduling?

24. How do you implement fair-share scheduling?

25. What is the drawback of fair-share scheduling?

26. How do you implement lottery scheduling?

27. What are the scheduling algorithms which may cause starvation? How do you reduce it if there is?

28. What will be the exponential average for predicting the next CPU burst value of a process, if constant weighting factor is 0, 0.5, and 0.9? Mention their significance as well.

29. Using $\alpha = 1/2$, what will be the prediction of the next CPU burst time, if five runs from oldest to most recent values of execution time are 30, 15, 40, 40, 20?

BRAIN TEASERS

1. Why does FCFS tend to favour long processes?

2. Why does FCFS tend to favour CPU-bound processes over I/O bound ones?

3. Which of the following events will cause process-scheduling and of which type? Explain what happens to the current running process:
   (a) Process creates its child.
   (b) Process executes a computation statement.
   (c) Process executes a read statement.
   (d) A resource is released for which no process is waiting.
   (e) A resource is released for which a blocked process is waiting.
   (f) A new job enters the job-queue.
   (g) A new process enters the ready-queue.
   (h) A process enters the blocked-queue.
   (i) A process enters the blocked-suspend queue.
   (j) An attached I/O fails.
   (k) An illegal instruction is executed in the process.
   (l) There is no process in the ready queue.
   (m) Some process need to be brought into the ready queue, but space in memory is not available.
   (n) A blocked process is suspended.
   (o) Process exits.
   (p) A process is dispatched from the ready queue.
   (q) A high priority process appears in the ready queue.
   (r) A lower priority process appears in the ready queue.
   (s) Process calls a module from library.

4. Demonstrate that a short quantum will increase the number of context switches in the system in RR scheduling.

5. Demonstrate that a long time quantum will lead RR scheduling to FCFS scheduling.

6. Can there be a situation in which a running process is selected again for execution?

7. What is the significance of normalized turnaround time? If it increases, what will be the effect on a scheduling algorithm?

8. Suggest an appropriate scheduling algorithm for the following software systems:
   (a) Online entrance examination system
   (b) Inventory control system
   (c) Missile tracking system
   (d) Railway reservation system
   (e) Traffic control system

9. What will be the effect on execution time estimation, if a simple averaging method is chosen, as compared to exponential averaging in SRN scheduling?

10. In interactive systems, the goal should be to minimize variance in response time as compared to minimizing the average response time. Explain the reason for this statement.

11. SRN is provably the best scheduling algorithm. Demonstrate.

12. Why can SRN not be used directly in practice?

13. If there are 7 processes in a system and 4 is the time quantum, what is the maximum and minimum time a process needs to wait for its execution?

14. A process changes its behaviour randomly. What kind of scheduling will you perform on this process?

15. A client process sends a message to a server requesting something, and then blocks itself. If scheduling is to be done, so that chances of running the server process next are to be increased, then which type of process-scheduling will you prefer?

16. A web server serves some audio files to its clients through various processes, which run at different frame rates. How will you ensure that scheduling of these server processes will serve clients perfectly?

17. There is a centralized system which is accessed by multiple groups. The first group accesses the general information for a very short time and there are 15 users in this group. Second group accesses the system for critical computation intensive work and there are only 2 users in this group. Which scheduling algorithm will suit this environment and how?

18. Consider the following scenario of processes with time quantum = 2.

Process	Arrival time	Execution time
P1	0	5
P2	1	9
P3	2	7
P4	3	2
P5	4	4

Draw the Gantt chart for the execution of the processes, showing their start time and end time using FCFS, RR, improved RR, and HRRN scheduling. Calculate turnaround time, normalized turnaround time, and waiting time for each process and average turnaround time, average normalized turnaround time, and average waiting time for the system.

19. Consider the following snapshot of the processes:

Process	Burst time	Arrival time	Priority
P1	8	0	1
P2	20	1	3
P3	3	2	2
P4	6	3	5
P5	12	4	4

Draw the Gantt chart for the execution of the processes, showing their start time and end time using FCFS, priority number-based scheduling (pre-emptive), SRN (without considering the priority), RR (with time quantum=5), improved RR, and HRRN scheduling. Calculate turnaround time, normalized turnaround time, and waiting time for each process and average turnaround time, average normalized turnaround time, and average waiting time for the system.

20. Consider the following scenario of processes with time quantum = 1 and 3.

Draw the Gantt chart for the execution of the processes, showing their start time and end time using FCFS, RR, improved RR, and HRRN scheduling. Calculate turnaround

time, normalized turnaround time, and waiting time for each process and average turnaround time, average normalized turnaround time, and average waiting time for the system.

Process	Arrival time	Execution time
P1	0	9
P2	2	20
P3	4	2
P4	7	14
P5	8	4

21. Consider the following scenario of processes with their priority.

Process	Arrival time	Execution time	Priority
P1	0	12	5
P2	2	25	1
P3	3	3	3
P4	5	9	4
P5	6	13	2

Draw the Gantt chart for the execution of the processes, showing their start time and end time, using priority number-based scheduling. Calculate turnaround time, normalized turnaround time, and waiting time for each process and average turnaround time, average normalized turnaround time, and average waiting time for the system.

22. Consider the following scenario of processes.

Process	Arrival time	Execution time
P1	0	9
P2	1	3
P3	1	14
P4	1	1

Draw the Gantt chart for the execution of the processes, showing their start time and end time, using SPN and SRN scheduling. Calculate turnaround time, normalized turnaround time, and waiting time for each process and average turnaround time, average normalized turnaround time, and average waiting time for the system.

23. Consider the following scenario of processes with time quantum = 1 and 2.

Process	Arrival time	Execution time
P1	0	9
P2	1	1
P3	2	7
P4	3	1
P5	4	6

Draw the Gantt chart for the execution of the processes, showing their start time and end time using FCFS, RR, improved RR, and HRRN scheduling. Calculate turnaround time, normalized turnaround time, and waiting time for each process and average turnaround time, average normalized turnaround time, and average waiting time for the system.

24. Which is the best non-pre-emptive scheduling algorithm? Prove it, taking an example set of processes.

25. Consider the following scenario of processes with time quantum = 3 ms.

Process	Arrival time	Execution time
P1	0	9
P2	1	5
P3	2	3
P4	3	4

Process P1 requires I/O after every 1 millisecond. P2 requires I/O after every 2 millisecond, and P4 after every 3 ms. The access of every I/O takes 2 milliseconds. The context switch time for every process switching is 1 millisecond. If RR scheduling is performed, what will be the CPU utilization in the system?

7 Process Communication and Synchronization

7.1 INTRODUCTION

Multi-programming environment poses many challenges. Some of them have been covered in the preceding chapters. As discussed in Chapter 5, there are concurrent processes that are natural outcomes of a multi-programming system. Independent processes are easy to implement than the interacting processes. Interacting processes may access shared data, produce deadlock while competing for resources and may starve for resources in some conditions. Moreover, they need to communicate some information among themselves. Therefore, there is a need to synchronize the activities of interacting processes and provide mechanisms through which they can communicate. This chapter discusses all the problems associated with interacting processes and their solutions. It provides some popular methods of process communication as well.

7.2 CONCURRENT PROCESSES

Independent processes are easier to manage, since they do not share any resources among them. The problem arises when the processes are interacting, that is, when they share some data structures or need to communicate. The root problem here is the concurrent processing. The concurrent access of some resources by these processes may cause problems in the system if not resolved. Therefore, there should be mechanisms to synchronize the processes so that they coordinate with each other, otherwise, multi-programming cannot be achieved. Moreover, the interacting processes must cooperate with each other and that is why they are known as co-operating processes. Let us discuss the issues related to concurrent processing:

7.2.1 Data Access Synchronization

While writing the code of processes, it is a general practice to take global variables that are shared by more than one process.

Learning Objectives

After reading this chapter, the reader should be able to understand:

- Concurrent processes and their problems
- Defining Critical section (CS) as a protocol for synchronization
- Algorithmic approach to CS implementation
- Semaphore as a synchronization tool and its implementation
- High-level language constructs for synchronization:
- critical region,
- conditional critical region (CCR),
- monitors, and
- protected objects
- Solution of classic synchronization problems:
- producer–consumer problem,
- reader–writer problem,
- dining-philosophers problem,
- cigarette smokers problem, and
- sleeping barber problem
- Hardware support for process synchronization

In a multi-programming environment, it may be possible that there is a concurrent access of a global variable by more than one process. However, this concurrent execution may not give the desired result. Let us see this with an example.

There are two processes, P1 and P2, sharing common variable *shared*. Suppose, P1 updates *shared* as

   shared = *shared* + *3*

and P2 updates *shared* as

   shared = *shared* − *3*.

If both processes reach the statement where *shared* is being updated and one process is interrupted in between and control switches to another process, then results may be wrong. Let us elaborate this problem.

At the time of implementation of the processes in a machine, the statements of a process are further broken down into a low-level language. Therefore, the two statements referred in P1 and P2 can be broken down as follows:

Process P1:

1. Load the value of *shared* in a register of the CPU
2. Add 3 to the value of the register
3. Load the new value of the register in *shared*

> *A1.* reg1 = *shared*
> *A2.* reg1 = reg1 + 3
> *A3. shared* = reg1

Process P2:

1. Load the value of *shared* in a register of the CPU
2. Subtract 3 from the value of the register
3. Load the new value of the register in *shared*

> B1. reg2 = *shared*
> B2. reg2 = reg2 − 3
> B3. *shared* = reg2

The single statements both in P1 and P2 have been divided into three equivalent statements. Suppose, P1 starts first and executes the Statements A1 and A2. At this time, P1 is interrupted and the execution is stopped. Then, P2 starts executing and completes all the statements, that is, B1, B2, and B3. After this, P1 is resumed and completes the execution of A3.

Suppose, the initial value of *shared* is 4; then after the execution of P2, the value of *shared* is 1; and after the execution of P1, it is 7. In fact, if Process P2 has completely updated the *shared* variable, then P1 will not get the correct result ever. This happens because P1 cannot update the new value of *shared* as it has already executed first two statements and only A3 is remaining. Here, the value of *shared* may be depending on the interleaved execution of the sequence of statements. The correct value cannot be predicted because there may be many combinations of execution of all the six statements of P1 and P2. This problem arises because both processes have been allowed to update the global variable at the same time. This leads to inconsistency of data, and the problem increases further if one process takes a decision or action based on the updated data. Let us elaborate this problem with an example.

Example 7.1

A web server services its clients by creating processes when it receives a client's request. All the processes are same in their function, that is, they are identical and each process updates a common data used to count the number of clients serviced. Thus, as soon as a client's request is received by a process, it updates the count.

In this example, it may be possible that when one process is updating the count, another client's request is received and another process is created. The new process will also update the count, making the data inconsistent.

Let us take the data variable as *count_client* and its current value as 4, that is, four clients have been serviced by the server. Now, a Client *x* requests and, corresponding to it, a Process x has been created. Process *x* then starts updating the *count_client*. While *x* is updating the *count_client*, another Client *y* requests and, corresponding to it, another Process *y* is created. Process *y* also starts updating the *count_client*. We can reverse this situation, that is, Process *y* starts first followed by *x*. The executions of both the cases are shown in the following table. In both the cases, the final *count_client* is 5, whereas the desired result is 6. It means that if we allow both the processes to update *count_client* concurrently, one client will not be counted leading to inconsistency of data.

The statements for two processes:

Process *x*	Process *y*
x.1 reg1 = *count_client* *x.2* reg1 = reg1 + 1 *x.3* count_client = reg1	*y.1* reg2 = *count_client* *y.2* reg2 = reg2 + 1 *y.3* count_client = reg2

Time	Case 1			Case 2		
	Process x	Process y	Current values	Process x	Process y	Current values
1	x.1		reg1 = 4		y.1	reg2 = 4
2	x.2		reg1 = 5		y.2	reg2 = 5
3		y.1	reg2 = 4	x.1		reg1 = 4
4		y.2	reg2 = 5	x.2		reg1 = 5
5		y.3	count_client = 5		y.3	count_client = 5
6	x.3		count_client = 5	x.3		count_client = 5

Now we can generalize that when more than one processes access and update the same data concurrently and the result depends on the sequence of execution of the instructions, the situation is known as a *race condition*. The two cases shown in Example 7.1 are examples of race conditions. Processes *x* and *y* are in a race to update the data first, and the result is incorrect in both the cases. Thus, race conditions lead to data inconsistency and, thereby, to wrong results. Data access synchronization is required when race conditions arise due to the execution of concurrent processes. It becomes necessary in database systems, where frequent queries and updating of data are required, that processes are not allowed to update global data concurrently. Therefore, these systems must adopt a mechanism through which data access synchronization is achieved.

7.2.2 Control Synchronization

If processes are interacting, it may be possible that one process needs an input from the other. In this case, the first process needs to wait until the required input is received from the other process. It means that the first process is dependent on the other. However, if there is no control on the execution of these interacting processes, then they will not be able to perform their functions in a correct manner. To have desired results, there should be a control over a process such that it is forced to wait until the execution of another process has been finished from which some data or information is expected. For example, there are two processes, *A* and *B*. The statement in *A* expects some information from *B*, which is possible only after the execution of the statement in *B*. Therefore, *A* needs to wait until the execution of the statement in *B* has been completed. This is known as control synchronization in interacting processes where the order of the execution of processes is maintained.

Example 7.2

There is a buffer in an application maintained by two processes. One process is called a *producer* that produces some data and fills the buffer. Another process is called a *consumer* that needs data produced in the buffer and consumes it. In this application, both the processes need control synchronization because they are dependent on each other. If the buffer is empty, then a consumer should not try to access the data item from it. Similarly, a producer should not produce any data item if the buffer is full. To track whether the buffer is empty or full, there should be a *counter* that counts the data items in the buffer. This *counter* variable will be shared between the two processes and updated by both. The consumer process before consuming the items from the buffer must check the value of the *counter*. If the counter is greater than or equal to 1, it means that there is some data item in the buffer. It starts executing for consuming it and updates the *counter* by decrementing it by one. Similarly, the producer process before adding the items to the buffer must check the value of the *counter*. If the *counter* is less than its maximum value, it means that there is some space in the buffer. It starts executing for producing the data item and updates the *counter* by incrementing it by one.

Let *max* be the maximum size of the buffer. There may be a situation that the buffer is full, that is, counter = *max*, and the consumer is busy executing other instructions or has not been allotted its time slice yet (see Fig. 7.1). At this moment, the producer is ready to produce an item in the buffer. Since the buffer is full, it needs to wait until the consumer consumes an item and updates the counter by decrementing it by one, that is, counter = *max* − 1. This is the control synchronization between the two processes, that one waits for the other and the sequence of processes needs to be maintained, otherwise, new item produced by the producer will be lost as the buffer is full.

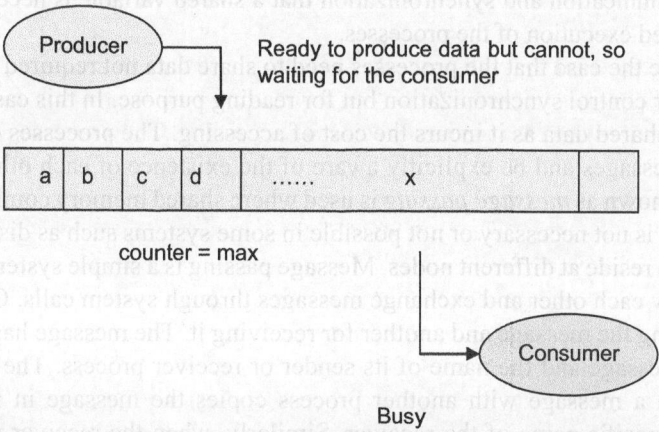

Fig. 7.1 Producer–consumer problem: Buffer is full

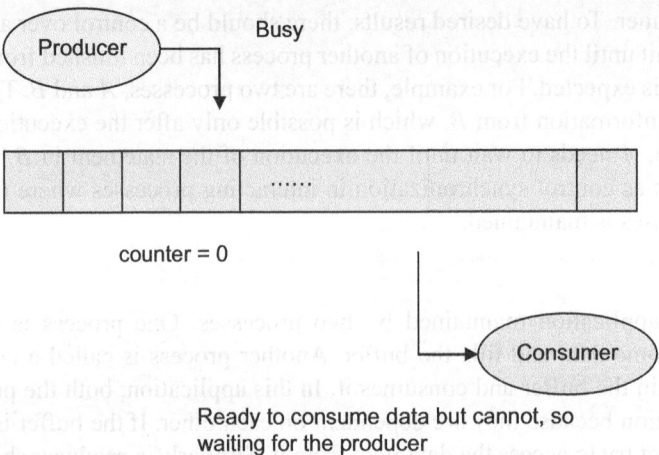

counter = 0

Fig. 7.2 Producer–consumer problem: Buffer is empty

Another situation may be that the buffer is empty, that is, counter = 0 (Fig. 7.2), and the producer is busy executing other instructions or has not been allotted its time slice yet. At this moment, the consumer is ready to consume an item from the buffer. Since the buffer is empty, it needs to wait until the producer produces an item and updates the counter by incrementing it by one, that is, counter = 1. This is the control synchronization between the two processes, that one waits for the other and the sequence of processes needs to be maintained, so that there is no inconsistency in the normal functioning of the processes.

7.2.3 Process Communication

In both the cases of synchronization discussed in Examples 7.1 and 7.2, the processes are interacting or communicating. There is a shared variable through which they communicate, that is, they are not aware of the existence of each other but coordinate with each other in the execution. In this way, there is an indirect communication through shared memory. It can be realized in both the cases of communication and synchronization that a shared variable is necessary to have a proper synchronized execution of the processes.

However, there may be the case that the processes need to share data not required for data access synchronization or control synchronization but for reading purpose. In this case, there is no need to maintain a shared data as it incurs the cost of accessing. The processes can also communicate through messages and be explicitly aware of the existence of each other. This type of communication known as *message passing* is used where shared memory communication among the processes is not necessary or not possible in some systems such as distributed systems, where processes reside at different nodes. Message passing is a simple system where processes explicitly know each other and exchange messages through system calls. One system call is used for sending the message and another for receiving it. The message has a fixed format consisting of a message and the name of its sender or receiver process. The process wishing to communicate a message with another process copies the message in its message structure with the specific name of the receiver. Similarly, when the receiver receives the message, it copies the message into its local variable and starts executing. Therefore, if there is no requirement to update the message concurrently, there is no need to maintain a shared variable; hence, a message-passing system is more appropriate. Due to its simplicity, a message-passing system can be implemented in distributed systems as well as in shared-memory systems.

The synchronization is also needed in a message-passing system. When a sender sends a message, it is not necessary that the receiver is ready to receive it. In this case, the sender will be blocked and the message will be copied to a buffer. It is activated only when the intended receiver will execute its system call for receiving the message. The message from the buffer is then sent to the process. Similarly, when a process is ready to receive a message, it is not necessary that the sender be ready to send it. In this case, the receiver will be blocked and activated only when the intended sender will send the message to it. Thus, there should be synchronization between the sender and the receiver process. The message-passing system is discussed in detail in Section 7.11. First, let us see an example of a message-passing system.

Example 7.3

Consider again Example 7.2, where producer and consumer processes communicate with each other. In this problem, both the processes need to know the maximum size of the buffer, denoted as *max*. Both the processes use *max* in their code but do not modify it; they use it only for knowing the size of the buffer. Therefore, there is no need to define *max* as a global variable. There can be one process or main () that can send the information about the size of the buffer to both the processes through a message passing system. Here, main () is the sender process and the producer and the consumer are the receiving processes.

Although shared memory and message passing systems are effective process-communication mechanisms, they are not suitable for emergency conditions. If a child process dies or is suspended, and this information is communicated through a message passing system, it may be possible that the parent process may not receive this message or receives it at the time when it has no relevance in the system. Similarly, if an arithmetic fault or illegal instruction has been executed in a process, it must be notified about this error by the kernel immediately. It means that there are some exceptional conditions and alarms that while occurring in the system must be communicated to the processes immediately without any delay. It becomes more important in the real-time systems because if a faulty process is not signaled at the right time, then the system may fail or behave erratically. It is worth mentioning here again that these kinds of exceptional notification messages cannot be communicated through message passing systems as they may not reach the desired process at the right time. Therefore, there should be another mechanism that catches the attention of the process to which the emergency message is to be passed. This form of process communication is known as a *signal*. Since communication should be established immediately without any delay, the receiving process must also respond to it by suspending what it was doing and execute the appropriate action. Therefore, the design of a signal-communication mechanism is just like an interrupt. Signals perform in a manner similar to the interrupts suspending the execution of a process. The only difference is that signals have no priority: All the signals are treated equally. The implementation details of signals will be discussed in detail later in this chapter.

7.2.4 Deadlocks

If there is no control on the competing processes for accessing multiple resources, then it can lead to a severe problem in the system. For example, a Process P1 is accessing a Resource R1 and needs another Resource R2 to complete its execution, but at the same time, another Process

P2 is holding a Resource R2 and requires R1 to proceed. Here, both the processes are waiting for each other to release the resources held by them. This situation is called a *deadlock*. There can be many situations like this causing deadlock problems in the system. Deadlocks will be discussed in detail in Chapter 8.

7.3   CRITICAL SECTION (CS)

An OS must be able to ensure co-operation among the processes such that the different speeds of the execution of concurrent processes do not cause any problems. If more than one co-operating process is sharing a data, then it must be protected from multiple accesses as discussed in data access synchronization. Similarly, when a process is given access to a non-shareable resource such as printer, another process cannot be given the access at the same time; otherwise, output of two processes will be mixed up and no process will get the desired result. This requirement is known as *mutual exclusion*. Mutual exclusion ensures that the processes do not access or update a resource concurrently.

The issues identified in the execution of concurrent processes lead to the design of a protocol that enforces mutual exclusion and does not cause race condition problem. The protocol demands that the code of a process where it modifies the data or accesses the resource be protected and not be allowed to be executed by concurrent processes simultaneously. Therefore, the first thing in the protocol is to identify a section of the code that must be protected. This section is known as a *critical section*. To protect the critical section, there should be some conditional criteria that a process must pass before entering the critical section. Only one process at a time is allowed to enter its critical section. If another process requests at this time, then the access will be denied so that mutual exclusion is maintained. The criteria for entering the CS are known as *entry criteria*. The protocol should also define that when one process has finished its execution, the other waiting processes must be informed so that one of them can enter the critical section. The criteria for exiting the CS are known as *exit criteria* (see Fig. 7.3).

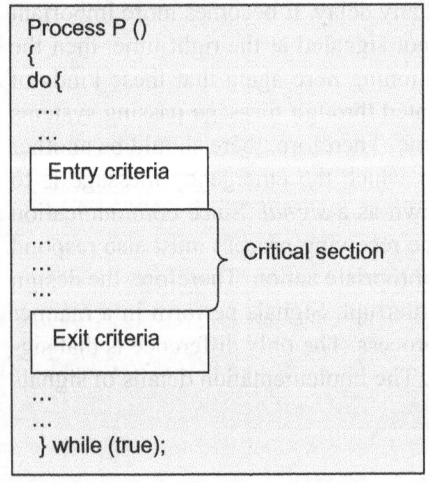

Fig. 7.3   Protocol for critical section

Example 7.4

We have seen in Example 7.1 that Processes x and y produce race condition if they try to update the global data *count_client*. The critical sections in this example are the instructions where the *count_client* is updated. According to the protocol designed to reduce race condition, both the processes cannot enter their critical sections at the same time. If Process x has entered its critical section, then Process y will have to wait until x exits. In this way, the process waiting to enter its CS will use the updated value of *count_client* and thus, there will be no data inconsistency. Both the cases of Example 7.1 have been shown again in table but with the critical section. No process is allowed to enter its CS unless the other process has exited. In both the cases the *count_client* is now equal to 6, which is correct as the two processes have been added.

Time	Case 1				Case 2			
	Process x	Process y	Current values	Status of process	Process x	Process y	Current values	Status of process
1	x.1		reg1 = 4	Process x appears first		y.1	reg2 = 4	Process y appears first
2	x.2		reg1 = 5	Process x continues		y.2	reg2 = 5	Process y continues
3	x.3		count_client=5	Process y appears but is not allowed to enter its critical section, that is, it could not update count_client			count_client = 5	Process x appears but is not allowed to enter its critical section, that is, it could not update count_client
4		y.1	reg2 = 5	Process x exits and Process y is allowed to enter its CS and starts updating count_client with new value 5	x.1		reg1=5	Process y exits and Process x is allowed to enter its CS and starts updating count_client with new value 5
5		y.2	reg2 = 6	Process y continues	x.2		reg1 = 6	Process x continues
6		y.3	count_client = 6	Process y updates count_client	x.3		count_client = 6	Process y updates count_client

The solution for CS problems should satisfy the following characteristics of protocol:

Mutual exclusion

The protocol should not allow more than one process at a time to update a global data.

Progress

The implementation of this protocol requires that the track of all the processes wishing to enter their critical sections be kept. If there are some processes in the queue waiting and, currently, no process is executing inside the critical section, then only the waiting processes must be granted permission to participate in the execution, that is, the CS will not be reserved for a process that is currently in a non-critical section.

Bounded wait

A process in its CS remains there only for a finite time because, generally, the execution does not take much time, so the waiting processes in the queue need not wait for a long time.

No deadlock

If no process is executing inside the CS and there are processes in the queue waiting for the execution but are not allocated the CS yet, then there may be a deadlock in the system. Therefore, the protocol must ensure that all the waiting processes are allotted the critical section.

7.4 ALGORITHMIC APPROACH TO CS IMPLEMENTATION

Initially, the CS was implemented through an algorithmic approach, that is, complex logical checks to implement mutual exclusion among processes. This section discusses some of them.

7.4.1 Two-process Solution

Let us take two processes, P1 and P2, and implement synchronization between them. Each process has a CS and needs to wait for the other if one of them has entered its critical section. The two-process solution has been implemented with a shared variable *process_turn* for providing mutual exclusion between the two (see Fig. 7.4). The variable is used to indicate which process is now able to enter its critical section. Here, the *while* statement acts as an entry criterion. P1 and P2 cannot enter the CS until the value of *process_turn* is one and two, respectively. If *process_turn* = 1, P1 will be allowed to execute in its critical section. At this time, if P2 is ready to enter its critical section, then it will not be granted permission since it does not meet its entry criterion, that is, *process_turn* = 2. After P1 completes its execution, it initializes *process_turn* as 2; hence, P2 will finally be able to execute. In this way, the two-process solution maintains mutual exclusion.

Let us now examine whether this algorithm follows other properties of the protocol. Suppose P1 is inside its CS and P2 is in its non-critical section. When P1 exits, it initializes *process_turn* as 2. However, P2 is still in its non-critical section and does not want to execute. On the other

```
Process P1
{
    int process_turn;

process_turn = 1;
do {

while (process_turn ! = 1);

    ┌─────────┐
    │ Critical │
    │ Section  │
    └─────────┘

process_turn = 2;
...
...
} while (true);
```

```
Process P2
{

do {

while (process_turn ! = 2);

    ┌─────────┐
    │ Critical │
    │ Section  │
    └─────────┘

process_turn = 1;
...
...
} while (true);
```

Fig. 7.4   Two-process solution: Attempt 1

```
Process P1
{
   int state_flag_P1, state_flag_P2

state_flag_P1 = 1;

do {

while (state_flag_P2 ! = 1);
state_flag_P1 = 0;

   ┌─────────────┐
   │ Critical    │
   │ Section     │
   └─────────────┘

state_flag_P1 = 1;
…
…
} while (true);
```

```
Process P2
{
   int state_flag_P1, state_flag_P2

state_flag_P2 = 1;

do {

while (state_flag_P1 ! = 1);
state_flag_P2 = 0;

   ┌─────────────┐
   │ Critical    │
   │ Section     │
   └─────────────┘

state_flag_P2 = 1;
…
…
} while (true);
```

Fig. 7.5   Two-process solution: Attempt 2

hand, P1 enters the wait state again. However, it cannot enter its CS since *process_turn* = 2. This is a violation of the protocol because the property of progress is not observed here.

The problem with this algorithm is that it does not save the state of the executing process. To store the state of the process, two more variables, namely, *state_flag_P1* and *state_flag_P2* are taken (see Fig. 7.5). If a process enters its critical section, it first sets this state flag to zero, and after exiting, it sets it to one. It indicates that if a process is using its CS, then the other process must wait until the state flag becomes one, that is, when the CS is available. In this way, the state flag variables eliminate the problem of progress observed in the first attempt of the algorithm. It can be seen in the second attempt that if a process is ready to enter its CS again, it may do so (Fig. 7.5).

This algorithm suffers from other problems as well. In the beginning, when no process is executing, both P1 and P2 will try to enter the critical section. This violates the mutual exclusion property of the protocol. To remove this problem, we should consider setting *state_flag_P1* and *state_flag_P2* to 0 before the while loop. This will solve the problem of mutual exclusion, but there still is one problem. Suppose, at the moment P1 starts and executes its first statement as *state_ flag_P1* = 0, P2 interrupts and gets the execution and executes its first statement, *state_ flag_P2* = 0. In this situation, if P2 continues and executes its while loop, then it will not be able to proceed as it is waiting for P1 to set *state_ flag_P1* to 1. Similarly, if P1 gets the execution and executes its while loop, then it will not be able to continue as it is waiting for P2 to set *state_ flag_P2* to 1. Both the processes are waiting for each other, thereby causing deadlock in the system.

This deadlock can be eliminated if a process before entering the CS checks whether the other process is ready or not. P1 checks whether *state_ flag_P2* = 0, then it sets *state_ flag_P1* = 1. Similarly, P2 checks whether *state_ flag_P1* = 0, then it sets *state_ flag_P2* = 1(see Fig. 7.6).

This solution for eliminating the deadlock causes another problem. It may be possible that both the processes are waiting for each other to execute and no process is proceeding. This situation is known as *livelock*. This situation arises because the variable *process_turn* has been ignored in this attempt of the algorithm.

```
Process P1
{
   int state_flag_P1, state_flag_P2

state_flag_P1= 1;

do {
state_flag_P1= 0;
if ( state_flag_P2== 0)
   state_flag_P1= 1;
while (state_flag_P 2 ! = 1);


   Critical
   Section


state_flag_P1= 1;
...
...
} while (true);
```

```
Process P2
{
   int state_flag_P1, state_flag_P2

state_flag_P2= 1;

do {
state_flag_P2= 0;
if ( state_flag_P1== 0)
   state_flag_P2= 1;
while (state_flag_P1! = 1);


   Critical
   Section


state_flag_P 2  = 1;
...
...
} while (true);
```

Fig. 7.6   Two-process solution: Attempt 3

7.4.2 Dekker's Solution

If both the turn and the state of a process are taken into consideration, the algorithm will not suffer from all the problems discussed in Section 7.4.1. The solution for the CS problem was given by Dekker (Fig. 7.7).

```
Process P1
{
  int state_flag_P,1
    state_flag_P2,
    process_turn ;

state_flag_P1 = 1;
process_turn = 1;
do {
state_flag_P1= 0;
while (state_flag_P 2 ! = 1)
{
    If (process_turn== 2)
    {
        state_flag_P1= 1;
        while (process_turn == 2);
        state_flag_P1= 0;
    }
}


   Critical
   Section


process_turn = 2;
state_flag_P1= 1;
...
...
} while (true);
```

```
Process P2
{
   int state_flag_P1
     state_flag_P2;
     process_turn ;

state_flag_P2 = 1;
do {
state_flag_P2= 0;
while (state_flag_P1! = 1)
{
    If (process_turn== 1)
    {
       state_flag_P2= 1;
       while (process_turn == 1);
       state_flag_P2= 0;
    }
}


   Critical
   Section


process_turn = 1;

state_flag_P 2 = 1;
...
...
} while (true);
```

Fig. 7.7   Dekker's solution for two-process synchronization

This algorithm satisfies all the rules of the designed protocol. Both the processes will not try to enter simultaneously due to the variable, *process_turn* and will satisfy the mutual exclusion property. If P1 starts first and finds that *state_flag_P2* = 0, that is, P2 wants to enter the CS, it will allow P2, only when *process_turn* = 2. Otherwise, it will wait for *state_flag_P2* to be one so that P1 can enter its CS. If *state_flag_P2* = 1 initially, then P1 will skip the while loop and straightway enter the CS. In this way, there will not be any deadlock or livelock. Moreover, the chance is given to only those processes that are waiting in the queue to enter the CS.

7.4.3 Peterson's Solution

The two-process solution for CS proposed by Peterson (Fig. 7.8) is an easier method compared to Dekker's solution. In this solution, *process_turn* takes the value zero for Process P1 and one for Process P2. For the process flag, a Boolean array *process_flag[]* is taken that consists of two values, zero for P1 and one for P2. The variable *process_turn* maintains the mutual exclusion and *process_flag[ ]* maintains the state of the process. Initially, both the processes make their flags true but to maintain the mutual exclusion, the processes before entering their critical sections allow other processes to run. The process that satisfies both the criteria, that is, its *process_flag* is true and its *process_turn* maintains mutual exclusion, is allowed to enter its critical section. After exiting the critical section, the process makes its flag false so that the other process can start if it wants. For example, P1 starts and executes *process_flag[0]* = true. At this time, P2 interrupts and gets execution and executes *process_flag[1]* = true and continues with *process_turn* = 0. At this time, if P1 is able to get the execution, then it can continue because P2 has given P1 another chance to execute by making *process_turn* = 0. If P1 continues, then it is able to enter the critical section. While P1 is inside the critical section, and P2 interrupts, it is not able to enter the CS unless P1 exits and makes *process_flag[0]* = false.

In this way, in this algorithm, processes do not wait for each other, thereby eliminating deadlock. There can be no situation that both the processes defer to each other. If one is deferring the other, then one of the processes is able to continue; therefore, there will be no livelock.

```
Process P1
{
    int process_turn;
    boolean process_flag[2];

do {
process_flag[0] = true;
process_turn= 1;

while (process_flag[1] &&
                process_turn==1);
    ┌─────────┐
    │ Critical│
    │ Section │
    └─────────┘
process_flag[0] = false;
...
...
} while (true);
```

```
Process P2
{

do {
process_flag[1] = true;
process_turn = 0;

while (process_flag[0] &&
                process_turn==0);
    ┌─────────┐
    │ Critical│
    │ Section │
    └─────────┘
process_flag[1] = false;
...
...
} while (true);
```

Fig. 7.8 Peterson's solution for two-process synchronization

A process cannot enter its CS while the other process is already in it, thereby maintaining the mutual exclusion. Obviously, there is also a bounded wait for every process.

The algorithmic implementation of critical-section solution poses many problems as we increase the number of processes for synchronization. If there are *n* number of processes, the status flags of the processes need to be maintained. Further, it must be known how many processes wish to enter their critical sections. The check for deadlock, livelock, and mutual exclusion becomes complex in case of *n* number of processes. There is a limitation to the algorithmic approach performed by the programmers. Programmers who have been hired to develop the software system are engaged in synchronizing the processes. Thus, it is not feasible that programmers provide the solution for CS in the system. There must be support from the hardware or the OS system to provide synchronization and communication among the processes. The operating-system and hardware-support mechanisms for synchronization will be discussed in succeeding sections.

7.5 SEMAPHORES

The problem of race conditions is avoided by not updating a global variable by more than one process at a time. The operations that cannot be overlapped or interleaved with the execution of any other operations are known as *indivisible* or *atomic operations*. It means that if the operations are made indivisible, then there will be no problem of race condition and this method can be implemented at the level of programming language and operating system.

Semaphore is a very popular tool used for process synchronization. Before understanding its implementation or physical structure, let us first understand its concept. The semaphore is used to protect any resource such as global shared memory that needs to be accessed and updated by many processes simultaneously. Semaphore acts as a guard or lock on the resource. The prerequisite for semaphore is that processes follow this guard to avoid any problem. Whenever a process needs to access the resource, it first needs to take permission from the semaphore. If the resource is free, that is, if no other process is accessing or updating it, the process will be allowed, otherwise permission is denied. In case of denial, the requesting process needs to wait until semaphore permits it, that is, when the resource becomes free. Semaphores can also be understood with our daily-life analogy. Let us take an example of a classroom where teachers take classes for students. A guard is sitting outside the room. Whenever a teacher comes to take the class, he or she asks the guard for permission to enter the class. The guard will allow the teacher only if the room is free, otherwise permission is denied. Thus, the room is used in mutually exclusive manner with the help of a guard. The semaphore works in the similar way.

The semaphore is implemented as an integer variable, say as *S*, and can be initialized with any positive integer values. The semaphore is accessed by only two indivisible operations known as *wait* and *signal* operations, denoted by *P* and *V*, respectively, after the Dutch notations. The simple implementation of these operations is shown in Fig. 7.9.

The implementation of a semaphore guarding the CS is shown in Fig. 7.10. Whenever a process tries to enter the critical section, it needs to perform *wait* operation. The wait is an entry criterion according to the designed protocol. If the CS is free or no other process is using it, then it is allowed, otherwise denied. The count of semaphore is decremented when a process accesses the available critical section; hence, the count of semaphore tells us the availability of the critical section. Initially, the count of semaphore is 1. If it is accessed by a process, then the count is decremented and becomes zero. Now, if another process tries to access the critical section, then it is not allowed to enter unless the semaphore value becomes greater than zero. When a process exits the critical section, it performs the signal operation, which is an exit

```
Operation Wait

P(S)
{
    while (S <= 0);
    S = S - 1;
}

Operation Signal

V(S)
{
    S = S + 1;
}
```

Fig. 7.9 Wait and signal operation in a semaphore

criterion. In this way, the solution to CS using semaphore satisfies the designed protocol. The semaphore whose value is either zero or one is known as *binary semaphore*. A resource having a single instance and which is to be used in a mutually exclusive manner can use binary semaphore for synchronization.

The semaphore can take any positive value as discussed in Section 7.4. Suppose, if there are three memory locations and each need to be updated in a mutually exclusive manner (see Fig. 7.11), then the semaphore is taken to guard all the three memory locations with value 3. It means that three processes at the same time can access the semaphore. After giving the access to the third process, the value of semaphore becomes 0. It will not allow any other process unless one of the running processes exits. This type of semaphore that takes a value greater than one is known as *counting semaphore*.

There is one more type of binary semaphore known as *mutex*, that is, in a binary semaphore, the CS locked by a process may be unlocked by any other process. However, in *mutex*, only the process that locks the CS can unlock it.

There is one problem in the implementation of such a semaphore. When a process does not get access to the critical section, it loops continually waiting for it. This does not produce any result but consumes CPU cycles, thereby wasting the processor time. This busy waiting is a problem in a multi-programming system where processor time is shared among the processes. This type of semaphore is known as a *spinlock*, since the process spins while waiting for the lock.

To save the processor time, the process that is not able to get the resource should be blocked. Since there may be many waiting processes, a queue is needed to store them. Therefore, a queue is maintained for storing all the waiting processes. A process is awakened from this queue when another process releases the resource and the semaphore allows it to enter its critical section. However, this solution incurs the cost of context switching as the process state needs to be switched from running to blocked, blocked to ready, and, then, ready to running. Therefore, when the busy waiting is of very short time compared to context switch time, there is no need to block the waiting process. In multi-processor systems also, there is no need to block the process due to multiple processors.

To incorporate this design, the implementation of the semaphore needs to be changed. Along with the integer value of semaphore, we need to take a queue or list storing the processes so that we can take a record or structure storing both of these elements. See this implementation in Fig. 7.12.

Example 7.5

There are three processes, P1, P2, and P3, sharing a semaphore for synchronizing a shared variable. The semaphore is guarding the CS of the processes where they update the shared variable. Initially, the value of the semaphore is one. P1 needs to access the CS and update the variable, so it accesses the semaphore first. It gets

```
do {

wait (Semaphore)
{

    Critical
    Section

}

signal (semaphore)
...
...
}
```

Fig. 7.10 Semaphore implementation: Attempt 1

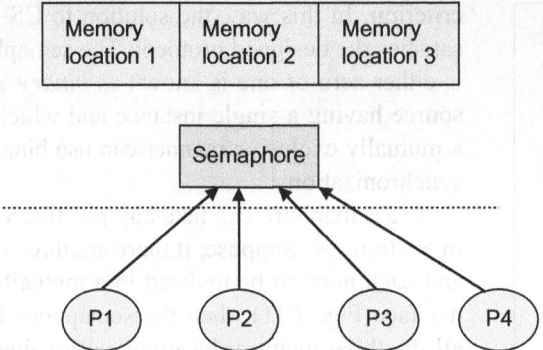

Memory location 1	Memory location 2	Memory location 3

Semaphore

P1 P2 P3 P4

Fig. 7.11 Counting semaphore

```
Struct {
        int sem_value;
        queue sem_q;
} semaphore;

semaphore S;

Operation Wait

P(S)
{
    S.sem_value = S.sem_value –1;
    if (S.sem_value < 0)
    {
        Add the process to S.sem_queue;
        Block the process;
    }
}

Operation Signal

V(S)
{
    S.sem_value = S.sem_value + 1;
    if (S.sem_value <= 0)
    {
        Remove the process from S.sem_queue;
        Wakeup the process;
    }
}
```

Fig. 7.12 Semaphore implementation: Attempt 2

permission as no one is using it, thereby making the value of the semaphore zero. After this, P2 needs to access its CS but is not allowed as the value of the semaphore is zero; hence, P2 is blocked and placed in the waiting queue. All other sequences of events and statuses are shown in the table. One point to be noted here is that the negative value of the semaphore tells us how many processes are waiting in the queue.

Time	Current value of the semaphore	Needs of process	Modified value of the semaphore	Current status
1	1	P1 needs to access.	0	P1 enters its critical section.
2	0	P2 needs to access.	−1	P1 continues and one process (P2) is waiting in the queue. P2
3	−1	P3 needs to access.	−2	P1 continues and two processes (P2 and P3) are waiting in the queue. P2 | P3
4	−2	P1 exits the critical section.	−1	P2 is waked up and enters its critical section. P3 still waits in the queue. P3
5	−1	−	−1	P2 continues and P3 still waits in the queue. P3
6	−1	P2 exits the critical section.	0	P3 is waked up and enters its critical section. The queue is empty now.
7	0	P3 exits the critical section.	1	No process is now using its CS and the queue is empty.

Example 7.6

Let S be the semaphore between three processes for mutual exclusion with an initial value one. Consider their executions in time instants in the following table and find out the final value of S.

Time	Process P1	Process P2	Process P3	Value of S	Processes in the queue of the semaphore
0	P(S)	−	−	0	−
1	−	P(S)	−	−1	P2
2	V(S)	−	−	0	−
3	−	V(S)	−	1	−
4	P(S)	−	−	0	−
5	−	−	P(S)	−1	P3
6	−	P(S)	−	−2	P3,P2

The final value of S is −2, that is, two processes are waiting in the queue. The change in value of S and the corresponding queue status, along with timeline, is depicted as follows:

7.6 SOLUTION OF CLASSIC SYNCHRONIZATION PROBLEMS USING SEMAPHORES

There are some classic synchronization problems in computer science. Programmers will face these synchronization problems during development of any application. The semaphore is the solution for all of them, for example, producer–consumer problem discussed in Examples 7.2 and 7.3. The synchronization among the processes can be obtained using semaphores. There are several synchronization problems such as these that are discussed in the subsequent sections.

7.6.1 Solution of Producer–Consumer Problem Using Semaphore

In the OS and in computer science in general, the problem of producer–consumer synchronization is common. For example, compilers and assemblers can be thought as producer and consumer processes, respectively. A compiler as a producer produces the object code and an assembler as a consumer takes the object code. Similarly, the process that gives command for printing a file is a producer process, and the process for printing them on the printer is a consumer process.

To solve the producer–consumer problem using semaphore, the following requirements should be met:

1. The producer process should not produce an item when the buffer is full.

2. The consumer process should not consume an item when the buffer is empty.
3. The producer and consumer processes should not try to access and update the buffer at the same time.
4. When a producer process is ready to produce an item and the buffer is full, the item should not be lost, that is, the producer must be blocked and must wait for the consumer to consume an item.
5. When a consumer process is ready to consume an item and the buffer is empty, it must be blocked and wait for the producer to produce the item.
6. When a consumer process consumes an item, that is, a slot in the buffer is created, the blocked producer process must be signaled about it.
7. When a producer process produces an item in the empty buffer, the blocked consumer process must be signaled about it.

The producer–consumer problem can be solved by placing a semaphore on the buffer. However, after analyzing these requirements, it is clear that we also need to check the status of the empty and the full buffer for the producer and the consumer, respectively. Moreover, the producer process after inserting the item in the buffer slot must increase the value of the full buffer to indicate that one slot of the buffer is filled. Similarly, the consumer process after taking the item from the buffer must increase the value of the empty buffer to indicate the empty slot in the buffer. For example, the three items have been produced by the producer, but nothing has been consumed by the consumer process. The empty and full pointers, along with their current values, are shown in Fig. 7.13. If the algorithmic solution mentioned for the checks is adopted, then again busy waiting will be there. The producer will be busy waiting for checking whether the buffer is empty. Similarly, the consumer will be busy waiting for checking whether the buffer is full. Instead of that, two more semaphores can be taken, which will count the number of empty slots and full slots in the buffer. Before accessing the buffer, the processes need to check its status. Therefore, the processes first wait on the semaphores used for status and then on the semaphores used for accessing the buffer. Thus, there are three semaphores to be used in the solution:

- Empty semaphore initialized to n, where n is the number of empty slots in the buffer
- Full semaphore initialized to zero
- *Buffer_access* semaphore initialized to one

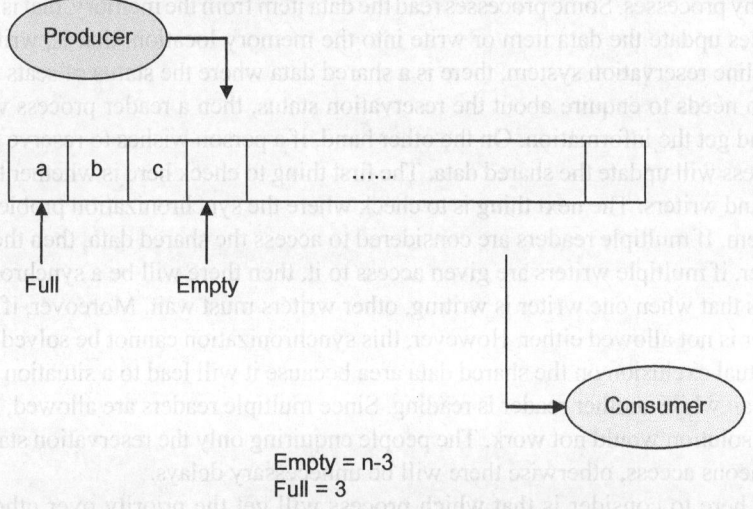

Empty = n-3
Full = 3

Fig. 7.13   Producer–consumer problem's solution with semaphores

```
Producer()                                  Consumer()
{                                           {

do {                                        do {
...                                         ...
Produce an item;                            P(Full); //Wait on Full semaphore
P(Empty); //Wait on empty semaphore         P(Buffer_access);
P(Buffer_access);                           // Wait on buffer_access semaphore
// Wait on buffer_access semaphore          Consume item from buffer;
Add item to buffer;                         V(Buffer_access);
V(Buffer_access);                           // Signal the buffer_access semaphore
// Signal the buffer_access semaphore       V(Empty);
V(Full);                                    // Signal the Empty semaphore
// Signal the Full semaphore                } while true;
} while true;
```

Fig. 7.14 Algorithms for producer–consumer problem's solution with semaphores

The producer process after producing the item waits on the empty semaphore because it needs to check whether there is an empty slot in the buffer. If there is a slot, the semaphore allows it to go further. Once it passes this condition, it waits on the *Buffer_access* semaphore to check whether any other process is accessing it. If any other process is already accessing it, then the semaphore will not allow it. After getting the permission, the process starts accessing and storing the item in the buffer. After storing, it signals the *Buffer_access* so that any other process in wait can access the buffer. Moreover, it also signals the full semaphore to indicate that the buffer now contains one item. In this way, the producer stores the item in the buffer and also updates the status of the buffer. Similarly, the algorithm of the consumer can be understood. Both the algorithms are given in Fig. 7.14.

7.6.2 Solution of Reader–Writer Problem Using Semaphores

There are several instances while designing a software system, for example, there is a data area shared among many processes. Some processes read the data item from the memory, that is, readers and some processes update the data item or write into the memory location, that is, writers. For instance, in an airline reservation system, there is a shared data where the status of seats is maintained. If a person needs to enquire about the reservation status, then a reader process will read the shared data and get the information. On the other hand, if a person wishes to reserve the seat, then a writer process will update the shared data. The first thing to check here is whether there are multiple readers and writers. The next thing is to check where the synchronization problems may occur between them. If multiple readers are considered to access the shared data, then there is no problem. However, if multiple writers are given access to it, then there will be a synchronization problem. It means that when one writer is writing, other writers must wait. Moreover, if a writer is writing, a reader is not allowed either. However, this synchronization cannot be solved by simply providing mutual exclusion on the shared data area because it will lead to a situation where a reader will also wait while another reader is reading. Since multiple readers are allowed, the pure mutual exclusion solution would not work. The people enquiring only the reservation status may be given simultaneous access, otherwise there will be unnecessary delays.

Another point here to consider is that which process will get the priority over others? If a writer is writing and multiple readers and writers are waiting, which process will get the priority? This may depend on some situations in the system. If a writer is critical, then all the writers must get the priority; otherwise, the readers may also be given a chance to read. Let us consider both the cases: When readers have the priority and when the writers have the priority.

Although mutual exclusion is not a good solution to the reader–writer problem, it is used here in the form of critical section. This is because when a writer is writing, a reader should not be allowed to access. Similarly, when a reader is reading or accessing, a writer should not be allowed to update. Therefore, a CS needs to be designed where the shared data will be accessed or updated, but not simultaneously.

Case 1: Readers have the priority

The priority to readers means that if a reader has gained the access to CS and there are multiple readers and writers waiting, then readers will be allowed to access the CS first. The writers will be allowed only after all the readers have finished accessing. It is obvious that we will use one semaphore for mutual exclusion between the readers and the writers. There may be the following scenarios on this semaphore:

1. A reader is inside the CS and multiple writers arrive, then they must wait on the semaphore.
2. A writer is inside the CS and multiple readers arrive, then they must wait on the semaphore.
3. A reader is inside the CS and multiple readers arrive, then they need not wait on the semaphore.
4. A writer is inside the CS and multiple writers arrive, then they must wait on the semaphore.

We need to count the number of readers also because writers, if waiting, will not be allowed unless all readers have accessed. Therefore, a counter is taken to count the number of readers arriving in the system. However, the processes should not be allowed to cause busy waiting to check the status of this counter and update this variable because this will be a shared variable among all readers. Therefore, another semaphore is used. The following semaphore and counter will be used in the solution:

ReadCount: integer variable as counter for readers; initialized as zero.
Sem_ReadCount: semaphore for ReadCount; initialized as one.
Sem_ReadWrite: semaphore for mutual exclusion between readers and writers; initialized as one.

See the algorithms for reader and writer in Fig. 7.15.

```
Reader()
{
   while(true) {
       wait(Sem_ReadCount);
       ReadCount++;
       If(ReadCount == 1)
          wait(Sem_ReadWrite);
       signal(Sem_ReadCount);

       Perform the read operation;
       wait(Sem_ReadCount);
       ReadCount--;
       If(ReadCount == 0)
          signal(Sem_ReadWrite);
       signal(Sem_ReadCount);
   }
}
```

```
Writer()
{
   while(true) {
       wait(Sem_ReadWrite);
       Perform the write operation;
       signal(Sem_ReadWrite);
   }
}
```

Fig. 7.15   Algorithms for reader–writer problem's solution with semaphores: readers have the priority

Case 2: Writers have the priority

Case 1 gives priority to readers. Writers cannot start unless all readers are finished. This may cause starvation of the writers. In fact, a writer is considered important as compared to a reader because it updates the data and the updating of data must be done in the system as soon as possible. Thus, writers must get priority over readers. The readers will also be served but only when there is no writer waiting. However, the solution to this case becomes complex as the readers need to be prevented from queuing on *Sem_ReadWrite* because if there is a long sequence of readers, then the system is forced to serve them first. Therefore, a solution must be designed such that a long queue of readers is not allowed where writers are waiting. For this purpose, let us consider one more semaphore, *Sem_Restrict*, which will restrict the readers from entering the queue. Only one reader is allowed in the queue of this semaphore. The following scenarios may arise in this case:

1. If no writer is accessing the CS currently, and a new writer arrives, then it will also wait on the *Sem_Restrict* so that readers do not monopolize and writers can also start.
2. Once a writer enters the CS and there are writers and readers waiting, then only writers will be allowed to access. The reader will start only after all the waiting writers are finished.
3. After all the writers finish their work, if a reader appears and then a writer, the reader will be given access first.

Another point to ponder here is where will the multiple readers wait when the writers have gained access to critical section? In addition, it is constrained that only one reader can queue on *Sem_Restrict*. In that case, if more than one reader is appearing, then they need to wait somewhere. Therefore, one more semaphore, Sem_ReaderWait, is needed.

Sem_ReadWrite will be used to provide mutual exclusion on the shared data. All the writers must queue on Sem_ReadWrite for mutual exclusion. However, if there is no writer waiting and multiple readers are there, then once a reader gains access, others need not wait on Sem_ReadWrite because multiple readers are allowed simultaneously.

```
Reader()
{
    while(true) {
        wait(Sem_ReaderWait);
        wait(Sem_Restrict);
        wait(Sem_ReadCount);
        ReadCount++;
        If(ReadCount = = 1)
            wait(Sem_ReadWrite);
        signal(Sem_ReadCount);
        signal(Sem_Restrict);
        signal(Sem_ReaderWait);
        Perform the read operation;
        wait(Sem_ReadCount);
        ReadCount--;
        If(ReadCount = = 0)
            signal(Sem_ReadWrite);
        signal(Sem_ReadCount);
    }
}
```

```
Writer()
{
    while(true)  {
        wait(Sem_WriteCount);
        WriteCount++;
        If(WriteCount = = 1)
            wait(Sem_Restrict);
        signal(Sem_WriteCount);
        wait(Sem_ReadWrite);
        Perform the write operation;
        signal(Sem_ReadWrite);
        wait(Sem_WriteCount);
        WriteCount--;
        If(WriteCount = = 0)
            signal(Sem_Restrict);
        signal(Sem_WriteCount);
    }
}
```

Fig. 7.16 Algorithms for reader–writer problem's solution with semaphores: Writers have the priority

Besides, all these semaphores, the readers, and the writers need to be counted in this solution. Obviously, one more semaphore, WriteCount, is required to update the count for writers.

The following semaphore and counters will be used in the solution:

ReadCount: integer variable as counter for readers; initialized as zero.

Sem_ReadCount: semaphore for ReadCount; initialized as one.

Sem_ReadWrite: semaphore for mutual exclusion between readers and writers; initialized as one.

WriteCount: integer variable as counter for writers; initialized as zero.

Sem_WriteCount: semaphore for WriteCount; initialized as one.

Sem_Restrict: semaphore to restrict the readers; initialized as one.

Sem_ReaderWait: semaphore where more than one reader appears; initialized as one.

See the algorithms for readers and writers in Fig. 7.16.

Case 3: No priority

Cases 1 and 2 consider the priority and are therefore not fair in the sense that the processes are not served in the sequence they appear in the system. Although a writer process must be given preference because it updates the value and thus the updated value is available to next processes, sometimes fair service to the processes is also required. Let us consider the following semaphores and counters used for the solution (see Fig. 7.17):

ReadCount: integer variable as counter for reader processes; initialized as zero.

Sem_Count: semaphore for mutual exclusion between ReadCount and WriteCount; initialized as one.

Sem_ReadWrite: semaphore for mutual exclusion between reader and writer processes; initialized as one.

WriteCount: integer variable as counter for writer processes; initialized as zero.

```
Reader()
{
  while(true) {
       wait(Sem_Count);
       If((WriteCount > 0 ) OR
           ReadCount = = 0)
       {
           signal(Sem_Count);
           wait(Sem_ReadWrite);
           wait(Sem_Count);
       }
       ReadCount++;
       signal(Sem_Count);
       Perform the read operation;
       wait(Sem_Count);
       ReadCount--;
       If(ReadCount = = 0)
           signal(Sem_ReadWrite);
       signal(Sem_Count);
   }
}
```

```
Writer()
{
  while(true) {
       wait(Sem_Count);
       WriteCount++;
       signal(Sem_Count);
       wait(Sem_ReadWrite);
       Perform the write operation;
       wait(Sem_Count);
       WriteCount--;
       signal(Sem_Count);
       signal(Sem_ReadWrite);
   }
}
```

Fig. 7.17   Algorithms for reader–writer problem's solution with semaphores: No priority

7.6.3 Solution of Dining-philosopher Problem Using Semaphores

This is a classic problem posed by Dijkstra to understand the synchronization among processes in an environment when there is insufficient number of resources. In this problem, there are five philosophers sitting around a round dining table. There is a bowl of rice placed in the centre of the table. Each philosopher gets a plate to eat and infinite supply of rice. Their work is to think and eat, whenever they are hungry. To eat, they must make use of two spoons, but there is scarcity of spoons with which they will eat (Fig. 7.18). The two conditions that need to be noted here are:

1. There are only five spoons available, each placed between two philosophers.
2. Philosophers can start eating only when they have two spoons. They cannot eat even if they have a single spoon. It means that every philosopher takes one spoon from his or her left and another from his or right and start eating. After eating, they have to put down both the spoons.

The problem here is obvious that all the philosophers cannot eat together as there are only five spoons, whereas there is a demand for 10 if all of them eat together. The solution should be such that if one philosopher is eating with two spoons, the adjacent philosopher must wait even if he or she is able to get one spoon. If all the philosophers pick up one spoon at the same time, then this leads to deadlock, since every philosopher is waiting for the other to release the spoon but no one is releasing. Therefore, a philosopher should not hold a spoon if he or she is not able to get the other. The philosopher must check the availability of both the spoons first and then pick up them. It is possible only when either of the neighbour philosophers is not eating.

The following conditions must hold for the solution of this problem:

- Only one philosopher can hold a spoon at a time.
- It must be impossible for a deadlock to occur.
- It must be impossible for a philosopher to starve waiting for a spoon.
- It must be possible for more than one philosopher to eat at the same time.

Let every philosopher be denoted by n and numbered from one to five. Similarly, spoons are numbered from one to five so that a philosopher n has a spoon n on the left and $n + 1$ on

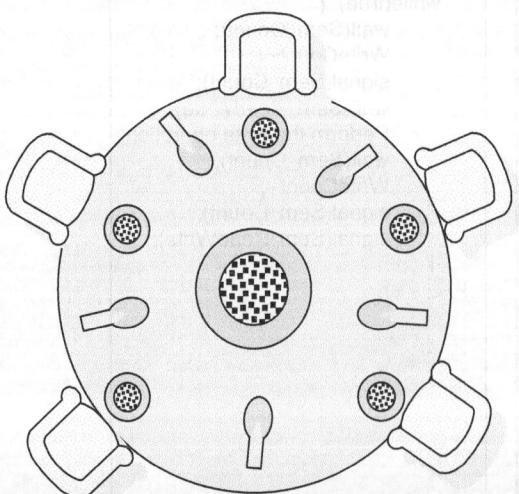

Fig. 7.18 Dining-philosopher problem

the right. However, in general how does a philosopher get spoons from either side? On his or her left, he or she gets a spoon by having number n and on his or her right, he or she gets it by calculating $(n +1)\% 5$. Since a spoon is mutually exclusive, consider a semaphore called Sem_Spoon to protect each spoon. We take an array of five elements of this semaphore type as

Semaphore Sem_Spoon[5];

The algorithm with this solution is given in Fig. 7.19.

The solution ensures that only one philosopher holds a spoon at a time. However, it is prone to deadlocks and livelocks. As discussed earlier, if all the philosophers hold the spoons on their left at the same time or hold the spoons on their right at the same time, it leads to deadlock. It may also be the case that all philosophers put down their spoons letting others to hold the spoons and try later. It may cause livelock. Thus, in any of these cases, the system will not progress.

To eliminate the deadlock, the root of the problem must be known. When five philosophers start picking up the spoons at the same time, it will always lead to a deadlock or livelock. If we allow only four philosophers to participate, then the deadlock will not happen. If four philosophers start at the same time, there is one spoon remaining on the table. Therefore, one of the philosophers will find this spoon on his or her one side and can start eating. Moreover, the philosopher after eating will put down both the spoons. Consequently, one of the adjacent philosophers will be able to start eating and so on. In this way, controlling the number of philosophers avoids deadlock.

To implement this solution, the fifth philosopher must be prevented from sitting with other four philosophers at the table. A semaphore, Sem_Philosopher, is required with an initial value of four because at the most, four philosophers must be allowed at a time. Philosophers must take their place at the table through this semaphore and after eating, they must leave the table. The solution is given in Fig. 7.20.

Another solution to the dining-philosopher problem to overcome deadlock is an asymmetric approach that states that there should be at least one left-handed and at least one right-handed philosopher at the table. Here, all five philosophers will participate but with the above condition. In this solution, there will not be any deadlock and one philosopher will be able to eat and eventually, all others will. In Fig. 7.21, two philosophers are left-handed and three are right-handed. There is one spoon available between the second and the third, even if they all

```
do{

        wait (Sem_Spoon[n]);
        wait (Sem_Spoon[(n + 1) % 5]);

        eat();

        signal (Sem_Spoon[n]);
        signal (Sem_Spoon[(n + 1) % 5]);
        ...
        think();
        ...
} while (true);
```

Fig. 7.19 Dining-philosopher problem's solution: Attempt 1

```
do{

    wait (Sem_Philosopher);
    wait (Sem_Spoon[n]);
    wait (Sem_Spoon[(n+1) % 5]);

    eat();

    signal (Sem_Spoon[n]);
    signal (Sem_Spoon[(n + 1) % 5]);
    signal (Sem_Philosopher);
    …
    think();
    …
} while (true);
```

Fig. 7.20   Dining-philosopher problem's solution: Attempt 2

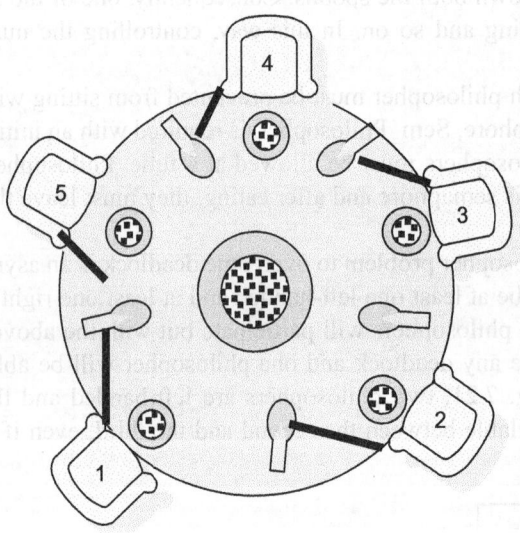

Fig. 7.21   Dining-philosopher problem's solution: Attempt 3

picked up one spoon at the same time. Either the second or the third can start eating. When the philosopher finishes eating, another can start and eventually, progress will be there.

In the line of asymmetric solution, there can be one more solution with the restriction that odd-numbered philosophers will first pick up spoons on their left and then the right one and even numbered philosophers will first pick up spoons on their right side and then the left one. In Fig. 7.22, all odd-numbered philosophers are able to pick up their first spoon that is on their left. In this case, all even-numbered philosophers are not able to pick up their first spoon on their right. Two spoons are free on the table, so Philosopher 1 and 3 can start eating. The solution algorithm given in Fig. 7.23 assumes that all the philosophers and the spoons have been numbered.

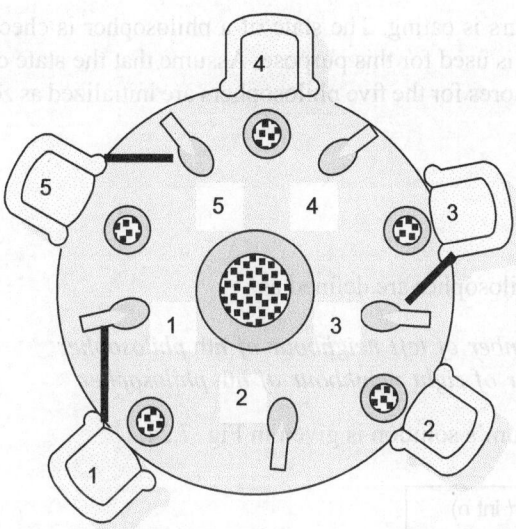

Fig. 7.22   Dining-philosopher problem's solution: Attempt 4

```
do{

        if (n % 2 ! = 0) // philosopher number is odd
    {
        wait (Sem_Spoon[n]);
          wait (Sem_Spoon[(n + 1) % 5]);

          eat();

        signal (Sem_Spoon[n]);
        signal (Sem_Spoon[(n + 1) % 5]);
        }
        else // philosopher number is even
        {
          wait (Sem_Spoon[(n + 1) % 5]);
          wait (Sem_Spoon[n]);

        eat();

        signal (Sem_Spoon[(n + 1) % 5]);
        signal (Sem_Spoon[n]);
        }
          ...
        think();
          ...
} while (true);
```

Fig. 7.23   Dining-philosopher problem's solution algorithm: Attempt 4

Another solution for dining-philosopher problem was given by Tanenbaum. He defines the states of a philosopher. The possible states are thinking, eating, and waiting (hungry). A semaphore is taken for all the philosophers, on which they wait to start eating. The philosophers can start eating only if neither of their neighbours is eating. The state of a philosopher is checked and updated; therefore, another semaphore is used for this purpose. Assume that the state of all the philosophers is thinking and all semaphores for the five philosophers are initialized as zero. The following are the data structures:

int state[5];
Semaphore Sem_State = 1;
Semaphore philosopher [5];
The left and right neighbour of a philosopher are defined as

#define LEFT (n + 5 − 1) % 5 // *number of left neighbour of nth philosopher*
#define RIGHT (n + 1)%5 // *number of right neighbour of nth philosopher*

The solution algorithm for Tanenbaum's solution is given in Fig. 7.24.

```
void philosopher( int n)
{
    do {
            think();
            get_spoons(n);
            eat();
            put_spoons(n);
    } while (true);
}
```

```
void get_spoons( int n)
{
    wait (Sem_State);
    state[n] = Hungry;
    test_state (n);
    signal (Sem_State);
    wait (philosopher[n]);
}
```

```
void put_spoons( int n)
{
    wait (Sem_State);
    state[n] = Thinking;
    test_state (LEFT);
    test_state (RIGHT);
    signal (Sem_State);
}
```

```
void test_state ( int n)
{
    if (state[n] == Hungry && state[LEFT] ! = Eating && state[RIGHT]!= Eating)
    {
        state[n] = Eating;
        signal (philosopher[n]);
    }
}
```

Fig. 7.24 Dining-philosopher problem: Tanenbaum's solution

7.6.4 Cigarette Smokers' Problem

This is another classic synchronization problem posed by Suhas Patil. The problem consists of three smokers S1, S2, and S3. All smokers prepare a cigarette themselves and smoke continuously with the help of three ingredients: tobacco, wrapping paper, and a match. Each smoker has infinite supply of only one ingredient. However, a smoker needs two more ingredients to prepare and smoke. For supplying the other two ingredients, there is a supplier having three vendors. Vendor V1 supplies tobacco and paper, V2 supplies paper and matches, and V3 supplies tobacco and matches. Every vendor supplies two ingredients to the smokers at random. Depending on the ingredients supplied, the smoker with the complementary ingredient takes them and prepares the cigarette. The smoker smokes it and signals to the supplier to supply the next lot of ingredients. For example, S1 has tobacco, S2 has paper, and S3 has matches. If a supplier offers paper and match, then S1 will take these two ingredients, prepare the cigarette, and smokes it.

Here, the supplier is the OS system and smokers are applications that require resources to execute. The problem is that if resources are available, then the OS system must provide these resources to the appropriate processes. Only the process that can be satisfied with the available resources should be woken up. In the example, if the ingredients are provided to S2, then it is of no use because the smoker cannot prepare a cigarette.

Let us discuss its solution now. All three vendors should not supply the materials at the same time. Therefore, a semaphore, Sem_Supplier is needed so that only one vendor supplies the materials and others wait. Three semaphores are required on three types of ingredients. There must be a mechanism for waiting and releasing the ingredients, so three semaphores for each ingredient are Sem_Tobacco, Sem_Paper, and Sem_Match. The algorithms for all vendors and smokers are given in Fig. 7.25. The semaphores are initialized as

Sem_Supplier = 1,
Sem_Tobacco = 0,
Sem_Paper = 0,
Sem_Match = 0;

```
Vendor V1()
{
    wait (Sem_Supplier);
    signal (Sem_Tobacco);
    signal (Sem_Paper);
```

```
Smoker with Tobacco()
{
    wait (Sem_Paper);
    wait (Sem_Match);
    signal (Sem_Supplier);
```

```
Vendor V2()
{
    wait (Sem_Supplier);
    signal (Sem_Paper);
    signal (Sem_Match);
```

```
Smoker with Paper()
{
    wait (Sem_Tobacco);
    wait (Sem_Match);
    signal (Sem_Supplier);
```

```
Vendor V3()
{
    wait (Sem_Supplier);
    signal (Sem_Tobacco);
    signal (Sem_Match);
```

```
Smoker with Match()
{
    wait (Sem_Tobacco);
    wait (Sem_Paper);
    signal (Sem_Supplier);
```

Fig. 7.25   Cigarette smoker problem's solution: Attempt 1

Problems, however, do exist in this solution. Suppose Vendor V1 supplies tobacco and paper. Since the smoker with matches is waiting for tobacco and paper, it might be unblocked, but the smoker with tobacco is waiting for paper, so it may also be unblocked. In such cases, one smoker will wait on paper and the other on matches. First, it is a wrong solution because only one smoker should start at a time. Second, if more than one smokers start, then there is a possibility of deadlock.

David Parnas provided the solution to these problems. He suggested three pushers that will respond to the signals from three vendors, keep track of the available ingredients, and signal the appropriate smoker. Suppose there are three Boolean variables to keep track of three ingredients and three more semaphores to signal the appropriate smokers. The smoker with tobacco will be signaled by one of the pushers. One more semaphore is needed so that all the pushers should not check and modify the status of Boolean variables at the same time. The additional data structures are

isTobacco = isPaper = isMatch = False
Semaphore Sem_Pusher_tobacco = 0,
Sem_Pusher_paper = 0,
Sem_Pusher_match = 0,
Sem_BooleanUpdate = 1;

Keeping the vendor algorithms same, the algorithms of each pusher and smoker are shown in Fig. 7.26. Suppose V1 supplies tobacco and paper, then Pushers A and B are activated. Pusher A first runs and finds that paper and match are not there yet. It makes is Tobacco = True. Then Pusher B runs and finds that paper and tobacco are there, signaling the smoker with matches. Similarly, the other pushers are activated.

7.6.5 Sleeping Barber Problem

This problem is related to synchronization between a barber and his or her customers. In a barber shop, there is one barber chair that the barber uses to sleep when there are no customers. A customer, who enters the shop, wakes up the barber and gets a haircut. If the barber is already busy with a customer and more customers arrive, they wait in the free

```
Pusher A()
{
    wait (Sem_Tobacco);
    wait (BooleanUpdate);
    if(isPaper)
    {
        isPaper = False;
        signal (Sem_Pusher_match);
    }
    elseif (isMatch)
    {
        isMatch = False;
        signal (Sem_Pusher_paper);
    }
    else
        isTobacco = True;
    signal (BooleanUpdate);
```

```
Pusher B ()
{
    wait (Sem_Paper);
    wait (BooleanUpdate);
    if (isTobacco)
    {
        isTobacco= False;
        signal (Sem_Pusher_match);
    }
    else if (isMatch)
    {
        isMatch = False;
        signal (Sem_Pusher_tobacco);
    }
    else
        isPaper= True;
    signal (BooleanUpdate);
```

```
Pusher C ()
{
    wait (Sem_Match);
    wait (BooleanUpdate);
    if(isPaper)
    {
        isPaper = False;
        signal (Sem_Pusher_tobacco);
    }
    else if (isTobacco)
    {
        isTobacco= False;
        signal (Sem_Pusher_paper);
    }
    else
        isMatch= True;
    signal (BooleanUpdate);
```

```
Smoker with Tobacco ()
{
    wait (Sem_Pusher_tobacco);
    PrepareCigarette();
    Smoke();
    signal (Sem_Supplier);
}
```

```
Smoker with Paper()
{
    wait (Sem_Pusher_paper);
    PrepareCigarette ();
    Smoke ();
    signal (Sem_Supplier);
}
```

```
Smoker with Match ()
{
    wait (Sem_Pusher_match);
    PrepareCigarette ();
    Smoke ();
    signal (Sem_Supplier);
}
```

Fig. 7.26   Cigarette smoker problem's solution: Attempt 2

chairs in the shop. If all the chairs are occupied, they leave the shop. When the barber is finished with one customer, he or she calls one of the waiting customers and starts hair cutting. If there are no customers waiting, the barber goes back to his chair and sleeps until a customer comes and wakes him up. This process continues. The problem here is to synchronize the activities of the barber and customers with predefined waiting chairs. It may be possible that the barber could end up waiting for a customer and the customer waiting for the barber, resulting in a deadlock. Alternatively, customers may not approach the barber in an orderly manner, leading to process starvation as some customers will not get a haircut even though they have been waiting. If two customers arrive at the same time when the barber is busy and there is only one chair vacant, then how will they synchronize with each other?

The solution needs two semaphores: Sem_Customer for customers and Sem_Barber for the barber. Sem_Customer is needed so that all customers wait properly and signal the barber that a new customer has arrived. Similarly, Sem_Barber is needed so that the barber waits for a customer and signals the customer when free. There are n chairs in the shop for waiting customers. On the basis of the number of occupied chairs, the number of customers waiting is estimated. Since the count of customers waiting needs to be updated, there should be one more semaphore, Sem_CountWaitingCustomers. The following are the data structures needed:

int NumberofCustomers = 0;

Semaphore Sem_Customer = 0,

```
Barber()
{
    wait (Sem_Customer);
    signal (Sem_Barber);
    cuthair ();
}
```

```
Customer ()
{
    wait (Sem_CountWaitingCustomers);
    if (NumberofCustomers == n + 1)
    {
    signal
(Sem_CountWaitingCustomers);
        leave the shop;
    }
    NumberofCustomers++;
    signal (Sem_CountWaitingCustomers);
    signal (Sem_Customer);
    wait (Sem_Barber);
    wait (Sem_CountWaitingCustomers);
    NumberofCustomers;
    signal (Sem_CountWaitingCustomers);
    gethaircut ()         ;
}
```

Fig. 7.27   Sleeping barber problem's solution

Sem_Barber = 0,

Sem_CountWaitingCustomers = 0;

The algorithms for customer and barber are given in Fig. 7.27.

7.7 CRITICAL REGIONS

The semaphore is an efficient tool for providing synchronization among processes as described in Section 7.6. However, in the solution of some complex problems, managing the semaphores is dangerous. If any sequence of wait and signal operations of a semaphore is missed or exchanged, it may lead to data corruption and deadlock. The programmer's effort is consumed in managing the semaphores instead of developing the application. Therefore, some high-level language constructs have been developed to make waiting and signaling operations much simpler as compared to semaphores. One of them is known as *critical region*.

In critical region, a global variable, *shared*, is used and accessed within a CS only. The CS is defined with the keyword *region*. If a shared variable S needs to be used among many processes inside a critical section, then the code should be written as shown in Fig. 7.28. Once S has been taken as a shared variable, it should be accessed inside a region, that is, critical section. If it is used somewhere else in the code, the compiler of high-level language will detect this as an error.

```
shared <type> S = <initial value>

while (true) {
    region S do
    {
        //Critical section
        //Access shared
        variable S here

    }
    ...
    ...
}
```

Fig. 7.28   Critical region

The critical region construct, however, is prone to busy waits because it is not able to block a process if it does not continue in a critical section. The next process in CS starts, but the previous process needs to loop to check whether the region is free to access. Therefore, the critical region is supported with one more keyword, *await (B)*. Whenever a process tries to enter a critical region, the Boolean expression B is evaluated. If B is true, then it is allowed to access the shared variable inside the region, otherwise the process is blocked until B becomes true. This type of critical region is called *conditional critical region* (CCR). The code given in Fig. 7.28 can be modified as given in Fig. 7.29. The *Edison* language for embedded applications supports CCRs.

```
shared <type> S = <initial value>
while (true) {
        region S do
        {
            await (B);

            //Critical section
            //Access shared
            variable S here

        }
        ...
        ...
}
```

Fig. 7.29   Conditional critical region

7.7.1 Producer–Consumer Problem's Solution with CCR

The producer–consumer problem can be solved with the help of CCR construct. We need to take some global variables as shared variables. The data structure is given by

Shared Struct {

Item buffer[n]; // buffer that stores items of type Item in n-sized buffer

int buffer_size = n;

int full = 0; // counter that keeps track of buffer items

} Bounded_buffer.

The producer produces an item in the buffer with the await condition that the buffer is not full, and similarly, the consumer consumes item with the await condition that the buffer is not empty. The algorithms for producers and consumers are given in Fig. 7.30.

7.8 MONITORS

The CCR can be dispersed throughout the program. The more structured critical regions are provided by monitors. The monitor is another high-level language construct used for shared

```
Producer ()
{
    while (true) {
        region Bounded_buffer do
        {
            await (full < buffer_size);
            produce (); // produce the item
            full++;
        }
    }
}
```

```
Consumer ()
{
    while (true) {
        region Bounded_buffer do
        {
            await (full > 0);
            Consume (); // consume the item
            full– –;
        }
    }
}
```

Fig. 7.30   Producer–consumer problem's solution with CCR

```
type <name of monitor type> = monitor
  ... data declaration
...
monitor entry <name and its parameters>
{
  ...
}
```

Fig. 7.31 Format of a monitor

data and process synchronization. The concept similar to encapsulation used in object-oriented languages for data hiding is applied in monitors. A monitor is same as a class type; like objects of a class are created, the variables of monitor type are defined. The monitor defines not only the shared data but also the operations that can operate on this data. The critical regions are written as procedures and encapsulated together in a single module. All procedure calls are mutually exclusive. In this way, monitors are superior to CCR and are more reliable to use in large concurrent systems because they provide data abstraction, control abstraction, and procedural abstraction through encapsulation. *Modula-1, Concurrent Pascal*, and *Mesa* are some languages that support monitors. The format of a monitor is shown in Fig. 7.31.

The synchronization among the processes is provided through the *monitor entry* procedures. There may be many processes that wish to enter the monitor at the same time, but it enforces mutual exclusion. Only one process will be allowed within the monitor; others will be blocked and made to wait at its boundary. Data inside a monitor may be shared among the processes or the local data of the procedure. However, the shared data cannot be accessed outside the boundary. Moreover, the *wait* and *signal* introduced in semaphores are also implemented in monitors through the use of *condition* variables. A process inside a monitor may wait till a specific condition occurs. This is known as blocking of the process on the condition. The first process in the queue is activated when the condition becomes true, which is explicitly signaled by the process inside the monitor. Thus, wait and signal are implemented inside the monitor through condition variables to enforce mutual exclusion and synchronization. Condition variables are different from normal variables because each of them has an associated queue. A process calling *wait* on a particular condition is put into the queue associated with that condition variable. It means that the process is waiting to enter a CS guarded by the monitor. A process calling the *signal* causes the waiting process in the queue to enter the monitor. The condition variable's declaration with wait and signal operations is defined as

Condition <name of variable>;
wait (condition variable);
signal (condition variable).

If the signaling process is still inside the monitor, then the waiting process in the queue cannot enter the monitor. To force the process to exit immediately after the signal operation, *signal-and-exit* monitor is used. However, in some cases, if the signaling process needs to be inside the monitor for some more time after signaling, then *signal-and-continue* monitor is used. It means that the signaling has been done by the process, but it still maintains a lock on the semaphore. Java programming language implements the signal-and-continue monitor.

7.8.1 Producer–Consumer Problem's Solution with Monitors

Let us revisit the producer–consumer problem to solve it with the help of monitors; buffer_full and buffer_empty have been taken as condition variables; and produce_info and consume_info are two monitor entry procedures through which synchronization between two processes is achieved. The algorithm is given in Fig. 7.32.

```
type Bounded_buffer = monitor
Item buffer[n]; // buffer that stores items of type Item in n-sized buffer
int full = 0;
Condition buffer_full;
Condition buffer_empty;

monitor entry produce_info ( );
{
        If (full = n)
                wait (buffer_empty);
        produce ();
        full++;
        signal (buffer_full);
}
monitor entry consume_info ( );
{
        if (full = 0)
                wait (buffer_full);
        Consume ();
        full− −;
        signal (buffer_empty);
}
```

```
Producer ()
{
        Bounded_buffer B;

        while (true)
        {
                B.produce_info ();
        }
}
```

```
Consumer ()
{
        Bounded_buffer B;

        while (true)
        {
                B.consume_info ();
        }
}
```

Fig. 7.32   Producer–consumer problem's solution with monitors

7.9 PROTECTED OBJECTS

Protected objects are another high-level constructs to implement monitors in Ada language. In this language, the data items are encapsulated into a protected object. The access to these data items is provided only via protected sub-programs on protected entries. Further, these sub-programs and entries are executed such that the data are mutually exclusively updated. Sub-programs are of two types: protected procedures and protected functions. The role of a *protected procedure* is to provide mutually exclusive read/write access to the encapsulated data. On the other hand, the protected functions provide concurrent read-only access to the encapsulated data. A *protected entry* is also a protected procedure having same features to update encapsulated data mutually exclusively and read/write access to the encapsulated data. However, the protected entry is guarded by a Boolean expression known as *barrier*. The barrier is inside the body of the protected object. While the entry call is made and barrier value is false, the calling function is suspended (queued) until the barrier value becomes true and there should be no other active task inside the protected object. Thus, the protected objects are used

```
protected type <Name of protected object> is
     entry <Name of protected entry>;
     procedure <Name of protected procedure>;
     function <Name of protected function>;
               return <return type>;
private
     Open : Boolean := False;
end <Name of protected object>;

protected body <Name of protected object>is

     entry <Name of protected entry> when Open is
     begin
       Open := False;
     end <Name of protected entry>;

     procedure <Name of protected procedure> is
     begin
       Open := True;
     end <Name of protected procedure>;

     function <Name of protected function>
               return <return type>is
     begin
       return Open;
     end <Name of protected function>;

   end <Name of protected object>;
```

Fig. 7.33   Format of protected objects in Ada

to implement conditional synchronization. In this way, protected objects make use of good points of both monitors and CCR. The method of defining the protected objects in Ada has been shown in Fig. 7.33. Since the protected object interface must provide all the information required by the compiler to allocate the required memory in an efficient manner, the state of the object is placed in the private part of the specification.

To call a protected object, the process names the object and the required sub-program or entry. For example, to call a protected entry the syntax is

Object_Name.Entry_Name (Parameters)

The barrier is thus executed on the call of a protected procedure or entry. On the completion of a protected procedure or entry, all barriers are re-evaluated. Barrier evaluation, protected-object queuing, and protected-object execution are collectively known as *protected actions*.

7.10 SYNCHRONIZED METHODS

This is a Java language construct to implement a monitor. A lock is associated with an object by the keyword *synchronized*. When a method is labeled with the synchronized modifier, access to it can be gained once the lock associated with the object has been obtained (see Fig. 7.34).

```
Synchronized void <name of method>
{
    ..
    ..
}
```

Fig. 7.34   Synchronized methods

```
void <name of method>
{
    synchronized (this)
    {
        ..
        ..
    }
    ..
    ..
}
```

Fig. 7.35   Synchronized method with *this*

Java also has the facility of making a block of statements as synchronized. The synchronized keyword takes an object as a parameter whose lock it needs to obtain before it can continue. The keyword *this* is used for obtaining the current object (see Fig. 7.35).

The conditional synchronization implementation is obtained with the following methods in Java:

1.   public void notify (): This method releases an object and sends a notification to a waiting process.

2.   public void notify All (): This method sends notification to all processes once the object is available.

3.   public void wait (): makes a process wait for the object till it receives a notification.

7. 11   MESSAGE PASSING SYSTEM

The message passing system allows processes to communicate through explicit messages as introduced earlier in process communication. In a message passing system, a sender or a source process sends a message to a known receiver or destination process. The message has a predefined structure through which the sender sends the message. In general, a message passing system is implemented through two system calls: send and receive. The general format of these two is given by

send (name of destination process, message);
receive (name of source process, message).

In these calls, the sender and receiver processes address each other by names. The addressing or mode of communication between two processes can take place through two methods. They are discussed in Sections 7.11.1 and 7.11.2.

7.11.1   Direct Addressing

In this type of communication, the two processes need to name each other to communicate. This becomes easy if they have the same parent. For example, Processes A and B communicate with each other through a message passing system. If Process A sends a message to Process B, then in this case, the format is

send (B, message);
receive (A, message).

In send () call, the sender process names the Recipient B, and at the same time, in receive () call, the receiver process names the Sender A. In this way, a link is established between A and B. Here, the receiver knows the identity of destination of message in advance. This type of arrangement in direct communication is known as *symmetric addressing*. The symmetric addressing is useful in concurrent processes where sending and receiving processes cooperate with each other. However, this type of addressing is not valid everywhere. For example, a print server receiving requests from many unknown processes may not be able to know the name or ID of the sending process in advance. For this purpose, another type of addressing known as *asymmetric addressing* is used. Here, the sending process's name is not mentioned in the receive call, but it possesses a value returned by a sending process when the receive operation has been completed.

7.11.2 Indirect Addressing

Another way of communication is indirect addressing where the processes need not name each other and send the messages directly. In contrast, the messages are sent to a shared area known as *mailbox*, which stores them. A mailbox can be regarded as an object where messages can be stored or removed by the processes. The receiver process that is not in synchronization with the sending process may receive the message after some time from the mailbox. The sender and receiver processes should share a mailbox to communicate (Fig. 7.36).

The following types of communication link are possible through mailbox:

One-to-one link: One sender wants to communicate with one receiver; a single link is established between two processes. No other processes can interfere in between.

Many-to-one link: Multiple senders want to communicate with one receiver. For example, in a client-server system, there are many client processes and one server process. The mailbox here is known as *port*.

One-to-many link: One sender wants to communicate with multiple receivers, that is, to broadcast a message.

Many-to-many link: Multiple senders want to communicate with multiple receivers.

7.11.3 Mailbox

A mailbox created among processes has a unique identity as there may be multiple mailboxes depending on the communication needs of the processes in the system. The mailbox implementation also has some design issues. The first issue is regarding its creation. Since the mailbox is a shared area, it needs to be created by a process. The kernel provides the system calls to create a mailbox. Another issue is about the ownership of a mailbox. The process that creates it becomes the owner, that is, the receiving process, by default. However, the ownership rights can also be transferred to other processes. In general, any process that knows the identity of a mailbox can send messages to it. However, there are some mechanisms to be provided by the kernel through which senders and receivers share a common mailbox to communicate. The mailbox can be deleted, or it gets terminated when its owner process terminates. In both the cases, the sending processes associated with the mailbox must be notified about it.

The assignment of a mailbox to the processes may not always be static. In case of one-to-one relationship, the mailbox assigned between the two processes are permanent. However, if there are multiple senders, then there will be dynamic assignment of the mailbox.

Since the mailbox is meant for storing messages, it has a queue to store them. In general, the message queue is implemented as first-in-first-out, but for some preferred messages, the queue may also be prioritized.

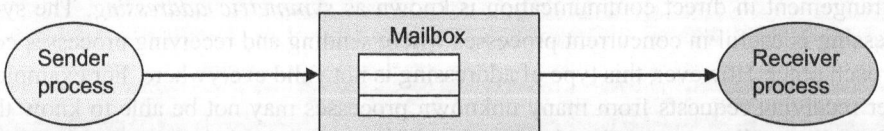

Fig. 7.36   Mailbox

7.11.4 Synchronization Protocols

The communication among processes need some type of synchronization between them. This synchronization is governed by rules known as synchronization protocols. The following are the two common protocols:

Blocking Protocol

In this protocol, both the sender and receiver are blocked until the message is delivered to the receiver. The advantage here is that the sender is ensured about the delivery of the message to its receiver. However, there is unnecessary delay in processing of the sender. When both the sender and receiver follow blocking protocol, they are said to be in *rendezvous*.

Non-blocking Protocol

In this protocol, both the sender and receiver are non-blocking, that is, they resume their operation without waiting for the message to get delivered. The advantage here is that the processing of the sender is not delayed, but it cannot ensure the delivery of the message to its receiver.

7.12 SIGNALS

Signals can be defined as the inter-process communication mechanisms that notify a process about any event but do not exchange the data as in message passing. For example, if a child process terminates or suspends, then this event should be notified to the parent process as a signal. Likewise, if a parent process wants to terminate its child process, then the signal about its termination will be sent. Signals can also be used to notify I/O completion. In this way, some signals are received by the running processes from other processes asynchronously. However, there are some events that when executed within the running process must be notified to it by the kernel synchronously. For example, a process tries to execute an illegal instruction, an invalid system call, or exceed file size limit, and so on. Thus, signals can be used either for process to process communication or kernel to process communication. Thus, a signal may notify a running process synchronously and asynchronously. Based on this concept, there are two types of signals: *synchronous* and *asynchronous*. A synchronous signal occurs due to an instruction executed by the process itself and is passed to this process by the kernel. An asynchronous signal occurs due to an external event and is passed from one process to another. The external event in an asynchronous signal is unrelated to any execution in the receiving process.

When a signal occurs, it is the job of the OS system to determine the process for which the signal is meant and the way the receiving process will respond to the signal. Generally, a process responds through a procedure known as *signal handler*. In other words, the exception generated in the form of a signal is caught by the process. Sometimes, a signal may be ignored by the process. In this case, the OS system takes some default action and executes a default signal handler. The default action may be to abort or suspend the process. The process may also mask or block a signal, which may be required if the process is already servicing another signal. The process of masking may be different in various operating systems.

The implementation of signals is similar to that of interrupts. The process receiving the signal is interrupted. The state of the process is saved before attending the signal handler so that it can resume its work after the execution of the signal handler. The process executes the

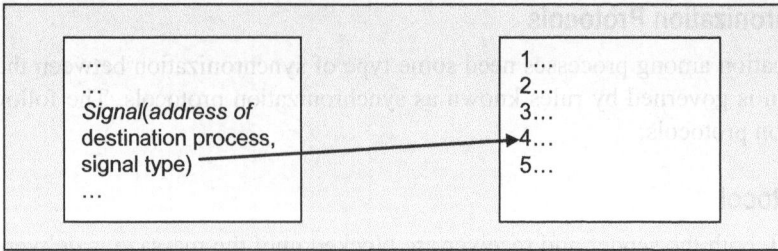

Fig. 7.37 Signal received by a process

signal handler for servicing the signal as interrupt service routine is executed for servicing the interrupt. After the execution, the process resumes its work from where it was interrupted. In fact, the signals are interrupted as a system call. The system call signal consists of two parameters: One is the address of the destination process and another is the type or the number of the signal to be sent (Fig. 7.37). Since the signal is a system call, the parameters of signal call are stored in CPU registers and an event-handling routine is executed. This event-handling routine extracts the information about the destination process and the signal type. It passes the signal to the destination process after which the control is passed to the signal handler. However, for this purpose, event-handling routine must know the address of the signal handler.

To know the address of the signal handler of a signal type, the process receiving the signal must initialize the signal before it receives the actual signal. The receiving process executes a system call for this initialization. The system call *init signal* is used for this purpose (see Fig. 7.38). The parameters of *init signal* are signal type and the address of its signal handler. When this system call is executed, the kernel enters the address of the signal handler in the *signal vector area* of the kernel. The signal vector area is similar to interrupt vector area and will be different for every process. It contains the addresses of the signal handlers

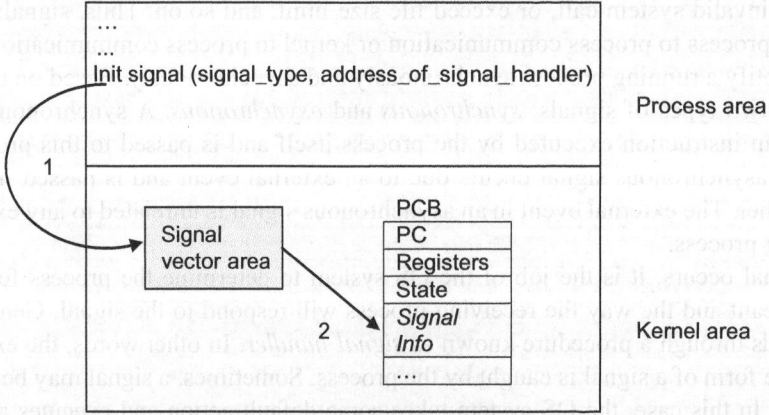

1. Address of the signal handler corresponding to its type is added in the signal vector area.
2. In the PCB of the process, Signal Info field is added and the address of the signal vector corresponding to the process is copied here.

Fig. 7.38 Preparation for signal implementation

corresponding to all the signals a process supports. Therefore, by executing init signal call, a process can store addresses of all the signal handlers in its signal vector area. For this implementation, the PCB will be modified to have a new field *signal info* containing the address of the signal vector area of the process.

When an event-processing routine corresponding to a signal system call is executed and sends the signal to its destination process, it locates the corresponding PCB. From the PCB, the address of the signal vector area is searched and then the address of the signal handler is searched in this signal vector area. Once the desired address is found, the control is passed to the signal handler and thereby it is executed. If the destination process is blocked, then the kernel may put it into a ready state and after executing the signal handler, it is moved back to its original state (see Fig. 7.39).

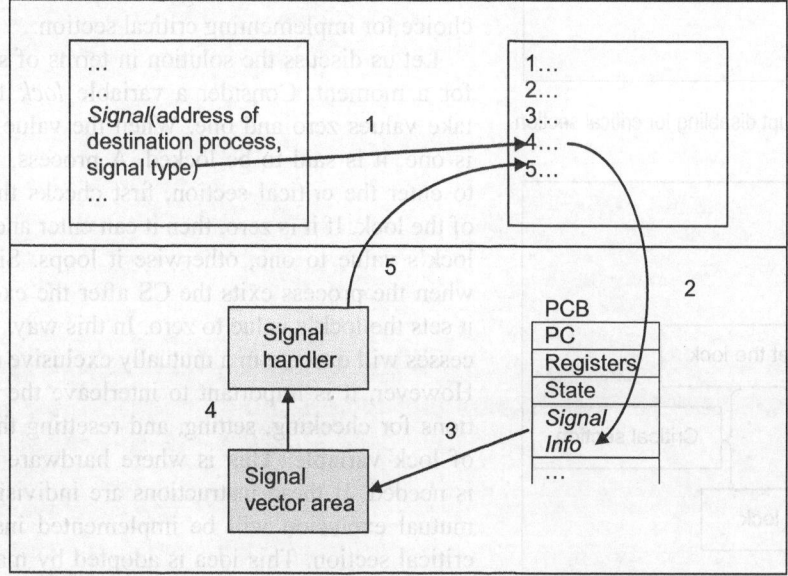

1. The sender sends the signal to the receiver. The process is interrupted.
2. The PCB of the receiver is searched and signal info field is searched for the address of its signal vector.
3. The address of signal handler is retrieved from signal vector and control is passed to the signal handler.
4. The signal handler is executed.
5. After executing the signal handler, the control is again passed to the receiver.

Fig. 7.39   Signal implementation

7.13 HARDWARE SUPPORT FOR PROCESS SYNCHRONIZATION

The CS implementation for avoiding race condition and thereby synchronizing the processes can be achieved if the hardware architecture support is there. In a uni-processor system, a process will continue to execute unless it is interrupted by a system call or an interrupt. If any system call or interrupt can be prevented, then the execution of a process in the CS will be mutually exclusive (see Fig. 7.40).

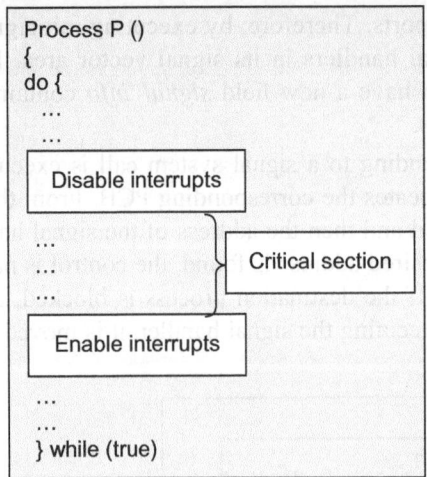

Fig. 7.40 Interrupt disabling for critical section

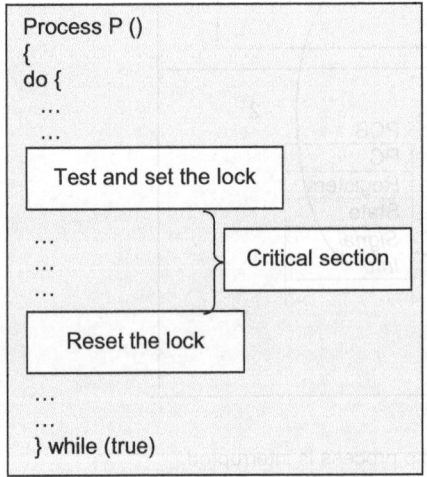

Fig. 7.41 Special instruction for critical section

However, interrupt disabling cannot be always adopted in a multi-programming environment. The first problem is that the system's efficiency is degraded as other processes are not allowed to be interleaved. Another problem is that this will only disable interrupts on a single processor; other processors may still allow the interrupts, and disabling interrupts on all processors may be time consuming and degrade the system efficiency. In addition, the kernel would not be able to update its data structures causing race conditions. Thus, it can be summarized that disabling interrupts is not a good choice for implementing critical section.

Let us discuss the solution in terms of software for a moment. Consider a variable *lock* that can take values zero and one. When the value of lock is one, it is said to be locked. A process, wishing to enter the critical section, first checks the value of the lock. If it is zero, then it can enter and set the lock's value to one, otherwise it loops. Similarly, when the process exits the CS after the execution, it sets the lock's value to zero. In this way, the processes will execute in a mutually exclusive manner. However, it is important to interleave the instructions for checking, setting, and resetting the value of lock variable. This is where hardware support is needed. If these instructions are indivisible, the mutual exclusion will be implemented inside the critical section. This idea is adopted by many systems. In IBM/370 systems, there is an indivisible instruction called Test-and-Set (TS). TS instruction performs two actions: First, it tests the value of a memory byte (for lock variable) to check whether it is zero or one. If it is zero, then it performs the second operation, that is, sets the byte to one. The initial value of a lock is zero. Now, to make these two operations indivisible, the processor executing these instructions locks the memory bus so that no other process may request to access the memory at this time. In this way, the indivisible operations are implemented using special machine instructions (see Fig. 7.41).

Compare-and-swap and Exchange are some other examples of hardware-supported indivisible instructions that have been implemented in systems such as x86, IA32, IA64, and so on.

SUMMARY

Interacting processes need to synchronize in various ways. The chapter discusses various classic synchronization problems and their solutions. Semaphores are one of the effective solutions to synchronization problems. However, in complex problems, semaphores may become difficult to implement. Therefore, some other methods, such as high-level language constructs, hardware support, and so on, are used. Synchronization among interacting processes also need to communicate. Shared memory, message passing systems, and signals are some of the means of communication discussed in the chapter.

Let us have a quick review of important concepts discussed in this chapter:

1. Concurrent processes may need to communicate data and information among themselves. Therefore, there should be some mechanisms for synchronizing the processes.

2. Data access synchronization is used to synchronize the concurrent processes so that they do not update a shared variable at the same time.

3. When more than one processes access and update the same data concurrently and the result depends on the sequence of execution in which it takes place, it is known as race condition.

4. Control synchronization is used to synchronize the sequence of execution of two processes where a process needs to wait for input from the other process.

5. When every process is holding a resource and waiting for another resource held by another process, the situation is known as deadlock in the system.

6. A section of code in the process where the shared data is accessed and updated is known as CS.

7. Critical section consists of three parts: entry criteria, CS code, and exit criteria.

8. When processes in a system are giving chance to one another and no process is proceeding, this situation is known as livelock.

9. The semaphore is a process-synchronization tool that protects any resource such as global shared memory that needs to be accessed and updated by many processes.

10. The semaphore is accessed with only two indivisible operations known as wait and signal operations. The wait and signal operations are also denoted by P and V, respectively, after the Dutch notations.

11. The semaphore whose value is either zero or one is known as binary semaphore.

12. A semaphore that may take values greater than one is known as counting semaphore.

13. In *mutex* semaphores, the process that locked the CS can only unlock it.

14. When a process does not get access to the resource, it loops continually waiting for it and wastes CPU cycles. This type of semaphore is known as a *spinlock*.

15. Process communication may take place in three ways: shared memory, message passing, and signals.

16. In shared variable communication, there is a shared variable among processes through which they communicate, that is, they are not aware of existence of each other but coordinate with each other in the execution.

17. The processes can also communicate through messages and be explicitly aware of the existence of each other. This type of communication is known as *message passing*.

18. A message passing system is implemented through two methods: direct addressing and indirect addressing. The classification of a message-passing system is given by

19. The direct addressing based communication demands that the sender and receiver processes know each other and explicitly name them.

20. Direct addressing is of two types: symmetric and asymmetric.

21. In symmetric addressing, both the sender and receiver know the names of each other in advance and use them for communication.

22. In asymmetric addressing, the sender knows the name of the receiver but the receiver does not know the name of the sender.

23. In Indirect addressing, the processes need not name each other and send the message directly to a shared area that stores them. This shared area for storing the messages is known as a *mailbox*.

24. The communication link through a mailbox is of the following types:
   (a) one-to-one   (b) one-to-many
   (c) many-to-one   (d) many-to-many

25. Exceptional notification messages cannot be communicated through message-passing systems as they may not reach the desired process at the right time. Therefore, there should be another mechanism that catches the attention of the process to which this emergency message is to be passed. This mechanism is known as a *signal*.

26. The operations that cannot be overlapped or interleaved with execution of any other operations are known as *indivisible* or *atomic operations*.

27. The high-level language constructs for implementing process synchronization are summarized as follows:

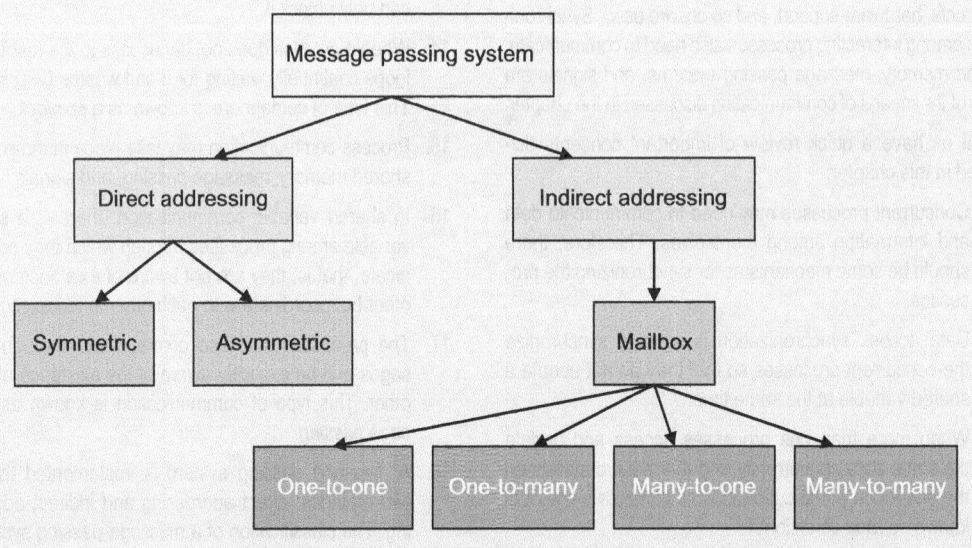

High-level language constructs	High-level language
Conditional critical region	Edison
Monitor	Modula-1, Concurrent Pascal, Mesa
Protected objects	Ada
Synchronized methods	Java

MULTIPLE CHOICE QUESTIONS

1. The situation where more than one processes access and update the same data concurrently and the result depends on the sequence of execution in which it takes place is known as
   (a) critical section
   (b) race condition
   (c) deadlock
   (d) none

2. Which one of the following is not a process communication method?
   (a) message passing
   (b) shared memory
   (c) signal
   (d) none

3. Which of the following is not a part of process synchronization protocol?
   (a) entry criteria
   (b) exit criteria
   (c) signal
   (d) critical section

4. When every process is waiting for the other to execute and no process is proceeding, the situation is known as
(a) deadlock   (c) critical section
(b) livelock   (d) none

5. The operations that cannot be overlapped or interleaved with execution of any other operations are known as
(a) atomic operations (c) messages
(b) system calls   (d) none

6. The semaphore whose value is either zero or one is known as
(a) binary semaphore   (c) guard
(b) counting semaphore (d) none

7. The semaphore that takes value greater than one is known as
(a) binary semaphore   (c) mutex
(b) counting semaphore (d) none

8. In a _____, the process that locks the CS will only unlock it.
(a) binary semaphore   (c) mutex
(b) counting semaphore (d) none

9. When a process does not get access to the resource, it loops continually for the resource and wastes CPU cycles. It is known as
(a) deadlock   (c) spinlock
(b) livelock   (d) none

10. A section of code in the process where the shared data is accessed and updated is known as
(a) critical section   (c) critical procedure
(b) critical region   (d) none

11. _____is a process synchronization tool that protects any resource such as global shared memory that needs to be accessed and updated by many processes.
(a) message passing system (c) semaphore
(b) signal   (d) none

12. In _____, a global variable is used with the keyword *shared* and accessed within a CS only.

13. Which one of the following languages does not support monitors?
(a) C   (c) Modula-1
(b) Java   (d) concurrent Pascal

14. Which high-level language construct uses the keyword *await (B)*?
(a) critical region   (c) monitor
(b) conditional critical region (d) synchronized method

15. Which language uses protected objects for synchronization?
(a) C   (c) Java
(b) C++   (d) Ada

16. A protected entry is guarded by a Boolean expression called _____ inside the body of the protected object.
(a) protected region   (c) barrier
(b) monitor   (d) critical region

17. Which language uses synchronized methods for synchronization?
(a) C   (c) Java
(b) C++   (d) Ada

18. In which type of link, a mailbox is known as a port?
(a) one-to-one   (c) many-to-one
(b) one-to-many   (d) many-to-many

19. When both the sender and receiver follow blocking protocol in a message passing system, they are said to be in
(a) concurrency   (c) rendezvous
(b) control   (d) none

20. ___ can be defined as the inter-process communication mechanisms that notify the exceptional conditions and alarms.
(a) A message passing system
(b) A signal
(c) A semaphore
(d) none

REVIEW QUESTIONS

1. What are concurrent processes? What are the problems associated with them?

2. What is a race condition? Write a program that shows the data access synchronization problem.

3. Write a program that shows the control synchronization problem.

4. Explain the shared memory method for process communication.

5. Explain the message passing system for process communication. What types of system is suitable for this method?

6. Explain the signal system for process communication. What types of system is suitable for this method?

7. Distinguish between deadlock, livelock, and spinlock.

8. Write a program that demonstrates a CS and its entry and exit criteria.

9. What are the characteristics of a protocol for having mutual exclusion in the form of critical section?

10. Explain the algorithms for two-process synchronization solution with shortcoming of every attempt.

11. What is the difference between Dekker's solution and Peterson's solution for two-process synchronization solution?

12. What is the difference between interleaved operations and indivisible operations? Explain with some program examples.

13. What is a semaphore? Explain its initial implementation.

14. What are the problems in initial implementation of a semaphore? How do you modify it?

15. Which type of systems a spinlock is useful for?

16. What is the difference between a binary semaphore, a counting semaphore, and a mutex?

17. What is the difference between symmetric and asymmetric solution of dining-philosopher problem using semaphore?

18. What is a critical region?

19. What is a CCR?

20. What is a monitor?

21. What are protected objects meant for?

22. What is a synchronized method?

23. What is the difference between a CCR and a monitor?

24. What is the difference between direct addressing and indirect addressing for the implementation of a message passing system?

25. What is the difference between symmetric and asymmetric addressing?

26. What is a mailbox? How is it used?

27. What is the difference between a blocking and a non-blocking protocol for the implementation of a message passing system?

28. What is a signal? What is the difference between a synchronous and an asynchronous signal?

29. Define signal handler, signal vector area, and signal info for the implementation of signals.

BRAIN TEASERS

1. Prove that all the CS protocol requirements are satisfied in Dekker's solution for process synchronization.

2. Prove that all the CS protocol requirements are satisfied in Peterson's solution for process synchronization.

3. Is nesting of critical sections possible in the system?

4. Is the reader–writer problem same as the producer–consumer problem?

5. Prove that there is a starvation problem in Tanenbaum's solution to the dining-philosopher problem.

6. Can you implement semaphores using monitors? If yes, write the code.

7. What are the problems faced by programmers in the implementation of a semaphore?

8. There are four processes sharing a semaphore for synchronizing a shared variable. The semaphore is guarding the CS of the processes where they update the shared variable. Initially, the value of the semaphore is three. The actions taken by the processes in time sequence are given below:

Time	Process	Operation
1	P1	P(S)
2	P2,	P(S)
	P3	P(S)
3	P4	P(S)

4	P1	V(S)
	P3	V(S)
5	P2	V(S)
	P1	P(S)
6	P2	P(S)
	P3	P(S)

Show and explain the current and updated value of a semaphore at every time instant and the processes in the wait queue.

9. A buffer has 10 slots. The initial value of empty = 10 and full = 0. What will be the value of empty and full in the following conditions?

(a) The producer has inserted five items and the consumer is not able to consume.

(b) The producer has inserted five more items and the consumer is not able to consume.

(c) The producer has produced three more items but cannot insert as the buffer is full.

(d) The consumer has consumed five items.

10. A system with three concurrent processes has a shared printer. Write a program to implement synchronization between the processes using a semaphore, a monitor, and a CCR.

11. Rendezvous is a point of synchronization where two processes wait for each other and neither is allowed to proceed until both have arrived. For example, see the Processes A and B in the following diagram. It needs to be confirmed that

A1 happens before B2 and B1 happens before A2. Write a solution for this rendezvous with semaphore. Can the solution be expanded to more than two processes?

Process A A1; A2;	Process B B1; B2;

12. The generalization of rendezvous mentioned in Problem 11 is in the form of a barrier. The synchronization requirement here is that no process executes a critical point until all the processes have executed the rendezvous. In other words, no process would execute the CS until all the processes have reached the barrier point. If there is any process left, all the other processes at the barrier point will be blocked. When all the processes reach at this point, they are allowed to execute. Can you provide a general solution for implementing this barrier?

13. There are two processes, oxygen and hydrogen. For a complete water molecule, two processes of hydrogen and one process of oxygen are required. To assemble these two processes in water molecules, a barrier is needed that makes each process wait until a complete molecule is ready to proceed. In other words,

(a) when an oxygen process arrives at the barrier, and no hydrogen process is there, it needs to wait for two processes of hydrogen;

(b) when a hydrogen process arrives, and no other process is there, it has to wait for one process of hydrogen and one process of oxygen.

Similarly, there may be other combinations. Provide a general solution to assemble the processes to prepare a water molecule.

14. There is a unisex salon where both males and females can get the salon service. However, there is a condition that males and females cannot come to the salon at the same time. The second condition is that there cannot be more than three persons in the salon at a time. Give a synchronization solution using semaphores.

15. There is a dining hall of capacity of 10 people at the most in a restaurant where families come to enjoy delicious food. On weekends, however, there is a great crowd in the restaurant. A person would be entertained only if there is a vacant chair. If all the seats are full, it means that there is a single family of 10 members enjoying the dinner. In this case, the person has to wait until the family leaves. Write a synchronization solution using semaphores for the customers entering and leaving the dining hall.

16. A working couple has three babies. The babies cannot be left unattended: Any one from the couple must be present at home for the babies. Write a solution for synchronizing the parents with the babies.

17. The passengers wait for a bus at a bus stop, and when the bus arrives, they board the bus. A passenger, who arrives when the bus is leaving, has to wait for the next bus. The capacity of the bus is 30. If there are more than 30 passengers waiting, only 30 will be allowed to board and others will have to wait for the next bus. Write a synchronization solution to this problem.

8   Deadlocks

8.1   INTRODUCTION

In the previous chapter, the problem of deadlock was introduced during the discussion of concurrent processes and their synchronization problems. In this chapter, deadlock will be discussed in detail. Deadlock is another critical problem in concurrent processes, and therefore, it must be known why it occurs in a system. There are some necessary conditions that give rise to a deadlock. If all of them hold true, the deadlock will certainly occur. If any one of the necessary conditions is prevented, the probability of deadlock becomes less. Some deadlock prevention methods have been discussed, but they are not always applicable. Deadlock avoidance is another approach to deal with deadlocks. Avoidance algorithms have been developed in order to have advance information about occurrence of deadlock. For that, it requires to know the maximum resource requirement of processes in advance, which is impractical. Therefore, this algorithm has low importance in practice. Deadlock detection is the method that a system must adopt if it is not able to prevent or avoid the deadlock. Finally, once a deadlock has been detected in a system, recovery methods are used. In this chapter, all these approaches have been discussed in detail.

8.2   DEFINING DEADLOCKS

The computer system uses several types of resources, such as consumable or non-consumable, and pre-emptable or non-pre-emptable. In a multi-programming environment, the problem starts with non-pre-emptable resources. These resources have to be used in a mutually exclusive manner. But the problem is that resources are always limited, compared to the number of processes. In this case, when the concurrent processes request the resources, a deadlock occurs.

Before defining a deadlock, let us understand how the resource allocation is done in a system. In general, the OS follows a protocol to use non-pre-emptive resources. The protocol consists of the following three events:

1. **Request**: Before using a resource, a process must request for it. This request is in the form of a system call, and it is passed on to the kernel. This uses a data structure *resource table* to store the information about all the resources in the system. Whenever the request is received, it checks the status of the resource.

Learning Objectives

After reading this chapter, you should be able to understand:

- Definition of deadlock
- Resource allocation graph (RAG)-based representation of deadlock
- Wait-for graph-based representation of deadlock
- Conditions for occurrence of deadlock
- Deadlock prevention methods
- Deadlock avoidance methods
- Banker's algorithm for deadlock avoidance
- Deadlock detection methods
- Recovery from deadlock
- Two-phase locking
- Starvation

If the resource is free, the requesting process will get it. Otherwise, the requesting process will be blocked, and it must wait until the resource is free.

2. **Use**: If a process gets the resource, the kernel changes the status of resource to *allocated* and the state of process to *ready*, if it has been blocked earlier. The process uses the resource in a mutually exclusive manner.

3. **Release**: After its use, a process releases the resource again through the use of a system call. The kernel can now allocate this resource to any blocked process or change the status of the resource to *free*.

The use of a non-pre-emptive resource may also follow the protocol of a critical section, which consists of the following criteria:

1. **Entry criteria**: The resource should be free while requesting, otherwise the requesting process must wait.

2. **Mutual exclusion:** The use of resource must be mutually exclusive.

3. **Exit criteria**: There must be some criteria for releasing the resources.

A semaphore can help the resources satisfy the above criteria. It will guard a resource and help in using it in a mutually exclusive manner (see Fig. 8.1).

Let us consider a system with two concurrent processes A and B, and with two resources such as one CD drive and one printer. Both the resources can be guarded using two semaphores (see Fig. 8.2).

As we know, in a multi-programming environment, there may be interleaving of concurrent processes. In this example of Fig. 8.2, if process A starts first and holds the CD, then process B will not be able to start,

```
Process A
{
semaphoresem_resource;

wait(sem_resource);
use the resource;  //CS
signal(sem_resource);
}
```

Fig. 8.1 Using resource with semaphore

as the CD is held by A. Thus, A will use both resources without any interruption. However, if there is a little change in the sequence of the instructions, the concurrent access of resources may not be as simple as shown in the figure.

It may be possible that B changes the sequence of requesting and releasing of the resources (see Fig. 8.3). It first requests the printer, and then the CD. It releases the CD first, and then the printer. With this change in the code sequence, there will be conflicting demands of both processes. In this scenario of concurrent processes, there may be interleaving of instructions as given in the following space:

1, 1', 2, 2'.

```
Process A
{
semaphoresem_CD;
semaphoresem_Printer;

  1 wait(sem_CD);
  2 wait(sem_Printer);
  3 use the resources;   //CS
  4 signal(sem_Printer);
  5 signal(sem_CD);
}
```

```
Process B
{
semaphoresem_CD;
semaphoresem_Printer;

  1' wait(sem_CD);
  2' wait(sem_Printer);
  3' use the resources;   //CS
  4' signal(sem_Printer);
  5' signal(sem_CD);
}
```

Fig. 8.2 Guarding two resources with two semaphores

```
Process A                          Process B
{                                  {
semaphoresem_CD;                   semaphoresem_CD;
semaphoresem_Printer;              semaphoresem_Printer;

  1 wait(sem_CD);                    1' wait(sem_Printer);
  2 wait(sem_Printer);              2' wait(sem_CD);
  3 use the resources;   //CS       3' use the resources;   //CS
  4 signal(sem_Printer);           4' signal(sem_CD);
  5 signal(sem_CD);                5' signal(sem_Printer);
}                                  }
```

Fig. 8.3   Guarding two resources with two semaphores: Request and release sequence changed

Here, process A has held the CD, and process B has the printer. Then A requests for the printer and is blocked. Similarly, Process B requests for the CD and is blocked. Thus, both processes hold one resource and are waiting for another resource held by the other process. It can be realized here that the system will not progress because both processes wait for an infinite time. This situation is known as a deadlock.

A deadlock can be defined as a situation when a set of concurrent processes in a system request for the resources in such a conflicting manner that there is an indefinite delay in resource allocation. In other words, every process in the system is blocked, and is waiting for the resources held by the other blocked processes. In this manner, no process is releasing any resource and cannot be awakened; therefore, the system is in a deadlock.

Deadlocks may occur with non-pre-emptable consumable resources as well. The consumable resources, like messages once received by a process, are considered as consumed. Fig. 8.4 shows the semaphore as a consumable resource. Another example with messages causing deadlock is shown in Fig. 8.5.

When a set of concurrent processes are in a deadlock situation, the degree of multi-programming in the system decreases. This affects the performance of a system. In turn, it

```
Process A                          Process B
{                                  {
semaphoresem_CD;                   semaphoresem_CD;

  1 wait(sem_CD);                    1 wait(sem_CD);
  2 use the resource;   //CS         2 use the resource;   //CS
  3 signal(sem_CD);                  3 signal(sem_CD);
}                                  }
```

Fig. 8.4   Deadlock using semaphores

```
Process A                          Process B
{                                  {
...                                ...
Receive_msg(B);                    Receive_msg(A);
...                                ...
Send_msg(B, message);              Send_msg(A, message);
}                                  }
```

Fig. 8.5   Deadlock using Messages

causes resource starvation because resources are tied up with deadlocked processes. Thus, deadlock situations are not favourable for a system. Moreover, deadlocks occur not only with user processes, but with OS processes as well. Thus, it becomes essential to identify and handle deadlock situations, whenever they occur, either with user processes or system processes.

It is obvious from the above examples that the problem is in the program, designed for the concurrent processes. Therefore, a careful approach for concurrent programming may avoid deadlocks. A proper ordering of allocation of resources to the processes may also help. There are many ways of handling deadlocks. However, let us first discuss how to model a deadlock, and also the conditions that cause a deadlock in a system.

8.3   MODELLING OF DEADLOCK

The deadlock situation becomes complex when there are multiple processes. It is difficult to find out which process has caused the deadlock. Therefore, a system needs to be represented using the processes and the state of resources in the form of a directed graph. This directed graph, known as a *resource allocation graph* (RAG), is a useful tool to represent the deadlock situation in a system. The RAG follows the following notations and rules:

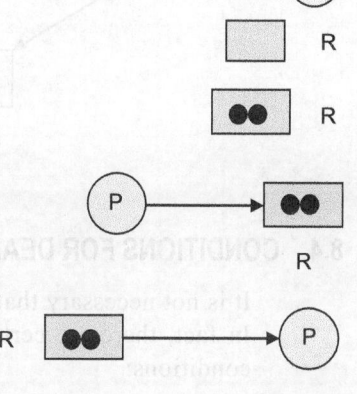

- The processes are represented as circular nodes.

- The resources are represented with a rectangle node.

- The resource node contains some dots to represent the number of instances of that resource type. The number of dots is equal to the number of instances.

- An edge, from a process to a resource, indicates that the process has requested this resource but it has not been allocated. This is known as a *request edge*.

- An edge, from a resource node dot (resource instance) to a process, indicates that one instance of this resource type has been allocated to the process. This is known as an *assignment edge*.

In Fig. 8.6 there are four processes and two resources. R1 has two dots, that is, there are two instances of R1. Similarly, R2 has a single instance. P1 has requested R1, and P3 has requested R2. One instance of R1 has been allocated to P2 and another one to P3. One instance of R2 has been allocated to P4.

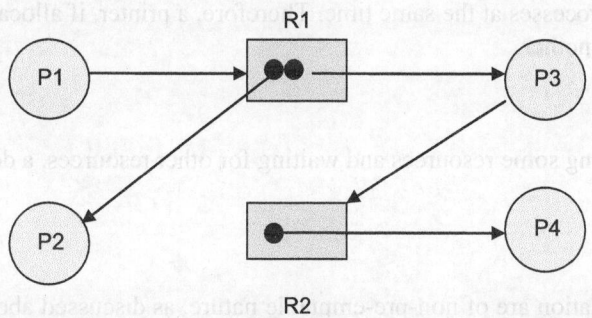

Fig. 8.6   Resource allocation graph

Example 8.1

In a system, the following state of processes and resources are given:

P1→R1, P2→R3, R2→P1, R1→P3, P4→R3, R1→P4

Draw the RAG for the system.

Solution

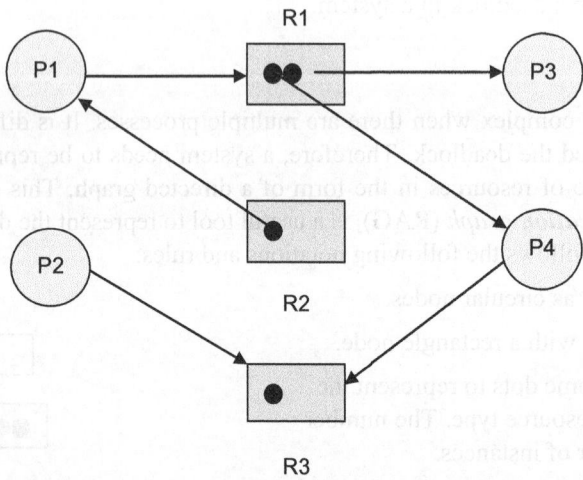

8.4 CONDITIONS FOR DEADLOCK

It is not necessary that a deadlock will always occur in concurrent process environments. In fact, there are certain conditions that give rise to a deadlock. The following are the conditions:

8.4.1 Mutual Exclusion

The resources which require only mutually exclusive access, may give rise to a deadlock. These resource types cannot allow multiple processes to access it at the same time. For example, a memory location, if allocated to a process, cannot be allowed to some other process. A printer cannot print the output of two processes at the same time. Therefore, a printer, if allocated to a process, cannot be allocated to another.

8.4.2 Hold and Wait

When all the processes are holding some resources and waiting for other resources, a deadlock may occur.

8.4.3 No Pre-emption

The resources in a deadlock situation are of non-pre-emptable nature, as discussed above. If a resource cannot be pre-empted, it may lead to a deadlock.

8.4.4 Circular Wait

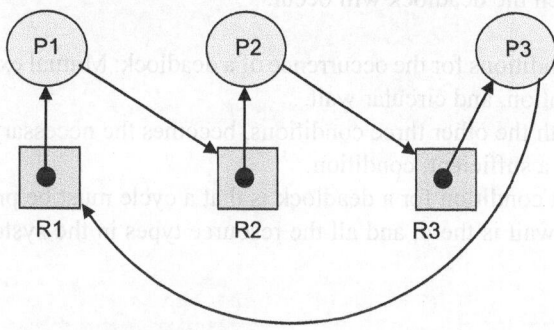

Fig. 8.7 RAG with deadlock

These three conditions together give rise to a fourth condition. A chain of processes may be produced, such that every process holds a resource needed by the next process. In this way, a circular chain of processes is built up in the system, due to mutually-exclusive and non-pre-emptable nature of resources. The RAG shown in Fig. 8.7 depicts a deadlock.

In this way, the four conditions mentioned above, are necessary for a deadlock to occur. In fact, the policies inherent in the first three conditions cause the fourth condition, circular wait.

Example 8.2

In a system, the following state of processes and resources are given:

R1→P1, P1→R2, P2→R3, R2→P2, R3→P3, P3→R4, P4→R3, R4→P4, P4→R1, R1→P5

Draw the RAG for the system and check for deadlock condition.

Solution

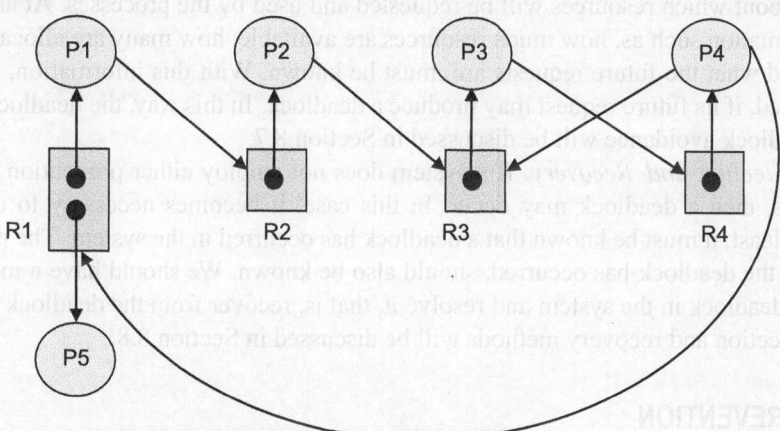

In this scenario, processes P1, P2, P3, and P4 are holding one resource each, and requesting for one more resource, which is held by the next process. From the RAG drawn above, it can be seen that there is a cycle, in the form of circular wait in the graph, thereby, causing a deadlock situation.

In Example 8.2, all the resource types have only a single instance, except R1. There is a possibility that P5 may release the instance of R1, because it does not want any other resource type. In that case, it will be allocated to P4. Consequently, the cycle will break and there will be no circular wait. It means the circular wait is a necessary, but not a *sufficient*, condition for a deadlock. If there are more than one instances of resource and there is a circular wait, there may or may not be a deadlock. Moreover, if each resource type consists of only single instance, and there is a cycle in the graph, then the deadlock will occur.

In general,

Fact 1: There are four necessary conditions for the occurrence of a deadlock: Mutual exclusion, hold and wait, non-pre-emption, and circular wait.

Fact 2: The circular wait, along with the other three conditions, becomes the necessary condition for a deadlock, but not a sufficient, condition.

Fact3: The necessary and sufficient condition for a deadlock is that a cycle must be present in the RAG, that is, a circular wait is there, and all the resource types in the system have only one instance.

8.5 DEALING WITH DEADLOCK

After characterizing the deadlocks, the question is how to deal with them. Every system may be prone to deadlocks in a multi-programming environment, with few dedicated resources. To deal with the deadlock, the following three approaches can be used:

Deadlock Prevention: This method is very idealistic. It is based on the fact that if any of the four necessary conditions is prevented, a deadlock will not occur. Although it is very difficult to achieve this kind of prevention, this method is better, in the sense that the conditions for deadlock will not be allowed to arise in the system. Moreover, a principle is established that a discipline is maintained, while the processes request for the resources. Deadlock prevention will be discussed in Section 8.6.

Deadlock Avoidance: Deadlock prevention is not always possible. Another method to deal with the deadlock is to avoid it. But avoidance is possible when there is complete knowledge in advance, about which resources will be requested and used by the processes. At any instant of time, information such as, how much resources are available, how many are allocated to the processes, and what the future requests are, must be known. With this information, a process may be delayed, if its future request may produce a deadlock. In this way, the deadlock may be avoided. Deadlock avoidance will be discussed in Section 8.7.

Deadlock Detection and Recovery: If a system does not employ either prevention or avoidance methods, then a deadlock may occur. In this case, it becomes necessary to detect the deadlock. At least, it must be known that a deadlock has occurred in the system. The processes, due to which the deadlock has occurred, should also be known. We should have a mechanism to detect the deadlock in the system and resolve it, that is, recover from the deadlock situation. Deadlock detection and recovery methods will be discussed in Section 8.8.

8.6 DEADLOCK PREVENTION

The deadlock prevention method is based on the philosophy-*'prevention is better than cure'*. The advantage of this method is that, it avoids the cost of detecting and resolving deadlocks because this method will make any of the four conditions false and hence, prevent the deadlock. Let us see one by one how any one of the conditions can be prevented.

8.6.1 Preventing Mutual Exclusion Condition

Non-sharable resources require mutually-exclusive access. It would be wrong to think that the mutual exclusion condition can be prevented! Rather, sharable resources should be examined. The reason for this is that, mutual exclusion is an inherent nature of a resource, which cannot be changed. If we have to use a resource among multiple concurrent processes, it has to be used in a mutually-exclusive manner. Otherwise, no process would be able to get the desired output. So, it is impossible to prevent mutual exclusion, but we can recognize resources which are sharable that can help us prevent the deadlock situation in the system. For example, read only files do not require mutually-exclusive access; any process can read this type of file. So, basically mutual exclusion cannot be prevented, but the idea here is to recognize and use sharable resources as much as possible.

8.6.2 Preventing Hold and Wait Condition

To prevent the hold-and-wait condition, two protocols can be used. The first protocol is that, instead of requesting a resource on a need basis, each process should request all its resources at one time, and in advance. No process will be allowed to execute until it gets all of its declared resources. In this way, there will not be any conflict, pertaining to the requesting of resources, and no hold-and-wait condition will be generated in the system. However, this protocol suffers from the following disadvantages:

1. A process may be idle for a long time, waiting for all the resources. This may decrease the degree of multi-programming.
2. Resource utilization will be reduced because all the resources are not used throughout the execution of the process. For example, a process copies some data from the CD to the hard disk and then sends the same for printing. In this case, it needs three resources, that is, the CD drive, hard disk space, and the printer. But if this process gets all the resources altogether, then the printer will be idle most of the time, because it will be used only at the end of the execution.
3. Some frequently-used resources will always be held up with a process, resulting in starvation of other processes.

The second protocol is that a requesting process should not be holding any resource. If a process needs another resource, it must first release the resource it is currently holding. This protocol may reduce the drawbacks of the first protocol to some extent.

8.6.3 Preventing No Pre-emption Condition

This condition is necessary to break because sometimes deadlock can be prevented easily by pre-empting the resources. In this method, if a process, holding some resources already, wants additional resources that are not free, then it should not wait. Rather, it should pre-empt all its resources, so that a deadlock situation can be avoided. After some time, when the resources are free, the process may request all its resources altogether and start the execution. However, there is a disadvantage. Imagine a situation, where a process is using a printer and the printer needs to be pre-empted in between. The problem with this method is that when a process releases its resources, it may lose all its work. Thus, this prevention method should be used with care and with the following guidelines:

1. The pre-emption is based on the execution of the processes. Suppose there are two processes, A and B. Each of them is holding a resource and needs another resource held by the other. This will give rise to a deadlock, if we do not pre-empt any of the resources. If A is about to complete its execution, while B has just started, the resource of B should be pre-empted, such that A finishes its execution without a deadlock.

2. The pre-emption is based on the priority level of the processes. If process B is of higher priority, the resource of process A should be pre-empted, and B should be allowed to complete first.

This method is costlier, in the sense that a process loses all its work and needs to start again. However, it is better and is applied in rare cases only.

8.6.4 Preventing Circular Wait

Since circular wait condition is the consequence of the other three conditions, it can be prevented, if any of these three conditions is prevented. The circular wait can be prevented independently also through *resource-ranking* or *ordering*. Resource ordering is a method, in which every resource type in the system is given a unique integer number as an identification. Whenever a process requests a resource, it is checked whether it holds any other resource. If it does, IDs of both resource types are compared. If the ID of a requested resource is greater than the ID of the resource it holds, the request is valid. Otherwise, it is rejected. Thus, following this resource-ordering, the processes can request resources in an increasing order of their IDs. This specific ordering of requests will not allow the circular wait condition to arise. We can represent resource-ordering as a one-to-one function, given in the following space:

$$F: R \rightarrow I$$

where, R is the set of resource type and I is the set of natural numbers for IDs.

This protocol implies that if a process wants to request a resource type with lower ID as compared to the ID of resource type it holds, it must release all its resources.

The protocol is good enough for preventing the circular wait condition, but at the same time, it is very difficult to implement it practically. Most of the resources are non-pre-emptable, and if they are released in between, in order to acquire other resources, a process will lose its work. The process then needs to acquire these released resources again. In this way, this protocol may lead to a degraded performance of the processes. Some guidelines that may help in implementing this protocol are:

1. The ordering of resource types should be done depending on its use in the system. For example, if a system is using a CD drive and a printer, the printer should be given a higher ID as compared to the CD drive, as it will be used at the end of the processing. Thus, careful numbering of resource types may help.
2. All processes should request the resources with lower ID, in the beginning itself.

Example 8.3

A system uses three types of resources: hard disk, CD drive, and printer. Each of the resource types are allocated an ID, as shown in Fig. 8.8, and processes can request the resources in an increasing order of their IDs, if they are already holding a resource.

In this example, processes P1, P2, and P3 hold and request resources, as shown in the figure. If P3 requests the CD drive or hard disk, the request will be denied, as the ID of these resources is less than the ID of the printer. This will generate a cycle or circular wait condition in the system, thereby, producing a deadlock situation. The problem can be resolved by following the guidelines listed in Section 8.6.4. Thus, this example illustrates that circular wait can be prevented by allocating to resource types and IDs in an increasing order, with the condition that processes will request resources only in an increasing order of their IDs.

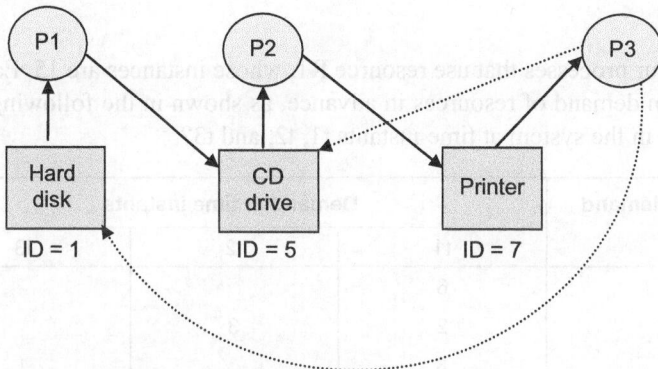

Fig. 8.8   Preventing circular wait

8.7 DEADLOCK AVOIDANCE

Deadlock prevention is used to prevent any of the conditions that cause deadlock. However, it results in degraded system efficiency and low device utilization. Therefore, this method cannot always be implemented.

Another mechanism for avoiding deadlocks is *deadlock avoidance*, which checks in advance, the condition that may give rise to a deadlock. It indicates the state of a system, such that if the request of a process for a resource gives rise to a deadlock condition, it is denied, and must wait. In this way, the deadlock is avoided. If the state of the system is such that it does not lead to a deadlock, then it is known as a *safe state*. The converse, that is, deadlock state is known as an unsafe state. The algorithm is run to check whether the requested resource changes the state of the system. If the resource will lead to an unsafe state, the request must wait, and if it does not affect the safe state, the request is granted. The deadlock avoidance algorithm, in the form of safe state protocol, must be run dynamically, whenever allocating a resource to a process. In this way, deadlock avoidance approach is better than deadlock prevention, because it does not constrain the resources or processes, and there is no system performance degradation or device underutilization.

The avoidance approach requires the knowledge of the maximum demand of all processes, all the resources available, the resources allocated presently, and the future requests of the processes. Whenever a resource request arrives, it is checked for its feasibility. A resource request is feasible, only if the total number of allocated resources of a resource type does not exceed the total number of that resource type in the system. For example, say, the maximum available instances of a resource type are 4. Suppose the current allocated resources are 3. If a request for the resource arrives, it can be granted. However, if another request for the same resource type arrives, it will exceed the total available instances of that resource type, and therefore, this request must be rejected.

With the advance knowledge of system resources and process requests, it is possible to define a safe state, which allows process requests without deadlock. However, if there is no possible safe state, the process is not allocated the resource, and it waits until there is a safe state in the system. For example, in a system there are three processes P1, P2, and P3. There are three resources, the CD drive, the hard disk, and the printer. P1 requires the CD drive and the printer. P2 requires the hard disk and the printer, and P3 requires all three resources. If the sequence of resources and releases for each process is known, the system can be maintained in a safe state.

Example 8.4

Consider a system with four processes that use resource R1, whose instances are 15. Each process declares its maximum demand of resources in advance, as shown in the following space. What will be the situation in the system at time instants t1, t2, and t3?

Process	Maximum demand	Demand at time instants		
		t1	t2	t3
P1	9	6		
P2	4	2	3	
P3	6	3		1
P4	8	2		

Solution

At time instant t1, all processes can be allocated the resources, because each process does not exceed its maximum demand, and the sum of their demands is less than the total number of instances, that is, 15. Further, the system will be in a safe state, because the remaining resource demands of all the processes can be satisfied in a safe sequence P2, P1, P3, P4. At t1, after allocating the current demands, the remaining numbers of instances are 2. So, only P2 can be satisfied at this moment. However, after allocating 2 instances to P2, the process execution will be finished and it will release all 4 instances. So we now have 4 instances, and P1 or P3 can be satisfied. Similarly, the process goes on for other processes, and finally all the processes can be allocated instances of resource without any delay.

At time instant t2, there is a request of 3 more instances from P2. But this will exceed the declared total number of maximum demand of P2. So it is not a feasible request and hence, it would be rejected.

At time instant t3, there is a request for one more instant from P3. This is a feasible request, but the remaining demands cannot be satisfied, and may lead to a deadlock. Since after allocating the demands of resources at t2, we have remaining one instance with which no process can be satisfied, the system may be in a deadlock state.

This example illustrates the fact that some resource request may convert a safe state into an unsafe state. So the idea is to check the state of the system, whenever a process requests for a resource. This will be dealt with in detail, in subsequent sections through deadlock avoidance algorithms. However, one point to be noted here is that an unsafe state does not always lead to a deadlock situation. In the above example, it may be possible that P2 does not demand its remaining resources, but releases all the resources it is holding. In this case, other processes may continue to execute, and there will be no deadlock. This happens only if the processes do not demand the maximum resources required and release their resources for the time being. Therefore, an unsafe state does not always cause a deadlock. But from the system's viewpoint, resources are not allocated to the processes that cause an unsafe state, and they need to wait until there is a safe state.

8.7.1 Deadlock Avoidance for Single Instance of Resources

To avoid a deadlock in a system, where every resource type has a single instance of resource, the RAG can be used again, but along with a new edge, known as *claim edge*. The claim edge is the same as request edge drawn from a process to a resource instance, but this does not mean that the request has been incorporated in the system. It is drawn in dotted lines. The RAG can be used in such a way that when a process requests for a resource, a corresponding claim edge is drawn, and the graph is checked before converting it to a request edge. That is, a process request will not be entertained until the cycle check has been done. After the cycle check, if it is confirmed that there will be no circular wait, the claim edge is converted to a request edge. Otherwise, it will be rejected. In this way, the deadlock is avoided.

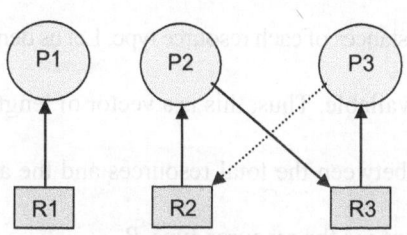

In Fig. 8.9, it can be seen, that if there is a request from P3 for R2, a claim edge is drawn. However, it can be observed that if this request is considered, a cycle will be generated and deadlock will occur. Hence, the request will be denied.

Fig. 8.9   RAG with claim edge

8.7.2 Dijkstra's Banker's Algorithm for Deadlock Avoidance in Multiple Instances of Resources

The RAG-based cycle check cannot be applied when there are multiple instances of resources, because in this case, it is not for certain that deadlock will occur. Therefore, an algorithm is designed to check the safe state, whenever a resource is requested. Dijkstra designed an algorithm, known as the *banker's algorithm*. The algorithm takes analogy of a bank, where customers request to withdraw cash. The banker has some data, based on which, cash is lent to a customer. The banker cannot give more cash than what a customer has requested for, and the total available cash. Similarly, to design the algorithm for checking the deadlock, some data structures are maintained, such that whenever a resource is requested, it can be checked whether the request maintains the safe state of the system. If it does, the request can be granted; otherwise, the process must wait until there are sufficient resources available.

The banker's algorithm has two parts. The first part is a Safety Test algorithm that checks the current state of the system for its safe state. The second part is resource request-handling algorithm that verifies whether the requested resources, when allocated to the process, affect the safe state. If it does, the request is denied. In this way, banker's algorithm avoids the deadlock.

Data Structures

1. *Total resources in a system*
   It stores the total number of resources in a system. Let us denote it as
   $Total\_Res[i] = j$
   It means, there are j instances of resource type R_i in the system. Thus, this is a vector of length r, that is, there are r numbers of resource types.
2. *Maximum demand of a process*
   Whenever a process enters the system, it declares its maximum demand of resources, which is stored in this data structure. Let us denote it as,
   $Max[i,j] = k$
   It means, process P_i has a total demand of k instances of resource type R_j. Thus, this data structure is a $p \times r$ matrix, where p is the number of processes, and r is the number of resource types.

3. *Current allocation of instances of each type of resource*

It indicates the current allocation status of all resource types to various processes in the system. Let us denote it as,

$Alloc[i,j] = k$

It means, process Pi is allocated k instances of resource type R_j. Thus, this is also a $p \times r$ matrix.

4. *Number of available resources*

This data structure stores the current available instances of each resource type. Let us denote it as,

$Av[i] = j$

It means, j instances of resource type R_i are available. Thus, this is a vector of length r, that is, there are r numbers of resource types.

This data structure is, in fact, the difference between the total resources and the allocated resources, that is,

$Av[i] = Total\_Res[i] - \sum_{all\ processes} Alloc[i]$ where i is the resource type R_i.

5. *Current need of a process*

This data structure indicates the current remaining resource need of each process. Let us denote is as,

$Need[i,j] = k$

It means, process P_i may require k more instances of resource type R_j, so that it can complete its execution. Thus, this is a $p \times r$ matrix.

This data structure is, in fact, the difference between the maximum demand of a process and the available resources, that is,

$Need[i,j] = Max[i,j] - Alloc[i,j]$

6. *Request for a process*

$Request_i$ is the vector to store the resource request for process P_i. Let us denote it as $Req_i[j] = k$

It means, process Pi has requested k instances of resource type R_j.

Safety Test Algorithm

Let *Current_Avail* and *Marked* be two vectors of length n and p, respectively. *Safe String* is an array to store the process IDs.

The algorithm is given by:

1. *Current_Avail = Av*
2. Initialize *Marked* as:
   for(i=1; $i<=p$;i++)
       Marked [i] = *false*;
3. Find a process Pi such that
   $Need_i \le Current\_Avail$ and $Marked[i] = false$
4. if(found)
   {
   Current_Avail = Current_Avail+ Alloc_i
   Marked [i] = *true*
   Save the process number in *SafeString*[]
   go to step 3.
   }

5. if($Marked[i] == true$) for all processes, then the system is in safe state.

Print *SafeString*.

Otherwise, the system is not in safe state, and is in deadlock.

Resource Request Handling Algorithm

Let Req_i be the vector to store the resource request for process P_i.

if($Req_i Need_i$)

the request is not a feasible request and is rejected.

elseif ($Req_i > Av$)

Resources are not available, so the process must wait.

Otherwise,

{

Z that the requested resource has been allocated to the process and update the state as:

$Av = Av - Req_i$

$Alloc_i = Alloc_i + Req_i$

$Need_i = Need_i - Req_i$

Execute the *Safety Test Algorithm*, assuming the state has been changed.

if (state is safe)

Change the state in actual and the resource will be allocated to the process.

Otherwise,

Keep the state unchanged and do not allocate the resource to the process.

}

Example 8.5

Consider a system with the following information. Determine whether the system is in safe state.

Total_Res

R1	R2	R3
15	8	8

Process	Max			Alloc		
	R1	R2	R3	R1	R2	R3
P1	5	6	3	2	1	0
P2	8	5	6	3	2	3
P3	4	9	2	3	0	2
P4	7	4	3	3	2	0
P5	4	3	3	1	0	1

With the information given above, let us find the available resources. The number of available resources is calculated by:

$Av[i] = Total\_Res[i] - \sum_{all\ processes} Alloc[i]$, where i is the resource type R_i

Hence, the available resources are:

Av

R1	R2	R3
3	3	2

Next, let us find the *Need* matrix by subtracting *Alloc* from *Max* as given in the following space:

Process	Max			Alloc			Need(Max – Alloc)		
	R1	R2	R3	R1	R2	R3	R1	R2	R3
P1	5	6	3	2	1	0	3	5	3
P2	8	5	6	3	2	3	5	3	3
P3	4	8	2	3	0	2	1	9	0
P4	7	4	3	3	2	0	4	2	3
P5	4	3	3	1	0	1	3	3	2

Now let us execute the Safety Test algorithm to find whether the new state is safe.
Current_Avail = *Av* = [3 3 2]

Marked	
P1	false
P2	false
P3	false
P4	false
P5	false

The sequence of processes should be such that each process satisfies the criteria, *Need≤Current_Avail*. A process, after finishing its execution, must release all the resources it is holding, so that the next process can avail them as per its need. The following table shows the process found, new value of *Current_Avail*, and *SafeString*. Repeat the procedure until all the processes complete their execution.

Process found	Current_Avail	SafeString []	Marked []
P5	[3 3 2] + [1 0 1] = [4 3 3]	P5	*Marked[P5]* = *true*
P4	[4 3 3] + [3 2 0] = [7 5 3]	P5, P4	*Marked[P4]* = *true*
P1	[7 5 3] + [2 1 0] = [9 6 3]	P5, P4, P1	*Marked[P1]* = *true*
P2	[9 6 3] + [3 2 3] = [12 8 6]	P5, P4, P1, P2	*Marked[P2]* = *true*
P3	[12 8 6] + [3 0 2] = [15 8 8]	P5, P4, P1, P2, P3	*Marked[P3]* = *true*

From the table, it can be observed that the *Marked* value for all processes is true. Therefore, the system is in safe state. The *Safe String* of processes is {P5, P4, P1, P2, and P3}, that is, the processes can be scheduled in this order, to have a safe state in the system.

Example 8.6

Consider the Example 8.5and assume that the system is in safe state. At this moment, if P4 requests two more instances of R1 and two instances of R3, will the system still be in safe state? According to the requests made by P4, we have the request vector as:

$$Req_4 = [2\ 0\ 2]$$

Now let us execute the resource request-handling algorithm, to find out whether the request can be granted.

First check that Req_4 is less than $Need_4$. We find that [2 0 2]<[4 2 3].

Next, check that Req_4 is less than Av. We find that $[2\ 0\ 2]\leq[3\ 3\ 2]$.

So, we pretend that we allocate these resources and update the following:

$$Av = Av - Req_4 = [3\ 3\ 2] - [2\ 0\ 2] = [1\ 3\ 0]$$
$$Alloc_4 = Alloc_4 + Req_4 = [3\ 2\ 0] + [2\ 0\ 2] = [5\ 2\ 2]$$
$$Need_4 = Need_4 - Req_4 = [4\ 2\ 3] - [2\ 0\ 2] = [2\ 2\ 1]$$

With the updated data structures, the state will be as given in the following space:

Av

R1	R2	R3
1	3	0

Process	Max			Alloc			Need		
	R1	R2	R3	R1	R2	R3	R1	R2	R3
P1	5	6	3	2	1	0	3	5	3
P2	8	5	6	3	2	3	5	3	3
P3	4	9	2	3	0	2	1	9	0
P4	7	4	3	5	2	2	4	2	3
P5	4	3	3	1	0	1	3	3	2

Now let us check again whether the system is in a safe state.

Current_Avail = Av = [1 3 0]

There is no process whose *Need≤Current_Avail*. Therefore, no process can be started, and thus, this state would be unsafe, if the request for P4 is granted. The unsafe state may lead to deadlock, so the OS should not grant the resources requested by P4, until the system is in a safe state.

Deadlock avoidance is a wonderful algorithm, as it alerts the system in advance that the system is switching from safe state to unsafe state, and that there may be a deadlock situation. But is it really possible to implement this algorithm? The answer is no. One reason is that it is almost impossible to have the knowledge of maximum demand of each process in advance. Without this information, the algorithm cannot be implemented. However, with some analysis on a stable system, the maximum demand of processes for resources can be estimated, and therefore, the deadlock avoidance algorithm can be implemented. Another reason is that in a multi-programming system, the number of processes is not fixed. In a time-sharing system, the processes are dynamic in nature; hence it may not be possible to have all the data structures required for deadlock avoidance algorithm. Another practical problem is the unavailability of resources at the required time. It is important that the resources must be available when a process requests for them, otherwise the algorithm cannot be implemented, even if the system knows in advance the total resources required by the process. Thus, the algorithm, due to these practical reasons, is rarely implemented. There is a lot of scope for researchers to investigate the problems inherent in this algorithm and make possible its implementation in order to avoid the deadlock.

8.8   DEADLOCK DETECTION

Despite its strength to avoid the deadlock, deadlock avoidance algorithm cannot be implemented, due to practical reasons. Thus, if a system is not able to implement neither deadlock prevention nor a deadlock avoidance algorithm, it may lead to a deadlock situation.

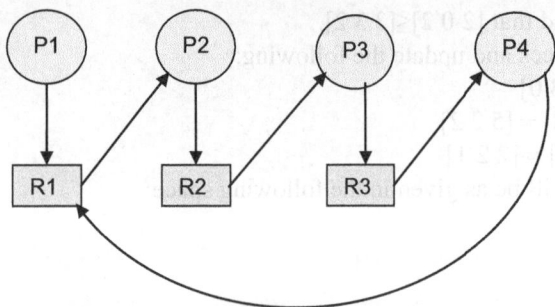

Fig. 8.10   RAG example

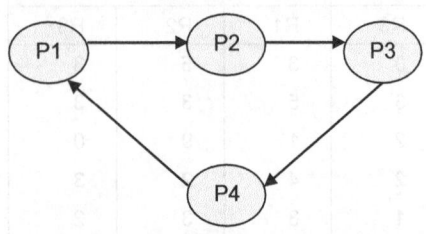

Fig. 8.11   Wait-for graph for Fig. 8.10

However, sometimes it is necessary to detect whether there is a deadlock in the system, and if there is, then which process is causing it. It is better to find the deadlock process, as it helps in recovering from the deadlock. The recovery process is the consequent action of deadlock detection, which will be discussed in the next section.

Deadlock detection algorithm also has two parts, such as avoidance, that is, detection of single instance of resource and detection for multiple instances of resources. Let us first discuss detection algorithm for single instance. But before discussing it, we need to have some modification in the RAG. We will use RAG for detecting the cycle as done in avoidance algorithm. It becomes difficult to store the information of request edge and assignment edge, as it is required to store all these information, in order to make a RAG detect a cycle in it. Therefore, in the graphical representation of RAG, some modification is done and a new graph, known as *wait-for graph*, is formed. In fact, RAG is optimized in wait-for graph by eliminating the resource nodes, and there are only edges between the processes. In Fig. 8.11, the wait-for graph has been shown, corresponding to the RAG shown in Fig. 8.10. There is an edge from P1 to P2, because P1 waits for R1, and R1 is held by P2. Therefore an edge exists between the processes, only if one process waits for another. For example, an edge $P_a \rightarrow P_b$ exists in wait-for graph only if there are edges $P_a \rightarrow R_i$ and $R_i \rightarrow P_b$ in RAG.

To detect the deadlock, it is checked whether the wait-for graph contains a cycle. If it does, there is certainly a deadlock in the system (see Fig. 8.11). In this way, this cycle detection can be done periodically or when required to detect a deadlock in the system.

8.8.1 Deadlock Detection in Multiple Instances of Resource Types

When there are multiple instances of resource types, then cycle detection is not sufficient to detect deadlock in a system. An algorithm, similar to the banker's algorithm, is designed. This will check the system state with some data structures maintained and signal whether the system is in deadlock. The data structures used to detect deadlock are almost the same as in avoidance algorithm. The following data structures are used:

1. *Total resources in system*
   It stores the total number of resources in the system. $Total\_Res[i] = j$
2. *Current allocation of instances of each type of resource*
   It indicates the current allocation status of all the resource types to various processes in the system.
   $Alloc[i,j] = k$
3. *Number of available resources*
   This data structure stores the current available instances of each resource type.
   $Av[i] = j$
   $Av[i] = Total\_Res[i] - \sum_{all\ processes} Alloc[i]$, where i is the resource type R_i.

4. *Request of each process*

This data structure stores the current request of each process in the form of $p \times r$ matrix, where p is the number of processes and r is the number of resource types. Let us denote it as $Req[i,j] = k$

It means, process P_i is requesting k instances of resource type R_j.

Detection Algorithm

Let *Current_Avail* and *Marked* be two vectors of length n and p respectively. *Safe String* is an array to store the process IDs.

1. *Current_Avail = Av*
2. For all $i = 1$ to p,
   Initialize *Marked* as *Marked* $[i] = false$;
   If $(Alloc_i = 0)$
   Initialize *Marked* as *Marked* $[i] = false$;
3. Find a process P_i such that
   $Req_i \leq Current\_Avail$ and *Marked* $[i] = false$
4. if (found)
   {
   *Current_Avail = Current_Avail + Alloc*i
   Marked $[i] = true$
   Save the process number in *Safestring*[]
   go to step 3.
   }
5. if (*Marked*[i] == *true*) is for all processes, then the system is not in deadlocked state.

   Print *Safe String*.
   Otherwise, the system is in deadlock caused by Process P_i.

Example 8.7

Consider a system with the following information. Determine whether the system is in dead-lock situation.

Total_Res

R1	R2	R3
5	6	4

Process	Alloc			Req		
	R1	R2	R3	R1	R2	R3
P1	1	0	2	1	0	0
P2	1	1	0	4	0	2
P3	1	1	0	0	1	2
P4	0	2	1	2	1	0
P5	1	2	0	3	1	4

With the information given above, let us find the available resources. The total number of available resources is calculated by:

$Av[i] = Total\_Res[i] - \sum_{all\ processes} Alloc[i]$, where i is the resource type Ri

Hence, the available resources are:

Av

R1	R2	R3
1	0	1

Now let us execute the detection algorithm.

$Current\_Avail = Av = [1\ 0\ 1]$

Marked	
P1	False
P2	False
P3	False
P4	False
P5	False

The sequence of processes should be such that each process satisfies the criterion, $Need \le Current\_Avail$. A process, after finishing its execution, must release all the resources it is holding, so that the next process can avail them as per its need. The following table shows the process found, new value of *Current_Avail*, and *SafeString*. Repeat the procedure until all the processes complete their execution.

Process found	Current_Avail	SafeString []	Marked []
P1	[1 0 1] + [1 0 2] = [2 0 3]	P1	Marked [P1] = true
P3	[2 0 3] + [1 1 0] = [3 1 3]	P1, P3	Marked [P3] = true
P4	[3 1 3] + [0 2 1] = [3 3 4]	P1, P3, P4	Marked [P4] = true
P5	[3 3 4] + [1 2 0] = [4 5 4]	P1, P3, P4, P5	Marked [P5] = true
P2	[4 5 4] + [1 1 0] = [5 6 4]	P1, P3, P4, P5, P2	Marked [P2] = true

From the table, it can be observed that *Marked* value for all the processes is true. Therefore, the system is not in a deadlock state. The *SafeString* of processes is {P1, P3, P4, P5, and P2}, that is, the processes can be scheduled in this order, and therefore, there will be no deadlock.

Example 8.8

In Example 8.7, if the process requests one additional instance of resource type R2, find out whether the system is in a deadlock state.

Let us see the changed state of the system, with additional request for the resource by P4.

Process	Alloc			Req		
	R1	R2	R3	R1	R2	R3
P1	1	0	2	1	0	0
P2	1	1	0	4	0	2
P3	1	1	0	0	1	2
P4	0	2	1	2	2	0
P5	1	2	0	3	1	4

Everything being same as in previous example, let us find the Safe String

Process found	Current_Avail	Safe String []	Marked []
P1	[1 0 1] + [1 0 2] = [2 0 3]	P1	Marked [P1] = true
P3	[2 0 3] + [1 1 0] = [3 1 3]	P1, P3	Marked [P3] = true
P4	-	-	Marked [P4] = false
P5	-	-	Marked [P5] = false
P2	-	-	Marked [P2] = false

It can be observed that after P3, no process request can be satisfied. Therefore, the system is in deadlock situation, due to processes P4, P5, and P2.

Deadlock detection is a costly algorithm to implement, as it incurs the cost of detecting the state of a system and affects system performance as well. Therefore, it is always a question of how often the algorithm should be run to detect the deadlock. It can be periodic, at regular intervals of time, or at arbitrary times, depending on the system's requirements, such as, if there is a decrease in CPU utilization. If the deadlocks are frequent in a system, it is necessary to run the algorithm periodically, otherwise it can be run on the demand of the system. Deadlocks generally occur when a request cannot be granted immediately. Therefore, it would be a good alternative if the detection algorithm is invoked, every time a process requests for a resource. The detection algorithm checks which process caused the deadlock. However, this solution is expensive, as it increases the overhead of computation time.

8.9   RECOVERY FROM DEADLOCK

The consequent action of deadlock detection is recovery from it. The aim of deadlock detection is to find out which process has caused the deadlock and resolve it, so that the system can resume its work. Imagine two cars approaching each other on a narrow bridge, through which only one car can pass at a time. If no car is ready to move back, then of course there will be deadlock situation forever. This is same as in a no pre-emption condition. So the only solution for resolving the deadlock is for one of the cars to move back (rollback) and allow the other car to pass through the bridge, thereby resolving the deadlock. An OS handles the deadlock in the same way. There should be pre-emption of resources from one process, so that the other process can continue and the deadlock is removed. Another solution is to abort the processes which cause the deadlock. There are various solutions, but each one should be adopted with a lot of care. Rollback or aborting a process cannot be implemented always, as there is a cost incurred in each solution. There are some factors which guide us to choose a particular recovery method. The following are some recovery methods:

8.9.1   Resource Pre-emption

Resource pre-emption is one of the methods with which to break a deadlock. In this method, resources are pre-empted from a process, which has caused the deadlock. These resources are then given to other processes, such that other processes execute their completion and in this way, the deadlock is removed. In other words, no pre-emption condition for deadlock must be broken, wherever applicable. However, there are various issues while adopting this solution. The first issue is to choose a process whose resources can be pre-empted and given to other processes. This decision is driven by the following cost factors:

Number and type of resources a deadlocked process is holding

If the number of resources is less compared to the requirement of other processes to break the deadlock, or if the process is not holding the desired type of resource, then those resources need not be pre-empted.

Execution span of a process

The process with the longest execution span should be pre-empted first. It may be possible that execution of a process is near completion, but it is in deadlock, due to shortage of just one resource instance. In this case, it is not feasible to pre-empt the process. A process, whose execution has just started and requires many resources to complete, will be the right victim for pre-emption.

Starvation of process

Based on the factors above, it may be possible that the same process is always chosen for resource pre-emption, resulting in a starvation situation. Thus, it is important to ensure that the process will not starve. This can be done by fixing the number of times a process can be chosen as a victim.

After resource pre-emption of a deadlocked process, what happens to this process? The process is not able to retain its position in execution, and cannot continue. This process either has to be rolled back or be aborted and restarted. The decision depends on the situation of the processes in the system. Both approaches involve cost. The abort solution involves the cost of execution of the process from the start. Rollback involves the cost of maintaining the checkpoints in the system and rollback to a safe state through the checkpoint.

8.9.2 Rollback

Checkpoints are also a good solution to recover from a deadlock, apart from using it in the resource pre-emption. The checkpoints save the state of a system at specified point in time. The resource state is saved in a separate file, along with the memory image. When a deadlock is detected, the state is analyzed and the deadlock process is detected. Further, the needed resource, which can break the deadlock, is also detected. The process, holding that resource, is rolled back to a safe checkpoint. After allocating the resource to the desired process, the system continues, thereby, recovering from the deadlock. The process, which was rolled back, restarts from the checkpoint.

There is another advantage of using the roll back method. The processes can be rolled back to a safe checkpoint and restarted from that point, such that, there is no deadlock.

8.9.3 Abort the process

Another method to recover from the deadlock is to abort some process, such that there is no deadlock in the system. However, it is a costly solution in terms of process computation. Alternatively, one process can be aborted at a time. After aborting a process, run the deadlock detection algorithm to confirm whether the deadlock still exists. Like resource pre-emption, here too, a victim process is chosen. Of course, the victim process should be such that the system is the least affected and runs without deadlock. There may be many factors to decide the victim process, which are as follows:

Number and type of resources a deadlocked process is holding

If the number of resources is less compared to the requirement of other processes to break the deadlock, it would be a waste, if we abort this process. Similarly, if the desired type of resource is not held by the process to be killed, then there is no use to kill it. Thus, this method is dependent on the number and type of resources the deadlocked process is holding.

Execution span of a process

If a process is just near completion, and is in deadlock, due to requirement of only one resource instance, it is not good to kill this process. A process, which has just started, or requires many resources to complete its execution, will be the right victim for termination. Thus, the execution span of a process may determine the victim process.

Process priority

If the process is of high priority, there is danger in aborting it.

Type of process

Aborting of interacting processes may affect the system's performance, as it will not able to interact with the user. Hence, it is always better to choose batch processes as victim.

8.10 PRACTICAL APPROACH FOR DEADLOCK HANDLING

All the methods, discussed above, can be employed in a system. However, the practical approach for handling deadlocks is to ignore it. Why? All the deadlock-handling strategies are costly to implement. The prevention methods, as discussed, are not applicable on every resource type. Only circular wait condition can be broken. The avoidance algorithm is also limited, because it is not possible to predict the maximum resources required by the processes in advance. The detection algorithm, employed in a system where there are too many processes, incurs cost. Thus a system, which is not mission-critical or business-critical, will ignore the deadlock, instead of employing any of the methods discussed.

However, the deadlock-handling methods have their importance in real-time systems. Real-time systems, where the system must work continuously, cannot afford to ignore the deadlock. Like a PC or any other system, a real-time system cannot reboot or restart, because it may result in data loss. Therefore, all deadlock methods are employed in a real-time system with modifications. Distributed database systems and web systems also require deadlock-handling methods, because they handle a large number of records of various users and websites.

No single method can be employed to handle the deadlock, instead an integrated strategy can be prepared for it. Some steps are given in the following space:

- Assign a resource to a process only when it is needed, that is, a process should not claim the resources in advance. This will reduce resources which need mutually-exclusive access. Mutual exclusion of some devices can also be handled with the help of creation of virtual devices. For example, spooling is used for making a virtual printer, and thereby, preventing the mutual exclusion condition.

- Apply the resource pre-emption, wherever possible. Some of the resources are pre-emptable by nature, for example, memory is a pre-emptable resource. In case of non-pre-emptable resources, depending on the nature of job of a process, there can be a forced pre-emption. For example, if a deadlocked process is using a printer, but the amount of job done by this process is very little, then we can pre-empt the printer forcibly and give it to some other process, so that the deadlock is broken.

- Always use a linear ordering of resource types, so that there is no circular wait, when processes request the resources. It is better to request the resources in an increasing order of their IDs, as discussed in Section 8.6.4.

- Deadlock detection is always a better choice in comparison with avoidance algorithm.

8.11 TWO-PHASE LOCKING

Two-phase locking is a concurrency control method in database deadlocks. In a database system, several processes need to lock the records, and then update them. In this environment, a deadlock may occur very easily. To avoid this type of deadlock, two-phase locking is used. This is done in two phases. In the first phase, known as *growing* or *expanding phase*, a process tries to lock all the records it needs, one at a time. After locking all the records, in the second phase, that is, the *shrinking phase*, it starts updating the records and releases the locks. If the process is unable to lock any of the records in the first phase, it releases all the records it has locked so far. It may start its first phase again and continue the procedure. In this way, two-phase locking and updating avoids the deadlock situation in database systems.

8.12 STARVATION

Starvation has been discussed at many points while discussing concurrent processes. In concurrent processes, starvation is another problem, which is closely related to deadlocks. It results when a process is not able to execute, as it is lacking enough resources due to process-scheduling or resource-scheduling. For example, if a high-priority process always gets the execution over a low-priority process, it causes the low-priority process to starve. To recover from a deadlock, as discussed earlier, the process can be aborted or rolled back repeatedly. This may again cause starvation in the system. Hence, starvation may occur in a system in many ways.

As in deadlocks, when the processes are not able to execute, it is the same case with starvation. The difference is that in deadlock, there is no future execution sequence that can get them out of it. But in case of starvation, there exists some execution sequence that is favorable to the starving process, although there is no guarantee it will ever occur. Thus starvation is not a deadlocked situation, but an indefinite postponement of getting the resources to the processes.

One solution to the problem of starvation in processes with priorities may be to temporarily increase the priority of a low-priority process gradually, so that it may also get the execution. This is known as *aging*. Aging helps lower-priority processes get rid of starvation. In case of starvation resulting from deadlock recovery methods, a complete detail, regarding processes, should be traced, for example, which process was last aborted or rolled back. The same process should not be aborted or rolled back again and again, to avoid its starvation.

SUMMARY

Deadlocks, if not detected properly, can harm a multi-programming system. The four necessary conditions have been discussed in this chapter to understand deadlocks completely. A deadlock is represented through a resource allocation graph (RAG) and wait-for graph. Both graphs have their importance in algorithms designed for deadlock handling. Circular-wait is the most important necessary condition for deadlock occurrence. In fact, it is the result of the first three conditions. If we are able to break the circular wait condition, the deadlock will not occur. A RAG representation easily detects a deadlock through cycle detection, where all resource types have a single instance. In case of multiple instances of resource types, there are other algorithms. Deadlocks can be

handled through prevention methods, that is, to prevent any of the four necessary conditions from occurring. But it may not be possible every time to prevent the necessary conditions. Another method to deal with a deadlock is deadlock avoidance algorithms. It requires information about the resources, processes, and demands of processes in advance and with this knowledge, it indicates whether a deadlock will occur. This approach is not practical, as it is not possible to know in advance the maximum resources required by a process in a system. The third approach to handle the deadlock is to detect it at an appropriate time, and recover from it. The detection algorithm is beneficial, if the system is able to recover from it. If there is no recovery, the system cannot proceed further, and is, therefore, useless. Therefore, the information acquired from the detection algorithm helps in recovering from the deadlock. The last method is to ignore the deadlock. All the methods discussed for deadlock handling are costly in terms of the system's performance.

Let us have a quick review of important concepts discussed in this chapter:

- Deadlocks can be defined as a situation in a system, in which a set of concurrent processes request the resources in such a conflicting manner, that there is an indefinite delay in resource allocation.
- Resource allocation graph (RAG) is a directed graph consisting of nodes and edges that represent the resources requested and held by the processes.
- The four necessary conditions for occurrence of a deadlock are: Mutual exclusion, hold and wait, no pre-emption, and circular wait. The necessary and sufficient condition for a deadlock is that a cycle must be present in the RAG.
- Deadlock prevention is a set of mechanisms, by which at least one of the four necessary conditions cannot hold.
- Deadlock avoidance algorithm indicates whether the state of the system is safe or unsafe. An unsafe state means the deadlock may occur, if the resource request is granted, otherwise it is safe.
- An unsafe state does not always lead to a deadlock situation.
- Deadlock detection algorithm is used to detect deadlocks in the system and the deadlock process.
- RAG is optimized in wait-for graph, by eliminating the resource nodes, and the edges are drawn between processes only.
- Recovery from deadlock can be done through resource pre-emption, roll back, and abortion of the process.

MULTIPLE CHOICE QUESTIONS

1. When a set of concurrent processes are in a deadlock situation, the degree of multi-programming in the system _____
   (a) increases
   (b) decreases
   (c) unaffected
   (d) none

2. RAG is a useful tool to represent a _____ in a system.
   (a) deadlock
   (b) race condition
   (c) resource allocation
   (d) none

3. An edge from a process to a resource in RAG is known as
   (a) assignment edge
   (b) request edge
   (c) claim edge
   (d) none

4. An edge from a resource instance to a process in RAG is known as
   (a) assignment edge
   (b) request edge
   (c) claim edge
   (d) none

5. The method based on future knowledge of process requests, is known as
   (a) deadlock prevention
   (b) deadlock avoidance
   (c) deadlock detection
   (d) none

6. A mechanism, by which we try to constrain the conditions for deadlocks, is known as
   (a) deadlock prevention
   (b) deadlock avoidance
   (c) deadlock detection
   (d) none

7. Which one of the following is not true?
   (a) Safe state means there is no deadlock.
   (b) Unsafe state always leads to a deadlock.
   (c) There are four necessary conditions for a deadlock.
   (d) All resources are not pre-emptable.

8. Which one of the following is correct?
   (a) $Need[i,j] = Av[i,j] - Alloc[i,j]$
   (b) $Need[i,j] = Max[i,j] - Alloc[i,j]$
   (c) $Need[i,j] = Alloc[i,j] - Max[i,j]$
   (d) None

9. To detect deadlock in single instance of resource types, which graph is used?
   (a) RAG
   (b) Wait-for graph
   (c) Directed graph
   (d) None

10. Which one of the following is not a deadlock recovery method?
   (a) Resource pre-emption
   (b) Abort the process
   (c) Rollback
   (d) Hold and wait

11. Deadlock may occur with
   (a) consumable resources
   (b) non-pre-emptable resources
   (c) non-pre-emptable and non-consumable resources
   (d) all of the above

12. Deadlock may occur with
   (a) system processes
   (b) user processes
   (c) both system and user processes
   (d) none of the above

13. Deadlock prevention is ___ possible.
   (a) always
   (b) not always
   (c) sometimes
   (d) none

REVIEW QUESTIONS

1. Give examples of deadlocks with every type of resource.

2. What is the effect of deadlock in a system?

3. What is a RAG? Explain all its components.

4. What are the necessary conditions for occurrence of a deadlock?

5. What is the necessary and sufficient condition for occurrence of a deadlock?

6. Explain all the methods for preventing a deadlock.

7. What is the difference between deadlock prevention and avoidance?

8. How do you use deadlock avoidance with a single instance of resource type?

9. How do you use deadlock avoidance with multiple instances of resource types?

10. What is a claim edge in RAG? What is its use in deadlock avoidance?

11. Explain all the steps in the banker's algorithm.

12. What is the difference between deadlock avoidance and detection?

13. What is the drawback of deadlock avoidance algorithm?

14. What is wait-for graph? Where is it used?

15. How do you use deadlock detection algorithm with a single instance of resource type?

16. How do you use deadlock detection algorithm with multiple instances of resource types?

17. What are the factors which must be considered in resource pre-emption method for recovery from deadlock?

18. What is rollback? What is its importance?

19. What are the guidelines to be followed while rolling back a process?

20. How do you select a victim process to abort a process, while recovering from a deadlock?

21. What is the practical approach for deadlock handling?

22. What is two-phase locking?

23. What is the difference between starvation and deadlock?

BRAIN TEASERS

1. 'Deadlocks are not always deterministic'. Comment on this statement.

2. Prove that circular wait condition may be produced, if all the other three necessary conditions of a deadlock are present in a system.

3. How many operations are required to detect a cycle in a RAG, assuming that there are p number of processes in the system?

4. How many operations are required to check a safe state in banker's algorithm, assuming there are p numbers of processes and r numbers of resources?

5. A system consists of three processes P1, P2, and P3. There is a single resource type *Printer* but with four instances. Each process declares the maximum resource demand of 3 instances. Is deadlock possible in this situation?

6. Can there be a deadlock in the main memory?

7. Demonstrate, with an example, how a safe state may become unsafe.

8. Does an unsafe state always lead to a deadlock? Demonstrate your answer with an example.

9. Name the deadlock handling method that can be applied for the following resource types:
   a) Tape drives b) Files c) Main memory d) Semaphores
   d) Disk space

10. Check whether a deadlock is present in the following:
    a) Two processes with two files
    b) Two processes access and lock database records
    c) Three processes with CD drive, printer, plotter

11. There is no practical use of deadlock avoidance approach. How can we benefit from this algorithm?

12. In a multi-programming and multi-user environment, the processes are dynamic, that is, the new users, and therefore, their processes log in and log out frequently. Does it affect the implementation of deadlock detection algorithm?

13. How do you recover a process from deadlock through roll-back, if it has updated some data in a website?

14. In a system, the following state of processes and resources is given:
    R2→P1, P1→R2, P2→R3, R1→P2, R3→P3, P3→R4, P4→R3, R4→P4, P4→R1, R1→P5

    Draw a RAG and wait-for graph for the system, and check the deadlock condition.

15. Consider a system with the following information. Determine whether the system is in safe state.
    Total_Res

R1	R2	R3	R4
10	5	7	8

Process	Max				Alloc			
	R1	R2	R3	R4	R1	R2	R3	R4
P1	4	2	0	2	4	2	0	2
P2	1	0	0	0	1	0	0	0
P3	3	1	2	1	0	1	3	1
P4	1	0	2	0	0	0	0	0
P5	0	1	1	3	1	0	1	2

Determine whether the system will be in safe state, if a request arrives from the following processes:
a) P1 requests two instances of R2, and one of R4.
b) P3 requests one instance of each resource type.
c) P5 requests one instance of R1, two instances of R3, and one instance of R4.

16. Consider a system with the following information. Determine whether the system is in a deadlock situation.

Total_Res

R1	R2	R3
8	5	7

Process	Alloc			Req		
	R1	R2	R3	R1	R2	R3
P1	1	0	2	1	0	0
P2	0	0	0	0	1	1
P3	2	1	1	2	0	0
P4	1	1	0	1	0	1
P5	2	2	2	1	1	0

17. Five processes are competing for resources R0, R1, R2, and R3 where (R1, R2, R3, R4) = (6, 4, 4, 2). The maximum claim of these processes and the initial resources allocated to these processes, are given in the following space:

Processes	Max				Alloc			
	R1	R2	R3	R4	R1	R2	R3	R4
P1	3	2	1	1	2	0	1	1
P2	1	2	0	2	1	1	0	0
P3	1	1	2	0	1	1	0	0
P4	3	2	1	0	1	1	1	0
P5	2	1	0	1	0	0	0	1

Does this initial allocation lead to a safe state? Explain with reason.
If P2 requests two instances of R1, one instance of R3, and one instance of R4, check whether the system is still in safe state. If it is, find out the safe sequence of process execution.

18. Explain the deadlock and starvation problems in dining-philosophers' problem.
19. Why can deadlock not happen in two-phase locking?
20. Two-phase locking can lead to starvation. How?
21. What will be the consequences of a deadlock in a real-time system?
22. What are the strategies that can be employed to handle deadlock in a real-time system?

9 Multi-threading

9.1 INTRODUCTION

In Chapter 1, many basic concepts of operating systems were discussed. The process concept described in previous chapters always contains a single thread. However, a process may also contain several threads giving rise to the concept of multi-threading. Multi-threading is implemented in modern operating systems for fast responsiveness and better efficiency. In this chapter, the difference between a process and a thread has been explained keeping in view why threads are required. All the issues related to the thread implementation have been discussed throughout the chapter.

9.2 PROCESS AND THREAD

In chapter 5, while learning the basic concepts of process management, it was established that the context switch time is proportional to the frequency of interrupted processes. If a running process is interrupted, theOS must save the context of that process and load the context of the next scheduled process. This context switch time incurs overhead in terms of the system's performance as no useful work is performed by the processor during this time. If the processes are interrupted frequently, the context switch time increases, thereby giving rise to a high overhead. This was the reason that in round robin process scheduling, the time quantum was not chosen as too short. A small time quantum will interrupt the processes very frequently causing more context switches of processes and thereby resulting in high overhead.

Learning Objectives

After reading this chapter, you should be able to understand:

- Difference between a process and a thread
- Difference between Multi-tasking and Multi-threading
- Thread control block and its fields
- Usage of multi-threading concept
- User threads
- Kernel threads
- Hybrid threads
- Thread Recycling
- Thread Pooling

Besides the frequent process switching, there is another factor that adds to the overhead. The factor is that a process is considered not only a unit of computation but also a unit of resource scheduling, resource accounting, and so on. The state saved in the PCB related to resource ownership increases the size of the PCB, thereby increasing the overhead. The more the information in the PCB the more time it will take in saving and restoring it. Thus, the context switch time is a problem in process management.

The context switch time can be reduced by reducing the information stored in the PCB. However, it is not possible to ignore the information for the sake of reducing the overhead. There is another solution. To elaborate the solution, let us take an example of a web server and client system. A web server needs to provide service to multiple clients concurrently. To meet this requirement, web server runs as a single process and then creates multiple processes that accept the clients' requests. Whenever a request is received by the server, it creates a new process. In this multi-programming environment, there are multiple processes serving various users accessing the web server, and there is process switching, which causes context switch overhead. The saved context of the current process and the restored context of the next scheduled process differ in the least. Both contexts differ only in their contents of CPU registers, PC value, and stack. Other information in both the processes is same. The reason is that all the processes have been created by the server process and share the code section, data section, and other resources. If the code and data section of two processes are same, then it is redundant to store and restore the same thing. This type of redundancy leads to high context switch overhead. If this is eliminated, then the context switch time can be drastically reduced.

To implement this solution, the concept of the thread is used. A process when scheduled for execution has a control thread known as thread of execution. Each process has a single thread of execution as shown in Fig. 9.1. When a client process requests the web server, the server creates its child processes. Every child process has same code section and data section as that of the parent process shown in Fig. 9.2. This way, the concurrency is achieved through multiple processes, but this process model has a high overhead as discussed in Section 9.2. In this sense, a process is also known as a *heavy weight process*.

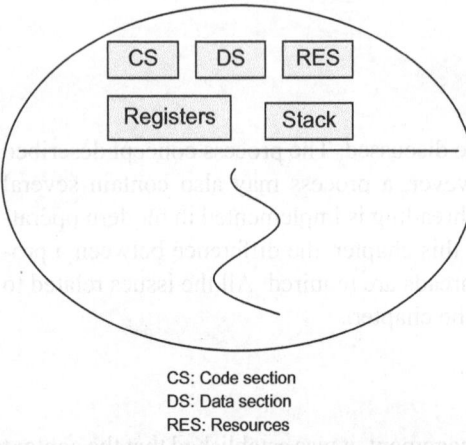

CS: Code section
DS: Data section
RES: Resources

Fig. 9.1 Process as a single thread of execution

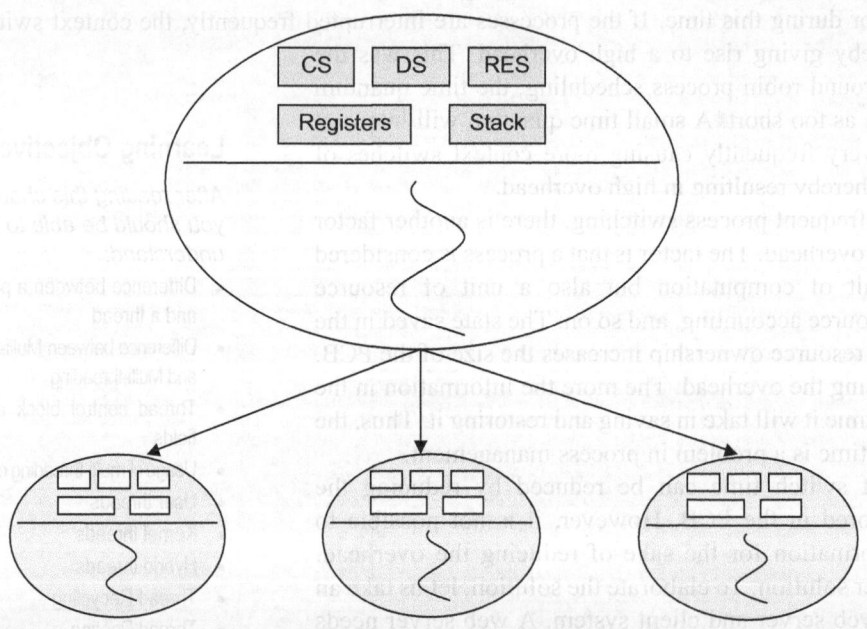

Fig. 9.2 Web server process divided into child processes

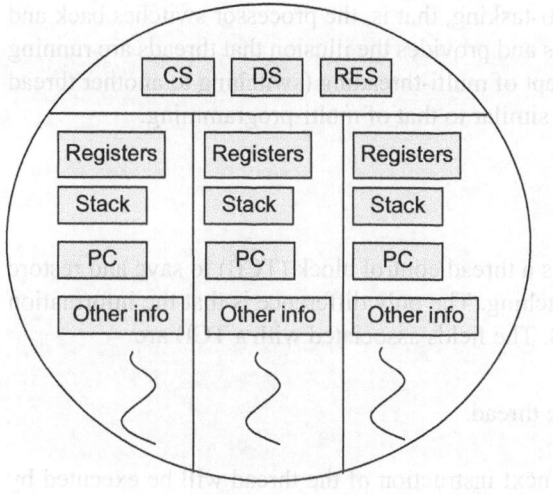

Fig. 9.3   A process divided into three threads of execution

If the functions of various child processes of web server are implemented as multiple threads of execution under a single (parent) process, then saving and restoring the redundant information can be avoided. In other words, threads of the same process share the code, data, and resources of the process. Therefore, a thread is a unit of concurrency within a process because it implements the various functions of the process and shares the address space as shown in Fig. 9.3. Therefore, whenever there is a need to switch between the threads of the same process, the context of a thread will be saved and restored in the form of its PC, CPU registers, and stacks, that is, code and data section are not part of the context of a thread. In this sense, a thread is known as a *light weight process* (LWP). There is no need to save or restore the code section, data section, or state of the resources. The code, data, and resource state is with the process only, but execution of a process is in the form of threads. This drastically reduces the context switch overhead.

The process concept is unaffected by the implementation of threads within it. A process still exists with its environment with code, data, stack, CPU registers, and PC. In addition, it has multiple threads that perform their designated tasks sharing the code section, global data, and resources of the process. Every thread consists of the following information that is not shared with a process:

Processor registers
Every thread works on its designated processor registers. Therefore, when there is a thread switch, these must be saved and restored.

Stack
Every thread has its own stack. Each frame of the stack stores local variables and returns address of the procedure called by the thread. It may be user stack or kernel stack depending on the type of the thread.

PC
Every thread has unique program counter value so that they execute independently.

Other info
The thread has some other unique information such as its state, priority, and so on.

9.3   MULTI-TASKING VS MULTI-THREADING

The concept of implementing multiple threads to achieve concurrency within a single process is known as *multi-threading*. This term should not be confused with multi-tasking or multi-user systems. Multi-user and multi-tasking, as discussed in Chapter 1, are similar as they both are implemented at the level of a process. Multi-threading, on the other hand, is implemented at the thread level. This is the major difference between multi-tasking and multi-threading. However, multi-threading works the same way as multi-tasking, that is, the processor switches back and forth among the threads as with the processes and provides the illusion that threads are running in parallel. In other words, the original concept of multi-threading (switching to another thread when one thread needs to wait for an I/O) is similar to that of multi-programming.

9.4 THREAD CONTROL BLOCK

Just like the PCB, in multi-threading, there is a thread control block (TCB) to save and restore the context of a thread in case of thread switching. The only difference is that the information in the TCB is lesser as compared to the PCB. The fields associated with a TCB are

1. **Thread ID (TID)**
   It is a unique identification number of the thread.
2. **PC**
   Indicates the address value at which the next instruction of the thread will be executed by the processor.
3. **Registers**
   CPU registers are used for the execution of a thread. While the thread is in execution, data registers, address registers, control registers, and status registers are used for executing and controlling the process. The information in registers must be saved when there is a change in the state of the threads so that it may resume its execution in its next turn.
4. **State**
   A thread also has a number of states just like a process. For scheduling the threads, the current state of a thread must be known.
5. **Priority**
   A priority number may be assigned to a thread as provided to a process.
6. **Event information**
   This is the event for which a blocked process is waiting. If the awaited event is over, the information regarding this event must be stored in this field so that the status of the blocked process is changed to ready.
7. **Information related to scheduling**
   The information related to scheduling of a thread, such as the waiting time and the execution span of the thread the last time it was running, is also stored.
8. **Pointer to owner process**
   The thread will be created within a process and it needs to access the execution environment of its owner process. Thus, the TCB contains a pointer to this information.
9. **TCB pointer**
   This is a pointer to another TCB that is used to maintain the scheduling list.

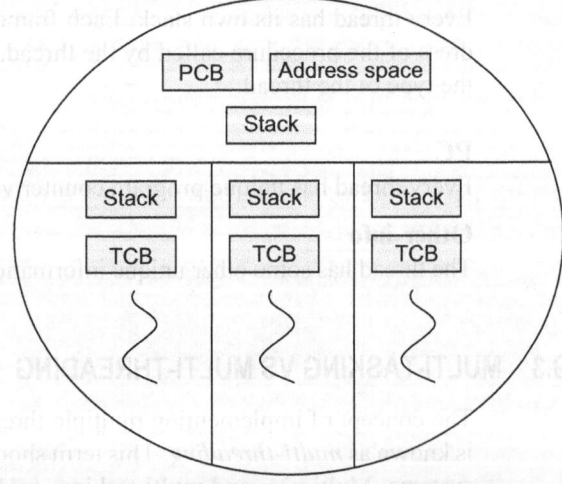

Fig. 9.4 Process's threads each with their stack and TCB

In a multi-threaded process environment, the process image is same as described in Chapter 5, but every thread within the process consists of its stack and TCB. Let us take an example. Suppose there are three threads in a process. Each thread contains its stack and TCB as shown in Fig. 9.4. The process has its address space, stack, and PCB as discussed in process image. It means that the process and its data structures are unaffected by the introduction of multiple threads but by the advantage that now there is no need to switch between various processes because the functions of these processes have been implemented within the process through the multiple threads.

9.5   USAGE OF MULTI-THREADING

The following are the usages of multi-threading:

1. **Low context switch overhead**

   This is the primary benefit of implementing multi-threading. In thread switching, the information to be saved and retrieved is less as compared to the process switching. Low context switch overhead increases the degree of concurrency and thereby improves the performance of the system.

2. **High computation speed up**

   Due to less information in the TCB and low context switch overhead, there is a tremendous increase in computation speed. As compared to the single-threaded process model, the computation speed up is high, even on a uni-processor system. On a multi-processor system, the concurrency can be increased further if the threads are executed in parallel.

3. **No need of IPC**

   Unlike the processes in a multi-programming environment, the threads in a multithreaded process do not require system calls to communicate with each other. This is because they share the code and data section of the process. Thus, it saves cost and time resulting in a high speed up.

4. **Decreased response time**

   As a consequence of the increased computation speed, the response time to a user decreases inspite of the execution of many other tasks. For example, in a multithreaded web server, every client gets immediate response due to a dedicated thread corresponding to each client.

5. **Sharing of resources**

   All the threads share the resources allocated to their owner process. Since the state of resources is maintained by the process, limited resources are utilized without maintaining their state.

6. **Efficient management**

   It is easy and economical in terms of memory and speed to create and destroy a thread as compared to a process. Some examples are as follows:

   (a) In UNIX, thread creation is 10 times faster than process creation. Similarly, it takes less time to terminate a thread as compared to a process termination.

   (b) In Solaris 2, thread creation is 30 times faster than process creation.

   It is easy to manage multiple activities within a process in the form of threads at a very low cost as compared to multiple-process creation because multi-threading comes with the advantage of low context switch overhead, no IPC, and zero state management of code and global data.

It may seem that a process and a thread have same effect in the system. In the case of a web server, either processes or threads can be used to serve the clients. Therefore, to a programmer, it is not clear when to use the multiple threads within a process. The following guidelines help to decide when multi-threading is to be used:

(a) The application will obviously be first divided into multiple processes. However, in the next stage, observe closely whether some or all the processes are using the same code and data section and their functions are same in the application. This guideline is similar to the example of the web server application discussed earlier. The web server needs to serve various clients for which it creates various processes whenever a client connection is established. Here, it can be observed that each process will use the same code and data section of the web server process and has the same function: to serve the clients' requests. For this type of applications, it is costly to create multiple processes as there will be high context switch overhead and more time will be taken to manage them. On the other hand, multiple threads within the web server process share the code section, data section, and resources of the process.

(b) There are several tasks inside a process, which if performed by a single thread of control, may affect its performance. These tasks if executed in parallel will enhance the speed of computation of the whole process. For example, a web browser performs several tasks: accepts request from the user, communicates with the server, displays an image on the screen, and so on. If the browser is a single-threaded process, some functions will be delayed. If the browser is currently displaying an image, and at the same time the user tries to enter his or her request, either the image will not be displayed or the response to the request will be delayed. Thus, if there are multiple functions in an application that can be run in parallel, multiple threads should be used.

(c) Some applications are highly interactive. If these applications are designed as a single-threaded process, the response time will be longer. To provide user with a quick response, the application must be designed as multithreaded. In a single-threaded process, only one user request can be served at a time, thereby delaying the response time. The Word or spreadsheet applications where the user expects a quick response should be designed as multithreaded. In Word application, while the user is typing the text, one thread should be there to accept the keyboard commands and text so that the user is able to see what he or she is typing. Another thread, known as *spell checker*, checks the typed texts for spelling. Similarly, there is a reformatting thread to perform functions such as deleting or changing the document setup. If any of the tasks is missed or delayed, the user will not get the desired performance from the application. This is the reason that all these tasks must be performed in the form of threads so that they can be performed concurrently.

As discussed, each thread has its own purpose in the application. Not all the threads are interactive. For example, in Word application, one thread serves the purpose of saving the contents of the Word file, that is, periodically saving the contents from RAM to disk. However, according to the guideline, the application with more interactive functions must be designed as a multithreaded application.

9.6 TYPES OF THREADS

As with the process model, threads can also be of two types:
1. User threads
2. Kernel threads

Let us discuss these in detail.

9.6.1 User Threads

The user threads are are managed by the application in user space. By default, an application starts running with a single thread of control, that is, as a process managed by the kernel. However,, the application may spawn new threads based on the requirements of the process. These threads are created and managed through a thread library provided by the OS so that application programmer need not write the routine for thread management. The thread library or thread package consists of the following functions related to the thread management:

- Thread creation and deletion
- Assigning priorities to the threads
- Thread scheduling
- Thread synchronization
- Communication between the threads
- Saving and restoring contexts of the threads
- Blocking and resuming the threads

These procedures need to be invoked by a procedure call, and the control is passed to the called procedure. However, these library procedures cannot directly execute privileged instructions or access kernel primitives. The thread management is quite similar to process management. A user thread, as discussed, is managed through the library functions. First of all, a process spawns a thread by calling a procedure. The thread-related data structures are then stored in the TCB. The process needs to keep track of all the threads within it. Therefore, just like the process table discussed in Chapter 5, a *thread table* is maintained. The thread table contains entries as a pointer to the TCB of each thread. Thus, each process in the application has its own thread table as shown in Fig. 9.5. Now, suppose a thread is running and it comes across an instruction for waiting for some resource. In this case, the library procedure is called that puts the running thread into a blocked state by saving its context in its TCB. The scheduling

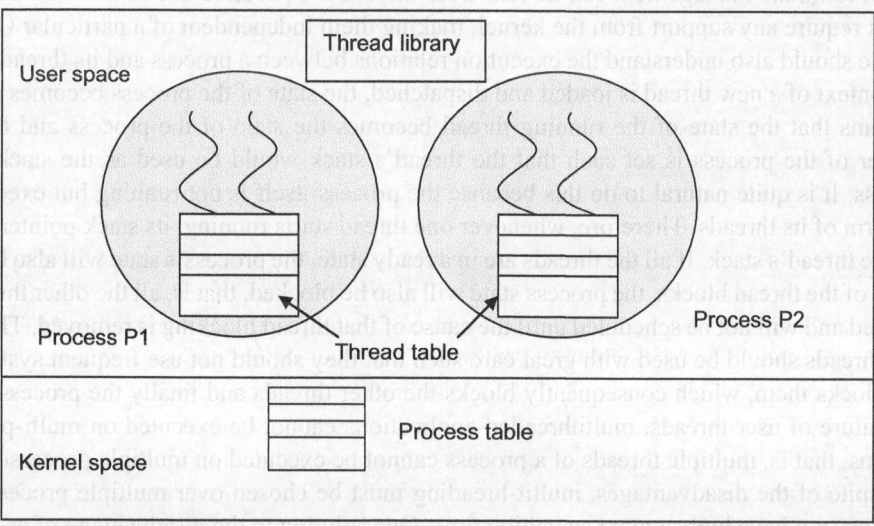

Fig. 9.5   User threads

is performed among ready threads and the context of the selected thread is loaded and it starts running. One can easily realize that all the functionalities related to thread management are same as that of process management.

The library procedures invoked for thread management in user threads are local procedures. There is no need to interface with the kernel, which is timeconsuming, and scheduling consumes less time to call and execute the local procedures. Moreover, the context of a thread to be saved and restored is lesser as compared to a process. Thus, creating and managing user threads are easy and much faster compared to a process and a kernel thread. Kernel threads will discussed in Section 9.6.2.

The point to be noted here is that all the thread-management activities are run in user space, that is, the kernel is not aware of them. It is concerned with the management of processes within the application as shown in Fig. 9.5. The kernel schedules and manages these processes in the kernel space without knowing the existence of multiple threads within each process. Therefore, the OS provides a single execution context to all the threads instead of each thread. This user-level thread implementation is known as *many-to-one* mapping as the OS maps all threads in a multithreaded process to a single execution context. Due to this, the process will get blocked as soon as a thread gets blocked. The multithreaded process consisting of user threads is responsible for maintaining thread-state information, scheduling threads within the process and synchronizing them as well.

Since the threads are part of a process, there will be some relation between process scheduling and thread scheduling. Suppose there are three processes, P1, P2, and P3, in an application. Each process consists of two threads. Some of the events in scheduling are shown in Table 9.1.

It is clear from Table 9.1 that the thread scheduling is application-specific. Taking the advantage of this concept, the scheduling algorithms can be tailored according to the need of the application without affecting the kernel scheduler. Therefore, it is not necessary that a thread scheduler will work only on one algorithm. One application may adopt round robin, whereas another may run priority-based scheduling algorithm. In fact, user threads can run on any type of OS. User threads do not require any support or modification in the underlying OS. The reason is that there is a thread library (shared by all applications) using which all the functions related to thread management can be run. User threads are portable due to their nature as they do not require any support from the kernel, making them independent of a particular OS.

One should also understand the execution relations between a process and its threads. When the context of a new thread is loaded and dispatched, the state of the process becomes running. It means that the state of the running thread becomes the state of the process and the stack pointer of the process is set such that the thread's stack would be used as the stack for the process. It is quite natural to do this because the process itself is not running but executing in the form of its threads. Therefore, whenever one thread starts running, its stack pointer is set to run the thread's stack. If all the threads are in a ready state, the process's state will also be ready. If any of the thread blocks, the process state will also be blocked, that is, all the other threads are blocked and will not be scheduled until the cause of that thread blocking is removed. Therefore, user threads should be used with great care such that they should not use frequent system calls that blocks them, which consequently blocks the other threads and finally the process. Due to this nature of user threads, multithreaded applications cannot be executed on multi-processor systems, that is, multiple threads of a process cannot be executed on multiple processors.

Inspite of the disadvantages, multit-hreading must be chosen over multiple process model as it does not have high context switching time. One solution to the disadvantage of user thread is to convert a blocking-system call executed by a thread into a non-blocking call. Instead of

Table 9.1 Relation between process scheduling and thread scheduling

Event	Process P1			Process P2			Process P3		
	Process state	Thread1 state	Thread2 state	Process state	Thread1 state	Thread2 state	Process state	Thread1 state	Thread2 state
Process P2 is scheduled and starts executing. Thread1 of P2 is scheduled to run by the thread scheduler.	Ready	Ready	Ready	Running	Running	Ready	Ready	Ready	Ready
Thread1 of P2 executes an I/O instruction, thereby causing it to wait for a resource.	Ready	Ready	Ready	Blocked	Blocked	Ready	Ready	Ready	Ready
Since P2 is blocked in the previous event, scheduler selects next ready process, that is, P1, and thread scheduler selects thread2 of P1.	Running	Ready	Running	Blocked	Blocked	Ready	Ready	Ready	Ready
Time slice of P1 expires.	Ready	Ready	Ready	Blocked	Blocked	Ready	Ready	Ready	Ready

directly calling a system call, an I/O routine known as *jacket routine* is called from the thread library. This jacket routine checks whether the I/O device is busy. If it is, then it becomes a blocking call. Therefore, it will not be executed and the control is passed to another thread within the process so that it is not blocked. If the device is not busy, then the system call is executed and the process is not blocked. This technique of checking the status of devices through an application-level jacket routine is known as *jacketing* or *wrapping*.

9.6.2 Kernel Threads

The kernel threads are managed by the kernel. Unlike user threads, there is no library routine facility. Kernel threads, implemented in the kernel space, are managed through system calls. Operations such as thread creation, deletion, context saving and restoring, synchronization, and so on are implemented through system calls. It is obvious that threads are implemented within a process, but there is no separate thread table corresponding to each process as in user threads. Here, all the threads are managed through a single thread table maintained in the kernel space as shown in Fig. 9.6. The thread table stores the same information as described for user threads. Thus, the kernel maintains a thread table in the kernel space, along with the process table to keep track of the processes. This concept eliminates the drawback of many-to-one mapping in user threads because the OS maps each thread to its execution context. Thus, there is a *one-to-one mapping* in kernel threads as shown in Fig. 9.7. The OS, to implement this type of mapping, provides each user thread with a kernel thread that it can dispatch. The user process requests a kernel thread using a system call and in turn the OS creates a kernel thread that executes user thread's instructions.

Since both process table and thread table are in the kernel space, there is a difference in thread scheduling of each kernel thread. The scheduler in the kernel schedules a thread on occurrence of an event. It is not necessary that the thread will be scheduled from the same process; it may be scheduled from any other process. The kernel checks whether the selected thread belongs to the same process as that of the interrupted thread or to a different process. If the thread is of the same process, then there is no issue and the kernel dispatches the thread for execution. However, if the thread belongs to a different process, then it saves and loads the context of the process to which the selected thread belongs and then dispatches it.

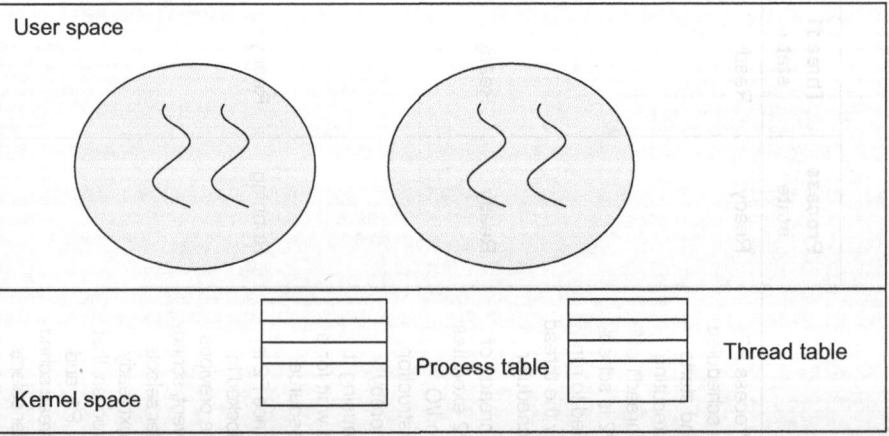

Fig. 9.6 Kernel threads

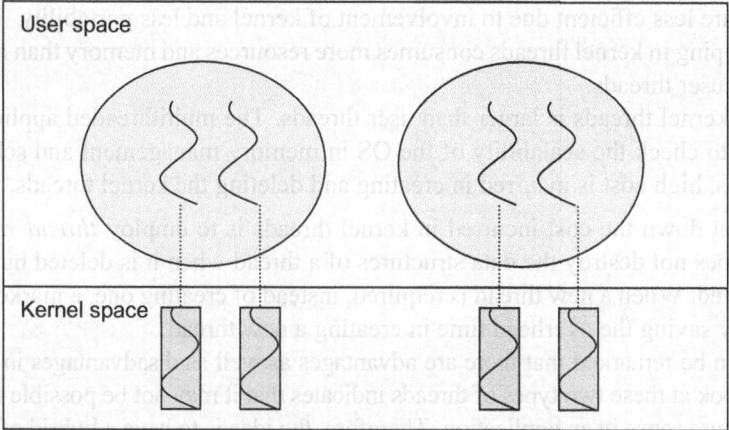

Fig. 9.7 One-to-one mapping in kernel threads

It can be realized that kernel threads are like processes because they interact with kernel as processes do. The kernel threads use system calls for any I/O requirement similar to the processes. Whenever there is a thread switching, the control is transferred from one thread to another by the kernel at the cost of a context switch. Thus, kernel threads make use of system calls and incur context switch overhead in thread switching within the same process. This increases the operational latencies of kernel threads, thereby making them slower compared to user threads. Thus, comparing processes, user threads, and kernel threads in terms of their operation latencies, it can be concluded that user threads have the lowest latency, followed by kernel threads and the processes are slower compared to both the types of threads.

Due to the design of kernel threads, the kernel is now able to schedule multiple threads of the same process on a multi-processor system. The OS recognizes each thread individually as the thread table is managed only by the kernel. Therefore, each thread can be prioritized depending on its service type. If a thread is interactive in nature, it should be given high priority compared to other threads. Thus, the OS may assign priority number to each of its threads. In addition, if a thread is blocked, it is possible to schedule another thread of the same process, that is, blocking a thread does not block the process. This improves the interactivity and efficiency of applications. Thus, kernel threads overcome the disadvantages of user threads.

9.7 HYBRID THREADS

After studying both types of threads, the question is how to select a type.

Let us first discuss the differences between user threads and kernel threads:

1. Due to short latencies, user threads are faster to execute. Kernel threads, on the other hand, are slower to execute.
2. Unlike kernel threads, user threads do not support priority-based scheduling. Therefore, if one user thread blocks, then the whole process blocks. The scheduler will not select another thread from that process even if it is of higher priority and may select a lower-priority thread from another process.
3. Since user threads do not support priority scheduling, it cannot be employed in a real-time system. A real-time system demands execution of all the high-priority processes and threads, whatever be the case.

4. Kernel threads are less efficient due to involvement of kernel and less portability.
5. One-to-one mapping in kernel threads consumes more resources and memory than many-to-one mapping in user threads.
6. The number of kernel threads is larger than user threads. The multithreaded application in this case needs to check the scalability of the OS in memory management and scheduling techniques. Thus, high cost is incurred in creating and deleting the kernel threads.

One approach to cut down the cost incurred in kernel threads is to employ *thread recycling*. Thread recycling does not destroy the data structures of a thread when it is deleted but instead marks them as deleted. When a new thread is required, instead of creating one, a marked thread is activated, thereby saving the overhead time in creating a new thread.

In this way, it can be remarked that there are advantages as well as disadvantages in both the threads. A critical look at these two types of threads indicates that it may not be possible to implement them in their pure sense in an application. Therefore, the idea is to have a hybrid of both the threads that combines the good features of both of them. In other words, instead of having many-to-one (user threads) or one-to-one thread mapping (kernel threads), it is better to have a combination of both, that is, *many-to-many thread mapping*. However, it depends on the nature of threads designed in an application to decide which mapping should be used. Threads that cannot be used concurrently should use many-to-one mapping because only one execution context is needed. Similarly, the threads that exhibit concurrency may use one-to-one mapping because separate execution context per thread is needed. In this combined approach, the application specifies the number of kernel threads required. For example, in Fig. 9.8, Processes P1 and P2 need two kernel threads and P3 needs only one. However, note that two threads, T1 and T2, of Process P1 have been mapped to a single-kernel thread. This decision about where the thread should be mapped depending on its purpose is taken by a programmer. P1 has many-to-one as well as one-to-one thread mapping, P2 has one-to-one mapping, and P3 has many-to-one mapping. Thus, multiple user-level threads of an application can be mapped to some or all kernel-level threads, taking the advantage of both the types of thread mapping. The overall advantage is that some threads may run in parallel on multi-processor systems and there is no need to block the whole process if one thread blocks. Moreover, due to the reduction in the number of kernel threads, less memory is consumed.

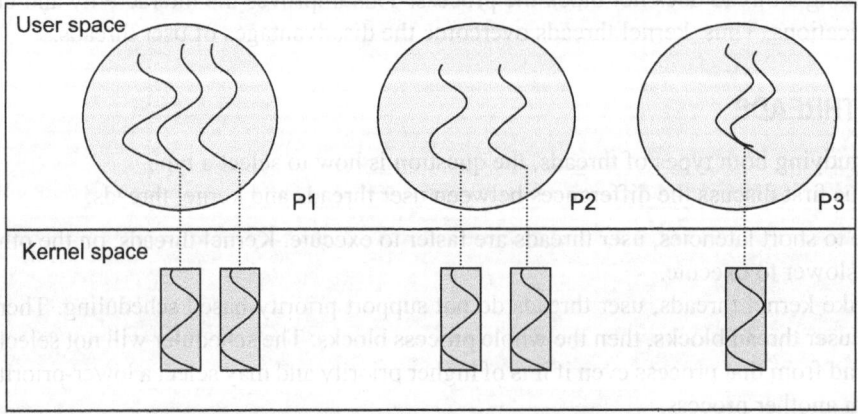

Fig. 9.8 Hybrid threads

9.8   THREAD OPERATIONS AND OTHER ISSUES IN THREAD IMPLEMENTATION

The thread operations correspond to process operations. All operations, such as create, terminate, suspend, resume, and so on, are also used in thread implementation. However, due to the differences in implementation of a process and a thread, the thread creation and termination are always faster when compared to process creation and termination.

A process or a thread may be terminated prematurely. There may be several reasons for cancellation of a thread, for example, illegal memory reference causing an exception is cancelled or a user wants to stop loading a web page. In general, a thread can be cancelled by *asynchronous cancellation method*, that is, the thread is cancelled immediately. However, if a thread that is modifying a shared variable is cancelled, then it may give an erroneous result. Therefore, for thread cancellation, some OSs choose another alternated method known as *deferred cancellation*. In this method, a *target thread* to be cancelled may periodically check when it should be cancelled. For this purpose, the target thread masks the cancellation signals except the abort signal while it is performing an operation that should not be interrupted.

9.8.1 Signal-handling Issues

Another issue in a multi-threading environment is signal handling. The signal handling in processes (single-threaded) has already been discussed in Chapter 7. It is difficult to handle signals of multiple threads. In case of synchronous signals, the signals are delivered to the thread that is executing at that time. However, in case of asynchronous signals, it is not clear which thread of the process will receive the signal. There are some options that are adopted by different OSs. The options may be to deliver the signal to all the threads, selected threads, or only one thread. The threads mask and accept only selected signals. In this way, signals are handled by the threads. However, the first thread that accepts the signal will execute its signal handler. Another option is to have a thread assigned by the process that will receive the signals. This thread in turn sends the signal to the first thread of the process that does not mask it.

9.8.2 Thread Pooling

The implementation view of user threads and kernel threads has given us an idea that creating and destroying threads incur cost. If there is a multi-threaded web server, then each time a client requests, a new thread is created. This thread is then destroyed after serving the web request. Moreover, if all the concurrent threads are allowed, then it may consume all the system resources.

To handle these issues, a fixed number of kernel threads are created in a pool. If there is a client request, the kernel thread is called to service from the pool. After serving the client, the thread is not destroyed but returned to the pool through thread recycling. In this way, the time taken to create and destroy the threads can be saved and at the same time, the system resources are not exhausted due to unlimited creation of threads in the system. On the application side, the response time of request decreases, thereby providing a better service to the clients.

9.8.3 Thread Scheduling

Thread scheduling differs according to the types of threads, that is, scheduling of kernel threads and scheduling of user threads. Since the kernel is not aware of the user-level threads, the scheduler works only for the processes. It means that multiple threads are not scheduled within a process. A scheduler schedules the threads as it does for processes. The thread scheduler is implemented through the thread library. However, the thread scheduler cannot allot time slice to the threads as there are no clock interrupts to stop it. Therefore, a thread may continue until it finishes or if it uses full quantum of its process. In this case, the kernel will select another process to run. Another method is to use a thread call known as *thread-yield*. On execution of this call, the running thread voluntarily gives up the processor so that other threads may run. This is an alternative solution to implement time sharing between the threads. Like this, other thread calls can be implemented so that a thread does not consume the full time quantum of a process and let other threads also share the processor time.

On the other hand, in case of kernel threads, the scheduler picks up a thread instead of a process. A thread may be given a time quantum. Thus, threads of different processes are scheduled. Threads can be scheduled in round robin fashion or according to the priority numbers assigned for them. However, the scheduler must consider the thread switching costs. The thread switching from one process to another will be costly as compared to thread switching within the same process. Therefore, a scheduler must consider all these factors while scheduling the kernel threads.

SUMMARY

The high context switch overhead in process switching has given rise to the multi-threading concept. an application that has multiple threads, responds quickly, and executes fast. The two types of threads, namely, user threads and kernel threads, have been discussed with their pros and cons. Another type of threads—hybrid thread—has also been explained keeping in view the advantages of both types of threads. Most of the issues regarding thread implementation and management (such as thread states, scheduling algorithms, and so on) are same as that of a process. Some of the differences in implementation of a thread and a process have also been discussed in the chapter.

Let us have a quick review of important concepts discussed in this chapter:

- Multi-threading is to have multiple concurrent paths of execution in the form of various threads of control within a single process.
- A thread is a unit of concurrency within a process because threads implement the various functions but share the address space of the process.
- Whenever there is a need to switch between the threads of the same process, the context of a thread will be saved and restored in the form of its PC, CPU registers, and stack: Code and data section are not the part of the context of a thread.
- Multi-threading works the same way as multi-tasking, that is, the processor switches back and forth among the threads as with the processes and gives the illusion that threads are running in parallel.
- The TCB saves and restores the context of a thread in case of thread switching.

- Threads are of two types: user threads and kernel threads.
- User threads are are only managed by the application in user space.
- Kernel threads implemented in the kernel space are managed through system calls.
- User threads are created and then managed through a thread library provided by the OS.
- A thread table is maintained for user threads. The thread table contains entries as a pointer to the TCB of each thread.
- Creating and managing a user thread is easier and much faster as compared to a process and a kernel thread.
- User threads are more portable due to their nature as they do not require the support of a kernel, making them independent of a particular OS.
- User-level thread implementation is known as *many-to-one mappings* as the OS maps all threads in a multi-threaded process to a single-execution context.
- Kernel threads are managed through a single-thread table maintained in the kernel space.
- There is one-to-one mapping in kernel threads that provides each user thread with a kernel thread that it can dispatch.
- Thread recycling is the concept that does not destroy the data structures of a thread when it is deleted but is marked as deleted and not runnable. When there is a requirement of a new thread, instead of creating a new thread, this marked old thread is activated from the thread pool, thereby saving the overhead time in creating a new thread.

MULTIPLE CHOICE QUESTIONS

1. Each process has at least ___ threads of execution.
   - (a) one
   - (c) three
   - (b) two
   - (d) none

2. A process is also known as ___.
   - (a) heavy weight process
   - (c) thread
   - (b) light weight process
   - (d) none

3. A thread is also known as ___.
   - (a) heavy weight process
   - (c) process
   - (b) light weight process
   - (d) none

4. Whenever there is a need to switch between the threads of the same process, the context of a thread will be saved and restored in the form of
   - (a) code, data, and stack
   - (b) code, CPU registers, and stack
   - (c) PC, CPU registers, and stack
   - (d) none

5. The information in the TCB is ___ as compared to the PCB.
   - (a) lesser
   - (c) much larger
   - (b) larger
   - (d) none

6. Low context switch overhead ___ the degree of concurrency.
   - (a) increases
   - (c) no effect
   - (b) decreases
   - (d) none

7. User threads are created and managed through ___.
   - (a) kernels
   - (c) shells
   - (b) thread library
   - (d) none

8. User threads can be ___ as compared to kernel threads.
   - (a) slower
   - (c) not comparable
   - (b) faster
   - (d) none

9. Which type of mapping is implemented in user threads?
   - (a) one-to-one
   - (c) many-to-one
   - (b) many-to-many
   - (d) one-to-many

10. Which type of mapping is implemented in kernel threads?
    - (a) one-to-one
    - (c) many-to-one
    - (b) many-to-many
    - (d) one-to-many

11. Which type of mapping is implemented in hybrid threads?
    - (a) one-to-one
    - (c) many-to-one
    - (b) many-to-many
    - (d) one-to-many

12. In may-to-one mapping, if a thread blocks, the whole process___
    - (a) blocks
    - (c) sleeps
    - (b) keeps running
    - (d) none

13. Multithreaded applications with ___ threads cannot be executed in multi-processor system.
    - (a) user
    - (c) hybrid
    - (b) kernel
    - (d) none

14. Which type has the lowest operational latency?
    - (a) kernel threads
    - (c) processes
    - (b) user threads
    - (d) none

15. Kernel threads consume ___ resources as compared to user threads.
    - (a) more
    - (c) equal
    - (b) less
    - (d) none

REVIEW QUESTIONS

1. What is the difference between a process and a thread?

2. What is the need to create a thread?

3. What is the difference between multi-tasking and multi-threading?

4. What is a TCB? Explain all its fields.

5. What is the difference between a PCB and a TCB?

6. Explain the benefits of the multi-threading concept.

7. Explain the implementation of user threads.

8. Explain the implementation of kernel threads.

9. What is wrapping?

10. What is the difference between one-to-one and many-to-one thread mapping?

11. What is the difference between a process table and a thread table?

12. List out the advantages and disadvantages of both user and kernel threads.

13. What is a thread library?

14. What are hybrid threads?

15. What is thread pooling?

16. How can a thread be cancelled?

17. Explain signal-handling methods in multi-threading.

18. What is a thread-yield?

BRAIN TEASERS

1. What are the key factors to be considered while choosing multi-threading for an application?

2. 'A multithreaded application with user threads cannot take the advantage of multi-processor systems.' Comment on this statement.

3. Why should user threads not use system calls frequently?

4. If a multithreaded process creates its child process, then will the child process get the same number of threads as the parent process?

5. Why is there no need of kernel for communicating between threads of the same process?

6. Explain how multi-threading can be implemented in a spreadsheet application.

7. If a thread opens a file with read privileges, then will another thread within the same process be able to read from that file?

8. You cannot afford to have an infinite number of threads for serving the clients' requests in a multithreaded web server. How do you limit the number of the threads?

9. How can scheduling be application-specific in case of user threads?

Case Study II: Process Management in UNIX/Solaris/ Linux/Windows

UNIX

In UNIX kernel, processes correspond with each other and rest of the UNIX entities via system calls. Every UNIX process (except process 0 or boot process) is created when another process executes the *fork* system call. The initiator process is called the parent process, and the initiated process is known as the *child* process. A single *parent* process can initiate multiple child processes. The child process receives a copy of its parent's address space.

States of a Process

A typical UNIX process switches between various states according to well-defined rules. The various states are shown in Table CS2.1.

Table CS2.1   Various states of a process in UNIX

State	Explanation
User running	Process executes in user mode.
Kernel running	Process executes in kernel mode.
Ready to run in memory	Process waits to be scheduled by short-term scheduler.
Asleep in memory	Process is in a sleep state in memory.
Ready to run, Swapped	Process waits for the swapper to swap it inside the memory so that the kernel can schedule it for execution.
Sleep, Swapped	The process is in the sleep state and has been swapped out to the secondary storage device.
Pre-empted	The kernel pre-empts it and does a context switch to schedule another process.
Created	The process is newly created and is in a transition state.
Zombie	The process executed the exit system call. Zombie state is the final state of the process.

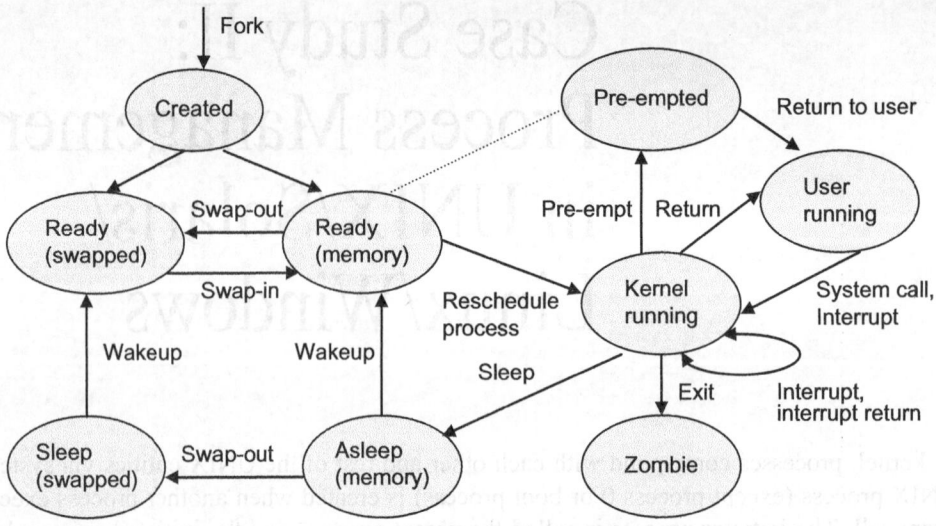

Fig. CS2.1 Process state transition diagram

Figure CS2.1 shows a state transition diagram of a process that describes various states and the events that cause the transition from one state into another.

The major features in process states of a process in UNIX are as follows:

- *Two ready states* When there is enough memory, the state is ready in memory.
  When there is not enough memory, the process is not in memory but waiting for swapper to swap it in memory.
- *Two running states* These include running in user mode and running in kernel mode.
- Basically, ready in memory and *pre-empted* are same as indicated by a dotted line in Fig. CS2.1. In UNIX, however, the distinction has been made between these two states. When a process running in kernel mode completes its execution and is ready to return control to the user process, it enters the pre-empted state. Thus, pre-emption occurs only when a process switches from kernel mode to user mode.

Context of a Process

Since UNIX is a multi-tasking OS, switching between various processes takes place very frequently. It first involves saving the information of the currently executing process and then transferring the control to the called process. The context in the realm of UNIX is amalgamation of the *user-*, *register-*, and *system-level context*.

Table CS2.2 summarizes the contents of these three contexts.

Table CS2.2 Process context in UNIX

User-level context	Text of the process
	Data of the process
	User stack
	Shared memory

(Cont)

(Table CS2.2 Contd)

Register-level context	Program counter
	Process status (PS) register
	Stack pointer
	General purpose register
System-level context	Process table entry
	User area
	Per-process region table
	Kernel stack

The user-level context contains the basic elements of a user's program. It contains the executable machine instructions of the program and the data content. While the process is executing, the processor uses the user stack area for procedure calls and returns and parameter passing. The shared memory area is a data area that is shared with other processes.

The register-level context refers to various registers that contribute during the course of processing, for example, the program counter contains the address of the next instruction the CPU will execute, whereas the process status register specifies the hardware status of the machine as it relates to a process.

The system-level context is related to OS that it needs to manage a process. It consists of two parts: static and dynamic. The static part is fixed in size and stays with a process throughout its existence. It contains the following:

- The process table entry in the process table consisting of the following information:
  - current state of the process
  - pointers to user area (U-area) and process memory area
  - process size
  - user identifiers (to determine various process privileges)
  - event descriptor(valid when the process is in the sleeping state)
  - scheduling parameters
  - signal (lists the signals sent to a process but not yet handled)
  - timers
  - process table pointer
- The U-area stores the process control information required by kernel in the context of a process.
- Per-process region table is used by the memory management system to define the mapping from virtual to physical addresses, thereby indicating the permission to a process for read/write/execute, and so on.

The system-level context as a dynamic part consists of kernel stack. This stack is used when the process is executing in kernel mode and contains the information that must be saved and restored as procedure calls and interrupts occur.

Implementation of Processes

When a user writes a command on the shell prompt, a new process is created using the fork() system call. This newly created process has associated with it its data structures along with the code. The values for two data structures associated with each process, that is, process table entry and U-area are being filled largely from the parent process of the currently executing 'child' process. The child is then given a PID (process ID), its memory map is set up, and it is given shared access to its parent's files. Then its registers are set up, and it is ready to run. Formally, a UNIX program can have one of the following statuses:

Foreground

Associated with one window, there can be one foreground process that can accept input from the keyboard and write its output to the screen.

Background

There can be multiple processes running in the background. These processes are also known as *daemons* and can be made to execute even when the user is not logged in or at some specified interval of time.

Scheduling of Processes

Like any other OS, UNIX too uses both long-term scheduler (to load processes from disk to memory) and short-term scheduler (to select among processes residing in memory). UNIX follows *round robin scheduling with multi-level feedback* to schedule multiple processes residing in memory, that is, the kernel allocates the CPU to a process for a given time slice, pre-empting the one that exceeds the quantum and feeds it back to one of the several priority queues. A typical UNIX process can execute both in user mode as well as kernel mode, and the two modes follow different criteria for scheduling processes for example, in user mode, the process that has recently used the CPU will be the last one to get it again. Thus, it will have the lowest priority value. The processes in this mode thus keep on moving among various priority values (Fig. CS 2.2). On the other hand, in kernel mode, processes with higher priority values are the ones that are not interruptible, whereas those with low priority values are interruptible.

Fair-share Scheduler

This type of scheduling is based on the fact that in a multi-user environment (i.e., an organization), the administrator is more concerned with determining which set of processes has completed its job rather than how many processes have been executed. The jobs are organized into pools by fair-share scheduler. The scheduler then shares the resources across all pools. A separate pool is allocated to each user by default.

In this scheduler, each user is assigned a weight of some sort that defines the user's share of system resources as a proportion of total usage of those resources. Scheduling is performed based on the following parameters:

- Base priority of process (the highest numerical value means the lowest priority).
- Recent processor usage by process.
- Recent processor usage of the group to which the process belongs.

The following formulas apply for each process in various groups:

Current processor usage = (Processor usage)/2
Current processor usage in group = (Processor usage in group)/2
Priority *(process) = (Current processor usage/2) + base level priority,*
where,
Processor usage is number of times a clock handler interrupts a processor;
Base level priority is threshold priority between kernel and user mode.

In case of the group utilization, the average is normalized by dividing by the weight of that group. The greater the weight assigned to the group, the less its utilization will affect its priority.

Let us see an example of fair-share scheduling (Fig. CS2.3). There are two groups of processes. Process *A* belongs to the first group whereas Processes *B* and *C* belong to the second

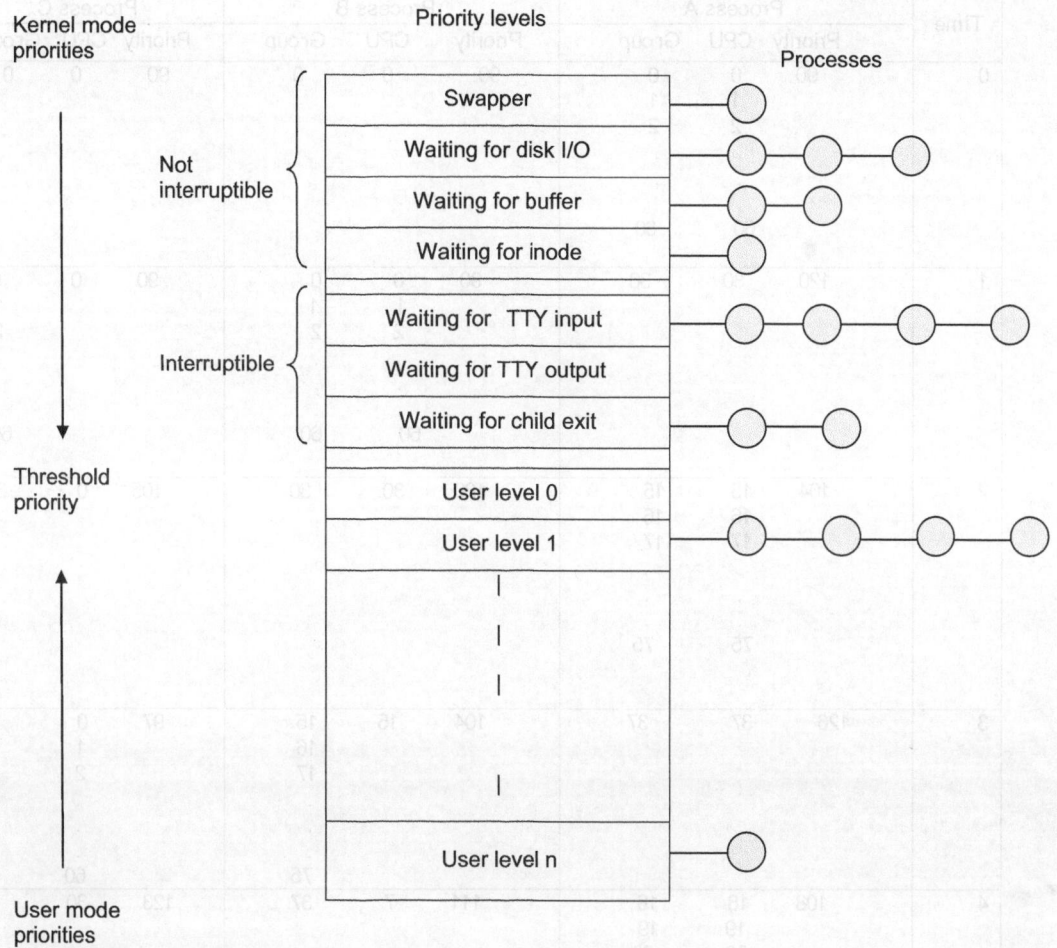

Fig. CS2.2   Process scheduling

group. Each group has a weighting of 50 per cent. We assume the following with regard to this example:

- All processes are processor-bound and are ready to run
- All processes have a base priority of 90.
- Periodically, the processor is interrupted 60 times per second.

Whenever there is an interrupt, the data structures, like processor usage related to present running process, and corresponding group are updated. The priorities are also recalculated after each interrupt, that is, after every second. As seen in Fig. CS2.3, Process *A* gets the processor first. However, it is pre-empted after 1 second. At this moment, Processes *B* and *C* have the higher priority. Therefore, Process *B* is next to run. After 1 s, Process *B* gets the processor. In this manner, the processor is allocated to processes of both the groups. The sequence of processes getting the processor in this example is as follows: *A, B, A, C, A, B,* and so on.

Time	Process A			Process B			Process C		
	Priority	CPU	Group	Priority	CPU	Group	Priority	CPU	Group
0	90	0 1 2 . . . 60	0 1 2 . . . 60	90	0	0	90	0	0
1	120	30	30	90	0 1 2 . . . 60	0 1 2 . . . 60	90	0	0 1 2 . . . 60
2	104	15 16 17 . . . 75	15 16 17 . . . 75	120	30	30	105	0	30
3	126	37	37	104	15 16 17 . . . 75	15 16 17	97	0 1 2 . . . 60	15 16 17 . . . 75
4	108	18 19 20 . . 78	18 19 20 . . 78	111	7	37	123	30	37
5	128	39	39	100	3	18	106	15	18

Fig. CS2.3   Process scheduling example

Inter-process Communication and Synchronization

UNIX allows several types of IPC mechanisms described as follows:

Pipe

This mechanism permits a stream of data acting as output to one process to act as input to second process. This method works in collaboration with I/O redirection concept. The method of piping can be extended to more than two processes depending upon the program need. It follows (FIFO) structure, that is, data are read in the order that it was written to the pipe and the system allows no deviation from that order. There are two types of pipes: named and unnamed. Only related processes can share unnamed pipes, whereas either related or unrelated processes can share named pipes. It is implemented via the system call:

Pipe (fildes)

Int fildes [2]

Pipe returns a read and write file descriptor (fildes[0] and fildes[1], respectively).

Messages

There are four system calls for messages: *msgget, msgctl, msgsnd,* and *msgrcv.* Each of them is described in Table CS2.3.

Table CS2.3   Messages-related system calls in UNIX

Syntax of system call	Explanation
msgqid = msgget (key,flag)	Returns a message descriptor that designates a message queue for use in other system calls.
msgctl (id,cmd,buf)	Allows process to set or query the status of the message queue ID or to remove the queue according to the value of cmd.
msgsnd (msgqid,msgp,size,flag)	Sends a message of size bytes in the buffer msgp to the msgqid.
msgrcv (id,msgp,size,type,flag)	Receives messages from the queue identified by ID.

Shared Memory

The system calls used for manipulating shared memory are shown in Table CS2.4.

Table CS2.4   Shared-memory system calls in UNIX

Syntax of system call	Explanation
Shmid = shmget(key,flag,size)	Creates a new region of shared memory or returns an existing one. Here, size is the number of bytes in the region.
Virtaddr = shmat(id,addr,flags)	Logically attaches a region to a virtual address space of the process.
Shmdt(addr)	Opposite to the previous system call, it detaches a region to a virtual address space of the process.
Shmctl(id,cmd,shmstatbuf)	Manipulates various parameters associated with the shared memory.

Signals

Each signal may be represented with an integer number or a symbolic name. Processes may send each other signals or the kernel may send signals internally. A signal is delivered by revising a field in the process table entry for the process to which the signal is being sent. The signal is processed in either of the following situations:

1. A process wakes up to run.
2. A process prepares itself to return from a system call.

A process responds to a signal by performing some default action, ignoring the signal, or calling the signal handler.

Semaphores

In UNIX, the operations involving semaphores are achieved by using three system calls shown in Table CS2.5.

Table CS2.5 Semaphore-related system calls in UNIX

Syntax of system call	Explanation
semctl(id,num,cmd,arg)	It does the specified cmd on the semaphore queue indicated by ID. Here, num gives the number of semaphores in the set to be processed.
Semget(key,nsems,flag)	It is used to initialize the semaphore set.
Semop(id,ops,num)	It does the set of operations (ops) on the semaphores identified by ID.

Intimate Shared Memory

Intimate shared memory (ISM) is a data-sharing technique which that helps to implement inter-process communication (IPC) in an optimized manner. This technique is being used in System V release of UNIX and Solaris 2.2 onwards. Extending the concept of just sharing the actual physical memory pages, this technique involves sharing of virtual-to-physical address translation for shared-memory pages. It is achieved by means of a data structure known as *translation tables*. Figure CS2.4 shows the difference between ISM and non-ISM shared segments

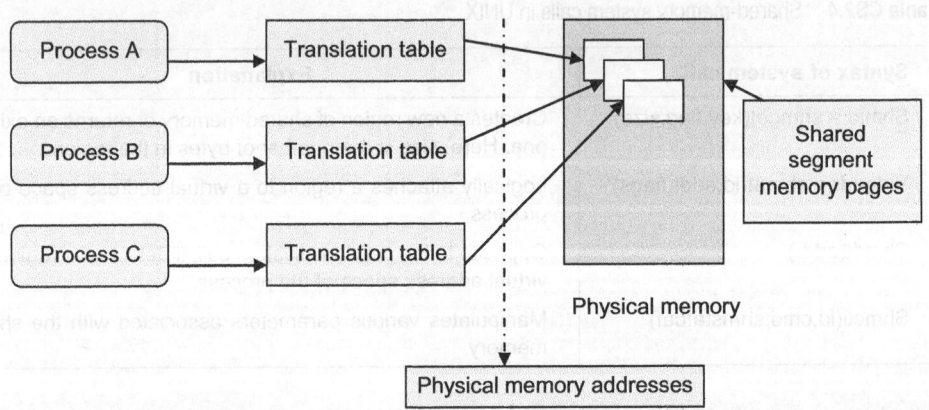

Fig. CS2.4 (a) Non-ISM shared segment

Intimate shared memory also provides a provision to lock the shared pages in memory that would never be paged out. This feature was added for the *relational database management system* (RDBMS) vendors. Solaris implements memory page locking by setting some bits in the memory page's structure. Every page of the memory has a corresponding page structure that contains information about the memory page. Page sizes vary across different hardware platforms.

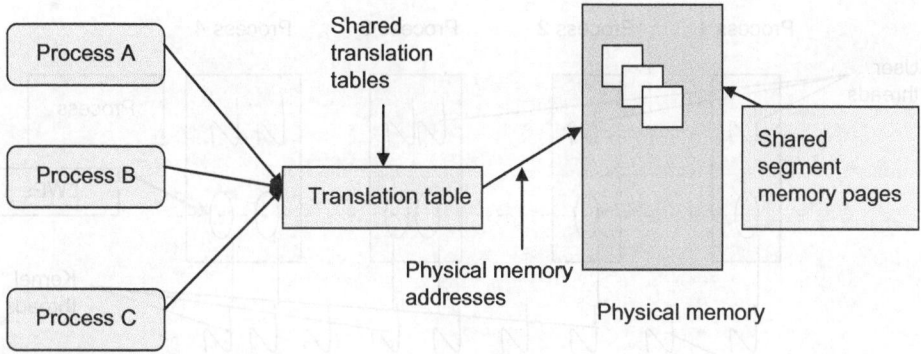

Fig. CS2.4 (b)   An ISM shared segment

SOLARIS

The Solaris kernel in comparison to UNIX has been extended as multi-threaded to allow concurrency across multiple processors. Within a single process, multiple threads of execution are allowed wherein each thread shares process' state. Furthermore, in Solaris, there is a two-level thread model, that is, thread abstractions are provided at the kernel and user level. Within a user process, thousands of threads can be created with a minimum overhead in kernel. The multi-threaded process model has the advantage that it can provide fine-grained application concurrency with less OS overhead that was high in UNIX as the concurrency was implemented with processes instead of threads.

In Solaris, each process has two kernel-level thread abstractions that are part of the two-level thread model. These abstractions in the process' address space are known as *lightweight process* (LWP) and kernel threads (kthreads; Fig. CS2.5). Lightweight process allows each kernel thread within a process to make system calls independent of other kernel threads within the same process. It consists of most information related to support system calls and to maintain hardware context information. If LWP is not there, only one system call is possible at one time. Each LWP has a stack to be used to place registers when a system call is made by a thread.

The kernel data structures implement these two kernel-level abstractions and link to the process structure. This model is able to isolate the kernel from user threads, that is, not visible to kernel. The user threads are distinct from LWP and kthreads. However, to execute a user thread, an LWP is required, which is created when a user thread is created. But this creation of LWP is not automatic and the user thread creation call explicitly asks the kernel to create the same. Every LWP has a corresponding kthread. In Solaris, the kernel itself is multi-threaded having multiple kernel threads.

The kthreads change state more frequently as compared to processes. Several kthreads belonging to the same process may be in different states. The following are the process states in Solaris (Fig. CS2.6):

- SIDL—process is being created.
- SRUN—process is runnable, waiting to be executed.
- SONPROC—process is running on a processor.

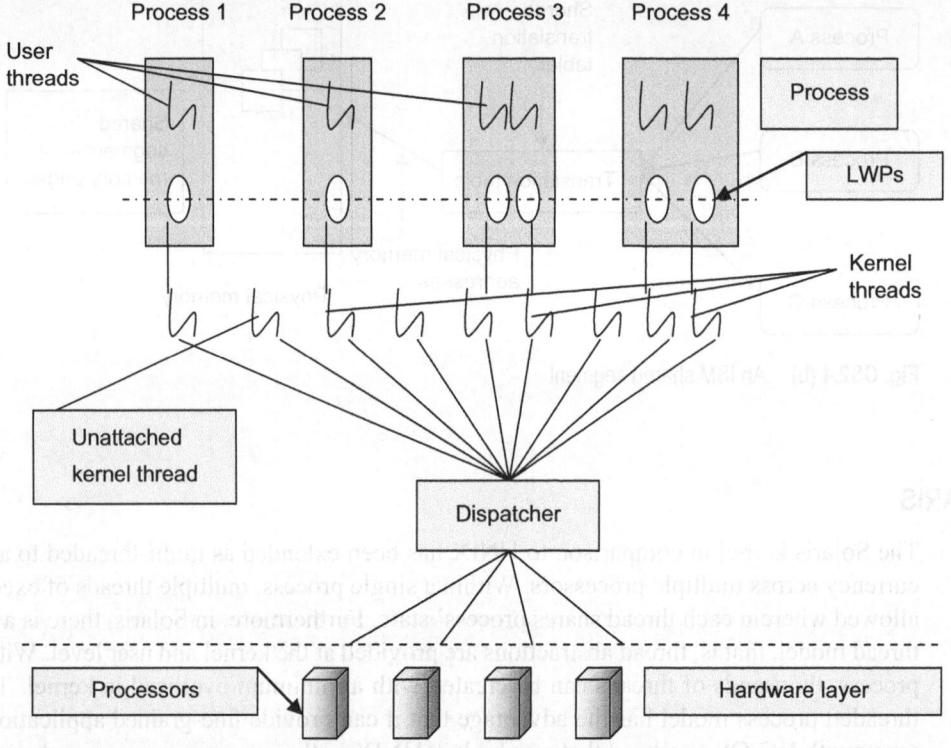

Fig. CS2.5 Multi-threaded process model

- SSTOP—process is stopped, typically because of debugger activity.
- SZOMB—process is in a zombie state.
- SSLEEP—process is in a sleeping state (i.e., waiting for an event).

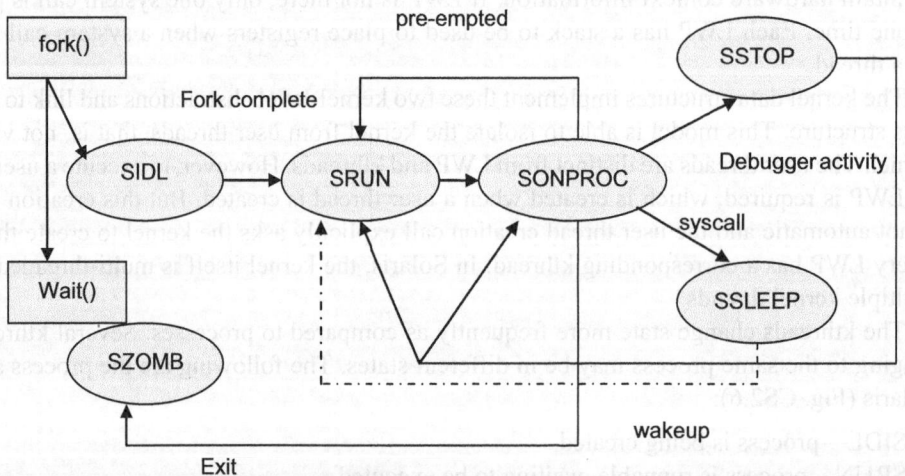

Fig. CS2.6 Process state transition diagram

Scheduling in Solaris

In Solaris, the kthreads instead of processes are put on the dispatch queue and get scheduled. The kthreads are prioritized with the help of various *scheduling classes*. For each scheduling, there is a *dispatcher table* to be used by the dispatcher to run a thread. To implement scheduling, dispatcher decides which kernel thread will execute next. It supports the concept of preemption. The kernel itself is pre-emptable. There are 170 global priorities ranging from 0 to 169 with the highest number being the highest priority. This priority-based scheduling is also adopted in UNIX SVR4.

The various scheduling classes are described as follows (Table CS2.6):

Time Share

The time-share (TS) scheduling class is the default class for processes and all the kthreads within the process. It uses the priority range from 0 to 59. The process priorities may be changed with the criteria of recent processor usage so that resources can be evenly allocated to the threads.

Time sharing scheduling governs the process priorities and time quanta at each clock tick or during wake up after sleeping for an I/O.

Interactive

Interactive (IA) is an enhanced TS class. It boosts up priority of threads within the window under focus. The priority range of this class is the same as that of TS class.

System

This class is for system threads. Its priority range is from 60 to 99. The threads in this class are known as bound threads as there is no time quantum, that is, they run until they get blocked.

Real Time

This class is for real-time threads. It uses fixed priority and fixed time quantum scheduling. Its range is from 100 to 159. The threads in the RT class have a higher priority over kthreads in the SYS class.

The interrupt priority levels shown in Table CS2.6 are available to be used by only interrupts. These have been placed in the priority scheme only to indicate that interrupts have priority over all other. The interrupts in the priority class scale have been placed in the range 100 to 109 if there are no real-time threads. Otherwise, they get placed in the range 160 to 169.

Table CS2.6 Scheduling priority classes

Priority range	Scheduling class
160–169	Interrupts, if there are real-time threads
100–159	Real time
100–109	Interrupts if there are no real-time threads
60–99	System class
0–59	TS/IA

Inter-process Communication

Solaris supports four different groups of IPC: basic IPC, System V IPC, POSIX IPC, and advanced Solaris IPC. In this section, Solaris specific method is described.

Solaris uses a new, fast, and lightweight mechanism for calling procedures between processes known as *doors*. The client and server processes are known as *door client* and *door server*, respectively. There is a thread in door server that sleeps waiting for an invocation from the door client. Thus, the client makes call to the server through doors along with a small (16 KB) payload. As soon as a door client makes a call to a door server, the scheduling control is passed to the thread in the door server. Once the door server has finished handling the request, it passes the control and responds back to the calling thread. This IPC mechanism has a low-latency turnaround as the client does not wait for the server thread to be scheduled.

LINUX

Process States

In Linux, both processes and threads are known as tasks and both are represented by a single data structure. A process in Linux may have the following states:

- Running
- Ready
- Suspended/waiting
- Zombie
- Stopped

The suspended/waiting states in Linux have been elaborated in two states: interruptible and uninterruptible. Interruptible is a blocked state wherein a process is waiting for an event. In an uninterruptible state, the process is waiting directly on for hardware conditions and, therefore, not waiting for an event or signal.

The details of other states are same as we discussed for UNIX/Solaris OSs.

In Linux, the threads are created with the cloning method besides fork method used in UNIX as discussed earlier. The Linux allows creation of clone of a process having duplicate address space in each clone. However, there is a difference. The clone processes are able to share the context with their parents. The process and its clone may have the following in sharing:

- Address space—share code and data segment.
- File system control information—share same root and current directories.
- Open file descriptor—share same open file descriptor.
- Process identifier—share the process number.

In clone method, there is an option to select exactly which elements are to be shared between the parent and the child process and which elements are to be copied. However, the process and its clone have separate stack and may be distinguished by their processor register values. Moreover, the access rights of clone are not shared. Since, a single copy of task management data structure is needed in Linux, the Linux threads simplify kernel code and reduce overhead.

When the fork method is used to create a thread, the kernel will create an identical copy of the parent process for the child. It results into the consumption of memory and time. This is reduced by copy-on-write (COW) method that prevents all the data of the parent process from being copied and instead, only page tables are copied. The copying of memory pages is delayed as long as possible, thereby saving time and memory.

Once a thread has been created using cloning method, it is placed in a run queue. All ready tasks are organized in a red-black tree (a binary search tree) as time-ordered, essentially with respect to their waiting time. In this tree, the leftmost entry is filled with the task that has been waiting for the CPU for the longest time and will be considered next by the scheduler. Tasks that have been waiting less long are sorted on the tree from left to right. The run queue is a processor's data structure that contains references to all the tasks competing for the execution on that processor. Like a multi-level feedback queue, the run queues assign tasks to priority levels, thereby forming a priority array of run queues. The priority array consists of pointers to a list of tasks. Each run queue has two priority arrays: active and expired. The active array consists of tasks whose time quantum has not been consumed. The expired array contains all the tasks for which time quantum has been expired. To avoid starvation of any process in the run queue, each process is run for an epoch having has fixed time duration at least once where an epoch is fixed time duration.

In Linux, processes adopt a hierarchical scheme wherein each process depends on a parent process. For instance, the kernel first starts the init process and then displays the login.

Process Scheduling/ Priority Levels

Since the Linux has pre-emptive process-scheduling mechanism, all processes are not of equal importance. The kernel serves two types of processes in the order of their priorities. The two classes of processes are real-time and normal. Real-time processes get priority over normal processes. There are 40 distinct priority levels recognized by Linux ranging from −20 to 19. As in UNIX, the smaller value indicates the higher priority. Whenever a task is created, it is assigned a static priority known as its nice value. This static priority, however, can be changed in the following two cases:

1. Static priority can be boosted by decrementing it for some I/O bound tasks so that they are able to get a processor before their time quantum expires. This modified priority of task is known as its *effective priority*. The effective priority also determines the level of the priority array in which a task is placed. Thus, the task that gets priority boost will get the place in priority array at a lower level.

2. The static priority can also be increased for some processor-bound processes so that other tasks with smaller effective priority can be run.

Schedulers, thus, compute time slices for each process in the system according to its wait time in the run queue and allow them to run until their time slice is used up. According to this policy, the task with great need of CPU time is scheduled. When a process forks off a child, the current static priority will be inherited from the parent.

The effective priority of the child is set to the normal priority of the parent.

The priority classes in the kernel range from 0 to 139. The lower values indicate higher priorities again. In this range, real-time processes range from 0 to 99. The nice values are mapped in this scale from 100 to 139 as shown in Fig. CS2.7. Real-time processes thus always have higher priority over normal processes.

Real-time processes	Normal processes
0 99	100 139

Fig. CS2.7 Scheduling classes in Linux

The Linux kernel has been updated recently in terms of process scheduling. The Linux Version 2.5 onwards and later versions consisting of O(1) scheduler have been adopted. This scheduler is able to schedule the processes in constant time, that is, scheduling is independent of the number of processes. Furthermore, another scheduler known as *completely fair scheduler* was adopted from Version 2.6.23. This scheduler is same as fair scheduler studied earlier. The completely fair scheduler is used for scheduling normal processes. In case of soft real-time processes, round robin and FIFO-scheduling algorithms are used.

SMP Scheduling

Since in multi-processor systems, load balancing is the major issue, Linux augments the run queue with one migration thread. The migration requests can be posted to this thread for which it maintains a migration queue. The kernel balances run queues periodically. Linux uses load_ balance function for load balancing. This function distributes multiple tasks from the busiest run queues to the current processor but not beyond a limit specified by the function max_load_move. The load_balance function works as follows:

1. It identifies which queue has the most work to do. Another sub-function known as *find_busiest_queue* is called for this purpose. This sub-function iterates over the queues for all processors and identifies the busy queues by comparing their load weights. The factor that determines the load weight is the average length of each run queue. The idea is to reduce the imbalance between the queues.

   While selecting the tasks from a run queue, it is checked whether a task is cache-cold or cache-hot. A cache-cold task does not contain much of the data in the processor's cache, whereas cache-hot task contains most of its data in the processor's cache. Therefore, migration of a cache-hot task may affect the performance of the task. Therefore, only cache-cold tasks are migrated from a run queue.

2. After finding the busy queue, its tasks are migrated to the current queue. The tasks from the larger queue are removed until the difference between the two queues has been halved.

Lazy Floating-point Unit Mode

The Linux uses lazy floating-point unit (FPU) mode to reduce the context switch time in the system. While saving the state of a task, floating-point registers (and other extended registers not used by the kernel, e.g., the SSE2 (Streaming SIMD [Single Instruction, Multiple Data] Extension 2) registers on IA-32 platforms) are not saved unless they are actually used by the application and are not restored unless they are required. This is known as *the lazy FPU technique*. Moreover, the contents of the floating-point registers are not saved on the process stack but in its thread data structure.

Synchronization

Linux provides the following methods for task communication among tasks:

- wait queues
- signals
- pipes
- sockets
- shared memory

- semaphores
- reader/writer locks

Linux provides the following methods for task synchronization among tasks:

- spinlocks
- reader/writer locks
- semaphores

Wait queue is a linked and circular list of descriptors. Each descriptor contains the address of a process descriptor and a pointer to the next element in the queue. The wait queues are manipulated by the functions add_wait_queue and remove_wait_queue.

Spinlocks are the mechanisms of synchronization on multi-processor systems for shorter durations. However, on a single-processor system, semaphores are used to lock the kernel. Semaphores are also useful in the case the lock needs to be held for a longer duration.

The details of other methods of synchronization and communication are the same as discussed for UNIX/Solaris.

WINDOWS

Windows processes are implemented as objects and any process may contain at least one thread of execution. A process in Windows has the following resources:

Security Access Token

This token is created by the OS when a user first logs on. The token consists of a security ID for the user. The OS validates the user accessibility to secured objects with the help of this token. The copy of this token is passed to every process created or run by this user.

Virtual Address Space

There is a series of blocks defining the virtual address space assigned to the process.

Object Table

The process may use some objects such as file and thread. So there must be object handles known to it. Therefore, the process has an object table consisting of object handles.

Threads are actual units of execution. A thread executes a part of process' code using the process' resources. A thread has its own execution context including its run time stack, state of registers, and attributes like scheduling priority.

The following data structures are maintained in Windows regarding process management:

Executive Process Block

It stores information that executive layer uses while manipulating a process object. It includes process ID, a pointer to the process's handle table, a pointer to the process' access token, and working set information used for page faults.

Kernel Process Block

It stores process information used by the microkernel. Since the microkernel manages thread scheduling and synchronization, this data structure stores the process base priority, default quantum for each of its threads, spinlock, and so on.

Process Environment Block

It is stored in the process' address space. This block is pointed by the executive process block. It stores information regarding user processes.

Executive Thread Block

It stores information that the executive layer uses while manipulating a thread object. The information includes the ID of the thread's process, its start address, its access token, and so on.

Kthread Block

It stores thread information used by the microkernel. It includes thread's base and current priority, its current state, and so on.

Thread Environment Block

It stores information about a thread in the address space of its process. This block is pointed by the kthread block. This block stores information such as thread ID, critical section owned by the thread, and so on.

Thread Local Storage

To maintain a thread data, a local storage known as *thread local storage* (TLS) is used.

In Windows, the parent and the child processes are completely independent, that is, a child process has a completely new address space. Therefore, when a child process terminates, the parent process is unaffected and vice versa. When all the threads of a process terminate, the process terminates. All the processes in the user context are terminated when a user logs off the system.

Fibers

Windows has the provision of creating further lightweight threads known as fibers. The fibers are created by the thread and scheduled by the thread that creates them. Thus, a fiber runs in the context of a thread. A single thread may schedule multiple fibers. The thread that creates a fiber specifies the starting address of the code that the new fiber is to execute. The starting address may be a user-supplied function in the code. The same function may be executed by more than one fiber. The difference between threads and fibers is that threads support pre-emptive multi-tasking whereas fibers use co-cooperative multi-tasking. The fibers also maintain their states such as process and thread. The state of a fiber is stored by the thread only. Fibers are user-level units of execution and are not visible to the kernel. Thus, the context switching between multiple fibers of a thread is fast in user mode. Like TLS, the fiber also has fiber local storage (FLS) to maintain its own data. A fiber can also access its thread's TLS.

The advantage of fibers is that they facilitate the porting of code written for other OSs to Windows. Otherwise, they are not advantageous over well designed multi-threaded application.

Thread Pooling

Thread pools are advantageous in case an application is highly parallel and can start a large number of small work items. These applications may create threads that spend much time in sleeping state, waiting for an event to occur or some threads to be awakened periodically. Thread pooling is the technique to manage threads efficiently by providing with a pool of worker threads managed by the system. The status of all wait operations is queued to the thread pool and is monitored by a thread. On the completion of a wait operation, a worker thread from the pool executes the corresponding function. A worker thread executes functions queued by user threads. In the absence of a request to be serviced, the worker thread is in sleep mode.

At the time of a process creation, the thread pool is empty. It is allocated space as soon as the process queues its first request.

Thread States

The following are the states in which a thread can be in Windows (Fig. CS2.8):

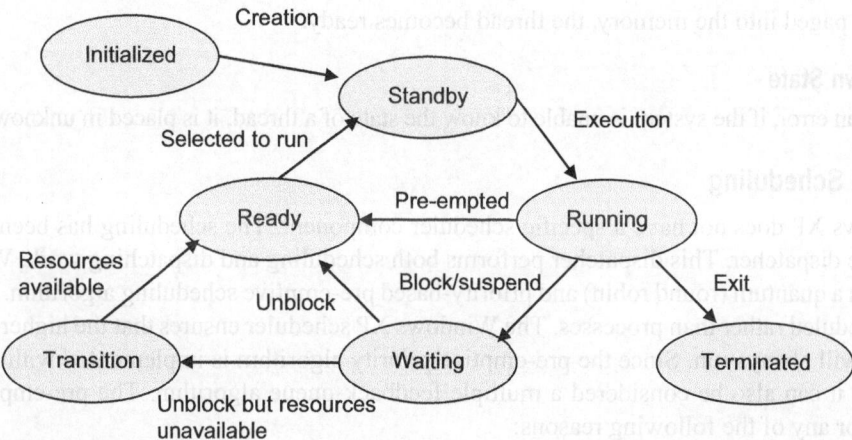

Fig. CS2.8   Thread state

Initialized

The thread when created is in initialized state.

Ready

The threads waiting in the queue to be executed are in this state.

Standby

When a thread has been selected by dispatcher and is waiting to be executed until the processor is made available, it is in a standby state. For example, Thread A is executing currently and Thread B has been selected to execute next. In this case, Thread B is in standby. If the priority of Thread B is high, it may pre-empt Thread A. However, it will be in standby state until Thread A's context will be saved and Thread B's context will be loaded.

Running

The thread starts execution.

Terminated

After the thread has finished its execution, it is put in terminated state. However, this thread object may be used by other threads in the system and, therefore, cannot be deleted. Otherwise, the threads may crash due to the object removed from the system. For this purpose, the object's reference count is maintained. The object manager does not delete a terminated thread until a thread object's reference count has become zero.

Waiting

When a running thread waits on an object handle or a thread suspend is suspended by another thread or system, the thread is in the waiting state.

Transition

A thread in wait state when becomes ready to execute but cannot start execution as the resources are not available is put in transition state. For example, kernel stack has been paged out of the memory. The thread therefore cannot start execution and is in transition state. As soon as the stack is paged into the memory, the thread becomes ready.

Unknown State

Due to an error, if the system is unable to know the state of a thread, it is placed in unknown state.

Thread Scheduling

Windows XP does not have a specific scheduler component. The scheduling has been merged with the dispatcher. This dispatcher performs both scheduling and dispatching work. Windows XP uses a quantum (round robin) and priority-based pre-emptive scheduling algorithm. Threads are scheduled rather than processes. The Windows XP scheduler ensures that the higher-priority thread will always run. Since the pre-emptive priority algorithm is implemented with multiple queues, it can also be considered a multiple feedback-queue algorithm. The pre-emption can occur for any of the following reasons:

- Higher-priority thread becomes ready.
- Thread terminates.
- Time quantum of thread expires.
- Thread performs a blocking system call, such as for I/O, in which case it leaves the ready state and enters a waiting state.

The dispatcher uses a 32-level priority scheme (denoted by integers from 0 to 31 and 0 being the lowest priority) to determine the order of thread execution. Each thread has a base priority defining the lower limit that it may occupy. In case of a user-defined thread, the base priority of the thread is affected by its process' base priority and the thread's priority level. The *process' base priority class* defines a narrow range so that the process' thread can be assigned a base priority. There are two broad categories of base priority classes:

Variable or Dynamic Class

This category encompasses priority levels 0 through 15. This category is known as variable or dynamic as the priority of thread is not static and can be altered by OS. This category is further divided into the following types:

1. Idle
2. Below normal
3. Normal
4. Above normal
5. High

Real-time Class

This category encompasses priority levels from 16 to 31, (plus a thread at Priority 0 managing memory). This category has static priorities to the threads.

Each scheduling priority has a separate queue of the corresponding processes. The dispatcher uses a queue for each scheduling priority and traverses the set of queues from the highest to the lowest until it finds a thread that is ready to run. The running thread is always one with the highest priority level. If no ready thread exists, the idle thread is run. When a thread's time quantum runs out, its priority is lowered, but is never less than its base priority. When a thread becomes ready after waiting, it is given a priority boost to execute it. Depending on the category of the process being run, the priority is boosted. For an instance, any thread of the process associated with the foreground process class is given a priority boost. The dispatcher scans the list of ready threads and boosts the priority of dynamic threads. It may also avoid starvation in case any lower-priority thread is indefinitely postponed.

Processes are assigned priorities belonging to normal priority class. There is also a special idle thread that is scheduled when no other threads are ready. Windows XP identifies the following seven priority levels within each priority class:

1. Idle
2. Lowest
3. Below normal
4. Normal
5. Above normal
6. Highest
7. Time critical

The combination of base priority class and level maps to a specific base priority is to be assigned to a thread.

Thread Synchronization

It is necessary to synchronize access by multiple threads, and the interdependent code is executed in the right sequence. The following are the thread-synchronization methods:

Dispatcher Objects

In Windows, there are *dispatcher objects* used for the synchronization. Each dispatcher object instance can be in two states: signaled and unsignaled. In an unsignaled state, a thread can be blocked. In signaled state, the thread is released. In general, a thread issues a wait request to the executive component of Windows using the handle of dispatcher object. When an object enters the signaled state, the executive releases one or all of the thread objects that are waiting on that dispatcher object. The following are some of the dispatcher objects:

Event objects
Threads may be synchronized with an event such as user I/O by using an event object. Using this method, the object notifies that an event has happened. When the events happen, the object manager sets the event object in the signaled state. The object is unsignaled when one or all threads awaken.

Mutex objects
These objects provide the synchronization for shared resources as discussed in 'binary semaphores'.

Semaphore objects
These objects provide the synchronization for shared resources as discussed in 'counting semaphores'.

Waitable timer object

Some threads may perform operations at regular intervals of time or at some fixed specific time. For this purpose, Windows provides waitable timer objects. These objects become signaled when the specified amount of time has elapsed.

Kernel Mode Locks

Kernel mode locks are the mechanisms to provide synchronization for shared-kernel data structures. Spinlock is one example of this type of locks. Windows provide queued spinlocks that enforce FIFO ordering of requests. A queued spinlock is more efficient than a spinlock because the processor to memory bus traffic associated with spinlock is reduced. In spinlock, the continual looping for lock is executed on the memory line, thereby creating bus traffic on the processor to memory bus. Instead of this, in queued spinlock, a thread after releasing the lock notifies the next thread in the queue. In this mechanism, the fairness through FIFO ordering is increased.

Slim Reader/Writer Locks

In Chapter 7, various types of reader/writer synchronization problems were discussed, wherein it was difficult to provide access to reader and writer threads with synchronization mechanisms such as critical section and mutex. Therefore, to access the shared resources by the threads of a single process, slim reader/writer (SRW) lock was introduced in Windows Vista. This lock is called slim because it consumes very less memory as of a pointer-sized. Due to this, it is fast to update the state of lock. Slim reader/writer lock has two modes to access a shared resource:

Shared mode

In this mode, read-only access to multiple reader threads is granted. Due to this, multiple reader threads are enabled to read data from shared resource concurrently.

Exclusive mode

In this mode, only one writer thread at a time is granted access. Once the access has been granted to one writer thread, no other thread can access the shared resource.

Wait Functions

These are specialized functions that allow a thread to block its own execution. These functions do not return until a specific criterion has been met. The thread that calls this function enters a wait state until the specific criterion has been met or a specified timeout interval elapses.

Barriers

Windows uses synchronization barriers to enable multiple threads to wait until all threads reach a particular point of execution.

Condition Variables

These are synchronous primitives that enable a thread to wait until a particular condition occurs. These variables are user-mode objects that are not sharable across processes. With the help of a condition variable, threads can release a lock and may enter the sleeping state. These variables may be used with critical sections or SRW locks. However, Windows XP does not support condition variables.

Deadlock Detection

In Windows, there is driver-verifier component that monitors Windows kernel-mode drivers to check the presence of any illegal function call or any action that might corrupt the system. In this driver verifier, there is an option known as *deadlock detection*. With this option enabled, the driver verifier monitors the driver's use of resources that need to be locked. It further detects code logic to check in advance that the code has the potential to cause a deadlock. This deadlock detection has been supported in Windows XP and later versions.

PART III

Memory Management

10 Basic Memory Management

10.1 INTRODUCTION

The multi-programming concept of an OS gives rise to another issue known as memory management. Process management needs the support of memory management. Memory, as a resource, needs to be partitioned and allocated to the ready processes, such that both processor and memory can be utilized efficiently. It is partitioned into two parts; one for the OS, and the other for the user area. Besides this, the user area needs to be divided into multiple parts for various user processes. This division of memory for processes needs proper management, including its efficient allocation and protection. Memory management needs hardware support also, therefore, the management technique also depends on the hardware available. The memory management issue extends from basic memory management techniques to virtual memory management, in order to meet the challenge of huge memory requirements of processes, since the size of the main memory is not sufficient. Therefore, there are two types of memory management: real memory (main memory) and virtual memory. This chapter discusses all the issues related to real memory management.

10.2 BASIC CONCEPTS

To understand memory allocation and other memory management schemes, some basic concepts are discussed in this section. These will be used throughout this chapter.

10.2.1 Static and Dynamic Allocation

Memory allocation is generally performed through two methods: *static allocation* and *dynamic allocation*. In static allocation, the allocation is done before the execution of a process. There are two instances when this type of allocation is performed:

1. When the location of the process in the memory is known at compile time, the compiler generates an absolute code for the process. If the location of the process needs to be changed on the memory, the code must be recompiled.
2. When the location of the process in the memory is not known at compile time, the compiler does not produce an actual memory

Learning Objectives

After reading this chapter, you should be able to understand:

- Static and dynamic memory allocation
- Basic concepts for memory management: logical and physical addresses, swapping, relocation, protection and sharing, fragmentation
- Fixed and variable memory partitioning
- Contiguous memory allocation
- Memory partition selection techniques: First fit, best fit, worst fit
- Non-contiguous memory allocation
- Paging concept
- Paging implementation with associative cache memory
- Page table and its structures
- Segmentation concept
- Hardware requirements for segmentation

address but generates a relocatable code, that is, the addresses that are relative to some known point. With this relocatable code, it is easy to load the process to a changed location and there is no need to recompile the code. In both cases of static allocation, size should be known before start of the execution of the process.

If memory allocation is deferred till the process starts executing, it is known as dynamic allocation. It means the process is loaded in memory initially with all the memory references in relative form. The absolute addresses in memory are calculated as an instruction in the process executed. In this way, memory allocation is done during execution of a program. Dynamic allocation also has the flexibility to allocate memory in any region.

10.2.2 Logical and Physical Addresses

To accommodate the multi-programming concept of modern OSs, dynamic memory allocation method is adopted. In this method, two types of addresses are generated. Since in dynamic allocation, the place of allocation of the process is not known at the compile and load time, the processor, at compile time, generates some addresses, known as *logical addresses*. The set of all logical addresses generated by the compilation of the process is known as *logical address space*. These logical addresses need to be converted into absolute addresses at the time of execution of the process. The absolute addresses are known as *physical addresses*. The set of physical addresses generated, corresponding to the logical addresses during process execution, is known as *physical address space*. There are now two types of memory: logical memory and physical memory. The logical memory views the memory from 0 to its maximum limit, say m. The user process generates only logical addresses in the range 0 to m, and a user thinks that the process runs in this logical address space. But the user process, in the form of logical address space, is converted into physical address space with a reference or base in memory. The memory management component of the OS performs this conversion of logical addresses into physical addresses. Thus, when a process is compiled, the CPU generates a logical address, which is then converted into a physical address by the memory management component, to map it to the physical memory.

10.2.3 Swapping

Swapping was introduced in Chapter 5 in concern with suspended processes. Swapping plays an important role in memory management. There are some instances in multi-programming when there is no memory for executing a new process. In this case, if a process is taken out of memory, there will be space for a new process. This is a good solution, but the following factors matter during the implementation.

- Where will this process reside?
- Which process will be taken out?
- Where in the memory will the process be brought back?

For the first question, the help of any secondary storage (generally, hard disk) known as backing store, is taken, and the process is stored there. The action of taking out a process from memory is called *swap-out*, and the process is known as a *swapped-out process* (see Fig.10.1). The action of bringing back the swapped-out processes into memory is called *swap-in*. A separate space in the hard disk, known as *swap space*, is reserved for swapped-out processes. The swap space should be large enough such that a swapped out process can be accommodated. The swap space stores the images of all swapped out processes. Thus, whenever a process is selected

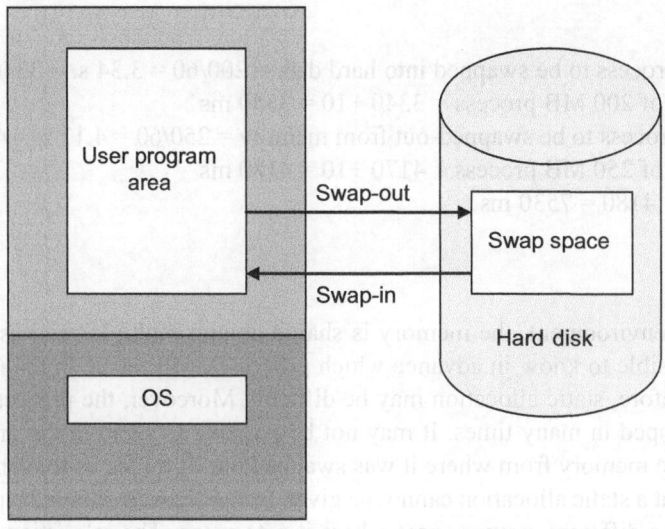

Fig. 10.1   Swapping

by the scheduler to execute, the dispatcher checks whether or not the desired process is in the ready queue. If not, a process is swapped out of memory and the desired process is swapped in.

For the second question, some of the processes that can be swapped-out are:

- In round robin process-scheduling, the processes are executed, according to their time quantum. If the time quantum expires and a process has not finished its execution, it can be swapped-out.
- In priority-driven scheduling, if a higher-priority process wishes to execute, a lower-priority process in memory will be swapped out.
- The blocked processes, which are waiting for an I/O, can be swapped out.

For the third question, there are two options to swap in a process. The first method is to swap-in the process at the same location, if there is compile time or load time binding. However, this may not be possible every time and it is inconvenient. Therefore, another method is to place the swapped-in process anywhere in the memory where there is space. But this requires the relocation, which is discussed in the next section.

Swapping incurs the cost of implementation. As discussed above, the swap space should be reserved in the secondary storage. It should be large enough to store images of the processes which are swapped out. Another cost factor is *swap time*, which is time taken to access the hard disk. Here, the transfer time from the hard disk matters. There is already some latency in data transfer from the hard disk, as compared to memory. So the swap time increases the transfer time. The transfer time is also affected by the size of the process to be swapped out from the hard disk. Hence, larger the size of the process, larger the transfer time.

Example 10.1

A process of size 200 MB needs to be swapped into the hard disk. But there is no space in memory. A process of size 250 MB is lying idle in memory and therefore, it can be swapped out. How much swap time is required to swap-in and swap-out the processes if:

Average latency time of hard disk = 10 ms

Transfer rate of hard disk = 60 MB/s

Solution

The transfer time of the process to be swapped into hard disk = 200/60 = 3.34 s. = 3340 ms
Therefore, the swap time of 200 MB process = 3340 +10 = 3350 ms
The transfer time of the process to be swapped-out from memory = 250/60 = 4.17 s. = 4170 ms
Therefore, the swap time of 250 MB process = 4170 +10 = 4180 ms
Total swap time = 3350 + 4180 = 7530 ms

10.2.4 Relocation

In a multi-programming environment, the memory is shared among multiple processes. Due to this, it may not be possible to know in advance which processes will reside in the memory and their locations. Therefore, static allocation may be difficult. Moreover, the processes may be swapped out and swapped in many times. It may not be possible to swap in the processes in the same location in the memory from where it was swapped out. It forces us to manage the memory in such a way that a static allocation cannot be given to a process. It should be possible to relocate the process to a different memory area where it gets space. The relocation process should be able to provide a new location to the process and translate all the memory references (either data reference or branch instructions) found in the process code into physical addresses, according to the current location in the memory. To translate all the memory references of the process, there must be an origin or base address in the memory. All relative addresses generated are added in this base address to get the new location in the memory.

To implement relocation, some hardware support is required. There should be a processor register which holds the base address. This register is known as the *base register* or *relocation register*. Base register holds the starting address in the main memory from where the process needs to be relocated. Along with the base register, there should be a register that stores the ending location of the process, that is, the knowledge of the limit of the process in the memory. The limit is stored in a *limit* or *bounce register* (see Fig. 10.2). Thus, with the help of base and limit registers, the process may be dynamically loaded or relocated. As soon as a process is loaded or swapped into the memory, these registers must be set by the OS.

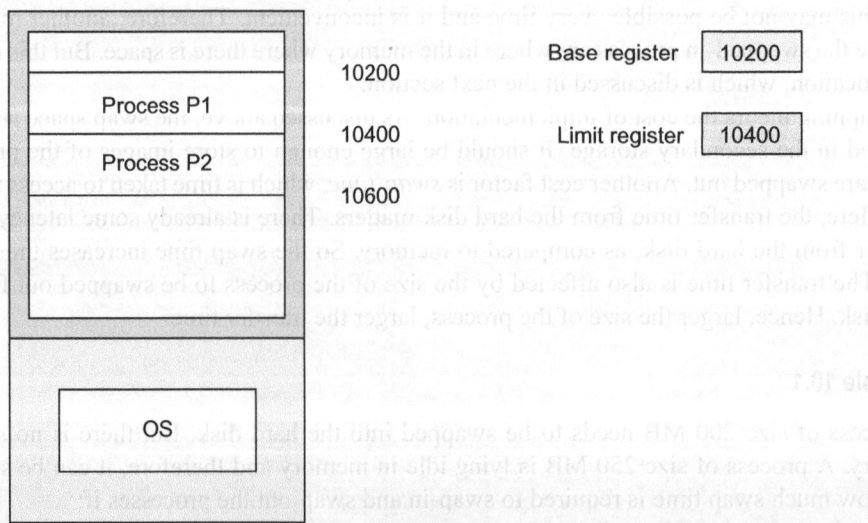

Fig. 10.2 Relocation with base and limit register

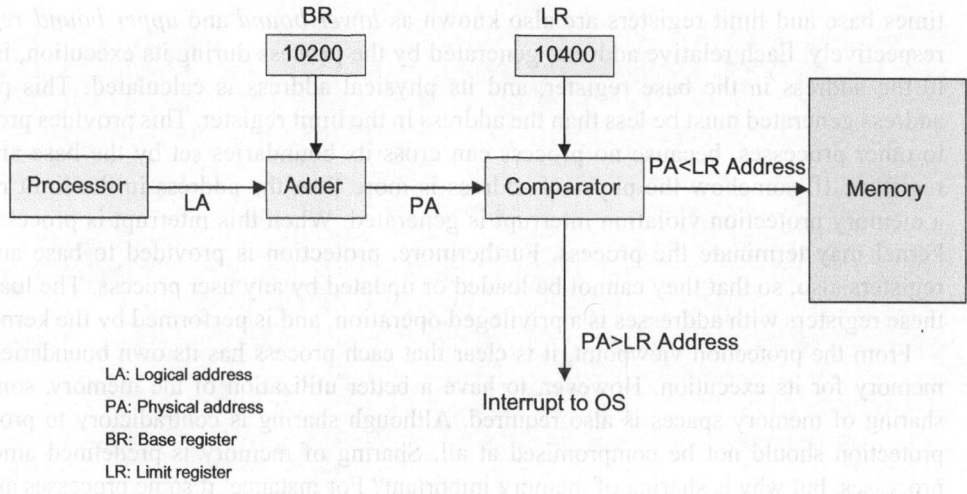

LA: Logical address
PA: Physical address
BR: Base register
LR: Limit register

Fig. 10.3 Memory mapping using base and limit registers

When the process starts executing, relative or logical addresses are generated by the CPU. These relative addresses are first added in the base register to produce an absolute address or physical address (see Fig. 10.3). Next, the address is compared with the address stored in the limit register. If the address is less than the limit register address, the instruction execution continues. It is clear that adder (to add the base and relative address) and comparator (to compare the generated physical address with the limit register address) are also required in the hardware of a Memory Management Unit (MMU). In this way, the MMU, with the help of base and limit registers, performs the memory mapping, by converting logical addresses into physical addresses.

Example 10.2

A process is to be swapped-in at the location 20100 in memory. If logical addresses generated by the process are 200, 345, 440, and 550, what are the corresponding physical addresses?

Solution

The relocation register will be loaded with the address 20100. So adding the logical addresses to the relocation register, the corresponding physical addresses are as follows:

$$20100 + 200 = 20300$$
$$20100 + 345 = 20445$$
$$20100 + 440 = 20540$$
$$20100 + 550 = 20650$$

10.2.5 Protection and Sharing

In a multi-programming environment, there is always an issue of protection of user processes, such that they do not interfere with others and even the OS. Therefore, it is required that the process should not be able to enter the memory area of other processes or the OS area. Each process should execute within its allocated memory. It means whenever a process executes, all the address generated must be checked, so that it does not try to access the memory of other processes. The base and limit registers serve this purpose. In protection terminology, sometimes base and limit registers are also known as *lower-bound* and *upper-bound registers*, respectively. Each relative address, generated by the process during its execution, is added to the address in the base register, and its physical address is calculated. This physical address generated must be less than the address in the limit register. This provides protection to other processes, because no process can cross its boundaries set by the base and limit registers. If, somehow the physical address is more than the address in the limit register, a memory protection violation interrupt is generated. When this interrupt is processed, the kernel may terminate the process. Furthermore, protection is provided to base and limit registers also, so that they cannot be loaded or updated by any user process. The loading of these registers with addresses is a privileged operation, and is performed by the kernel only.

From the protection viewpoint, it is clear that each process has its own boundaries in the memory for its execution. However, to have a better utilization of the memory, sometimes sharing of memory spaces is also required. Although sharing is contradictory to protection, protection should not be compromised at all. Sharing of memory is predefined among the processes, but why is sharing of memory important? For instance, if some processes are using the same utility in their execution, it would be wastage of memory, if same kind of utility is given space in the memory for each process. Therefore, the better idea is to have a single copy of that utility in the memory and processes will share it, when required. Thus, memory management techniques must consider memory-sharing, but with protection.

Example 10.3

A process has relocatable code of size of 900 K. The relocation register is loaded with 40020 K and the limit register contains the address 41000 K. If the processor generates a logical address 990, where will it be located in the physical memory?

Solution

The physical address corresponding to logical address 990
    = relocation register address + logical address
    = 40020 + 990 = 41010
But the process will not be allocated, because it is greater than the address in the limit register, hence, violating the criterion for protection. Consequently, an interrupt will be generated.

10.2.6 Fixed and Variable Memory Partitioning

The memory space is divided into fixed or variable partitions, which will be described in detail in the subsequent sections. Fixed partitioning is a method of partitioning the memory at the time of system generation. In fixed partitioning, the partition size can be of fixed size as well as variable, but once fixed, it cannot be changed. Variable partitioning is not performed at the system generation time. In this partitioning, the number and size of the memory partition vary and are created at run time, by the OS.

10.2.7 Fragmentation

When a process is allocated to a partition, it may be possible that its size is less than the size of partition, leaving a space after allocation, which is unusable by any other process. This wastage of memory, internal to a partition, is known as *internal fragmentation*.

While allocating and de-allocating memory to the processes in partitions through various methods, it may be possible that there are small spaces left in various partitions throughout the memory, such that if these spaces are combined, they may satisfy some other process' request. But these spaces cannot be combined. This total memory space fragmented, external to all the partitions, is known as *external fragmentation*.

10.3 CONTIGUOUS MEMORY ALLOCATION

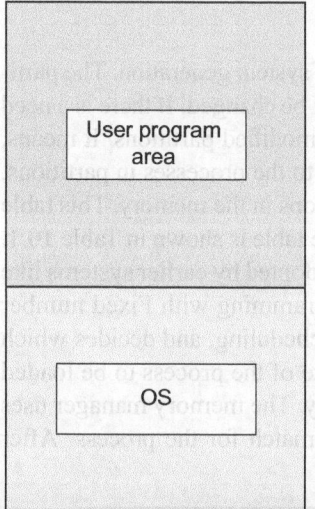

In older systems, memory allocation is done by allocating a single contiguous area in memory to the processes. When there was multi-programming or a multi-user system, memory was divided into two partitions, - one for the OS, and the other for the user process (see Fig. 10.4). The user process in its partition has a single contiguous region of memory.

After the invention of multi-user and multi-programming systems, more processes need to be accommodated in the memory (see Fig. 10.5). Multiple processes are accommodated by having multiple partitions in the memory. However, multiple partitioning has an effect on the OS partition. It is still present in the memory. The OS area is generally placed in the lower memory addresses. It can be in high memory also, but interrupt vector is often in lower memory addresses.

The contiguous allocation method was implemented by partitioning the memory into various regions. The memory can be partitioned, using either fixed memory or variable memory partitioning.

Fig. 10.4   Single partition in memory

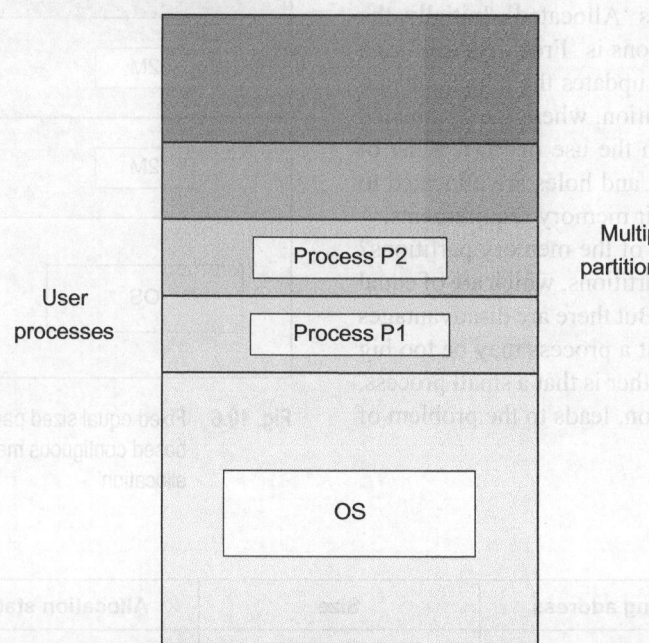

Fig. 10.5   Multiple partitioning of memory

In this method, a process is allocated a contiguous memory in a single partition. Thus, the memory partition, which fits the process, is searched and allocated. The memory partition, which is free to allocate, is known as a *hole*. Thus, an appropriate hole is searched for allocating it to a process. When the process terminates, the occupied memory becomes free and the hole is available again. Initially, all the holes are available. When all the holes are allocated to the processes, the remaining processes enter wait state. As soon as a process terminates, a hole becomes free, and is allocated to a waiting process.

10.3.1 Contiguous Allocation with Fixed Partitioning

Fixed partitioning is a method of memory partitioning at the time of system generation. The partition can be of fixed as well as variable size, but once fixed, it cannot be changed. If there is a need to change the partition size, the OS must be generated again with modified partitions. It means, the partitions, once fixed, are static in nature. To allocate memory to the processes in partitions, the OS creates a table to store the information, regarding the partitions in the memory. This table is called the *partition description table* (PDT). The structure of the table is shown in Table 10.1.

The contiguous allocation method with fixed partitioning was adopted by earlier systems like IBM mainframe OS/360, which was called OS/MFT (Multi-programming with Fixed number of Tasks). In this method, the long-term scheduler performs job scheduling, and decides which process is to be brought into the memory. It then finds out the size of the process to be loaded and requests the memory manager to allocate a hole in the memory. The memory manager uses one of the allocation techniques (discussed later) to find a best match for the process. After getting a hole, the scheduler places the process in the allocated partition. Next, it enters the partition ID in the PCB of the process, and then PCB is linked to the chain of the ready queue. Memory manager marks the status of the partition as 'Allocated'. Initially, the status of all memory partitions is 'Free'. As soon as a process terminates, the OS updates the allocation status (in the PDT) of the partition, where the terminated process resided. Thus, with the use of PDT, a list of available holes is obtained, and holes are allocated to the processes, based on their memory requirements.

What should be the size of the memory partitions? One approach is memory partitions, which are of equal size, as shown in Fig 10.6. But there are disadvantages to this approach. One is that a process may be too big to fit into the partition. Another is that a small process, occupying the entire partition, leads to the problem of internal fragmentation.

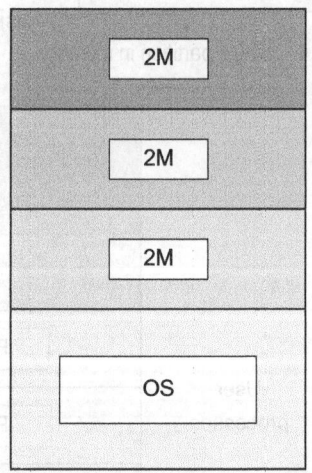

Fig. 10.6 Fixed equal sized partitioning based contiguous memory allocation

Table 10.1 Partition description table

Partition ID	Starting address	Size	Allocation status

Example 10.4

Three processes P1, P2, and P3 of size 21900, 21950, and 21990 bytes, respectively, need space in the memory. If equal-sized partitions of 22000 bytes are allocated to P1, P2, and P3, will there be any fragmentation in this allocation?

Solution

After allocating the partitions to the processes, the leftover space in each partition is estimated by the difference between partition size and process size. Hence,
The leftover space in the first partition = 22000 – 21900 = 100 bytes
The leftover space in the second partition = 22000 – 21950 = 50 bytes
The leftover space in the third partition = 22000 – 21990 = 10 bytes.
This leftover space in each partition is nothing but internal fragmentation, as shown in the following figure:

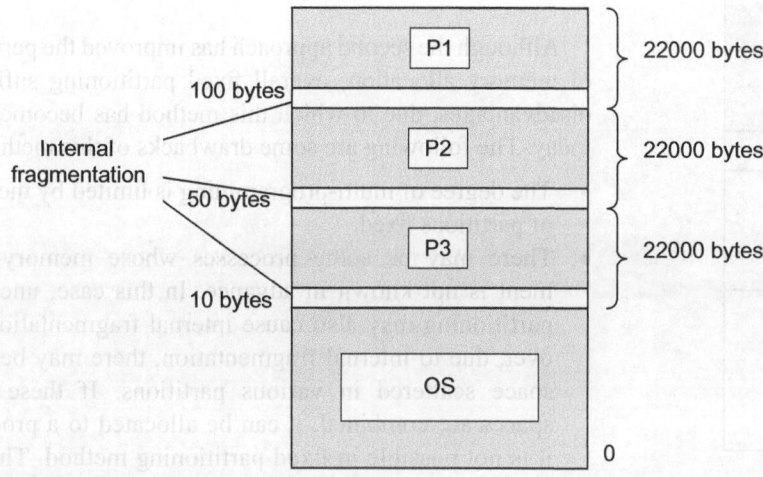

Example 10.5

Three processes P1, P2, and P3 of size 67000, 65000, and 60000 bytes, respectively, need space in the memory. If partitions of equal size, that is, 70000 bytes, are allocated to P1, P2, and P3, will there be any fragmentation in this allocation?

Solution

After allocating the partitions to the processes, the first, second, and third partitions are left with 3000 bytes, 5000 bytes, and 10000 bytes, respectively. This leftover space in each partition is internal fragmentation, as shown in the figure.

In the above two examples, fixed memory partitioning, with equal partitioning size, leads to wastage of a large space in the memory. The second approach is to use unequal-sized partitions in the memory. Unequal-sized partitions can be chosen, such that smaller to bigger size processes can be accommodated, thereby, wasting less memory, as shown in Fig. 10.7. Keeping in view the average size of the processes, the size of partitions in the memory can be fixed.

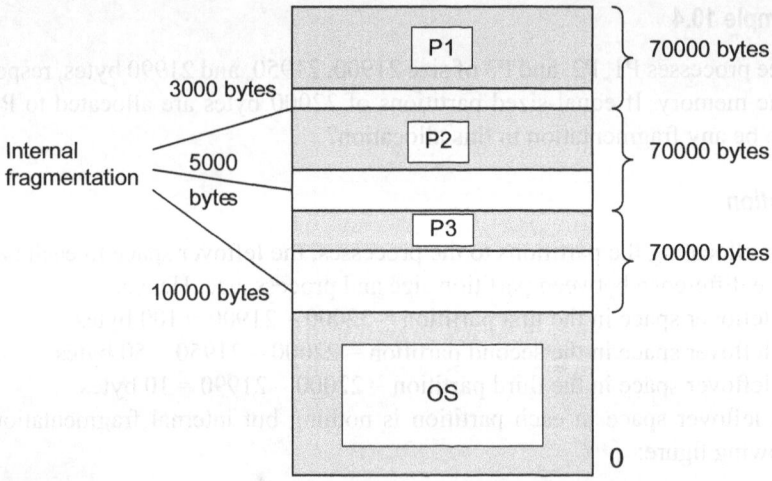

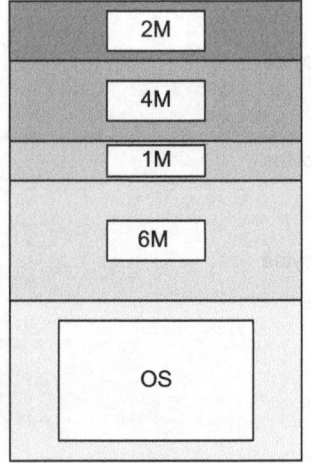

Fig. 10.7 Fixed unequal-sized partitioning-based contiguous memory allocation

Although the second approach has improved the performance of memory allocation, overall fixed partitioning suffers from disadvantages, due to which this method has become obsolete today. The following are some drawbacks of this method:

- The degree of multi-programming is limited by the number of partitions fixed.
- There may be some processes whose memory requirement is not known in advance. In this case, unequal-size partitioning may also cause internal fragmentation. Moreover, due to internal fragmentation, there may be memory space scattered in various partitions. If these memory spaces are combined, it can be allocated to a process. But it is not possible in fixed partitioning method. This results in external fragmentation also. Thus, fixed partitioning method suffers from both types of fragmentation.

Example 10.6

Three processes P1, P2, and P3 of size 19900, 19990, and 19888 bytes, respectively, need space in memory. If partitions of equal size, that is, 20000 bytes, are allocated to P1, P2, and P3, will there be any fragmentation in this allocation? Can a process of 200 bytes be accommodated?

Solution

After allocating the partitions to the processes, the first, second, and third partitions are left with 100 bytes, 10 bytes, and 112 bytes, respectively. This leftover space in each partition is internal fragmentation.

The total space left = 100 + 10 + 112 = 222 bytes

Process of 200 bytes cannot be accommodated, even if the total space left is more than 200 bytes. This is because the space left is not contiguous. Hence, this partitioning also leads to external fragmentation.

10.3.2 Contiguous Allocation with Dynamic/Variable Partitioning

Contiguous allocation with fixed partitioning suffers from drawbacks, as discussed above. To overcome these drawbacks, contiguous allocation with variable partitioning was devised. It is also known as dynamic partitioning. Instead of having static partitions, the memory partition will be allocated to a process dynamically. In other words, the number and size of partitions are not fixed at the time of system generation. They are variable and are created at run time by the OS. The procedure for memory allocation in this method is the same as fixed partitioning. The only difference is that partitions for processes are created at run time, when they are brought to the ready queue. PDT is maintained in variable partitioning as well. In the same way as discussed in fixed partitioning, a hole is searched for in the process. Initially, there is only a single large hole, that is, a partition allocated to user processes. The first process is allocated the required memory, out of this large hole, and the rest of the memory is returned. It means there are two partitions of the original hole: one allocated to the process and the other partition, which is available. In this way, the processes are allocated the required space in the hole and variable-sized partitions are produced. Two contiguous free holes can be combined into a single partition.

The IBM mainframe was developed as Multi-programming with Variable number of Tasks (OS/MVT). The advantage in variable partitioning is that the process is given exactly as much space as it requires, reducing the internal fragmentation faced in fixed partitioning. Although variable partitioning reduces memory wastage, it can still cause fragmentation. Eventually, there are small holes in the memory partitions. These holes cannot be allocated to any process, because they are not contiguous, and hence, cause external fragmentation.

Example 10.7

Let us understand dynamic partitioning with an example. Consider three processes P1, P2, and P3, as shown in Fig. 10.8. Initially, 120M hole is available in the memory. P1 of 30M consumes memory from the first hole and leaves 90M space. Similarly, P2 and P3 are allocated 40M and 48M of memory, respectively, leaving a hole of 2M. In Fig. 10.8(e), P2 releases the memory, leaving a hole of 30M. In Fig. 10.8(f), P4 arrives and acquires 28M, leaving a hole of 2M. In Fig. 10.8(g), P3 releases the memory, leaving a hole of 48M. In Fig. 10.8(h), P1 arrives again, and now requires 30M space. Since P4 resides in the space, which was earlier allocated to P1, it will consume 30M from the hole left by P3.

10.3.3 Compaction

External fragmentation in dynamic partitioning can be reduced, if all the small holes formed during partitioning and allocation, are compacted together. Compaction helps to control memory wastage, occurring in dynamic partitioning. The OS observes the number of holes in the memory and compacts them after a period, so that a contiguous memory can be allocated for a new process. The compaction is done by shuffling the memory contents, such that all occupied memory region is moved in one direction, and all unoccupied memory region in the other direction. This results in contiguous free holes, that is, a single large hole, which is then allocated to a desired process.

Compaction, however, is not always possible. One limitation is that it can be applied, only if the memory is relocated dynamically at the execution time, so that it is easy to move one process from one region to another. Another limitation is that compaction incurs cost, because it is time consuming and wastes CPU time.

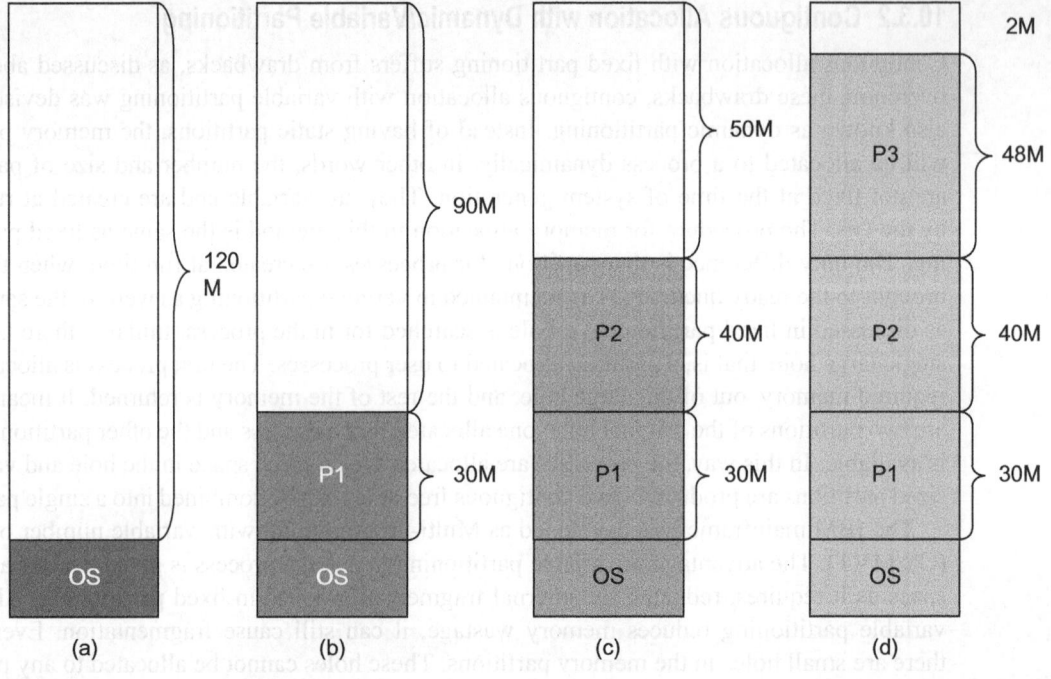

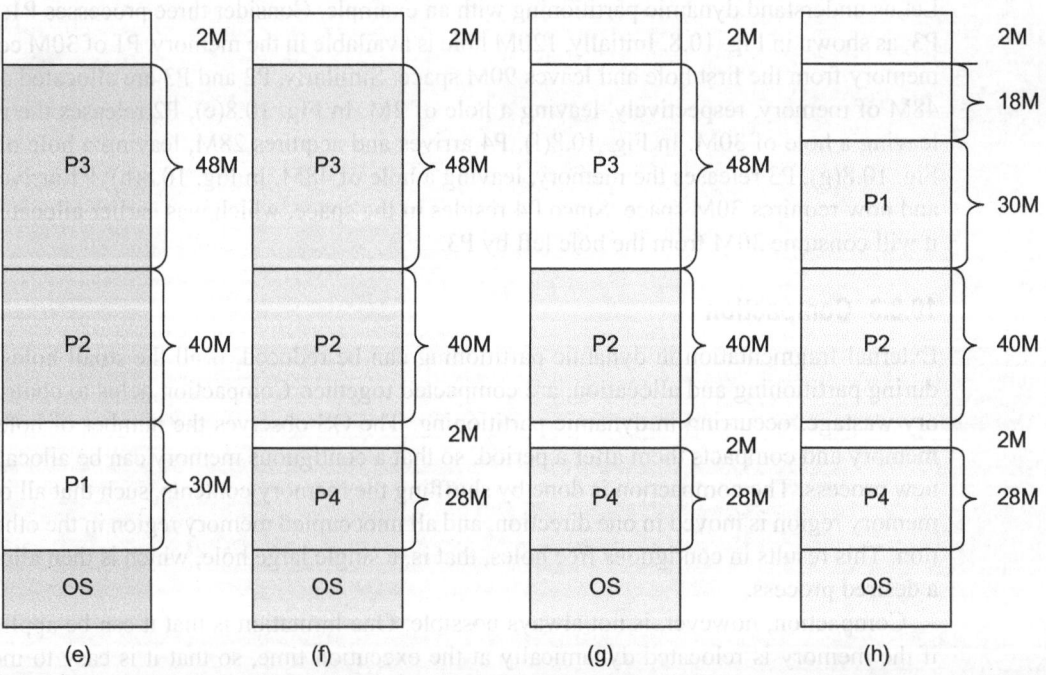

Fig. 10.8 Variable partitioning

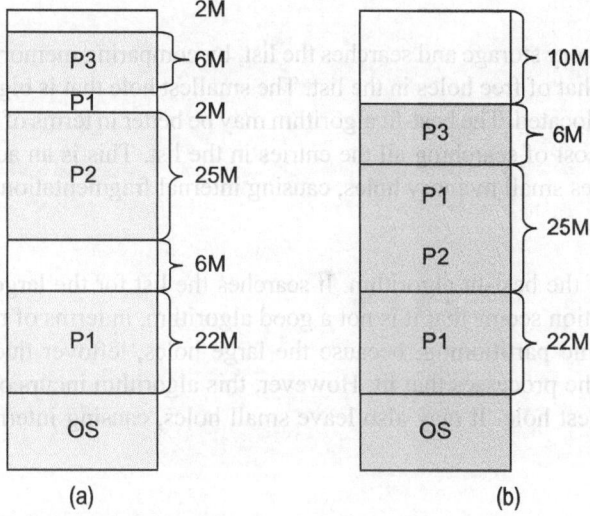

Fig. 10.9 Compaction

Example 10.8

Fig. 10.9(a) shows the state of three processes in memory. Here, the wastage of memory is 6M + 2M + 2M = 10M. No process can be allocated to this space. However, through compaction, that is, by merging these memory spaces, 10M space can be obtained contiguously, and can be used for the allocation of a process, which is less than or equal to 10M (see Fig. 10.9 (b)). For compaction, the processes should be relocated to different addresses. This may consume time, thereby making this method costly.

The contiguous allocation method, with fixed as well as variable partitioning method, suffers from fragmentation and wastes memory, as discussed above. The alternate method is non-contiguous partitioning, which will be discussed later.

10.3.4 Memory Allocation Techniques

Memory allocation techniques are algorithms that satisfy the memory needs of a process: they decide which hole from the list of free holes must be allocated to the process. Thus, it is also known as partition selection algorithms. In fixed partitioning with equal-sized partitions, these algorithms are not applicable, because all the partitions are of the same size and therefore, it does not matter which partition is selected. These algorithms, however, play a great role in fixed-partitioning with unequal-sized partitions and in dynamic partitioning, in terms of system performance and memory wastage. There are primarily three techniques for memory allocation.

First-fit Allocation

This algorithm searches the list of free holes and allocates the first hole in the list that is big enough to accommodate the desired process. Searching is stopped when it finds the first-fit hole. The next time, searching is resumed from that location. The first hole is counted from this last location. In this case, it becomes the *next-fit* allocation. The first-fit algorithm does not take care of the memory wastage. It may be possible that the first-fit hole is very large, compared to the memory required by the process, resulting in wastage of memory.

Best-fit Allocation

This algorithm takes care of memory storage and searches the list, by comparing memory size of the process to be allocated with that of free holes in the list. The smallest hole that is big enough to accommodate the process is allocated. The best-fit algorithm may be better in terms of wastage of memory space, but it incurs cost of searching all the entries in the list. This is an additional overhead. Moreover, it also leaves small memory holes, causing internal fragmentation.

Worst-fit Allocation

This algorithm is just reverse of the best-fit algorithm. It searches the list for the largest hole. This algorithm in its first perception seems that it is not a good algorithm, in terms of memory. But it may be helpful in dynamic partitioning, because the large holes, leftover due to this algorithm, may be allocated to the processes that fit. However, this algorithm incurs overhead of searching the list for the largest hole. It may also leave small holes, causing internal fragmentation.

Example 10.9

Consider the memory allocation scenario as shown in Fig. 10.10. Allocate memory for additional requests of 4K and 10K (in this order). Compare the memory allocation, using first-fit, best-fit, and worst-fit allocation methods, in terms of internal fragmentation.

Solution

First-fit allocation: It allocates the first hole in the list that is big enough. Hole of 10K is allocated to the process of 4K, leaving a hole of 6K in memory. The next request is of 10K. So, the next hole in the list is of 5K and it cannot accommodate the process. Hence, the next available hole of 15K is allocated, leaving a hole of 5K (see Fig. 10.11). It leaves fragmentation of 6K +5K = 11K.

Best-fit allocation: It allocates the smallest hole that is big enough. Hole of 5K is allocated to the process of 4K, leaving a hole of just 1K. The next request is of 10K. After comparing the size of all the holes, hole of 10K is allocated. It leaves fragmentation of 0K +1K = 1K (see Fig. 10.12).

Worst-fit allocation: It allocates the largest hole in the list. For the process of 4K, the largest hole of 22K is allocated. This leaves a hole of 18K in the memory. The next request is of 10K.

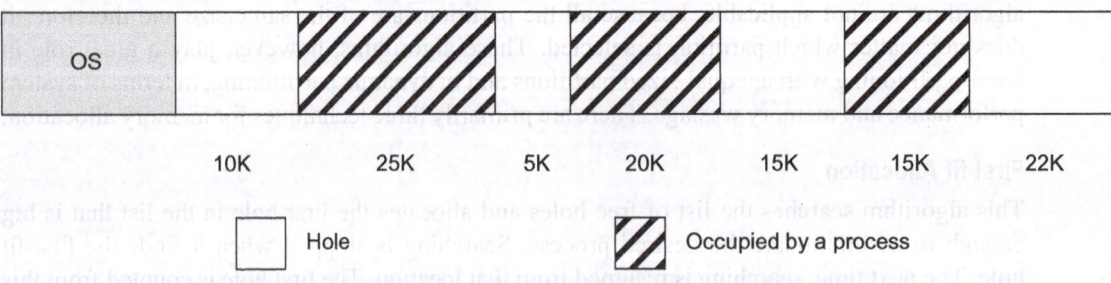

| 10K | 25K | 5K | 20K | 15K | 15K | 22K |

☐ Hole   ▨ Occupied by a process

Fig. 10.10   Example memory allocation scenario

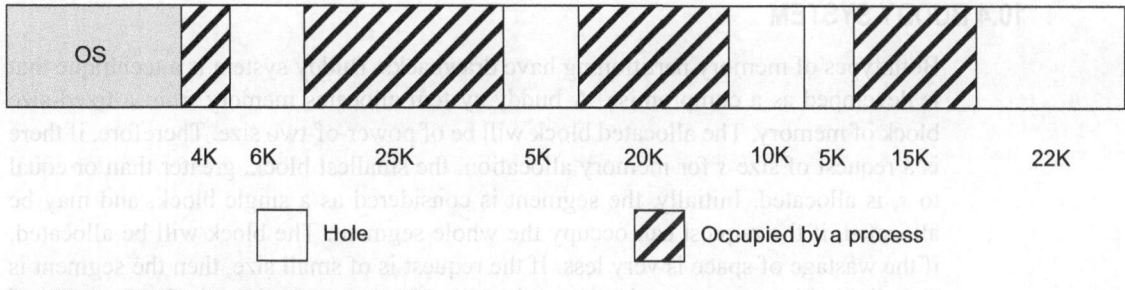

Fig. 10.11   First-fit allocation for Example 10.9

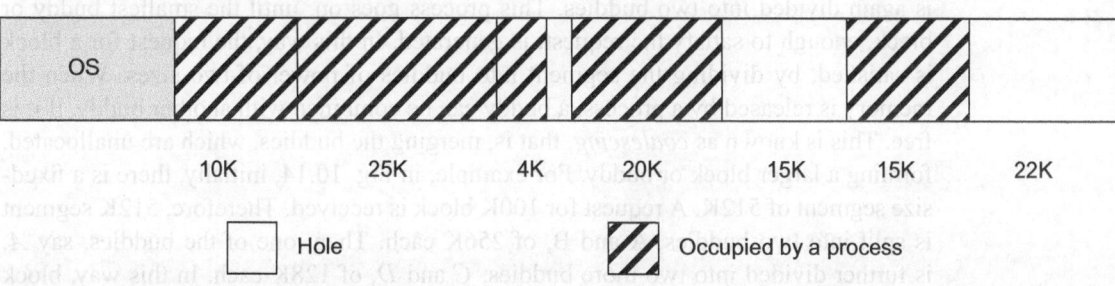

Fig. 10.12   Best-fit allocation for Example 10.9

Comparing the size of all holes, the 18K hole is the largest hole in the list. Hence, it is allocated to the process. It leaves fragmentation of $22K - 4K - 10K = 8K$ (see fig. 10.13).

By comparing all the algorithms on the basis of internal fragmentation, the best-fit allocation is the best method, as it wastes least memory. The worst-fit is better than the first-fit allocation, as it provides more holes of appropriate sizes for future requests. Also, memory wastage is comparatively less.

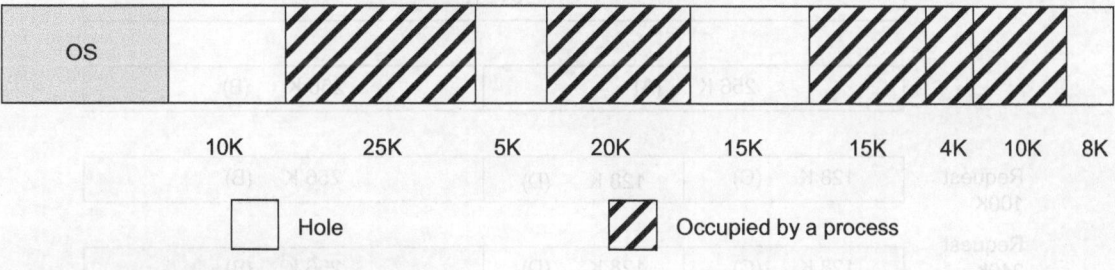

Fig. 10.13   Worst-fit allocation for Example 10.9

10.4 BUDDY SYSTEM

Both types of memory partitioning have drawbacks. Buddy system is a technique that is developed as a compromise. A buddy system allocates memory from a fixed-size block of memory. The allocated block will be of power-of-two size. Therefore, if there is a request of size s for memory allocation, the smallest block, greater than or equal to s, is allocated. Initially, the segment is considered as a single block, and may be allocated, if the request can occupy the whole segment. The block will be allocated, if the wastage of space is very less. If the request is of small size, then the segment is first divided into two parts, known as buddies. One of the buddies is then considered for allocation. If the size of the buddy is large, compared to the request, then this buddy is again divided into two buddies. This process goes on, until the smallest buddy or block, enough to satisfy the request, is generated. In this way, the request for a block is satisfied, by dividing the segment into buddies of power-of-two sizes. When the memory is released by a process, a buddy can be combined with another buddy, if it is free. This is known as *coalescing*, that is, merging the buddies, which are unallocated, forming a larger block or buddy. For example, in Fig. 10.14, initially, there is a fixed-size segment of 512K. A request for 100K block is received. Therefore, 512K segment is split into two buddies, A and B, of 256K each. Then, one of the buddies, say A, is further divided into two more buddies, C and D, of 128K each. In this way, block C is allocated to the request. After this, suppose a request of 240K block is received. B is allocated for this request, as its size is 256K. After some time, A releases the memory. Another request of 240K block is fulfilled by coalescing A (128K) and B (128K), making a larger block to accommodate the new request.

The buddy system is efficient, compared to fixed and variable partitioning. The good feature of this method is coalescing of blocks. UNIX kernel memory allocation is done using the buddy system. However, this is not used in any contemporary OS, as this may also suffer from fragmentation, if the system rounds up the size of a block

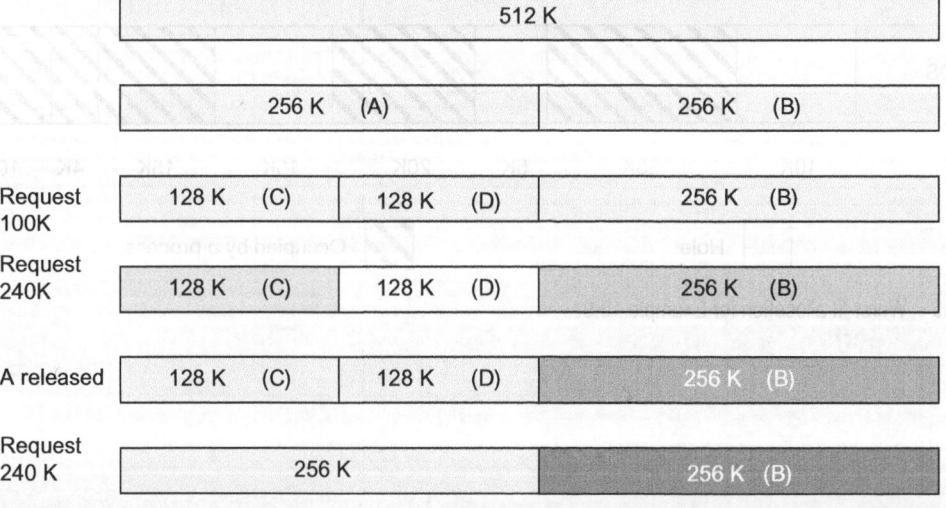

Fig. 10.14 Buddy System

to the next higher power of 2. For example, a request for 65K, which cannot be satisfied with a block of size 2^5, will be satisfied with a block of 2^6, but there will be a large wastage of memory. Therefore, for any modern OS, paging and segmentation are used for memory allocation. These methods will be discussed later in this chapter and the next chapter.

10.5 NON-CONTIGUOUS MEMORY ALLOCATION

Contiguous memory allocation method suffers from many drawbacks. Both types of this method cause internal as well as external fragmentation. Moreover, the fragmentation is also in the secondary storage, where the swapped-out processes of variable sizes need space. Thus, the contiguous allocation method wastes a lot of memory space. These drawbacks lead us to the non-contiguous allocation method. In this method, the holes do not need to be contiguous. They may be scattered in the memory, and can be allocated to a process. The non-contiguous memory allocation is also classified as fixed partitioning and variable partitioning. The former is known as paging, and the latter is known as segmentation. These are discussed in the subsequent sections.

10.6 PAGING CONCEPT

The first non-contiguous allocation method is paging, where memory is divided into equal-size partitions. The partitions are relatively smaller, compared to the contiguous method. They are known as *frames*. Since the idea is to reduce external fragmentation, the logical memory of a process is also divided into small chunks or blocks of the same size as frames. These chunks are called *pages* of a process. In this way, whenever a frame in memory is allocated to a page, it fits well in the memory, thereby eliminating the problem of external fragmentation. Moreover, the hard disk is also divided into *blocks*, which are of same size as frames. Thus, paging is a logical concept that divides the logical address space of a process into fixed-size pages, and is implemented in physical memory through frames. All the pages of the process to be executed are loaded into any available frame in the memory.

Let us understand the paging concept in detail and the benefits of a non-contiguous method with an example.

Example 10.10

In Fig. 10.15(a), it is given that there are 10 free frames in the memory. There are four processes P1, P2, P3, and P4, consisting of three, four, two, and five pages, respectively. All three pages of P1 have been allocated to frames (see Fig.10.15 (b)). Similarly, all the pages of P2 and P3 have been allocated, as shown in Fig. 10.15 (c) and 10.15 (d). Now only one frame is free in the memory, whereas P4 requires 5 frames. After some time, P2 finishes its execution and therefore, releases memory. Therefore, frames 3 to 6 are free now, making the total number of free frames as five. These five frames, though non-contiguous, are allocated to P4. Four pages are allocated frames 3, 4, 5, and 6 and one page gets frame 9 (see Fig 10.15 (f)). Suppose after some time, P1 releases page 1, P4 releases page 2, and P3 releases page 1, as shown in (see Fig. 10.15(g)), as they are swapped out into the disk. At this time, another process, say P5, is introduced in the system with five pages, but needs only three pages to be accommodated in the memory. As shown in the figure, three non-contiguous frames are available. These will be then allocated to P5 (see 10.15 (h)), through paging.

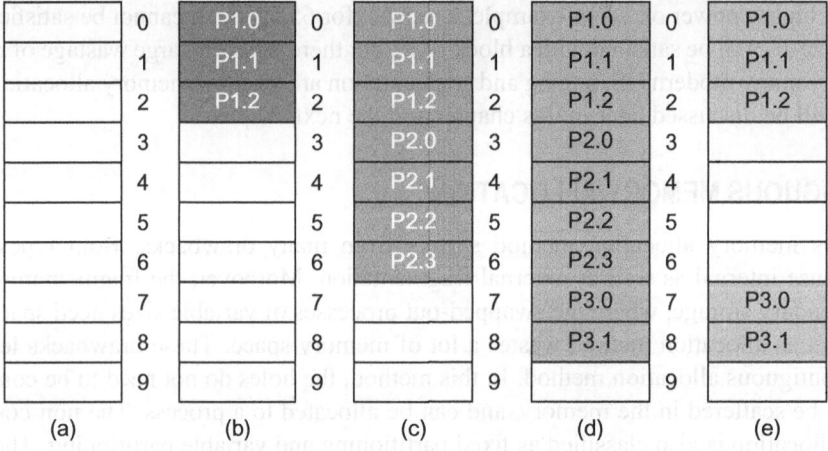

Fig. 10.15   Paging concept example

One can realize that a logical address in the paging concept has two parts: a page number and its displacement or offset in the page. Consequently, this logical address is converted into a physical address. For that, the start address of the page in the memory, that is, address in the base register, must be known. In this way, every page will have one start address in the memory. But a single base register will not suffice for this purpose, unlike contiguous allocation. Instead of a base register for every page, the start addresses of pages are stored in the form of a table, known as a *page table*. A page table is a data structure used to store the base addresses of each page in the process, that is, the entry in the page table indicates the frame location of pages in the memory. Thus, the paging concept involves the logical memory division into pages, page table to keep the base addresses of pages, and physical memory divided into frames (see Fig. 10.16).

Example 10.11

Design page tables for all the processes at the time instant of Fig. 10.15(h).

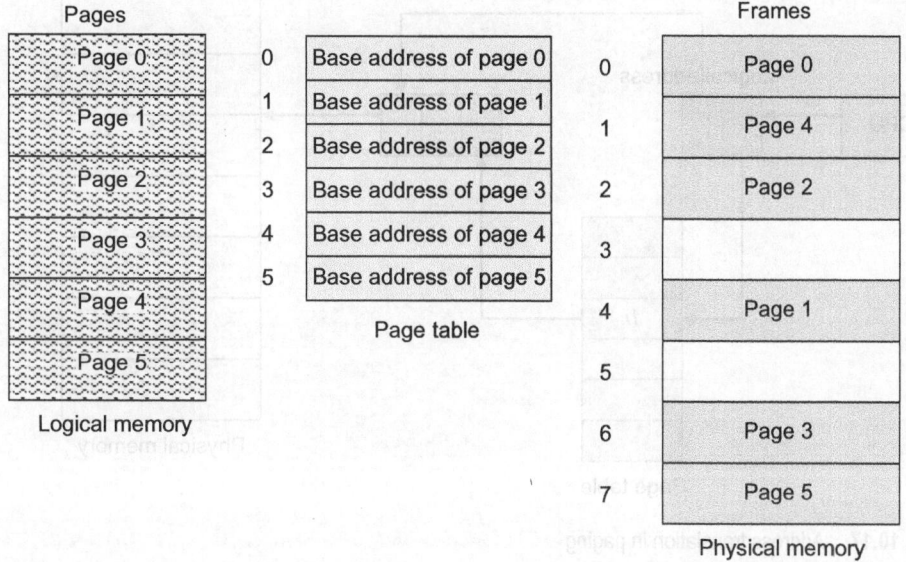

Fig. 10.16 Paging concept

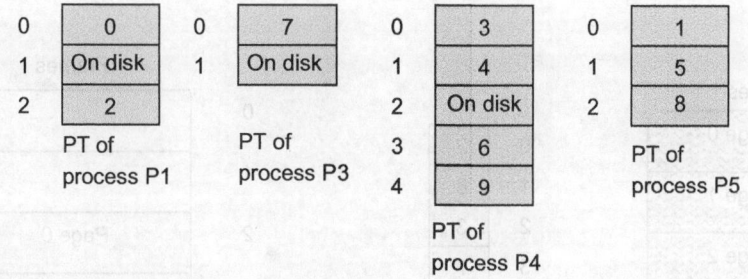

Solution

After reaching the start location of a page, its displacement or offset is added to map the complete logical address into physical address and then, the particular instruction in a page can be executed. Thus, the processor, in case of paging, generates the logical address in the form:

(Page number p, Offset d)

The logical address is converted into a physical address by the MMU. The hardware must be updated such that it must know how to access the page table for conversion. The steps for logical to physical address conversion (see Fig. 10.17) are as under:

1. The processor generates a two dimensional logical address, (p, d).
2. The page number p is extracted from the logical address, and is used as an index in the page table.
3. The base address b, corresponding to the page number, is retrieved.
4. b is added to the offset d to get the corresponding physical address.

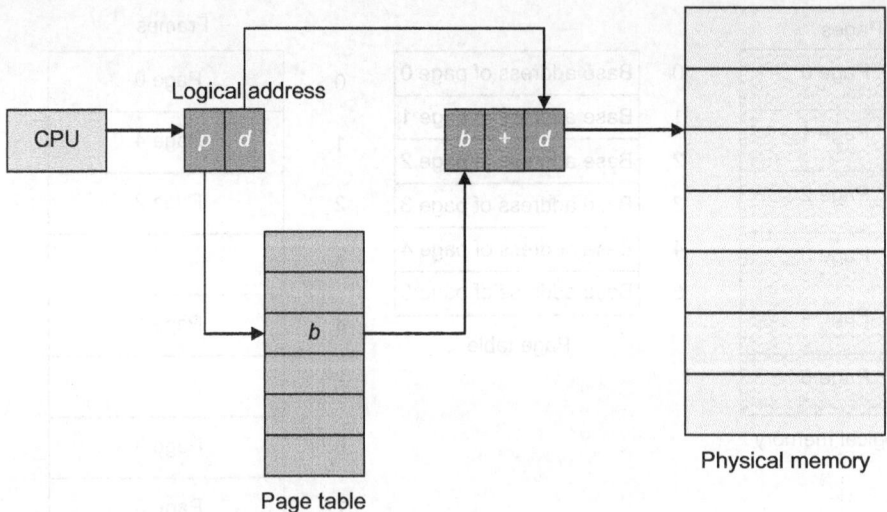

Fig. 10.17   Address translation in paging

Example 10.12

A program's logical memory has been divided into five pages and these pages are allocated frames, 2, 6, 3, 7, and 5. Show the mapping of logical memory to physical memory.

Solution

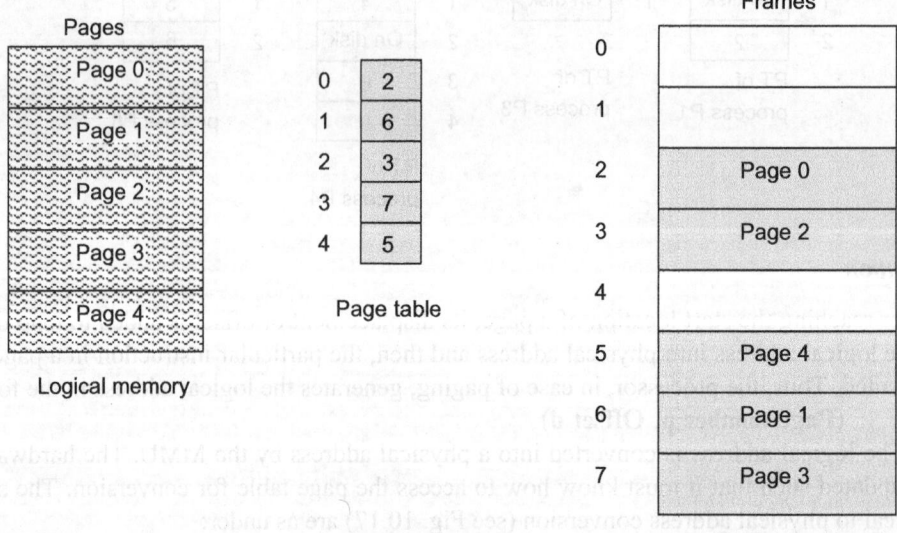

Example 10.13

A program's logical memory has been divided into four pages. The pages are allocated frames 5, 3, 1, and 2. Assume that each page size is 4 bytes. Show the mapping of logical memory to physical memory in bytes.

Solution

Since the page size is of 4 bytes, the frame size will also be the same. Therefore, a logical address needs to be converted accordingly. Suppose the logical address is (2, 2) (page number = 2 and offset = 2). After the page number is used to index into the page table, page 2 is in frame 1. The actual location of frame 1 is at $1 \times 4 = 4^{th}$ byte in physical memory. So the logical address will map to $4 + 2 = 6^{th}$ byte in physical memory. Similarly the logical address page number = 0 and offset = 3, will map to $(5 \times 4) + 3 = 23^{rd}$ byte in the memory.

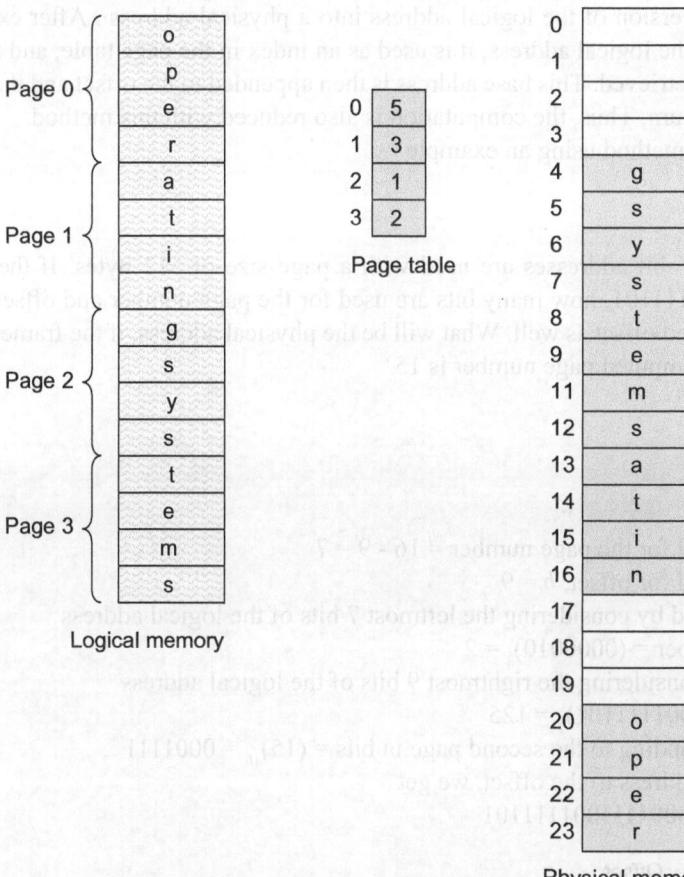

Logical memory / Page table / Physical memory

The logical address will not be generated as two-dimensional address by the processor. The processor generates only a simple single-dimensional binary address, but the page number and offset is separated out from the bits of the logical address. Some lower bits (rightmost) are for offset and higher bits (leftmost) are for page number. The question is how many bits in the address should be fixed for the page number and offset. This is decided by the page size. If a process is of size 65536 bytes (2^{16}) and the page size is taken as 1024 bytes (2^{10}), then the number of pages will be 64 (2^{6}). It means the page number has 6 bits (leftmost) and the remaining 10 bits (rightmost) are for offset. In this way, the page size decides the division of the logical address into a page number and offset. Thus, if the size of a logical address space is 2^{a}, and the page size is 2^{b}, then the high-order bits (a-b) indicates the page number and the low-order bits b gives the page offset (see Fig. 10.18).

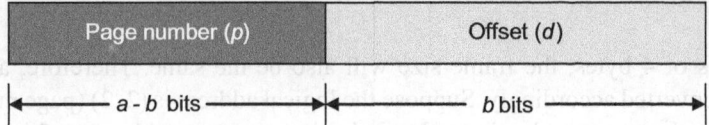

Fig. 10.18   Logical address format in paging

But this scheme is only possible if page size is taken as power of 2. Otherwise, it is not possible to divide the logical address in this fashion. The page size, as power of 2, also conventionally facilitates the conversion of the logical address into a physical address.. After extracting the page number from the logical address, it is used as an index in the page table, and the base address of that page is retrieved. This base address is then appended to the offset and there is no need to calculate their sum. Thus, the computation is also reduced with this method.

Let us illustrate this method using an example

Example 10.14

In a paging scheme, 16-bit addresses are used with a page size of 512 bytes. If the logical address is 0000010001111101, how many bits are used for the page number and offset? Compute the page number and offset as well. What will be the physical address, if the frame address corresponding to the computed page number is 15.

Solution

Logical address space = 2^{16}
Page size = $512 = 2^9$
Number of bits required for the page number = $16 - 9 = 7$
Number of bits required for offset, $b = 9$
Page number is obtained by considering the leftmost 7 bits of the logical address
      i.e., Page number = $(0000010)_2 = 2$
Offset is obtained by considering the rightmost 9 bits of the logical address
      i.e., Offset = $(001111101)_2 = 125$
Frame address corresponding to the second page in bits = $(15)_{10} = 0001111$
Appending the frame address to the offset, we get
the physical address = **0001111**001111101

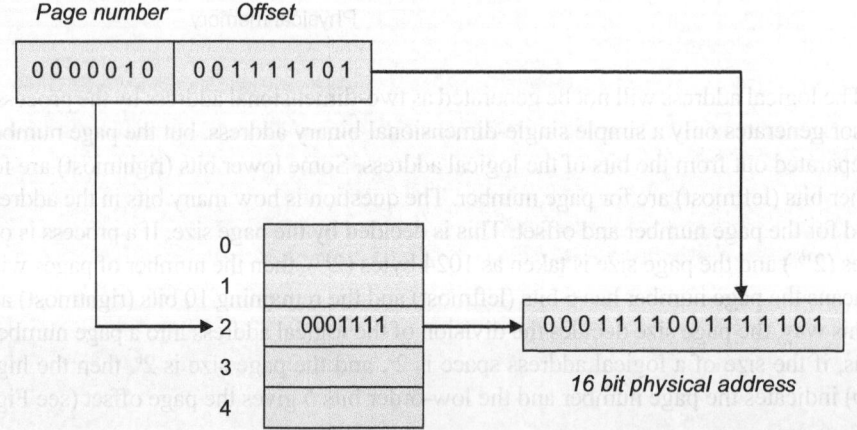

16 bit physical address

Example 10.15

There are 128 pages in a logical address space, with a page size of 1024 bytes. How many bits will be there in the logical address?

Solution

The logical address space contains 128 pages i.e., 2^7 pages.
That means the number of bits required for the page number, $p = 7$
Page size, $2^b = 1024$ bytes $= 2^{10}$, and
That means the number of bits required for the offset, $b = 10$

$$p = a - b$$
$$7 = a - 10$$
$$a = 17$$

Therefore, 17 bits are required in the logical address.

Example 10.16

There is a system with 64 pages of 512 bytes page size and a physical memory of 32 frames. How many bits are required in the logical and physical address?

Solution

Given, page size = 512 bytes = 2_9 i.e., $b = 9$
No. of pages = 64 = 2_6 i.e., $p = 6$
Since $p = a - b$, $a = 15$
Therefore, 15 bits are required in the logical address.
Since the number of bits required for offset, $b = 9$ and
The number of bits required to address 32 (2^5) frames = 5
Therefore, after appending the number of bits required for the frame size to the offset, 14 bits are required in the physical address.

10.6.1 Paging Implementation and Hardware Requirements

To implement the paging concept, the memory management component of the OS maintains a list of status of all the frames in the memory. Initially, all the frames are empty in the user area of the memory. As soon as a process loads its pages, the empty frames are allocated, and their status is marked as allocated. As the pages are loaded to the frames, the page table of that process is also updated correspondingly. The frame address of a page, where it has been allocated, is entered in the page table. In this way, a page table must be updated as soon as the frame address of a page changes. Furthermore, the address of a page table, where it is stored in the memory, is also stored in the PCB of the process. This information is useful at the time of execution of a process. As soon as a process is scheduled for execution, its appropriate page table is referred for execution, if there is a page table address entry in its PCB.

It is clear from the above discussion that paging will incur cost and increase the access time, because the page table will also be stored in the memory. To reduce the access time, some systems (like DEC PDP-11) were developed, with the help of fast access registers at the hardware level. These registers were used to store the page table entries. These registers were developed with very high-speed logic, so that address translation in paging is efficient and does not affect the access time. However, this register-based page table entries method could not be successful, because such entries increased (more than million entries) with the later architecture of the system. The large number of page table entries was not feasible to implement with fast access registers. Therefore, the page table is stored in the memory only in any contemporary OS. The hardware support needed in this case is to have a register just like the base register, so that the page table address can be stored. This base register is known as *Page Table Base Register* (PTBR). So, whenever a process is scheduled to be executed, the page table address from its PCB is loaded into PTBR, and the corresponding page table is accessed in the memory. Thus, a page table per process, along with one PTBR in hardware, is sufficient to implement the paging concept. When the current process is suspended or terminated, and another process is scheduled to execute, then the PTBR entry is replaced with the page table address of a new process.

Another problem in paging is an increased number of memory accesses. To execute an instruction in a page of a process, first its page table is accessed in the memory to find the frame address of the desired page. This frame address is then combined with the offset, and then the actual frame is accessed in the memory for the operation. Therefore, there are two memory accesses that slow down the execution.

Total memory access time = Time to access page table + Time to access memory location

This problem can be reduced if some of the page table entries are cached in a high-speed cache memory. High speed associative cache memory known as *Translation Look-aside Buffer* (TLB) is used for this purpose. The TLB consists of some recently-used page table entries with page number (p) and its corresponding frame address (b). Whenever the CPU generates a logical address, TLB is first searched for the page frame address. If the page number is found in the TLB, it is known as a *TLB hit*, otherwise it is a *TLB miss*. This type of memory mapping through TLB is known as *associative mapping*. In case of a TLB hit, the frame address of the desired page number is retrieved from the TLB, and there is no need to access the page table, thereby reducing to one memory access. However, in case of a TLB miss, the page table must be searched for the frame address, and then the physical address is mapped. Furthermore, this page table entry must be entered in the TLB as well, so that the next reference to this page number can be found in the TLB. In this way, the solution to reduce the two-memory accesses in paging with TLB may be costlier, if the TLB miss ratio is high. To make it successful, the TLB hit ratio must be high, otherwise Effective-memory Access Time (EAT) will increase further (see Fig. 10.19). The total access time, in this case of a system with TLB, will be increased as compared to that without TLB as in the following:

Total memory access time = Time to access TLB + Time to access page table + Time to access memory location

The effective memory access time can be calculated, if TLB is used for paging address translation. It is calculated, based on the probability of TLB hit or miss, as in the following:

Effective memory access time (EAT) = $P(H)$ × *(Time to access TLB + Time to access the memory location)* + $[(1 - P(H))$ × *(Time to access TLB + 2 (Time to access the memory location))]*

where P(H) is TLB hit ratio.

If the hit ratio is high, the EAT is reduced. So, there should be a mechanism, such that the hit ratio is high, in order to have a low EAT. The performance of the system with TLB is highly dependent on the high value of hit ratio, otherwise its performance will be worse

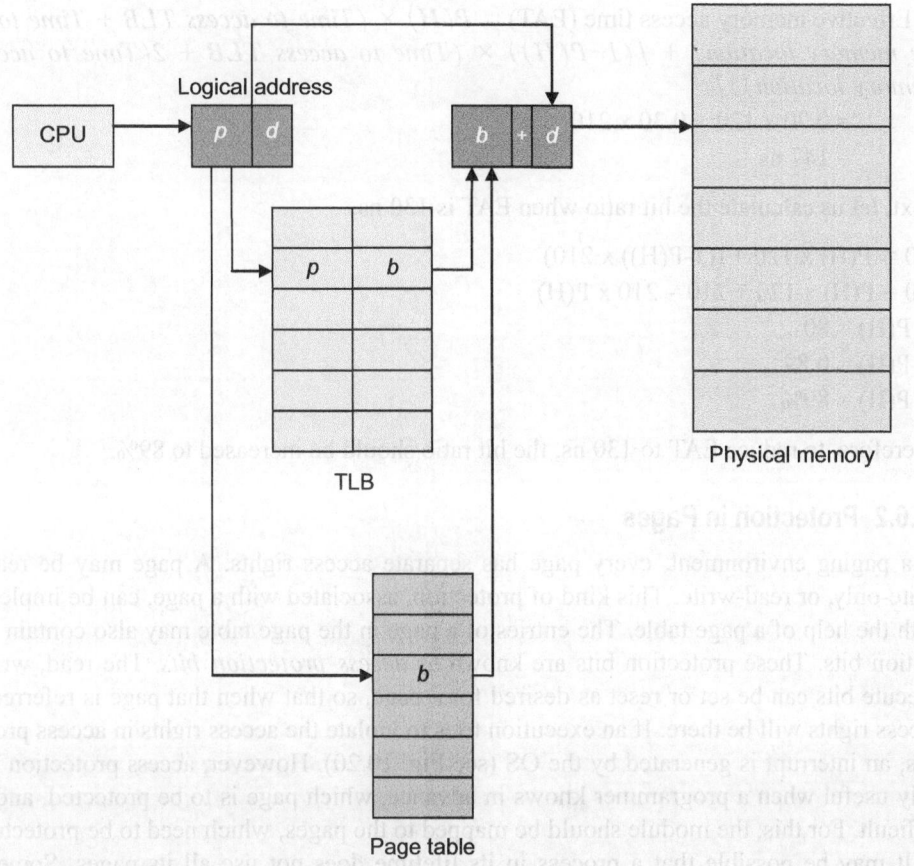

Logical address

Fig. 10.19   Paging implementation with TLB

than the system without TLB. Therefore, the TLB entries should be designed to have the most frequent page table entries. Associative registers can also be added to have more number of frequent page table entries.

Example 10.17

In a paging system with TLB, it takes 30 ns to search the TLB and 90 ns to access the memory. If the TLB hit ratio is 70%, find the effective memory access time. What should be the hit ratio to achieve the effective memory access time of 130 ns?

Solution

Time taken in case of TLB hit = Time to access TLB + Time to access memory

= 30 + 90 = 120 ns

Time taken in case of TLB miss = Time to access TLB + Time to access page table + Time to access memory

= Time to access TLB + 2(Time to access the memory location)

= 30 + 2 (90) = 210 ns

Effective memory access time (EAT) = $P(H) \times$ *(Time to access TLB + Time to access the memory location) + [(1−P(H)) × (Time to access TLB + 2(Time to access the memory location))]*

$$= 0.70 \times 120 + 0.30 \times 210$$
$$= 147 \text{ ns}$$

Next, let us calculate the hit ratio when EAT is 130 ns.

$$130 = P(H) \times 120 + ((1\text{-}P(H)) \times 210)$$
$$130 = P(H) \times 120 + 210 - 210 \times P(H)$$
$$90\ P(H) = 80$$
$$P(H) = 0.89$$
$$P(H) = 89\%$$

Therefore, to reduce EAT to 130 ns, the hit ratio should be increased to 89%.

10.6.2 Protection in Pages

In a paging environment, every page has separate access rights. A page may be read-only, write-only, or read-write. This kind of protection, associated with a page, can be implemented with the help of a page table. The entries of a page in the page table may also contain its protection bits. These protection bits are known as *access protection bits*. The read, write, and execute bits can be set or reset as desired for a page, so that when that page is referred to, its access rights will be there. If an execution tries to violate the access rights in access protection bits, an interrupt is generated by the OS (see Fig. 10.20). However, access protection bits are only useful when a programmer knows in advance, which page is to be protected, and that is difficult. For this, the module should be mapped to the pages, which need to be protected.

It may be possible that a process in its lifetime does not use all its pages. Some of the pages, at a given time, may not be valid. However, the page table entries for these invalid pages are still there, and therefore, may be accessed. To make these pages invalid, another protection bit known as *valid-invalid* bit can be added to the page table. This bit is used in the page table to mark a page as valid or invalid. Valid means the page is being referred by the process, and invalid means the page is not in use by the process and it is illegal (see Fig. 10.21). Another method to have protection against these invalid pages is to have a *Page Table Length Register* (PTLR), just like the PTBR. Any access beyond the PTLR causes an interrupt in the OS. However, it would be a waste to have page entries of those pages, which are not in use. As page tables consume space in the memory, it is not recommended to have these invalid pages in the page table entries.

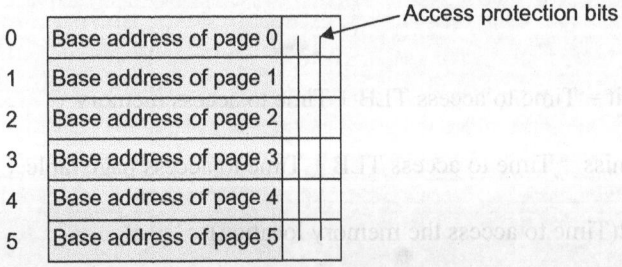

Fig. 10.20   Page table with access protection bits

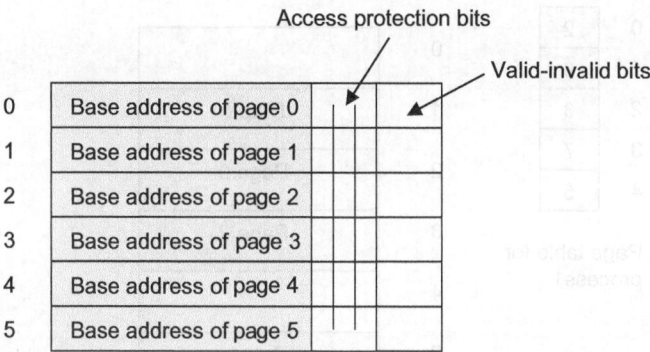

Fig. 10.21   Page table with valid-invalid bits

Example 10.18

In Example 10.12, assume that page 4 is invalid, page 0 is read-only, page 2 is read-write, and other pages have read, write, and execute permissions. Draw the page table, incorporating the protection bits for the pages.

Solution

The page table is given by:

Base Address	Read	Write	Execute	Valid/Invalid bit
2	1	0	0	1
6	1	1	1	1
3	1	1	0	1
7	1	1	1	1
5	1	1	1	0

10.6.3 Shared Pages

In a multi-user time-sharing environment, different users may need to use the same software. However, this does not mean that each user has copies of the desired software. To save memory space, there should be a single copy of the software in the memory, instead of multiple copies. Paging can be used here by means of shared pages. Suppose, if a compiler consuming 1500 KB memory is shared between two users, then all the pages, related to the compiler, can be shared among all users. In the memory, there will be only one copy of the compiler. The page table corresponding to all user processes will map the compiler to the same location in the memory, except the data page of the process (see Fig. 10.22). If each user process uses a separate copy of the compiler, 3000 KB memory will be consumed, whereas with shared pages concept, only 1500 KB memory will be consumed, thereby, saving the memory space.

However, not all the pages can be shared. The data areas of processes cannot be shared, as the processes will need separate data areas to run the same software. Moreover, the sharable code page should be of re-entrant type. A re-entrant code never changes during execution, and thus can be shared easily by multiple users. Thus, all the processes, sharing the same software, can execute the same code in the memory in the form of shared pages, and each process has its own copy of registers and data storage in the memory as non-sharable pages. The page table of each process maps to the same location in the memory for the shared pages.

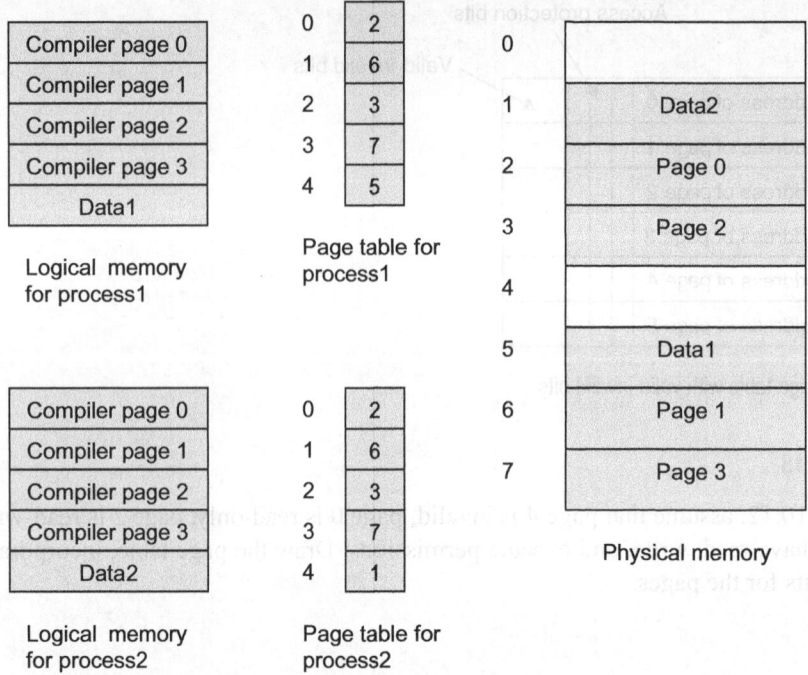

Fig. 10.22 Shared pages

10.6.4 Fragmentation

The paging concept was developed to reduce external fragmentation. However, it suffers from internal fragmentation, as it may leave some bytes of memory, if the process does not fit in a page size. If the size of a process is an exact multiple of the page size chosen, there will not be any internal fragmentation, because each frame will be utilized completely. In practice, it may not be possible that process size is an exact multiple of page size. Therefore, there will be some internal fragmentation. Paging eliminates external fragmentation, because even if there is sufficient space that is non-contiguous in the memory, it will be allocated to a process utilizing the memory space.

10.7 PAGE TABLE STRUCTURES

The page tables in the paging concept may have various page table structures, depending on different requirements.

10.7.1 Hierarchical/Multi-level Page Table Structure

Modern computer architecture supports a larger address space, such that a page table consisting of page entries, consumes a large memory, even in megabytes. Most of the systems are of 32-bit logical address space. If the page size is 4 KB (2^{12}), and a page table entry consumes 4 bytes, then the page table will consume 4 MB of memory. Thus, if a single page table, corresponding to a single process, consumes memory in megabytes, a large space is required to accommodate page tables of all the processes in the system. It is obvious that this much space cannot be accommodated in the memory contiguously. The solution is to allocate the memory to page tables as non-contiguous. The page table of a process may also be scattered in the memory, if it does not find contiguous space. Another table must be maintained to keep the record of the page table, where it occupies the space in the memory. It means the page table is also paged and is called two-level paging. Furthermore, if this second level page table also cannot be accommodated in a contiguous space, it may again be divided and memory is allocated non-contiguously. In this way, there may be several levels to manage the page tables in the memory. This is known as *multi-level* or *hierarchical page table structures*.

Let us discuss in detail how the multi-level page structures are implemented. In a two-level page table structure, the page table is paged, such that its entries are scattered in the memory and allocated non-contiguous memory. But another table is maintained that will contain the entries of the page table, where these are stored in the memory. This table is known as *outer page table* or *directory* of page table (see Fig.10.23).

To implement a two-level page table structure, the logical address needs to be modified, in order to have the outer page table entries. To perform an operation in the process' page, first the outer page table will be searched for the address of a page table, and then the page table is searched for the address of the page. So, the page number field in the logical address is divided into two parts: one for the outer page table and another for the page table. The modified logical address is shown in Fig. 10.24 for a 32-bit logical address space. Using this modified logical address, the address translation starts from the outer page table bits p1, and then continues using p2 and offset d, as shown in Fig. 10.25.

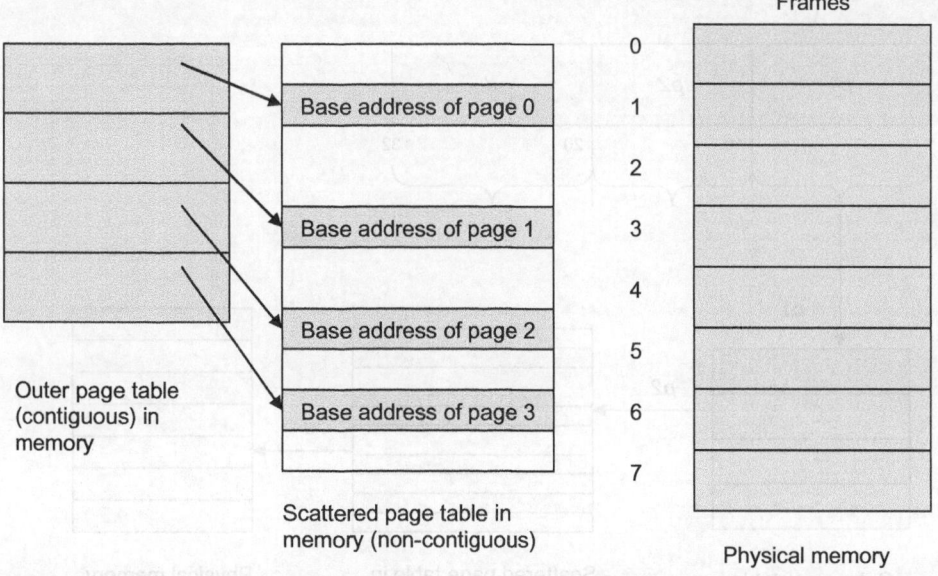

Fig. 10.23   Two-level page table structure

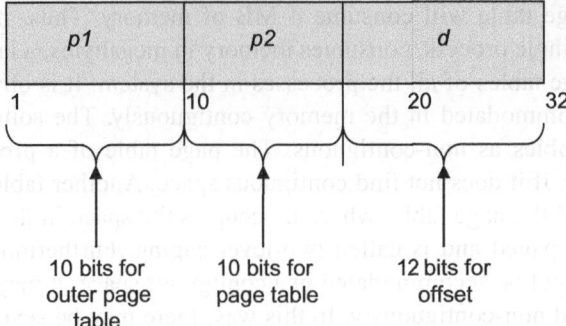

Fig.10.24   32-bit Logical address corresponding to two-level page table structure

Example 10.19

A system with 32-bit logical address uses a two-level page table structure. It uses page size of 2^{10}. The outer page table or directory is accessed with 8 bits of the address.

  i) How many bits are required to access the page table?
 ii) How many entries are there in the directory?
iii) How many entries are there in the page table?

Solution

  i) Since the page size is 2_{10}, therefore, 10 bits are required for the offset. It is given that 8 bits are required to access the outer page table, so bits required to access the page table = 32 − (10 + 8) = 14.

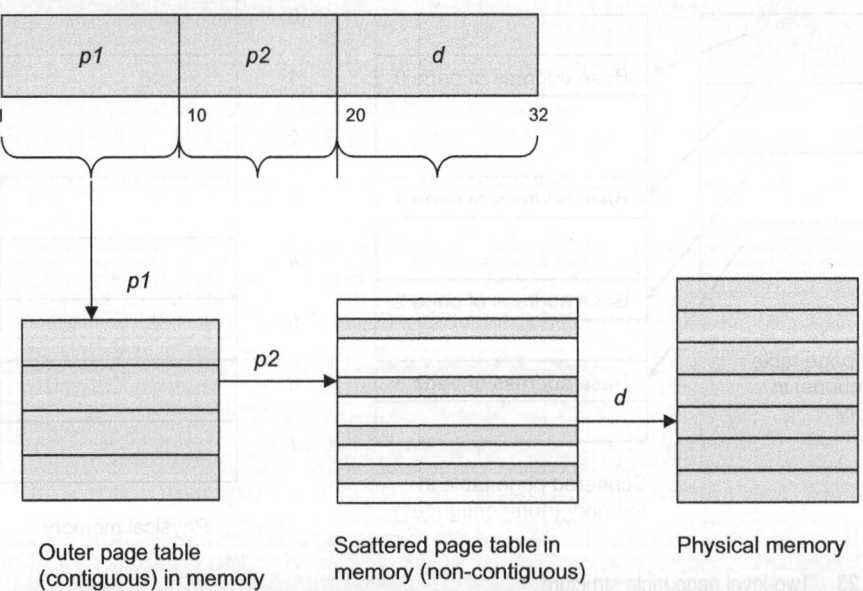

Fig. 10.25   Address translation using two-level page table structure

ii) Since directory is accessed with 8 bits,
It can have $2^8 = 256$ entries
iii) Since page table is accessed with 14 bits.
It can have $2^{14} = 16, 384$ entries

Example 10.20

A system with 32-bit logical address space uses 512 bytes page size. A page table entry takes 4 bytes. If a multi-level scheme is to be used for the page table structure, how many levels are required?

Solution

Page size $= 512 = 2^9$
Therefore, page offset requires $= 9$ bits
The page number required $= 32 - 9 = 23$ bits
A single-level page table can handle 9 of 23 bits. That means three levels are required: Dividing 23 bits into 9 for the first level, 9 for the second level, and 5 for the third level, page table at the first level and second level will have 2^9 entries each, and the third level will have 2^5 entries.

The two-level paging may not be valid for 64-bit systems. The directory or outer page table entries may be too large, such that these entries cannot be allocated contiguously. Therefore, the directory should also be divided so that these entries are allocated non-contiguous space as available. This results in three-level paging. To implement three-level paging, logical address needs to be modified to accommodate another outer page table. In this paging, there will be two outer page tables and one page table (see Fig.10.26). In this way, multiple levels can be formed, if the size of page table entries is high, resulting in hierarchical or multi-level page table structures.

The disadvantage of hierarchical or multi-level paging is that it increases the memory accesses. As the number of levels increases, the number of memory accesses also increases. There are two memory accesses in a simple page table implementation, as discussed earlier. If there is a two-level paging structure, there are three memory accesses. Similarly, if there is a three-level paging structure, there are four memory accesses, and so on. Multi-level paging, though, manages the memory non-contiguously; and the number of memory accesses is large. However, this number of accesses can be reduced with the help of associative mapping, by having TLB as associative memory, and the performance of execution can be increased.

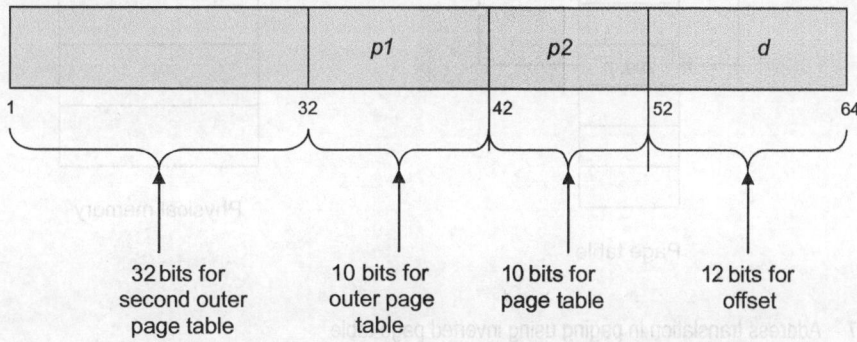

Fig. 10.26   64-bit Logical address corresponding to three-level page table structure

10.7.2 Inverted Page Table Structure

The page table size is a serious issue for an OS designer. The page table size is directly proportional to the virtual address space. There is another way to design it: using an inverted table structure. In this design, instead of a virtual page, a real page frame is taken as the page table entry. In other words, an inverted page table has one entry for each real page frame of memory. Each entry consists of the virtual address of the page stored in the real memory location. It consists of information about the process that owns the page. Since the process and page information is stored together in one entry, there is no need to prepare a separate process table for each process. There is a standard page table for all the processes that contains only one entry for each physical page frame of the memory. This saves memory space, but inverted page table structures are not appropriate for shared pages, as there is more than one virtual address for one physical page frame.

The inverted page table is indexed by the page frame number of the physical memory, rather than the virtual page number. The logical address in this page table structure consists of process ID (*pid*), page number (*p*), and the displacement (*d*): (*pid, p, d*) (see Fig. 10.27). Once the logical address is generated, the inverted page table is then matched for the required *pid* and *p*. As soon as a match is found, the frame address is obtained, which is then merged with the offset to get the physical mapping address.

10.7.3 Hashed Page Table Structure

Inverted page table is efficient in memory saving, but searching the table for a match of process ID and page number is a disadvantage. Searching the inverted page table may adversely affect the performance of paging in the system. Therefore, hashing is used to speed up the page table lookup. An appropriate hash function is used and applied on the page number of the virtual address to locate the page table entry. The hash function on the page number results in a value

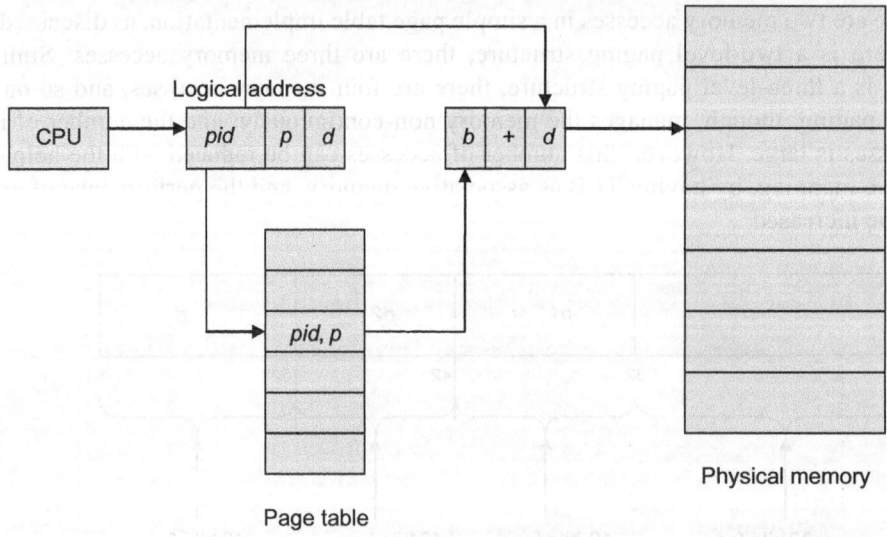

Fig. 10.27 Address translation in paging using inverted page table

that is used as an entry number for the page table to be searched and mapped. If this entry contains the page table, its frame address is used to map the virtual address. Otherwise, the system checks the value of the chaining pointer, as the chaining mechanism is used with hashing. If the chaining pointer is null, it means the page is not in memory, and therefore, it is a page fault. Otherwise, there is a collision at that page table entry.

10.8 SEGMENTATION

A programmer writes programs not in terms of pages, but modules, to reduce the problem complexity. There may be many modules: main program, procedures, stacks, data, and so on. So, it would be better if memory management is also implemented in terms of these modules. Segmentation is a memory management technique that supports the concept of modules. The modules in this technique are called segments. Now the memory management is implemented in the form of segments, instead of pages (see Fig.10.28). The segments are logical divisions of a program, and they may be of different sizes, whereas pages in the paging concept are physical divisions of program, and are of equal size.

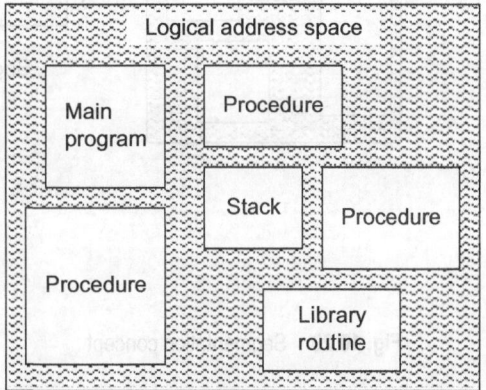

Fig. 10.28   Logical address space divided into segments

Managing memory in the form of segments has two obvious advantages: one is that, segments as logical memory are closer to a programmer's way of thinking, and the other is that the segments need not be of the same size, compared to pages. All the modules or segments in the programs are of different sizes. Therefore, it is advantageous to divide the logical address space into blocks of different sizes as required. This division of logical address space into variable-sized segments eliminates the problem of internal fragmentation that occurred in the paging concept. Thus, segmentation can be defined as a memory management technique, where the logical address space is divided into variable-sized segments, as required. Each segment is identified by a name and its length. The logical address is in two parts: the segment name and its offset, in order to know the location within a segment. There are three major segments in an executable program: code segment, data segment, and stack segment. Each of these segments might use another segment. For example, a program may use segments for precompiled library routines and for any other sub-routines. The segmentation does not require a programmer to specify the segments and their sizes.

The logical address in segmentation has two parts: segment number (segment name is replaced by segment number for the convenience of implementation), and offset in the segment. Consequently, this logical address is converted into physical address. To convert it into physical address, the starting address of segment in the memory, that is, address in the base register, must be known. The starting addresses of all the segments are stored in a table, known as *segment table*, as shown in Fig.10.29. The compiler/linker creates the segments at the time of compilation/linkage, numbers them, builds a segment table, and finally an executable image is produced by assigning two-dimensional addresses. In segmentation, there is a need to know

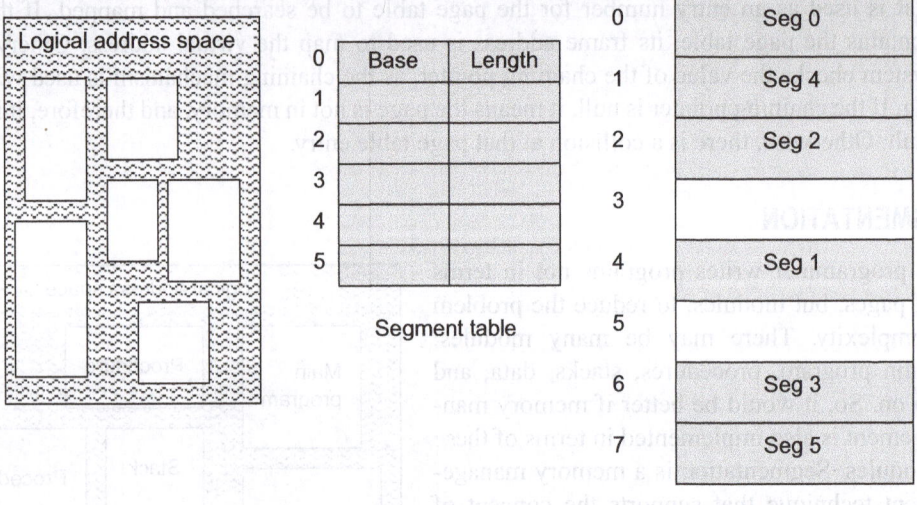

Fig. 10.29   Segmentation concept

the length of each segment, as every segment may be of a different size. Therefore, another field known as *limit*, is added to the segment table to check the length of the segments. Thus, a segment table is a data structure used to store the base addresses of each segment in the process, along with their limits. After reaching the start location of a segment through the segment table, its offset is added to it in order to map the complete logical address onto the physical address, and the instruction in a segment can be executed. The processor, in case of segmentation, generates the logical address as:

(Segment number s, Offset d)

The logical address in segmentation is generated by the compiler, unlike in paging. In paging, the two-dimensional address is extracted from a single dimensional address generated by the compiler, as the page size is always to the power of 2. But in segmentation, the size of a segment varies, and the compiler itself has to generate the two-dimensional address.

The logical address in segmentation is converted into a physical address by MMU. The hardware must be updated, such that it must know how to access the segment table for conversion. The steps for logical to physical address conversion (see Fig. 10.30) are as under:

1. The processor generates a two-dimensional logical address that consists of s and d.
2. The segment number s is extracted from the logical address, and is used as an index of the segment table.
3. After reaching the desired segment number in the segment table, its offset d is checked with the limit of the segment. If $d \leq$ length, then go to the next step. Otherwise, an interrupt is generated to indicate that the address in the segment is not valid.
4. The base address, corresponding to the segment number, is retrieved.
5. The base address is added to d to get the physical address.

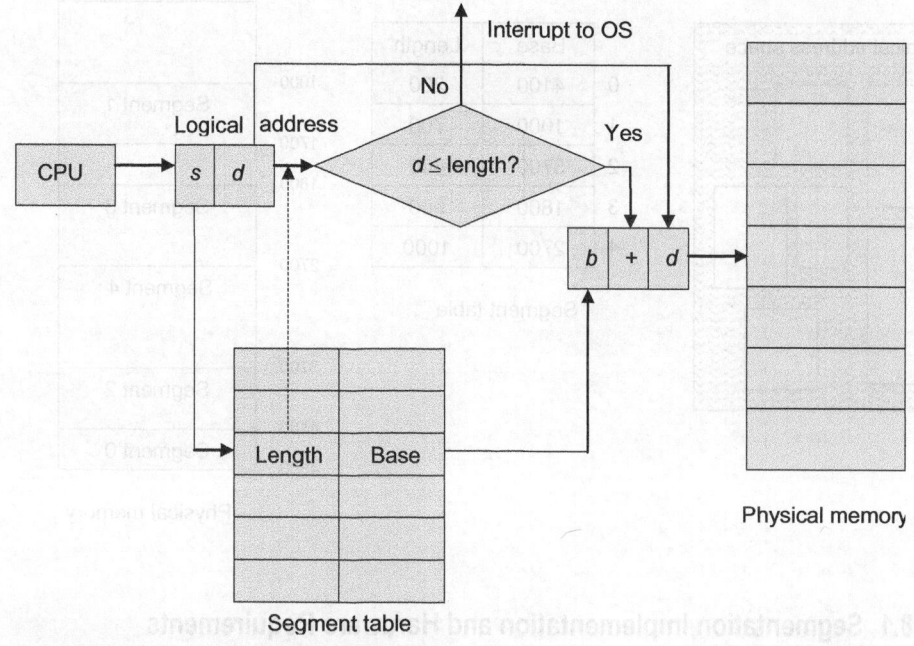

Fig. 10.30 Address translation in segmentation

Example 10.21

A program has been divided into five modules. Their lengths and base addresses are stored in the segment table, as depicted in the following space:

Show the physical memory mapping for the segments. What will be the physical memory address for the following logical addresses?

Segment number	Length	Base address
0	200	4100
1	700	1000
2	400	3700
3	900	1800
4	1000	2700

Solution

The physical mapping of all the segments, along with the segment table, is shown in the following space:

The physical addresses of logical addresses are shown in the following space:

s	d
1	665
3	906
4	770

s	d	Physical address
1	665	1000 + 665 = 1665
3	906	Not a valid address, as offset is larger than the length of the segment.
4	770	2700 +770 = 3470

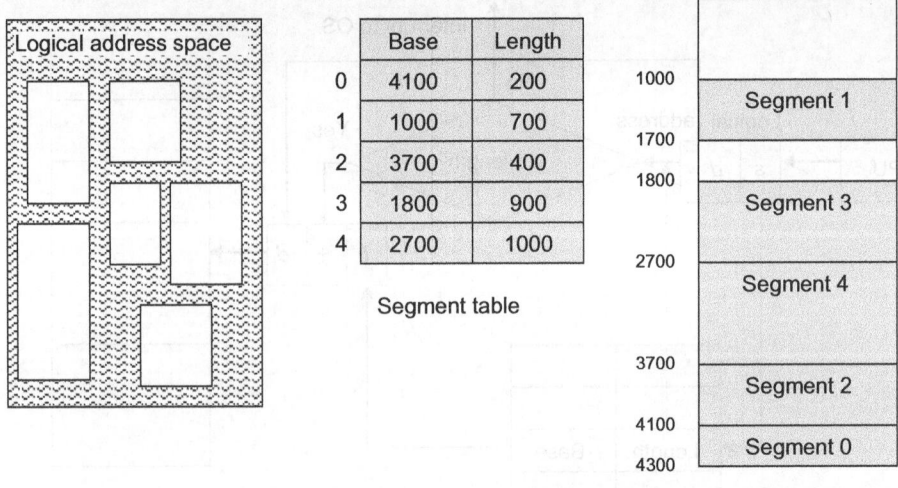

Physical memory

10.8.1 Segmentation Implementation and Hardware Requirements

To implement segmentation, the memory management component of an OS maintains a list of status of all the holes in the memory, as done for the paging concept. The only difference is that the OS needs to check the sizes of holes as well, as there is a different memory requirement for various segments. As soon as a process loads its segments, the holes are allocated, and their status is marked as 'allocated'. As the segments are loaded, the segment table of that process is also updated correspondingly. The base address of a segment, where it has been allocated, is entered into the segment table. In this way, a segment table must be updated as soon as the base address of a segment changes. When a program is compiled, the compiler keeps the segment table address and the maximum number of segments of the segment table in the header of the executable file of the program. The address of the segment table, where it is stored in the memory, and the maximum limit of the segments are copied to the PCB of the process at the time of process creation. This information is useful at the time of execution of a process. As soon as a process is scheduled for execution, the appropriate segment table is referred for execution, if there is a segment table address entry in its PCB. The segment table address is retrieved from the PCB and needs to be stored somewhere, so that during the execution, its segment table can be referred to. The hardware support needed for this purpose is to have a register to store the segment table address. This register is known as a *Segment Table Base Register* (STBR). Similarly, to check the validity of a segment number, another register known as a *Segment Table Limit Register* (STLR) is used (see Fig 10.31). So, whenever a process is scheduled to be executed, its segment table address from its PCB is loaded to the STBR, and the limit of the segment table is stored in the STLR. When the process starts executing, the logical address, consisting of a segment number and its offset, is generated. But the validity of this segment number is first checked against the value of the STLR. If the segment number is less than, or equal to, the value of STLR, the processing continues, otherwise interrupt is generated to the OS. Thus, a segment table per process, along with one STBR and STLR in hardware, is sufficient to implement the segmentation concept. When the current process is suspended or terminated, and another process is scheduled to execute, then the current STBR is replaced with the segment table address of the new process.

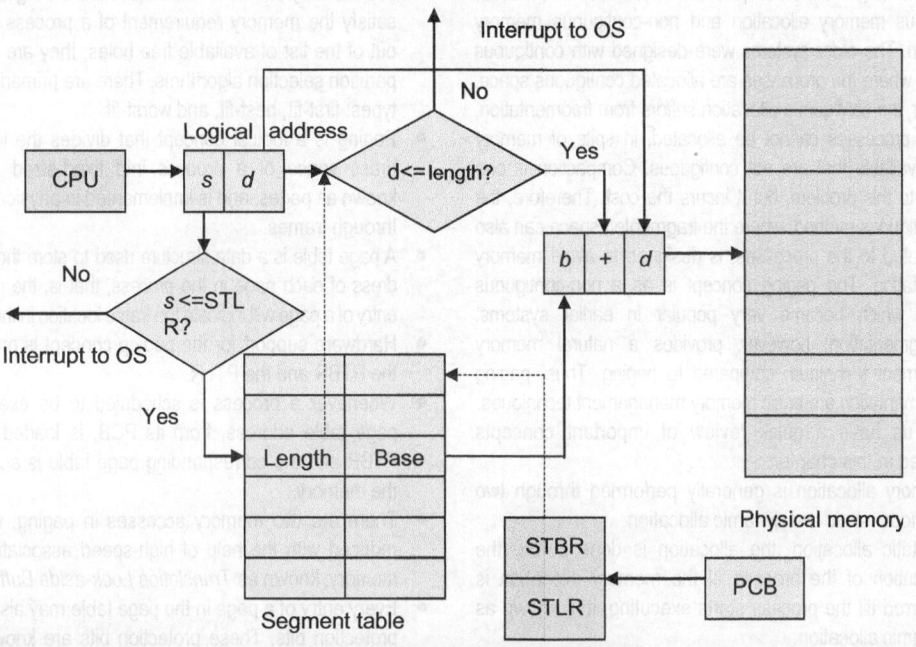

Fig. 10.31 Hardware requirements for address translation in segmentation

10.8.2 Protection and Sharing

In a segmentation environment as well, every segment may have separate access rights, like paging. A segment may have permission to read, write, execute, or append. There can be many combinations of these access rights, such as read-only, write only, read-write, and so on. This kind of protection is again implemented using the segment table. Every entry of a segment in the segment table may have its access protection bits as well. If an execution tries to violate the access rights in access protection bits, an interrupt is generated in the OS (see Fig.10.32). In segmentation, a programmer

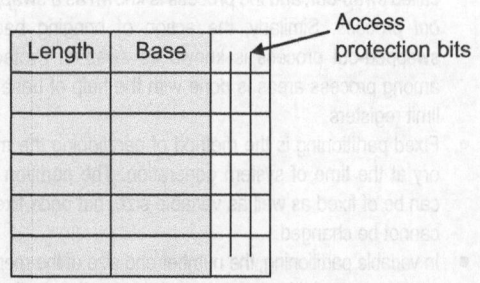

Fig. 10.32 Segment table with access protection bits

knows, in advance, which segment is to be protected, unlike paging and therefore, it is easy to implement protection on segments.

Like pages, segments also help in memory optimization. Owing to this, they can also be shared. Sharable segments are prepared with the help of a re-entrant code. The segment table of each process should map to the same location in the memory, so that the segment table of every process maps to the same segment, which needs to be shared.

SUMMARY

Memory management techniques of two types were discussed: contiguous memory allocation and non-contiguous memory allocation. The older systems were designed with contiguous method, where the processes are allocated contiguous space. However, the contiguous allocation suffers from fragmentation, and the processes cannot be allocated, in spite of memory space available that are not contiguous. Compaction is one solution to this problem, but it incurs the cost. Therefore, the non-contiguous method, where the fragmented space can also be allocated to the processes, is designed to avoid memory fragmentation. The paging concept is as a non-contiguous method, which became very popular in earlier systems. The segmentation, however, provides a natural memory management technique, compared to paging. Thus, paging and segmentation are basic memory management techniques.

Let us have a quick review of important concepts discussed in this chapter:

- Memory allocation is generally performed through two methods: static and dynamic allocation.
- In static allocation, the allocation is done before the execution of the process. If the memory allocation is deferred till the process starts executing, it is known as dynamic allocation.
- When a process is compiled, the CPU generates a logical address, which is then converted into a physical address, by the memory management component, to map it to the physical memory.
- The action of taking out a process from the memory is called *swap-out*, and the process is known as a *swapped-out process*. Similarly, the action of bringing back a swapped-out process is known as *swap-in*. Protection among process areas is done with the help of base and limit registers.
- Fixed partitioning is the method of partitioning the memory at the time of system generation. The partition size can be of fixed as well as variable size, but once fixed, it cannot be changed.
- In variable partitioning, the number and size of the memory partition are variable, and are created at run-time by the OS.
- The memory partition that is free to be allocated, is known as a *hole*.
- To allocate memory to the processes in partitions, the OS creates a table to store information, regarding the partitions, known as *partition description table* (PDT).
- Fixed partitioning method suffers from both types of fragmentation: external and internal.
- Variable partitioning method suffers from external fragmentation.
- Compaction method is used to reduce memory wastage in variable partitioning.

- The memory allocation techniques are the algorithms that satisfy the memory requirement of a process of size *n*, out of the list of available free holes; they are known as partition selection algorithms. There are primarily of three types: first-fit, best-fit, and worst-fit.
- Paging is a logical concept that divides the logical address space of a process into fixed-sized partitions, known as pages, and is implemented in physical memory through frames.
- A page table is a data structure used to store the base address of each page in the process, that is, the page table entry of a page will indicate the frame location in the memory.
- Hardware support for the paging concept is provided by the PTBR and the PTLR.
- Whenever a process is scheduled to be executed, its page table address, from its PCB, is loaded in to the PTBR and the corresponding page table is accessed in the memory.
- There are two memory accesses in paging, which are reduced with the help of high-speed associative cache memory, known as *Translation Look-aside Buffer* (TLB).
- Every entry of a page in the page table may also have its protection bits. These protection bits are known as *access protection bits*.
- The *valid-invalid* bit is used in the page table to mark a page as valid or invalid. Valid means the page is being referred to by the process, and invalid means the page is not in use by the process and is illegal.
- A re-entrant code is that which never changes during execution, and thus, can be shared easily by multiple users. Thus, all the processes sharing the same software can execute the same code in the memory, with the help of shared pages.
- The huge size of a page table is handled with the hierarchical page table structure or inverted page table structure.
- Segments are logical divisions of a program, and therefore, may be of different sizes, whereas pages in the paging concept are physical divisions of the program, and are of equal size.
- Segmentation can be defined as a memory management technique, where a logical address space is divided into variable sized segments, as required.
- A segment table is a data structure used to store the base address of each segment in the process, along with their limits.
- Hardware support for segmentation is provided by the STBR and the STLR.
- Whenever a process is scheduled to be executed, its segment table address from the PCB is loaded to the STBR, and the limit of segment table is stored in the STLR.

MULTIPLE CHOICE QUESTIONS

1. The swap space is reserved in _____.
   - (a) The main memory
   - (b) The hard disk
   - (c) any secondary storage
   - (d) none

2. A memory management unit performs memory-mapping by converting a logical address into a physical address, with the help of _____.
   - (a) base registers
   - (b) limit registers
   - (c) base and limit registers
   - (d) none

3. Fixed partitioning is a method of partitioning the memory at the time of _____.
   - (a) system generation
   - (b) compilation
   - (c) run-time
   - (d) none

4. In fixed partitioning, the partition size can be of
   - (a) fixed size
   - (b) variable size
   - (c) fixed as well as variable
   - (d) none

5. The OS is generally in the _____ memory addresses in the memory.
   - (a) higher
   - (b) lower
   - (c) any fragmented space
   - (d) none

6. Fixed partitioning method suffers from _____ fragmentation.
   - (a) internal
   - (b) external
   - (c) both internal and external
   - (d) none

7. Pages and frames are _____ in size.
   - (a) unequal
   - (b) equal
   - (c) none

8. _____ is a data structure used to store the base address of each page in the process.
   - (a) PDT
   - (b) Page table
   - (c) Frame table
   - (d) none

9. A page table entry provides _____
   - (a) offset
   - (b) base address
   - (c) limit address
   - (d) none

10. A page table must be updated as soon as the _____ address of a page changes.
    - (a) frame
    - (b) logical
    - (c) virtual
    - (d) none

11. What is the minimum number of memory accesses needed in paging?

12. Memory mapping through TLB is known as _____.
    - (a) associative mapping
    - (b) physical mapping
    - (c) TLB mapping
    - (d) none

13. TLB hit ratio must be _____ to decrease the effective memory access time.
    - (a) low
    - (b) high
    - (c) no effect
    - (d) none

14. The _____-related areas of processes cannot be shared.
    - (a) code
    - (b) data
    - (c) page table
    - (d) none

15. If the size of a process is an exact multiple of page size chosen, there will not be any _____ fragmentation.
    - (a) internal
    - (b) external
    - (c) internal and external both
    - (d) none

16. If there is a two-level paging structure, there are _____ memory accesses.
    - (a) four
    - (b) two
    - (c) three
    - (d) none

17. Rather than having the page table entry for a virtual page, _____ is taken as a page table entry in the inverted page table.
    - (a) process number
    - (b) PTBR
    - (c) PTLR
    - (d) real page frame

18. The paging concept _____ context switch time.
    - (a) decreases
    - (b) increases
    - (c) no effect
    - (d) none

19. Which of the following decreases the overhead of processing?
    - (a) paging
    - (b) segmentation
    - (c) compaction
    - (d) none

20. A buddy system is a compromise between _____.
    - (a) internal and external fragmentation
    - (b) paging and segmentation
    - (c) fixed and dynamic partitioning
    - (d) none

(a) Three   (c) Four
(b) Two   (d) Five

REVIEW QUESTIONS

1. Distinguish between:
   (a) Static and dynamic allocation
   (b) Logical and physical addresses
   (c) Swapping and paging
   (d) Fixed and variable partitioning
   (e) Internal and external fragmentation
   (f) Contiguous and non-contiguous allocation
   (g) Page, frame, and segment

2. What are the advantages and disadvantages of contiguous allocation with fixed partitioning?

3. What are the advantages and disadvantages of contiguous allocation with variable partitioning?

4. What is the requirement of relocating the processes?

5. How do unequal-sized fixed partitions improve the performance of memory allocation? Explain with an example.

6. What is the use of PDT?

7. Explain contiguous allocation with variable partitioning with an example.

8. Discuss the disadvantages of contiguous memory allocation. What are its solutions?

9. Discuss the performance of all memory partition selection algorithms.

10. What is a buddy system? Explain its role in memory allocation with an example.

11. A process is to be swapped-in to the location 40100 in the memory. If the logical addresses generated by the process are 100, 245, 140, and 350, what are the corresponding physical addresses?

12. A process has relocatable code of size 700 K. The relocation register is loaded with 30010 K and the limit register contains the address 31000 K. If the processor generates logical addresses, 990 and 1020, where will they be located in the physical memory?

13. Illustrate the paging concept with an example.

14. Discuss the role of PTBR and PTLR in the implementation of paging.

15. How does the paging concept increase memory accesses?

16. How do you reduce two-memory accesses in paging?

17. Discuss the role of access protection bits in paging? Where do you implement these bits?

18. Does paging support sharing?

19. How does paging eliminate external fragmentation?

20. Discuss the address translation in the two-level page table structure.

21. Discuss the address translation in the inverted page table structure.

22. What is the need for segmentation?

23. Discuss the address translation in segmentation concept.

24. What are the hardware requirements in the implementation of segmentation?

BRAIN TEASERS

1. A process of size 300 MB needs to be swapped-in from the hard disk. But there is no space in the memory. After observing the memory, it was found that two processes of size 150 MB and 200 MB are lying idle, and therefore, can be swapped out. How much swap-time is required for swap-in and swap-out of the processes, if the following is given:
   Average latency time of the hard disk = 10 ms
   Transfer rate of the hard disk = 60 MB/s

2. Three processes P1, P2, P3, and P4 of size 18900, 19500, 19990, and 20990 bytes, respectively, need space in memory. The equal partitions of size 20000 bytes are allocated to P1, P2, P3, and P4. Is there any

fragmentation in this allocation? Can a process of 600 bytes be accommodated?

3. Design an example of variable partitioning that reduces internal fragmentation, and then analyze the situation when it may cause external fragmentation.

4. Analyze the costs associated with compaction.

5. Assume the memory allocation scenario, as in the following, and allocate memory for additional requests of 10K and 20K (in this order). Compare the memory allocation using first-fit, best-fit, and worst-fit allocation methods, in terms of internal fragmentation.

OS	(diagram showing memory partitions)

5K   30K   20K   5K   15K   15K   22K

☐ Hole   ▨ Occupied by a process

6. Design a scenario that illustrates that the worst-case allocation may prove to be a good algorithm for dynamic partitioning.

7. A program's logical memory has been divided into 7 pages, and these pages are given frame numbers, 4, 10, 3, 7, 6, 8, and 2. Show the logical memory mapping to the physical memory.

8. In a paging scheme, 16-bit addresses are used with page size of 256 bytes. If the logical address is 0011010101110101, how many bits are used for the page number and offset? Also, compute the page number and offset. What will be the physical address, if the frame address corresponding to the computed page number is 20?

9. There is a system with 2^{32} bytes of memory and fixed partitioning of size 65536 bytes. What is the minimum number of bits required for an entry in the process table to store the partition to which a process has been allocated?

10. On a system with 1MB of memory that uses a buddy system, show a diagram that illustrates the following requests:

    (a) P1 requests 256 K   (e) P2 releases
    (b) P2 requests 210 K   (f) P1 releases
    (c) P3 requests 50 K   (g) P5 requests 410 K
    (d) P4 requests 60 K

11. In Problem 10, after allocating memory to P5, how much is the internal and external fragmentation?

12. How many bits are there in a logical address in a paging system with 2^{32} bytes of physical memory, 512 pages of logical address space, and a page size of 2^8 bytes?

13. Analyze the searching efficiency of first-fit, next-fit, best-fit, and worst-fit algorithms.

14. The address of a block under current allocation in a buddy system is 011011000011. If the block is of size 16, what is the binary address of its buddy?

15. How many bits are there in a logical address, where page size is of 2^{10} bytes and 256 pages are there in the logical address space?

16. A system with 32-bit logical address uses a two-level page table structure. It uses page size of 2^6. The outer page table or directory is accessed with 10 bits of the address.

    i) How many bits are required to access the page table?
    ii) How many entries are there in the directory?
    iii) How many entries are there in the page table?

17. A program has been divided into four modules. Their lengths and base addresses are stored in the segment table, as depicted in the following space:

Segment number	Length	Base
0	400	200
1	100	3000
2	700	1400
3	300	800

Show the physical memory mapping for the segments. What will be the physical memory address for the following logical addresses?

    (a) 1, 200   (c) 0, 134
    (b) 2, 345   (d) 3, 453

18. There is a system with a two-level paging scheme. It has 2^{10} bytes page size and 32-bit virtual addresses. If the first level page table uses first 10 bits of the address to specify a page table entry, then

    (a) How many bits are required to specify the second-level page table?
    (b) How many pages are there in the first level page table?
    (c) How many pages are there in the second level page table?
    (d) How many pages are there in the virtual address space?

19. In a paging system with TLB, it takes 40 ns to search the TLB and 70 ns to access memory. If the TLB hit ratio is 50%, find the effective memory access time. What should

be the hit ratio to achieve an effective memory access time of 220 ns?

20. Design a page table that illustrates the behaviour of an inverted page table structure. Analyze its performance compared to the general page table structure.

21. Design a page table that illustrates the behaviour of a hashed page table structure. Analyze its performance compared to the general page table structure.

22. Study the architecture of some recent OSs and analyze how the large size of the virtual address space and page table is handled.

23. A system with 32-bit logical address supports 2^6 bytes page size and 2^{20} bytes of physical memory. How many page table entries are there in a single level and inverted page table?

24. There is a system with 64 pages of 512 bytes page size and physical memory of 24 frames. How many bits are required in the logical and physical addresses?

11 Virtual Memory

11.1 INTRODUCTION

In Chapter 10, basic memory-management techniques were discussed. The discussion was based on the real (main) memory. However, the main memory extends to the concept of virtual memory.

Virtual memory targets the organization of the memory when the process size is too large to fit in the real memory. Therefore, a virtual memory is created that does not limit the size of the real memory and a programmer is free to write a large-size program. This is a general method of memory management used in today's OSs. In virtual memory, combined approach of paging and segmentation is used. The virtual memory implementation is complex as compared with real memory. It needs the assistance of hardware support known as *paging hardware*. Moreover, OSs have a module known as *virtual memory handler* (VM handler) that takes care of various algorithms needed to implement the virtual memory. The implementation and management of a virtual memory system, along with paging hardware and VM handler will be discussed in detail in this chapter.

11.2 NEED FOR VIRTUAL MEMORY

Paging and segmentation are two basic memory-management techniques that require an entire process to reside in the main memory before its execution. However, in modern systems that require a high degree of multi-programming, this becomes a limitation. The increase in the degree of multi-programming means that more number of processes should be accommodated in the memory. Consequently, the degree of multi-programming is limited with the size of the memory. This limitation may lead to several problems. There may be a situation where a demand to increase the number of processes in the memory is unable to be fulfilled due to the limit of memory size. Another situation may be that a programmer writes a process that is too large to fit in the memory. It may not be executed due to its large size. If there is no size limit, then maximum number of processes can be accommodated in the memory and a programmer need not worry about the size of the process.

Is it necessary to have the whole process in the main memory before execution? If the execution of some real programs is observed closely, it can be noticed that the processes are not required entirely in the main memory. Only certain portions of a

Learning Objectives

After reading this chapter, you should be able to understand:

- Need of virtual memory
- Virtual addresses and virtual address space
- Implementation of VM system through demand loading
- Demand paging
- Page-replacement algorithms
- Stack property of page-replacement algorithms
- Thrashing and its solutions
- Paging hardware and its components
- VM handler and its components

process are required for its execution. While declaring the variables, a large memory is allocated, which is never used. An array of 100 memory locations may not be used for all 100 locations. Some code in a process is reserved for some exceptional conditions that may not be used every time the process is executed. There may be some portion devoted for initialization, which is necessary only at the start of an execution. If a process is divided into several portions and only one portion is required in the memory, then there is no need to load the entire process in the main memory. Therefore, more number of processes can be accommodated in the memory.

This solution was adopted many years ago in the form of *overlays*. An overlay is a portion of a process. A program is first divided into many overlays and stored in the disk. A program containing overlays is called an *overlay structured program*. This program consists of a set of overlays and a permanently resident portion known as *root*. Overlays are identified as mutually exclusive modules of a program as they do not call each other and thus, need not be loaded simultaneously in the memory. The root is first loaded in the memory and control is passed to it for execution. As the root executes, the overlays are loaded as and whenever required. The required overlays are swapped in the memory and later on swapped out when the memory is full. The loading of an overlay overwrites a previously loaded overlay with the same load origin. This benefits the memory management by reducing the memory requirements of a program. Although the swapping was done by the system only, the division of process into overlays was done by the programmer. It is a difficult task for a programmer to divide a process into small overlays. Moreover, today, overlay is an obsolete technique. This gives rise to the concept of virtual memory in modern systems. *Virtual memory* is a method that manages the exceeded size of larger processes as compared to the available space in the memory. It means that the degree of multi-programming can be increased without worrying about the size of the memory. Further, a programmer is relieved from the tight constraints of memory size when writing a process. A large process will be accommodated in the memory. Suppose, a system has 2-MB size memory and a programmer writes 8-MB size process. A VM system carefully divides the process into 2-MB portions and loads the appropriate portion into the memory for execution.

11.3 PRINCIPLE OF LOCALITY

In virtual memory, the entire process is not loaded in the memory. Instead, only required portions of the process are loaded. This is also supported with the principle of locality. The *principle of locality of reference* states that during the course of execution of a program, memory references by the processor tend to cluster. This is true for both instructions and data in a program. Over a long period of time, the cluster of memory references changes, otherwise, the same set of instructions is repeated. The memory references cluster due to the following reasons:

i) Most of the time, the program execution is sequential except for branch and call instructions, and the ratio of these branch and call instructions is lesser as compared to sequential instruction. For example, GOTO instruction in various languages is rarely used and its use in programming is often discouraged. The frequency of call instruction is also very less.

ii) The loop constructs in a program consist of very small set of instructions that are repeated many times. During the loop execution in a program, the processor generates memory references confined to a small contiguous portion of a program.

iii) The nesting depth of loops in a program is also confined to a small level in structured programs. The moral of good programming is to have a very small nesting depth of loops that again causes the clustering of memory references.

iv) When performing operations on data structures in a program, it has been observed that it involves access to a clustered set of data locations. When an array or table is accessed, then its data locations are accessed in sequence resulting in fixed clustered references.

Analyzing these facts of programming, locality of reference can be observed at two levels: *temporal locality* and *spatial locality*. Temporal locality means that the recently referenced memory locations are likely to be referenced again. In this way, loops, subroutines, and data variables used to count or for summation are all examples of temporal locality. Spatial locality means that nearby memory locations are also referenced. In this way, all sequential statement execution and array traversal are examples of spatial locality. Both the types of locality tend to generate clustered-memory references.

The principle of locality of reference thus promotes the idea of virtual memory implementation and concludes that only a few portions of a process are needed over a period of time in its execution. The programmer must learn the structured programming techniques, otherwise, frequent changes in clusters of memory references may be harmful for the system.

11.4 VIRTUAL MEMORY SYSTEM

On the light of principle of locality of reference, it is now possible to implement a system with virtual memory. The system with virtual memory is known as virtual memory (VM) system. The implementation of a VM system requires both hardware and software components. The software implementing the VM system is known as *VM handler*. Virtual memory may be realized with paging or segmentation as it requires a non-contiguous memory allocation method. The simple paging and segmentation concepts have been discussed in Chapter 10. All the basics of these concepts are also applicable to VM systems. The logical address here is known as *virtual address*, and the logical address space is known as *virtual address space*. The address translation using paging and segmentation is applied in the same way as discussed Chapter 10. The only difference of applying paging and segmentation in relation to virtual memory is that there is no need to load all the pages or segments of a process into the main memory. The VM system requires only those pages or segments of a process in the memory that are needed at a certain time of execution. This approach benefits a large process that does not fit within the limited size of the memory. Even the process that can fit into the memory is not entirely loaded. Thus, the approach of VM system is to load only those pages or segments of a process in the memory that are required for execution at an instant of time. Therefore, there will be space for loading components of other processes. This approach is known as *demand loading* of process components.

11.4.1 Demand Loading of Process Components

From the observation of location of reference, it would be wasteful to load all the components of a process into the memory. A process can be executed without loading all its components. Thus, in a VM system, only required components are loaded first in the memory. The other components are loaded as and whenever required. The thumb rule of demand loading is that *never load a component of a process unless it is needed*. The components of a process that are present in the memory are known as *resident set* of the process as shown in Fig.11.1. The execution of a process takes place smoothly as long as the logical address generated by the processor is in the resident set of the process. However, a situation may occur when a component (page or segment) corresponding to a generated logical address is not in the resident

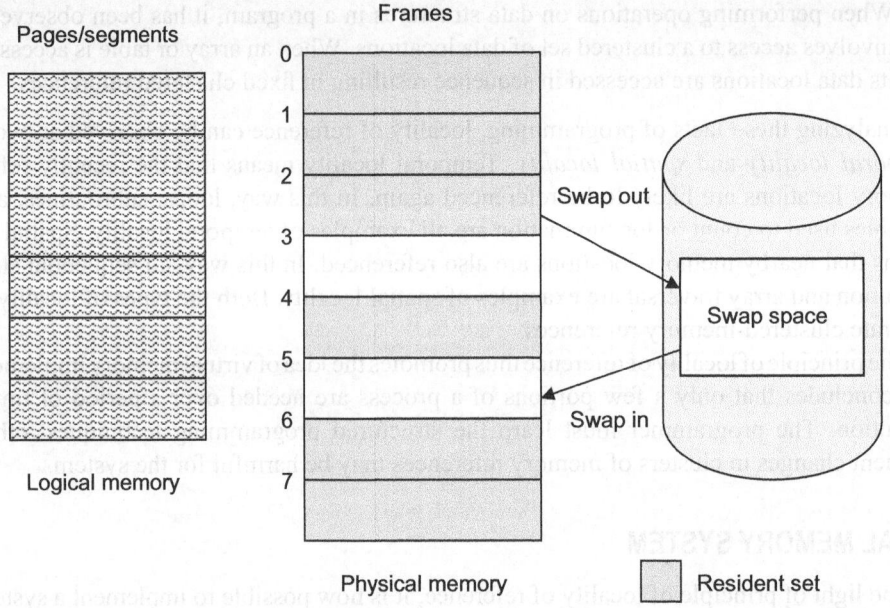

Fig. 11.1 Demand loading

set of the process. Therefore, to execute the process, the components that are not in memory need to be brought in. Where are these components stored then? For this, a secondary storage, generally a hard disk is used. The components that are not in the memory are stored in the hard disk in a separate area. If the processor generates a logical address that is not found in the memory after address translation, a memory-access-fault interrupt is generated. It means that a component corresponding to the generated logical address is not present in the memory at that time. The process being executed is interrupted and is put into a blocked state by the OS. To resume its execution, the component needs to be swapped in the memory. For this, the OS issues a disk I/O read request and dispatches another process to run while the disk I/O read operation is being performed. As soon as the disk I/O read operation is finished, an I/O interrupt is issued and the control is passed to the OS. The OS then puts the blocked-state process back into the ready state so that it can be executed again.

The issues related to the implementation of demand loading in a VM system are as follows:

i) How will one recognize which component is in the memory and which one is not?
ii) How many processes will be resident in the memory?
   This is related to the degree of multi-programming. The low degree as well as high degree of multi-programming may cause problem to the VM system. If there are only a few processes, then it may be possible that all the processes are blocked. On the other hand, if there are too many processes, then the resident set of each process will get very less space, and most of the time, components will be replaced for bringing in the desired components.
iii) How much main memory is allocated to a process?
   A fixed or variable number of frames may be allocated to the process depending on many factors.
iv) When a required component from the hard disk is to be brought into the memory, it may be possible that there is no free frame to be allocated. Where will this component be stored in the memory then? The idea is to replace some component already stored there and make room for the new component. In this way, an already existing component is swapped out and a new one is swapped in. This is known as *component replacement*. However, what

will be the strategy for replacing a component? The strategies are known as *component replacement algorithms* discussed later in the chapter.

v) The VM system realizes a huge memory only due to the hard disk. With the help of the hard disk, the VM system is able to manage larger-size processes or multiple processes in the memory. For this purpose, a separate space known as *swap space* is reserved in the disk. The components of the processes are swapped in and swapped out of this swap space. Swap space requires a lot of management so that the VM system woks smoothly. This is known as *swap space management*, which will be discussed later.

11.5 DEMAND PAGING

As discussed in Section 11.4, a VM system can be implemented using either paging or segmentation. In this section, virtual memory implementation with paging concept is discussed. All the details discussed in this section with reference to paging are also applicable to segmentation. To understand this, demand loading of a component is renamed as demand paging. The concept is same as discussed in demand loading of components, but it has been specified in terms of virtual address space. In demand paging, only pages that are needed at an instant of the time of execution are loaded. The benefit is that some pages corresponding to some exception-handling or error-handling code, which may not be executed, are not loaded. It results in efficient utilization of memory and efficient execution in terms of time. Paging system with swapping was discussed in Chapter 10. Demand paging is also the same except that an entire process is not swapped in or swapped out. Rather a *lazy swapper* is used here that loads only those pages that are needed. The *swapper* term is used for swap-in and swap-out. Here, the term *pager* will be used. The swapping operations will hence be known as *page-in* and *page-out* operations.

Like demand loading, demand paging also has some issues related to its implementation. The first issue with demand paging is how to recognize whether a page is present in the memory. The page table with valid–invalid bit can be used for this purpose. In demand paging, a valid bit means that the page is in the logical address space of the process and is in memory at the time. Similarly, an invalid bit means that the page is either not valid or not present in the memory. The page table entry for a valid bit (1) will contain the frame address of the page. In case of an invalid bit (0), the page table entry will not contain any frame address (see Fig. 11.2).

The second issue with demand paging is the situation when a process execution does not get a page in the memory. A situation will occur in demand paging when the page referenced is not present in the memory. This is known as a *page fault*. Consequently, the page fault must be noticed by the system and be serviced appropriately. Paging hardware while translating the address through the page table notices that the page-table entry has an invalid bit. It causes a trap to the OS so that a page fault can be noticed.

0	Base address of page 0	← Valid–invalid bit
1	Base address of page 1	
2	Base address of page 2	
3	Base address of page 3	
4	Base address of page 4	
5	Base address of page 5	

Fig. 11.2   Page table with valid–invalid bit

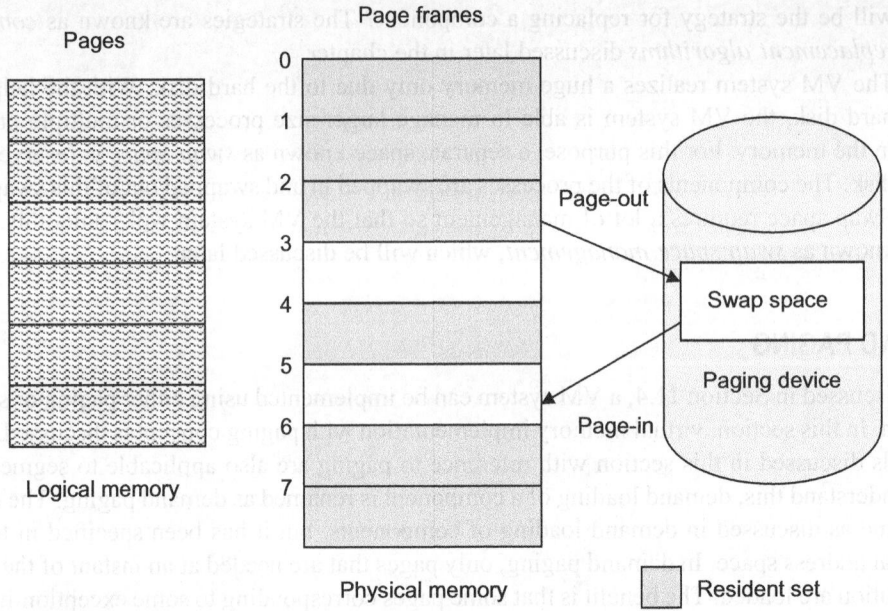

Fig. 11.3 Demand paging

The page fault once detected must be handled immediately. The page fault handling is to page in a page from the disk known as a *paging device*. However, for a page-in operation, a free frame should be available in the memory. If the free frame is there, a disk operation to read the desired page is initiated. When the desired page is paged into the memory, the page-table entry must also be updated as valid as the page is now in the memory. The process can now be executed again without a page fault. The demand paging with page-fault handling is shown in Fig. 11.3.

Example 11.1

A logical address in a paging system generates the page number 5. After looking at the page-table entry, it is found that its invalid entry is 0. After passing the control to the OS, it is found that the page is legal on the paging device. This is a page fault as the required page number is not in the memory. The page number 5 from the disk is then paged-in as depicted in the following diagram.

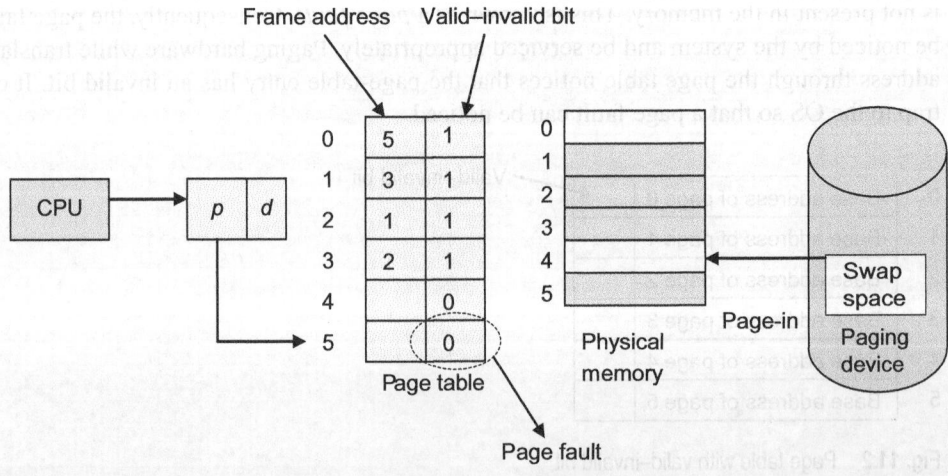

Third issue is that there may be a situation when there is no free frame. In this case, to make room for the page to be paged in, the existing page in the memory needs to be paged-out. In other words, the existing pages may be replaced so that a page can be paged-in from the disk. However, which page will be replaced is another issue? A strategy must be devised that will guide the page replacement. Page-replacement strategies are known as *page-replacement algorithms*. The page-replacement algorithms may affect the performance of the system. Therefore, these algorithms must be optimized and chosen carefully. Page-replacement algorithms will be discussed later in this chapter.

Example 11.2

Consider Example 11.1: If there are no free page frames in the memory as all the frames are occupied with other pages, then any of the page frames needs to be replaced so that page number 5 can be paged-in. Here comes the need of page-replacement algorithm that chooses a victim page frame out of the resident set as depicted as follows.

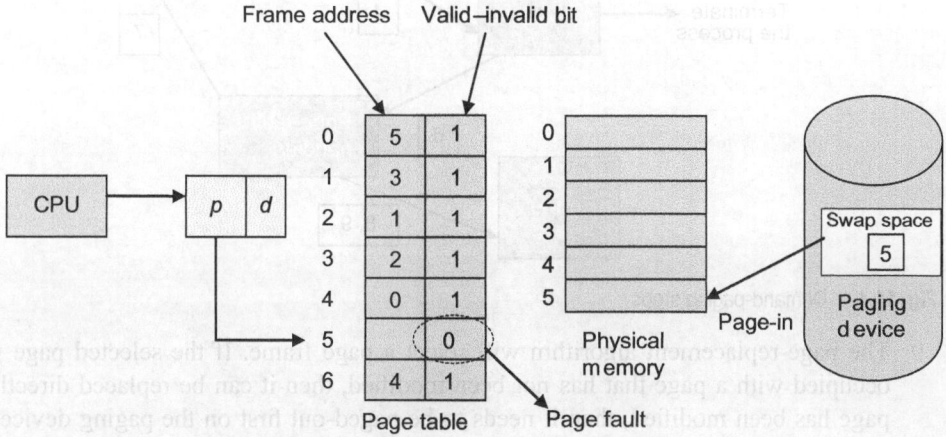

The sequence of operations in demand paging, along with page fault handling, is summarized in the following steps (see Figs 11.4 and 11.5):

1. Extract the page number from the generated logical address.
2. Check the page table and look for the corresponding page-number entry in the page table.
3. If the corresponding valid–invalid bit corresponding to the page number is 1, then the desired page is in the memory and the address translation unit of paging hardware translates it into a physical memory as described earlier.
4. If the corresponding valid–invalid bit corresponding to the page number is 0, then an interrupt is generated and the control is passed to the OS.
5. The OS saves the registers and state of the process and checks whether the page is in the legal boundary. If not, then the process may be terminated.
6. If the page is found to be in the logical memory, then it is a page fault and a page-fault handler module of the VM handler is invoked to tackle the page fault.
7. The page-fault handler reads the disk address of the page number stored in the page table and locates the required page on the paging device.
8. The page-fault handler checks whether there is a free frame through a free frame list that maintains the status of all the free frames in the memory. If the memory is full and there is no free frame, then a page-replacement algorithm is run to select a victim page frame so that the desired page from the paging device can be paged-in.

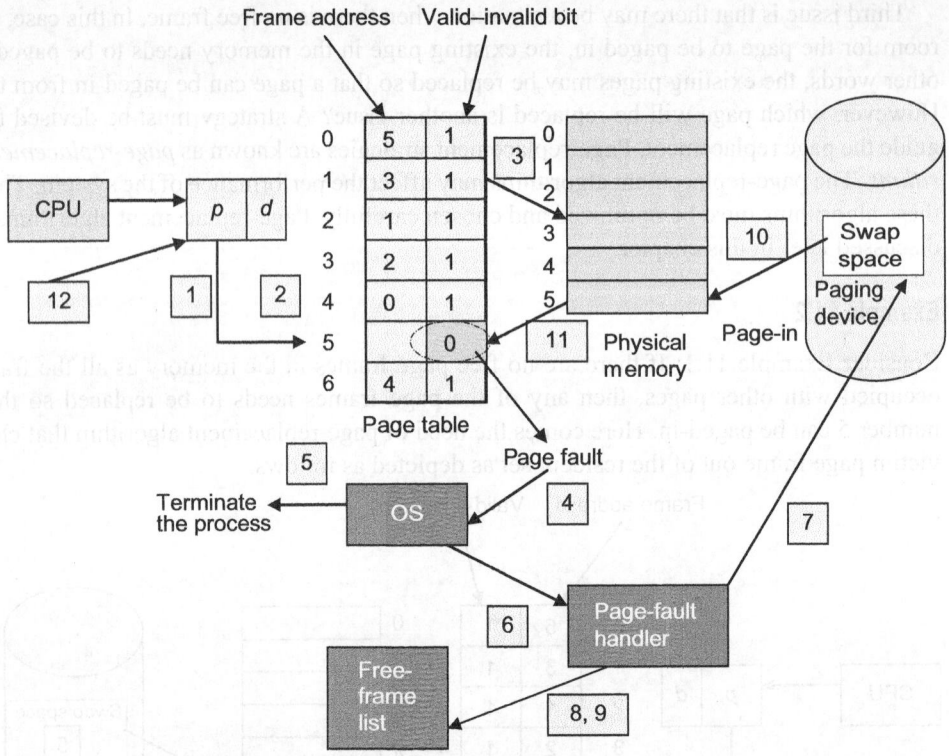

Fig. 11.4 Demand-paging steps

9. The page-replacement algorithm will select a page frame. If the selected page frame is occupied with a page that has not been modified, then it can be replaced directly. If the page has been modified, then it needs to be paged-out first on the paging device. Therefore, a disk-write operation is performed. The page-modification information is maintained through a modify bit (M-bit) in the page table (discussed in detail in Section 11.7)

10. When the page frame has been made free, the page-fault handler starts a disk-read operation to page-in the desired page.

11. After the page has been paged into the memory, its page-table entry is updated by marking the corresponding valid–invalid bit as 1 and adding frame address of the page indicating that the page resides in the memory.

12. The instruction is restarted from the logical address where the page fault has happened.

It is to be noted that during every read/write operation on disk, there may be a queue of waiting processes that need access to the device. While waiting for the device in the queue, the CPU may switch to another process and the current process is blocked. As soon as the disk I/O read/write request is finished, an I/O interrupt is issued and the OS gets the control back. The blocked process is moved back into the ready state so that it can be executed again. In this way, page-fault-service time will be increased due to the device-waiting time.

11.6 VIRTUAL MEMORY SYSTEM WITH TRANSLATION LOOK-ASIDE BUFFER

VM system also uses TLB to reduce the memory accesses and increase the system performance. The hardware implementation is the same as discussed in Chapter 10. The only difference is the software mechanism in the OS by which a page fault is generated if the desired page is not

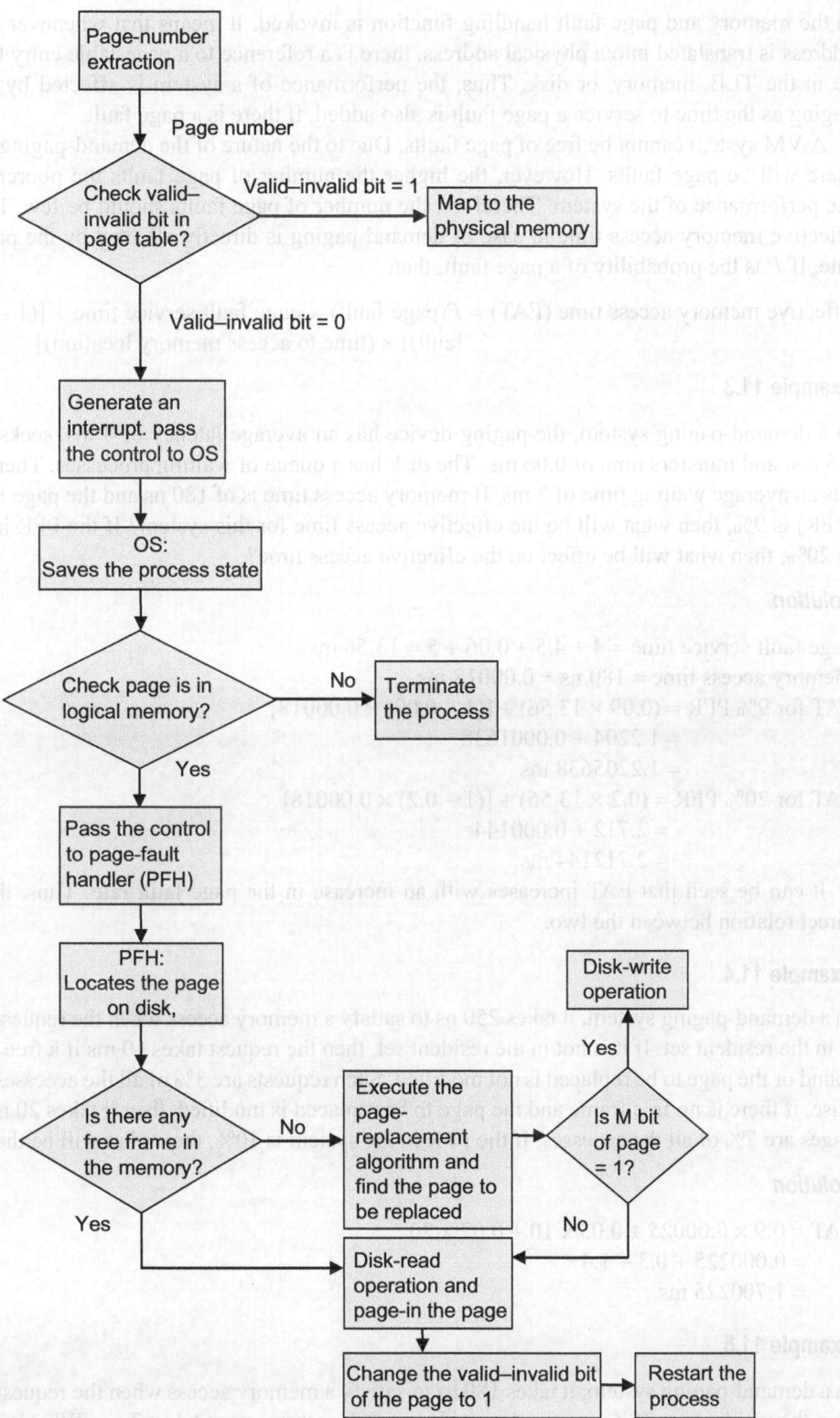

Fig. 11.5 Flow of sequence of events in demand paging

in the memory and page-fault handling function is invoked. It means that whenever a virtual address is translated into a physical address, there is a reference to a page-table entry that may be in the TLB, memory, or disk. Thus, the performance of a system is affected by demand paging as the time to service a page fault is also added, if there is a page fault.

A VM system cannot be free of page faults. Due to the nature of the demand-paging system, there will be page faults. However, the higher the number of page faults the poorer will be the performance of the system. Therefore, the number of page faults should be few. Thus, the effective memory access time in case of demand paging is directly affected by the page fault rate. If P is the probability of a page fault, then

$$\text{Effective memory access time (EAT)} = P(\text{page fault}) \times \text{page fault service time} + [(1 - P(\text{page fault})) \times (\text{time to access memory location})]$$

Example 11.3

In a demand-paging system, the paging device has an average latency of 4 ms, seeks time of 4.5 ms, and transfers time of 0.06 ms. The disk has a queue of waiting processes. Therefore, it has an average waiting time of 5 ms. If memory access time is of 180 ns and the page fault rate (PFR) is 9%, then what will be the effective access time for this system? If the PFR increases to 20%, then what will be effect on the effective access time?

Solution

Page fault service time = $4 + 4.5 + 0.06 + 5 = 13.56$ ms
Memory access time = 180 ns = 0.00018 ms
EAT for 9% PFR = $(0.09 \times 13.56) + [(1 - 0.09) \times 0.00018]$
            = $1.2204 + 0.0001638$
            = 1.2205638 ms
EAT for 20% PFR = $(0.2 \times 13.56) + [(1 - 0.2) \times 0.00018]$
            = $2.712 + 0.000144$
            = 2.712144 ms

It can be seen that EAT increases with an increase in the page fault rate. Thus, there is a direct relation between the two.

Example 11.4

In a demand-paging system, it takes 250 ns to satisfy a memory access when the requested page is in the resident set. If it is not in the resident set, then the request takes 10 ms if a free frame is found or the page to be replaced is not modified. Such requests are 3% of all the accesses. Otherwise, if there is no free frame and the page to be replaced is modified, then it takes 20 ms. Such pages are 7% of all the accesses. If the PFR in the system is 10%, then what will be the EAT?

Solution

EAT = $0.9 \times 0.00025 + 0.03 \times 10 + 0.07 \times 20$
    = $0.000225 + 0.3 + 1.4$
    = 1.700225 ms

Example 11.5

In a demand-paging system, it takes 180 ns to satisfy a memory access when the requested page is in the resident set. If it is not in the resident set, then the request takes 7 ms. What will be the

EAT if the PFR is 8%? What would be PFR to achieve an EAT of 400 μs? Convert all the units to microseconds.

Solution

Case I

EAT = 0.92 × 0.18 + 0.08 × 7000
    = 0.1104 + 560
    = 560.1104 μs
    = 0.5601104 ms

Case II

EAT = 400 = (1 − PFR) × 0.18 + PFR × 7000
400 = 0.18 − PFR × 0.18 + PFR × 7000
400 = 0.18 + 6999.82 × PFR
399.82 = 6999.82 × PFR
PFR = 5.7%

11.7 PAGE-REPLACEMENT ALGORITHMS

Due to the concept of demand paging, the degree of multi-programming can be increased, that is, more number of processes can be allocated in the memory as compared to the simple paging concept. If there are five processes with five pages each, but only four pages of all processes are used, then it makes room for another process with five pages to be accommodated. However, the memory will be over-allocated in this case. Moreover, the memory is used not only for holding pages but also contains page tables, buffers for I/O, and so on. Therefore, when a page fault occurs during the execution of a process, a page needs to be paged into the memory from the disk. However, it may be the case that there is no free frame in the memory. In such case, an already existing page should be replaced so that there is room for a page that needs to be paged. This is known as a *page replacement*. A page replaced randomly may affect the performance of the system. Suppose a page is used frequently during the execution of a process. If this page is replaced by a random approach, then it may be needed very soon and need to be paged-in again resulting in more page faults and degrades the performance of the system. Thus, instead of replacing any page, the use of pages in the memory is to be observed and a page should be replaced such that the effect on performance of the system is the least. The strategy to choose the best page to be replaced in the memory is called a page-replacement algorithm.

The page replacement increases the overhead because there are two page transfers: page-in and page-out. Therefore, these two page transfers will increase the page-fault service time, thereby increasing the overhead. This overhead can be reduced if it is known whether a page has been modified. It is not necessary that all the pages in the memory have been modified at a certain instant of time. Some pages may have been modified and some may not be. Moreover, some pages may be read-only. If a page has not been modified and is chosen as the victim page, then there is no need to replace it. It can simply be overwritten by another page because its copy is already on

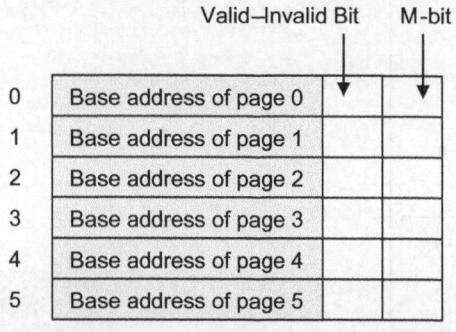

Fig. 11.6   Page table with valid–invalid and M-bits

the disk. In this way, one page-transfer time can be reduced. This is implemented by including a an M-bit) or a *dirty bit* with each page (see Fig.11.6) or frame in the hardware. Whenever there is a change in a page, the modify bit is set by the hardware. If the modify bit is set, then it indicates that the page has been modified since it was read in the memory. If the modify bit is not set, then it means that the page has not been modified. It need not be paged-out for replacement and can be overwritten. This mechanism reduces the page-fault service time.

How does one select a page-replacement algorithm? The evaluation criterion for the algorithm is to have the lowest PFR. The algorithm that will produce less page faults will be considered a good page-replacement algorithm. To select an algorithm, consider which memory reference has caused the page fault during the execution of a process. Therefore, to evaluate an algorithm, it is a must have a particular string of memory references. A string of memory references is known as a *reference string*. The algorithm will be run on this string. The reference string can either be generated artificially or a snapshot can be taken from an actual running process. However, the reference string in the form of actual memory addresses will be inconvenient for the evaluation of the algorithm. Therefore, the memory reference is considered in the form of a page. The page number containing the memory reference is taken in the reference string. In this way, it is easy to know the page number where the memory reference has produced a page fault.

For a page-replacement algorithm experimental evaluation, it is important to know the number of page frames available in the memory. The number of page frames plays an important role in producing the number of page faults and in the performance of the system. The more the number of page frames the less is the probability of page faults and increased performance of the system. This is because with the increase in the number of page frames, more number of required pages can be accommodated in the memory. Therefore, the required pages will be in the memory most of the times, thereby reducing the number of page faults. Thus, in general, it is expected that as the number of page frames increases the number of page faults decreases to a minimum level as shown in Fig. 11.7.

A page replacement algorithm must satisfy the following requirements:

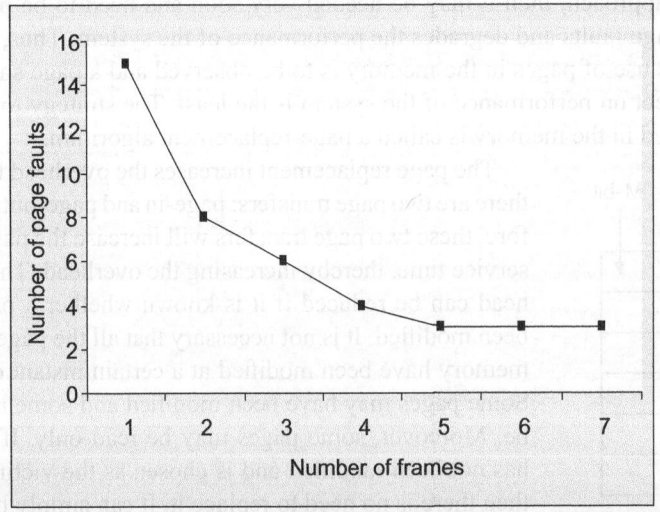

Fig. 11.7 Relation between PFR and the number of page frames

- The algorithm must not replace a page that may be referenced in the near future. This is known as *non-interference with the program's locality of reference*.
- The PFR should not increase with an increase in the size of the memory.

11.7.1 FIFO Page-replacement Algorithm

This strategy is used very often in daily life. Let us take an analogy of a shelf, which is used to keep several things. When there is no place in the shelf to keep a new item, the oldest item is replaced. The same strategy known as *first-in first-out* (FIFO) is also used for page replacement. According to FIFO, the oldest page among all the pages in the memory is chosen as the victim. The question is how to know the oldest page in the memory. One approach may be to attach the time while storing a page in the memory. However, an easier approach is to store all the pages in the memory in a FIFO queue. The page at the head of the queue will be paged-out first and a new page will be inserted at the tail of the queue. Let us understand this algorithm with some examples.

Example 11.6

Calculate the number of page faults for the following reference string using FIFO algorithm with frame size as 3.

   5 0 2 1 0 3 0 2 4 3 0 3 2 1 3 0 1 5

Solution

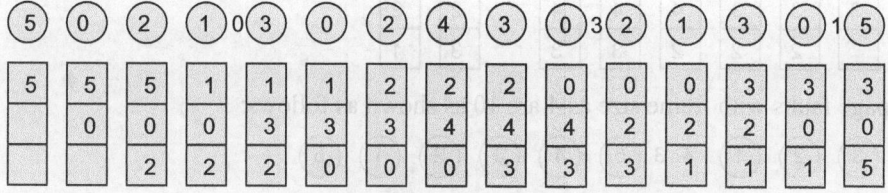

Initially, all the three frames are empty. Page number 5 is first referenced, and it is a page fault. After handling the page fault, the page is brought into the memory in one of the frames. Similarly, Page numbers 0 and 2 occupy the other two frames. Next, Page number 1 is referenced but there is no free frame. Here, the FIFO algorithm comes into the picture and replaces the page that was brought first, that is, Page number 5. The next referenced Page number 0 is already in the memory; therefore, it will not fault. After this, the next referenced page number is 3, which is a page fault. Therefore, Page number 0 is replaced. This process goes on resulting in 15 page faults. All the page references causing page faults have been circled to show the page faults.

Example 11.7

Calculate the number of page faults for the following reference string using FIFO algorithm with frame size as 4.

   5 0 2 1 0 3 0 2 4 3 0 3 2 1 3 0 1 5

Solution

Eleven page faults occur in the same reference string as in the previous example. The difference is in the number of frames in the memory. With frame size 4, the number of page

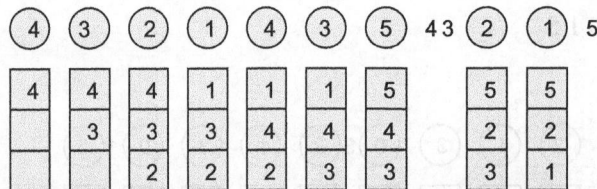

faults decreases as discussed earlier that the number of page faults will decrease with an increase in the number of page frames.

Example 11.8

Calculate the number of page faults for the following reference string using FIFO algorithm with frame size as 3 and then as 4.

4 3 2 1 4 3 5 4 3 2 1 5

Solution

The page faults with frame size as 3 are 9 as shown as follows:

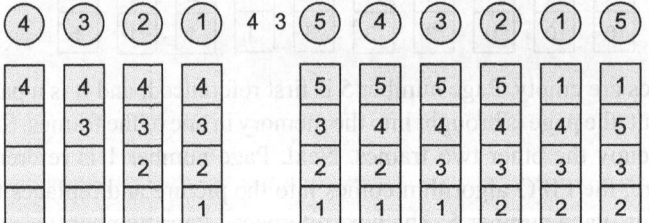

The page faults with frame size as 4 are 10 as shown as follows:

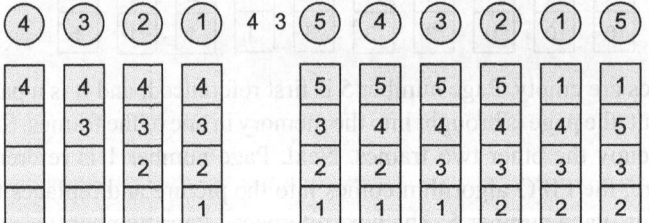

Belady's Anomaly

In Example 11.8, with frame size 3, the number of page faults is 9, whereas with frame size 4, it is 10. This is contradictory to the established principle that the number of page faults decrease with an increase in the number of frames in the memory. This anomaly was observed by a researcher, Belady, and is known as *Belady's anomaly* that shows the unexpected behaviour of FIFO page-replacement algorithm. This unexpected behaviour is seen in some of the reference strings but not always. This anomaly therefore decreases the reliability of the replacement algorithm. Moreover, it will soon be discussed that this algorithm produces a large number of page faults compared to other algorithms. Thus, this algorithm cannot be a good choice for page replacement.

11.7.2 Optimal Page-replacement Algorithm

The FIFO algorithm produces a large number of page faults. Moreover, it suffers from Belady's anomaly as discussed in Section 11.7.1. An algorithm is required that produces the least number of page faults and does not suffer from Belady's anomaly. An optimal policy is formed according to which a page that will not be referenced for the longest time will be replaced. This policy produces a minimal number of page faults. Let us understand this algorithm with an example.

Example 11.9

Calculate the number of page faults for the following reference string using optimum algorithm with frame size as 3.

  5 0 2 1 0 3 0 2 4 3 0 3 2 1 3 0 1 5

Solution

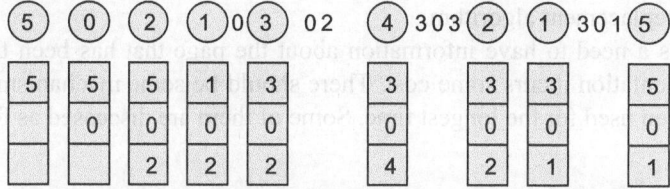

The Page numbers 5, 0, and 2 are page faults as shown earlier. The next page reference is 1, which is a page fault. At this moment, it is observed which page out of 5, 0, and 2 will not be referenced for a long time in the reference string. This is Page number 5. Therefore, Page number 5 will be replaced in the memory. The next reference Page number 0 is not a page fault. Page number 3 is again a page fault. Again, it is observed which page out of 1, 0, and 2 will not be referenced for a long time. This is Page number 1. Therefore, Page number 1 is replaced. The process goes on resulting in 9 page faults. The number of page faults in this algorithm is very less compared to FIFO algorithm.

Although the optimal page-replacement algorithm provides the minimum number of page faults, it cannot be implemented. The reason is that there is no provision in the OS to know the future memory references. Thus, this algorithm has no practical use in page replacement. However, it can be used to measure the performance of an algorithm in comparison with this algorithm. A new algorithm, although may not be optimal, can be compared with the minimum number of page faults found in this algorithm. In this way, the efficiency of an algorithm can be assessed.

11.7.3 Least Recently Used Page-replacement Algorithm

The optimal algorithm is not realizable as discussed in Section 11.7.2. The optimal algorithm was designed to replace a page that will not be referenced for the longest time. In other words, this was meant to have a low number of page faults. This algorithm may also be approximated with another view. The idea is to predict future references based on the past data, that is, a page that has not been referenced for a long time in the past may not be referenced for a long time in the future either. In this way, LRU page-replacement algorithm replaces a page that has not been used for the longest period of time in the past. Let us understand this algorithm with an example.

Example 11.10

Calculate the number of page faults for the following reference string using LRU page-replacement algorithm with frame size as 3.

  5 0 2 1 0 3 0 2 4 3 0 3 2 1 3 0 1 5

Solution

⑤ ⓪ ② ① 0 ③ 0 ② ④ ③ ⓪ 3 ② ① 3 ⓪ 1 ⑤

5	5	5	1	1	2	2	2	0	0	1	1	1
	0	0	0	0	0	3	3	3	3	3	3	5
		2	2	3	3	4	4	4	2	2	0	0

The page references 5, 0, and 2 will result in page faults. The next page reference 1 needs page replacement. Out of 5, 0, and 2, Page number 5 has not been used in the past. Therefore, it will be replaced. This process goes on resulting in total 13 page faults, which is again less compared to FIFO page-replacement algorithm.

Since in LRU, there is a need to have information about the page that has been the least recently used, its implementation incurs some cost. There should be some mechanism to find out a page that has not been used for the longest time. Some of them are discussed as follows:

Stack Implementation

To implement LRU, a linked list of all the pages in the memory can be maintained. The list can be structured as a stack such that whenever a page is referenced, it is placed at the top of the stack. This way, the most recently used page will always be at the top and consequently, the least recently used page will be at the bottom of the stack. This implementation requires removing one entry from the middle and placing it at the top of the stack. Thus, the stack needs to be updated with every memory reference, which incurs a cost. However, the advantage is that only the bottom of the stack needs to be searched for this purpose, which saves time.

Example 11.11

A page reference string is given by
5 0 2 1 0 3 0 2 4 3 0 3 2 1 3 0 1 5

The stack implementation that records the most recent reference at the top and the least-used page reference at the bottom of the stack. The following figure shows the state of the stack after the first reference of Page number 3 in the reference string.

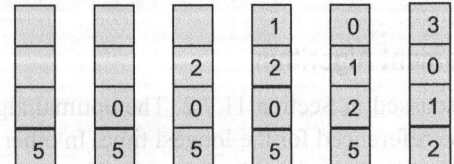

Counter Implementation

The stack implementation is costly because of constant updating of data in the linked list. If it is possible to note the time when a memory reference was made, then the time when a page was referenced can be known. For this purpose, a counter is taken in hardware, which is incremented after every memory reference. Further, the contents of this counter should be copied to the page table. For this, there must be another column, say counter, in the page table (see Fig. 11.8). Therefore, whenever there is a reference to a page, the counter (time of the last use) is incremented and the value of counter is copied into the counter field in the page-table entry for that page. In this way, the time of the last reference of a page is obtained. Whenever a page fault occurs, the page table is searched for the smallest value of the counter. The page with the

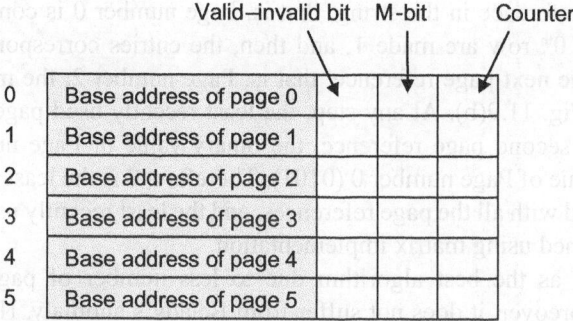

Fig. 11.8   Page table with counter

smallest value is replaced according to LRU policy. Counter implementation requires hardware assistance for counter, page table searching, and a write operation to the memory for copying the counter value into the page table.

Matrix Implementation

In this implementation, a matrix of $n \times n$ is maintained, where n is the number of page frames in the system. All the entries in the matrix are initialized to 0. Whenever a page, say m, is referenced, all the entries of mth row in the matrix are set to 1 and all the entries of mth column are then set to 0. This process is repeated with every memory reference. The page corresponding to the least binary value of the row is the least recently used page. This implementation, however, needs hardware assistance: All the matrix operations are implemented in hardware.

Example 11.12

A page reference string is given by

    0 2 1 0 3 0 2 3 0 3 2 1 3 0 1

The matrix implementation of this string for some of the page references is shown in Fig. 11.9.

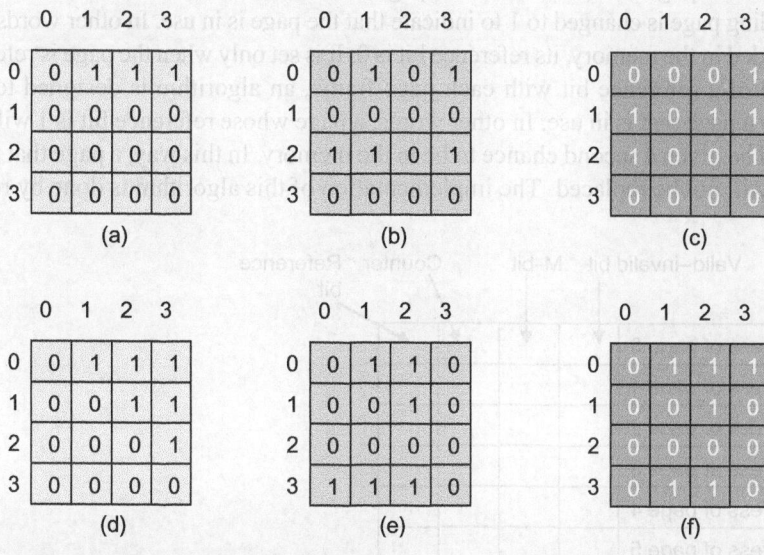

Fig. 11.9   Matrix implementation of LRU

In Fig. 11.9(a), the first page reference in the string, that is, Page number 0 is considered. The entries corresponding to the 0th row are made 1, and then, the entries corresponding to the 0th column are made 0. For the next page reference, that is, Page number 2, the matrix of Fig. 11.9(a) is used resulting in Fig. 11.9(b). At any step, the least recently used page can be obtained. For example, after the second page reference, the binary value of Page number 2 (1101) is more than the binary value of Page number 0 (0101). Therefore, 0 is the least recently used page. This process is repeated with all the page references, and the least recently used page to be replaced can be easily obtained using matrix implementation.

LRU algorithm is considered as the best algorithm due to less number of page faults compared to FIFO algorithm. Moreover, it does not suffer from Belady's anomaly. However, the implementation of LRU demands hardware assistance. Moreover, there is a need to update the clock or stack for every memory reference. This slows down every memory reference in the system. Thus, inspite of being good in performance, LRU is difficult to implement and incurs overhead. Therefore, some other algorithms are required for page replacement. The researchers have tried to approximate the nature of the LRU and developed some other algorithms that incur the least overhead or require the least hardware assistance. These algorithms are discussed in the subsequent sections.

11.7.4 Second Chance Page-replacement Algorithm

This algorithm is a modification of FIFO algorithm. The FIFO algorithm inspite of its poor performance is a low-overhead algorithm. The major drawback of this algorithm is that even if a page is in use, it may be replaced due to its arrival time. It means that there is no consideration of the use of a page in FIFO algorithm. The performance of FIFO algorithm can be increased and can be approximated to LRU if information regarding how much a page is in use in the system is added. For this purpose, some additional bits are required to keep the information. A *reference bit* or *use bit* is used to give information regarding whether the page has been used (see Fig. 11.10). This information is entered into the page-table entries. Initially, all the reference bits of the pages are set to 0 to indicate that the page is not in use. As the page is referenced, the status of the reference bit of the corresponding page is changed to 1 to indicate that the page is in use. In other words, whenever a page is loaded in the memory, its reference bit is 0. It is set only when the page is referenced.

With the help of a reference bit with each page frame, an algorithm is designed to give a second chance to a page that is in use. In other words, a page whose reference bit is 1 will not be replaced and will be given a second chance to be in the memory. In this way, a page that is being frequently used will not be replaced. The implementation of this algorithm is done by resetting

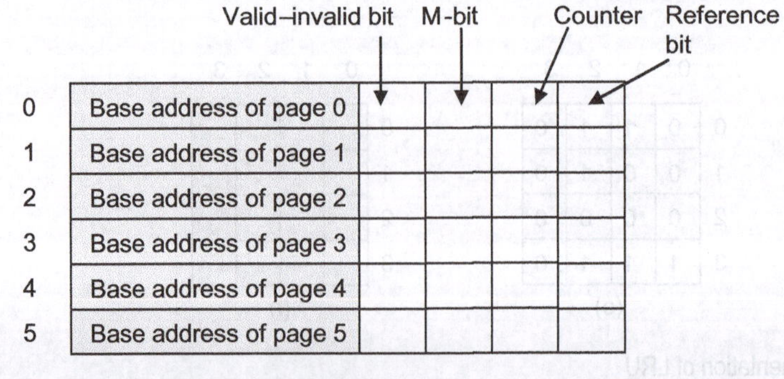

Fig. 11.10   Page table with reference bit

its reference bit to 0 and arrival time to the current time. Thus, a page that is given a second chance will not be replaced until all the other pages have been replaced. Generally, FIFO list is maintained through a queue. Therefore, this page is appended at the end of the queue of pages by the OS. If a page is being frequently used, then its reference bit is always set to 1 and will never be replaced. There may be a situation when all the pages in the memory are in use, then this algorithm degenerates into pure FIFO algorithm. In this case, it scans all the pages once and reaches to the first page again.

Example 11.13

Calculate the number of page faults for the following reference string using second-chance algorithm with frame size 3 and compare the result with FIFO algorithm.

    5 0 2 1 0 3 0 2 4 3 0 3 2 1 3 0 1 5

Solution

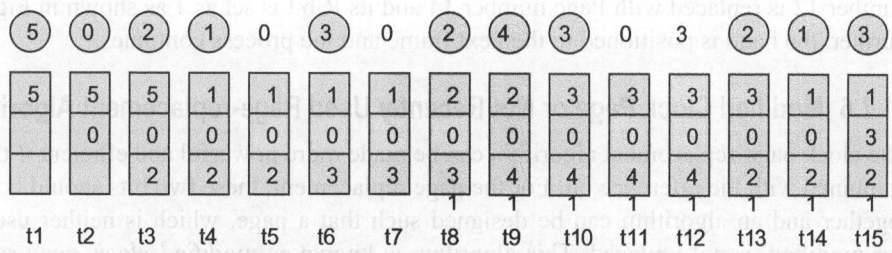

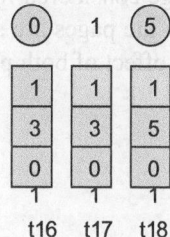

The page whose reference bit is 1 has been shown in grey color, otherwise, the reference bit of the page is 0.

If we compare the number of page faults here as compared to FIFO in Example 11.6, then second-chance algorithm is better as there are only 13 page faults in the second chance as compared to 15 in FIFO.

11.7.5 Clock Page-replacement Algorithm

Implementation of the second-chance algorithm in the form of a queue may be inefficient as it incurs the cost of moving the pages with reference bit 1 at the end of the queue. Therefore, the pages are moved around in the queue unnecessarily. A better approach is to have a circular queue instead of a general queue. The circular queue will store all the pages with their status bits as before, but now, there is a hand (a pointer) that indicates the next page in the circular queue. This circular queue is known as a *clock*. Whenever there is a page fault, the page indicated by the hand of the clock is inspected. If the reference bit of the page being inspected is 1, then it is reset to 0, that is, the page is given a second chance and the position of the hand is advanced to the next page in the clock. Otherwise, if the reference bit is 0, the page is replaced with the new one. The reference bit for this page is set to 1, and the hand is advanced to the next page in the queue. It may be possible that the reference bit of all the pages is set as 1. In that case, the hand scans all the pages one by one and resets all of them to 0. Finally, it reaches the first page in the clock where it started, but this time, the reference bit is 0. Therefore, the first page can be considered for the replacement.

Example 11.14

The circular queue implementation as a clock has been shown for some pages in the queue with a hand (see Fig.11.11(a)). Currently, the hand points to frame 1 containing Page number 4 and its reference bit R is set as 1. The clock algorithm is executed. Since the R bit is 1, the page cannot be replaced but its R bit is set as 0. The hand is advanced to the next frame. The next frame contains the Page number 12 and its R bit is 0. This page can be replaced with an incoming page. Suppose the page to be brought in is the Page number 14. Therefore, Page number 12 is replaced with Page number 14 and its R bit is set as 1 as shown in Fig. 11.11(b). Further, the hand is positioned to the next frame and the process continues.

11.7.6 Modified Clock Page or Not Recently Used Page-replacement Algorithm

The clock page-replacement algorithm can be made more powerful and efficient if the M-bit is combined with the reference bit. For the page replacement, these two bits should be combined together and an algorithm can be designed such that a page, which is neither used recently nor modified, is not replaced. This algorithm is known as *modified clock page-replacement algorithm* or *not recently used algorithm* (NRU). The modified page considered for the page replacement needs to be written to the disk so that changes done in the pages are saved. The combination of reference bit and M-bit can be exploited to have the effect of both page access

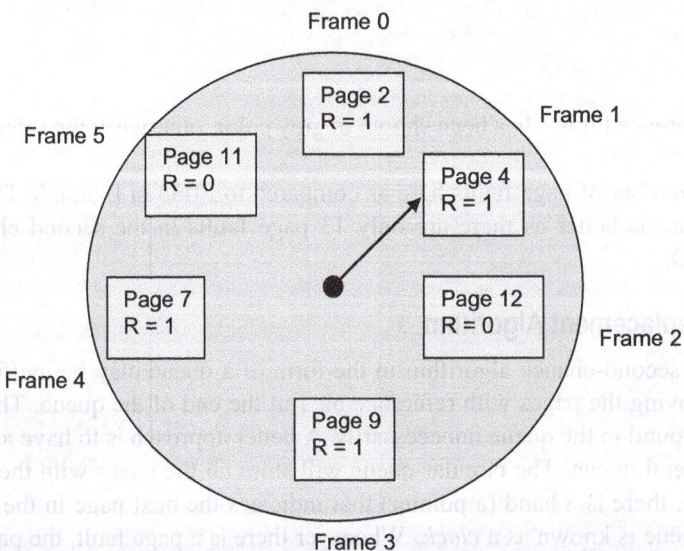

Fig. 11.11 (a) Circular queue clock page replacement

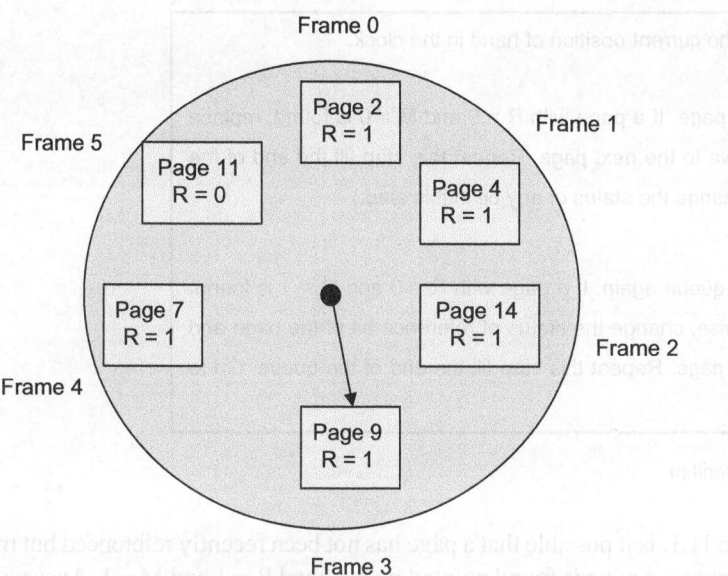

Fig. 11.11 (b) Clock page replacement

and page modification. The combination of the bits is shown in Table 11.1, where R is reference bit and M is M-bit. R and M bits are set by the hardware. When a page is referenced, the R bit is set, and if the page is modified, its M bit is set.

For page replacement, a page that has been recently used or modified will not be considered. Therefore, the Classes 2 and 3 in Table 11.1 are invalid for page-replacement algorithm. Therefore, the Classes 0 and 1 can be considered. In these two cases, Class 0 is more suitable because it has not been used recently and is not modified. Thus, the clock algorithm is designed such that the hand scans the pages in the clock and replaces the first page with R = 0 and M = 0. Note that the R bit of any page is not modified in this step. If such a page is found, then the algorithm executes fast as there is no need to transfer the page to be replaced to the hard disk, thereby reducing the I/O time required. On the other hand, if the desired page is not found, then the hand scans the clock again, but this time the strategy is changed, that is, R = 0 and M = 1. If such a page is found, then replace it; otherwise, R bit is reset and the hand is advanced to the next page. This process continues until the desired page is obtained. If not, then scan the queue again; this time, a page that satisfies either of the two strategies, as discussed earlier, will be found. In this modified-clock algorithm, multiple sweeps of the circular queue may be needed to perform that may improve the performance of the algorithm. The algorithm is shown in Fig. 11.12.

Table 11.1 R bit and M bit combinations

Class	R	M	Meaning
0	0	0	Page is not being used recently and is unmodified.
1	0	1	Page is not being used recently and is modified.
2	1	0	Page is being used recently and is unmodified.
3	1	1	Page is being used recently and is modified.

Step 1: Find out the current position of hand in the clock.

Step 2: Scan the page. If a page with R = 0 and M = 0 is found, replace it. Otherwise, move to the next page. Repeat this step till the end of the queue. (Do not change the status of any bit in this step.)

Step 3: Scan the queue again. If a page with R = 0 and M = 1 is found, replace it. Otherwise, change the status of reference bit of the page and move to the next page. Repeat this step till the end of the queue. Go to Step 1.

Fig. 11.12   NRU algorithm

As given in Table 11.1, is it possible that a page has not been recently referenced but modified? This is possible. Suppose, a page is found pointed by the hand R = 1 and M = 1. According to the algorithm given in Fig. 11.12, the status of the R bit is changed to 0 to differentiate between the recently referenced and the earlier ones. Therefore, it may be possible that whenever the hand of the clock comes back to this page, its R bit is 0 whereas M bit is still 1. This is because the status of the R bits is only changed in the algorithm and M bit is untouched. Therefore, it is possible that one page is with R bit set to 0 and M bit as 1.

Example 11.15

A circular queue shown in Fig. 11.13 (a) uses R bit as well as M bit. The hand is positioned currently on the Page number 4 whose R bit and M bit are set as 1. Therefore, this page cannot be replaced. According to the algorithm, the R bit of this page is set to 0 and the hand is

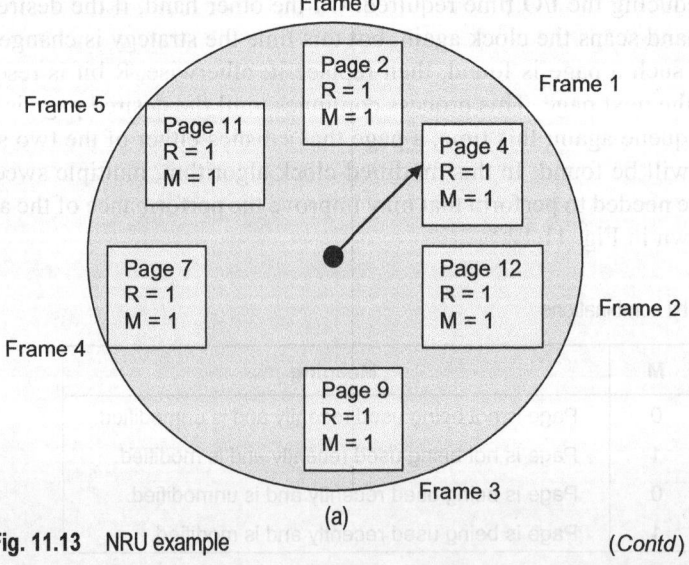

Fig. 11.13   NRU example   *(Contd)*

(*Fig. 11.13 Contd*)

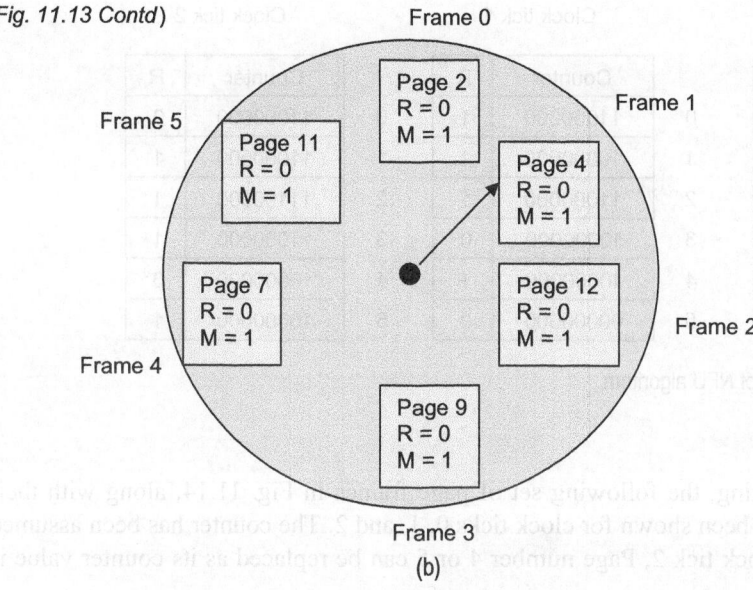

(b)

advanced to the next frame. Coincidently, all the frames in the queue have R and M bits set as 1. Therefore, one round of the algorithm does not find any page to be replaced. However, in the next round, all pages have R bits reset to 0. Therefore, the first page, that is, Page number 4, can be chosen for the replacement as shown in Fig. 11.13(b).

11.7.7 Not Frequently Used Page-replacement Algorithm

Another approximation for LRU algorithm is *not frequently used (NFU) algorithm*. In this algorithm, one counter is taken with every page frame. The counter variable is used to count how many times the page has been used. R bit is also considered as used before, that is, it is set or reset according to its use. The counter for each frame is initially 0. At each clock interrupt, the OS scans all the pages. The R bits (either 0 or 1) of all the pages are added to their corresponding counters. If a page is used, then its R bit is set as 1. Therefore, its counter will be incremented by 1. If a page is not used during a clock tick, then its counter will be unchanged as its R bit is 0. This is done for all the page frames in the memory. Thus, the counter value for a page frame indicates how many times a page has been used. When a page fault occurs, the algorithm chooses a page with the lowest value of counter, that is, the page that has been used least.

This algorithm suffers from a problem. it does not take into account the time span of the pages being used. It may be possible that in a particular time frame, some pages are frequently used and therefore, their counter will provide a high count. These pages will not be replaced even though in another time frame, they are not frequent and have a low count. Similarly, in-spite of their heavy use in the current time frame, the new pages that are useful for execution may be replaced due to their low counter value in the previous time frame.

This algorithm can be modified to rule out the problem. The solution is called *aging*. The first modification is to shift all the counters to right by 1 bit after the clock interval and before adding the R bit. The second modification is to add the R bit to the leftmost position of the corresponding counter rather than the rightmost. These two modifications in the counter value help to indicate not only the frequency but also the time span of reference of a page frame. Let us illustrate this with an example.

Clock tick 0

	Counter	R
0	10000000	1
1	00000000	0
2	10000000	1
3	10000000	1
4	00000000	0
5	00000000	0

Clock tick 1

	Counter	R
0	11000000	1
1	10000000	1
2	11000000	1
3	10000000	0
4	10000000	1
5	00000000	0

Clock tick 2

	Counter	R
0	11000000	0
1	11000000	1
2	11100000	1
3	11000000	1
4	10000000	0
5	10000000	1

Fig. 11.14 Implementation of NFU algorithm

Example 11.16

Using the NFU with aging, the following set of page frames in Fig. 11.14, along with their counters and R bits, has been shown for clock ticks 0, 1, and 2. The counter has been assumed to be of 8 bits. After clock tick 2, Page number 4 or 5 can be replaced as its counter value is the lowest.

11.8 STACK PROPERTY OF PAGE-REPLACEMENT ALGORITHMS

The Belady's anomaly observed in FIFO page-replacement algorithm forced researchers to analyse the page-replacement algorithms. Their investigations resulted into a property known as *stack property of page-replacement algorithms*. An algorithm that satisfies this property does not suffer from the Belady's anomaly. The property considers the execution of an algorithm with two different page-frame sizes, say m and n where $n < m$. At an instant of time, all the pages that are in the memory when the page-frame size is n would also be in the memory when the page frame size is m. In other words, the set of pages when the page-frame size is n is a subset of the set of pages when the page-frame size is m as follows:

$$\{page\_set_i\}^t_n \subseteq \{page\_set_i\}^t_m$$

where $n < m$, t is the time instant

$\{page\_set_i\}$ is set of pages in memory of process i

The implication of stack property is that the number of page faults in page-frame size n is more compared to that of m. It means that it holds the page fault characteristic, that is, the number of page faults decreases as the page-frame size increases.

Example 11.17

Using the following page-reference string and frame size as 3 and 4, show whether FIFO, optimal, LRU, and second-chance algorithm satisfy the stack property of page-replacement algorithms:

t1	t2	t3	t4	t5	t6	t7	t8	t9	t10	t11	t12	t13	t14	t15	t16	t17	t18
5	0	2	1	0	3	0	2	4	3	0	3	2	1	3	0	1	5

Compare the performance of algorithms with both the frame sizes based on the PFR.

Solution

FIFO

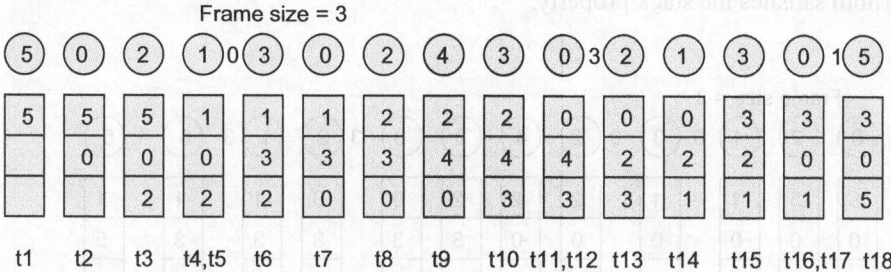

Frame size = 3

|t1|t2|t3|t4,t5|t6|t7|t8|t9|t10|t11,t12|t13|t14|t15|t16,t17|t18|

Frame size = 4

|t1|t2|t3|t4,t5|t6,t7,t8|t9,t10|t11,t12|t13|t14|t15,16,17|t18|

In FIFO, at time instants t9 and t18, the page_set in execution with page-frame size = 3 is not the subset of page_set in execution with page-frame size = 4. Thus, this algorithm does not satisfy the stack property.

Optimal

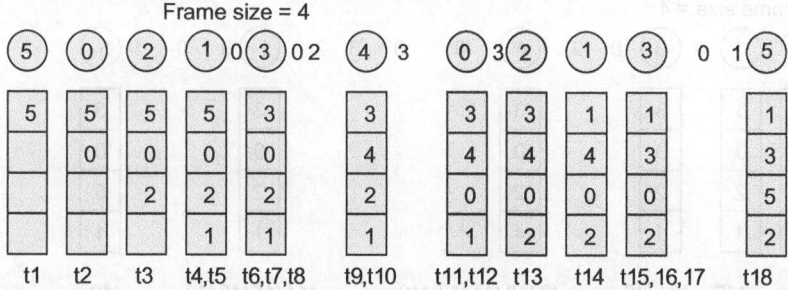

Frame size = 3

|t1|t2|t3|t4,t5|t6,t7,t8|t9,t10,t11,t12|t13|t14,t15,t16,t17|t18|

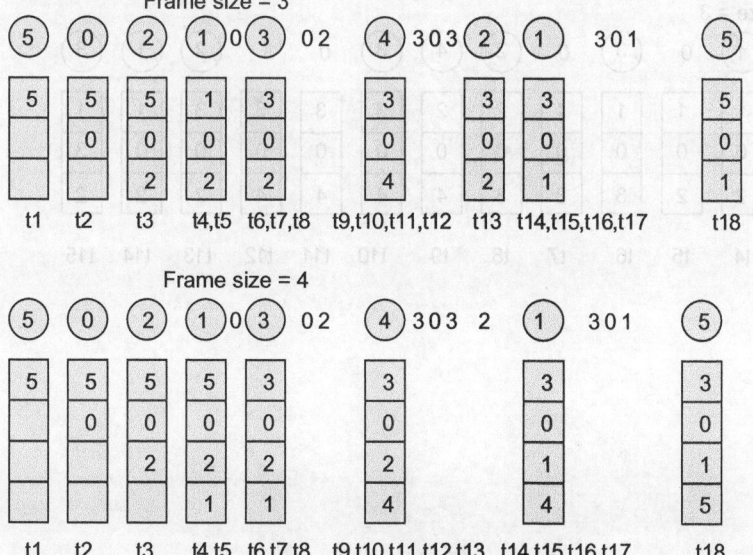

Frame size = 4

|t1|t2|t3|t4,t5|t6,t7,t8|t9,t10,t11,t12,t13|t14,t15,t16,t17|t18|

Here, in optimal algorithm, at every instant of time, the page_set in execution with page-frame size = 3 is the subset of the page_set in execution with page-frame size = 4. Thus, this algorithm satisfies the stack property.

LRU

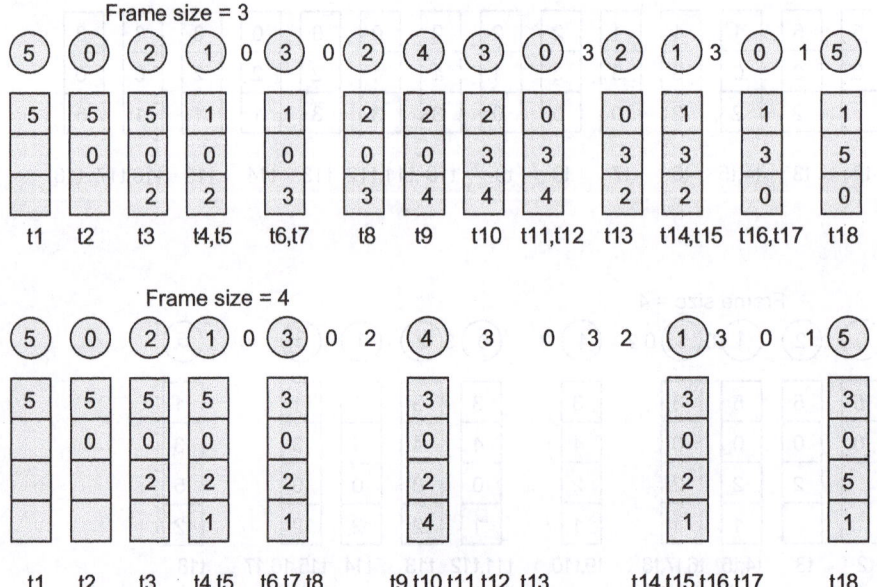

Here, in LRU algorithm, at every instant of time, the page_set in execution with page-frame size = 3 is the subset of the page_set in execution with page-frame size = 4. Thus, this algorithm satisfies the stack property.

Second-chance algorithm

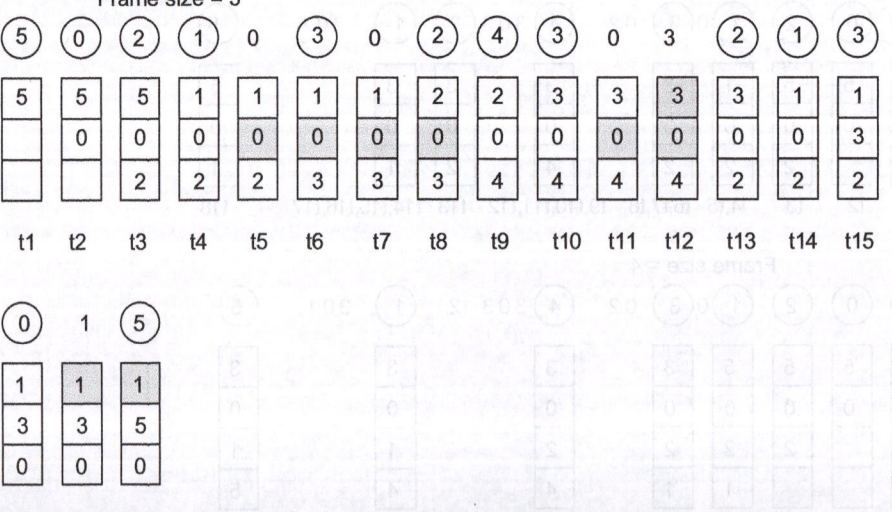

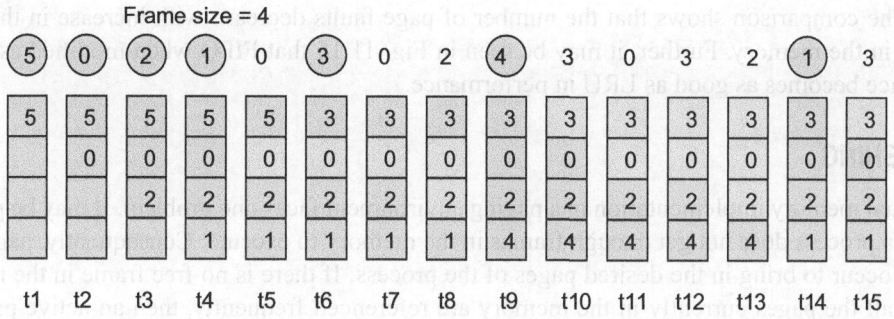

Frame size = 4

5	5	5	5	5	3	3	3	3	3	3	3	3	3	3
	0	0	0	0	0	0	0	0	0	0	0	0	0	0
		2	2	2	2	2	2	2	2	2	2	2	2	2
			1	1	1	1	4	4	4	4	4	4	1	1

t1 t2 t3 t4 t5 t6 t7 t8 t9 t10 t11 t12 t13 t14 t15

0   1   5

3	3	3
0	0	0
2	2	5
1	1	1

t16 t17 t18

Similarly, in second-chance algorithm, at every instant of time, the page_set in execution with page-frame size = 3 is the subset of the page_set in execution with page-frame size = 4. Thus, this algorithm also satisfies the stack property.

The performance comparison of all the algorithms is as follows:

Algorithm	No. of page faults with frame size = 3	No. of page faults with frame size = 4
FIFO	15	11
Optimal	9	8
LRU	13	8
Second chance	13	8

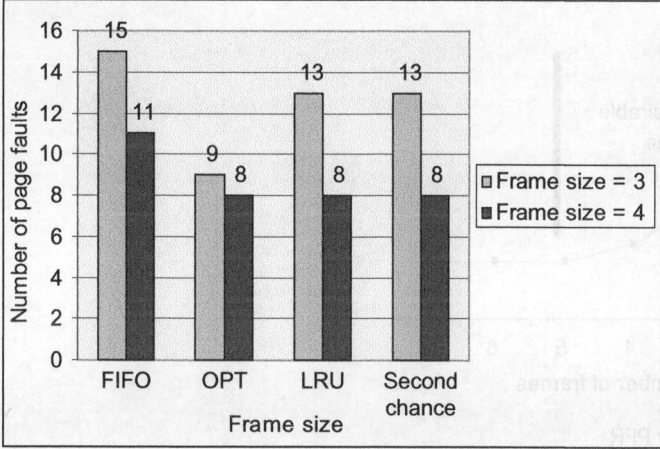

Fig. 11.15 Performance comparison of page-replacement algorithms

The comparison shows that the number of page faults decrease with increase in the frame size in the memory. Further, it may be seen in Fig. 11.15 that FIFO when modified as second chance becomes as good as LRU in performance.

11.9 THRASHING

Virtual memory implementation in a paging environment faces one problem. It may be possible that a process does not get enough frames in the memory to execute. Consequently, page faults will occur to bring in the desired pages of the process. If there is no free frame in the memory and all the pages currently in the memory are referenced frequently, then an active page will be replaced to bring in the desired pages. When an active page is replaced, it will be needed again, right away resulting in a page fault. After some time, the processes will try to replace the active pages of another process to get a free frame in the memory causing a large number of page faults. This results in a high PFR known as *high paging activity*, and this high paging activity is known as *thrashing*. A process is said to be thrashing if most of the time is consumed in paging rather than in its execution.

The process of thrashing can be understood with the help of the relation between the number of page frames and that of page faults as described earlier in Fig. 11.7. This relation is reproduced in Fig. 11.16 by showing two zones in the graph. One zone is where the processes execute with low number of page faults, and another is where the processes execute with high number of page faults. The former is a desirable zone where low paging activity occurs. On the other hand, in the latter case, processes are in high paging situation where they are busy in paging activity rather than execution.

It should be clear that accessing the disk may take a few milliseconds compared to the instruction execution that takes few nanoseconds. When there are a number of page faults and, consequently, page replacements, the processes need to queue up on the hard disk because one page transfer to and from the secondary storage takes time. Most of the processes are in waiting queue of the hard disk and the main memory starts emptying as shown in Fig. 11.17. When a process page faults, it is blocked. Therefore, most of the processes in high-paging activity are in blocked states, that is, waiting for the hard disk for its service (page-in or page-out). Consequently, the average service time for a page fault increases due to longer queue on the paging device. Therefore, no useful work other than page-in or page-out is being done by the processor. In other words, CPU utilization decreases.

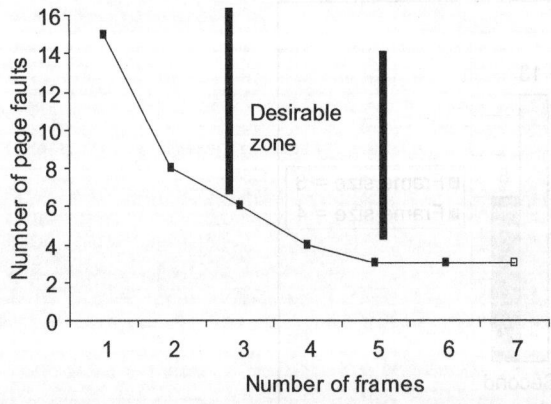

Fig. 11.16   Desirable zone for PFR

point has reached the system and the degree of multi-programming must be decreased to stop thrashing in the system. Thus, it can be said that thrashing is a situation of coincidence of high paging activity and low CPU utilization.

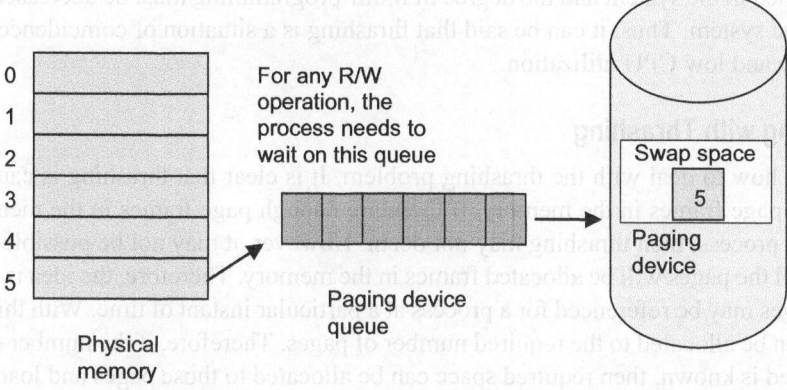

Fig. 11.17   Paging device queue

The long-term scheduler observes the low CPU utilization and therefore, increases the degree of multi-programming by pushing a new process from the job queue to the ready queue. As soon as a new process arrives in the ready queue, it causes page fault because being a new process it demands frames for its pages. This further decreases the CPU utilization instead of increasing it. The scheduler may try to further increase the degree of multi-programming, thereby causing more page faults. In this situation, there is a tremendous increase in the number of page faults and all the processes are busy paging rather than executing. The system throughput is reduced to almost zero, and this is the point of thrashing. At this time, it must be understood that if CPU utilization does not increase inspite of increasing the degree of multi-programming and drops down, then the degree of multi-programming should be decreased instead of increasing because thrashing point in the system has been reached. In Fig. 11.18, the normal behaviour of CPU utilization can be seen, that is, CPU utilization increases with the increase in the degree of multi-programming. However, it may be possible that the CPU utilization suddenly starts dropping with the increase in the degree of multi-programming. It means that the thrashing

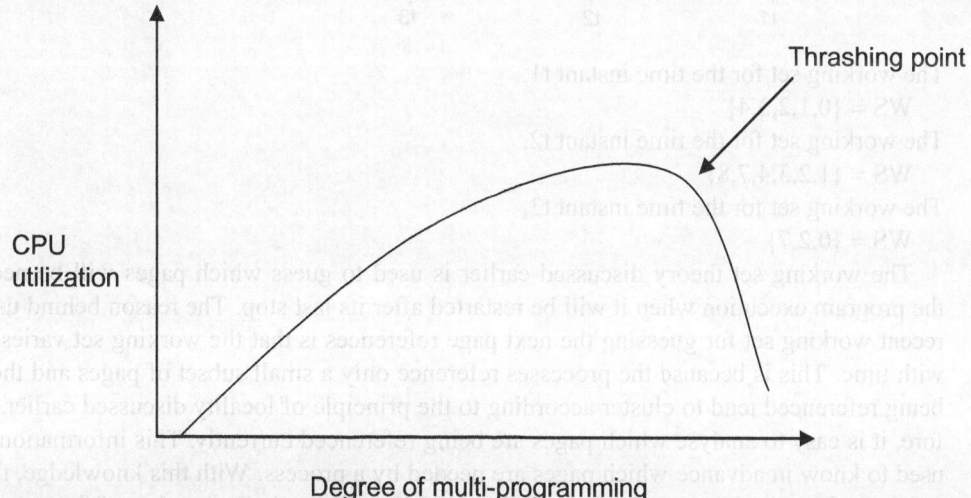

Fig. 11.18   Thrashing

point has reached in the system and the degree of multi-programming must be decreased to stop thrashing in the system. Thus, it can be said that thrashing is a situation of coincidence of high paging activity and low CPU utilization.

11.9.1 Dealing with Thrashing

Let us discuss how to deal with the thrashing problem. It is clear that thrashing is caused due to shortage of page frames in the memory. If there are enough page frames in the memory for execution of a process, then thrashing may not occur. However, it may not be possible most of the time that all the pages will be allocated frames in the memory. Therefore, the idea is to guess how many pages may be referenced for a process at a particular instant of time. With this guess, some space can be allocated to the required number of pages. Therefore, if the number of pages to be referenced is known, then required space can be allocated to those pages and loaded. The set of pages a process is using is known as a *working set*. The working set is a set of *m*, that is the most recent page references. If a page is in use, then it will be in the working set, otherwise, it will be dropped from it at a particular instant of time.

Let *m* =10, that is, the working set has 10 most recent page references. At a particular instant of time, look for the recent 10 page references. The pages that are in use in these recent 10 references will be the part of the working set. The duplicate entries are omitted.

Example 11.18

A process executes with the following page reference string:

1 3 4 3 2 3 4 2 0 3 4 3 1 2 3 7 2 8 7 4 7 2 7 2 7 0 2 7 2 0 7 0 2

Taking the working set window size as 10, what will be the working set for the time instant t1, t2, and t3?

Solution

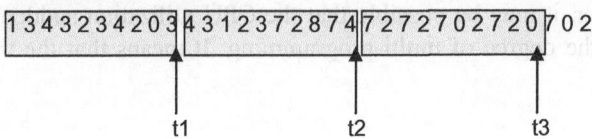

The working set for the time instant t1,
   WS = {0,1,2,3,4}
The working set for the time instant t2,
   WS = {1,2,3,4,7,8}
The working set for the time instant t3,
   WS = {0,2,7}

The working set theory discussed earlier is used to guess which pages will be needed in the program execution when it will be restarted after its last stop. The reason behind using the recent working set for guessing the next page references is that the working set varies slowly with time. This is because the processes reference only a small subset of pages and the pages being referenced tend to cluster according to the principle of locality discussed earlier. Therefore, it is easy to analyse which pages are being referenced currently. This information can be used to know in advance which pages are needed by a process. With this knowledge, the total number of required frames can be calculated. If *NumFrame* is the number of frames required by a process, then the total demand for the frames by all processes in the system are

$$TotalFramesDemand = \sum_{i=1}^{n} NumFrame_i$$

where n is the number of processes.

Let *TotalFramesAvail* be the number of frames available. If *TotalFramesDemand* is larger than *TotalFramesAvail*, then thrashing may occur as some processes do not have enough frames that cause chain of page faults. The OS observes the working set of each process while executing and allocates the number of frames required by it. If there are enough frames, then another process in the system must be allowed to execute. Otherwise, if the *TotalFrames Demand* is larger than *TotalFramesAvail*, then a process is selected to suspend. The pages of the process thus chosen are paged-out and frames are allocated to other processes that are short of frames. In this way, the system does not allow all the processes in the ready queue to execute and keep a limit on them to prevent thrashing; hence, working set strategy not only prevents thrashing but also keeps the CPU utilization high.

The working set strategy needs to keep track of the number of pages in the working set. This can be implemented through a shift register of length m that shifts the register left by one position with every memory reference and inserts the most recently referenced page number on the right. The set of m page numbers in the shift register represents the working set. However, maintaining and updating the shift register with every memory reference is quite expensive. Therefore, this technique is not used in practice. Another technique is to use a time interval instead of the number of memory references. In other words, the working set will not be based on the number of memory references but on a time interval. The set of pages being referenced during the time interval is the working set. This can be implemented through a fixed-interval timer interrupt.

11.9.2 Working-set-based Page-replacement Algorithm

The working set theory can also be used for page replacement. The strategy to replace a page in the memory is to find a page that is not in the working set and replace it. This algorithm needs two items of information in the page table. Therefore, a page table must use the following, along with its other items (see Fig. 11.19):

(a) reference bit R
(b) time of last use (TLU)

It must be noted that on each interrupt, the reference bits of the pages in the memory are set to 0 and the pages that are in the working set being referenced are set to 1. According to this

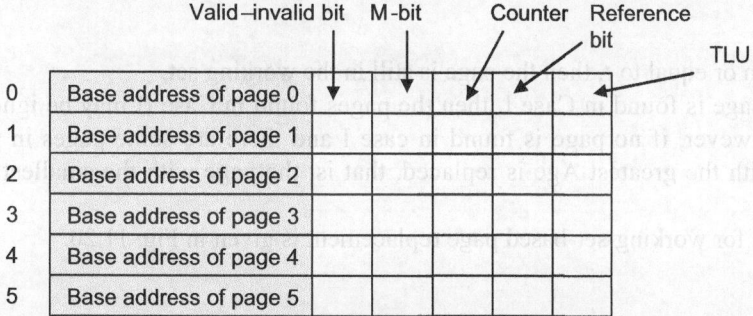

Fig. 11.19   Page table with R bit and TLU

```
On every Page_fault
{
    while (page table entry)
    {
        If R bit = 1
            TLU = Cur_time
        Else
        {
            If Age > t
                Replace the page
            Else if Age <= t
                Store its Age
        }
    }
    If no page is found for replacement and there
        are pages with R = 0 and Age <= t
            Replace the page with the greatest Age
}
```

Fig. 11.20 Algorithm for working-set-based page replacement

algorithm, on every page fault, the page table is scanned to find a page whose R bit is not 1 and that is in the memory. If the R bit of the page is 1, then the current value of time is written into the TLU field of the page table. It indicates that the page was in use when the page fault happened. This page has been obviously referenced recently during the current clock interrupt. It is in the working set and cannot be replaced. On the other hand, if the R bit of a page is 0, then the page has not been referenced recently and is in the memory and can be considered for replacement. Nevertheless, there are further conditions to check for its replacement.

Let t be the time frame of the working set, that is, the number of pages being referenced during past t seconds.

Cur_time = Current time in the system

TLU = Time of last use

Using these parameters, calculate the age of a page whose R bit is 0 as the following:

Age = Cur_Time − TLU

There may be two cases in the algorithm:

Case I:

If Age is greater than t, then the page is no longer in the working set and can be replaced with the new page.

Case II:

If Age is less than or equal to t, then the page is still in the working set.

If a suitable page is found in Case I, then the pages found in Case II may be ignored for replacement. However, if no page is found in case I and there are some pages in Case II, then the page with the greatest Age is replaced, that is, the page with the smallest TLU is replaced.

The algorithm for working-set-based page replacement is given in Fig. 11.20.

Example 11.19

In the following table, if a page is to be replaced on a page fault, which page will it be?

Page number	TLU	R bit
0	1002	1
1	1100	1
2	980	1
3	1020	0
4	1102	0
5	990	1
Cur_time = 1200		
t = 60		

Solution

On scanning the page table, for all the entries with R =1, TLU is replaced with Cur_time.

For the entries with R = 0,

Age = Cur_time – TLU

i.e., Age for page 3 = 1200 – 1020 = 180 and

Age for page 4 = 1200 – 1102 = 98

Given, t = 60

Therefore, Page number 3 has Age > t, that is, 180 > 60, and therefore, the page can be replaced.

11.9.3 WSClock Page-replacement Algorithm

The working-set-based page replacement algorithm is good but expensive to implement as the whole page table needs to be searched for a suitable page. The scanning of the entire page table takes time. The working-set-based algorithm can be modified according to the clock-based algorithm and thus can be implemented efficiently. Therefore, the modified clock algorithm when implemented along with working set information is known as WSClock page-replacement algorithm. As discussed in clock algorithm, the pages are stored in the circular queue as they are loaded in the memory. The difference is that each entry in the queue for a page consists of the following information:

i) R bit
ii) M bit
iii) TLU

Along with these fields of information in the queue, the algorithm also uses *Age* and *t*. The hand position in clock is used to start the algorithm. The R bit of the page being examined is checked first. If the R bit is 1, then it means that the page has been referenced recently and therefore, cannot be used for replacement. Therefore, the page is not replaced and the hand is positioned to the next page after resetting the R bit of the current page as 0. On the other hand, if the R bit of a page is 0, then *Age* is checked. If *Age* of the page is greater than *t*, then it is not in the working set. Further, the M bit of the page is also checked. If M bit is 0, it means that the page has not been modified and its copy is already there on the disk and therefore, need not to be transferred to the disk. Thus, a page whose *Age* is greater than *t* and M bit is 0 is the best to be replaced because it is the oldest and can be replaced immediately without transferring it to the disk. However, if the M bit is 1, then it means that the page has been modified and therefore, needs to be saved on the disk. The write-to disk is scheduled to save the modifications in the page and the hand is positioned to the next page to find a suitable page in the queue. There may be a worst case that all the pages in the queue have been modified. It may lead to high disk traffic as all the pages need to be saved on the disk. Therefore, a limit must be put on the pages to be written back to the disk. Further, it may be possible that the hand comes back to the first position in the clock. It means that either there is no page with R = 0 or there is a page with R = 0 but not with M = 0. In the former case, all the pages are in the working set; therefore, no page can be replaced. In the latter case, the page found is not in the working set but has been put on the disk queue to be written back. Thus, by the time the hand comes back to the first position in the queue after completing one cycle around the clock, it may be possible that the write-to

```
On every page fault
{
    while (page table entry)
    {
        If R = 1
        {
            R = 0
            Position the clock hand to the next page in the queue
        }
        Else
        {
            If (Age > t)
            {
                If (M = 0)
                        Replace the page
                Else
                {
                        Schedule the disk writeoperation
                        Position the clock hand to the next page in the queue
                }
            }
            Else if Age <= t
                Store its Age
        }
    }
    If no page found for replacement and there are pages with R = 0 and Age <= t
        Replace the page with the greatest Age
}
```

Fig. 11.21   Algorithm for WSClock page replacement

operation scheduled for the page has been completed and thus, can be chosen for replacement after making its M bit as 0. The algorithm for WSClock page-replacement algorithm has been shown in Fig. 11.21.

Example 11.20

Which page will be replaced in the clock shown in the following daigram with Cur_time = 1210, t = 50 using WSClock page-replacement algorithm?

Solution

1. The clock hand is positioned on Frame 1. Here, R = 1. Therefore, it is reset to 0 and the hand is moved to the next frame.
2. The R bit of Frame 2 is also 1. Again, the R bit is reset and the hand is moved to the next frame.
3. The R bits of all the pages are 1. Therefore, in the first round through the clock, they are reset to 0.
4. In the second round, on the first frame, now, the R bit is 0. The Age is 1210 − 1008 = 202, which is greater than t. But the M bit is 1, that is, the page has been modified and needs to be written to the disk. Therefore, the hand is moved on to the next frame.
5. On Frame 2, R = 0, M = 0, and Age = 1202 − 1160 = 42. Again, the page cannot be replaced as Age is less than t. The hand is moved to the next frame.

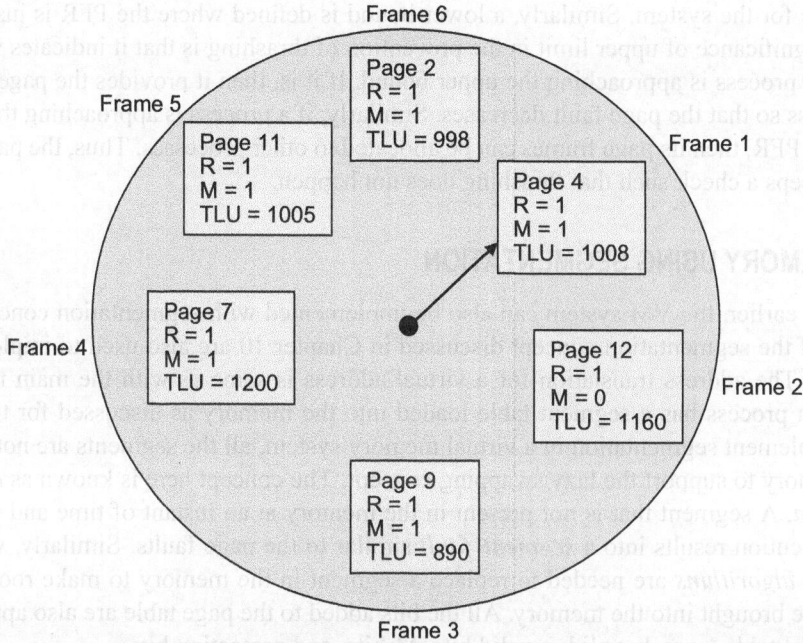

Frame 6

Page 2
R = 1
M = 1
TLU = 998

Frame 5

Page 11
R = 1
M = 1
TLU = 1005

Frame 1

Page 4
R = 1
M = 1
TLU = 1008

Page 7
R = 1
M = 1
TLU = 1200

Frame 4

Page 12
R = 1
M = 0
TLU = 1160

Frame 2

Page 9
R = 1
M = 1
TLU = 890

Frame 3

6. Again, in this round, no page can be replaced because now, all the pages have M = 1.

7. On the next round, again search for a page to be replaced. For the first frame, the page was scheduled to be written to the disk. Therefore, if the write operation has been finished by this time, then the M bit will be 0. Therefore, this page can be chosen for replacement. If the write operation has not been finished yet, then the hand advances to the second frame and the page can be chosen for replacement as a last option.

11.9.4 Page Fault Frequency

Another method in dealing with thrashing is to measure the page fault frequency. The idea behind measuring the page fault frequency is to establish an upper bound of page faults as well as a lower bound (see Fig. 11.22). The limits in the form of page fault bound help to know the status of the PFR. An upper bound is a limit of the PFR, which is too high and

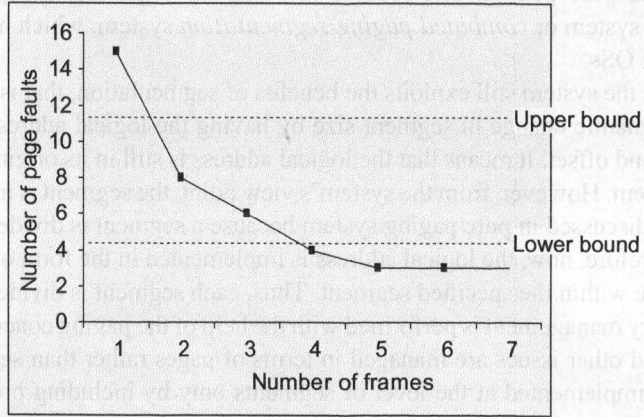

Fig. 11.22   Page fault frequency

unacceptable for the system. Similarly, a lower bound is defined where the PFR is just negligible. The significance of upper limit in the prevention of thrashing is that it indicates whether the PFR of a process is approaching the upper bound. If it is, then it provides the page frames to this process so that the page fault decreases. Similarly, if a process is approaching the lower bound of the PFR, then its page frames can be allocated to other processes. Thus, the page fault frequency keeps a check such that thrashing does not happen.

11.10 VIRTUAL MEMORY USING SEGMENTATION

As indicated earlier, the VM system can also be implemented with segmentation concept. All the details of the segmentation concept discussed in Chapter 10 are also used to implement a VM system. The address translation for a virtual address is same as with the main memory system. Each process has a segment table loaded into the memory as discussed for the page table. To implement segmentation in a virtual memory system, all the segments are not loaded into the memory to support the lazy swapping concept. The concept here is known as *demand segmentation*. A segment that is not present in the memory at an instant of time and requirement for execution results into a *segment fault* similar to the page faults. Similarly, *segment replacement algorithms* are needed to replace a segment in the memory to make room for a segment to be brought into the memory. All the bits added to the page table are also applicable to the segment table, namely valid–invalid bits, M-bits, and protection bits.

11.11 COMBINED PAGING AND SEGMENTATION

Both paging and segmentation have advantages and disadvantages. The paging concept, being transparent to the programmer, divides the logical memory into pages and avoids external fragmentation, thereby providing an efficient memory-management strategy. However, it may result into internal fragmentation. Moreover, it is not a natural division done by the programmer. Segmentation, which is visible to the programmer, avoids internal fragmentation and supports natural modularity, along with sharing and protection. However, pure segmentation further leads to external fragmentation. Moreover, if a segment is too large to keep it in the memory, then it is better to load only some portions of it. Thus, either pure paging or pure segmentation cannot be adopted in practical. Therefore, to have the advantages of both the memory-management techniques, they are combined. Segments are partitioned into pages to have the benefits of both pure segmentation and pure paging. The idea of dividing the segments into pages is called *paged segmentation* system or *combined paging/segmentation* system, which has been adopted in many significant OSs.

In this combined system, the system still exploits the benefits of segmentation, that is, avoids the fragmentation due to dynamic change in segment size by having the logical address in the form of a segment number and offset. It means that the logical address is still in its original form as in pure segmentation system. However, from the system's view point, the segment is managed with the paging concept as discussed in pure paging system because a segment is divided into a fixed number of pages. Therefore, now, the logical address is implemented in the form of a page number and offset for a page within the specified segment. Thus, each segment is divided into a number of pages and memory management is performed with the help of the paging concept. The page faults, working set, and other issues are managed in terms of pages rather than segments. However, the protection is implemented at the level of segments only by including protection bits as discussed earlier in the segment table. This combined mechanism provides the benefits

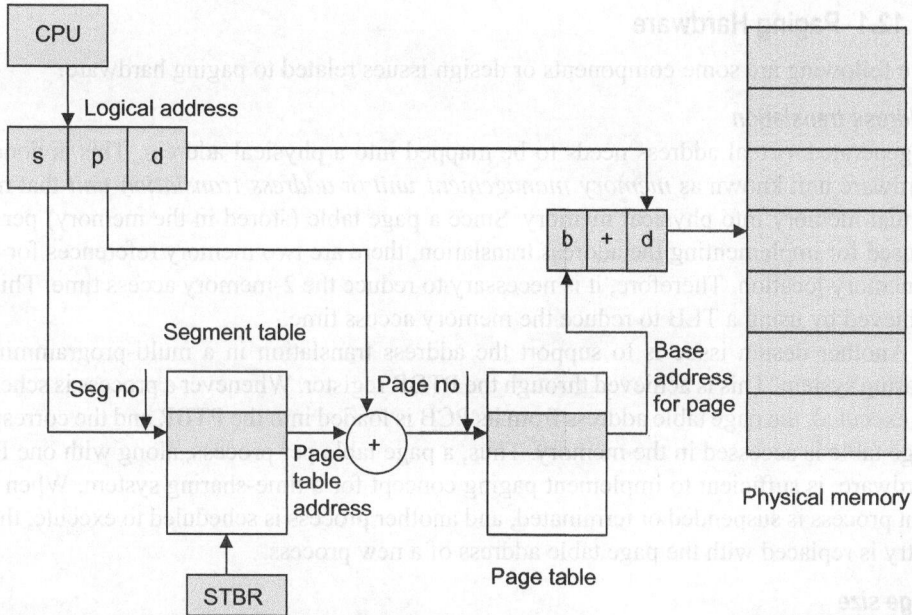

Fig. 11.23   Address translation in paged segmentation

of pure segmentation or paging because only required portion of a segment is retained in the memory, thereby utilizing the memory and making it a better memory-management technique.

In the combined segmentation/paging system, there is a segment table with each process as in pure segmentation but with many page tables, because now, every segment of the process consists of a page table. If a process has five segments, then this process consists of one segment table and five page tables—one per segment. The virtual address in this system is of the following form:

(Segment number *s*, page number *p*, offset *d*)

When a process executes, the STBR holds the starting address of the segment table for that process as discussed in pure segmentation system. After getting the location of the segment table, the processor uses the segment number to index into the segment table to find the page table for that segment. After this, the page number *p* in the virtual address is used to index into the page table of the segment and get the address of the page. Finally, the address of the page thus found is used with offset in the virtual address to get the physical address in the memory. In this way, paged segmentation system maps a virtual address to a physical memory as shown in Fig. 11.23 using two levels of address translation: the first level when the segment table is referenced and the second when the page table is referenced. This address translation involves three memory references as segment table and page table both are in the memory. This slows down the address translation process. To speedup, TLBs can be used for frequent entries in both the segment table and page table.

11.12   DESIGN AND IMPLEMENTATION ISSUES

As discussed earlier, a VM system is composed of both hardware and software components. The design of a VM system is not easy to implement, and therefore, this section is devoted to various design and implementation issues to have a better understanding. The following sections will discuss issues related to the paging hardware and OS–VM handler.

11.12.1 Paging Hardware

The following are some components or design issues related to paging hardware:

Address translation

A generated virtual address needs to be mapped into a physical address. This is done by the hardware unit known as *memory management unit* or *address translation unit* that maps the virtual memory into physical memory. Since a page table (stored in the memory) per process is used for implementing the address translation, there are two memory references for locating a memory location. Therefore, it is necessary to reduce the 2-memory access time. This can be achieved by using a TLB to reduce the memory access time.

Another design issue is to support the address translation in a multi-programming/time-sharing system. This is achieved through the PTBR register. Whenever a process is scheduled to be executed, the page table address from its PCB is loaded into the PTBR and the corresponding page table is accessed in the memory. Thus, a page table per process, along with one PTBR in hardware, is sufficient to implement paging concept for a time-sharing system. When the current process is suspended or terminated, and another process is scheduled to execute, the PTBR entry is replaced with the page table address of a new process.

Page size

The size of a page is pre-defined in the architecture of a computer system, which in turn determines the number of bits required to represent the word in a page. The paging hardware implicitly uses this hardware information to implement the paging in a virtual system. In virtual memory using paging concept, however, the page size is a major design issue. The page size cannot be taken as random but decided carefully depending on various factors. The page size if not chosen appropriately may affect the performance of the system. In general, the page size is taken as power of two varying from 2^{12} to 2^{22}. If it is too small, then a process will have more number of pages and therefore, more number of entries in a page table that will consume more memory. Thus, a larger page size causes smaller page table as there will be less number of page-table entries in the page table. Therefore, there is an inverse relationship between the page size and page-table size. A larger page table is too difficult to store in the memory and the searching time increases. A smaller page size will also increase the number of page faults.

Small page size increases the number of pages in the logical memory. Therefore, I/O time required to read or write pages also increases with the increase in the number of pages, as each page demands separate seek, latency, and transfer time. On the other hand, large page size may cause memory-space wastage. It is not necessary that a process always fits exactly on the boundary of a page. Some space remains unused on the last page while allocating memory to a process in the form of pages. Therefore, the larger the page size the more will be the wastage causing larger internal fragmentation in the system. On average, the last page would be half empty causing fragmentation. Thus, there is a direct relationship between page size and internal fragmentation. Further, it may be possible that as the size of a page increases, the whole page may not be in the execution but only a small part of the page that is in execution. Therefore, the page size chosen should not be too large such that it does not appropriately cover the locality of a page. Thus, the page size cannot be chosen as too small or large but is decided depending on the memory space and process size.

The page size also affects the PFR. The number of pages in the memory will be increased if the page size is reduced. The more the number of pages the less the PFR, as the most of the memory references will be found in the memory. On the other hand, if the page size is increased, then the number of pages will be decreased causing more page faults as the memory references may not occur in the pages present in the memory. Thus, there is an inverse relationship between page size and PFR, already shown in Fig. 11.7.

Support for page replacement

As discussed in page-replacement algorithms, it is necessary to have information when a page was last used to select a page to be replaced. This information is then collected by the paging hardware and provides the same to the VM handler, so that an appropriate page replacement algorithm can be implemented.

Support for memory protection

A valid–invalid bit is used in the page table to see whether a page exists in the logical address space. The address translation unit checks for an illegal logical address, that is, a page number generated in the address may not be in the current logical address space. In this case, this unit checks the page number in the logical address generated against the PTBR and PTLR. It raises a memory protection interrupt if the page number exceeds the PTLR to protect the processes from one another. Another case may be that a process violates its access privileges stored in accessprotection bits. Again, the address translation unit checks the access of the process with its allowed access protection bits. If these do not match, then a memory protection interrupt is raised to protect the page against any misuse.

Paging device

Another issue in implementation regarding hardware is the selection of a paging device, which is, in general, a disk. The paging device may affect the performance of a VM system as the disk access is much slower as compared to the memory. Moreover, there may be a number of page-in and page-out operations in the system depending on the PFR, thereby increasing the device access time, if the data transfer rate of the device is low. Therefore, the paging device selected should be of high speed and also of high capacity to have a larger portion of swap space.

Each process is allocated a fixed space in the disk reserved as swap space. The process table contains the disk address for each process. The page offset of a process is added to this disk address to write a page in the swap space. It means that the pages of a process are allocated contiguous space in the swap space. The pages in the memory have a shadow copy in the disk. However, this copy may be outdated if the pages have been modified since being loaded and therefore, must be updated before replacing it in the memory.

Page-frame allocation

A minimum number of page frames ensures good performance of the system as the PFR increases with a decrease in the number of page frames. Therefore, it becomes necessary that processes are allocated a minimum number of page frames. One method is to allocate the processes equal number of frames. This is known as an *equal allocation*. However, this strategy may not be appropriate where there is a large variation in process sizes. Some processes may be small compared to other processes. For example, a process of size 10 KB may not need many frames as compared to a process of size 150 KB. Therefore, it is obvious not to allocate frames to the processes using the equal allocation method, but use a proportional method according to the sizes of the processes. This is known as *proportional allocation*. Using this method, the number of frames allocated is calculated as

Alloc_frames $(P_i) = (P\_Size_i / S) \times n$

where i is the ith process,
P_Size is memory size of ith process
S is the total memory size, which is sum of size of all processes
n is the total number of available frames

Example 11.21

In a system, there are three processes, P1, P2, and P3, divided into 32, 189, and 65 pages, respectively. If there are 115 frames in the memory, then calculate the proportions in which the frames will be allocated to the processes.

Solution

$n = 115$
$S = 32 + 189 + 65 = 286$
Alloc_frames (P1) = $(32 / 286) \times 115 = 12.86 = 13$
Alloc_frames (P2) = $(189 / 286) \times 115 = 75.99 = 76$
Alloc_frames (P3) = $(65 / 286) \times 115 = 26.13 = 26$

11.12.2 Virtual Memory Handler

As discussed earlier, VM handler is the software part that implements the VM system. This VM handler is only a part of the OS. It starts functioning right from the process creation time till its exit. Its main design issue is the PFR. All the components of a VM handler are designed with the goal that the PFR should be the least because all the performance-related issues become complex when the PFR becomes high. The following are components/design issues of a VM handler:

Logical address space manager

This component of VM handler starts functioning at the time of a process's creation. When a process is created, it first determines how large the process and its initial data will be. Based on this, it creates a page table for the process, and consequently, space is allocated to it in the memory. Similarly, the space for the process is allocated on the disk as swap space. After this, the logical address space of the process is initialized with the process's text and data on this swap space so that when the new process starts getting page faults, the pages can be paged-in from the disk. When a page fault occurs, the page is paged-in and its status is modified in the page table. Similarly, when there is a need to replace a page in the memory, the selected page is paged-out and again, its status is modified in the page table. Thus, the logical address space manager maintains the page table and performs the page-in and page-out operations.

Physical memory manager

This component keeps track of free page frames in the memory. It uses a data structure known as *frame table* (FT). FT consists of status and page ID of the page of a process as shown in Table 11.2. The status of a free frame is simply marked as 0, and when a page is loaded, it is marked as 1.

Table 11.2   Frame table

Page_ID (process no, page no)	Status
P1,3	0
P2,5	1
P3,2	1
P4,4	0

Protection initializer

This module is used to initialize the protection information as required to implement the protection among various processes. First, it stores the access privileges of all the pages of a process in the page table. This information remains there until the process is terminated. After this, the protection hardware is initialized by loading the page table start address and size information in the PTBR and the PTLR, respectively, while dispatching the process. In this way, the hardware is reset after initializing according to the new process. The TLB is also flushed so that there is no trace of the previous process.

Page fault handler

This module acts when a page fault occurs. It reads out the hardware registers to determine which virtual address and, hence, page has caused the page fault. After this, it checks whether it is a valid address. Then, its access privileges are checked out. If the page is not valid or access privileges do not match, then a memory protection interrupt is generated. On the other hand, if it is valid and access privileges are matching, then the module checks whether a page frame is free in FT. If not, the page-replacement algorithm is run and a page is selected as the victim. The page-replacement algorithm may need to access R bits of the page table. The M bit of the selected page is then checked to determine whether it has been modified. If it is, then it is scheduled to be transferred to the disk, that is, the page is paged-out to save its changed contents. Since this page-out operation is an I/O operation and the disk needs to be accessed, there are process switching and scheduling of another process. It means that the page fault handler for the current process is blocked. If the page is not modified, then it means that the page frame is ready to accomodate the required page. Therefore, this module looks up the disk address where the required page is stored in the swap space and the page-in operation is scheduled. Again, this being an I/O operation, the process is blocked. When the process is waked up, the page table is updated to make it a valid page.

Prepaging

Due to the nature of demand paging, a number of page faults occur when a process starts executing to load the initial required pages in the memory. Similarly, when a swapped-out process is restarted, it results in many page faults. Therefore, to load the initial locality of a process, the pages are loaded from the disk, thereby increasing the number of page faults in the system in the beginning of execution. It would be better if the page faults due to the nature of demand paging can be reduced. Pre-paging is the solution for this. Loading the initial required pages in the memory before execution of a process is known as *pre-paging*. The question is how to determine which pages will be required so that they can be loaded in the memory in advance. The working set theory may help here. It is kept along with each process. Whenever a process is swapped out, its working set is saved. When it is swapped in again for execution, its working set is retrieved, and all the required pages are first loaded in the memory and then it starts executing.

Page-replacement policy

When a page is replaced as discussed in page-replacement algorithms, there are two choices. One is that a page to be replaced is chosen from the set of page frames allocated only to the running process. This is known as *local page-replacement policy*. Another approach is to choose the page from the set of page frames of any of the processes. It means that a process may take up the page frames of any other processes. This is known as *global page-replacement policy*. Suppose, there are three processes in the system and they have been allocated the pages in the memory as shown in Fig. 11.24(a). If the process A is executing and it needs to page in A3, then according to the local page-replacement policy, only pages allocated to the running process A can be replaced. Therefore, A4 is selected as the victim page for replacement (see Fig. 11.24(b)). If the replacement policy is global, then the whole set of page frames in the memory will be considered for the page replacement. Suppose the victim page in this policy is C2, then it will be evicted from the memory (Fig. 11.24(c)), even though A is executing.

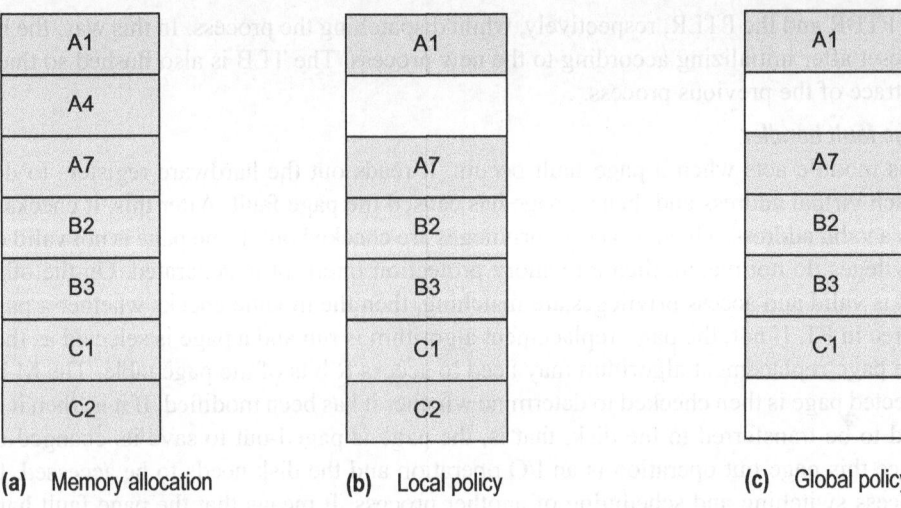

(a) Memory allocation   (b) Local policy   (c) Global policy

Fig. 11.24 Page-replacement policy

The global policy of allocating frames is better compared to local policy because there is a constrained set of frames in local policy, whereas there is a large set of page frames in global. The local policy is not appropriate when the working set size varies over a period of time in the system. Thrashing may occur in case of local policy when the working set size increases even if there are free page frames, and the memory is wasted if the working set size decreases. On the other hand, global policy works fine in both the cases because there is no restriction in choosing the page frame. A higher-priority process can take advantage of this global policy by taking the frames of a lower-priority process to execute smoothly without any page faults. Since a process can use the frames of other processes, the performance of a process depends on the paging behaviour of other processes. The process execution time may vary in two executions of the same process due to change in page frames of other processes, affecting the global allocation of a process.

Page-frame locking

According to the page-replacement policy, any page can be replaced. However, some pages if replaced cause problems in the system. These pages can be I/O buffers, kernel pages, key control structures, and so on. The locking is implemented by adding a lock bit in the page table corresponding to the page frame. When the lock bit of a page is set to 1, it cannot be replaced. The locking bit can be used in some critical situation. For example, it can be used where higher-priority process preempts a lower-priority process and replaces the pages again and again. The pages of the lower-priority process can be locked until it executes and is unlocked after the execution.

Page-frame cleaning

It has been discussed that whenever a page fault occurs, the required page is brought into the memory, and if there is no space in the memory, then a page is chosen to be replaced. However, it is always better to have in advance, sufficient page frames to handle the situation of page faults. In this approach, the page fault service time decreases and no time is wasted in finding a free page frame in the memory. For this purpose, a background process is designed that periodically inspects the state of the memory. This process is known as *paging daemon*. A limit is fixed for the number of page frames. If the number of page frames available in the memory is less than this limit, then the process starts evicting pages from the memory using the page-replacement algorithms. If the pages have been modified, then they are written back to the disk.

In this way, paging daemon cleans up the memory so that enough page frames are available to service the page fault and provide space to the incoming pages.

Page buffering/page caching

It has been observed in page-replacement algorithms that an active page should not be replaced, otherwise, it page faults again and again. In some situations, a replaced page should not be moved out of the memory. Similarly, the cost of performing page-out operation on a modified page is costlier. In this case also, modified page should not be moved out of the memory. For these situations, a buffer or cache is optimized to store the replaced pages. In fact, the pages are replaced according to the page-replacement policy or algorithms but are not removed from the memory: Their entries in the page tables are deleted. The page has been shown to be replaced, but in actual, it resides in the memory in the form of a buffer or cache. This buffer or cache is implemented as a list. The list is of two types: *free page list* and *modified page list*. The free page list stores the pages that have not been modified. This list can be used for reading the pages. In this way, when an unmodified page ID is replaced, it is added to the tail of the free page list. Similarly, the modified page list stores the pages that have been modified. The page that has been modified and replaced is added to the tail of this list. Thus, these two lists act as a cache of pages. The cache is useful where the page is active and is referenced after replacement. In this case, the page is returned to the resident set of the process at less cost because the cost of page-in and page-out operations is saved. Another use of the modified page list is that after having a number of pages in this list, all can be paged out so that their modified copy can be saved on the disk. The advantage is that pages are written out in a cluster rather than one at a time. It greatly reduces the I/O operations and disk-access time.

Load control

Whenever the working set of all processes exceed the total system memory, thrashing may occur. The page fault frequency method indicates if the processes are page faulting too high. In this case, each process is in need of page frames so that the page fault reduces. In this situation, if no remedy is taken, then the system thrashes. On the other hand, if we control the load, that is, allocate the page frames to a limited number of processes, then thrashing can be handled. The solution is to get rid of some processes so that the number of competing processes for page frames decreases and the page fault reduces. The processes are swapped out to the disk and their page frames are shared among processes in need. The processes can be swapped out one by one. For example, if one process is swapped out, then its page frames are shared among other processes and it is checked for thrashing. If not, then another process is swapped out and checked for thrashing again. This process is repeated until the thrashing stops. In this way, swapping is used along with paging to reduce the demand for page frames, thereby removing the thrashing situation in the system. The only question in this method is which process will be the victim to be swapped out. This may depend on many factors such as priority, its nature of CPU bound or I/O bound, and so on.

Shared pages

Shared pages, discussed in Chapter 10, have some design issues in their implementation. Since there is a single address space allocated to both code and data, the pages need to be identified for the code portion that are to be shared and for the data portion that cannot be shared. Therefore, it would be easy if there are separate address spaces for code and data. These separate address spaces are known as *I-space* (*instruction-space*) and *D-space* (*data-space*). Both the address spaces can be further paged and each one has its own page table. An instruction is referenced through the I-space page table, and similarly, data is referenced through the D-space page table. The processes share pages using the same I-space page table but have different D-space page tables. Each process has two pointers in its page table: one for the I-space page table and another for the D-space page table.

Another design issue with shared pages is that the pages being shared should not be allowed to be paged out simply because of one process that needs to be suspended. For example, two processes, x and y, share the pages of a utility. Suppose, x needs to be removed from the memory, then its pages may also be evicted from the memory. However, this will cause y to page fault. Therefore, shared pages should not be allowed to be evicted or selected for replacement when one of the processes needs to be removed from the memory.

SUMMARY

The VM system is implemented through paging/segmentation hardware and VM handler. The demand loading is the key concept behind virtual memory. However, it gives rise to many other issues. Since all the pages or segments of a process are not loaded in the memory, the memory allocation to processes becomes difficult. Further, page faults occur when the pages or segments are not found in the memory. Therefore, the page fault must be handled appropriately. Consequently, the page to be brought into the memory should get a free frame. It may need to replace an existing page. Thus, many page/segment-replacement algorithms have been discussed in detail. The VM system gives rise to thrashing problem when there is high paging activity. Similarly, various issues related to paging hardware and VM handler, as well as their solutions, have also been discussed.

Let us have a quick review of important concepts discussed in this chapter:

- *Virtual memory* is a method that manages the exceeded size of a larger process or processes as compared to the available space in the memory.
- The *principle of locality of reference* states that during course of execution of a program, memory references by the processor tend to cluster.
- *Temporal locality* means that the recently referenced memory locations are likely to be referenced again.

Spatial locality means that nearby memory locations are referenced.

- The system with virtual memory is known as a *virtual memory (VM) system*. The software implementing the VM system is known as *VM handler*.
- VM system requires only those pages or segments of a process in the memory that are needed at a certain time of execution.
- The thumb rule of demand loading is that *never load a component of a process unless it is needed*.
- The components of a process that are present in the memory are known as *resident set* of the process.
- Demand paging is to load only those pages in the memory that are needed at an instant of time of execution.
- A *pager* term is used in connection with demand paging concept as compared to *swapper*. The swapping operations are renamed as *page-in* and *page-out* operations as compared to swap-in and swap-out.
- In demand paging, when the page referenced is not in the memory, it is known as a *page fault*.
- A strategy to replace an existing page so that a page that causes page fault can be paged in is known as *page-replacement algorithm*.
- The various page-replacement algorithms with their features are as follows:

Page-replacement algorithm	Features/imple mentation	Advantage/disadvantage
FIFO	The oldest page is chosen.	Page fault rate is high.
	Implemented through a FIFO queue.	Suffers from the Belady's anomaly.
Optimal	The page that will not be referenced for the longest time is replaced.	No way of knowing the future memory references and therefore cannot be implemented.
LRU	Replaces a page that has not been used for the longest period of time in the past.	Provides less number of page faults.

(Contd)

(*Table Contd*)

	Implemented through a stack/counter/matrix.	Difficult to implement and incurs overhead.
Second chance	A page that is being frequently used will not be replaced and given a second-chance.	When all the pages in the memory are in use, this algorithm degenerates into pure FIFO algorithm.
	Implemented through a FIFO queue and reference bit.	Incurs the cost of moving the pages with reference bit 1 at the end of the queue.
Clock	Another implementation of the second-chance algorithm.	
	Implemented through a circular queue.	
Modified clock or not recently used (NRU)	modify bit is combined with reference bits.	
Not frequently used (NFU)	One counter is taken with every page frame to count how many times the page is used. The algorithm chooses a page with the lowest value of counter.	

- Belady's anomaly is observed in the FIFO algorithm that violates the general page fault behaviour: The number of faults does not decrease with the increase in the number of page frames.
- An LRU can be implemented with three approaches: stack, counter, and matrix.
- According to stack property, the set of pages when the page-frame size is *n* is a subset of the set of pages when the page-frame size is *m*, where *n* < *m*.
- A process is said to be thrashing if it spends maximum time in paging rather than its actual execution.
- The working set is a set of *m* most recent pages a process references.
- The working set theory is used to guess which pages will be needed in the program execution when it will be restarted after its last stop.
- The OS observes the working set of each process while executing and allocates the number of frames required by it.
- Another method to deal with thrashing is to measure the page fault frequency. The idea behind measuring the page fault frequency is to establish an upper bound and lower bound of page faults.
- Segments are partitioned into pages to have the benefits of both pure segmentation and pure paging. The idea of dividing the segments into pages is called *paged segmentation* system or *combined paging/segmentation* system.
- The page table may consist of various fields as depicted in the following table:

	Valid–invalid Bit	M-bit		Counter	Reference bit	Time of last use	Protection bits	
0	Base address of page 0							← Lock bit
1	Base address of page 1							
2	Base address of page 2							
3	Base address of page 3							
4	Base address of page 4							
5	Base address of page 5							

- A larger page size causes smaller page table as there will be less number of page-table entries in it. Therefore, there is an inverse relationship between the page size and page-table size.
- Smaller page size increases the number of pages in the logical memory. I/O time required to read or write pages also increases with the increase in the number of pages as each page demands separate seek, latency, and transfer time.
- The larger the page size the more the wastage causing larger internal fragmentation in the system.
- The number of frames allocated to a process is
  Alloc_frames $(P_i) = (P\_Size_i / S) \times n$

where i is the ith process,
P_Size is memory size of ith process
S is the total memory size, which is sum of size of all processes
n is the total number of available frames

- Loading the initial required pages in the memory before execution of a process is known as *pre-paging*.
- When the victim page to be replaced is chosen from the set of page frames allocated to the running process, it is known as *local page-replacement policy*. When it is chosen from the set of page frames of any process, it is known as *global page-replacement policy*.

MULTIPLE CHOICE QUESTIONS

1. The degree of multi-programming is limited with the size of the _____
   (a) disk
   (b) memory
   (c) processes
   (d) none

2. Loops, subroutines, and data variables that are used to count or for summation are all examples of _____
   (a) spatial locality
   (b) principle of locality
   (c) temporal locality
   (d) none

3. All sequential statement execution and array traversal are examples of _____
   (a) spatial locality
   (b) principle of locality
   (c) temporal locality
   (d) none

4. VM system's implementation requires _____
   (a) hardware
   (b) software
   (c) both hardware and software
   (d) none

5. The software implementing the VM system is known as _____
   (a) pager
   (b) swapper
   (c) virtual software
   (d) VM handler

6. Virtual memory may be realized with _____
   (a) paging only
   (b) segmentation only
   (c) combined paging and segmentation only
   (d) paging or segmentation

7. _____ is to load only those pages in the memory that are needed at an instant of time of execution.
   (a) Paging
   (b) Demand paging
   (c) Pre-paging
   (d) None

8. The effective memory-access time in case of demand paging is directly affected by the _____
   (a) degree of multi-programming
   (b) number of pages
   (c) PFR
   (d) size of the memory

9. The overhead of a page-replacement algorithm can be reduced with
   (a) R bit
   (b) M bit
   (c) counter
   (d) none

10. Which of the following algorithms suffers from Belady's anomaly?
    (a) LRU
    (b) Optimal
    (c) FIFO
    (d) Second chance

11. Which of the following algorithms does not satisfy the stack property?
    (a) Second chance
    (b) LRU
    (c) Optimal
    (d) None of the above

12. The optimal algorithm is impractical because it is impossible to know
    (a) the future memory references
    (b) the page size in advance
    (c) the page fault frequency
    (d) none

13. Which of the following bits of a page table is used by the second-chance page-replacement algorithm?
    (a) R bit
    (b) M bit
    (c) Both R and M bits
    (d) None

14. Clock page-replacement algorithm is another implementation of _____.
    (a) LRU
    (b) optimal
    (c) FIFO
    (d) second chance

15. Which of the following bits of a page table is used by NRU page-replacement algorithm?
    (a) R bit
    (b) M bit
    (c) Both R and M bits
    (d) None

16. Which of the following bits of a page table is used by NFU page-replacement algorithm?
    (a) R bit
    (b) M bit
    (c) Both R and M bits
    (d) TLU

17. Which of the following bits of a page table is used by work-ing-set-based page-replacement algorithm?
    (a) R bit   (c) Both R and M bits
    (b) M bit   (d) TLU

18. Which of the following bits of a page table is used by WSClock page-replacement algorithm?
    (a) R bit   (c) TLU
    (b) M bit   (d) All of the above

19. Page fault frequency may be used to keep a check on

20. A larger page size causes _____ page table.
    (a) smaller   (c) no effect
    (b) larger   (d) none

21. Larger the page size _____ will be the memory wastage.
    (a) the more   (c) no effect
    (b) the less   (d) none

(a) paging   (c) thrashing
(b) segmentation   (d) none

REVIEW QUESTIONS

1. What is the need of a virtual memory?

2. What is an overlay structured program?

3. What is the principle of locality? What are temporal and spatial localities?

4. What is the thumb rule for demand loading?

5. How do you implement demand paging?

6. When does a page fault occur? What are the steps to handle a page fault?

7. What is a free frame list?

8. What is a paging device?

9. What is the role of valid–invalid bits in a page table?

10. What is the difference between resident set and working set?

11. What will be the effect of adopting a TLB in a VM system?

12. What is the relation between effective access time and PFR?

13. How do you reduce the 2-page transfers during the page replacement?

14. What is the relation between memory size and PFR?

15. What is Belady's anomaly? Give an example of a page reference string that illustrates this anomaly.

16. What is the problem in implementing optimal page-replacement algorithm?

17. Discuss the implementation of LRU page-replacement algorithm using a counter, a stack, and a matrix using an example.

18. Demonstrate that LRU does not suffer from Belady's anomaly.

19. Compare the performance of second-chance algorithm with FIFO.

20. Show the stack implementation of LRU on the following string:

    1 0 5 1 1 3 5 1 5 3 4 5 2 1 3 0 1 4 0 5

21. Show the matrix implementation of LRU on the following string: 0 1 0 0 2 0 3 3 2 1 1 2 2 3 2 1 3

22. Show that a page-replacement algorithm that satisfies the stack property cannot suffer from Belady's anomaly.

23. How do you implement a clock page-replacement algorithm?

24. Discuss the implementation of NRU algorithm with an example.

25. How many types of data structures are used by a VM handler?

26. What are various functions performed by a VM handler?

27. What is stack property of page-replacement algorithms?

28. What is the relation between the degree of multi-programming and CPU utilization?

29. What is thrashing? Why does it occur?

30. Using the NFU with aging, the set of page frames, along with their counters and R bits, has been shown as follows for clock tick 0. Calculate the value of page frames after clock tick 3.

    Clock tick 0

	Counter	R
0	0000000	1
1	00000001	0
2	110000000	1
3	00000000	1
4	00000011	0
5	10000000	0

31. Discuss the solutions for handling the thrashing.

32. How is a working set theory developed in the page-replacement algorithm?

33. Explain the algorithm for working-set-based page-replacement algorithm.

34. How is a working-set-based algorithm modified into WSClock page-replacement algorithm?

35. Explain the algorithm for WSClock page-replacement algorithm.

36. How does the combined approach of paging and segmentation work? Explain the address translation in this combined system.

37. How are page frames allocated to different processes?

38. Explain the functions of a page fault handler.

39. What is pre-paging? What is its use?

40. Explain the two types of page-replacement policy with examples.

41. What is the need of locking a page frame?

42. What is a paging daemon process?

43. What is page buffering?

44. What are the issues in the design of shared pages?

BRAIN TEASERS

1. Prepare some guidelines of structured programming using the principle of locality that helps in avoiding the thrashing.

2. In a demand-paging system, it takes 150 ns to satisfy a memory request while the page is in the memory. Otherwise, it takes 8 ms if the free frame is available or page to be replaced is unmodified. However, the request takes 20 ms if the free frame is not available and the page to be replaced is modified. The chances that the page has been modified are 50%. What is the effective access time if the PFR is 12%? If the PFR increases to 16%, then what will be the effect on effective access time?

3. In a demand-paging system, the paging device has an average latency of 10 ms, seek time of 5 ms, and transfer time of 0.15 ms. The disk has generally the queue of waiting processes. Therefore, it has an average waiting time of 10 ms. If memory-access time is 200 ns and the PFR is 9%, then what will be the effective access time for this system?

4. In a demand-paging system, it takes 220 ns to satisfy a memory access when the requested page is in the resident set. If it is not in the resident set, then the request takes 10 ms. What will be the EAT if the PFR is 10%? What would be the PFR to achieve an EAT of 350 µs? Convert all the units to microseconds.

5. Design a scenario in a virtual memory wherein all the fields of page table mentioned in the chapter are used. Analyze the performance of the system using all these fields.

6. Calculate the number of page faults for the following reference string using FIFO, optimal, LRU, and second-chance algorithm with frame size as 3 and 4.
   1 0 5 1 1 3 5 1 5 3 4 5 2 1 3 0 1 4 0 5
   Which algorithm performs better in terms of the PFR? Which of the algorithm satisfies the stack property?

7. Consider the following page table. If a page is to be replaced on page fault, then which page will it be?

Page number	TLU	R bit
0	1020	0
1	950	1
2	1230	0
3	1000	1
4	878	1
5	990	0
Cur_time = 1278		
t = 50		

8. Which page will be replaced in the following page table with Cur_time = 1278, t = 50 using WSClock page-replacement algorithm? The clock hand is presently at frame 2.

Frame number	Page number	R bit	M bit	TLU
1	12	1	0	1020
2	3	1	1	950
3	4	1	1	1230
4	9	1	1	1000
5	7	1	1	878

9. What is the effect of paging on the context switch time?

10. Why is the page size always taken as power of 2?

11. Do you find a VM system suitable for a real-time system?

12. The size of a working set may increase or decrease with the execution of a program. How?

13. In a system there are five processes divided into 23,117, 45, 8, and 98 pages. If there are 200 frames in the memory, calculate the proportion in which the frames will be allocated to the processes.

14. Check whether second-chance algorithm suffers from Belady's anomaly.

15. A system uses 64-bit virtual address space with 2K page size. If a single-level page table is used, then what problem would one face? What is the remedy for this?

16. The optimal page size should be lesser than 1K. However, computer systems tend to use larger page size of the order of 1K bytes. What is the reason for this?

17. Is it possible to design FIFO, optimal, and LRU segment-replacement algorithms similar to page-replacement algorithms?

18. Based on the two parameters in the following table, when should be the degree of multi-programming increased? Which case will give rise to thrashing?

CPU Utilization	Paging-device utilization
80%	3%
7%	78%
8%	14%

19. Write a program that reads the page reference string from a file and calculates the number of page faults using FIFO, optimal, LRU, and second-chance page-replacement algorithms. The user should be asked to choose a page-replacement algorithm. The program should be able to graphically compare the performance of all the algorithms.

20. Write a program to implement LRU using stack and matrix methods.

21. Write a program that implements the second-chance algorithm using the circular queue.

22. Write a program that simulates the NRU page-replacement algorithm.

23. Write a program that simulates the NRU page-replacement algorithm with aging.

24. Write a program that simulates the working-set-based page-replacement algorithm.

25. Write a program that simulates the WSClock page-replacement algorithm.

26. Write a program that maps the virtual address to physical address in paged segmentation.

Case Study III: Memory Management in UNIX/Solaris/ Linux/Windows

UNIX

UNIX memory-management policies have evolved from simple swapping process to a more efficient demand paging process, which is being implemented from *Berkeley Software Distribution* (BSD) Version 4 onwards. As in any other OS, demand paging in UNIX frees the process from the size constraints of physical memory, that is, the process need not be bound to the size of physical memory. Demand paging is generally implemented by machines that have page-based memory architecture and whose CPUs have instructions that can be restarted. Demand paging is transparent to the user programs except for the virtual size permissible to a process.

Data Structures for Demand Paging

For the purpose of implementing demand paging, memory has to maintain various kinds of information such as the page mappings for a particular process (the page table; PT), the location of swapped pages on disk, and the state of the actual physical pages in memory. Memory in UNIX thus maintains four major data structures to implement demand paging. Each of them is described as follows:

Page Table Entry

This data structure is used to map the virtual address to physical address. The various fields and their descriptions are given in Table CS3.1.

Table CS3.1 Page table entry fields

Field name	Description
Frame number	It refers to the frame in physical memory.
Age	This is the time period that a page has been in the memory without being referenced.
Copy on write	Used when a page is being shared by more than one processes. If any of the processes writes into the page, a separate copy of the page must first be made for all other processes that share the page.
Modify	It indicates that the page has been modified.
Reference	It indicates that the page has been referenced.
Valid	A valid page is in main memory, an invalid one is swapped out.
Protect	It contains the permission information for the page and is also hardware dependant.

Disk Block Descriptor

This data structure contains the information mapping a virtual page to a spot on disk. The OS maintains a table of descriptors for each process. Its fields are shown in Table CS3.2.

Table CS3.2   Disk block descriptor fields

Field name	Description
Swap device number	It is basically a pointer to the disk that this page was swapped to.
Device block number	It is the actual block that the page is stored on. This is why most UNIX systems prefer to have a separate swap partition, so that the block size can be set to the page size.
Type of storage	It indicates that the storage may be a swap unit or an executable file.

Page Frame Data Table

Also known as *pfdata table*, the page frame data table holds information about each physical frame of memory (indexed by frame number). This table is of primary importance for the page-replacement algorithm. Its fields are shown in Table CS3.3.

Swap Use Table

This data structure contains an entry for every page on the swap device. Its fields are shown in Table CS3.4.

Figure CS3.1 shows the relationship between the various data structures described in Tables CS3.3 and CS3.4. A virtual address of 5678K of a process maps into a page table entry (PTE) that points to a Physical page 123. The disk block descriptor for the PTE shows that the copy of the page exists at Disk block no. 4554 on Swap device 1. The pfdata table entry for Physical page 123 also shows that a copy of the page exists at the same block on the same swap device and its in-core reference count is 1. The swap use count for the virtual page is 1, meaning that one PTE points to the swap copy.

Table CS3.3   Page frame data table fields

Field name	Description
Page state	It indicates whether the frame is available or not or has an associated page (i.e., whether it has been allocated to a process or not).
Reference count	It holds the number of processes that refer to this page.
Logical device	It contains the device number of the disk that holds a physical copy of the page
Block number	It holds the block number on that disk where the page data is located.
pfdata pointer	It points to other pfdata table entries.

Table CS3.4   Swap use table fields

Field name	Description
Reference count	It holds the number of page table entries that point to the page on the swap device.
Page/storage unit number	It is a page identifier on storage unit.

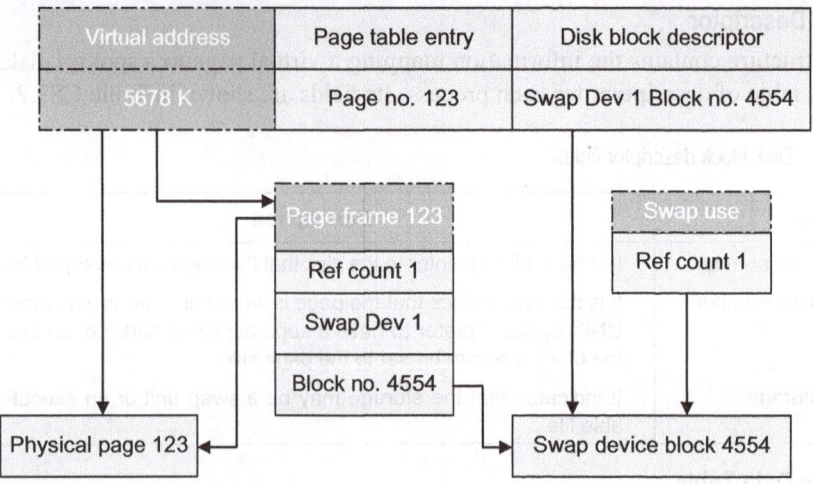

Fig. CS3.1   Relationship of data structures for demand paging

Page Replacement

UNIX System V uses the page stealer process as a solution to page replacement. The page stealer is a kernel process that swaps out memory pages that are no longer part of the working set of a process. The kernel creates the page stealer when the system boots and invokes it throughout the lifetime of the system when it lacks free pages. For this purpose, the kernel sets two threshold values for the number of free frames:

- minimum number of free frames
- maximum number of frames

As soon as the number of free frames is less than the minimum number of free frames, the kernel awakens the page stealer to swap out the eligible pages on the swap space of the disk. On the other hand, when the number of free frames is higher than the maximum threshold, the page stealer goes to sleep. The two threshold values can be configured to reduce thrashing by system administrators.

When the page stealer process is activated, it looks for the age of the page. If a particular page is not referenced by any process since, say, last n examinations done by the page stealer process, its age field in the PTE is subsequently increased. When the value of the age field reaches the predefined threshold, it is considered to be ready for swapping. Table CS3.5 shows the interaction between process accessing a page and examinations by the page stealer process. Here, the page stealer process makes three rounds of examination. As shown in the table, if the page is referenced during examination by the page stealer process, its age field is set to zero. Otherwise, it is incremented, and when it reaches the threshold, the page is swapped out.

When the page stealer process decides to swap out a page, it considers whether its copy exists on the swap device. There are three possibilities as follows:

1. If no copy of the page is on a swap device, the kernel swaps the page. The page stealer process thus places the page on a list of pages to be swapped. When the list of pages to be swapped reaches a limit (dependent on the capabilities of the disk controller), the kernel writes the pages to the swap device.

2. If a copy of the page is already on a swap device and no process had modified its in-core contents (the PTE *modify* bit is clear), the kernel clears the PTE *valid* bit, decrements the reference count in the pfdata table entry, and puts the entry on the free list for future allocation.

3. If a copy of the page is on a swap device but a process had modified its contents in memory, the kernel schedules the page for swapping and frees the space it currently occupies on the swap device.

Table CS3.5   Example of aging a page

Page state	Time	Last reference
In memory	0	
	1	
	2	
	0	Page referenced
	1	
	0	Page referenced
	1	
	2	
	3	Page swapped out
Out of memory		

Another page replacement policy is *two-handed clock algorithm* implemented in System V Release 4 (SVR4) version. This is a modified form of clock-based replacement algorithm implemented by the *pageout daemon process*. It uses the reference bit in the PTE to select a page to be swapped out. This bit is zero when the page is first brought in the memory. Furthermore, it is set to 1 on its reference for read or write. The hands in this algorithm are *fronthand* and *backhand*. The fronthand sweeps through the set of eligible pages in the list and sets the reference bit to zero on each page. After some time, the second clock hand, that is, backhand, sweeps through the same list and finds out which pages have not been referenced in the time span between the first scan by fronthand and the second sweep by backhand, that is, whose reference bit is still zero. These pages are then moved to the list of pages that need to be swapped out. The algorithm depends on two parameters: scan rate and hand spread. Scan rate determines the rate at which two hands scan through the page list. Hand spread is the gap between the two hands.

The scan rate varies with the amount of free memory. There are two system parameters for this purpose known as *lotsfree* and *minfree*. If the amount of memory is approaching minfree, it means that there are very less few numbers of pages. In this case, the clock hand moves more rapidly, that is, the scan rate is high. Similarly, the scan rate becomes low as the amount of memory approaches lotsfree. The page daemon process has the responsibility to check whether there is sufficient number of free frames available. Periodically, it runs every 250 ms with the coordination of lotsfree and minfree parameters. However, the page daemon process should not consume more than 10 per cent of the processor time.

SOLARIS

The linear virtual address space in Solaris kernel is represented as segments. There is a segment for each type of memory area in the address space. For instance, there are separate segments for process binary and scratch memory (known as *heap space*). Each segment manages the mapping for the virtual address range mapped by that segment and converts that mapping into MMU pages. The MMU then maps these pages into physical memory with the help of translation tables.

Each process is divided into segments, so that each part of the address space can be treated differently. For example, machine-code portion of the executable binary is mapped by the kernel as read-only, so that the process is prevented from modifying its machine code instructions. Solaris has read, write, and executable protection modes implemented by the hardware MMU. The virtual address space consists of at least the following four segments (Fig. CS3.2):

Fig. CS3.2 Virtual address space

Executable Text

The executable instructions in binary reside in this segment.

Executable Data

The initialized variables in the executable code reside in this segment.

Heap Space

Heap segment allocates virtual memory (VM) of a process for user data structures. The heap starts with small allocation but grows as VM is expanded. It grows in units of pages. In fact, this is a large area available for reading and writing.

Process Stack

The stack also grows like heap but downwards. It is mapped into the address space with an initial allocation as a single page and then grows as the process executes and calls functions. The program counter, arguments, and local variables are pushed onto the stack. When the stack grows larger than one page, the process causes a page fault and the kernel notices that this is a stack segment page fault and grows the stack-segment.

The Solaris kernel uses a combined demand-paged and swapping model for memory management. By default, demand paging is used while swapping is adopted when the system needs memory that cannot be managed without swapping.

Solaris VM is implemented through three layers as shown in Fig. CS3.3. The layers are described as follows:

Hardware Address Translation Layer

This layer is about implementing the hardware-dependent address translation. Having this as a separate layer minimizes the amount of platform-specific code that must be written for each new platform.

Address Space Management Layer

The segments created by device drivers are mapped into address spaces in the form of memory pages. The drivers then call for *hardware address translation* (HAT) layer to create the translations between the address space they are managing and the underlying physical pages.

Global Page-replacement Manager

This is memory-management daemon that steals pages when there is need of memory. It steals pages from the address space that have not been run recently, that is, it follows LRU for page replacement. There is a system threshold, say 1/64th of total physical memory, i.e., if the memory goes down beyond this threshold, the page scanner runs and looks for pages to be replaced. The *two-handed clock algorithm* is implemented for this purpose that views the page list as a circular list. The two hands, that is, fronthand and backhand rotate clockwise in page order around the list. The fronthand that rotates ahead of the backhand clears the reference bit and modified bit for each page. After some time, the backhand observes both the bits for the pages. The pages that have not been referenced or changed are swapped out and freed. This layer uses a page scanner that implements the page replacement.

Page Scanner

The page scanner is implemented as a thread along with two other threads, namely, callout thread and page-out thread (Fig. CS3.4). The callout thread scans the pages, and the page-out thread pushes the dirty pages (explained in Chapter 10, Memory Management) waiting for I/O to the swap device. The callout thread scans the pages by cal-

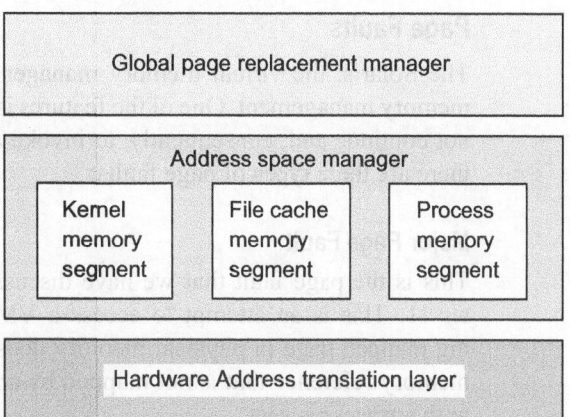

Fig. CS3.3 Virtual memory management in Solaris

culating two scanning parameters: the number of pages to scan and the number of processor ticks that the scanner can consume while doing so. The callout thread uses a function that checks whether free memory is below the threshold and triggers the page scanner thread. The page scanner thread scans the physical page list that is progressing by the number of pages requested each time the page scanner thread is triggered with the help of two hands already mentioned. The fronthand progresses first and clears the referenced and modified bits of the page pointed presently. After some time, the backhand starts and scans the status of the page. If the page has been modified, it is placed in the dirty page queue that will be processed by page-out thread. Otherwise, the page is freed. The page-out thread then writes these modified pages to the disk.

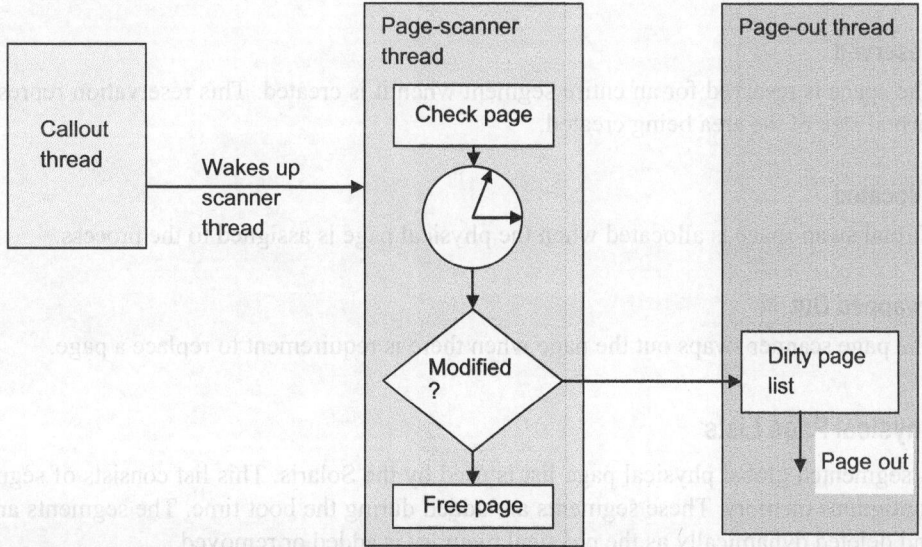

Fig. CS3.4 Implementation of page scanner

Page Faults

The Solaris, the virtual memory manager (VMM) uses features of the hardware MMU for memory management. One of the features is to generate exceptions when a memory access cannot continue and, consequently, to invoke appropriate memory-management code. In Solaris, there are three types of page faults:

Major Page Fault

This is the page fault that we have discussed while studying the VM management in Chapter 11. This is an attempt to access a VM location mapped by a segment, but corresponding mapped page in physical memory does not exist. Another case of major page fault is the memory reference that is not mapped by any segment. In this case, a segment violation signal to the process is sent.

Minor Page Fault

Minor fault occurs when there is an attempt to access a VM location that resides within the segment and the page is also in the physical memory but it is not possible to translate the MMU address from the physical page to the address space.

Page Protection Fault

This is a page fault that occurs when there is an attempt to access a memory location such that it violates the access protection of a memory segment.

Swap Space Allocation States

The swap space is reserved as we create VM. The partial swap space is allocated only when real pages are assigned to the address space. The remaining swap space remains unused. Thus, the swap space allocation is performed through the following three states:

Reserved

The space is reserved for an entire segment when it is created. This reservation represents the virtual size of the area being created.

Allocated

Virtual swap space is allocated when the physical page is assigned to the process.

Swapped Out

The page scanner swaps out the page when there is requirement to replace a page.

Physical Page Lists

A segmented global physical page list is used by the Solaris. This list consists of segments of contiguous memory. These segments are added during the boot time. The segments are added and deleted dynamically as the physical memory is added or removed.

A free list is maintained to have the pages that are not mapped to any address space. The pages are put in this list when a process exits.

Large Page Support

The Solaris supports large pages of the size of 4 MB. Since the memory performance of a modern system is directly influenced by the effectiveness of the TLB used, the TLB should have a high hit ratio. This can be increased with the large page size. The amount of memory the TLB can address concurrently is known as the *TLB reach*. If the TLB reach is low, the TLB miss ratio will become high. So the idea is to increase the TLB reach to increase its effectiveness. One method is to have a large number of entries in TLB. However, this will add complexities to the hardware. Another method is to increase the page size. The higher the size of the page, the higher will be the TLB reach.

LINUX

The MMU in Linux divides a system's physical address space into nodes. A node is associated with each processor of the system. Each node is then further divided into three zones. The size of each zone depends on the architecture. The three zones are:

DMA Memory Zone

This is the reserved memory area legacy architecture. It may be allocated for user processes if free memory is scarce or full. Kernel data are also stored in this zone.

Normal Memory Zone

This zone is used to store user and most of the kernel pages along with data from devices.

High Memory Zone

This memory is used to allocate user processes, by any devices that can access memory in this zone, and for temporary kernel data structures. Some devices cannot access this zone as their addressing capacity is limited. In this case, a bounce buffer is maintained in DMA memory to perform I/O operation. Whenever the I/O operation is complete, the modified pages in buffer are copied to high memory.

Depending on the compile-time configuration, some zones need not be considered. For example, 64-bit systems do not require high memory zone. Figure CS3.5 shows the memory zones for IA-32 architecture.

The physical memory is allocated in the form of page frames by *zone allocator*. According to the requests, the page frames are allocated from an appropriate zone. For user processes, any memory area can be allocated in various zones but the kernel first attempts to allocate the space from high memory zone. In case this zone is full, it attempts to allocate space from normal zone. If both high memory and normal zones are full, DMA memory zone is used. In each zone, a *free_area* vector is used to identify contiguous block of memory that is free. The blocks of page frames are allocated in groups of power-of-two.

Linux maintains a list of free pages in the memory by using the *buddy system* wherein the kernel maintains a list of page groups of fixed size. The sizes may be 1, 2, 4, 8, 16, or 32. These page groups

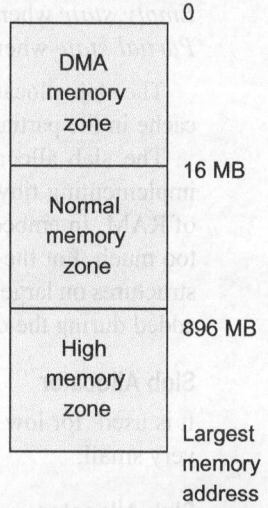

Fig. CS3.5 Memory zones in IA-32 architecture

refer to contiguous pages in the memory. The buddy algorithm enhances the efficiency of reading in and writing out pages to and from the memory.

With buddy system allocation, there can be internal fragmentation if the requests are for very small amount of memory. The kernel wastes time in the allocation, initialization, and de-allocation of various objects that consume small memory. Thus, to reduce the internal fragmentation and to have speed improvement, *slab allocator* is used. A slab allocator uses

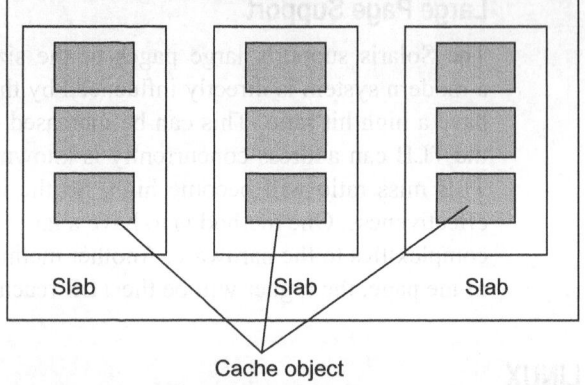

Fig. CS3.6   Components of a slab allocator

a slab that is one or more physical contiguous pages of memory. A slab is used as a container for storing kernel data structures. Slab allocator also serves as a *slab cache* that consists of a number of frequently allocated and released objects called slabs spanning one or more pages (Fig. CS3.6). The cache may consist of one or more slabs. There is a single cache for each unique data structure. Each cache is populated with initialized instances of the concerned data structure. By means of a slab cache, the kernel is able to store the objects ready for subsequent use. The number of objects in a slab cache depends on the size of the associated slab.

When the memory is released, the slab allocator keeps it in an internal list and does not immediately return them to the buddy system. A recently returned block is then used when a new request is received for a fresh instance of the object. Initially, all the objects in the cache are marked as *free*. The object when assigned from the slab cache is marked as *used*. This approach results into shorter handling time, as the kernel accesses the slab cache and does not approach the buddy system.

There can be three states of a slab as follows:

Full state where all the objects are used.
Empty state where all the objects are free.
Partial state where both used and free objects are present.

The slab allocator first attempts to allocate the cache from partial slab. If it does not find the cache in the partial slab, the empty slab is used.

The slab allocator may not perform optimally when slab allocation is used on systems, implementing tiny embedded systems and large parallel systems consisting of huge amounts of RAM. In embedded systems, the total footprint and complexity of slab allocation could be too much. For the second case, many gigabytes of memory are required only for the slab data structures on large systems. Therefore, two replacements, as follows, for the slab allocator were added during the development of Linux kernel 2.6:

Slob Allocator

It is used for low code size. With roughly 600 lines, the total footprint of the slob allocator is very small.

Slub Allocator

It minimizes the required memory overhead by dividing page frames into groups.

Virtual Memory Management

The virtual address space in Linux is of 4 GB on 32-bit systems and 2 PB (petabytes) on 64-bit systems. The total address space is usually split in a 3:1 ratio. For example, on IA-32 systems, the kernel is assigned 1 GB, whereas 3 GB is available to *each* user space process.

Linux implements memory management that is largely independent of the processor on which it is executing. The VM system supports three-level page table structure. The three level page tables are as follows:

- The first level of page table is *page global directory* that stores addresses of second-level page tables.
- The second level is known as *page middle directory* that points to pages in the page table of third level.
- The third level is known as *page table* that points to pages of the process.

To accommodate real-time processes that must not be interrupted or suspended, Linux provides for the locking of the pages. Through locking, a memory zone can be defined that will not be transferred to the secondary memory to free the memory.

To implement the VM, the pages are swapped out to make room for new requests in case the memory is full. There is a kernel thread known as *kswapd* (swap daemon). It periodically replaces the pages and reclaims the dirty pages by swapping out and writing on the secondary storage. On the secondary storage, the *system swap file* is there as a swap space. To avoid slow I/O operations while writing the dirty pages on the secondary storage, a *swap cache* is maintained. The kswapd thread first checks the page in swap cache before writing it onto swap file. If it is found in swap cache, the page frame is freed immediately without writing the page to the secondary storage as the page is already in swap file.

While performing page replacement for page faults, the page that has been chosen for replacement must be first checked for its references to avoid inconsistencies. It may be the case that a page chosen for replacement may be referenced by more than one process, that is, it is shared or the case may be that it has been modified. It may also be possible that the page is locked. For the first case, the kswapd thread must know all its references and then unmap all the references. The unmapping is done by zeroing its PTE values. To do this, the kernel needs to search every page table in the system to find page table entries mapping the victim page for replacement. Linux uses *reverse mapping* to find out all page table entries referencing to a page. For this purpose, a linked list of page table entries that references the page is maintained in page structure. This reverse mapping increases the size of page object but enhances the performance.

The page-replacement algorithm in Linux is based on clock algorithm. In this algorithm, an 8-bit variable known as *age* is used. The age determines how much a page has been used. Therefore, this variable is incremented after every page is accessed. The algorithm is executed in multiple passes. Linux periodically sweeps through global page pool in every pass and decrements the age value for each page as it rotates through the pages. The victim page to be replaced will be the page whose age count is the lowest. A larger value of age for a page means that it is a frequently accessed page and cannot be the choice for page replacement.

WINDOWS

In Windows, the VMM component is responsible for allocating memory and other memory management functions. Depending on the processor, Windows provides either 32 or 64-bit virtual address space. On 32-bit Windows, each process can address up to 4 GB of memory.

Similarly, each process on 64-bit Windows, can address virtual address space up to 8 TB. All the threads belonging to a process can also access the corresponding process' virtual address. Windows XP allocates 4 GB virtual address space to each process. However, this space is divided into two parts:

- The first 2 GB is for use of process.
- The second 2 GB is reserved for the system for kernel-mode components

Depending on the versions of Windows, the physical memory ranges from 2 GB to 2 TB. The subset of virtual address space residing in physical memory is called *working set*. The data stored on the disk in the form of files is known as *pagefiles*. The physical memory is divided into fixed-size page frames having page size of 4 KB on a 32-bit system.

The VMM creates two types of memory pools located in the address space reserved for the system to manage the memory: non-paged and paged pools. The virtual addresses are in non-paged pool, whereas the page pool consists of VM.

Memory Allocation

Memory allocation is done in the following three steps:

- A process first *reserves* space in its virtual address space.
- The process cannot access the page until it *commits* it. The commit is performed when the process is ready to write to the page.
- Finally, the ready process *accesses* the committed VM.

This type of memory allocation has an advantage that it uses only the required memory.

Memory Mapping

Windows XP uses two-level page table structure. Therefore, the virtual address is composed of the following:

- The offset in page directory table (PDT)
- The offset in page table
- The offset on a page in physical memory

Each process is assigned a page table directory. Whenever, there is a process switching, the location of new process' page table directory is loaded into the *page directory register*. Each entry in PDT points to the page table. The value of page directory register is added with the first portion of the virtual address that determines the location of page directory entry in PDT. The value in page directory entry is then added to a second component of virtual address that points to the PTE that contains the page frame number corresponding to the virtual page's location in the memory. Finally, the PTE is concatenated with the third component of the address to form the physical address.

The five protection bits in PTE out of 32 bits are for protection indicating whether a process can read, write, or execute the page. These protection bits may also inform whether a page is copy-on-write page. When a page is to be shared, the system uses only one page with both processes sharing that same copy of the page. However, when one of the processes writes onto the page, a private copy is made for that process, which can then be manipulated individually. This is known as *copy-on-write*. This gives a lot better efficiency.

Large Page Support

A large page is formed as a set of contiguous pages that OS treats as one single page. Windows XP allows allocating a large page to the applications. When the system has been running for a long time and at this time applications allocate large pages, it may affect the system performance as the memory may get fragmented by this time. Therefore, applications should not allocate repeated large pages in between. The large page allocation should be allowed only at start up. The large page memory should be non-pageable.

Virtual Memory Management

When there are much less number of page frames in the memory, Windows XP does not allow multiple requests to be serviced. It has a process known as *I/O throttling* that manages one page frame at a time and retrieves one page at a time from disk also. It slows down the system but avoids crashing of the system.

In Windows XP, each page's state is also maintained in a database known as *page frame database*. This database lists the state of each page frame sorted by the page frame number only. The system has a singly linked list known as *page list* for each state of the page frame. For example, there is a page list of free page frame that contains all page frames having the state as free. Table CS3.6 lists all the possible states of a page frame. As per the states, various page lists are maintained. When Windows is started, all memory is in the free page list. As a process requires memory, it is faulted in from zeroed page list. Zeroed means the page is free but has been filled with zeroes so that there is no dirty bit. When a process exits, its pages are moved back to free page list. There are two threads that move threads from one list to another:

Zero page thread   that is responsible for zeroing out free pages before they are moved from free page list to zeroed page list;

Modified page writer   that is responsible to move pages from modified page list to standby page list.

Table CS3.6   Page frame states in Windows

Page frame state	Meaning
Valid	Page is in the working set of process and PTE is set to valid.
Standby	Page has just been removed from working set and is not modified. The PTE points to physical page but has been marked as invalid and is in transition.
Modified	Page has just been removed from working set. The page has been modified but the changed contents have not been written to the disk. The PTE points to unchanged physical page but has been marked as invalid and is in transition. The VMM must write modified page to the disk.
Modified No-write	It is the same as modified but has been marked as No-write, that is, not to write it to the disk.
Free	Page is free but may contain some dirty data.
Zeroed	Page is free and does not contain any dirty data but has been filled with zeros. Page is not part of any working set.
Bad	Page has generated parity or other hardware errors and should not be used.

Windows XP is able to predict the requests for pages on disk and then move these pages into the memory such that there is less number of page faults in the system. The API functions can be invoked to know process' future memory requirements.

Windows uses *clustered demand paging* instead of demand paging. The idea is to load several nearby pages along with the page for which the system gets a page fault. In Windows, the disk is divided into clusters of bytes. Windows taking the advantage of this spatial locality loads all the pages in a cluster at once. Any kind of prefetching, however, must be carefully handled as it may bring in some unrequired pages in the memory, leaving less space for required pages and thereby increasing the page faults.

Page Replacement

The page-replacement policy of Windows XP is based on working set model. The working set is the set of pages a process is currently using. There is a minimum and maximum range for a working set of a process. The VMM assigns a default minimum (50 for the Windows XP) and maximum working set. There is a component known as *balance set manager* that is responsible to move pages to pagefiles. Windows XP uses localized LRU page-replacement policy. Whenever the working set size of a process becomes equal to its maximum working set size, it requests an additional page. In this case, the balance set manager pages out a page on the disk. The balance set manager checks the free space in memory once per second and adjusts the working set size as per the maximum one. Furthermore, it also performs *page trimming*, that is, the process of moving out the pages that are not required by a process.

Prefetching

Prefetching may also reduce the loading time of application, files, and even the OS. The system adopts the recording system that monitors which pages have been accessed. While loading a new application, it retrieves its history and loads all required pages. The Windows OS creates prefetch files in a special prefetch folder to speed up the booting of the system and to increase the application response time. There are some scenarios such as booting time and application loading in the OS, and for prefetching facility, the users have to specify to Windows for which scenarios they need services of a prefetcher. For each scenario, a scenario file is created. The memory traces of the scenario files are stored by the Windows. For booting, the prefetcher observes which files are required for booting. After this, it optimizes the locations of these files on the disk in such a manner that reduced disk I/O time is required. Moreover, it issues large asynchronous I/O requests overlapped with device initialization process during boot time. This is the reason that Windows XP offers fast boot-up time. Once the application is loaded, the prefetcher checks the traces and finds whether any data or code specified in the trace is present in memory. If not, then it prefetches from the disk. After successful loading of application, the scenario files are updated every 10 s periodically. To optimize the application load time, the prefetcher organizes the files that have been previously fetched in contiguous manner on the disk so that the seek time is minimized. In Windows XP, the prefetcher is called *logical prefetcher*, and in Windows Vista and Windows 7 it is called *superfetcher*.

PART IV

File Management

12 File Systems

12.1 INTRODUCTION

Disks are used as a primary storage medium for information. The file system provides a convenient mechanism to store and retrieve the data and programs from this medium. In fact, files are used as a collection of related information, the meaning of which is defined by its creator. These files are mapped to the disks or other storage media by the OS. Files themselves are organized in the form of a directory. This chapter discusses files and the file system concept, along with details about the internal structure of a file and directory.

12.2 FILES AND FILE SYSTEM

A file is the most obvious thing used in computers. Through the use of files, a convenient environment is created that allows one to write, read, save, and retrieve the program and data on any type of storage media. Moreover, the file concept is independent of the type of device. In other words, a user or programmer need not be worried about the hardware complexities of the device while writing a program or data in a file. A file, thus, is a collection of related information that is mapped on to a secondary storage. The information stored in a file is in bits, bytes, lines, or records, and so on. The meaning of the content is specified by its creator.

However, as a logical concept, a file is not stored on permanent media. Therefore, after saving all the work, a file needs to be mapped on to the storage device. This is the background work which is not seen by a user. The user only sees the logical view of the files. The system views all the work required to map the logical file to the secondary storage. In other words, a file is used to store the programs and data on the secondary storage. The benefit of storing files on the secondary storage is the facility provided by the file system: to create, store, and retrieve the information in the form of files. The OS abstracts the actual storage of the program and data from the user, and provides a logical and convenient file concept.

A user may want some files to be sharable among the members of a group. The file system also provides explicit sharing of files when the user wants. The files can be organized by the way they are accessed, for example, sequential, direct, and so on. Moreover,

Learning Objectives

After reading this chapter, you should be able to understand:

- The logical concept of file and file system
- Internal structure of a file
- Record blocking
- File-naming conventions
- Various types of files
- Various attributes of a file
- Different operations performed on a file
- How files are implemented
- Methods in which a file can be accessed
- The concept of directory
- The logical structuring of directories
- How files can be shared
- File protection issue
- The concept of file system mounting

they may be structured in a hierarchical manner. Thus, file organization and structure are also the constituents of a file system. The following are the primary constituents of a file system:

- **File Management**
  It manages how the files are stored, referenced, shared, and secured.
- **File Allocation**
  It provides the methods to allocate files on the disk space.
- **File Access Methods**

  It provides the methods to access stored files.

12.3 FILE STRUCTURE

The basic element of data, *field*, is a single valued item, for example, name, date, employee ID, and so on. Obviously, it is characterized by its length and data type. When multiple fields are combined to form a meaningful collection, it is known as a *record*. For example, a student's information (see Fig. 12.1) can be one record, consisting of fields such as roll number, name, qualification, and so on. When such similar records are collected, it is known as a *file*. File has also a name similar to a field or record. Thus, a file is treated as a single entity that may be used by a programmer or application.

The files can also be flat in the form of an unstructured sequence of bytes, that is, the structure has no fields or records. Thus, a file, composed of bytes, has no fields or records, and is looked upon as a sequence of bytes by the programs that use it. UNIX and Windows use this kind of file structure.

Nevertheless, the OS must support a required structure for a certain type of file. For example, an executable file must have a defined structure, so that the OS can determine the location in the memory to load the file and locate the first instruction to be executed. Some OSs support a single file structure, but may opt for multiple file structures as well. In the latter case, the size of the OS increases, as it needs to support multiple file structures.

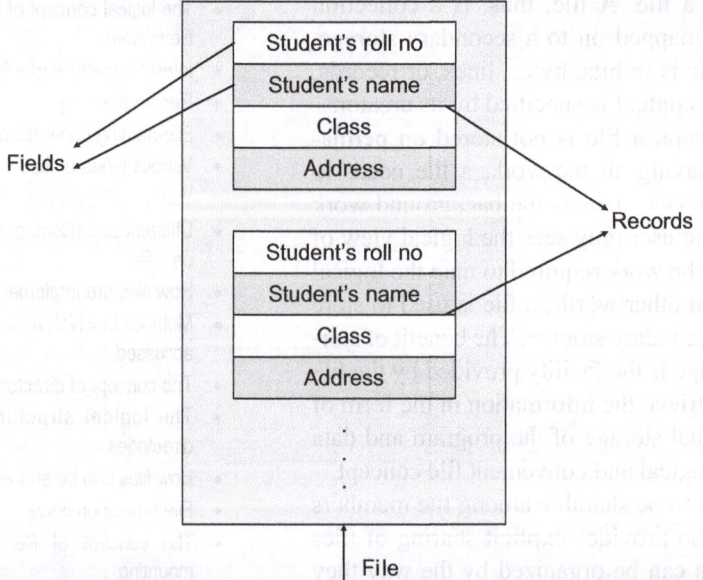

Fig. 12.1 File structure

12.3.1 Internal Structure and Record Blocking

Locating an offset within a logical file may be difficult for an OS. Since the logical file will be mapped to the secondary storage, it is better to define the internal structure of a file in terms of the units of secondary storage. In general, the disk is used for secondary storage and hence, *block* is a unit taken for the storage. The block unit needs to be mapped to the logical file structure as well. For example, a file is considered a stream of bytes in UNIX. Each byte in the file can be found having a start address of the file. Consider the logical record size as 1 byte. Now, assume the packing of some bytes or records in the file into the disk blocks. For example, a group of 512 bytes is packed into one block of disk. In this way, a file may be considered as a sequence of blocks, and therefore, all basic I/O functions are performed in terms of blocks. This is known as *record blocking*. The larger the size of a block, the more number of records will be mapped on to the block of disk. In turn, larger number of bytes will be transferred in one I/O operation. This is more advantageous, in case the file is searched sequentially, thereby, reducing the number of I/O operations as well.

Another issue regarding record blocking is whether the blocks should be of fixed- or variable size. Based on this issue, there are three methods of blocking (see Fig. 12.2):

Fixed Blocking

In this blocking, fixed sized records are used. Therefore, there may be a mismatch between the sizes of a record and block, leaving some unused space in the last block. This causes internal fragmentation. In Fig. 12.2(a), R1, R2, and R3 fit in the fixed blocks but R4 does not, leaving some space in the last block. The space may be left unused, if there is not enough space to allocate a block at the end of the track of the disk space, as shown in the figure. This method is advantageous when sequential files are used.

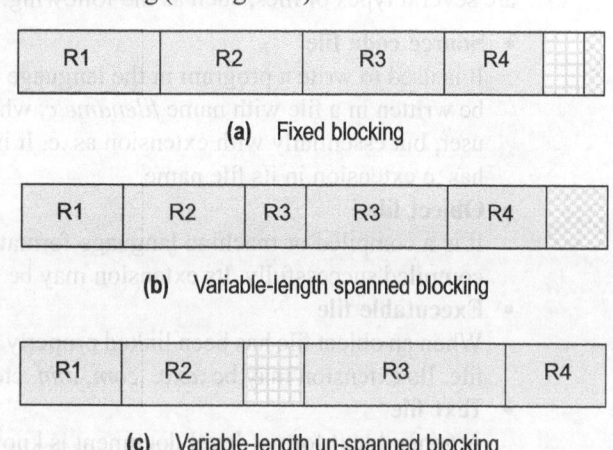

(a)   Fixed blocking

(b)   Variable-length spanned blocking

(c)   Variable-length un-spanned blocking

Fig. 12.2   Methods of blocking

Variable-length Spanned Blocking

In this blocking, variable length records may be considered instead of fixed size. Therefore, some records may span more than one block in continuation. It happens when one block is smaller in size as compared to the size of records. In this case, the records, after consuming this block, may continue in another block. For example, R3 spans two variable-sized blocks in Fig. 12.2(b). This method of blocking will not cause any fragmentation.

Variable-length Unspanned Blocking

In this blocking, records of variable lengths are used, but spanning is not considered in case of small-size blocks. A small-size block is left unused, causing wastage of memory space, and the records are allocated to a bigger block. In Fig. 12.2(c), R3 does not fit in a small block and therefore, it is allocated to the next block, which is bigger. It causes wastage of block space.

12.4 FILE NAMING AND FILE TYPES

A file needs to be named, so that a user can store and retrieve the information from the storage device. Through the name of a file, the work, which was saved on the disk, can be recognized and retrieved easily, without knowing the actual storage details on the hardware. There are rules for naming the files, which may vary from system to system. Some systems distinguish between uppercase and lowercase letters, while some do not. Some systems support length of file names as long as 255 characters. In some conventions of file naming, some special characters are also allowed.

In general, the file name has two parts, separated by a period (.). The first part is the name of the file, defined by the user, and the second part is known as an *extension*. The extension part usually indicates what type of file has been created. Some of the extensions have been shown in Table 12.2. The extension part is generally composed of three letters, as in MS-DOS. Sometimes there may be two or more extensions in the file name as in UNIX.

An OS must recognize the type of the file, because the operations performed on it depend on its type. For example, a zip file cannot be printed. Based on the extensions of a file name, there are several types of files, such as the following:

- **Source code file**
  It is used to write a program in the language chosen. For example, C language program will be written in a file with name *filename.c*, where filename is the name given to the file by its user, but essentially with extension as .c. It is recognized as a source program file, only if it has .c extension in its file name.
- **Object file**
  It is a compiled or machine language format-based, file when the source code file has been compiled successfully. Its extension may be *.obj* or *.o*.
- **Executable file**
  When an object file has been linked properly and is ready to run, it is known as an executable file. Its extension may be *.exe*, *.com*, *.bin*, etc.
- **Text file**
  A general text format-level document is known as a text file. Its extension is *.txt* or *.doc*.
- **Batch file**
- It is a file consisting of some commands to be executed and given to command interpreter. Its extension is *.bat*.

Table 12.2   Different Extensions in a file name

Extension	Meaning
.c	C source file
.cpp	C++ source file
.jpg	Picture file encoded with JPEG standard
.pdf	Portable document format file
.ps	Postscript file
.txt	Text file
.zip	Compressed file
.bak	Backup file

- **Archive file**
  When a group of files is compressed in a single file, it is known as an archive file. It extension may be *.zip*, *.rar*, and so on.
- **Multimedia file**
  It is a file containing audio or video information. Its extension may be *.mpeg*, *.mov*, *.mp3*, *.jpg*, etc.

Many other types of files may also exist today, depending on the necessity and support provided by the OSs. But in general, files are of the following types:

- **Regular**
  Regular files contain the user information. The internal structure of the file type may be of any type, as we discussed in file structures. Regular files may be either of ASCII or binary type. The advantage of ASCII format is that they can be displayed and printed as it is, and can be edited, using any text editor. On the other hand, binary files need to have an internal structure, otherwise, they cannot be displayed or printed in their right form.
- **Directory**
  Directory is a file type used to organize the list of files in a group, that is, it organizes the files in a hierarchy. Directory file is an ordinary file which can be read by any user, but write operation is permitted in file system only. A created file is entered in a directory.
- **Special**
  A special file contains no data but provides a mechanism that maps physical devices to file names, that is, these are used to access I/O devices. There are two types of special files namely, *character special files* to map serial I/O devices like terminals, printers, and so on, and *block special devices* to model devices like disks.

12.5 FILE ATTRIBUTES

Besides name and data, a file has other attributes as well. These attributes also vary from system to system. But some of the attributes are very common in every system, for example, data and time of creation of a file. Some of the attribute types are as the following:

- **General information**
  Some attributes of a file are general for example. name, type, location, size, time, and date of creation.
- **Protection-related attributes**
  A file may be enabled with access protection. Users cannot access it in their own way. Before accessing, they must know its access rights, for example, read, write, and execute permissions. Password of the file and creator/owner of the file also contribute to protection attributes.
- **Flags**
  Some flags control or enable some specific property of the file. Some of them are:
  - i) *Read-only flag*: It is used for making a file read-only. It is 0 for read/write and 1 for read-only.
  - ii) *Hidden flag*: It is used to hide a file in the listing of the files. It is set for hiding the file, otherwise, the file is displayed.
  - iii) *System flag*: It is used to designate a file as system file. It is set for making a file a system file, otherwise, the file is a normal one.

iv) *Archive flag*: It is used to keep track of whether the file has been backed up or not. The OS sets it whenever a file is changed. The flag is 0, when the changed file has been backed up.

v) *Access flag*: It is used to convey how the file is accessed. It is set when the file is accessed randomly, otherwise, the file is accessed sequentially.

- **Time of last change and last access**
  It is used to provide information about the time when the file was last modified, and when it was last accessed.

12.6 FILE OPERATIONS

Because a file is of an abstract data type, the kind of operations that can be performed on it must be known. The OS provides system calls for each operation to be implemented on the file. The following are some operations that are performed on a file:

- **Create a file**
  It is a file creation operation. The OS must look for the space needed to create the file, and the related attributes are set or created.

- **Write a file**
  The write operation needs the name of the file, wherein the data are to be written. The OS must have a pointer in the file for reading or writing. This is known as *current position pointer*. If the pointer is at the end of the file, the size of the file increases. If the pointer is in between, the contents of the file are overwritten with the data to be written.

- **Saving a file**
  The contents of the file must be saved on the disk. For this, the OS must look for space on the disk, and then save it. The appropriate entry in the directory, where the file is created, is also done.

- **Deleting a file**
  When the file is not needed, it can be deleted. Now, the OS has some free space after deleting it. The entry in the directory is also removed.

- **Open a file**
  Before a process uses a file for any operation, the file must first be opened. The OS fetches its attributes and list of disk addresses into the main memory for rapid access to open the file.

- **Close a file**
  A file, when not needed, for any access may be closed. The close operation frees memory space for attributes and disk addresses, and the file is updated on the disk. But closing a file does not mean deleting it, because the file has not been removed from the disk. A process may open many files at a time, consuming space in the memory. Therefore, a limit is put on a process to open multiple files.

- **Read a file**
  The read operation also needs the name of the file and the pointer, from where the bytes will be read. The current position pointer is maintained for this operation as well. After reading the data, the pointer is updated to the position where the last read finished.

- **Append a file**
  This is another version of the write operation. The only difference here is that the write operation is performed only at the end of the file. The OS locates the end of the file, using the pointer, and then appends the data to be written in the file.

- **Repositioning the current position pointer**

  The current position pointer used to read and write in the file can be repositioned to any desired position. The general system call for this operation is *seek* in some OSs. Therefore, it is also known as *seek* operation.

- **Get/Set attributes**

  The attributes of a file can be read, or even changed by a user, if necessary. A user may need to look when the file was last changed or created. Similarly, the user might want to change the access permission of a file. The system calls of an OS help to get/set the attributes of a file.

12.6.1 Implementation of File Operations

Although the implementation of file systems will be discussed in the next chapter, let us just go through its basics. To perform any operation on a file, the file needs to be opened. The following data structures are used for opened files:

Open File Table

Since the open operation fetches the attributes of the file to be opened, the OS uses a data structure known as *open file table* (OFT), to keep the information of an opened file. When an operation needs to be performed on the file, it is specified via an index into this table, and therefore, it need not be searched in its directory entry every time. OFT is maintained per process basis, that is, it maintains the detail of every file opened by a process. OFT stores the attributes of the opened file. Thus, each process has an OFT for this purpose. The OFT, per process, may help in an environment, where several processes open files simultaneously. The OFT maintains a counter known as *open_count* that keeps the count of opened files. Each open operation increments this counter, and similarly each close operation decrements this counter. When the counter reaches zero, the file is no longer in use, and is closed.

System-wide Open File Table

System-wide open file table (SOFT) is another data structure, which is used to maintain the status of open files, but on the system basis rather than the process. The status of the open files is now counted for the system. An entry in the OFT points to a SOFT, where the process-independent information about the open file is maintained, for example, location of a file on the disk, file size, and so on. Thus, once a process opens a file, the file gets entry in both OFT and SOFT.

Address of the File on Disk

The address of the file, where it resides on the disk, may be needed every time the file is opened. Therefore, to avoid reading the address from the disk again and again, its address is kept in the memory.

12.7 FILE ACCESS

The files stored on the disk are required to be retrieved by the user. But there are many ways to access a file. The file access depends on the blocking strategy on the disk and the logical structuring of records. The following are some file access methods:

Sequential File Access

The file is accessed sequentially, that is, the information in the files is accessed in the order it is stored in the file. This is a simple and commonly-used access method. The sequential access is possible only when there are fixed-length records consisting of fixed set of fields in a

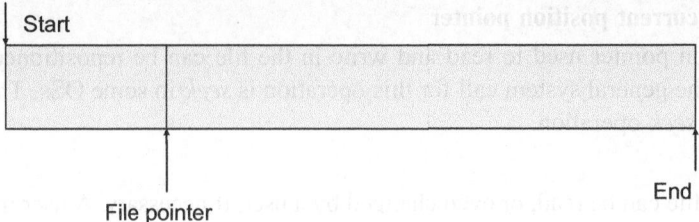

Fig. 12.3   Sequential access

particular order. There is a *key field*, usually the first field in the record, by which the sequential order is maintained (see Fig. 12.3). To read or write on such a file, a file pointer is maintained. Whenever there is a request for a read or write operation, the current position of the file pointer is seen, and advanced to the next position after the read or write operation. The pointer can be reset to the beginning of the file by assigning zero value to it.

Sequential access of a file is not suitable for all types of applications. If the application is a batch type and need to process all the records, then sequential access is a good option, as it will be beneficial for batch processing. On the other hand, if the application is of interactive type, then access and additions may be difficult. A sequential file access needs a proper match of the key field in every record, resulting in considerable processing time and delay, especially when the size of a sequential file is large. The sequential file is best suited to sequential access devices, like tapes.

Indexed Sequential File Access

Another approach for accessing a file is indexed sequential. In this type, a key field is maintained just like the sequential file access, that is, records are organized in a sequence, based on a key field. Instead of locating a record sequentially, a random access approach is followed here by incorporating an index. The index stores the key field and a pointer on the main file (see Fig. 12.4). To find a specific field, the index is searched for the highest key value, equal to or less than the desired value. The search is continued in the main file, after getting the pointer from the index. In this way, the index takes the pointer to the vicinity of a desired record, and reduces the number of lookups in the main file. The average search length may be reduced from millions to thousands. The advantage of the indexed sequential access is that the sequential nature of a file is not modified. The file stored is still sequential, and by this access method, the time to search a record is greatly reduced. If the index file is too large for the main file, it will be better to have a second-level index file. The second-level index will have pointers to the first level index, and the first level index will have pointers to the actual record in the main file.

Example 12.1

A file, consisting of students' records, each occupying 16 bytes, is stored on a disk. The block size on disk is 512 bytes. Therefore, each block can have 32 records. A file of 80,000 records would occupy 2,500 blocks. If a particular record is to be retrieved on a sequential access file, thousands of records need to be searched. Instead of this, an index can be defined, consisting of last name of the students (each 10 bytes), and the logical record number, as a pointer to various blocks in the file. The index will be sorted on the basis of last name. To search a student record, the index with the last name, can be searched for the file pointer. The pointer will point to the required block and the block can be searched sequentially.

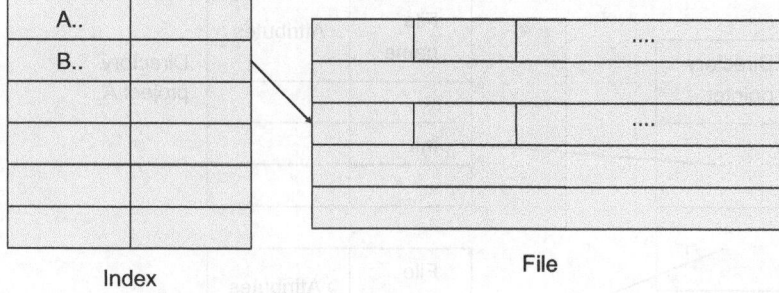

Fig 12.4 Indexed sequential File

Indexed File Access

It is not necessary to store the data in a file sequentially and to search a record by its key field. There may be other attributes by which a user wants to find a record. Thus, when the sequential nature and a single key field for searching are not required, the sequential and indexed sequential accesses are not found suitable. For this purpose, indexed file access is considered. The idea here is to prepare multiple indexes, each for an attribute, by which the user wants to search a record in the main file. There is no restriction of placing the records in sequence and they can be of variable lengths as well. There are two types of indexes: exhaustive index and partial index. The exhaustive index will contain one entry for every record in the main file. The partial index consists of entries of the records indexed by a particular attribute.

Direct File Access

Direct access is meant for a random structure of secondary storage, like in disks. This type of file is most suitable for disks to access a particular record randomly. It is not necessary to store and access the records in sequence, but they must be of fixed-length. Since the block is a unit on a disk, the key field, as in case of sequential and indexed sequential, may also be the block number. Thus, by having a block number, the block can be accessed directly, instead of a sequential access. The direct access method is suitable for applications, where rapid access of data from large amount of information is required.

12.8 DIRECTORIES

The directories are used to maintain the structure of a file system. A user, if working in a flat file system, may not be able to sort different tasks. One task may have 10 files, but all scattered in the file system. Similarly, other tasks may have multiple files, but cannot be grouped together. Thus, there is a need to group files related to a category or task. If a user performs different tasks, then each file must move in its related task group. In this way, different groups, according to the tasks, are obtained. These groups are known as directories or folders. The directory is also a file, but it lists all the files stored in it. The listing displays various attributes that may vary from system to system. The general attributes displayed may be name of the file, its location, its access rights, its date and time of creation, and so on.

Directories are convenient for users, as they can separate their work into different directories, related to different tasks. For example, if a student works on two projects, A and B, then he/she can make separate directories for Project A and Project B, such that the files related to a project will only be stored in the related directory. The directories also give flexibility such that files can

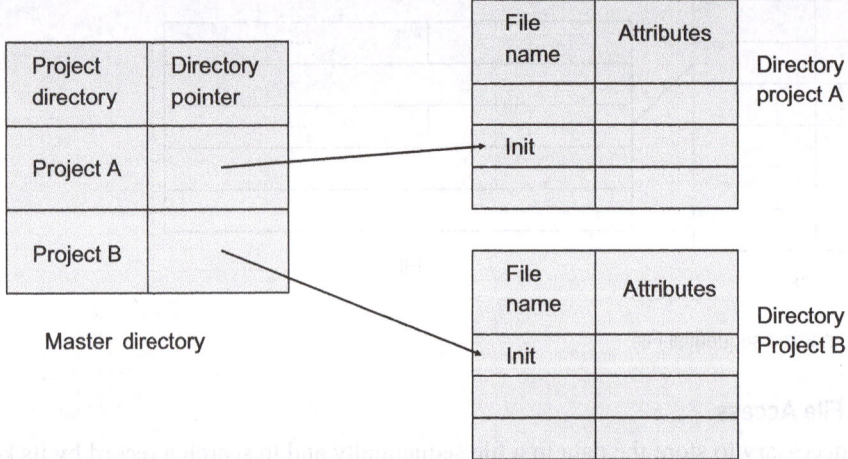

Fig. 12.5 Naming freedom through master directory

have same names in different directories. Thus, the name of every file need not be unique. In a folder, however, every file must have a unique name. The same name facility in different directories is implemented by having a master directory associated with the file system. The master file directory stores the pointer to every directory the user has made. For example, Project A and Project B are two different directories of a user. He can give same name, say *Init*, to the files in both directories. In this case, the file system will use master directory, storing the pointers of both directories, as shown in Fig. 12.5. There is no conflict in the name Init, because when the desired file is referred to, the file system will search the pointer in its corresponding directory.

The logical structuring of directories can be done in many ways, according to the requirements of a user. These are discussed in the following sections.

12.8.1 Single Level

The first logical structuring of directories can be done in a very simple manner that is, having a single level of directory structure under which all the files will be stored. It means there is a single directory in the system, known as root director, and all the files are stored only under this directory (see Fig. 12.6). It is easy to work under this structure as searching a file is easy. This kind of structure was used in earlier systems when there was no concept of multi-users. A single-level directory, therefore, is not suitable for multi-user systems, because of duplicate naming of file. If a user by mistake takes the same name of an existing file, it will be overwritten, and the old contents of the file are lost forever. If a user writes programs in many languages, it is not possible to have separate directories for each language in a single level directory structure. Thus, this structure is not used in modern systems. It may be applicable in the system where the number of files is less, as in case of an embedded system.

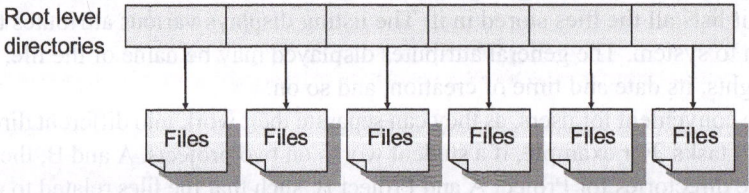

Root level
directories

Fig. 12.6 Single-level directory

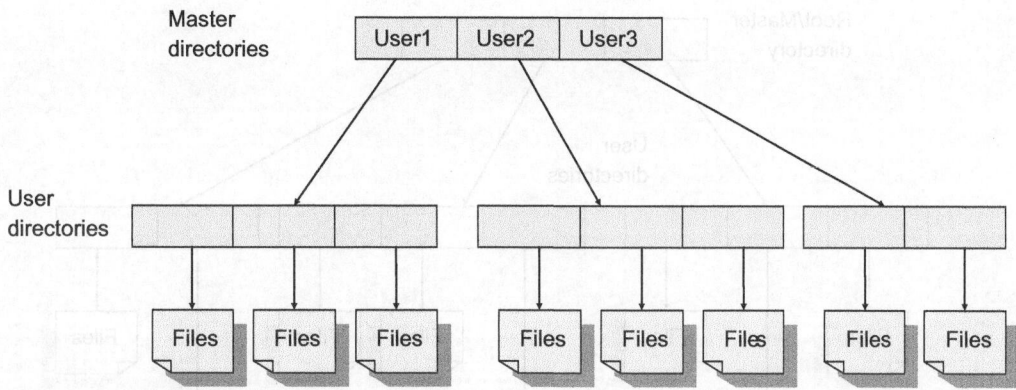

Fig. 12.7 Two-level directory

12.8.2 Two Level

The disadvantage of duplicating file names by different users in a single-level directory gives rise to the idea of having separate directories for each user, or for each task. In the two-level directory, there are two levels: master directory and user directory (see Fig. 12.7). The master directory stores the user ID and its address. The user directory is simply a list of files, as seen in a single-level. When a user starts, the system's master directory is searched for the entries of this user, through user name or account number. After searching the appropriate entry, the address of its user directory is retrieved. It means, when a user refers to a particular file, its own user directory is searched in the master directory. Thus, different users may have files with the same name in their respective directories, as seen before. The addition and deletion of a file also require searching of the file in the user directory, therefore, a file with the same name in other user directories cannot be deleted.

12.8.3 Hierarchical or Tree Structure

In a two-level directory structure, a user is limited to have a single personal directory. What will happen if a user wants more levels to divide the work in more than one group and access other users' files? In that case, the two-level structure is not suitable. An extended design of two-level structure allows a user to have sub-directories, so that the work can be divided among these sub-directories. Thus, a directory, where there is no limit on sub-directories of a single user, is known as a tree-structure directory. Thus, a large set of files can be further divided, and then grouped into sub-directories, as shown in Fig. 12.8. In the tree-structure directory, there is a root or master directory, consisting of user directories. Each user directory can be further divided into sub-directories, or it may have files. Thus, a directory has both sub-directories and files. The primary advantage of this structure is that a user can access another user's files. This facility is provided by a pathname. A pathname is a sequence of one or more path components in the tree structure that uniquely identifies a file. The pathnames, thus, can be used to access another user's file and to uniquely identify files with same names in different directories.

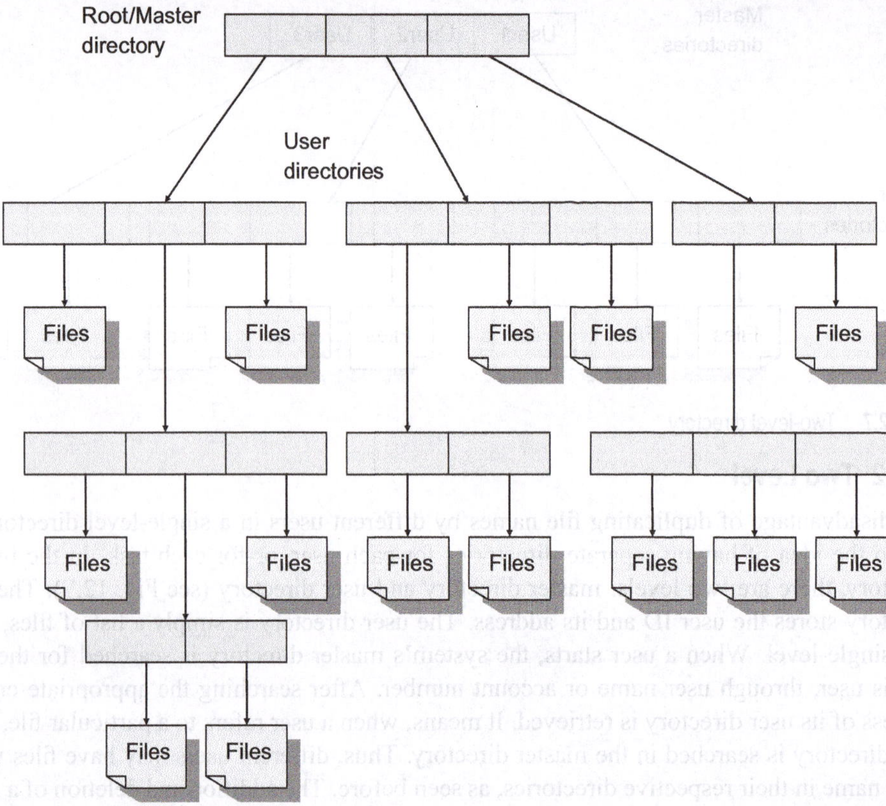

Fig. 12.8 Tree directory

Paths

There are two types of paths in a tree structure: *absolute path* and *relative path*. An absolute path is a path that always starts from the root directory, and follows the path descending to the specified file in a particular directory. To define a relative path, first let us define a term known as *current directory* or *working directory*. A current directory is a directory, where a process or user normally works. Any file specified by a user is first searched in its current directory. If the user wishes to access a file, which is not in the current directory, then a path must be provided to access it. However, it is not necessary that the path is absolute. The path provided may be relative to the current directory, that is, the path starts from the current directory, instead of the root. This is known as a relative path. Although the relative path is more convenient, as the absolute path need not be specified every time, it does exactly what an absolute path does.

The relative path does not work every time. A user may be at his/her current directory, such that the file to be accessed cannot be specified, using a relative path. In this case, the path of the file to be accessed must be specified using an absolute path. Absolute path always works, because it is an unambiguous way of referring to a file in the tree-hierarchy. A user, however, may feel inconvenient to specify the absolute path every time, if the number of files to be accessed is more. In this case, the user may change the current directory explicitly and specify the relative path. Whenever a process or user changes its current directory, it must know its location in the tree structure of the file system.

Example 12.2

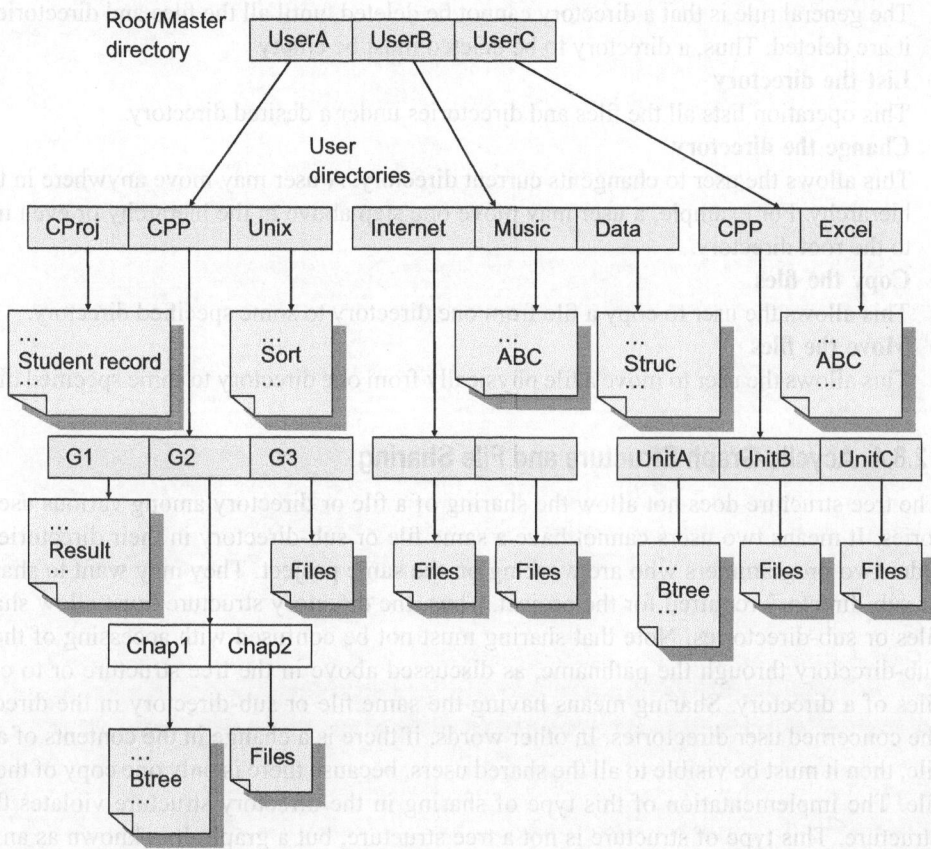

The tree-directory structure, shown above, consists of files having identical names. But the files can be easily accessed using pathnames. Both user A and user C consist of a file named 'Btree'. The files, however, can be distinguished and accessed using the following path names:

UserA/CPP/G2/Chap1/Btree

UserC/CPP/UnitA/Btree

Since the pathnames are unique to both files, the same name is allowed in the tree structure.

If the working directory of a user is G2 and the user wants to access any file in the hierarchical structure below it, then an absolute path need not be specified. The relative path, Chap1/Btree, is sufficient to access the Btree file.

Operations

Considering the directory as a tree structure, there are a number of operations that can be performed through commands or system calls. Some of them are as the following:

- **Create a directory**

  This allows the user to create a directory, according to the tree-hierarchy.

- **Delete a directory**
  This allows the user to delete a directory. There are certain rules for deleting it in most OSs. The general rule is that a directory cannot be deleted, until all the files and directories under it are deleted. Thus, a directory to be deleted must be empty.
- **List the directory**
  This operation lists all the files and directories under a desired directory.
- **Change the directory**
  This allows the user to change its current directory. A user may move anywhere in the tree-hierarchy. For example, a user may move one step above in the hierarchy or even move up to the root directory.
- **Copy the files**
  This allows the user to copy a file from one directory to some specified directory.
- **Move the files**
  This allows the user to move a file physically from one directory to some specified directory.

12.8.4 Acyclic Graph Structure and File Sharing

The tree structure does not allow the sharing of a file or directory among various user directories. It means two users cannot have a same file or sub-directory in their directories. Consider two programmers who are working on the same project. They may want to share a file or sub-directory required for the project. Thus, the directory structure must allow sharing of files or sub-directories. Note that sharing must not be confused with accessing of the file or sub-directory through the pathname, as discussed above in the tree structure or to copy the files of a directory. Sharing means having the same file or sub-directory in the directory of the concerned user directories. In other words, if there is a change in the contents of a shared file, then it must be visible to all the shared users, because there is only one copy of the shared file. The implementation of this type of sharing in the directory structure violates the tree-structure. This type of structure is not a tree structure, but a graph. It is known as an acyclic graph (see Fig. 12.9).

An acyclic graph structure is implemented through a pointer, known as a *link*. A link is a pointer that points to a file or directory. If a directory entry is marked as a link, the real file information is in the link. The link is implemented as a pathname of the shared file. Thus, when a file is needed, the directory entry is searched. If the directory is found as a link, then the link is resolved to have the access of the real file. This is known as a *symbolic link* or *soft link*. In UNIX, file-sharing is done with the help of *link* and *unlink* commands. The link system call is specified with two parameters: the existing file name and the pathname as a link. It creates a link between the existing file and the file specified in the link. Similarly, an unlink system call is used to remove the link between two files. However, unlink does not affect the shared file in any way. It just removes the symbolic link between the files. Symbolic links can also be used to link to files on any machine in the network, by providing the network address and pathname of the machine.

There are, however, some problems in implementation of the symbolic linking. It may be possible that a file has multiple absolute paths referring to the same file. The problem also occurs when the structure needs to be traversed for some purpose, like copying all files for backup. The problem in traversing the structure is that, it results in duplicate copies of the same file. Another problem is that symbolic links incur an extra overhead. Since the symbolic link

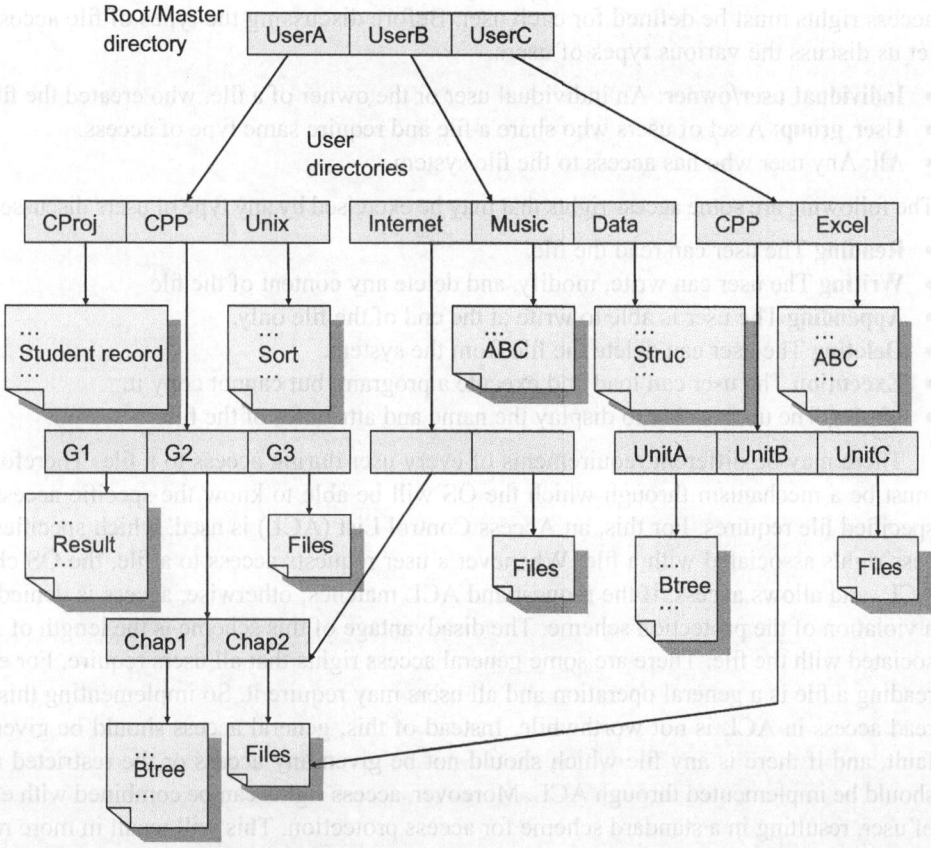

Fig. 12.9   Acyclic graph-based directory structure

execution requires reading of path in link, parsing of path, and following the path step by step, the overhead includes both time and disk space, as extra disk accesses and space are required. Contrary to soft links, a directory entry may have an entry that specifies the location of a file on the storage device. In this case, the file is accessed by directly accessing the physical blocks that are being referenced to. This is known as a *hard link*. But a hard link needs to be updated, whenever there is a change in physical addresses on the disk.

File sharing is of two types: *sequential sharing* and *concurrent sharing*. Sequential sharing allows a file to be shared by multiple users but one by one in a sequence. On the other hand, concurrent sharing allows multiple users to share a file over the same period of time. Sequential sharing is implemented with the help of a lock system, known as *file-locking*. File-locking restricts the access to a file by allowing only one user at a time.

12.9   FILE PROTECTION

The file-sharing discussed in the last section poses a protection problem. The file-sharing facility in the system does not mean that any user can access the file and modify it. There may be a file-system that prohibits any sharing of files among users. On the other hand, some file-systems may allow access to all users. But both kinds of systems represent two extremes of file protection. Instead of having total prohibition or full flexibility of access,

access rights must be defined for each user. Before discussing the types of file access rights, let us discuss the various types of users.

- **Individual user/owner**: An individual user or the owner of a file, who created the file.
- **User group**: A set of users who share a file and require same type of access.
- **All**: Any user who has access to the file system.

The following are some access rights that may be exercised by any type of users discussed above:

- **Reading** The user can read the file.
- **Writing** The user can write, modify, and delete any content of the file.
- **Appending** The user is able to write at the end of the file only.
- **Deleting** The user can delete the file from the system.
- **Execution** The user can load and execute a program, but cannot copy it.
- **Listing** The user is able to display the name and attributes of the file.

There may be different requirements of every user during access to a file. Therefore, there must be a mechanism through which the OS will be able to know the specific access right a specified file requires. For this, an Access Control List (ACL) is used, which specifies the access rights associated with a file. Whenever a user requests access to a file, the OS checks its ACL, and allows access, if the request and ACL matches; otherwise, access is denied, as it is a violation of the protection scheme. The disadvantage of this scheme is the length of ACL associated with the file. There are some general access rights that all users require. For example, reading a file is a general operation and all users may require it. So implementing this general read access in ACL is not worthwhile. Instead of this, general access should be given by default, and if there is any file which should not be given any access or the restricted accesses should be implemented through ACL. Moreover, access rights can be combined with each type of user, resulting in a standard scheme for access protection. This will result in more restricted protection, having only three fields of protection. Each field may be of several bits, representing access protection. For example, in UNIX, there are three fields: owner, group, and all. Each field has three bits, specifying read, write, and execute access permissions. Thus, only 9 bits are required per file.

Example 12.3

A leader of a group on a project wants all group members to be able to read and write, but not delete data on the project directory. Other users may be allowed only to read the files under the project

Type of user	Permissions
Owner	All
Group	Read and write
All	Read only

directory. Besides this, the project leader should have all access rights. So the mapping of every type of user in the project with their access rights is as depicted in the following space:

12.10 FILE SYSTEM MOUNTING

There are several types of storage devices like CD-ROMs, hard disks, USB storage and so on. Hard disks may have several partitions as well. In Windows, the devices and/or partition can be accessed by opening *My Computer* on the desktop. The hard disk partitions are D: and E: and other devices may be represented as F:, G:, and so on. It means that it is possible to access these devices. On the other hand, in case of a Linux or UNIX OS, the CD or hard disk partitions cannot be accessed. The reason is that the user needs to mount all the devices or hard disk partitions explicitly, whereas in Windows, the OS does the mounting of all attached devices and partitions of the hard disk; every file-system is accessible in the root directory of the system. Therefore, every storage device/partition must be attached to the root directory of the system, before they can be used. This attaching of the device is known as *mounting*, and the directory where the device is attached, is known as a *mount point*. Similarly, *unmounting* is done to remove the device from the mount point. To mount a device, the OS requires the name of the device and the mount point. The OS then reads the device directory and verifies that the directory has a valid file-system. After this, it records the entry of a new device directory in its directory structure at the desired mount point.

SUMMARY

The fundamental issues of the file structure and directory structure, along with their implementations have been discussed in this chapter.

Let us have a quick review of important concepts discussed in this chapter:

- A file may be considered as a sequence of blocks, and therefore, all basic I/O functions are performed only in terms of blocks. This is known as *record blocking*.
- The larger the size of a block, the more number of records will be mapped to the block on the disk.
- There are three types of files: regular, directory, and special.
- Regular file is one that contains the user information.
- Directory is a file type used to organize the list of files in a group, that is, it organizes the files in a hierarchy.
- Special file contains no data, but provides a mechanism that maps physical devices to file names, that is, these are used to access I/O devices.
- To implement the file operations, there are three major data structures:
  open file table (OFT) to keep the information of an opened file,
  System-wide open file table (SOFT) to maintain the status of an opened file, but on the system basis, rather than the process,
  Address of the file on disk.
- The files may be accessed through:

Sequential file access where the file is accessed sequentially, that is, the information in the files is accessed in the order it is stored in the file.

Indexed sequential file access where random access approach is followed by incorporating an index. The index stores the key field and a pointer to the main file.

Indexed file access prepares multiple indexes, each for an attribute, by which a record is searched in the main file.

Direct file access is meant for the random structure of secondary storage, like a disk.

- The logical structuring of the directories can be done through single level, two level, and tree structure.
- There are two types of paths in a tree structure: *absolute path* and *relative path*.
- An absolute path is a path that always starts from the root directory, and follows the path descending to the specified file in a particular directory.
- A current or working directory is a directory, where a process or user normally works.
- A relative path is relative to the current directory, that is, the path, instead of starting from the root, starts from the current directory only.
- A tree structure does not allow sharing of a file or sub-directory among various user directories.
- Acyclic graph allows the sharing of files or sub-directories among different users.

MULTIPLE CHOICE QUESTIONS

1. When multiple fields are combined to form a meaningful collection, it is known as a _____.
   (a) file
   (b) block
   (c) record
   (d) none

2. The larger the size of a block, _____ number of bytes will be transferred in one I/O operation.
   (a) smaller
   (b) larger
   (c) zero
   (d) none

3. When the object files have been linked properly and are ready to run, they are known as _____.
   (a) archive files
   (b) object files
   (c) batch files
   (d) executable files

4. A file consisting of some commands to be executed and given to command interpreter, is known as _____.
   (a) archive files
   (b) object files
   (c) batch files
   (d) executable files

5. When a group of files is compressed in a single file, it is known as _____.
   (a) archive files
   (b) object files
   (c) batch files
   (d) executable files

6. _____ file contains the user information.
   (a) Regular
   (b) Directory
   (c) Special
   (d) none

7. _____ is a file type used to organize the list of files in a group.
   (a) Regular
   (b) Directory
   (c) Special
   (d) none

8. _____ contains no data, but provides a mechanism that maps physical devices to file names.
   (a) Regular
   (b) Directory
   (c) Special
   (d) none

9. _____ in a file attribute is used to keep track of whether file has been backed up or not.
   (a) Hidden flag
   (b) System flag
   (c) Access flag
   (d) Archive flag

10. Multiple indexes are prepared in a _____.
    (a) Sequential file
    (b) Indexed sequential file
    (c) Indexed file
    (d) Direct file

11. Sharing of a file or directory is allowed in a _____ directory structure.
    (a) single level
    (b) two-level
    (c) tree
    (d) acyclic

REVIEW QUESTIONS

1. What are the constituents of a file system?
2. What is a record blocking? Explain its types.
3. Explain various formats of a file.
4. Define regular, directory, and special types of a file.
5. Explain different types of flags used in a file's attribute.
6. What are the various operations that can be performed on a file?
7. Distinguish between OFT and SOFT.
8. Explain different types of file-accessing methods.

9. Explain the ways by which the logical structuring of a directory can be done.
10. What is the concept of a working directory?
11. Distinguish between an absolute and a relative path in a tree-directory structure.
12. Distinguish between a tree and an acyclic graph directory structure.
13. What is symbolic linking?
14. What is an access control list?
15. What is the purpose of file -system mounting?

BRAIN TEASERS

1. Sunil and Rajesh are working on Project A and B, respectively, by maintaining separate directories. However, there is a utility which may be used by both. Which type of directory structure would be the best for this case?

2. The Projects A and B need to have a file named "Utility", but with different contents. Can both projects use the same file name? If yes, which directory structure would be the best for this case?

3. Can a two-level directory structure be considered as a tree-structure directory?

4. In a LAN environment, some users are working on a project. The project leader, with his four members working on the project, wants that all group members should be able to read and write on the project directory, but should not be able to delete it. Other users may be allowed only to read and execute the files under project directory. Besides this, the project leader should have all the access rights. Prepare a file access protection scheme for this.

13 File System Implementation

13.1 INTRODUCTION

The fundamentals of the files and file system were discussed in Chapter 12. In this chapter, the implementation details of the file system have been described. The file system accepts the user request for any disk I/O and sends it to the device through various intermediate layers. Various data structures are used on disk as well as in the memory for implementation of the file system. The implementation details of various file-related operations and how the files are allocated on the disk are discussed in this chapter. Besides this, some issues regarding the file system, such as backup and recovery of critical data, file system inconsistencies, and some performance issues have also been discussed.

13.2 FILE SYSTEM STRUCTURE

The file system is structured in various layers to incorporate various operations. Each layer uses the operation of its lower layer. The various layers as depicted in Fig. 13.1 are discussed as follows:

13.2.1 Logical File System

The logical file system is concerned with the logical structure of the file. This module manages all the information about file attributes. The file structure is maintained in a data structure generally known as a *file control block* (FCB). This layer manages the directory structure where a file is located and provides information about the file location to the file organization module.

13.2.2 File Organization Module

This module knows about the logical blocks of the file and translates them to physical blocks so that the basic file system gets the physical blocks and proceeds further. For this translation, it needs to know the location of the file and its allocation type. The file is allocated the disk space in some specified manner known as *file allocation methods*, which will be discussed later in this chapter. Further, it also must know which blocks are free. This information is provided by the free space manager that tracks unallocated blocks and provides them to the file organization module so that the translation of logical blocks can be performed. Free space manager will be dealt in detail later.

Learning Objectives

After reading this chapter, you should be able to understand:

- Layered structure for file system
- On-disk file system implementation data structures
- In-memory file system implementation data structures
- File mapping on disk
- Implementation of file-related operations
- File allocation methods: contiguous, linked, indexed
- Free space management
- Directory implementation
- Backup and recovery methods for file system
- File inconsistencies and the checks against them
- File system performance issues
- Log structured file system

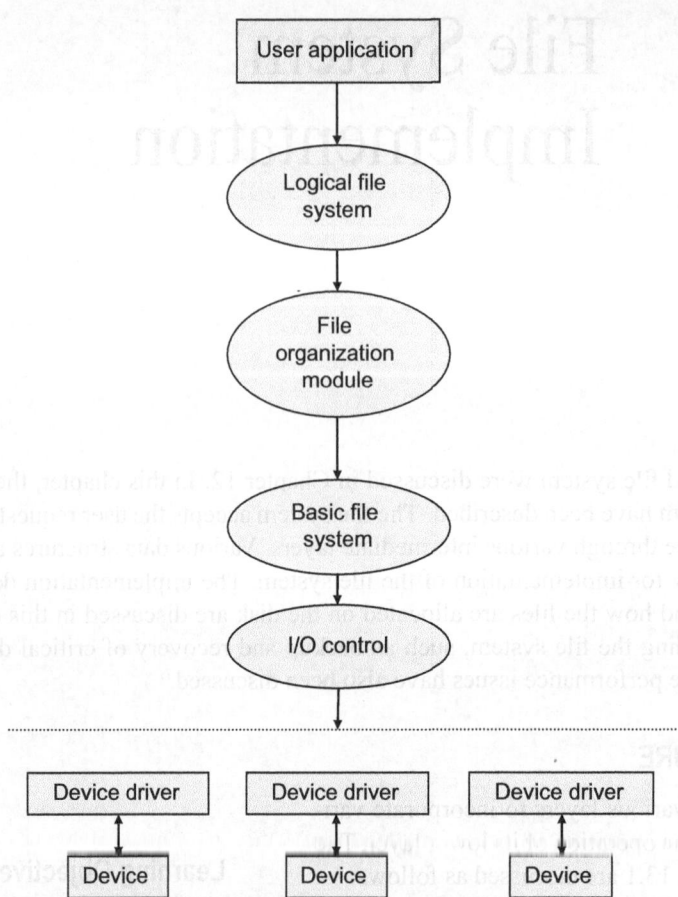

Fig. 13.1 Layered structure of the file system

13.2.3 Basic File System/Physical Input–Output Level

The basic file system issues the generic commands to the device drivers of the corresponding devices to read and write physical blocks. The physical blocks are identified with their disk addresses. The blocks are first allocated in a buffer. When there is an I/O request, the blocks are transferred either to the disk or the memory and buffer becomes free. The buffer management is also done at this level.

13.2.4 Input–Output Control

This is the lowest level in the layered design of the file system. This module communicates with the actual device (disk or tape drive), starts operation on the device, and processes the I/O request. It consists of device drivers and interrupt handlers to transfer information between the main memory and the device.

The benefit of layered structure of a file system is that the code of one layer can be used by different file systems. For example, the basic file system or I/O control module can be reused by various file systems. On the other hand, the number of layers should be decided wisely. If it is large, then there is a possibility of decreased performance. Thus, the number of layers may affect the performance of an OS.

13.3 IMPLEMENTATION OF DATA STRUCTURES

The file system implementation involves various data structures to manage its data and meta-data. Since the secondary storage used

Boot block	Super block	I-nodes	Files and directories

Fig. 13.2 Disk layout implementing the file system

for the file system implementation is generally a disk, some of these data structures are on-disk or in-memory. The on-disk data structures are organized by dividing the disk into blocks of some size: The disk space is partitioned into a series of blocks. In general, the block size is 4KB. Most of the disk space, that is, the blocks are reserved for storing the data. These blocks are known as *data blocks*. Some of the blocks are reserved for on-disk data structures. Although the data structures may vary as per the implementation of different OSs, the general on-disk data structures are discussed as follows (see Fig. 13.2):

1. **Boot block**

   Every partition on the disk starts with the boot block. The program in the boot block loads the OS in that partition.

2. **File control block**

   It is required to track the information such as which data blocks comprise a file, and the file's size, owner, access rights, date of creation, access or modification, and so on. All this information is stored in FCB, which is an array of data structures per file. It is also known as *Inode* (*Index node*). It contains all the accounting information and the information to locate all the disk blocks that hold the file's data.

3. **Super block/volume control block**

   It stores the key information about the file system on every partition (or volume) of the disk, which is read into memory after the system is booted, protecting the integrity of the file system. Thus, when mounting a file system, the OS will first read the superblock to initialize various parameters and then attach the volume to the file-system tree. When files within the volume are accessed, the system will thus know exactly where to look for the needed on-disk structures.

   The superblock consists of the following information:

   - *File system identifier*: It is also known as a *magic number that uniquely identifies the file type*
   - Number and size of data blocks in the file system
   - Addresses of the free blocks
   - Free block count
   - Free FCB count
   - Addresses of the FCB
   - Address of the root directory
   - Date and time of last modification to the file system

4. **Free list**

   It is used for tracking unallocated blocks. It points to the first free block, which then points to the next free block and so forth.

5. **Files and directories**

   To organize the files, the directory structure on each file system is used. It may consist of file names and their corresponding FCB.

Mount table	Directory-structure cache	SOFT	OFT	Buffer area

Fig. 13.3 In-memory data structures implementing the file system

Table 13.1 Structure of the SOFT

File name	FCB	Open_count
C:/admin/dbase/fileA.doc	File permissions File access dates File owner File size Address of file on disk	

Some data structures reside in memory instead of disk. These data structures may be used at the time of mounting or for updating a file system required during the file operations. The following are some in-memory data structures (see Fig. 13.3):

1. **Mount table**

   It stores the information about each mounted file system on each partition.

2. **Directory-structure cache**

   It stores the information about the recently accessed directories.

3. **SOFT**

   As discussed in Chapter 12, it maintains the information about the open files in the system. It keeps the copy of the FCB of each opened file for this purpose. Since this is a process-independent system-wide data structure, it has a count of the times a file has been opened by various processes. This count is incremented every time a specific file is opened. The structure of the SOFT is shown in Table 13.1.

4. **OFT**

   As discussed in Chapter 12, an OFT maintains the detail of every file opened by a process and an entry in the OFT points to a SOFT wherein the process-independent information about the open file is maintained. An OFT is a data structure maintained per process basis. When a process accesses a file, the access position of the file may change. The next time when the same process opens the file, it must resume its access from the last position. Therefore, a current position pointer is maintained for every process in this table so that a process can read or write from where it accessed the last time. The access rights for a file are also stored in this table such that a file can be granted permission for appropriate operations. The structure of the OFT is shown in Table 13.2.

5. **Buffer area**

   This is a temporary storage area in the memory that is used to hold the data while performing any I/O operation with the disk.

13.4 FILE MAPPING THROUGH FCB

A logical file is a continuous stream of bytes, but the file data inside the blocks may not be contiguous on the disk. The file system uses the logical position in a file stored by the FCB to map

Table 13.2   Structure of per-process OFT

Process name	File name	Current position pointer	Access rights	Other information	Pointer to the SOFT
Process A	C:/admin/dbase /fileA.doc				
	D:/admin/cpp /fileB.doc				

it to a physical location on the disk as shown in Fig. 13.4. The FCB contains a list of blocks of a file and their corresponding disk block addresses. Thus, to retrieve the data at some position in a file, the file system first translates the logical position to a physical location in the disk. After this, the request is made to transfer that mapped location (block) in the disk and the data is passed to the user after retrieving the block from the disk.

An FCB stores between 4 and 16 direct block references. However, if we keep on storing large number of block references in it, then the FCB needs more memory space as it needs to be copied in the memory for every file to be opened. Thus, there is trade-off between the size of the FCB and the amount of data it can map. This limitation does not allow us then to have a file of a bigger size. To overcome the space constraints for storing block addresses in the FCB, it can use *indirect blocks*. An indirect block contains pointers to the blocks that make up the data of the file as shown in Fig. 13.5. Through the use of indirect blocks, the FCB instead of storing the block addresses of the data blocks now stores the block address of the indirect block. The use of indirect blocks allows the FCB to extend the amount of data a file can address. The number of data blocks an indirect block can refer is given as,

File system block size/size of disk block addresses

Given a block size of 1024 bytes and the disk block address size of 8 bytes, the number of data blocks an indirect block can refer is 128.

Although indirect blocks increase the amount of data a file can access, they are limited to a few bytes in size.

The idea of indirect blocks can be extended further to accommodate files of even bigger sizes. Another level of indirect blocks when extended is known as *double indirect blocks*.

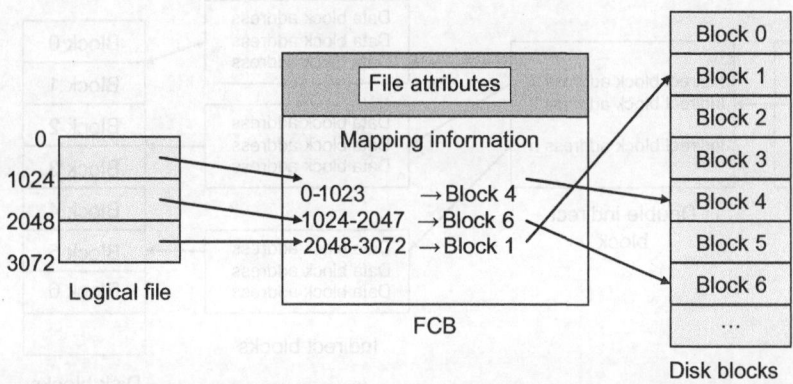

Fig. 13.4   File mapping through FCB

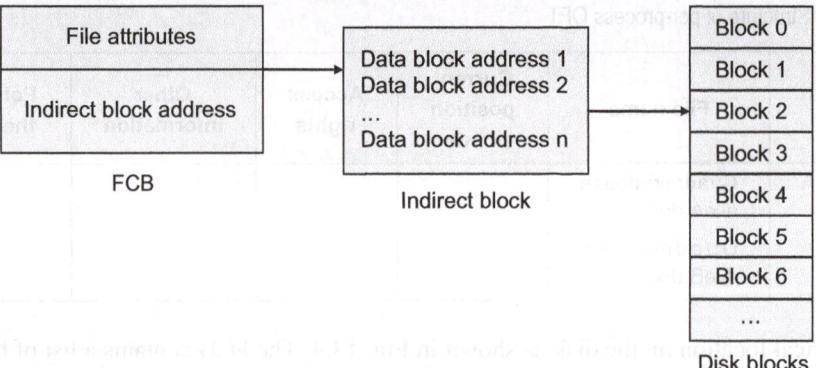

Fig. 13.5   File mapping through indirect block

In double indirect blocks, the FCB contains the address of double indirect block (see Fig. 13.6) and, in turn, double indirect block contains pointers to indirect blocks. The indirect blocks contain pointers to the data blocks of the file. This can be extended further to the third level called *triple-indirect blocks*, if required.

13.4.1 Extents

Instead of using multiple levels of indirect blocks, extents can be used to support a large-sized file. The extent is also a simple list of block addresses, but the difference is that each address in the list is not for a single block rather for a range of blocks. In other words, one address in the list will represent the multiple blocks of the disk. Thus, an extent is a compact way to refer to large amounts of data represented in the form of pointer-length pair where the pointer is the address to the start address of the range of blocks and length is the number of blocks. Although the size of an extent is larger than the block address as used in the simple block address list, it is able to map a larger number of consecutive blocks onto the disk. Moreover, they allow disk I/O in units of multiple blocks if storage is in consecutive blocks. For sequential access, multiple block operations are considerably faster than block-at-a-time operations.

However, if the blocks on the disk are fragmented, the extent cannot address them. In this case, the indirect blocks are the only solution. Therefore, extents with indirect blocks can also be

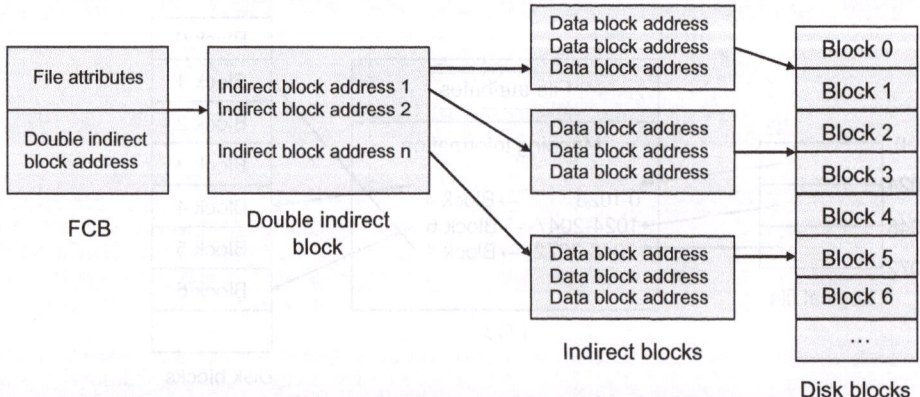

Fig. 13.6   File mapping through double indirect block

implemented. Another limitation in using the extent list is that searching a particular position in the file requires starting at the first extent and scanning through all of them until the desired location is found.

13.5 IMPLEMENTATION OF FILE OPERATIONS

In Chapter 12, we saw that various operations can be performed on the files. On the light of the file system basics and the data structures, let us discuss how various file-related operations are implemented.

13.5.1 Create a File

To create a new file, a system call is passed to the logical file system. It reads the appropriate directory structure where the new file will be created. For this, it calls the file organization module to map the directory information to its corresponding block. After that, the basic file system issues the disk read operation to the disk device driver. I/O control layer implements the read operation on the disk and copies the result in the memory. In this way, the disk read operation is performed for directory read operation. After reading the directory structure, it needs to be updated for the new file. For this, the new file name and its corresponding FCB are added in the directory structure. The FCB block is assigned by the free space manager. The directory structure is then finally written to the disk in the same hierarchy as used for disk read operation.

13.5.2 Open a File

The system call for opening an existing file is passed to the logical file system. The logical file system searches the SOFT to find out whether this file is already in use by another process or not. If it is, then an entry in the OFT is created pointing to the SOFT. If the file is not found in the SOFT, then the FCB of that file is read in the memory. However, at this moment, the file system has only the path of the desired file. To locate the FCB of the desired file, the FCB of the directory is required wherein the file resides. Therefore, the FCB of the directory is read in the memory. However, it may be possible that this directory again lies inside some other directory or the root directory. In this case, the FCB of the previous directory or the root directory is located. In this way, the FCBs of all the directories or sub-directories are searched until the desired FCB is found. Once it is found, it is copied to the SOFT in the memory. An entry in OFT pointing to the entry in SOFT is also created. After checking the file permissions, the file system returns a pointer to the appropriate entry in the OFT. This pointer is known as a *file descriptor* or *file handle*.

Example 13.1

A file is to be opened whose full path is given as *C:/project/code/system.c*. Assuming that there are no FCBs in the memory except the superblock, the following operations are performed:

(a) Search the SOFT to find an entry of the file.
(b) If found, create an entry in OFT pointing to the entry in the SOFT. Otherwise, move to the next step.
(c) Read the FCB of the root directory from the disk.

(d) Read the data blocks of the root directory from the disk.
(e) Read the FCB of the Project sub-directory.
(f) Read the data blocks of the Project sub-directory.
(g) Read the FCB of the Code sub-directory.
(h) Read the data blocks of the Code sub-directory.
(i) Read the FCB of the *system.c* file.
(j) Create an entry of the FCB by copying it to the SOFT.
(k) Create an entry in the OFT pointing to the entry in the SOFT.

In this way, to read in the FCB of the desired file, we need to perform six read operations on the disk. These read operations may affect the performance of the system. Therefore, the FCB of root directory and other subdirectories including the file may be cached in memory if the file is frequently in use. In this way, many disk I/O operations can be saved and the system performs quickly.

13.5.3 Read a File

For reading a file, it must be opened. After that, the file can be read by using the file handle in OFT and the FCB in SOFT. The block to be read in the file is known with the help of the FCB. After read operation, the current position pointer in the OFT is updated so that the next read/write operation can be performed.

13.5.4 Write a File

There are two cases in write operation. One is to update the existing file. Second case is that the file is appended to an existing file or a new file is written. For the first case, the procedure is same as for reading a file. Therefore, the desired block is read in the memory, updated, and then written back to the disk. In the second case, new blocks are required to be allocated to the new file or to append a file. Since a bit map is used to track free and allocated blocks, it must be first read to know which new block can be allocated. When the block is allocated, the status of the bit map is modified and updated on the disk. After this, the newly allocated block is written. After the write operation, the current position pointer in the OFT is updated so that the next read/write operation can be performed.

Example 13.2

In Example 13.1, suppose the file contents are being written and one additional block is required. In this case, bit map is read into the memory to check which block can be allocated to this file. After checking the status in bit map and allocating the new block to the file, the bit map needs to be modified to change the status of the block allocated. The modified bit map is then updated on the disk. Thus, two additional disk I/O operations are required to write in a file. The third disk I/O operation is, of course, the actual writing in the file.

13.5.5 Close a File

For closing a file, OFT entry is removed and the count in SOFT, discussed earlier, is decremented. When all the processes have closed the file, SOFT entry is removed and any updates on the file are written back to the disk. It is obvious that I/O operations are very less in the file closing as compared to other file operations.

13.6 FILE ALLOCATION METHODS

It is clear now that files as a logical concept will be mapped into the secondary storage such as disk. While mapping the file, the desired number of blocks is required to store the whole file. The file system is responsible to allocate the blocks to the file. The files may be allocated in two ways: *static allocation* and *dynamic allocation*. The static allocation is to allocate the maximum size of a file in advance when it is created. The dynamic allocation allocates the blocks as per requirement. Obviously, the dynamic allocation is better as there is space wastage in static allocation.

The files need to be stored on the hard disk as part of their implementation. However, the file allocation must ensure that there is quick access to the contents of the file and storage space is utilized efficiently. There are three methods of file allocation.

13.6.1 Contiguous File Allocation

This type of file allocation allocates contiguous blocks on the disk at the time of file creation. In contiguous file allocation, there is no or minimum head movement when a job is accessing the blocks of the file. On the disk, suppose a file is stored on one track but continues on the next track. To access a block on a different track, head movement is needed only from one track to the next. Thus, seek time will be minimal. Consequently, access time of a file and I/O performance by reading in multiple blocks can be improved.

The contiguous allocation is implemented through a *file allocation table* (FAT) that defines the start address and length of a file. The start address is the address of the block where the file starts and the number of blocks thereafter defines the length of a file. Since the file allocation is contiguous, the length is sufficient to indicate how many blocks will be required to store the file.

Example 13.3

FAT

File name	Start address	Length
C:/project/OS/FileA	2	5
C:/project/OS/FileB	10	3
C:/project/OS/FileC	18	7
C:/project/OS/FileD	7	3

To implement the file as shown above in its FAT, the contiguous allocation can be seen in Fig. 13.7. FileA starts from the block address 2 and since its length is five, it consumes Block number 3, 4, 5, and 6 in continuation. Similarly, FileB consumes the Blocks 11, 12, and 13 and similarly, all other files consume contiguous space on the disk.

The contiguous file allocation is simple to implement. There is only one disk-seek required for the start address of the file and after that, there is no seek or latency to find the next block and the whole file can be read from the disk in one operation. Thus, contiguous allocated file is suitable for sequential as well as direct access files. It is easy to access the next block sequentially as the file system has an entry for the last block referenced. For direct access, the start address and the block number are required. To access the *n*th block whose start address is *s*, block $s + n$ can be accessed.

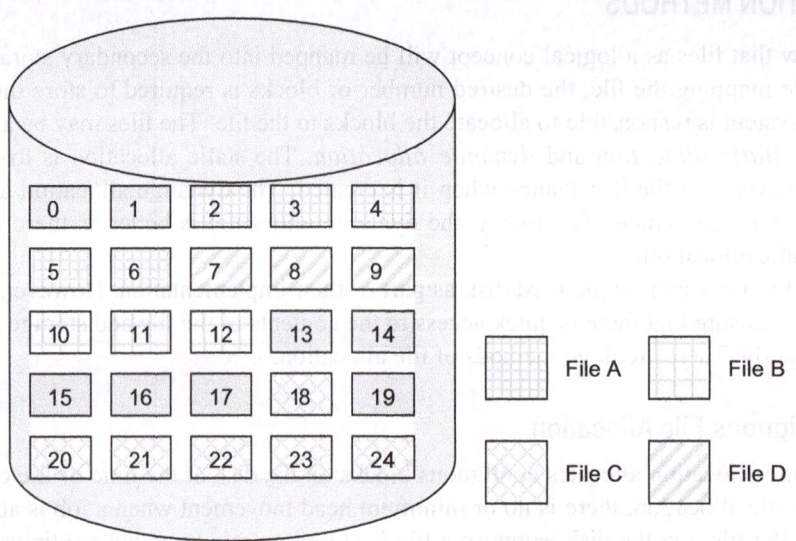

Fig. 13.7 Contiguous file allocation

The contiguous allocation is a pre-allocation strategy. The problem is to decide how much space is required for a file. The file owner, in fact, does not know the size of the file. There may be two cases: The allocated space for the file may be too small or too large. In the first case, the user may not be able to execute the program, and in the second case, there will be wastage of space resulting in fragmentation. Moreover, there may be some space in the form of external fragmentation that will not suffice as a contiguous space for storing a file. The fragmentation can be reduced through compaction method, but it is a costly affair.

Example 13.4

In Fig. 13.7, if FileD is deleted, the blocks consumed by it will be free, that is, Blocks 7, 8, and 9 as shown in Fig. 13.8. Suppose another file needs to be created whose length in blocks is nine. Although the required number of blocks on the disk are available (Block number 0–1, 7–9, 13–17), they cannot be allocated to the new file as the blocks are not contiguous leading to fragmentation. However, if compaction is done, then the blocks on the disk become contiguous and can be allocated to the new file as shown in Fig. 13.9. However, in this case, the start address of the files should be changed in the FAT of every file.

13.6.2 Linked/Chained File Allocation

In linked allocation, two strategies are followed: dynamic allocation and non-contiguous allocation. In the first strategy, the blocks are allocated as per the requirement of the files. In the second strategy, non-contiguous blocks are allocated, saving the space created by the fragmentation as in case of contiguous allocation. To implement this allocation, each entry of the FAT corresponding to a file has a pointer (initialized to nil) to the first disk block and the length of the file. As the file grows, a free block on the disk is found and this block is linked to the end of the file. In this way, one block points to another block resulting in a chained allocation for the file. The linked allocation eliminates the drawbacks of the contiguous file allocation. Now, there is no need to declare the size of a file in advance, and since any free block on the disk can be allocated, there will not be any problem of external fragmentation either.

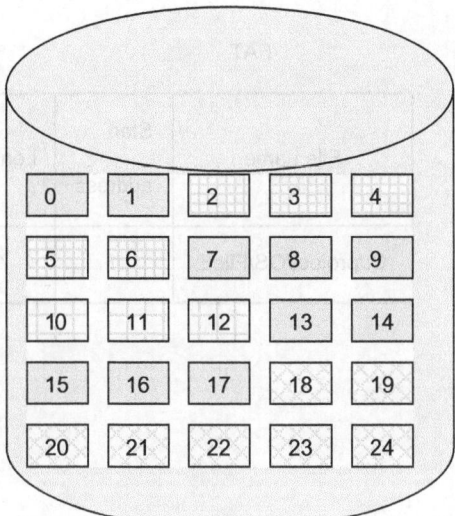

Fig. 13.8 Fragmentation in contiguous file allocation

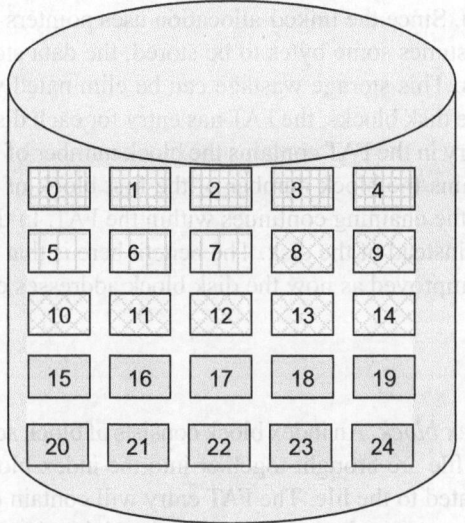

Fig. 13.9 Compaction

Example 13.5

Suppose a disk has been fragmented and there are some free blocks on the disk as shown in Fig. 13.10. A new file, whose length is seven, needs to be allocated on the disk. In this case, the linked allocation will be appropriate as the non-contiguous free blocks can be linked together and allocated to the new file.

The linked allocation supports sequential access files but is not suitable for direct access files. We cannot access the nth block efficiently as in contiguous allocation because the blocks are scattered on the disk. Each access of a block consumes some time in disk-read and disk-seek. The lookup starts from the first address following the pointers for the next disk-read until the nth block is found. This results in multiple block reads, slowing down the random access of disk blocks. Thus, the linked-allocation is not suitable for direct-access files.

Fig. 13.10 Linked file allocation

There is another drawback of this allocation. Since the linked-allocation uses pointers to point to the next disk block and each pointer consumes some bytes to be stored, the data storage of each block is wasted in storing the pointers. This storage wastage can be eliminated with the help of FAT. Instead of having pointers to the disk blocks, the FAT has entry for each disk block and is indexed by the block number. The entry in the FAT contains the block number of the next block. The directory entry for the file contains the block number of the first block of the file. The first block points to the next block and the chaining continues within the FAT. In this way, pointer storage is consumed in the memory instead of the disk. The benefit here is that the random access performance of the file can be improved as now the disk block addresses can only be read from the FAT in the memory.

13.6.3 Indexed File Allocation

In this allocation, each file is allocated an *index block*. An index block consists of block addresses of the file. In this way, all the pointers of a file are brought together into the index block. The index block is one separate disk block allocated to the file. The FAT entry will contain only the address of the index block of the file. The ith entry in the index block is the ith block of the file. In other words, to retrieve the ith block in the file, the ith pointer in the index block is retrieved. When a file is created, a block is found from the free space and the address of that block is written in the ith index block. In this way, an index block contains information of all the disk blocks of the file, and hence, supports both sequential as well as direct access of the files.

Example 13.6

The file shown in Fig. 13.11 has been allocated Block number 14 as index block that contains the addresses of the blocks that makes the file. In this case, the Block numbers 8, 2, 12, 18, 19, and 23 have been allocated to the file. However, instead of having pointers in each block, the index block contains the addresses of all the blocks.

The problem with indexed file allocation is in deciding the size of an index block. In general, the index block will be one disk block. The pointer entries in the index block are too small or too large in number. When there are only two or three entries in the index block, the space of

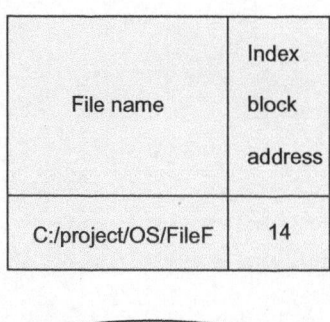

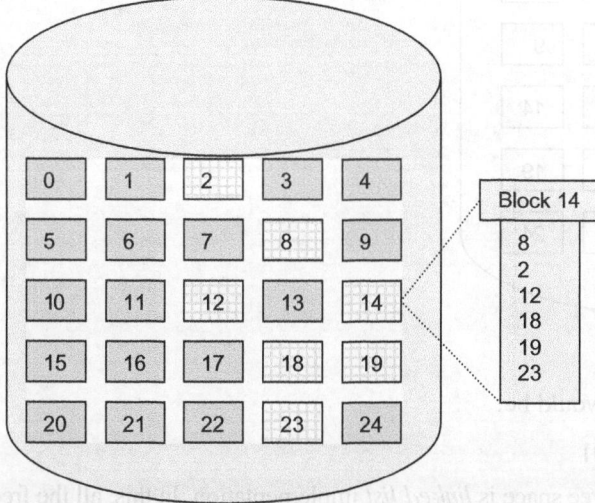

Fig. 13.11 Indexed file allocation

a disk block is wasted. On the other hand, if entries are large in number, then one disk block is not sufficient to store all the entries. In that case, a mechanism is required that can store all the entries in the index block. For example, the size of an index block can be increased by linking one disk block to another.

13.7 FREE SPACE MANAGEMENT

Since the file allocation methods find a free disk block for the file, it is important to keep track of free space. It is necessary to have an account of the location of a free disk block. Therefore, a data structure known as *free space list* is required to store the information of free or unallocated disk blocks. After allocating a free disk block to a file, the entry corresponding to that block is removed from the free space list. When a file is deleted, its disk blocks are added to the free space list.

The free space list can be implemented as a *bit map* or *bit table*. The status of a disk block is represented with binary value, that is, zero or one. When a disk block is free, it is zero, otherwise, when the block is allocated to a file, it is one. The bit table is easy to access for sequential access file or direct-access file. However, the space required to store the bit map may be too large (may be in MBs). If the bit map is stored on the disk, then the large space required to manage the free space may not be affordable for the system. For a free block, the bit map is accessed first. It increases the I/O required to access the disk. Due to this reason, it may be inefficient to put the bit map on the disk. It would be better if it was in the memory. However, if the disk is of high capacity, then the bit map will be huge in size. Moreover, it would be very time consuming to search a large-sized bit map in the memory.

Example 13.7

Give the bit map for the disk shown in the figure.

Solution

The bit map for the given disk would be:

1010111010111101110111101

Another method to manage the free space is *linked list* implementation. In this, all the free blocks are linked together so that there is no need to maintain a bit map separately. A special pointer on he disk is reserved that points to the first free disk block. The first free block points to the second free block, the second block points to the third one, and so on (see Fig. 13.12). In this way, every free block will contain a pointer to the next free block on the disk. However, this implementation will incur the cost of storing the pointers, and accessing the linked list involves substantial I/O time.

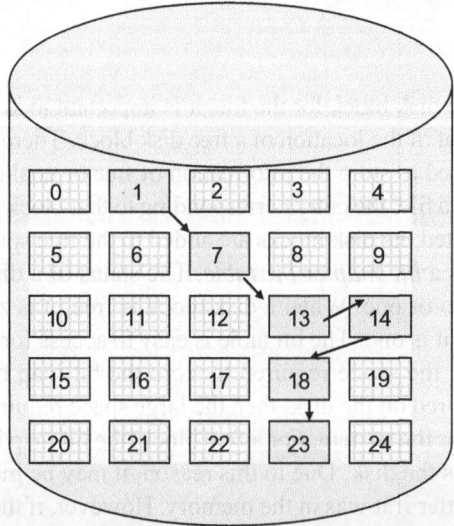

Fig. 13.12 Linked list implementation for free space management

13.8 DIRECTORY IMPLEMENTATION

As discussed in Chapter 12, a file system uses directory to provide a way to name and organize multiple files. The primary purpose of directory is to manage a list of files and to connect the name in the directory with the associated file. There is a handler associated with each file name in the directory that refers to the contents of that file. The directory therefore stores both the name of the file and the pointer to the FCB of the file. Since the FCB stores the meta-information about the file and pointer to the actual contents of the file, it becomes the handler of the file in the directory. To look for a file in a directory, the directory searches its name as key and the FCB is a reference that allows the file system to access the contents of the file and other meta-data of the file.

The simplest technique to implement a directory is to have a linear list. However, unsorted linear list containing directory entries may become inefficient when there are large numbers of file names as it needs to have a scan of entire directory, thereby consuming a significant lookup time. In spite of the drawbacks of linear list implementation, it is used widely due to its simplicity. Keeping in view the drawbacks of the linear list to store the directory entries, the data structure chosen must fulfil the following:

- It should perform efficient lookups on the list.
- It should have reasonable cost for insertions or deletions in the list.

Therefore, the directory implementation can be better done with B-tree, hash tables, or radix sorting methods.

13.9 BACKUP AND RECOVERY

There may be several reasons for data loss; disk crash is one of them. Therefore, it becomes necessary to backup data such that they can be recovered in case of any data loss. There are three types of backups discussed as follows.

13.9.1 Physical Backup

This is the simplest type of backup. The copying of data on backup medium is done bit by bit without any interpretation of where the file belongs. In other words, there is no meta-data information about the files or logical structure of the file system. Since the logical structure of the backup data is not known, the selected data cannot be restored while recovering from the backup. The entire file system needs to be restored. Moreover, the backed-up data may be in corrupted form or the backed-up block may not contain any data.

13.9.2 Logical Backup

This type has the interpretation of the files that need to be backed-up. For example, it inspects the directory structure for the files. Since the logical structure of the file system is known here, the selected files may be restored while recovering the data from the backup.

13.9.3 Incremental Backup

It is not necessary that the information or data changes every day. The incremental backup does not support the backup of whole data either for physical or logical backup. It takes the backup of only those data that have been changed since the last backup. How much data changes in which duration can be surveyed. For example, the data changes weekly. In this case, a weekly backup of the data that have changed since last week is done. Thus, the incremental backup is fast as less data need to be backed-up.

13.10 FILE SYSTEM INCONSISTENCY

The file system maintains some data structures that get updated on the file-related operations, or the data blocks of a file get updated. However, the changes are done in a buffer as described earlier, and the disk is updated asynchronously. It means that the state of the file system on the disk lags behind what it represents in the buffer. If the data are not updated properly, the file system will result into some inconsistencies that may lead to wrong file operations or no operation. Some of the file system inconsistencies are described as follows:

- In case of delayed write operation, if the modified blocks are still in the cache and if the system crashes at that moment, then the file system will result into an inconsistent state as the modified blocks have not been written on the disk. This problem of inconsistency increases if these modified blocks are directory blocks, free-list blocks, and so on.
- Several file-related operations update multiple data structures and if there is a system crash in between, then it will cause inconsistency. For example, while creating a new file, an FCB is created by allocating space for it. After this, the appropriate directory is read in the memory, updated for the new file name and its FCB, and written back to the disk. Now, if the system crashes due to any reason in between these operations for creating a new file, then it may be possible that the file is created but not shown in the directory, leading to inconsistency. In another example, if a data block is allocated for a growing file, then its bit map also needs to be updated. However, if the system crashes after allocating the data block, then its bit map will not be updated and will again, lead to inconsistency in the system.
- If a system is not shut-down properly, then it may also cause inconsistency in the file system.
- Inconsistencies may also result due to defective hardware. It may be the case that blocks are damaged on the disk drive or a disk controller is not functioning properly.

In the light of this discussion, it can be said that inconsistencies in the file system may result in some catastrophic situations in the system. Therefore, there must be some checks against these inconsistencies and action must be taken if they are found. There are some tools that can perform this function. These tools can check for the consistency of files and blocks while the system is booted. Some of the checks are as follows:

13.10.1 Superblock Check

Since the superblock is a data structure used to store the key information regarding a file system, it gets updated with every operation on the files. For example, if a file is allocated a new data block, the free block count field of the superblock should be decremented. Similarly, the date/time of the last modification field should also be updated. If these are not updated, then there may be several inconsistencies in the file system. The superblock may be checked for all the static parameters mentioned in it such as:

- number and size of data blocks in the file system
- number of FCBs and
- free FCB count.

Further, any of the free blocks should not be claimed by any file as it also leads to inconsistency. Therefore, free block count is also checked.

13.10.2 File Control Block Check

The FCB may also be checked for many parameters that may cause inconsistency if these are changed somehow. When a file system is created, a fixed number of FCBs are created but not allocated to any file. They are allocated as per the needs of a file created. An FCB that has not been allocated must be checked for whether it is pointing to any file or directory. It is possible that due to some hardware failure, some bad data may get written into the FCB. Therefore, a check is required here. The following types of checks can be done in an FCB to avoid inconsistency:

- A file may get an entry in multiple directories due to hard links. Therefore, there is a count in FCB that indicates its entry in multiple directories and must be checked for consistency. It is possible that the FCB count differs from the count of directories a file has entered. For example, the FCB count is four but in actual, the file has entries in three directories. This happens when a file has been deleted in a directory but the FCB has not been updated accordingly.
- The FCB contains the pointers to the blocks that make a file. It may be possible that a block is claimed by two FCBs resulting in duplicate block allocation. Therefore, each block number must be checked that only a single FCB claims it. Similarly, inconsistencies may happen when the FCB contains indirect blocks.
- The FCB can also be checked for bad blocks allocated to a file. If the block pointed by the FCB lies within the range supported by the file system, then there is no inconsistency; otherwise, the block number is a bad one.
- The FCB also contains a field for count of data blocks it points to. This must be also checked for consistency. If the count in an FCB does not match with actual number of blocks, then it means that it has not been updated since deletion in a file.

13. 11 FILE SYSTEM PERFORMANCE ISSUES

Since the file system performance is critical to the user and resources, several issues must be considered while designing and running the file system. Some of the issues are discussed as follows:

13.11.1 Block Size

The block size on the disk is one of the issues that affect the performance of the file system. If the block size is too large, then the smaller files (say, 1KB in size) will waste much space in the block. On the other hand, if the block size is too small, then the file system will need more number of disk blocks to store the file. This in turn increases seek time, rotational delay, and so on, increasing the access time of a file. Thus, smaller block size will affect the performance of a file system. Thus, there is a conflict between performance of the file system and space utilization on the disk. Therefore, the designer who decides the size of a block must keep in mind the average size of a file in an environment and should take a medium size such that space wastage and access time are minimal. In general, the block size used is 4KB.

13.11.2 Input–Output Transfer Time

It is a known fact that a disk access is slower (generally measured in milliseconds) as compared to the memory access that corresponds to several millions of clock cycles spent waiting for data to be fetched from the disk. If there is too much usage on file system to access data from the disk, then the system gets slow. To handle this, first, it needs to be identified where and how much is the dependence of the file system. The aim is to prevent heavy usage of the file system, that is, to reduce the disk I/O time. For this purpose, the system is checked to know whether there is a heavy use of file-system-related system calls. There are tools available that point out the places of heavy use of these system calls. After recognizing the problem area, an appropriate remedy can be found out. For example, a slow application reads some data from a server. In this case, rather than reading from the server each time, the desired data may be cached in the memory. The tools are helpful in detecting redundant file operations, discovering which files are being used by the user application, consuming much time in reading, and so on. The following are some methods through which the number of I/O transfers can be reduced:

Cache

One of the methods to reduce I/O transfer is to use buffer cache. It would be better if the frequent disk block accesses were placed in the memory as cache and retrieved from the memory itself to increase the performance of the file system. Whenever there is a requirement to access the file contents from the disk, the cache will be searched first. If it is not in the cache, then only the contents will be retrieved from the disk. Therefore, care should be taken in designing a cache such that only frequently accessed contents are stored in it, thereby making hit ratio high. The performance will be degraded if the hit ratio is very low. Another issue in cache design is to update the cached data blocks (on the disk) that have been modified. There may always be a possibility that the system crashes while the critical updated data is still in the cache. Therefore, a policy can be established to update any block on the disk immediately or to update the data blocks periodically. The file system can also reserve data blocks to be allocated on the disk but are stored in buffer cache for some time. A virtual extent can be prepared in the memory for the reserved blocks. In this way, the I/O transfers with the disk are reduced. To flush out the buffer, the real blocks on the disk are allocated to the virtual extent.

The cache implemented for disk blocks is implemented as *page cache* by some systems. The page cache is implemented with paging memory management. The VM system implements a page cache, and the file system uses this facility to cache files. Thus, it uses VM techniques to cache file data as pages rather than file data blocks.

Optimal Buffer Size

A buffer is needed to store the data read from the disk after which, the data is processed. The size of the buffer plays an important role in reducing the I/O transfer. If buffer size is very small, say 1K, and a large file is to be read from the disk, then it would require larger number of disk-reads to read the entire file. On the other hand, if the size of the buffer is large, then it would take less number of disk-reads. In this way, several smaller I/O transfers can be grouped into one large transfer. Thus, an optimal buffer size should be chosen such that a larger file should not consume much time in data transfers.

Some OSs use multiple read-ahead buffers to increase the parallel accessing of disk contents.

Sequential Reads

Another way to reduce I/O transfers is to perform sequential reads wherever possible. If there are small amounts of data scattered on the disk, then it would take much time in reading them as more number of I/O transfers are needed. On the other hand, if all these small data are compacted in one place and accessed sequentially in one or more transfers, then it will increase the system's performance. The future need for pages of a file can be predicted by observing the pattern in which a process accesses the file. Suppose if a process accesses two successive blocks of the file, the file system may assume that the process will continue to access the file sequentially and therefore, schedule the additional sequential reads.

Deferred I/O

When a disk space is allocated to a file, there is a possibility that contents of the new file will get mixed with the previous file that has been deleted now. To avoid this, the space allocated to the new file is filled with zeros to prevent interloping of data leftover from a previously deleted file. However, this will increase unnecessary write operations on the disk, decreasing the performance. The solution is to delay these write operations. When a file is read, the file system should write zeros to new areas only when there is an attempt to read from that area or when the file is closed. In this way, the delayed disk-write operations will help in reducing the I/O transfers for some time. The advantage here is that any I/O operation can be deferred until the time the application actually needs it. At some instances, if the I/O on a disk is delayed, contiguous range of blocks on the disk can be obtained and the file can be stored contiguously, which in turn increases the file system performance.

13.12 LOG-STRUCTURED FILE SYSTEM

The methods or tools chosen to check and repair the file system inconsistency may have limited use. It may be possible that the problem of inconsistency identified by the checker need not be repaired by it. Even the checker may miss some fields to check, thereby losing the file, directory, or any other data.

From another perspective, there are some technical problems with the traditional file systems some of which are described as follows:

- The memory sizes have been increased, increasing the buffer cache size for read-ahead purpose. Consequently, this will increase the traffic load on disk-write operation when there is time to flush out the cache contents and update the changes to the disk. However, the disk access and transfer bandwidth have not improved much in the years of time as the memory size has been increased or the processor has become so fast. Therefore, disk-write operations are sometimes very slow due to heavy load on the system.
- The traditional file systems spread the data on the disk such that the random accesses to them become slow. Further, the FCB and the file contents may be at some wide locations on the disk. This increases disk-seek and I/O time.
- The traditional file systems tend to write synchronously, that is, the changes are updated to the disk at the same time. This may affect the performance of the application in the system.

Keeping such problems in view, another file system known as *log-structured file system* (LFS) was devised. The LFS aims to improve the disk-write performance by writing all modifications to disk sequentially in a log structure, thereby avoiding all disk-seeks. A log is a sequential structure on the disk to store the last updates and an LFS stores data permanently in the log. The log consists of a series of segments where each segment contains file data and its meta-data information, and it also contains indexing information so that the files can be read back efficiently.

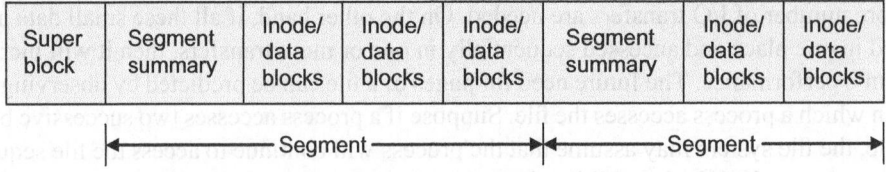

Super block	Segment summary	Inode/ data blocks	Inode/ data blocks	Inode/ data blocks	Segment summary	Inode/ data blocks	Inode/ data blocks

|← Segment →|← Segment →|

Fig. 13.13 General layout of an LFS

An LFS gathers a segment worth of data in the memory and appends the segment at the end of the log. For an LFS to operate efficiently, it must ensure that there are always large portions of free space available on the disk so that the recent updates can be maintained in the log. Initially, the log is allocated a single contiguous space on the disk but after some time, the free space may get fragmented into many small holes corresponding to the files that were deleted or overwritten. A segment cleaner is used to combine the holes and compact the file system allowing large extents of free blocks to be found. There are two methods for cleaning: *threading* and *copying*. In threading, the holes are not combined physically; rather, some data structure is used to note the location of the holes in free extents. However, this method is not feasible for the log as the fragmented holes will again add the cost in writing as in normal disk-write operation. In copying, the blocks are compacted together to form a large extent of free blocks. The compaction brings the holes together as sequential blocks.

As discussed earlier, when the system crashes while updating the disk, it may leave the system in an inconsistent state. It is very difficult to find where the last changes were made in a traditional file system. Since the recent updates are at the end of the log in an LFS, it is easy to determine the last changes. Thus, an LFS also helps in faster crash recovery by examining the most recent portion of log instead of scanning the entire disk to restore consistency after a crash.

The layout of an LFS consists of a superblock and a series of segments. Each segment at its start location has a data structure known as *segment summary* to identify the blocks in that segment as shown in Fig. 13.13. A segment may contain inodes (discussed in Section 13.3) as well as data blocks.

In an LFS, inodes are written to the log as compared to a fixed location on the disk. An inode map is used to maintain the current location of an inode corresponding to a file. Thus, for a given file, inode map is indexed to give the disk address for the inode of that file. The inode map is also written to the log as a file known as inode map file.

When a file is created, the new blocks are written at the end of the log. The sequence of writing is as follows: data blocks and inode blocks, directory data blocks, and inode map file blocks. While appending something to an existing file, new data blocks are added at the end of the log, and the corresponding meta-data are updated accordingly.

The superblock in an LFS consists of the following information:

- Number of allocated inodes in the system
- Block address for inode map file
- Block number of the next segment
- Segment size

The segment summary includes the following information:

- Number of blocks in the segment
- Data blocks in the segment
- Inode blocks in the segment

SUMMARY

All the implementation-related issues have been discussed in the chapter. The required data structures to implement the file system, along with the techniques of mapping the files on the storage, are given in detail. The file system needs to allocate the files on the secondary storage. The file allocation methods with their implementation have also been discussed. In contrast to traditional file systems, the LFS improves the disk-write performance.

Let us have a quick review of important concepts discussed in this chapter:

- The layered structure of the file system consists of four layers: logical file system, file organization module, basic file system, and I/O control.
- The FCB is an on-disk data structure that tracks the information such as which data blocks comprise a file, the size of a file, its owner and access rights, date of its creation, its access or modification, and so on.
- An extent is a simple list of block addresses wherein each address in the list is for a range of blocks.
- An extent is a compact way to refer to a large amount of data represented in the form of a pointer-length pair where the pointer is the address to the start address of the range of the blocks and the length is the number of blocks.
- The file system returns a pointer to the appropriate entry in the OFT known as *file descriptor* or *file handle*.
- The files may be allocated in two ways: *static allocation* and *dynamic allocation*. The static allocation is to allocate the maximum size of a file in advance when it is created. The dynamic allocation allocates the blocks as per the requirement.
- Contiguous file allocation is based on the fact that a file will be allocated contiguous blocks of storage on the disk at the time of its creation. It is suitable for both sequential as well as direct access files.

- In linked file allocation, any free block on the disk can be allocated, eradicating the problem of external fragmentation. It supports sequential access file.
- In indexed file allocation, each file is allocated an index block. An index block consists of block addresses of the file. In this way, all the pointers of a file are brought together at one place in the index block. This allocation is suitable for both sequential as well as direct access files.
- A free space list is a data structure that stores the information of free disk blocks.
- The bit map is a data structure used to implement the free space list by showing the status of a disk block with binary values.
- There are three types of backup: physical, logical, and incremental.
- In physical backup, the copying of data on backup medium is done without any interpretation of where the file belongs. In other words, there is no meta-data information about the files or logical structure of the file system.
- Logical backup has the interpretation of the files that need to be copied as backup.
- Incremental backup takes the backup of only those data that have been changed since the last backup.
- If the block size is too large, then the smaller files will waste much space in the block. On the other hand, if the block size is too small, then the file system will need more number of disk blocks to store the file.
- Caching frequent disk block accesses in memory and retrieving them from memory increase the performance of the file system.
- An optimal buffer size should be chosen such that a large file should not consume much time in data transfers.
- An LFS aims to improve the disk-write performance by writing all modifications to the disk sequentially in a log structure, thereby avoiding all disk-seeks.

MULTIPLE CHOICE QUESTIONS

1. _____ layer manages the directory structure where a file is located and provides the information about the file location to its lower layer.
   - (a) File organization module
   - (b) I/O control
   - (c) Logical file system
   - (d) Basic file system

2. _____ layer knows about the logical blocks of the file and translates them into physical blocks so that basic file system gets the physical blocks and processes further.
   - (a) File organization module
   - (b) I/O control
   - (c) Logical file system
   - (d) Basic file system

3. _____ layer issues the generic commands to the device drivers of the corresponding devices to read and write physical blocks.
   - (a) File organization module
   - (b) I/O control
   - (c) Logical file system
   - (d) Basic file system

4. _____ layer consists of device drivers and interrupt handlers so that the information between the main memory and the device can be transferred.
   - (a) File organization module
   - (b) I/O control
   - (c) Logical file system
   - (d) Basic file system

5. _____ tracks the information such as which data blocks comprise a file, the size of a file, its owner and access rights, and so on.
   (a) Superblock   (c) Free list
   (b) FCB   (d) File system identifier

6. _____ stores the key information about the file system on every partition (or volume) of the disk and is read into the memory after the system is booted, thereby protecting the integrity of the file system.
   (a) Superblock   (c) Free list
   (b) FCB   (d) File system identifier

7. _____ is also known as a magic number that uniquely identifies the file type.
   (a) Superblock   (c) Free list
   (b) FCB   (d) File system identifier

8. _____ is a process-independent data structure.
   (a) The SOFT   (c) The FCB
   (b) The OFT   (d) None

9. When using an indirect block, the FCB stores the block address of (i.e., a pointer to) _____.
   (a) data blocks   (c) the FCB
   (b) indirect block   (d) none

10. _____ is a compact way to refer to large amount of data represented in the form of pointer-length pair.
    (a) The FCB   (c) Extent
    (b) Indirect block   (d) None

11. The file system returns a pointer to the appropriate entry in the OFT. This pointer is known as
    (a) *file handle*   (c) *indirect pointer*
    (b) file descriptor   (d) none

12. There is minimum disk head movement in _____ file allocation.
    (a) contiguous   (c) indexed
    (b) linked   (d) none

13. The contiguous allocation is a _____ strategy.
    (a) post-allocation   (c) random
    (b) pre-allocation   (d) none

14. Which of the file allocation methods is suitable for both sequential as well as direct access files?
    (a) Contiguous only   (c) Indexed only
    (b) Linked Only   (d) Contiguous as well as indexed

15. In the indexed allocation, all the pointers of a file are brought together at one place in the___.
    (a) data block   (c) index block
    (b) indirect block   (d) none

16. In _____ backup, the copying of data on backup medium is done without any interpretation of where the file belongs.
    (a) a logical   (c) an incremental
    (b) a physical   (d) none

17. _____ backup has the interpretation of the files that need to be copied as backup.
    (a) Logical   (b) Physical
    (c) Incremental   (d) none

18. _____ backup takes the backup of only those data that have been modified since the last backup.
    (a) Logical   (c) Incrementall
    (b) Physica   (d) none

REVIEW QUESTIONS

1. Discuss all the layers in the layered structure of a file system.

2. Suppose a new file needs to be created. Discuss the role of all layers in this case.

3. Define the following:
   (a) Boot block   (b) Data block
   (c) Superblock   (d) Inode

4. Discuss and compare the roles of the SOFT and the OFT in file system implementation.

5. Discuss the file mapping on the disk using indirect blocks.

6. What is an extent? How is it different from the indirect block?

7. Explain various on-disk data structures while opening a file.

8. Explain various in-memory data structures while writing a file.

9. Explain and compare different file allocation methods.

10. What is a free-space list? How do we implement it?

11. What are the issues in implementing a directory?

12. What are the various ways for the backup of a file system?

13. Explain various types of superblock checks for file system inconsistencies.

14. Explain various types of FCB checks for file system inconsistencies.

15. How should the designer choose the block size in a file system?

16. How should the designer choose the buffer size in a file system?

17. How can cache reduce the I/O transfer time?

18. How can sequential reads reduce the I/O transfer time?

19. How can deferred I/O reduce the I/O transfer time?

20. What is an LFS? Discuss its general layout.

BRAIN TEASERS

1. What should be the inconsistency check against the bitmap?

2. In a file system, the bitmap itself consumes large space, (in megabytes). Moreover, the searching for the status of a disk block in bitmap is slow due to its large size. What can be the remedy for this problem and to increase the search efficiency?

3. Which file allocation method is appropriate for a long file that is accessed sequentially?

4. Which file allocation method is appropriate for a long file that is accessed randomly?

5. Which file allocation method is appropriate for a short file that is accessed sequentially?

6. How many disk I/O operations are required to read into the FCB of the following file? Assume that the memory does not have the FCB of root directory.

    D:/OS/kernel/FS/fileA.c

7. Following is a bitmap in a file system:

Block no.	0	1	2	3	4	5	6	7	8
Bitmap	0	0	0	1	0	0	1	1	1

Due to system crash, there is some inconsistency in the bitmap. The tool that checks inconsistency found the following bitmaps. Explain the meaning of these inconsistencies in the bitmaps.

(a)

Block no.	0	1	2	3	4	5	6	7	8
Bitmap	0	0	0	0	0	0	1	0	1

(b)

Block no.	0	1	2	3	4	5	6	7	8
Bitmap	0	0	2	1	0	0	1	0	1

8. Explain the meaning of the following file system inconsistencies found when checked with a tool:
   (a) FCB count for a file is found to be six but in actual, the file has entry in only four directories.
   (b) The FCB for FileA and the FCB for FileB point to the same data block.
   (c) The count of data blocks in the FCB is found to be six while the FCB points to only four blocks.

9. In what circumstances does compaction will be advantageous to eliminate the fragmentation in contiguous file allocation?

10. The linked file allocation eliminates the drawbacks of the contiguous file allocation. However, the linked allocation may consume more time as compared to the contiguous allocation. How can it be improved?

11. What can be the worst case in the performance of a system in the indexed file allocation?

Case Study IV: File Management in UNIX/ Solaris/Linux/Windows

UNIX

Files in UNIX are of the following types:

Ordinary/regular file

This type of file contains arbitrary data that is internally represented as a stream of bytes. It can be further categorized as follows:

Text file
It contains only printable characters.

Binary file

It contains both printable and non-printable characters that cover the entire ASCII range, for example, Picture, sound, video files, and so on.

Directory file

This type of file contains details of all the files and subdirectories underneath it. Directory files are actually regular files with special write protection privileges so that only the file system can write into them, whereas read access is available to user programs. For each file/subdirectory, it contains two things :
- a filename
- a unique ID for that file/subdirectory also known as its *index node* (*inode*) number

Device file

This type of files contains the details of various peripheral devices required during I/O. This information is stored in the file called /dev.

Named pipes

A pipe file buffers data received in its input, so that another process can read from the pipe's output. It receives the data on a first-in-first-out (FIFO) basis.

Links

A link is nothing but another file name for an existing file.

Symbolic links

This is a data file that contains the name of the file it is linked to.

Inode Structure and File Allocation in UNIX

System V Release 4 and almost all the other releases of UNIX identify each file using a distinctive inode number. When a system call is executed to access a file, its inode number is being referred. This inode number is nothing but an index into the inode table where the information about the file is stored. An inode table of a file is a data structure associated with each file that contains the metadata (data about data) for each file. Several file names may be associated with a single inode, but an active inode is associated with exactly one file, and each file is controlled by exactly one inode. The contents of a typical inode table residing in the disk are as follows:

- **File owner identifier and access permissions**

This identifier identifies both individual and group owners, and defines the set of users who have access rights to a file. Each class has access rights to read, write and execute the file, which can be set individually.

- **File type identifier**

A file can be of any of the types described in the previous sections.

- **File access time**

This identifier contains the time when a file was last accessed , when it was last modified, and when the corresponding inode was last modified.

- **Number of links to a file**

It includes the number of names the file has in the directory hierarchy.

- **Table of contents for the disk addresses of data in the file**
- **Size of file (in bytes)**
- **Address of the blocks where the file is physically present**

A typical inode entry of System V is shown below in Fig. CS4.1. Among other information, each inode entry in the inode table consists of 13 addresses that specify where the contents of a file are stored on the disk. These addresses may be numbered 0 to 12. Of these, the first 10 addresses(0–9) directly point to 1 KB blocks on the disk. The last three blocks, that is, 11 to 13 indirectly contain addresses of the blocks of files that have sizes greater than 10 KB.

As shown in Fig. CS4.1, the first 10 addresses point to the first 10 data blocks of the file. Each of the blocks is not necessarily stored on the contiguous location. If the file requires more than 10 data blocks, one or more levels of indirection are used as follows:

- The eleventh address in the inode table does not contain an address of a block. Instead it points to a block on the disk that contains the next portion of the index. It is capable of referring 256 more addresses. This is known as the *single indirect block*. This block can thus handle a file of maximum size 256 KB (256 × 1 KB).
- In case the file contains more blocks, the 12th address in the inode points to a block known as a *double indirect block*. This block points to a block of 256 addresses, each of which in turn points to another set of 256 addresses. These are the addresses of 1 KB chunks, making the maximum size accessible to be 256 × 256 KB = 64 MB.

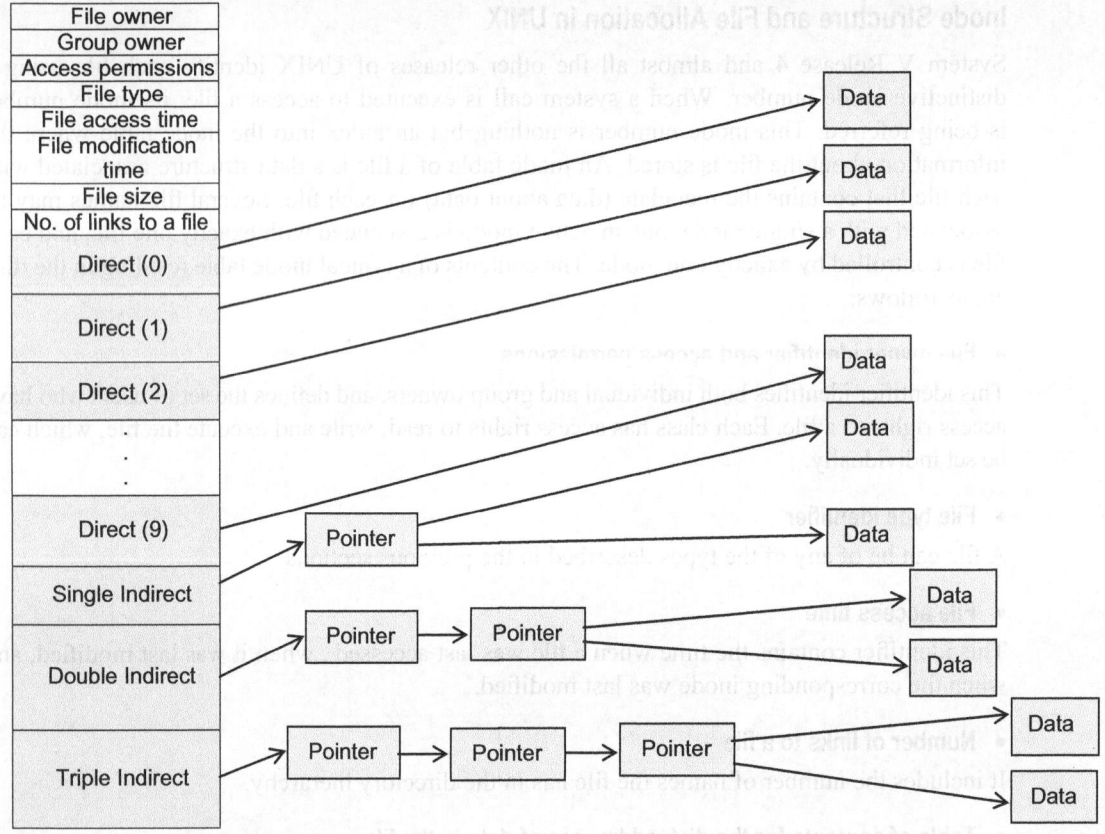

Fig. CS4.1 File allocation in UNIX

- If the file still contains more blocks, the 13th address in the inode points to a block known as a *triple indirect block*. It is a third level of indexing. This block also points to additional double indirect blocks. This level of addressing can support a file of maximum size 256 × 256 × 256 KB = 16 GB.

  In this way, SVR4 can together handle a file of 10 KB + 256 KB + 64 MB + 16 GB capacity.

File System Contents

A UNIX file system (UFS) is logically divided into the following four parts:

- **Boot block**

  This block marks the beginning of the file system. It contains 'bootstrap loader' that is the program used for booting the OS.

- **Super block**

  It describes the status of the file system such as its size, and current capacity.

- **Inode block**

  It contains the collection of inodes for each file.

- **Data block**

  It contains the actual file contents and subdirectories.

Directories

Directories are special files that give the file system its hierarchical structure. Its data content is a sequence of entries, each consisting of an inode number and the name of a file contained in the directory. When the file or directory is accessed, its i-number is used as an index into the inode table. The main reason for creating directories is to keep related files together and separate them from other group of files. A hierarchical directory structure followed by almost all the versions of UNIX is shown in Fig. CS4.2.

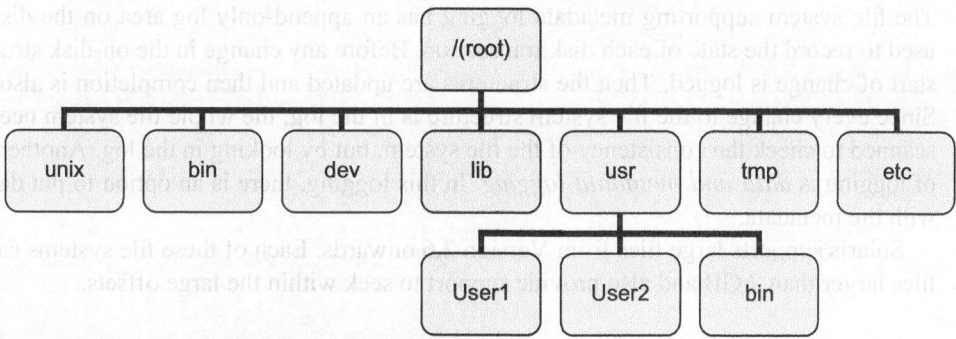

Fig. CS4.2   Hierarchical structure of UNIX file system

SOLARIS

Solaris provides multiple and different file systems. The default file system is UFS that holds all of the files in the root directory hierarchy of the file system. The UFS uses a storage device to store file data. That is why it is also known as *on-disk* or *regular* file system. In contrast to on-disk, there are some file systems that represent virtual devices such as processes and network sockets. These are known as *pseudo* file systems.

There are different file allocation methods for different file systems. However there are two common allocation methods supported by Solaris:

Block-based Allocation

This method is used by the traditional UFS. According to this method, it creates incremental disk space for a file. The disk blocks are allocated as the need arises so that there is a minimum allocation to conserve the space on the disk. When a file requires space, blocks are allocated from a free block map. However, sometimes blocks are allocated in a random order. Random block allocation can be avoided by optimizing the block allocation policy such that the blocks are allocated in a sequential manner. This reduces the disk seek time but results in fragmented disk blocks on the system. A file system block structure is maintained wherein address of the new block allocated and other information are stored. This data structure is known as *metadata*.

Extent Allocation

This method creates a large series of contiguous blocks. When a new file is created, it is allocated a large number of blocks, also known as an *extent*. On the subsequent demand also, the file is allocated extent of sequential blocks. The metadata is maintained as discussed in block allocation. However, the metadata here is just the starting block number and length for each extent. On the other hand, for block allocation, a lot of metadata for each file are maintained as block address of each disk block is required. Thus, the metadata write operations are reduced in this method as compared to the block allocation method. Since an extent is a group of sequential disk blocks, this allocation method optimizes the seek pattern.

The robustness of a file system can be increased by logging or journaling. Logging helps in preventing the file system structure corruption during a power or system failure. Logging logs changes to on-disk data in a separate log area such that an accurate structure of the file system is maintained. In case of any kind of failure, the state of the file system is known from file system log. *Metadata logging* is the type of logging used in most of the Solaris versions. The file system supporting metadata logging has an append-only log area on the disk that is used to record the state of each disk transaction. Before any change in the on-disk structures, a start of change is logged. Then the structures are updated and then completion is also logged. Since every change to the file system structure is in the log, the whole file system need not be scanned to check the consistency of the file system, but by looking in the log. Another method of logging is *data and metadata logging*. In this logging, there is an option to put data along with the metadata.

Solaris supports large files from Version 2.6 onwards. Each of these file systems can reside files larger than 2 GB and also provide support to seek within the large offsets.

LINUX

Since a user may work on various types of platforms, there may be a need to support various file systems. Linux supports a variety of file systems through a single, uniform file system interface through a *virtual file system* (VFS). The kernel supports more than 40 file systems of various origins. Linux kernel includes a layer between user processes (or the standard library) and the file system implementation. In this system, a user can view all the files and directories in the system under a single directory tree. It is intended to provide uniform ways of manipulating files, directories, and other objects. The user is not concerned about the location of file data and type of the file system. Thus, there is a VFS layer where all the user requests in the form of system calls related to the file are sent first. The VFS system layer acts as an interface through which a file of any file system can be accessed. The VFS layer after receiving a user request determines the file system to which the request actually belongs known as the *target file system*. For this purpose, a mapping function is called in the kernel that maps the call from the VFS into a call to the target file system. The target file system in turn converts the initial user request into device-specific instructions that are then passed to the concerned device driver (Fig. CS4.3).

The VFS is implemented as an object-oriented technology. The objects in its implementation are known as *VFS objects*. The following are VFS objects used in the VFS:

Superblock Object

The superblock contains the information about a mounted file system. It is created by the kernel and resides exclusively in the memory. Whenever a file system is mounted, the superblock data must be provided to the VFS. The superblock data are file system dependent. It may consist of the following data:

1. Pointer to the root inode, that is, the root of the file system
2. Type of the file system
3. Number of free blocks

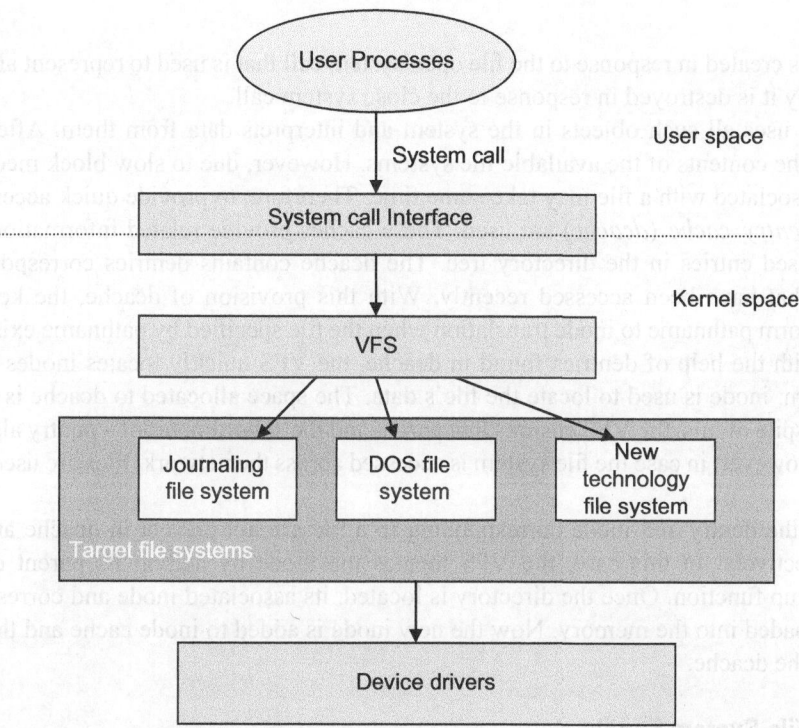

Fig. CS4.3.   Virtual file system

4. Number of free inodes
5. Basic block size
6. Function pointers to read, write, and manipulate inodes

Inode Object

Inode object associated with each file provides the information about a file or directory along with its location and data contents. This object does not contain the name of the file but is rather represented by a tuple containing an inode number and a number that identifies the file system that contains the inode.

Directory Entry Object

Each file in the VFS is represented as a file descriptor. This file descriptor contains the following information:

1. The inode being accessed,
2. The position in the file being accessed
3. The manner in which the data are being accessed, that is, which permission is executed (read/write/append-only, etc.)

To map file descriptors to the corresponding inodes, the VFS uses another object known as directory entry (dentry) object. A dentry object contains the name of file or directory an inode represents. Thus, a file descriptor points to a dentry and dentry in turn points to the corresponding inode. It also includes pointers to the parent dentry and subordinate dentries.

File Object

This object is created in response to the file open system call that is used to represent an opened file. Similarly it is destroyed in response to the close system call.

The VFS uses all such objects in the system and interprets data from them. After this, it determines the contents of the available file systems. However, due to slow block media, finding inode associated with a file may take some time. Therefore, to provide quick access, *inode cache* and *dentry cache* (*dcache*) are used. These caches provide related information for the frequently used entries in the directory tree. The dcache contains dentries corresponding to directories that have been accessed recently. With this provision of dcache, the kernel can quickly perform pathname to inode translation when the file specified by pathname exists in the memory. With the help of dentries found in dcache, the VFS quickly locates inodes in inode cache. In turn, inode is used to locate the file's data. The space allocated to dcache is not very large but in spite of this, the VFS ensures that parent and the subordinates of a dentry also reside in dcache. However, in case the file system is accessed across the network, files are used instead of dcache.

Initially, the dentry and inode corresponding to a file are not present in dcache and inode cache, respectively. In this case, the VFS locates the inode by calling its parent directory inode's lookup function. Once the directory is located, its associated inode and corresponding dentry are loaded into the memory. Now the new inode is added to inode cache and the dentry is added to the dcache.

Extended File System Family

Initially, Linux kernel had adapted the MINIX file system but could not evolve with this. The file system for Linux kernel was developed known as the *extended file system*. Many versions of this extended family have been released now. The following is the description of all these versions.

Second Extended File System

Its second version was released commercially, named as the *second extended file system* (ext2). This was the first file system using the VFS API. It solved major problems encountered in the MINIX file system. For example, in MINIX, there was limit of file name as of 14 characters maximum. The ext2 file system supports maximum data size of 4 TB and maximum file name length of 255 characters. Like this, there was much advancement in the ext2 file system.

Ext2 is a *block-based* file system that divides the hard disk into several blocks. The blocks are of the same size and files may occupy only integer multiples of the block size. The block size may range from 1KB to 8 KB. Since the blocks with big sizes require fewer I/O requests, I/O operations will speed up as less number of head seeks are required. The file size may range from 16 GB to 2 TB. The file system may be of size ranging from 4 TB to 32 TB. Ext2 is able to manage file systems on much bigger partitions.

It supports basic objects such as superblock, inodes and directories with their extended features. The disk space corresponding to ext2 file system is divided into fixed-size blocks of data. As discussed earlier, an inode represents files and directories in the ext2 file system. In each ext2 inode, there are 15 data block pointers. The first 12 data blocks are directly located by first 12 pointers. The remaining pointers are indirect pointers. The 13th pointer is a single indirect pointer, 14th is double indirect and 15th is triple indirect. If a file is smaller in size, that is, it consumes less than 12 blocks of data, it does not need any indirect pointer otherwise it needs some indirect pointers according to its size.

Ext2 has the provision of fast symbolic links. The reason for the fast symbolic links is that it does not use any data block on the file system but stores the target name on the inode itself. In this way, it speeds up link operation and saves disk space also. However, this implementation cannot be done for every link as the space available on inode is limited. The maximum size that can be supported in a fast symbolic link is 60 characters.

The central element of the ext2 file system is block group that is a cluster of contiguous blocks. The idea is to reduce seek time to access large groups of related data by storing related data in the same block group. The structure of a block group is shown in Fig. CS4.4.

Superblock	Group descriptors	Data bitmap	Inode bitmap	Inode table	Data blocks

Fig. CS4.4   Structure of a block group

Superblock

This block stores all characteristic data of the file system that the kernel first views while mounting the file system. Some of the data stored in superblock are as follows:

1. Total number of blocks in the file system
2. Total number of inodes in the file system
3. Total number of free blocks
4. Total number of free inodes
5. Total number of reserved blocks
6. Size of a block
7. Number of blocks per group
8. Number of inodes per group
9. The time at which the file system was mounted

Group descriptor

These blocks store the information about the contents of each block group of the file system, that is, the block numbers of inode bitmap, data bitmap and inode table. Besides these, they also contain some accounting information such as number of free block in the group, and number of free inodes in the group, number of directories in the group.

Inode table

It contains an entry for each inode in the block group.

Inode bitmap

The inode bitmap is a block used to provide an overview of the used and free inodes of a block group.

Each inode is represented as 'used' or 'free' by means of a single bit in inode bitmap. Thus, to track use of inode in a block group, an allocation bitmap is maintained wherein each bit corresponds to an entry in the group's inode table. At the time of file allocation, an available inode is selected from inode table to represent the file. At the same time, the bit in the inode bitmap corresponding to the inode's index in the inode table is turned on to reflect that the inode is in use. For example, if a file has been assigned 10th entry in inode table, the 10th bit in inode bitmap is turned on.

Data bitmap

To track the use of each group's block usage, another bitmap known as data bitmap or block allocation bitmap is maintained in the same manner as inode bitmap.

Data blocks

They contain useful data of the files in the file system.

Directories and Files

As described for UNIX, directories in ext2 are special files with pointers to inodes and their file names to represent files and subdirectories in the current directory. Each directory is represented by an inode to which data blocks are assigned. The blocks contain structures to describe the dentries. Each dentry consists of the following fields:

- inode number
- dentry length
- file name length
- file type
- file name

The ext2 file system is also able to represent objects such as devices and sockets as files.

Pre-allocation

The ext2 file system uses a new mechanism called pre-allocation. When there is demand for new blocks to be allocated for a file, it allocates the required blocks along with some additional blocks in the consecutive allocations. These extra blocks are kept for later use. This mechanism may save time when allocating the blocks to a file and also in preventing fragmentation. However, pre-allocated blocks may be overwritten if required.

Third Extended File System

Ext2 was later extended as the third extended file system (ext3) with more advanced features. It was ported into Linux kernel Version 2.4.15 in 2001. The block size in this file system ranges from 1 KB to 8 KB. The file size ranges from 16 GB to 2 TB. The file system size ranges from 2 TB to 32 TB. The ext3 file system was extended as a log-structured file system to have a consistent file system wherein the file data is logged in a log, also known as a *journal*. There are three modes by which the kernel may access the file system:

Writeback mode

In this mode, only changes to the file metadata are logged to the journal. In other words, the operations on useful data are not considered. Therefore, this mode provides the highest performance but does not provide any protection to the useful data.

Ordered mode

In this mode, only changes to the file metadata are logged to the journal, but changes to useful data are grouped and are always made *before* operations are performed on the metadata. This mode is therefore slightly slower than the writeback mode but provides data protection.

Journal mode

In this mode, along with the changes to metadata, useful data are also written to the journal. Thus, it provides the highest level of data protection.

The journal may reside in a special file with its inode or on a separate partition. The kernel includes a layer called a *journaling block device* (JBD) layer to handle journals and associated operations.

To accommodate the structure of a file system and for performance reasons, the transactions are broken down into the following smaller units:

Log records
These are the smallest units that can be logged.

Handles
Several log records when grouped together are known as a *handle*.

Transactions
Several handles when grouped together are known as a *transaction*.

In inspite of the advanced log facilities in the ext3 file system, ext2 is the preferred file system for flash and USB drives as it does not support logging. Since logging requires more writes to the storage unit, it can slow down the performance.

Forth Extended File System

The fourth extended file system (ext4) file system was developed as an extension to ext3. The stable version started from Linux version 2.6.28 in 2008. It uses a 48-bit addressing system that allows a maximum file size of 16 TB.

The maximum file system size it can support is 1 EB (Exabyte; 1 EB = 1024 PB and 1 PB = 1024 TB). Some of the features of ext4 are as follows:

1. Files stored on an ext4 file system are stored in extents that reduces fragmentation and improves performance. The contiguous space of 128 MB can be mapped with a single extent having block size of 4 KB. In the inode, there can be four extents. In case there are more than four extents, the rest of the extents are stored in an HTree (a specialized version of B-tree).
2. A directory can contain maximum 64,000 subdirectories, whereas ext3 supports 32,000.
3. It also uses multi-block allocation method that writes multiple blocks at once to increase the performance.
4. Along with multi-block allocation, delayed allocation is also used that flushes cache at a regular fixed time interval.
5. To improve performance, logging feature can be turned off, if required.
6. To improve the reliability, journal checksumming has been used.
7. An improved time stamp has been implemented in this file system. Since the Linux system may be used in mission critical systems, it provides time stamps measured in nanoseconds. Moreover, two more bits have been added in the seconds field of timestamp.
8. Pre-allocation is also supported in ext4.

Proc File System

This file system does not grant access to data stored on disk but provides certain kernel information in the form of virtual files. The purpose of this file system is to provide real-time information about the status of the kernel and processes in the system. Some of the available files or directories in the file system are as follows:

- Description of processor
- List of device controllers included in the kernel

- List of file systems supported
- Memory allocated to the kernel
- List of modules loaded in the kernel
- List of file systems mounted
- Kernel version
- Information on network protocols

Using this information, kernel behaviour can be modified without the need to recompile the sources, load modules, or reboot the system. This is quite useful to driver developers and system administrators who can refer this detailed information about system usage.

WINDOWS

Windows XP has a layer of file system drivers. File system drivers are responsible to implementing a particular file system format. Whatever the facilities a user uses from the file system are implemented through file system drivers only. Thus, they are interfaced between the user's view of file system and the actual representation of files on the storage. Furthermore, these drivers also perform some high level functions, such as virus protection and compression. Windows XP supports New Technology File System (NTFS) as its native file system format. It also supports some other formats to support various devices such as compact disk file systems for CDs and universal disk format for CDs and DVDs.

New Technology File System

Windows NT 3.1 onwards, the developers of Windows adopted a new file system known as NTFS. Now it is a default file system for Windows XP. It is a flexible and powerful file system intended to meet high-end requirements for workstations and servers. It addresses all the limitations of the file allocation table (FAT) file system previously used in Windows. It uses the concept of clusters along with the sector for disk storage, but the cluster is the fundamental unit of allocation in NTFS instead of sectors. The contiguous sectors on the same track form a *cluster*. A logical partition on the disk consisting of one or more clusters forms a *volume*. A volume consists of information about the file system. The clusters allocated to a file need not be contiguous. The maximum file size in NTFS can be 232 clusters. The use of clusters makes it possible to support non-standard disks that do not have 512-byte sector size (as NTFS does not recognize a sector). Another benefit is that it is possible to support large disks and large files by using a larger cluster size.

The NTFS considers every element on the volume as a file. Every file in turn consists of various attributes including data contents of a file. The layout of an NTFS volume consists of the following regions (Fig. CS4.5):

Partition boot sector	Master file table	System files	File area

Fig. CS4.5 Layout of NTFS volume

Partition Boot Sector

The size of this region is equal to the size of 16 sectors, that is, 512x16 containing the information about volume layout, file system structures, boot startup information, and so on.

Master File Table

This region has the information about all the files and directories on the volume including the metadata. The metadata may be the time of creation, file name, file permissions, archives, and so on. Each file has an entry in the master file table (MFT). Thus, the MFT is a list of files and their attributes. It is organized as 1024-byte rows called records. Each row describes a file. The required file attributes are as follows:

- **Standard information**

  It includes access attributes such as read and write, along with time stamp and link count (i.e., how many directories point to the file).

- **File name**

- **Security descriptor**

  It specifies the owner of a file and who can access it.

- **Data**

  It is the contents of a file.

  It may be possible that a file attribute does not fit into the file's first MFT record. In this case, the NTFS creates a special attribute that stores pointers to the attributes located in different records. On the basis of this, the attributes that fit into the file's first MFT record are known as *resident attributes* whereas the second category is called as *non-resident attributes*.

System Files

These are hidden files from the view of NTFS volume. This region is of 1 MB length consisting of the following files:

- **MFT2**

  It is a mirror of the first three rows of an MFT to access the information in case of single-sector failure.

- **Log file**

  It contains a list of transaction steps to recover any information in case of sector failure. Its size depends on the volume size.

- **Cluster bitmap**

  It shows which clusters are in use.

- **Bad cluster file**

  It consists of information about the bad clusters on the volume.

- **Security file**

  It contains a unique security descriptor for all files.

- **Attribute definitions**

  It is a table consisting of attribute names, numbers and description.

Data Streams

A data stream is a file attribute that stores file data. The NTFS allows multiple data streams for a single file and these streams store metadata about a file.

File Compression

The NTFS allows compressing of files and folders in Windows. For compressing a file, the NTFS divides the file's data into blocks of 16 contiguous clusters known as *compression units*. For this, the NTFS mainly uses Lempel–Ziv compression algorithm that is a lossless compression algorithm. It uses segmented compression by dividing files into compression units. It compresses one unit at a time. One unit may be of 16 clusters. Segmented compression is better observed in large files. The compressed files enable the decreased file access time. The benefit of segmented compression is that the file can be compressed even if it is being modified by an application.

File Encryption

Like compression, the NTFS encrypts the files in the unit of 16 clusters. Each unit is encrypted separately. It uses a public/private key pair to encrypt the files. The NTFS creates recovery keys that can be used to decrypt the files. The recover keys are helpful when a user forgets the private keys. The encryption keys are stored in the non-paged memory pool in the system due to security reason such that these are not written to the disk. Furthermore, these keys are stored in encrypted manner to increase the security.

Sparse Files

Although the compression reduces the space, decompression is a time-consuming process. As an alternative, the concept of sparse files has been taken. A sparse file is a file that has most of the data as zero (white spaces). If we store this file on the disk, it wastes most of the space in storing only zero entries. The scientific and database files may be sparse files containing very few data. A thread may be assigned the job of explicitly specifying the sparse file. This thread indicates areas of the file that contain large number of zeroes. The NTFS uses sparse files to store them on disk such that only non-zero data are stored consuming less space. The NTFS does not store zero data but keeps track of them using a *zero black list* for the file.

PART V

Input–Output Management

Case Study V: *Input/Output Management in UNIX/Solaris/Linux/Windows*

PART V

Input–Output Management

14. Basics of I/O Management

15. Disk Management

Case Study: F: Input–Output Management in
UNIX Solaris/Linux/Windows

14 Basics of I/O Management

14.1 INTRODUCTION

The most challenging task for an OS is to manage the I/O devices in a computer system. It acts as an interface between devices and other computer systems. This interface should be simple, user-friendly, and preferably, same for any type of device. However, today there are myriad input and output devices. Each I/O device has its own detail and complexity. In this case, the OS needs to be changed to incorporate every newly-introduced device. Therefore, the I/O operations should be treated separately in the OS, so that the other parts of the OS are not affected. The software which deals with the I/O, is known as *I/O software*. In I/O software, there are two types of modules. The first module deals with general functionalities when interfacing with any type of device, that is, these functions are common while interfacing with any I/O device and are known as *device-independent I/O softwares*. For example, there should be a general interface for any type of device. The second module provides device-specific code for controlling it and is known as *device driver*. The second module, in fact, takes care of the peculiarity and details of a particular device, that is, how to read or write data to the device. In this way, the OS need not change its code again and again to incorporate any new device. Its I/O software takes care of all the I/O devices to be interfaced with the system, without changing the OS code.

In this chapter, some basic concepts related to device management, such as various types of devices, how the I/O requests are implemented on devices, and so on, have been reviewed. To manage the devices, a layered structure has been discussed. It consists of two parts: I/O software and I/O hardware. The I/O software consists of user I/O software, kernel I/O sub-system, and device driver. Kernel I/O sub-system primarily provides the device independence, along with other functions, such as I/O scheduling, buffering, and so on. Device driver acts as an interface with the hardware consisting of device-specific functionalities. I/O hardware consists of two parts: device controller and the hardware device. The chapter discusses how the system call, as an I/O request, is implemented through the hierarchical layers on the devices.

14.2 TYPES OF DEVICES

There are various types of devices available today. They may vary depending on their operation, speed, data transfer, and so on. Some devices may be categorized based on these characteristics.

Learning Objectives

After reading this chapter, you should be able to understand:

- Various types of devices
- The need of device management
- Layered structure for I/O software
- The need of kernel I/O sub-system
- How the kernel I/O sub-system provides device independence
- Role of buffering in device management
- Types of buffering: single buffering and double buffering
- Role of caching in device management
- Life cycle of an I/O request

Even within a category, the devices may vary. This is the reason that device management is necessary as part of OS function. Some of the criteria, by which the devices are classified, are the following:

- *Human-readable* and *machine-readable*: The human-readable devices are mouse, keyboard, monitor, and so on, and the machine-readable devices are sensors, controllers, disks, tapes, and so on.
- Transfer of data: The devices transfer the data as a stream of bytes or in the form of a block. On the one hand, if the device accepts and delivers the data as a stream of characters/bytes, it is known as *character-oriented device*. Character-oriented devices are suitable where linear stream of bytes are required. For example, while accepting input data from the keyboard, a block of characters cannot be expected in one instance. Therefore, input devices like keyboard, mouse, modems, and so on, are all examples of character devices. Output devices of this kind, like printers, are also character devices. On the other hand, if the device accepts and delivers the data as fixed-size blocks, it is known as *block-oriented device*. Disk is the example of a block device.
- Type of access: On the basis of accessing data sequentially and randomly, the devices are called *sequential device* such as a tape drive, and *random access device*, such as a disk, respectively.
- *Network device*: Network devices, unlike conventional devices such as disk, need special I/O interfaces to send or receive data on a network. For example, a socket is a major I/O interface used for network devices.
- Complexity of control, data representation, error conditions, and so on.

14.3 TYPES OF I/O

There are three techniques by which an I/O operation can be performed on a device. These are known as I/O communication techniques. These techniques are used to have a mode of communication between the user request and the device, taking device characteristics into account.

14.3.1 Programmed I/O

Whenever a process is being executed and the processor finds an I/O instruction, it issues the commands to the appropriate device controller (discussed in Chapter 2). The device controller performs the operation by interfacing with the physical device, and then sets the status of the operation in a status register. But it is the job of the processor to check whether the operation has been done or not. For this purpose, it continually checks the status of the operation, until it finds that it is complete. Therefore, the process is busy waiting, until the I/O operation has been performed.

The I/O operation is performed using a processor register and a status register. On the one hand, when input operation is required, the device puts the data in the processor register. On the other hand, when output operation is required, the device reads the data from the register. After completion of the I/O operation, the status of the operation is written into the status register as a flag. In this way, the processor executes the instruction in such a way, that it is in direct control of the I/O operation, that is, sensing a device status, sending read/write command to the device, and transferring the data.

There is one disadvantage of this technique. During the I/O operation, the processor is not executing other instructions of the same process or any other process, and is being tied up for only one I/O operation. Programmed I/O is better for I/O operations that consume little time or systems where the CPU has no other job to do. However, for a multi-tasking environment, where there are several processes in queue waiting for the processor, it is a time-consuming procedure.

14.3.2 Interrupt-driven I/O

In programmed I/O technique, the processor time is wasted, as it continually interrogates the status of an I/O operation, while waiting. It would be better if the processor switches to another process to be executed, instead of waiting for the I/O operation to complete. Therefore, the processor issues an I/O command to the device controller for performing the operation, and switches to another processor by calling the scheduler that schedules the process to it. Then how does the processor know when the I/O is complete? This is done through an interrupt mechanism. When the operation is complete, the device controller generates an interrupt to the processor. In fact, the processor checks for the interrupt after every instruction cycle. After detecting an interrupt, the processor will stop what it was doing by saving the state of the current process and resumes the previous process (where I/O occurred), by executing the appropriate interrupt service routine. The processor then performs the data transfer for the I/O operation. For example, when a user requests a read operation from an input device, the processor issues the read command to the device controller. The device controller, after receiving this command, starts reading from the input device. The input data from the device need to be stored in the controller's registers. But it may take some time, and this time is sufficient to serve any other process. Therefore, the processor is scheduled to execute any other process in the queue. As soon as the data become available in the controller's register, the controller signals an interrupt to the processor. The appropriate interrupt handler is run, so that the processor is able to get the data from the controller's register, and save the same in the memory.

I/O management takes the help of interrupt-driven I/O. Modern OSs are interrupt driven, that is, they service the I/O requests, using the interrupt mechanism.

14.3.3 Input–Output Using DMA

When a user wants to input some data through the keyboard or some data are printed on the screen, after every character to be input or output, the processor intervention is needed, to transfer the data between the device controller and the memory. Suppose, a user inputs a string of length 50 characters, and to input each character, a time period of 10ms is required. It means, between two inputs, there is a gap period of 10ms, causing an interrupt. It results in a number of interrupts, just to enter a 50 characters-long string. Thus, when the data are large, interrupt-driven I/O is not efficient. In this case, instead of reading one character at a time through the processor, a block of characters is read. This operation is known as *direct memory access* (DMA), that is, operation done without processor intervention. In DMA, the interrupt will not be generated after every character input; rather, a block of characters is maintained, and this block is read or written. So, when a user wishes to read or write this block, the processor sends the command, and rest of the responsibility to do I/O operation for one block to the DMA controller. The processor passes the following information to the DMA controller:

- The type of request (read or write)
- The address of the I/O device to which I/O operation is to be carried out
- The start address of the memory, where the data need to be written or read from, along with the total number of words. The DMA controller then copies this address and the word count to its registers.

Therefore in DMA-based I/O, instead of generating multiple interrupts after every character, a single interrupt is generated for a block; reducing the involvement of the processor. The processor just starts the operation and then finishes the operation, by transferring the data between the device controller and memory.

14.4 INPUT–OUTPUT MANAGEMENT ISSUES

Since there are various types of devices available today, I/O management becomes difficult. Let us first understand the issues in I/O management.

System Response

A user interacts with the devices, that is, it provides input to the computer system and expects output from it. Therefore, the system must respond within a stipulated time. Thus, in this case, an interrupt-driven I/O, or programmed I/O, is required to implement communication between the user and the devices.

Transfer of Information

Some devices cannot be interfaced on a character basis, as in the case of a keyboard. For example, the disk cannot be read character by character. Therefore, the information is transferred in the form of blocks. A block is read or written from/to the device.

Uniform Interfacing

All the devices are not same in structure or provide/access the same information. For example, a disk is different from a CD, and it is different from a tape drive. But a user is unaware of the hardware details of the devices it is accessing. For the user, read is a general operation required for every device, that is, the user will give the read command to the device, irrespective of its type or version. Therefore, uniform interfacing is an issue in I/O design. There should be a mechanism by which the user can issue some general commands to the device and interface them.

Device Independence

With the introduction of new varying devices, it is not possible to modify the OS code frequently. Therefore, I/O should be device-independent, such that the OS need not be modified. However, the kernel cannot achieve this. Therefore, I/O is designed as a layered structure that hides the hardware details in lower layers, and the user processes, and some upper layers access the I/O devices, using some general functions like read, write, and so on. In this way, the I/O function can be divided into two parts: general and the device-specific or device-dependent. This hierarchy will abstract the general functions of the kernel separate from the device-specific details, and changes will be done only in those layers.

Speed Mismatch

Despite the availability of different types of I/O devices, they are still slower than the processors and the main memory that are available today. This affects the performance of I/O operations. Suppose a user is reading from the disk and processing the data. The data, accessed from the disk, are processed quickly by the processor, and it waits for the next data. However, the device has not accessed the data yet. In this case, the process needs to wait and the processor sits idle, decreasing the efficiency of the system. To resolve this issue, buffering is used.

Multi-tasking

In a multi-tasking environment, there may be multiple tasks assigned to a device. There must be some mechanism to order their requests and schedule them such, that performance of the system is not affected. The system should not allow a device to hold a process for a long time, or a slow-speed device to execute a critical process. For this purpose, various I/O requests are maintained in the device queue. For example, to serve the I/O requests on the disk efficiently, disk scheduling is done.

Communication Medium

The network devices available today are faster, and demand better management of communications traffic across the network. But the types, characteristics, and performance issues of the network devices are different from the general block or character-oriented devices. For example, the read() or write() system call, used for accessing the conventional devices, cannot be used to access the network devices. In UNIX, the I/O interface is in the form of sockets. Moreover, the wireless devices need to have different mechanisms for different I/O operations. Thus, either wired networking devices or wireless networking devices demand that the OS must negotiate with the medium to communicate. The I/O design, in this case, depends upon the nature of the medium being used.

Protection

The most important issue in I/O design is the protection of I/O devices. They must be protected from any illegal use, and in case of any error, they must be notified. Moreover, the resources that have been shared must be protected from concurrent use, by multiple tasks.

14.5 INPUT–OUTPUT SOFTWARE

Keeping in view the goal of I/O to be device-independent, it needs to have a layered design to incorporate its functionality; such that there is no change in the kernel code with the introduction of new devices. I/O is designed as a hierarchical layered structure, wherein different layers perform I/O functions. Each layer has its own specified function, provides its services to its next higher layer, and conceals the details of services provided by its lower layer. The design of the layers is defined in such a way, that changes in one layer do not affect the other layers. The functions of the layers and the interfaces may differ from system to system. A general layered structure of I/O is shown in Fig. 14.1.

14.5.1 User-level Input–Output Software

This is a part of the I/O software situated in the user space (see Fig. 14.1). When the user requests an I/O through a system call in a program, there is a library routine corresponding to the system call. The library routine, when called, is linked to the program, and becomes a part of the object program in the memory. Thus, all the library routines are part of the I/O software. In fact, there is a standard I/O library, consisting of a number of routines for I/O.

14.5.2 Kernel Input–Output Sub-system

This part of the I/O software is provided in the kernel space. The user interacts with this layer to access any device. Since the user does not know the hardware details of the devices or its

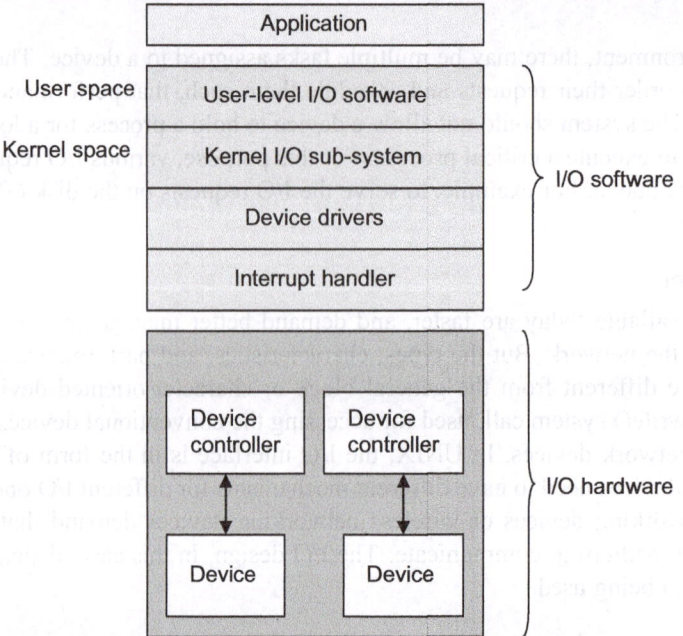

Fig. 14.1 Layered structure of I/O

controllers, this layer provides uniform interfacing to all devices. The user need not worry about the devices, the device drivers, or controllers. So through the system call for a specific I/O function, the user is able to interact with the device. It has another advantage by which I/O devices are protected from any illegal I/O request. Since the device is referenced through a symbolic name, instead of its hardware configuration, thereby hiding its hardware details, the I/O software takes care of mapping the symbolic names to their actual hardware.

Besides being device-independent, it is also responsible for providing access control to I/O devices. A device cannot perform all the I/O operations. So the I/O software needs to check the type of access a device provides, thereby providing operational control. After providing the right access to the device, it may be possible that multiple processes are waiting to access the same device. Therefore, there may be a queue on the device. In this case, the device is busy, and the processes in wait must be scheduled in some order, such that the efficiency of the system increases. This is known as *device scheduling*. Thus, the kernel I/O sub-system must also check the device status to find whether it is busy or available.

To avoid mismatch between the speed of the processor and access speed of I/O devices, some methods are necessary for accessing I/O devices, and hence increase performance of the system. These methods include buffering, caching, spooling, and so on. For example, to cope with the slow access speed of the device, one buffer is introduced between the process and the device, to store the input or output data. It is then sent to the process (for input data) or to the device (for output data) asynchronously.

It is possible that some errors may prevent the access to I/O devices. These errors must be notified and handled properly by I/O software, so that the system runs properly.

Thus, the kernel I/O sub-system performs all the necessary functions to access the I/O devices, but the hardware details of the devices are not shown or required here. As we move down the hierarchy of the layers, as shown in Fig. 14.1, we will find that hardware devices comprise the lower layers.

14.5.3 Device Driver

Each device needs a device-specific code for controlling it, and this code is known as the device driver of that device. Each device has a device controller that has some device registers for performing I/O operations on the device. But the number of device registers and the nature of commands for performing I/O operations vary from device to device. Therefore, to communicate with each type of device controller, a device driver is written. This takes care of the specific device controller registers and the commands. Thus, the device drivers act as a layer that hides the differences among the device controllers.

The first function of a device driver is to accept the I/O requests from the kernel I/O sub-system. It checks the input parameters provided in the I/O requests. If there is something wrong with the parameters, such as invalid parameter, it may generate an error. Otherwise, it translates the logical address to the actual hardware details. For example, for a disk read, a logical block number is converted into the disk address in the form of a cylinder, track, and sector.

Before starting an I/O operation, the device driver also needs to check the availability of a device and informs the same to its upper layer, that is, kernel I/O sub-system. If the device is busy, the request is queued on the device queue. The device may not be available to the system, due to some failure or other reason. An error code is returned, if the device is not available. If the device is available, the device driver starts the operation. The scheduling of I/O requests, in case of busy device, is performed according to the scheduling algorithm chosen by the kernel I/O sub-system. Once the device is scheduled, the device driver can start the I/O operation after initializing the device, if there is such a need.

The next function of the device driver is to control the I/O operation. To perform an I/O operation, there may be more than one command. The sequence of these commands is determined according to the operation required to be performed. After fixing the commands' sequence, the device driver interfaces with the device controller and writes the sequence of commands to its registers, one by one. After writing one command, the device driver checks to see whether the device controller is able to accept it or not. If it is ready, other commands follow. Otherwise, the device driver waits and blocks itself, until an interrupt unblocks it. If the commands are written to the device controller, I/O operation is performed by interacting with the actual device. There may be some data, as a result of I/O operation, which the device driver may retrieve again, from the controller's registers, and send them to the layer above it.

It may be possible that many applications need to interact with various devices, which are of the same type. For this purpose, all such devices have a common device driver. In this case, the device driver must know which application needs to interface with what device. Therefore, it uses a *mapping table* that keeps track of which application uses what device. In this environment, the common device driver may use more than one resource. Therefore, it needs to keep a track of use of the resources. Sometimes, it may desire to have a mutually-exclusive access to a resource. Therefore, the device driver uses a *resource table* that keeps track of which resources are being used by the device driver. Thus, the common device driver uses two data structures-mapping table and resource table- to select an appropriate I/O through an *I/O channel*, as shown in Fig. 14.2. An I/O channel is primarily a small computer, basically used to handle the I/O from multiple sources. It ensures that I/O traffic is smooth.

14.5.4 Interrupt Handling

The device driver communicates with the device controllers, and then the device, with the help of the interrupt-handling mechanism. The last layer in this I/O software hierarchy is, therefore,

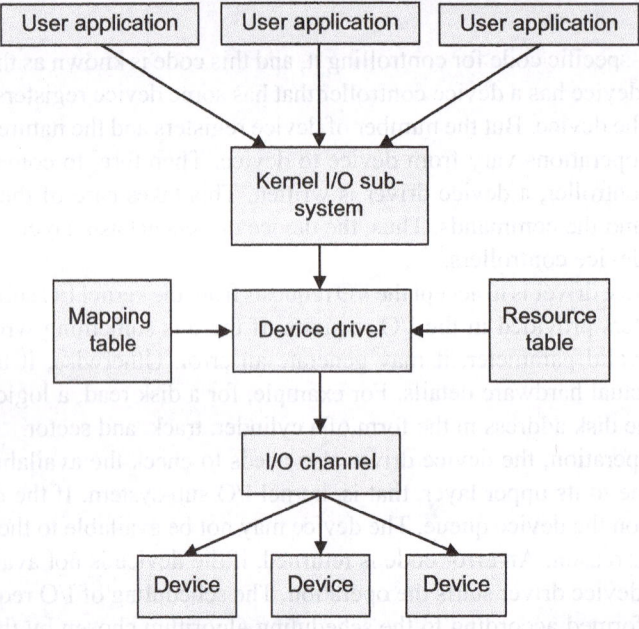

Fig. 14.2 Device driver interface

the interrupt handler. When the device controller interacts with the actual device, the data are transferred between the actual device and the controller, according to the I/O operation; that is, the data from the device are written to the controller's register, in case of an input operation, or the data from the controller's register are sent to the device, in case of an output operation. After the completion of the I/O operation at the level of device and device controller, the device controller generates an interrupt to the device driver. The Interrupt Service Routine (ISR) is executed in order to handle a specific interrupt for an I/O operation. This routine extracts the required information from the device controller's register and performs the necessary action. After the completion of an ISR, the blocked device driver is unblocked, and it may run again.

14.6 KERNEL I/O SUB-SYSTEM

The different functions of the kernel I/O sub-system are discussed in the following subsections.

14.6.1 Uniform Interface

The kernel hides all the hardware details of the devices, and then presents the OS interface to its lower layer, that is, device drivers as a uniform interface. It means when the system call from the first layer is passed to this layer, it requires interfacing with the device driver of the desired device. Since there are different device drivers for various devices, the code of the kernel needs to be changed for every interface with the device drivers. There may be different driver functions available for the system to call, and different kernel functions that the driver needs to interface with. In this case, there will be no uniform interface and therefore, it will require changing the kernel code, according to the available device drivers. To avoid this, the device-independent I/O software layer attempts to make uniform the interface, such that all the drivers interface through a common interface. The layer uses the fact that not all the devices are different. There are some common functions or devices which belong to the same type. Although the exact system call to access the device may differ in various OSs, the device types are standardized based on the common functions.

By identifying a few general types of devices, a uniform interface for a specific type can be designed. The differences in the devices are encapsulated in the device drivers of the devices. Since this layer is independent of the hardware details, the OS designer need not worry about the device's actual details. The hardware manufacturers of the device also benefit from this, as they design new devices that are compatible with the existing interface type or they write device drivers to interface the new devices to popular OSs. In this way, new devices can be easily supported by the system, without changing its kernel code.

The user, who requests access to a device, does not know its location or its device controller. The request is made through a symbolic name. In this way, there is a uniform naming scheme, by which the application is interfacing with the devices. However, the symbolic names must be mapped to their respective device drivers and device controllers. The mapping to devices and their controllers is done by the device-independent layer, so that the uniform symbolic naming is visible to the user, hiding the details of where it will be mapped to the actual device. For example, in DOS, the filename starts with the disk symbolic name. C:/ represents the hard disk. It is defined in the OS that 'C' represents the primary hard disk. The 'C' symbolic name is then mapped to its port address through a device table. Similarly, in UNIX, there is a mount table, consisting of the names of the devices. These names also have the form of a name in file system name space. The inode for the special files for these devices provides two numbers: the major and minor device numbers. The major device number locates the device driver to handle the I/O on this device. The minor device number is passed to the device driver that uses this number to index into a device table, which locates the corresponding device controller.

14.6.2 Input–Output Scheduling

Since the speed of I/O device access is slow, as compared to the memory, or the execution speed of the processor, the order of I/O requests can be changed to increase the efficiency of the system. For this purpose, a device queue is maintained for every blocking I/O request. This device queue indicates how many requests are pending on that device. But the question is how to schedule the requests from the device queue, such that performance of the system, due to slow access speed of the device, is compensated. An FCFS order for serving the requests can be used, but that may degrade the system's performance. Therefore, some scheduling algorithms should be devised, keeping in view the structure of the I/O device, so that the efficiency and performance can be enhanced. For example, in case of disk, it matters where the disk arm is presently positioned. If the disk arm is near the end of the disk, it would be beneficial to access the request that wants the block near the end. Thus, an I/O scheduler schedules the I/O requests, according to the selected I/O scheduling algorithm and orders them. It not only increases the efficiency of the system, but also decreases its response time to the user. Before allocating the device to the I/O request in the device queue, the status of the device is checked. If the device is idle, it can be allocated, otherwise, it remains in the queue.

14.6.3 Buffering

Buffering is done for several reasons. Some of them will be discussed in this section. Before detailing the I/O buffer, let us first discuss the issues that lead to the concept of buffering.

When an I/O operation starts, the process waits for the result, that is, for reading the data from the device or writing the data to the device. This is due to the speed mismatch as discussed in I/O management issues. Suppose, a process needs to read the data from the disk, it issues a read system call, and then blocks, to wait for the data from the disk. But in this case, if a byte arrives, an interrupt is generated. The corresponding ISR unblocks the user process, and provides the byte to it. The process stores this byte somewhere in the memory, and reads another byte from the disk, and blocks again. This causes another interrupt. The ISR is executed, the process is unblocked, and the byte is handed to it, and this process is continued. Since the speed mismatch is too large between the user application and the devices, and even transfer between the devices, starting the user process for reading or writing a byte becomes a slow and tedious job using the interrupts.

Another problem is the availability of memory space. The memory locations in the memory area of a user process must be available, while data are being transferred. However, if the page containing the target locations is swapped out during the transfer time, the data being transferred are lost. One remedy to this problem is to lock the page containing the target locations for data transfer. But, there may be many processes locking the pages, and therefore, the number of available pages will reduce, resulting in poor performance. Thus, this approach of I/O transfer will interfere with virtual memory decisions.

An *I/O buffer* is a memory area where data are stored temporarily during an I/O operation. The problems discussed above can be resolved using buffers. A buffer is an area where the data, being read or written, are copied in it, so that the operation on the device can be performed with its own speed. Where in the memory will this buffer occupy space? If it is stored in the user memory (see Fig. 14.3(a)), the page containing the buffer needs to be locked. Therefore, the buffer should be given space in kernel memory. The buffer in the kernel space solves the problem of I/O transfers. When a user process initiates an I/O operation, the OS assigns a buffer in the kernel (see Fig. 14.3(b)). Now the data, to be read or written, are first copied to the buffer at the speed of the device. In this case, now the process is not blocked every time the byte is read or written from/to the device. Once the buffer is full, the buffer is copied to the user area in the memory. For example, if data are to be read from the disk, these continue to be stored in the buffer, until it is full. Once the buffer is full, these are copied to the user area, and then executed. Thus, the I/O operation is performed in one operation, instead of several operations, while there is no buffering, thereby increasing the performance of the system. Depending on the nature of the devices, buffers can be used to hold the bytes or lines, in case of a stream-oriented device, or a block, in case of a block-oriented device.

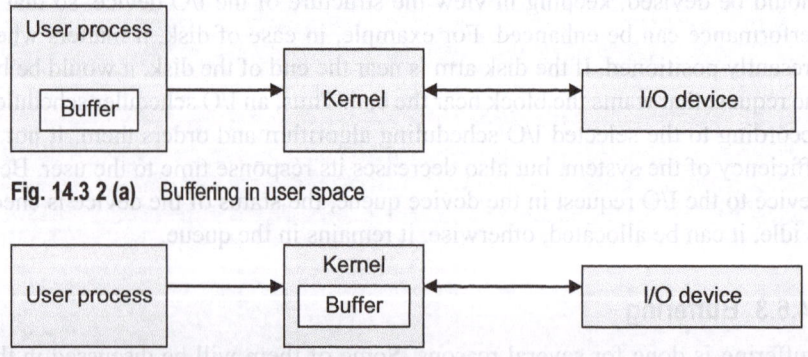

Fig. 14.3 2 (a)   Buffering in user space

Fig. 14.3 (b)   Buffering in kernel space

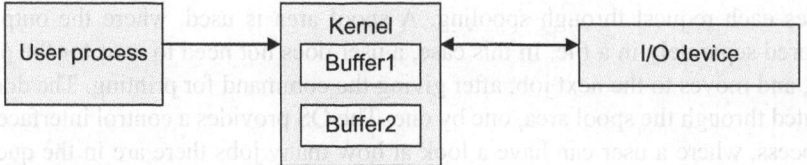

Fig. 14.3 (c)   Double buffering

While the buffer is full during an I/O operation, the full buffer is copied to the user space. However, when the buffer is being copied, I/O operation is continued. In that case, what will happen to the data that are still arriving? Obviously, those will be lost. Therefore, another buffer should be there, so that when one full buffer is being copied to the user area, the operation continues with the second one (see Fig.14.3(c)). This method is known as *double buffering*, and the earlier approach, wherein a single buffer is used, is known as *single buffering*. Double buffering, thus, smoothes out the flow of data between I/O devices and a process. The number of buffers may be increased, if needed, in case a process processes rapid bursts of I/O. However, this comes at the cost of maintaining the information by the OS to keep records of the buffers that are allocated to the processes.

14.6.4 Caching

While performing I/O operations, cache may be used between the devices and user application, to improve the efficiency of the operations. For example, some frequently-accessed data from the disk, which are stored in the cache, need not be read from the disk. In this way, a slower disk-to-memory operation is replaced with a faster memory-to-memory operation. Caching is also performed by the device-independent I/O software.

Cache memory is different from the buffer. A buffer is used to hold the data received from any input or output device, until they are flushed out to the process for reading or writing; a cache contains the copy of frequently-accessed data (that is already in the secondary storage) on a faster storage to be accessed quickly. Although caching and buffering are different, they can be merged for improving the I/O efficiency. When a disk-read operation is performed, the contents are first checked in the cache. If not found, the contents are read through the buffer, but must be copied to the cache also, such that the next read operation will find the contents in cache itself. Sometimes the buffer and cache share the same memory area, known as a *buffer cache*. The buffer cache is used for both buffering, as well as, caching. When a disk-read operation is initiated, the kernel will first check the buffer cache (used as a cache). If found, the operation can be performed, otherwise the data from the disk are read into the buffer cache (used as a buffer). Similarly, in case of a disk-write operation, the data to be written to the disk are accumulated in the buffer cache for a long time, but not written to the disk. Meanwhile, if there is a disk-read operation for the contents presently in the buffer cache, but not written to the disk, the buffer cache provides the contents. In this way, the buffer cache may be used for write operations also, using the delayed-write concept. Thus, the common memory area acts as both buffer as well as cache.

14.6.5 Spooling

The kernel I/O sub-system also performs the spooling function. It may be possible that many user requests arrive simultaneously for a shared resource. For example, multiple users send print requests concurrently. In this case, the kernel I/O sub-system queues up all the print requests and schedules each request through spooling. A spool area is used, where the output to be printed is stored separately in a file. In this case, a user does not need to wait for the printer to be available, and moves to the next job, after giving the command for printing. The documents are then printed through the spool area, one by one. The OS provides a control interface for this spooling process, where a user can have a look at how many jobs there are in the queue. The user may further suspend or delete the print job, if he/she wishes to do so.

14.6.6 Error Handling

The I/O functions, when performed, may sometimes result in errors. Though the device-specific errors are appropriately handled by the device drivers, the strategy to handle them is device-independent. Therefore, they are handled by device-independent I/O software, during I/O processing. There are two types of errors:

Transient Errors

These are temporary reasons that cause any I/O processing to fail. For example, there could be a problem in the network, due to which the packet could not be delivered to its destination. The problem is temporary, and the packet is delivered, as soon as the problem is eliminated.

Permanent Errors

These are permanent errors, due to the failure of any device or wrong I/O request. For example, if a disk is defective, no I/O operation can be performed on it.

The major task for the kernel I/O sub-system here is to handle I/O related errors, such that after knowing a specific error, it should be reported to the user process. Sometimes, the device-specific error is handled by the device driver. But, if the device driver does not handle the same, it is again passed on to the device-independent I/O software layer. It reports back to the user and gives options (retry, ignore, or cancel) for the next action. Sometimes it is not sufficient to display an error message to the user, but some action must also be taken as part of error handling. For example, in case of a corrupted root directory, an appropriate error message is displayed, and the system is also terminated.

14.7 LIFE CYCLE OF I/O REQUEST

Based on the layered structure of I/O software, the life cycle of an I/O request, from the software to the hardware level, is discussed in the following list (see Fig. 14.4):

1. A user issues an I/O system call in the program.
2. The shell part of the kernel receives it, checks its parameters for correctness, and interprets it.
3. The kernel I/O sub-system blocks the calling process, and maps the symbolic name of the device, mentioned in the I/O request, to its actual hardware.
4. If the system call is for an input data, the kernel I/O sub-system will check the contents of buffer cache. The data, if found, will be returned to the calling process and the I/O request is serviced.
5. If the input data are not found in the buffer cache, or the request is for an output, the I/O sub-system initializes the corresponding device driver of the device to be communicated, and sends the I/O request to it.
6. Kernel I/O sub-system checks the status of the device to find out whether it is busy or not, through the device driver. If it is busy, the I/O request is queued on the device queue, and scheduled accordingly.

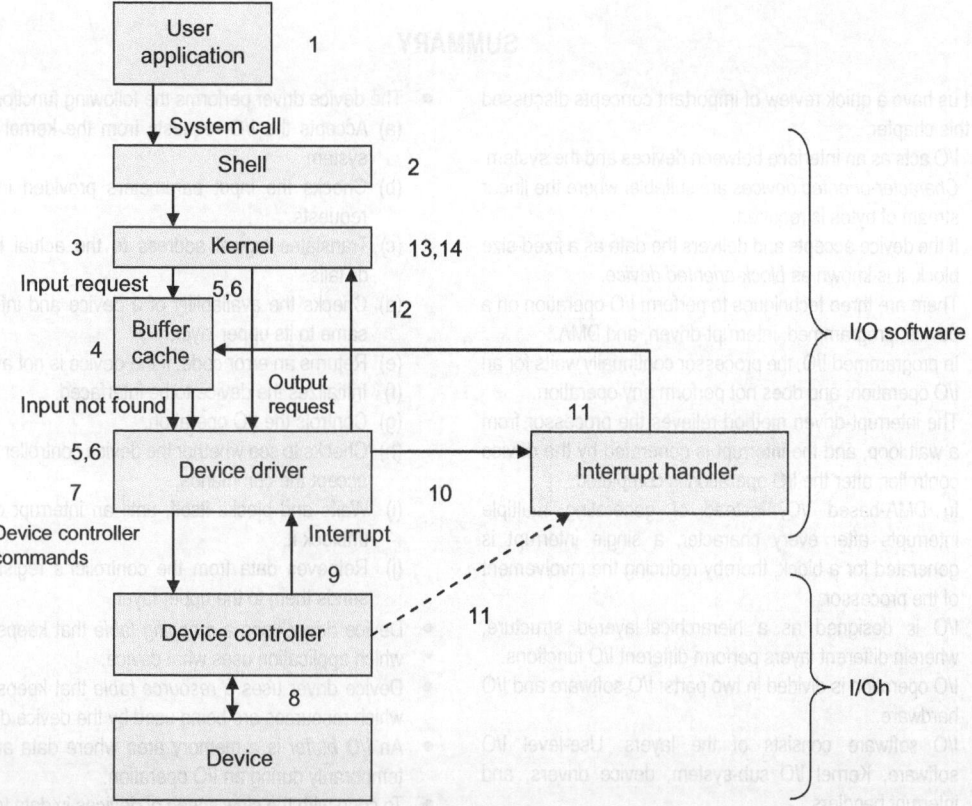

Fig. 14.4 Life cycle of an I/O request

7. Once the I/O request is scheduled on the device, the device driver processes the request, translates it into the device controller's specific commands, and writes them into its device-controller registers.

8. The device controller, in turn, interfaces with the actual device, and performs the data transfer. The data, from the device, are written to the controller's register, in case of input operation, or the data from the controller's register are sent to the device, in case of output operation.

9. The device controller, on completion of the data transfer, interrupts the device driver.

10. The device driver receives the interrupt and passes the control to an appropriate interrupt handler.

11. The interrupt handler extracts the required information from the device controller registers and stores the data in the buffer.

12. The device driver determines which I/O operation has been completed, in case there are multiple I/O requests pending, and signals the kernel I/O sub-system about it.

13. The kernel I/O sub-system unblocks the process that issued the system call and refreshes its status as ready, by moving it from the blocked queue to the ready queue.

14. The kernel I/O sub-system transfers the data from the buffer to the address space of the process, in case of input operation.

SUMMARY

Let us have a quick review of important concepts discussed in this chapter:

- I/O acts as an interface between devices and the system.
- *Character-oriented devices* are suitable, where the linear stream of bytes is required.
- If the device accepts and delivers the data as a fixed-size block, it is known as *block-oriented device*.
- There are three techniques to perform I/O operation on a device: programmed, interrupt-driven, and DMA.
- In programmed I/O, the processor continually waits for an I/O operation, and does not perform any operation.
- The interrupt-driven method relieves the processor from a wait loop, and the interrupt is generated by the device controller, after the I/O operation is completed.
- In DMA-based I/O, instead of generating multiple interrupts after every character, a single interrupt is generated for a block, thereby reducing the involvement of the processor.
- I/O is designed as a hierarchical-layered structure, wherein different layers perform different I/O functions.
- I/O operation is divided in two parts: I/O software and I/O hardware.
- I/O software consists of the layers: Use-level I/O software, Kernel I/O sub-system, device drivers, and interrupt handlers
- I/O Hardware consists of the layers: Device controllers and devices.
- Kernel I/O sub-system provides the following functions:
  (a) Uniform interfacing to all the devices.
  (b) Access control to the I/O devices.
  (c) I/O scheduling.
  (d) Buffering, caching, and spooling.
  (e) Error handling.
  (f) Configuring and initializing the device driver.
- The device-specific code is known as a device driver of that device. It acts as a layer that hides the differences among the device controllers.

- The device driver performs the following functions:
  (a) Accepts the I/O requests from the kernel I/O sub-system.
  (b) Checks the input parameters provided in the I/O requests.
  (c) Translates logical address to the actual hardware details.
  (d) Checks the availability of a device and informs the same to its upper layer.
  (e) Returns an error code, if the device is not available.
  (f) Initializes the device to be interfaced.
  (g) Controls the I/O operation.
  (h) Checks to see whether the device controller is able to accept the commands.
  (i) Waits and blocks itself, until an interrupt comes to unblock it.
  (j) Retrieves data from the controller's registers, and sends them to the upper layer.
- Device driver uses a *mapping table* that keeps track of which application uses what device.
- Device driver uses a *resource table* that keeps track of which resources are being used by the device driver.
- An *I/O buffer* is a memory area where data are stored temporarily during an I/O operation.
- To cope with the slow speed of devices in data transfer, a buffer, known as single buffering, is used.
- When one full buffer is being copied to the user area, the data may be lost, if coming continuously. In this case, another buffer is used to hold the data when the first buffer is emptied out. This is known as double buffering.
- The buffer cache is used for both buffering, as well as, caching.
- The kernel must notify the user about errors, and take further action as well.

MULTIPLE CHOICE QUESTIONS

1. For a multi-tasking environment, _____ is not a better choice.
   - (a) Programmed I/O
   - (c) DMA
   - (b) Interrupt-driven I/O
   - (d) None

2. _____ is not efficient in case of large data transfer.
   - (a) Programmed I/O
   - (c) DMA
   - (b) Interrupt-driven I/O
   - (d) None

3. Device independence is achieved through the _____.
   - (a) Device driver
   - (c) Device controller
   - (b) Kernel I/O sub-system
   - (d) none

4. The device-specific code is written into the _____.
   - (a) Device driver
   - (c) Device controller
   - (b) Kernel I/O sub-system
   - (d) none

5. _____ translates the logical address to the actual hardware details.

(a) Device driver   (c) Device controller

(b) Kernel I/O sub-system   (d) none

6. _____ generates an interrupt after the I/O operation.

(a) Device driver   (c) Device controller

(b) Kernel I/O sub-system   (d) none

7. _____ uses mapping table and resource table data structures.

(a) Device driver   (c) Device controller

(b) Kernel I/O sub-system   (d) none

8. _____ takes care of mapping the symbolic names of the devices to their actual hardware.

(a) Device driver   (c) Device controller

(b) Kernel I/O sub-system   (d) none

9. _____ acts as a layer that hides the differences among the device controllers.

(a) Device driver   (c) Device controller

(b) Kernel I/O sub-system   (d) none

10. _____ increases the I/O performance of the system, through buffering, caching, and spooling.

(a) Device driver   (c) Device controller

(b) Kernel I/O sub-system   (d) none

11. _____ is a memory area, where data are stored temporarily, during an I/O operation.

(a) cache   (c) RAM

(b) buffer   (d) none

12. _____ waits and blocks itself, until an interrupt unblocks it.

(a) Device driver   (c) Device controller

(b) Kernel I/O sub-system   (d) none

13. _____ notifies and handles errors properly, so that the system runs properly, despite errors

(a) Device driver   (c) Device controller

(b) Kernel I/O sub-system   (d) Interrupt handler

14. _____, on completion of the data transfer, interrupts the device driver.

(a) Device driver   (c) Device controller

(b) Kernel I/O sub-system   (d) Interrupt handler

15. _____ checks to see whether the device controller is able to accept the commands.

(a) Device driver   (c) Device controller

(b) Kernel I/O sub-system   (d) Interrupt handler

16. _____ extracts the required information from the device controller registers and stores the data in buffer.

(a) Device driver   (c) Device controller

(b) Kernel I/O sub-system   (d) Interrupt handler

REVIEW QUESTIONS

1. Differentiate between character- and block-oriented devices.

2. Differentiate between caching and buffering.

3. When should we adopt the DMA approach for I/O operations?

4. Explain various types of techniques used to perform an I/O operation.

5. Explain various functions of an I/O software.

6. What is the need of a kernel I/O sub-system?

7. What is the device-independent feature for an I/O software?

8. How does a device driver interact with devices?

9. How does a device driver interact with the kernel I/O sub-system?

10. What is the role of mapping table and resource table in the functioning of a device driver?

11. What is an I/O channel?

12. How does kernel I/O sub-system provide a uniform interface?

13. What is the need of buffering? Discuss ingle- and double-buffering.

14. How does a cache, introduced in kernel I/O sub-system, improve the I/O efficiency?

15. What is a buffer cache?

16. Suppose a user wishes to perform write operation on the disk. Explain the steps, using life cycle of an I/O request.

BRAIN TEASERS

1. Interrupt-driven I/O is a better approach for I/O handling. However, this approach incurs the cost of context switching. Is it possible to replace this approach with programmed I/O? Explain with reason.

2. While the device driver is busy reading from a device, a user suddenly removes the device. What will happen to the current I/O transfer and the pending requests on the device queue?

3. Suppose a user has used a local machine to log on to his/her machine, remotely. In this case, the data entered on the local machine must be transported to the remote machine through the network devices. Will this network I/O increase the context switches?

4. Frame the guidelines for designing an I/O-scheduling algorithm?

5. If a process performs rapid bursts of I/O, double buffering will not suffice. Is it feasible to have more number of buffers? What would be the limit on the number of buffers?

6. Name the layer where the following function will be implemented:

   (a) Converting a logical block address to a physical disk configuration, that is, track, sector, and so on.

   (b) Checking an invalid operation defined by the user in the program.

   (c) Checking the access permissions to a file.

   (d) Checking if the input data are in buffer cache.

   (e) Processing the interrupt after I/O operation.

   (f) Checking the status of a device.

   (g) Reading or writing in a buffer.

15   Disk Management

15.1 INTRODUCTION

In Chapter 14, the basics of device management were discussed. Efficiency is a major concern while accessing any I/O device due to speed mismatch between the processor and the devices. This chapter discusses some efficiency and performance issues of the disk as it is a widely used I/O device. Disk scheduling is one of the major parts of disk management that schedules the I/O requests arriving on the disk. This chapter explains various disk-scheduling algorithms, disk formatting, and bad sectors. The discussion extends to swap-space management and RAID structures.

15.2 DISK SCHEDULING

Disk scheduling schedules the I/O requests arriving on the disk. There are several reasons disk scheduling is important for I/O operations.

- In a multi-programming environment, many processes may send I/O requests for the disk. Since the processor can service only one I/O request at a time, others may need to wait on the disk queue. When the current request is finished, another request from the disk queue is scheduled to be serviced.
- While accessing a particular location on the disk, the current position of the disk arm matters. If the next request is far from the current position, then the seek time is more as compared to other requests having less seek time.
- When the disk storage becomes a bottleneck, disk scheduling may help loading a large request on small set of disks.
- Random requests from the users may also need disk scheduling so that various types of requests of different users are serviced. For example, in case of web servers and data base servers, the users may request smaller to larger data in size. Moreover, the requests may not be on the same cylinder.

Keeping in view such facts, there is a need to schedule the requests on the disk to improve the performance of the system. In this direction, various scheduling algorithms have been developed.

Learning Objectives

After reading this chapter, you should be able to understand:

- Disk scheduling criteria
- FCFS disk-scheduling algorithm
- Shortest seek time first (SSTF) disk-scheduling algorithm
- SCAN disk-scheduling algorithm
- Circular scan (C-SCAN) disk scheduling algorithm
- Freeze-SCAN (F-SCAN) disk-scheduling algorithm
- N-SCAN disk-scheduling algorithm
- LOOK disk-scheduling algorithm
- C-LOOK disk-scheduling algorithm
- Rotational optimization
- Disk-scheduling algorithms based on rotational optimization
- Disk formatting
- Bad sectors
- Swap space management
- Redundant array of independent disks (RAID) structure

15.3 DISK-SCHEDULING CRITERIA

Disk I/O operation is a major aspect of the computer system. Since it is dependent on the movement of the disk arm, the disk scheduling is performed such that the arm movement is utilized to service more I/O requests efficiently. For accessing the disk, the logical blocks are converted into the disk physical blocks. However, the disk physical block address is in the form of cylinder, track, and sector: First, the cylinder is identified, then track within the cylinder, and finally, sector within the track.

Thus, before discussing the scheduling algorithm, let us look at the criteria of disk-scheduling algorithms.

Seek Time

Seek time is the time taken by the disk head to move from one cylinder to another. It is therefore dependent on the seek length, that is, the length between the current and the next position of the head. For example, if the disk head is currently at Cylinder number 13 and it has to move to 34. The seek length in this case is 21, that is, to reach its target, the head needs to pass 21 cylinders. The average seek time can be calculated if the average time to move from one cylinder to another is estimated. Based on the mechanical characteristics of the disk, the seek time is affected by two factors: mechanical settling time and acceleration factor. The seek time is thus given as

$$\text{Seek}(n) = 0 \text{ if } n = 0$$
$$= a + bn \text{ if } n > 0,$$

where n is the seek distance, a is the mechanical settling time, and b is the acceleration factor. Thus, seek time may affect the performance of the system. The scheduling algorithm that provides the minimum average seek time is better.

Rotational Latency

Rotational latency is the time taken by the addressed sector of the track to rotate into a position such that read/write head is accessible to it, that is, the sector comes under the head. The disk-scheduling algorithm that provides minimum rotational latency is better.

Transfer Time

Transfer time is the time for data transfer. For example, if it needs to read some data from the disk, then the transfer time is the time taken to transfer the data from the disk to the application. It depends on the rotational speed of the disk and the number of bytes to be transferred.

Disk Access Time

It is the time to perform any operation on the disk. It is the sum of seek time, rotational latency, and transfer time.

Disk Bandwidth

It is the total number of bytes transferred divided by the total time between the first request of the service and completion of the last transfer of the data. The scheduling algorithm should provide a high bandwidth.

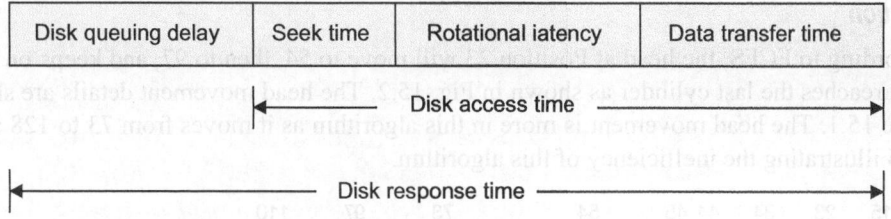

Fig. 15.1   Disk I/O performance time factors

Throughput

It is the total number of disk requests serviced per unit time. A scheduling algorithm must provide maximum throughput.

Response Time

It is the average time spent by a request in waiting. A request must be serviced within a predictable response time; otherwise, it may have adverse effects on the application. There are two parameters in response time: One is the *average response time* that shows the response time of the whole system, and another is *variance of response time*. Variance of response time is the measure of how individual requests are serviced relative to the average system performance. If the variance is low, then it means that most of the requests are serviced after waiting for a similar amount of time. In this way, the variance is a parameter for measuring the fairness and predictability. To avoid irregularity in service time of the requests, the scheduling algorithm should minimize the variance of response time.

The time parameters of the disk are illustrated in Fig. 15.1.

15.4 DISK-SCHEDULING ALGORITHMS

This section discusses the various types of disk-scheduling algorithms.

15.4.1 FCFS

It is the simplest scheduling algorithm, as seen in case of CPU scheduling. The requests are scheduled in the order they arrive in the disk queue. Thus, every request gets a fair chance to be executed and indefinite postponement of requests does not occur.

This may, however, not be a good choice for a scheduling algorithm. It may be possible that the first request in the queue is very far from the current position of the disk head. In this case, the seek time will be high and throughput will be low. The algorithm may be good in performance when the load on the disk is low and the requests are uniformly distributed. However, as the load on the disk increases, FCFS provides poor performance as it increases the average response time. However, the FCFS will provide low variance of response time due to random seek, that is, the arriving disk requests cannot get ahead of already pending requests.

Example 15.1

Consider a disk queue with I/O requests on the following cylinders in their arriving order: 54, 97, 73, 128, 15, 44, 110, 34, 45

The disk head is assumed to be at Cylinder 23. Calculate and show with diagram the disk head movement using FCFS-scheduling algorithm.

Solution

According to FCFS, the head at Position 23 will move to 54, then to 97, and keeps on moving till it reaches the last cylinder as shown in Fig. 15.2. The head movement details are shown in Table 15.1. The head movement is more in this algorithm as it moves from 73 to 128 and 128 to 15 illustrating the inefficiency of this algorithm.

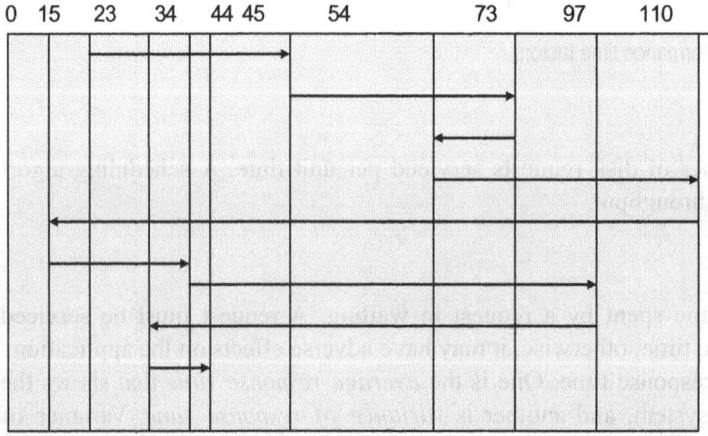

Fig. 15.2   FCFS disk scheduling for Example 15.1

Table 15.1   FCFS head movement for Example 15.1

I/O request for cylinder	Head movement	Total head movement for the request
54	23–54	31
97	54–97	43
73	97–73	24
128	73–128	55
15	128–15	113
44	12–44	32
110	44–110	66
34	110–34	76
45	34–45	11
Total head movement = 451		

15.4.2 SSTF

In this algorithm, the request with the shortest seek time will be executed first. Therefore, it calculates the seek time of all the requests in the queue, selects the appropriate request, and schedules it for the execution. In this way, the requests that are near to the current head position get serviced first, thereby improving the performance of the system. This will increase the throughput of the system and decrease the average response time as compared to FCFS.

Since it needs to calculate the seek time from the current disk head position, it will also incur the cost of computation. Another drawback in this algorithm is that a request very far away from the current head position will not get scheduled if the arriving requests have less seek time compared to this request. In this case, the request will starve.

Since the algorithm services the requests whose seek time is less, the requests that are concentrated in one region will be served the most. This may cause in low response times for the requests whose seek time is high, that is, the track for the request is at the other end of the disk. Further, it may be difficult to predict the response time as the algorithm favours only some requests. Thus, it causes high variance of the response time.

The SSTF algorithm may be best suitable for batch-processing systems where high throughput and average response time are required. However, it may not be efficient for interactive and online systems where high response time and its predictability are required.

Example 15.2

Calculate and show with diagram the disk-head movement using SSTF-scheduling algorithm in Example 15.1.

Solution

Since in SSTF, the head movement is based on the shortest seek time, calculate the shortest distance that a head needs to move. From the current position, the next request whose movement distance is the shortest is serviced, as shown in Table 15.2 and Fig. 15.3.

Table 15.2   SSTF head movement for Example 15.2

Head movement	Total head movement for the request
23–15	8
15–34	19
34–44	10
44–45	1
45–54	9
54–73	19
73–97	24
97–110	13
110–128	18
Total head movement = 121	

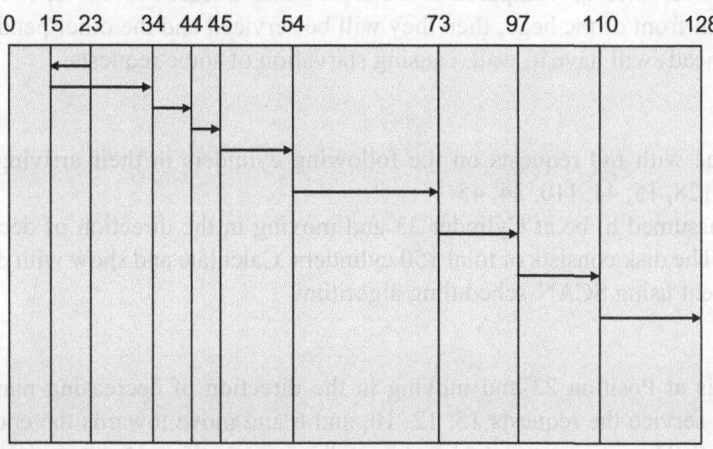

Fig. 15.3   SSTF disk scheduling for Example 15.2

The total head movement drastically reduces in the SSTF algorithm compared to FCFS. Moreover, the head does not change its direction of movement frequently as was seen in case of FCFS. This shows that this algorithm increases the performance of the system as the head movement is reduced by following the shortest seek length.

Example 15.3

In Example 15.2, suppose when the head is processing request at Cylinder 73, a request at Cylinder 75 arrives. Since the new request will have the shortest seek length, the head will move to it and service the request. After this, the head will move to Cylinder 97 and processes the request. While processing, two new requests arrive at Cylinders 99 and 100. Again, these new requests have the shortest seek lengths, the head will move to Cylinder 99 and then to 100. This will make some requests in the queue such as 110 and 128 to starve if more requests whose seek lengths are short continue to arrive in the system.

15.4.3 SCAN

This algorithm uses the property that the disk arm after reaching the end of the disk moving in one direction, that is, the outermost or the innermost cylinder, reverses its direction. It services the requests in the direction of its head movement and continues until it reaches the end of the disk or the last cylinder. After this, it reverses the direction and services the requests in its path. According to this algorithm, the preferred direction of the head movement has to be found first and all the requests in that direction will be serviced. It may be possible that some requests appear while processing a request. If these new requests are in the path of the preferred direction of movable disk head, then these requests will also be serviced. However, if they arrive just behind the head, then they will have to wait until the head reverses its direction and services them. In this way, the head moves back and forth across the disk and services the requests in its path. Hence, the algorithm is also known as *elevator algorithm* taking the analogy of an elevator that continues in one direction servicing each floor as per the requests and reverses its direction after reaching the top or ground floor.

Since the behaviour of this algorithm is similar to SSTF, it also provides high throughput and average response time. Moreover, it will provide low variance of response time as compared to SSTF as it services all requests in a given direction. In this algorithm, the requests at the midrange will be visited more as compared to outer or inner tracks. Moreover, if the new requests are arriving in front of the head, then they will be serviced and the other pending old requests (behind the head) will have to wait, causing starvation of some requests.

Example 15.4

Consider a disk queue with I/O requests on the following cylinders in their arriving order: 6, 10, 12, 54, 97, 73, 128, 15, 44, 110, 34, 45

The disk head is assumed to be at Cylinder 23 and moving in the direction of decreasing number of cylinders. The disk consists of total 150 cylinders. Calculate and show with diagram the disk head movement using SCAN-scheduling algorithm.

Solution

Since the disk head is at Position 23 and moving in the direction of decreasing number of cylinders, it will first service the requests 15, 12, 10, and 6 and move towards the end of the disk, that is, Cylinder 0. Then it reverses its direction and services other requests in its path till

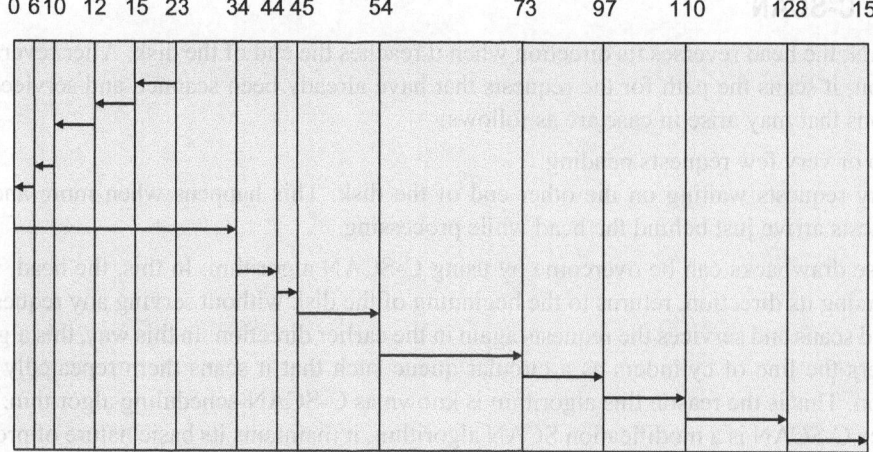

Fig. 15.4 SCAN disk scheduling for Example 15.4

it reaches Cylinder 150 as shown in Fig. 15.4. The total head movement in this algorithm is $23 + 150 = 173$. However, in this algorithm, the disk movements from Cylinders 6 to 0 and from Cylinders 128 to 150 are unnecessary as there are no requests in these paths.

Example 15.5

In Example 15.4, suppose some new requests arrive at Cylinders 60, 65, and 70 while the disk head is processing Cylinder 54. What will happen to these new requests according to the SCAN-scheduling algorithm?

Solution

Since the new requests arrived are in the preferred direction of disk-head movement, all these requests will be serviced just after the processing at Cylinder 54 as shown in the highlighted portion in Fig. 15.5. However, due to arrival of these new requests, the waiting time of pending requests in the queue increases.

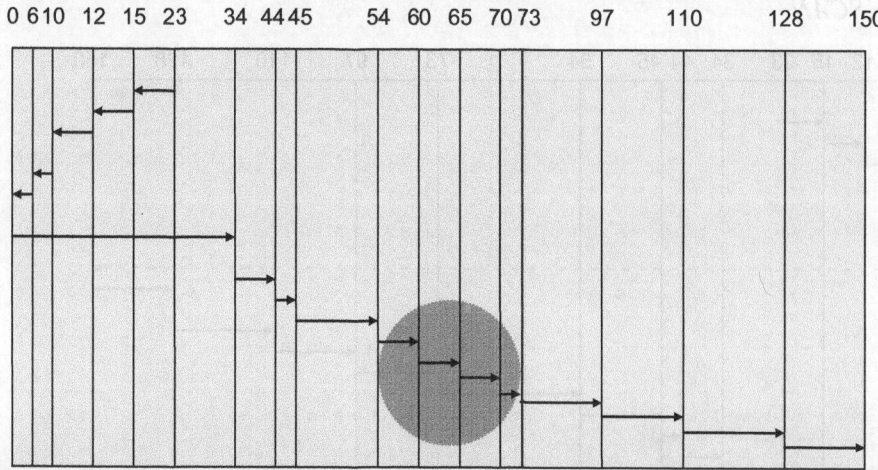

Fig. 15.5 SCAN disk scheduling for Example 15.5

15.4.4 C-SCAN

In SCAN, the head reverses its direction when it reaches the end of the disk. After reversing its direction, it scans the path for the requests that have already been scanned and serviced. Two situations that may arise in case are as follows:

- Zero or very few requests pending.
- Many requests waiting on the other end of the disk. This happens when more and more requests arrive just behind the head while processing.

These drawbacks can be overcome by using C-SCAN algorithm. In this, the head, instead of reversing its direction, returns to the beginning of the disk without serving any request in its path and scans and services the requests again in the earlier direction. In this way, this algorithm considers the line of cylinders as a circular queue such that it scans them repeatedly in one direction. This is the reason this algorithm is known as C-SCAN-scheduling algorithm.

Since C-SCAN is a modification SCAN algorithm, it maintains its basic nature of providing high throughput. Further, it provides the low variance in response time as compared to SCAN algorithm as the pending jobs on the other side of the disk may get chance to be executed and centre cylinders are not favoured. However, the starvation may still occur as in SCAN algorithm if more and more new requests arrive on the same cylinder or in front of the head.

Example 15.6

Solve Example 15.4 using C-SCAN-scheduling algorithm.

Solution

The disk head after reaching Cylinder 0 reverses its direction, and starts scanning from Cylinder 150 and services the requests in its path as shown in Fig. 15.6. The total head movement in this algorithm will be reduced to 139 as compared to 173 of SCAN algorithm.

15.4.5 F-SCAN and N-step SCAN

In all the algorithms discussed earlier, if new I/O requests arrive while the disk head is processing one request, then some requests may starve and are denied fair chance to be serviced. To resolve this problem, some variants of scan algorithm have been developed: *F-SCAN* and *N-step SCAN*.

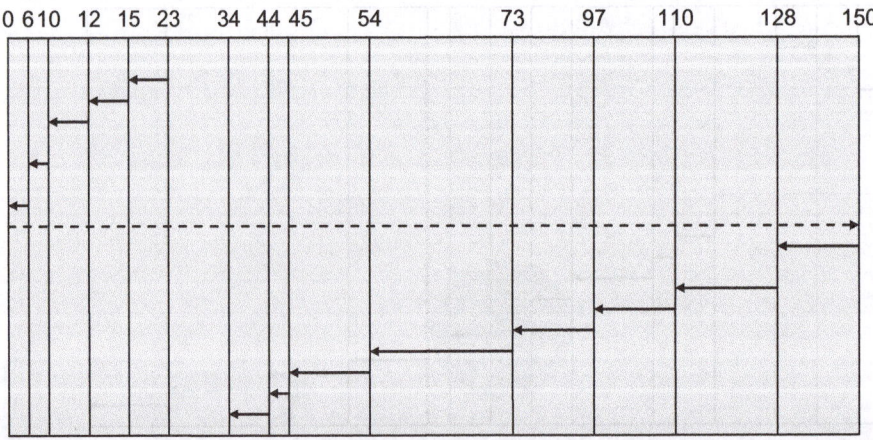

Fig. 15.6 C-SCAN disk scheduling for Example 15.6

FSCAN: It maintains two queues. One queue is for storing the requests that have arrived and another queue is initially empty. The disk arm starts servicing the requests from the first queue. However, if there are any new requests arriving while old requests from the first queue are being processed, then they will reside in the second queue; they will not be allowed to enter the first queue and thereby change the order of the queue. In this way, the new requests are deferred until all the pending old requests have been processed. However, this freezing of requests is for the period till the disk head reaches the end of the disk. As the disk head reaches the last cylinder and changes its direction, the second queue is merged with the first queue and sorted for optimum service. The disk head now starts servicing the requests according to this new queue of the requests.

N-step SCAN: The idea here is to serve the requests at the interval of n in the queue in a sweep when the head is moving in one direction. For example, if n is four, the first four requests are serviced first. When the sweep is complete, the next four requests in the queue are considered for service. In this way, a large queue is divided into subqueues, each containing n requests. When a new request appears while a subqueue is being processed, it will be added at the end of the original queue. This helps to avoid starvation, thereby guaranteeing the service of the requests. The value of n should be chosen carefully for the maximum performance of the algorithm. If value of $n = 1$, then it becomes a first-in-first-out (FIFO) algorithm. On the other hand, if the value of n is very large, then it is as good as SCAN algorithm.

Neither of the variants of SCAN algorithms therefore postpones the service of any old pending requests and thereby reduces the variance of the response times as compared to SCAN algorithm. The F-SCAN may prove to be better as compared to N-SCAN algorithm. N-SCAN algorithm may decrease the throughput as it adds the new arriving requests at the end of request queue and these cannot be serviced until all sub-queues have been serviced. However, F-SCAN algorithm considers the new requests in its original queue after every sweep when the disk head changes its preferred direction. The following are the benefits of F-SCAN over N-SCAN:

- High throughput
- Low variance of the response time
- Good average response time
- Reduced starvation

Example 15.7

Consider a disk queue with I/O requests on the following cylinders in their arriving order:
54, 97, 73, 128, 15, 44, 110, 34, 45

The disk head is assumed to be at Cylinder 23 and moving in the direction of decreasing number of cylinders. The disk consists of total 150 cylinders. Suppose when the head is processing at 15, a new request arrives at Cylinder 10. Similarly, when the head is processing request at 73, a request on Cylinder 75 arrives. While processing at 97, new requests arrive at Cylinders 35, 99, and 100. Apply the F-SCAN algorithm for this situation.

Solution

F-SCAN

Using F-SCAN, two queues are maintained as shown in Fig. 15.7.

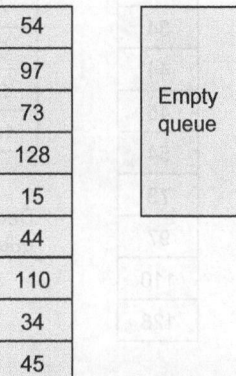

Fig. 15.7   F-SCAN initial queues for Example 15.7

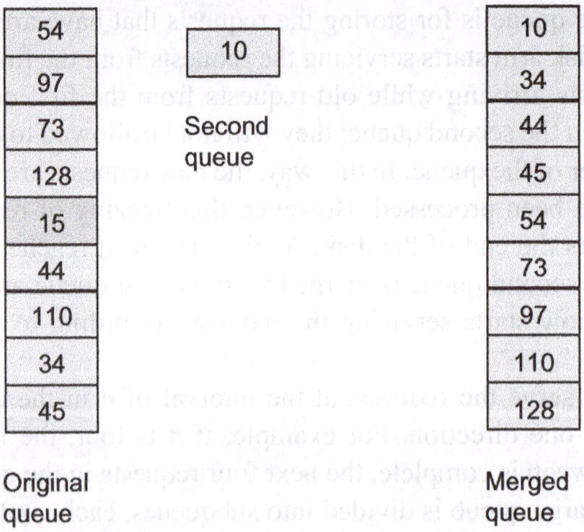

Original queue: 54, 97, 73, 128, 15, 44, 110, 34, 45

Second queue: 10

Merged queue: 10, 34, 44, 45, 54, 73, 97, 110, 128

Fig. 15.8 F-SCAN first pass for Example 15.7

When the head processes at 15, a request arrives at Cylinder 10. However, this will not be processed as the original queue is frozen and hence, it is added to the second queue. As the head reaches the end of the disk, that is, at Cylinder 0, it reverses its direction. At this point, the original queue is merged with the second queue and sorted in the ascending order as shown in Fig. 15.8. This sorted queue is now the original queue.

When the head processes at 73, a request arrives at Cylinder 75. The request is added in the second queue. Further, while processing at 97, new requests arrive at Cylinders 35, 99, and 100. The requests are again added in the second queue. The new status is shown in Fig. 15.9. However, no new requests present in the second queue will be processed as the head has not reached the end of the disk.

As soon as the head reverses its direction, the original list is merged with the second queue and sorted and processed again. The statuses of the queues are shown in Fig. 15.10.

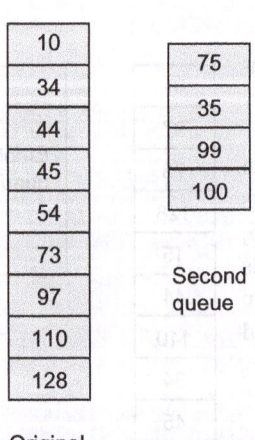

Original queue: 10, 34, 44, 45, 54, 73, 97, 110, 128

Second queue: 75, 35, 99, 100

Fig. 15.9 F-SCAN status of queues after first pass for Example 15.7

Original queue	Second queue	Merged queue
10	75	10
34	35	34
44	99	35
45	100	44
54		45
73		54
97		73
110		75
128		97
		99
		100
		110
		128

Fig. 15.10   F-SCAN second pass for Example 15.7

Since in our example, all the requests are serviced in the original queue, the second queue is the remaining queue that needs service. This queue is sorted and then serviced as shown in Fig. 15.11.

Example 15.8

Consider a disk queue with I/O requests on the following cylinders in their arriving order: 6, 10, 12, 54, 97, 73, 128, 15, 44, 110, 34, 45

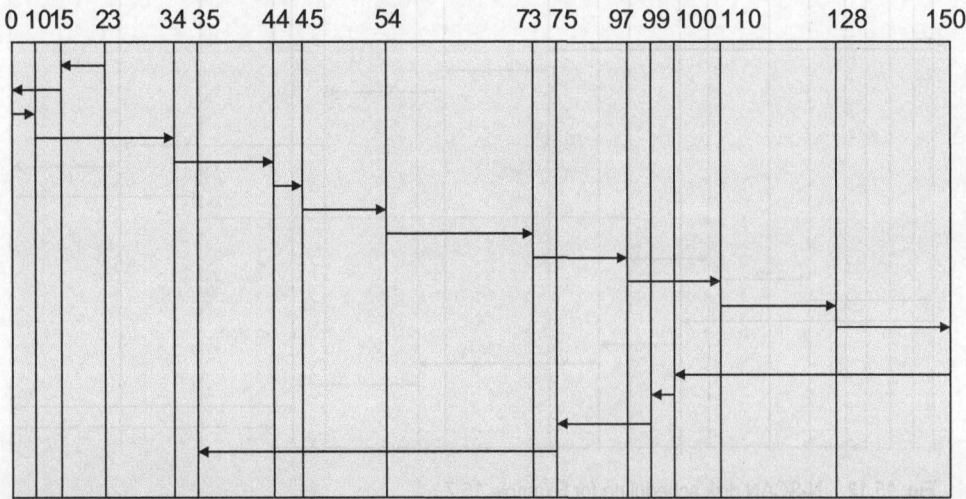

Fig. 15.11   F-SCAN disk scheduling for Example 15.7

The disk head is assumed to be at Cylinder 23 and moving in the direction of decreasing number of cylinders. The disk consists of total 150 cylinders. Suppose when the head is at 15, a request arrives at Cylinder 11 and when it is at 73, a request arrives at Cylinder 75. While at 97, new requests arrive at Cylinders 35, 99, and 100. Apply the N-SCAN algorithm for this situation for $n = 4$.

Solution

Since the $n = 4$, the first four requests in the queue, that is, 6, 10, 12, and 54 are considered for processing. Now, the head is presently at 23 and moving towards 0. Therefore, it processes the requests 12, 10, and 6 in its scan towards 0 and then reverses its direction for the next sweep. The request 54 though is in the consideration but could not be serviced as it was not found in its previous sweep. Therefore, it is considered in the next sub-queue. The next four elements in the sub-queue, 54, 97, 73, and 128, are serviced. When the head was processing request at 73, a request for Cylinder 75 arrived. Although it was in the path of the last sweep, it could not be serviced as the algorithm does not allow and was added at the end of the queue. Similarly, while processing at 97, new requests arrived for Cylinders 35, 99, and 100 but could not be processed. These are also added at the end of the original queue. The head again reverses its direction. The next sub-queue having the elements 15, 44, 110, and 34 is serviced. When the head was servicing at 15, a new request for Cylinder 11 appears. However, it was not considered for service and was added at the end of the original queue. In this way, the next sub-queue consisting of 45, 75, 35, and 99 is serviced. Finally, we have only two requests, 100 and 11, in the queue, which are serviced as shown in Fig. 15.12.

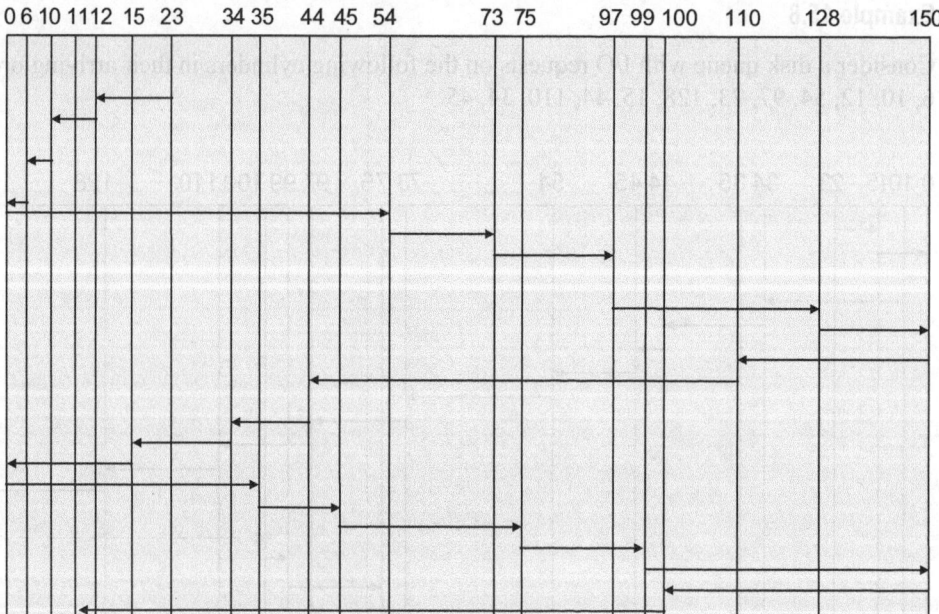

Fig. 15.12 N-SCAN disk scheduling for Example 15.7

15.4.6 LOOK and C-LOOK

In SCAN and its variants, the disk head moves to the last cylinder and then reverses its direction. In this case, the head moves unnecessarily, thereby increasing the delay. Therefore, another modification is made in these algorithms such that the head moves in one direction only till the last request in that direction. LOOK algorithm solves this deficiency. According to this, the disk head looks ahead in its direction of movement for the last request. It moves to the last request and changes its preferred direction there without moving to the last cylinder and continues servicing the request in the other direction. Thus, it eliminates unnecessary seek operations and hence decreases the average response time and lowers the variance of response time.

Like SCAN algorithm, LOOK can also be designed as C-LOOK that treats the request queue as circular. It is similar to C-SCAN except that the head moves till the last request instead of last cylinder. Thus, C-LOOK achieves the benefits of both C-SCAN- and LOOK-scheduling algorithms. C-LOOK lowers the variance of the response time as compared to LOOK algorithm but incurs cost of reduced throughput. It may increase the average response time also.

Example 15.9

Consider a disk queue with I/O requests on the following cylinders in their arriving order: 6, 10, 12, 54, 97, 73, 128, 15, 44, 110, 34, 45

The disk head is assumed to be at Cylinder 23 and moving in the direction of decreasing number of cylinders. The disk consists of total 150 cylinders. Calculate and show with diagram the disk head movement using LOOK-scheduling algorithm.

Solution

Since the disk head is at Position 23 and moving in the direction of decreasing number of cylinders, it will first service the requests at 15, 12, 10, and 6. It reverses its direction at 6 and services other requests in its path as shown in Fig. 15.13. The head stops at 128 without continuing to the last cylinder and reverses its direction, if there are any new requests pending. The total head movement in this algorithm is 139.

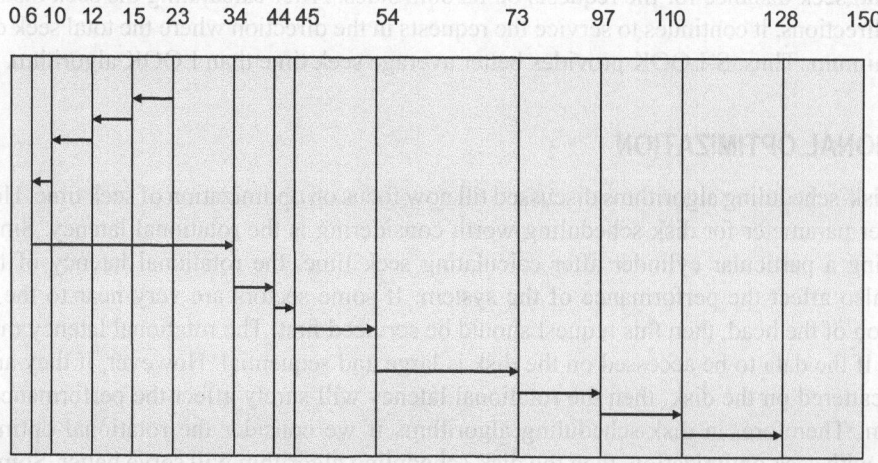

Fig. 15.13 LOOK disk scheduling for Example 15.9

0 6 10 12 15 23   34 44 45   54   73   97   110   128   150

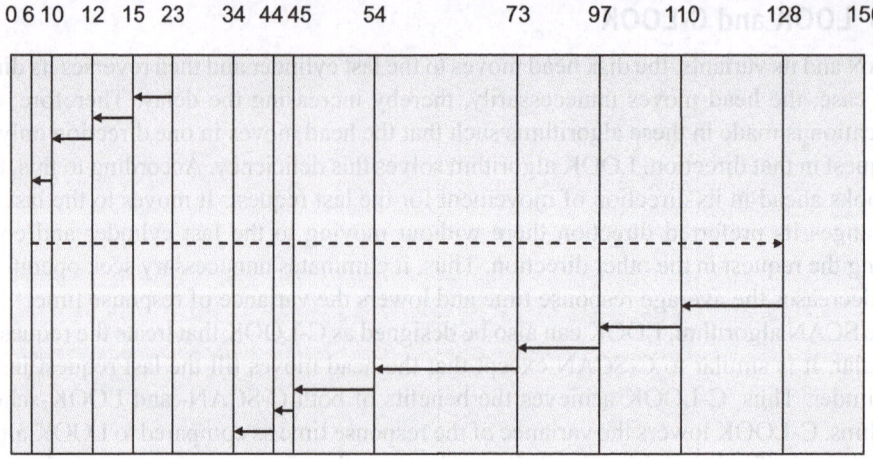

Fig. 15.14   C-LOOK disk scheduling for Example 15.10

Example 15.10

Apply C-LOOK-scheduling algorithm in Example 15.9.

Solution

The head will first service the requests 15, 12, 10, and 6 and changes its direction. Then it moves to the other end of the disk but looks for the first request there, that is, 128. At Cylinder 128, it reverses its direction and services the requests in its path as shown in Fig. 15.14. The total head movement in this algorithm will be reduced to 111 as compared to 139 of LOOK algorithm.

Another variant of LOOK algorithm is S-LOOK. The shortest-LOOK (S-LOOK) algorithm is an extension of the LOOK algorithm to handle the cases where the disk head is located among the far-end requests. The algorithm decides which direction should be served first instead of only continuing to seek in the same direction before the new requests have arrived. It calculates the total seek distance for the requests on its both sides. After calculating the seek distances in both directions, it continues to service the requests in the direction where the total seek distance is minimum. Thus, S-LOOK provides better average seek time than LOOK algorithm.

15.5 ROTATIONAL OPTIMIZATION

The disk-scheduling algorithms discussed till now focus on optimization of seek time. However, another parameter for disk scheduling worth considering is the rotational latency. Since after reaching a particular cylinder after calculating seek time, the rotational latency of the disk may also affect the performance of the system. If some sectors are very near to the current position of the head, then this request should be serviced first. The rotational latency might not affect if the data to be accessed on the disk is large and sequential. However, if they are small and scattered on the disk, then the rotational latency will surely affect the performance of the system. Therefore, in disk-scheduling algorithms if we consider the rotational optimization along with seek optimization, then the disk-scheduling algorithm will serve better. Some of the algorithms devised for rotational optimization are discussed in subsequent sections.

15.5.1 SLTF-scheduling Algorithm

After the disk head has been positioned on a cylinder, there may be requests on many sectors. A request queue is maintained for the requests that will store the sector numbers so that the rotational optimization can be performed. The shortest latency time first (SLTF) algorithm first examines all the requests in the queue and selects the request having the shortest rotational delay. In other words, the requests whose sectors are positioned neart the head are serviced first.

15.5.2 SPTF-scheduling Algorithm

This algorithm considers the seek time as well as rotational latency. It means that for a disk address in a request, both seek time and rotational latency are calculated and added together to obtain irts positioning time. Thus, for each request, a positioning time is calculated and the shortest one is selected for the service. This algorithm results in higher throughput and good average response time but may cause starvation as in case of SSTF.

15.5.3 SATF-scheduling Algorithm

In SPTF algorithm, the throughput may be increased if data transfer time is also taken into consideration along with positioning time. The positioning time and data transfer time form the total access time for a request. In this way, the total access time is calculated for each request and the one with the shortest time is scheduled first. This algorithm increases the throughput as compared to SPTF but suffers from the starvation problem as requests on outermost and innermost cylinders may be postponed for servicing the requests on the cylinders lying between them.

SPTF and SATF disk-scheduling algorithms, however, are dependent on the knowledge of disk characteristics. For example, to calculate the transfer time, rotational speed, size of the disk, and so on must be known. The major problem is that the modern disk drives do not provide the actual details of the disk configuration. For instance, the sectors on the disk may not be contiguously allocated. Sometimes bad sectors are also allocated space from the reserved sectors. Therefore, the rotational optimization-based disk-scheduling algorithms are dependent on the availability of disk configuration and other details.

15.6 DISK FORMATTING

The disk formatting prepares the raw disk to be used. There are three levels in disk formatting: *low-level formatting*, *disk partitioning*, and *logical formatting*. The low-level formatting is performed by the manufacturer and the other two steps are performed by the OS and therefore are linked to it. The manufacturer of the disk performs the low-level formatting and is able to test the disk and later on use it for storage. The low-level format may decide the sector size on the track. The second step is disk partitioning, where the disk is divided into multiple partitions. The OS treats each disk partition as a separate disk. In most of the systems, Sector 0 contains the master boot record containing boot code. The partition that contains the boot code is known as *boot partition*. The disk that contains the boot partition is called a *boot disk* or *system disk*. The information regarding each partition is stored in a data structure known as *partition table*. The partition table stores the information such as starting sector, size, and so on. The partition table is also stored at Sector 0. More than one OS may also be loaded on the system by making use of partitions. Suppose there are three partitions in a disk. Two partitions may be used for Windows and one partition for Linux.

Another step in disk formatting is logical formatting, which is concerned with the OS. This is also known as high-level formatting. This operation is performed on each partition. The logical formatting operation lays down a boot block in the partition and creates a file system. The initial file system data structures, such as free and allocated lists or bitmaps, root directory, and empty file system are also stored. Since different partitions contain different file systems, the partition table entries will indicate which partition contains which file system.

15.7 BAD SECTORS

While working with disks, there may be many types of errors or failures. The mechanical parts used in disk and disk controller cause some failures. For example, disk crash is a common failure. It occurs when the disk head touches the disk surface. The remedy to this problem is to replace the faulty disk with a new one. Another frequently occurring error is read error, that is, the disk head is not able to read a sector. This may be a *transient error* occurring due to presence of some dust particles under the head. It may be possible that this type of error does not appear if given a second chance to read. However, sometimes these read errors become *permanent*. Inspite of several attempts to read, the error remains there. This error is of permanent nature and indicates that a particular sector is not readable or writable. These kinds of sectors are known as *bad sectors* or *bad blocks*. The sectors may become bad sectors due to manufacturing defect, improper write, virus, or errant program. These types of sectors can be repaired with some programs (Norton Disk Doctor, etc.), or a low-level format. A low-level format will remove all the data from the drive. Bad Sectors can also be reported if there is a noise in the data from faulty cables or other components, but they may also be of transient nature.

It may be possible that only some bits of a sector are erroneous, that is, the error is very small. In this case, the error-correcting code (ECC) will correct it. However, if many bytes of a sector are defective, then the sector must be designated as a bad sector so that some remedy must be taken. The remedy to bad blocks can be done at two levels: either at disk-controller level or at the OS level. Whatever it may be, it is kept completely transparent to the user. While the disk is tested by the manufacturer at the time of low-level formatting, a list of bad sectors is maintained on the disk by the disk controller. For each bad sector, a substitution is also

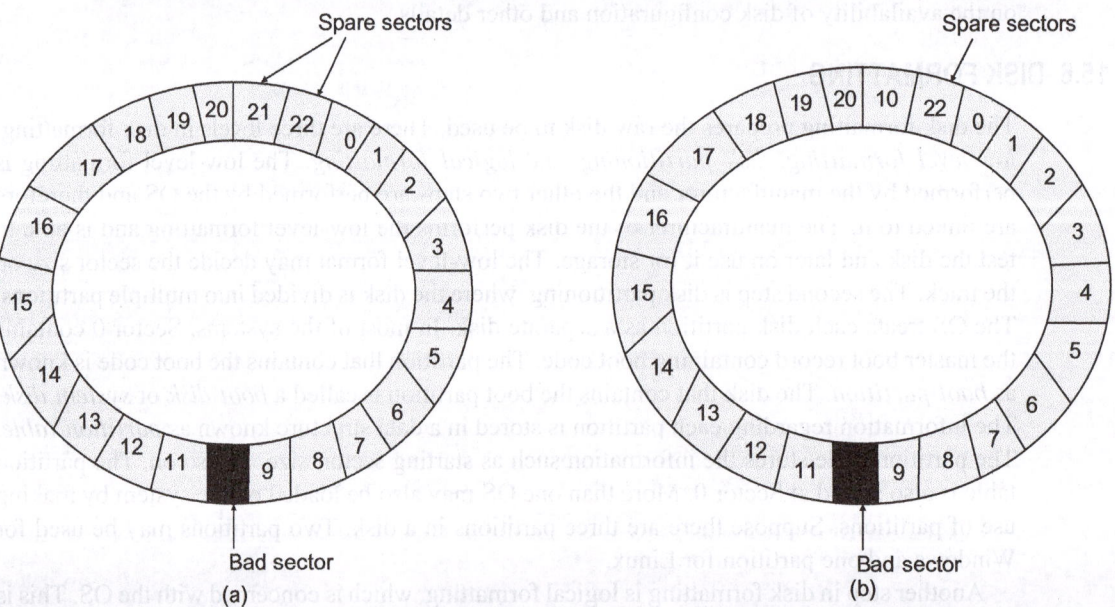

Fig. 15.15 Sector sparing

given. In fact, some predefined spare sectors are provided to be given as substitution. The disk controller maps the bad sector to the spare sector. This is known as *sector sparing* or *forwarding*. For example in Fig. 15.15(a), Sector 10 is found as bad sector by the disk controller. The Sectors 21 to 22 are reserved as spare sectors. The disk controller maps the bad sector with Sector 21 as substitution as shown in Fig. 15.15(b).

Instead of mapping the bad sector to the spare sector provided in the reserved area, we can ignore the bad sector and continue the storage from the next sector onwards. For this, we can just shift all the sectors to bypass the bad one. This is known as *sector slipping*. Sector 10, instead of mapping into Sector 21, can be continued from the next sector after the bad sector as shown in Fig. 15.16 by shifting all the sectors by one. In this way, the last Sector 20 will occupy the position in spare sector. The advantage of the sector slipping is that the performance of the system will increase as the work is performed in one rotation of the track only. Comparing with the previous approach, the head will move to Sector 21 for bad sector and again move back to Sector 11. This will increase the delay in reading the sectors. Therefore, sector slipping may enhance the performance. However, this is achieved at the cost of re-mapping the sectors that have been shifted by one. Another problem is that it is implemented only if the spare sector is on the same track as the bad sector so that the work is completed in one rotation. If the spare sector is on a different track, then shifting method does not gain any performance factor.

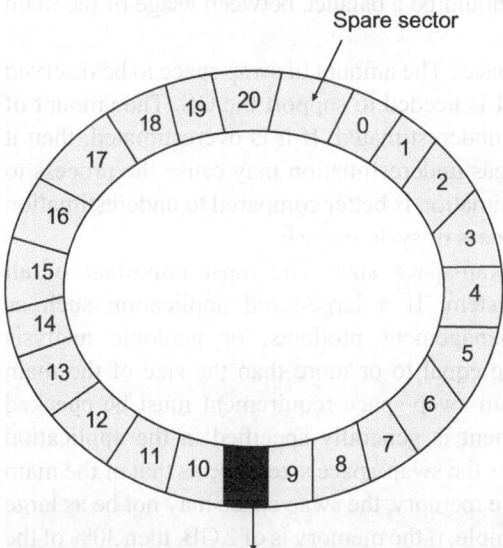

Fig. 15.16   Sector slipping

The sector sparing or slipping requires separate sectors on each cylinder or sometimes even a spare cylinder. This is because any unused sector cannot be used as spare sector, as this may cause problems in memory management. Therefore, separate sectors or cylinder are reserved for sparing. Thus, the disk controller will map the bad sectors from the space reserved for only sparing.

The sectors may also become defective during the normal operation. At the first instance, the ECC may correct the error. However, if the error repeats again and again on a sector, then that sector must be declared as a bad sector. In that case, the disk controller maps init to a spare sector using sector sparing or sector slipping.

At the OS level, the disk can also be tested and a list of bad sectors can be obtained. Further, the sector sparing and sector slipping discussed earlier can also be implemented by the OS. The OS must ensure that bad sectors do not occur in any file or the free list. A separate file may be prepared that consists of all bad sectors and should not be included in the file system.

15.8 SWAP-SPACE/PAGING-SPACE MANAGEMENT

As discussed in Chapter 11, the implementation of virtual memory (VM) is done by reserving some space on the disk where a process or its pages can be swapped-out or paged-out and retrieved back when required. Thus, swap space can be defined as a temporary storage location on the disk to implement the VM when system's memory requirements exceed the size of available main memory. In main memory, a process is swapped-out or swapped-in, but in VM, the process is divided into pages and therefore, the pages are paged-in or paged-out. Hence, the term *paging space* is used for the space reserved for the page-in and page-out operations.

The use of swap space may decrease the performance of the system. This happens when there is frequent transfer between the main memory and swap space on the disk, that is, when the program repeatedly accesses more VM than is available in the main memory. As the number of page faults increases, the performance decreases. At one instant of time, it leads to thrashing due to high paging frequency. Therefore, there should be a balance between usage of the main memory and swap space/paging space.

How much space must be reserved for swap space? The amount of swap space to be reserved out of the disk space depends on how much VM is needed to support the OS. The amount of swap space estimated may be overestimated or underestimated. If it is overestimated, then it may lead to wastage of space on the disk, whereas underestimation may cause the process to abort or the system to crash itself. Hence, overestimation is better compared to underestimation as there will be no chance of abortion of any process or system crash.

There are many factors that decide the swap-space size. The most important of all is the application size being used on the system. If a large-sized application such as computer-aided-design simulators, database-management products, or geologic analysis systems is used, then it may require swap space equal to or more than the size of the main memory. In this case, the application's minimum swap-space requirement must be checked before running it on the system. This requirement is generally specified in the application software manuals. Some OSs such as Solaris takes the swap-space size same as that of the main memory. However, with the increase in size of the memory, the swap space may not be as large as the memory but some percentage of it. For example, if the memory is of 2 GB, then 30% of the memory may be taken as swap space. The number of concurrent applications may also require some additional space in the swap space. Moreover, some trivial applications, light-weight applications, and heavy-weight applications must also be considered for estimating the size of swap space. Another requirement to be considered is the space for crash dumps resulting from fatal system failures. A crash dump is a copy of the kernel memory of the computer at the time of a fatal system error. The OS generates the crash dump and by default stores it to the swap space on the disk to know the cause of the system error. Kernel memory holding the crash dump accounts for around 20% of total memory. For example, if we have 1 GB of memory, then 256 MB of space must be reserved or added in the swap space for crash dumps.

Where should the swap space be allocated? A fast local disk is chosen for swap space, if available. If the swap space is allocated on a disk of remote computer, then it may affect the performance of the system while implementing VM. On a local disk, it may be implemented out of the existing file system or in a separate disk partition. In the separate-disk-partition method, the disk partition is taken as a raw partition, that is, no file system is implemented on this partition. This disk partition is known as *swap partition*. From the raw partitions, the blocks are allocated or de-allocated for swap-space management, that is, the blocks are allocated to store pages in the swap space or the blocks are de-allocated when there is no requirement to store the pages. Thus, the efficiency to access the blocks on the swap space increases as compared to the file system implementation since swap partition will use direct reads and writes to the disk and there is no overhead for accessing inodes, indirect blocks, and so on.

What will happen if more swap space is required? The swap space is implemented as a large file known as *swap file* if sliced out of the file system. All the file system commands such as create the swap file, space allocation, delete the swap file, and so on are used for the swap-space creation and management. For example, a swap file is created using *mkfile* command in some OSs. However, the access to the swap space using the swap-file implementation may be slow as it needs to access the directory structure and other data structures related to the file system. Therefore, the swap-file method is not generally recommended but it would be useful as a temporary solution if more swap space is required.

Through the installation program, swap space is initially configured during software installation. However, due to changes in system configurations and installation of some new software packages, more swap space is added using the commands provided in the OS. Alternatively, the existing disk can be repartitioned or another disk may be added.

15.9 RAID STRUCTURE

Although the disk is widely used for storage purposes, its slow access as compared to the processor and memory is a critical factor in overall computer system performance. There has been a performance gain in the disk access in the last few years, but this is not sufficient compared to the access speed of processor and memory. To bridge this gap, an idea was coined by a group of researchers at the University of California; they considered the concept of parallel processing in disk management. Patterson et al. suggested the use of an array of disks instead of one that could be accessed simultaneously to improve the speed as well as reliability. These multiple disks may operate independently and in parallel. With multiple disks, it was possible to organize the data in various ways and redundancy of data helps in increasing the reliability. The researchers named this new I/O as *RAID*. The idea of this multipledisk database design was accepted by the industries but changed the 'inexpensive' to 'independent'. This structure then became popular as RAID.

The RAID structure is a set of physical disk drives, and RAID controller (instead of a disk controller). However, the RAID structure is a single logical drive for the OS. The RAID structure is organized in seven levels (zero to six) of disk arrays. These levels do not represent any hierarchical organization but are different design architectures proposed by the researchers. In RAID, the data is distributed among various disks such that the data is accessed simultaneously from multiple drives, thereby having quick access. While designing the RAID structure, the following two aims are set:

Increased performance
Multiple disks can be accessed in parallel. Therefore, a file may be organized in such a way that the data is spread across multiple disks. Therefore, a file stored on RAID structure is accessed from multiple disks simultaneously, thereby improving the traditional disk accesses. Suppose, if two requests belong to two different disks, they can be served in parallel. In this way, more number of requests can be serviced as compared to a single-disk system, increasing the throughput of the system. Moreover, the response time in accessing a large data is reduced.

Increased reliability
In some applications such as database design or real-time system design, reliability is a critical requirement in the system. In these types of systems, the data loss cannot be afforded. Here, the design of RAID can utilize the multiple disk drives to improve the reliability by putting redundant copies of the data. Moreover, the use of multiple drives increases the probability of failure. So the RAID addresses the redundancy issue effectively so as to reduce the chance of loss of data.

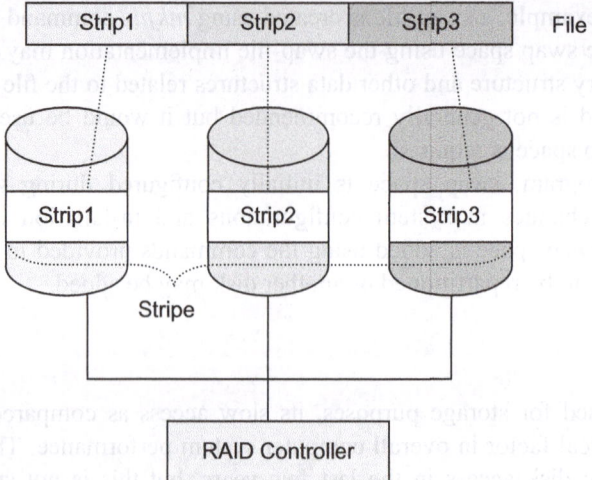

Fig. 15.17   Data striping

Improvement in performance and reliability is achieved via the following:

Data striping

In RAID, the data is stored on separate disks as a strip. A strip may be a fixed size block on the disk. A file is viewed as an array of contiguous strips, that is, the file data is split among multiple disks in the form of strips. The contiguous strips of a file are stored on separate disks at the same location. The set of strips stored on the disks in the array is known as a *stripe*. In this way, a file is stored in the form of strips across multiple disks along a stripe. Thus the OS views the array of multiple disks as a logical/virtual single disk. The file data can be processed in parallel depending on the length of the stripe, that is, the number of disks participating. If there are three disks in a stripe, the speed of accessing the data may increase by three times as the file data can be accessed simultaneously as shown in Fig. 15.17.

The strip size may affect the access time, throughput, and data transfer time. If the strip size is small, then the number of participating disks in the stripe will be increased. The smaller-sized strips are known as *fine-grained strips*. Fine-grained strips will reduce the access time as compared to a single disk and thereby increase the throughput and data transfer rate. If we increase the strip size, then it may be possible that a request will map only one or two strips. These large-sized strips known as *coarse-grained strips*, therefore, service more requests but may reduce the data-transfer rate.

Disk mirroring

As discussed earlier, the RAID structure provides redundancy of data in some systems where the failure of access or loss of data cannot be afforded. The redundancy is provided through the disk-mirroring concept where the duplicate of a strip is placed on a separate disk such that every disk has a mirror copy. If one of the disks fails, then the mirrored copy is accessed. However, mirroring will reduce the storage capacity on RAID structure.

RAID controller

Since the RAID structure consists of multiple disks, a normal disk controller is not able to handle this structure. Instead, RAID controllers are used to manage the disks. They perform data stripping and disk mirroring and maintain redundancy as necessary. For example, if a read request consists of three consecutive strips, then the RAID controller will break this request into three different read commands, mapping them on three disks so that they can be read in parallel.

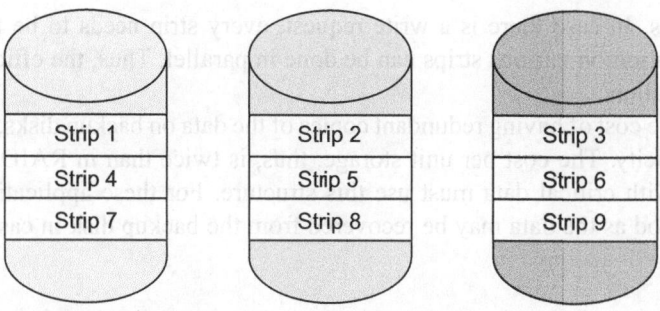

Fig. 15.18   RAID level 0

15.9.1 RAID Levels

The various RAID levels are discussed as follows:

RAID Level 0 (Striping)

It is the simplest form of RAID structure wherein the data is distributed across all the disks in the form of strips. RAID is like a logical disk that is divided into strips. These strips are mapped into an array of consecutive disks in round robin manner, that is, the first n logical strips are stored as the first strip on each of the disks, and the next n logical strips are stored as the second strip on each disk and so on, forming multiple stripes as shown in Fig. 15.18.

However, this structure does not provide any redundancy. If one of the disks in the array is not accessible, then the data or strips in that disk are lost. Consequently, all the other data retrieved from other disks may become unusable if they are related to a single request or the lost data. Due to this reason, this level is not considered as a true member of RAID structure.

RAID level 0 is simple to implement as it does not incur any cost for redundancy. Moreover, it increases the performance of disk access by the factor n where n is the number of disks in the disk array. This structure is more appropriate for the applications that do not require reliability but performance and low cost.

RAID Level 1 (Mirroring)

This structure includes striping as well as redundancy. The redundancy is achieved via disk mirroring, as shown in Fig. 15.19. When there is a read request, the disk with the shortest seek time and rotational latency can be accessed, thereby having the advantage of distributing

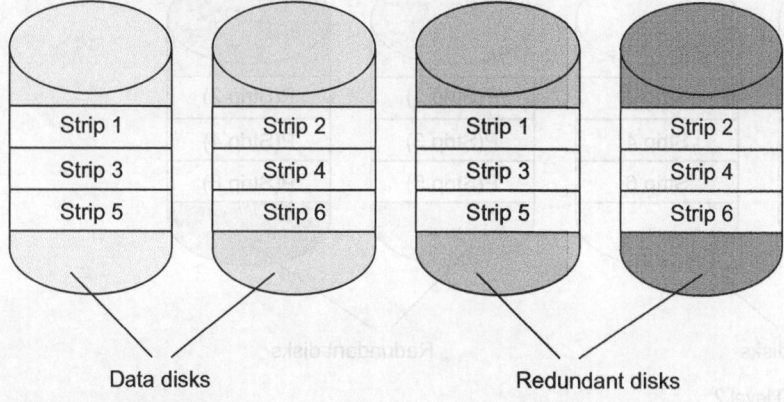

Data disks   Redundant disks

Fig. 15.19   RAID level 1

the load over more drives. In case there is a write request, every strip needs to be updated. However, this write operation on various strips can be done in parallel. Thus, the efficiency is not affected in write operation.

This structure incurs the cost of having redundant copies of the data on backup disks, thereby reducing the storage capacity. The cost per unit storage, thus, is twice than in RAID level 0. Therefore, applications with critical data must use this structure. For these applications, the fault tolerance is quite good as the data may be recovered from the backup disk in case of any disk failure.

RAID Level 2 (Fine-grained Striping and ECC Parity)

This structure uses fine-grained strips. Another modification in this structure is that instead of disk mirroring, an ECC scheme is implemented, thereby reducing storage overhead and cost. ECC is used to detect and correct the errors on the data. Hamming ECC is used for this purpose. Hamming code is calculated across corresponding bits on each disk. It uses parity bits to check for errors in data transmission from disks and possibly corrects them. The parity bits of the hamming code are stored in separate disks. For example, there is a data of four bits to be written and each strip stores one bit. In this case, the stripe consisting of four bits is written on four separate data disks where each strip stores one bit. RAID structure then calculates the parity bits corresponding to the data stored in the stripe and then stores them in separate parity disks as shown in Fig. 15.20. Thus, this structure reduces data storage, but even then, it is very less as compared to RAID level 1. The increase in number of parity disks is proportional to the log of number of data disks.

In case of a read operation, all the disks need to be accessed as the request data is spread over all the disks and moreover, the hamming code is calculated and compared with the values retrieved from the parity disks. Similarly, in case of a write operation even on a single strip, all the disks including data and the parity disks must be accessed to calculate the Hamming code and then write the data. Therefore, this structure may degrade the performance. Due to this reason, multiple requests cannot be serviced in this structure. Some systems therefore relax the condition of calculating the Hamming code in write operation but not on the read operation.

The RAID level 2 is applicable where more disk errors appear. However, today, the modern disk drives come with fault-tolerance mechanisms or with built-in error-detection such as Hamming code. Therefore, this level is not used nowadays.

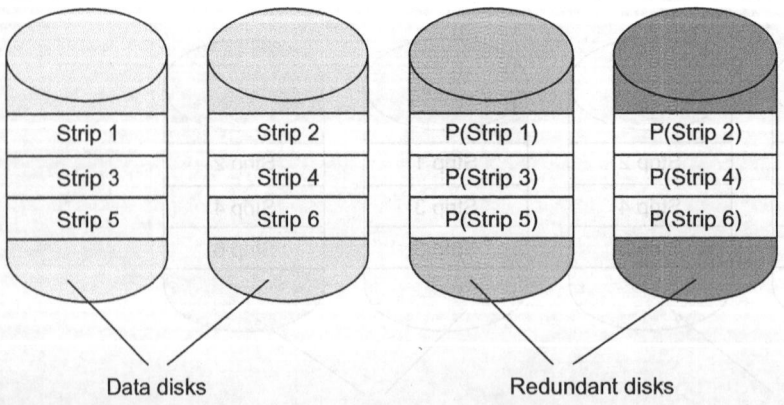

Data disks   Redundant disks

Fig. 15.20   RAID level 2

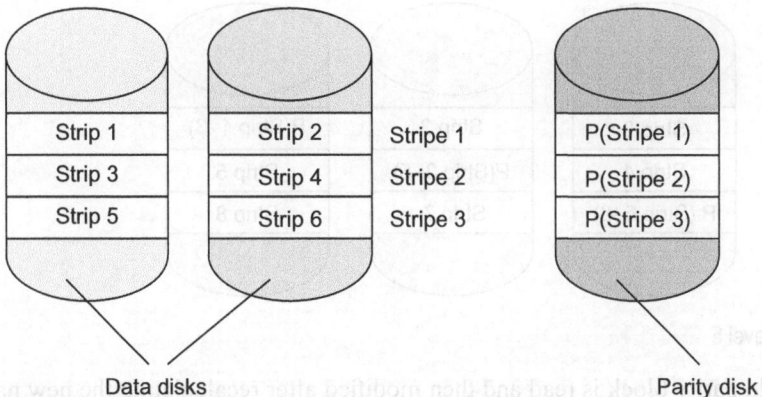

Fig. 15.21   RAID level 3

RAID Level 3 (Fine-grained Striping and Single-parity Disk)

This structure is also based on bit-level or byte-level striping. However, instead of Hamming code, it uses XOR ECC. The XOR code exploits the exclusive-OR operation to compute the parity of each strip. Suppose, a strip X = {1010}, the parity bit is 0 as there are even number of 1s. Suppose X = {1110}, the parity bit here is 1 as there are odd number of 1s. The parity for the ith strip on each data disk is calculated by applying XOR operations on the contents of ith strip of each disk. In case of a disk failure, the data on the disk can be reconstructed from the contents of the corresponding strips on remaining disks in the disk array by applying XOR operation on the strips. This structure uses only single-parity disk to store the parity of strips, thereby reducing the redundant storage space as shown in Fig. 15.21. Since the strip size is very small, the data transfer rate is high as parallel access on separate disks is possible especially in large files, but, multiple requests in parallel cannot be serviced.

Example 15.11

There are three data disks D1, D2, and D3, each consisting of a strip of single bit. The parity bit of ith strip is stored on the separate parity disk D4 and can be calculated as
D4(i) = D3(i) D2(i) D1(i).
 Suppose, disk D2 fails and the data on it is lost. In this case, the data of D2 can be regenerated as follows:
D2(i) = D4(i) D3(i) D1(i)

RAID Level 4 (Block Level XOR ECC Parity)

This structure uses large-sized strips and the data is striped as fixed-sized blocks, generally larger than a byte. In effect, each strip stores more data, thereby allowing multiple I/O requests to be serviced in parallel. The drawback is that the data-transfer rate becomes slow due to coarse-grained strips. It uses exclusive-OR ECC as used in RAID level 3. The parity bit for the strip on each disk is calculated and stored on the parity disk. Since the parity calculation is required for all read and write operations, the parity calculation can be eliminated for multiple read requests so that they can be accessed faster. However, it cannot be ignored in case of write operations. The large data read or write operations are fast in this structure as parallel access is possible. However, a small data read or write access may become slow due to parity bit calculation. Any write operation needs to read the old data block, update it, and then write the new data block. This read-update-write cycle may affect the performance of the system.

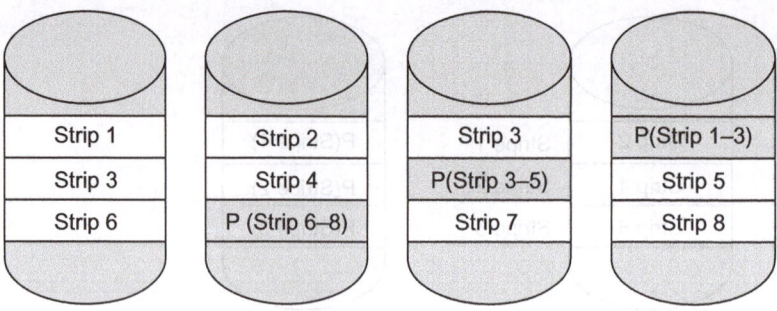

Fig. 15.22   RAID level 5

Moreover, the old parity block is read and then modified after recalculating the new parity bit. Thus, any write operation involves two reads for old blocks and two writes for the new blocks. Therefore, in case of small write requests, the overhead increases, thereby reducing the performance. Further, in case of multiple write requests, either small or large, the parity disk becomes a bottleneck as each write request needs to write on the disk for new parity bit.

RAID Level 5 (Block Level Distributed XOR ECC Parity)

In this structure, the parity bits are not stored in a single devoted disk. Rather each disk in the disk array participates to store the parity strip in a round robin fashion as shown in Fig. 15.22. This reduces the bottleneck seen in RAID level 4, and now the parity bits can be updated in parallel. However, the read-update-write cycle still exists for each write operation. There are different methods to reduce this overhead. One method is to cache the recently accessed data and parity strip. Second method is to store only the difference between the old parity and new parity bits in the memory. This is known as *parity logging*. The third method is to reduce the I/O operations during write operation to defer the parity generation in case of multiple small write operations at once and perform parity calculation only when the system load is light. This technique is known as *A Frequently Redundant Array of Independent Disks (AFRAID)*. This structure is frequently used RAID level due to its balanced features of reliability, performance, and cost.

RAID Level 6 (Block Level Dual Parity)

This structure enhances the reliability by including two types of parity calculations. One of them is XOR as used in previous structures. The other calculation method is based on an algorithm that is independent of data stored on the disks, providing higher reliability on the disks failure. The two types of parity strips (say, P1 and P2) calculated are stored on two separate

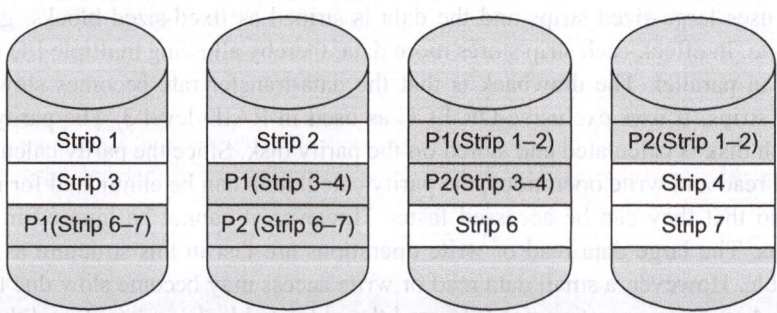

Fig. 15.23   RAID level 6

disks (see Fig. 15.23), thereby increasing the redundant storage. Thus, RAID level 6 may suffer in performance due to two parity disks for a single write operation.

To obtain better features of different RAID levels, RAID levels are combined. For example, RAID levels 0 and 1 have been combined to obtain RAID 0 + 1. It gives better performance and reliability. In this scheme, a set of *n* disks are striped, and then the stripe is mirrored on *n* redundant disks. The other structure that is available is RAID 1 + 0. The difference in 0 + 1 is that each data disk is first mirrored on the redundant disk and then the data disk, as well as the mirrored disk, is striped. The advantage in 1 + 0 is that in case of failure of a single disk, the mirror copy of the whole disk is available, while in case of 0 + 1, only mirrored strip of the failed disk is available. Therefore, RAID 1 + 0 provides better reliability. Other RAID levels such as 0 + 3, 0 + 5, and 1 + 5 have also been developed.

SUMMARY

Let us have a quick review of important concepts discussed in this chapter:

- The seek time is the time taken by the disk head to move from one cylinder to another.
- The rotational latency is the time taken by the addressed sector to rotate into a position such that it comes under the head.
- The transfer time is the actual time when the data to be read or written is transferred. The transfer time depends on the rotational speed of the disk and the number of bytes to be transferred.
- Disk bandwidth is the total number of bytes transferred divided by the total time between the first request of the service and completion of the last transfer of the data.
- Throughput is the total number of disk requests serviced per unit time.
- Response time is the average time spent in waiting by a disk request.
- Variance of response time is to measure how individual requests are serviced relative to average system performance. If the variance is low, then it means that most of the requests

- are serviced after waiting for a similar amount of time.
- The desired disk performance parameters are summarized as follows:

Parameter	Desired performance
Seek time	Minimize
Rotational latency	Minimize
Transfer time	Minimize
Bandwidth	Maximize
Throughput	Maximize
Average response time	Minimize
Variance of response time	Minimize

- The various disk-scheduling algorithms with their criteria and pros and cons are summarized as follows:

Algorithm	Criteria	Pros/cons
FCFS	the requests are scheduled in the order as they have arrived in the disk queue.	Fair Low throughput High average response time Low variance High seek time
SSTF	the request whose seek time is the shortest will be executed first.	Reduced seek time High variance High throughput Starvation Unfair

(Contd)

(Table Contd)

SCAN	services the requests in the direction of its head movement and continues until it reaches the end of disk	Good average response time Low variance High throughput Starvation
C-SCAN	considers the queue of cylinders as a circular queue such that after reaching the last cylinder, it starts scanning again from the first cylinder.	High throughput Low variance Starvation
F-SCAN	the new requests are deferred until all the pending old requests in the queue have been processed.	High throughput Good average response time Low variance
N-SCAN	serves the *n* requests in the queue in a sweep when the head is moving in one direction.	High throughput but low as compared to F-SCAN Good average response time Low variance
LOOK	the disk head looks ahead in its direction of movement for the last request, moves to the last request, and changes its preferred direction there only and continues servicing the request.	Reduces seek time High throughput Low variance Good average response time
C-LOOK	Combines the features of LOOK and C-SCAN algorithm.	Low variance as compared to LOOK High throughput but low as compared to LOOK Reduces seek time Good average response time

- Rotational optimization is to consider the effect of rotational latency on the performance of the I/O operation on the disk. The various disk-scheduling algorithms that take into consideration the rotational optimization are summarized as follows:

Algorithm	Criteria	Pros/cons
SLTF	examines all the requests in the queue and finds out the request having the shortest rotational delay.	Reduces the rotational latency High throughput Starvation
SPTF	considers the seek time as well as rotational latency.	Reduces the rotational latency High throughput Starvation
SATF	the total access time is calculated for each request and the shortest one is scheduled first.	

- The rotational optimization-based disk-scheduling algorithms are dependent on the availability of disk configuration and other details.
- There are three steps in disk formatting: low-level formatting, disk partitioning, and logical formatting.
- The rotational optimization-based disk-scheduling algorithms are dependent on the availability of disk configuration and other details.
- There are three steps in disk formatting: low-level formatting, disk partitioning, and logical formatting.
- The *low-level formatting* is performed by the manufacturer and the other two steps are performed by the OS.
- The partition that contains the boot code is known as *boot partition*.
- The disk that contains the boot partition is called a *boot disk* or *system disk*.
- The information regarding each partition is stored in one data structure known as a *partition table*. The partition table stores the information about each partition such as its starting sector, size of each partition, and so on.
- The logical-formatting operation lays down a boot block in the partition and creates a file system.
- The disk controller maps the bad sector to the spare one out of pre-defined spare sectors. This is known as *sector sparing* or *forwarding*.

- The *low-level formatting* is performed by the manufacturer and the other two steps are performed by the OS.
- The partition that contains the boot code is known as *boot partition*.
- Instead of mapping the bad sector to the spare sector, just shift all the sectors to bypass the bad one. This method is known as *sector slipping*.
- The sector sparing and sector slipping can also be implemented by the OS.
- Swap space can be defined as a temporary storage location on the disk to implement the VM when system's memory requirements exceed the size of available main memory.
- The multiple disks operate independently and in parallel to organize the data in various ways, and redundancy of data increases the reliability. This is known as *RAID*.
- In RAID, the data is stored on separate disks as a strip. A strip may be a fixed size block on the disk.
- The set of strips at the same location on each disk in the array is known as a *stripe*. The small-sized strips are known as *fine-grained strips*, whereas the large-sized strips are called *coarse-grained strips*.
- The RAID structure is organized in seven levels (zero to six) of disk arrays, which are summarized as follows:

RAID level	Description	Pros/cons	Disks required
0	Striped Non-redundant	Simple to implement High data transfer High I/O request rate	n
1	Mirrored Redundant	Increases data transfer capacity for read operation but not for write operation. Increases I/O request rate twice for read but not for write.	2n
2	Fine-grained striping Redundancy through Hamming ECC	Highest data transfer capacity Increases I/O request rate twice	n + m
3	Fine-grained striping Single-parity disk Redundancy through XOR ECC	Highest data transfer capacity Increases I/O request rate twice	n + 1
4	Coarse-grained striping Single-parity disk Redundancy through XOR ECC	Low data transfer capacity Low I/O request rate	n + 1

(Contd)

(*Table Contd*)

5	Coarse-grained striping Distributed parity Redundancy through XOR ECC	Low data transfer capacity Low I/O request rate	n + 1
6	Coarse-grained striping Dual distributed parity	Low data transfer capacity Low I/O request rate	n + 2

MULTIPLE CHOICE QUESTIONS

1. _____ is the time taken by the disk head to move from one cylinder to another one.
   - (a) Seek time
   - (b) Rotational latency
   - (c) Transfer time
   - (d) None

2. _____ is the time taken by the addressed sector of the appropriate track to rotate into a position such that read/write head is accessible to it.
   - (a) Seek time
   - (b) Rotational latency
   - (c) Transfer time
   - (d) None

3. _____ depends on the rotational speed of the disk and the number of bytes to be transferred.
   - (a) Seek time
   - (b) Rotational latency
   - (c) Transfer time
   - (d) None

4. Which algorithm is better when the load on the disk is low and the requests are uniformly distributed?
   - (a) SCAN
   - (b) LOOK
   - (c) FIFO
   - (d) SSTF

5. _____ algorithm may be best suitable to batch-processing systems where high throughput and average response time are required.
   - (a) SCAN
   - (b) LOOK
   - (c) FIFO
   - (d) SSTF

6. _____ will provide low variance of response time due to random seek.
   - (a) SCAN
   - (b) LOOK
   - (c) FIFO
   - (d) SSTF

7. _____ is also known as *elevator algorithm*.
   - (a) SCAN
   - (b) LOOK
   - (c) FIFO
   - (d) SSTF

8. _____ eliminates unnecessary seek operations and thereby increases average response time.
   - (a) SCAN
   - (b) LOOK
   - (c) FIFO
   - (d) SSTF

9. C-LOOK achieves the benefits of both

   - (a) SCAN and LOOK
   - (b) SCAN and FCFS
   - (c) C-SCAN and LOOK
   - (d) C-SCAN and SSTF

10. The information regarding each partition is stored in one data structure known as
   - (a) *partition table*
   - (b) boot partition
   - (c) bad partition
   - (d) None

11. _____ formatting operation lays down a boot block in the partition and creates a file system.
   - (a) High-level
   - (b) Low-level
   - (c) Both high-level and low-level
   - (d) None

12. _____ formatting is performed by the manufacturer.
   - (a) High-level
   - (b) Low-level
   - (c) Both high-level and low-level
   - (d) None

13. While the disk is tested by the manufacturer at the time of low-level formatting, a list of bad sectors is maintained on the disk by
   - (a) manufacturer
   - (b) disk controller
   - (c) the OS
   - (d) none

14. The set of strips at the same location on each disk in the array is known as a
   - (a) *strip queue*
   - (b) stripe
   - (c) striping
   - (d) none

15. Which of the following does not provide redundancy?
   - (a) RAID level 0
   - (b) RAID level 1
   - (c) RAID level 2
   - (d) RAID level 4

16. Block level XOR ECC parity is used in
   - (a) RAID level 1
   - (b) RAID level 4
   - (c) RAID level 5
   - (d) RAID level 6

17. Block level distributed parity is used in
   - (a) RAID level 1
   - (b) RAID level 4
   - (c) RAID level 5
   - (d) RAID level 6

18. Block level dual parity is used in
   - (a) RAID level 1
   - (b) RAID level 4
   - (c) RAID level 5
   - (d) RAID level 6

REVIEW QUESTIONS

1. Discuss the system parameters that decide the need for disk scheduling.

2. Define seek time, rotational latency, transfer time, response time, and variance of response time.

3. Explain the criteria and situation where the following disk-scheduling algorithms will perform better:
   (a) FCFS
   (b) SSTF
   (c) SCAN
   (d) C-SCAN
   (e) N-SCAN
   (f) F-SCAN
   (g) LOOK
   (h) C-LOOK
   (i) S-LOOK

4. Differentiate between the following:
   (a) SCAN and C-SCAN
   (b) SCAN and N-SCAN
   (c) SCAN and F-SCAN
   (d) LOOK and C-LOOK
   (e) LOOK and S-LOOK
   (f) S-LOOK and C-LOOK
   (g) N-SCAN and F-SCAN

5. What is rotational optimization?

6. Explain the criteria and situation where the following disk-scheduling algorithms will perform better:
   (a) SLTF
   (b) SPTF
   (c) SATF

7. Define the following:
   (a) boot partition
   (b) bad sector
   (c) paging space
   (d) swap partition
   (e) data striping

8. Differentiate between the following:
   (a) sector sparing and sector slipping
   (b) seek optimization and rotational optimization
   (c) low-level and high-level disk formatting

9. What are transient and permanent errors on disk?

10. What is the role of disk controller and the OS in reference to bad sectors?

11. What are the factors that decide swap-space size?

12. What is RAID? Explain its various levels.

13. What is the difference between RAID 0 + 1 and 1 + 0?

14. Compare and contrast F-SCAN- and N-SCAN-scheduling algorithms.

15. What is XOR ECC?

16. How many I/O operations are required for a write operation in RAID level 4?

17. How does RAID level 5 reduces the bottleneck of single parity disk for write operations?

18. What are different methods to reduce the read-update-write cycle overhead for write operations?

Additional differentiate items (continuation of question near top right):
(f) coarse-grained and fine-grained striping
(g) disk mirroring
(h) RAID controller
(i) parity logging
(j) AFRAID

BRAIN TEASERS

1. Is the rotational latency same for each disk access?

2. What will be the criteria or situations to choose seek-optimization-based and rotational-optimization-based disk-scheduling algorithms?

3. What will be the requirement for average response time and variance of response time in the case of a web server that serves multiple user requests frequently?

4. FCFS is considered to be a fair algorithm and reduces variance of response time. Then why is it not a preferred algorithm?

5. The overhead in SSTF is proportional to the number of requests in the queue. Explain how.

6. SCAN performs unnecessary seek operations. Explain how.

7. SCAN is a biased scheduling algorithm. Is it true? Explain.

8. Both SSTF and SCAN may cause indefinite postponement of the requests. Which one of the two is better in this regard?

9. F-SCAN is an improvement over SCAN algorithm. However, it may lead to lower throughput. Explain how.

10. C-LOOK is an improvement over LOOK-scheduling algorithm. However, it may lead to increased average response time and lower throughput. Explain how.

11. Consider a disk queue with I/O requests on the following cylinders in their arriving order: 37, 56, 98, 32, 108, 78, 44, 78, 67, 69, 100

   The disk head is assumed to be at Cylinder 40 and moving in the direction of decreasing number of cylinders. The disk consists of total 150 cylinders. Calculate and show with diagram the disk head movement using FCFS-, SSTF-, SCAN-, F-SCAN-, N-SCAN- (n = 3), LOOK-, and C-LOOK-scheduling algorithms.

12. In Problem 11, suppose some new requests arrive as given

   (a) Requests on Cylinders 60, 85, and 90 arrive while processing at 37.

   (b) Requests on Cylinders 70, 40, and 130 arrive while processing at 78.

   What will happen to these new requests according to all the scheduling algorithms?

13. Consider a disk queue with I/O requests on the following cylinders in their arriving order:

67, 12, 15, 45, 48, 50, 109, 89, 56, 59, 34, 88, 130, 24, 109, 22

The disk head is assumed to be at Cylinder 80 and moving in the direction of increasing number of cylinders. The disk consists of total 150 cylinders. Calculate and show with diagram the disk head movement using FCFS-, SSTF-, SCAN-, F-SCAN-, N-SCAN- (n = 3), LOOK, and C-LOOK-scheduling algorithms.

14. In Problem 13, suppose some new requests arrive as given

(a) Requests on Cylinders 60, 85, and 90 arrive while processing at 50.

(b) Requests on Cylinders 70, 40, and 128 arrive while processing at 130.

What will happen to these new requests according to all the scheduling algorithms?

Case Study V: Input/Output Management in UNIX/ Solaris/Linux/Windows

UNIX

In UNIX, I/O devices are associated with special files and the file system manages these special files. Thus, the I/O operations are performed on the devices in the same manner as of files. There are three main kinds of I/Os in Free Berkely Software Distribution (FreeBSD): block devices, character devices, and socket interface. Input/Output requests can be handled with buffer cache. In UNIX, buffer cache is basically a disk cache. There are two types of buffers used: system buffer cache and character queues. The DMA is used to transfer data between the buffer cache and the user process space. Buffer cache is maintained further with three more queues described as follows:

Free list   It is a list of all available slots in the cache.

Device list   It is a list of the buffers that are presently associated with each disk.

Driver I/O queue   It is a list of buffers that are waiting for an I/O.

The size of buffer cache affects the performance of the system, so it should be decided appropriately. The size should be large enough such that the cache hit ratio is high and the number of actual I/O transfers is low. In FreeBSD, buffer cache is optimized by adjusting the amount of memory used by programs and disk cache continuously.

Character Queues

Character queues, also known as C-lists, are smaller buffers as compared to buffer cache. All free character buffers are placed in a single free list. When there is a write system call for a device, the characters are placed in an output character queue for it. The hardware interrupts start de-queuing of characters and thereby transfer the characters. If there is no space in the output queue, the system call is blocked unless there is sufficient space. The input is also interrupt driven as discussed for output. However, for input, two character queues are maintained: raw queue and canonical queue. Raw queue is to collect characters coming from the terminal port. The canonical queue is where the input is being processed.

SOLARIS

Asynchronous I/O

Asynchronous I/O in Solaris is dealt with two interfaces known as aioread() and aiowrite() routines. These routines do not block a calling process or thread when it issues a read or write but allows it to continue. A signal known as SIGIO is sent to the calling thread as a notification of completion of

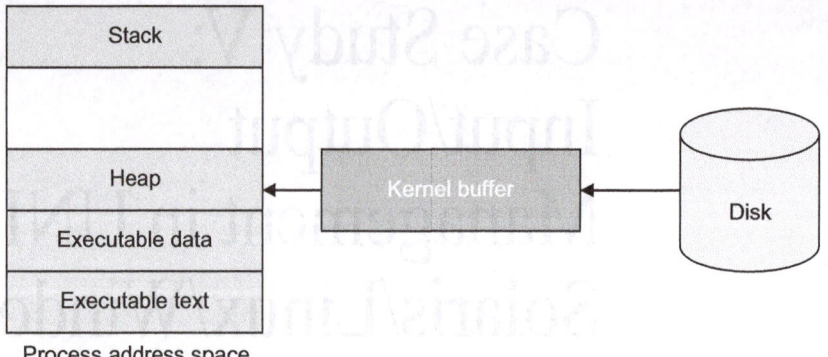

Fig. CS5.1   File I/O with kernel buffer

I/O operation or about the error encountered. However, this type of dealing with asynchronous I/O does not provide optimal performance for applications that extensively make use of this asynchronous I/O. In case of extensive use, there are overheads involved in creating, managing, and scheduling of user threads. In response to this, a low overhead implementation to deal with asynchronous I/O was devised known as *kernel asynchronous I/O* (kaio). The kaio is the method available in Solaris 2.4 onwards. However, kaio works only when the target of asynchronous I/O is a character device.

File I/O, as we know, is performed with system calls that perform I/O on behalf of a process with the help of a kernel buffer (Fig. CS5.1).

Another way to perform file I/O is implemented in the form of memory mapping. This is done by mapping a file directly into the process's address space (Fig.CS5.2). There is a system call known as *mmap*() that allows to map a range of a file into a process's address space and the file can be accessed by referencing to memory locations. This method reduces the overhead of read and write system calls, and there is no need to handle the data twice as in buffer method.

Fig. CS5.2   Memory mapped file I/O

Solaris Page Cache

When we use traditional buffer cache method for file data caching, the file system looks up the corresponding disk direct/indirect block for the file the process has requested in its system call. After having the block number, it requests that block from file I/O system. If the request is for the first time, the I/O system retrieves the block from the disk and the subsequent requests are satisfied by the buffer cache (Fig.CS5.3). The disadvantage here is that every time we need to invoke the file system and look up physical block number for every cached I/O operation.

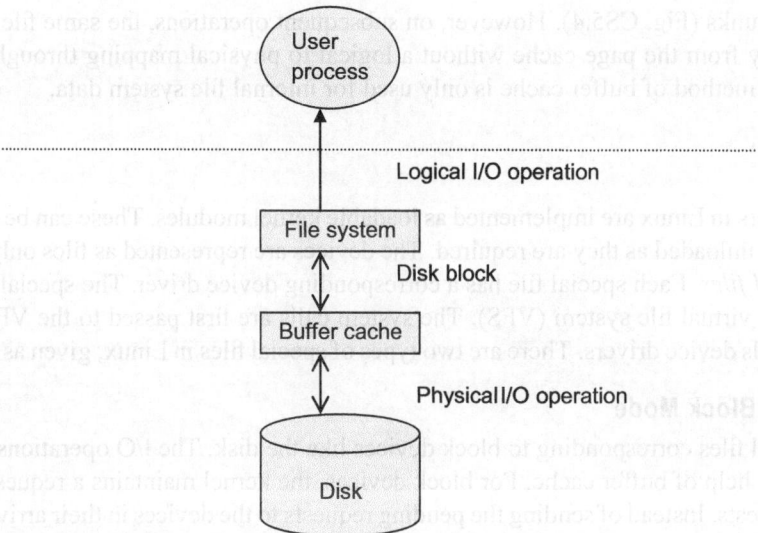

Fig. CS5.3   Buffer cache-based I/O

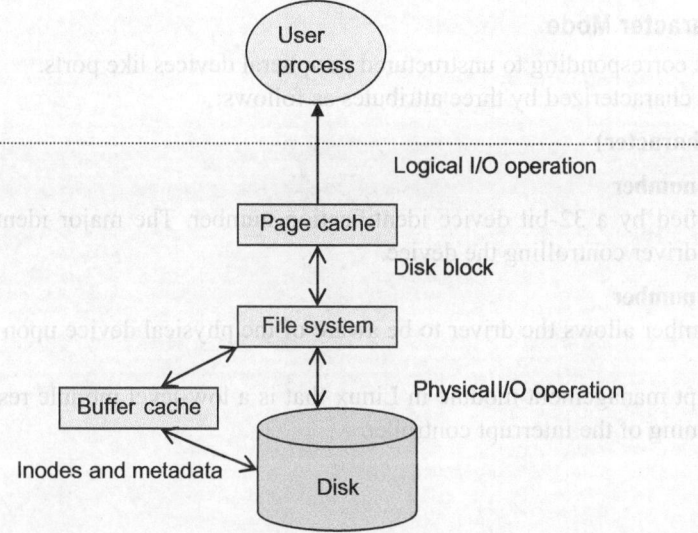

Fig. CS5.4   Page cache-based I/O

Instead of traditional caching file system data, Solaris has a new caching method known as *page cache*. The limitation of old caching method is that its size is limited, that is it cannot be expanded. Moreover, the old method is not efficient. The page cache, as an improved caching method, is dynamically sized and can use all the memory that is presently not in use. It is basically a virtual file cache rather than a physical block cache. Thus, it caches file blocks in the form of page caches rather than disk blocks. The OS retrieves the file data efficiently by looking up the file reference and seek offset. In the older method, on the other hand, the OS invokes the file system, looks up the physical disk block number corresponding to the file, and retrieves that block from the physical block cache. When a process requests an I/O operation through system call, the file data are retrieved from disk through the file system into memory in page-sized chunks (Fig. CS5.4). However, on subsequent operations, the same file data are retrieved directly from the page cache without a logical to physical mapping through the file system. The old method of buffer cache is only used for internal file system data.

LINUX

The device drivers in Linux are implemented as loadable kernel modules. These can be dynamically loaded and unloaded as they are required. The devices are represented as files only known as *device special files*. Each special file has a corresponding device driver. The special files are accessed via the virtual file system (VFS). The system calls are first passed to the VFS. After this, the VFS calls device drivers. There are two types of special files in Linux, given as follows:

Special File in Block Mode

These are special files corresponding to block devices like the disk. The I/O operations are carried out with the help of buffer cache. For block devices, the kernel maintains a request list for the pending requests. Instead of sending the pending requests to the devices in their arrival order, these are sent to the request list. The kernel now can order the requests (based on some factors like location of disk head) in request list, so that I/O operations performance can be increased.

Special Files in Character Mode

These are special files corresponding to unstructured peripheral devices like ports.

Each special file is characterized by three attributes as follows:

File type (block or character)

Major identification number

Each device is identified by a 32-bit device identification number. The major identification number identifies the driver controlling the device.

Minor identification number

This identification number allows the driver to be aware of the physical device upon which it should act.

There is an interrupt management module in Linux that is a low-level module responsible for physical programming of the interrupt controller.

Disk Scheduling

Linux adopts two improved disk-scheduling algorithms discussed as follows:

Deadline Scheduling

This scheduling algorithm prevents starvation problem occurring in disk scheduling. A deadline scheduler has been designed, which services each request within a given deadline. The deadline scheduler attempts to service the request before its deadline expires. To meet the deadline of each request, the scheduler has to process quickly. For this purpose, a single queue for requests does not suffice as linear search of requests in this queue would lead to poor performance and missed deadlines. Therefore, deadline scheduler uses the following three queues:

- Sorted elevator queue
- Read first-in-first-out (FIFO) queue
- Write FIFO queue

When a new request arrives, the request is placed in this queue. The queue is sorted according to the disk head positions. Each incoming request is also placed at the tail of a read or write queue depending on the type of request. Thus, two separate queues based on the operations are maintained to improve the efficiency. There is a deadline period with each request. For a read request, the expiration time is 0.5 s, whereas for a write request, it is 5 s. These values provide better performance in general but can be changed by system administrator. When a request gets serviced, it is removed from the sorted queue as well as from the corresponding read/write queue.

Anticipatory Scheduling

In case there are a number of synchronous read requests, the deadline scheduling may not perform well. The deadline scheduler after servicing a read request may switch to another request, thereby causing delay in read requests. It would be nice if all the read requests are serviced first and then the other requests. Due to the principle of locality, it is possible that successive read requests by a process may lie on the disk near to each other. There are chances that the process requesting a read operation will further issue another read request to the same region on the disk. The performance of the system may be increased if there is a delay for a short time after servicing a read request to look whether there is a nearby read request. Thus, this scheduler anticipates the future requests. The standard delay between the read requests is 6 milliseconds.

WINDOWS

In Windows, I/O management involves many kernel components. The user processes interact with environment subsystem that passes I/O requests to the I/O manager (Fig. CS5.5). The I/O manager in turn interacts with device drivers to process an I/O request. The I/O manager keeps

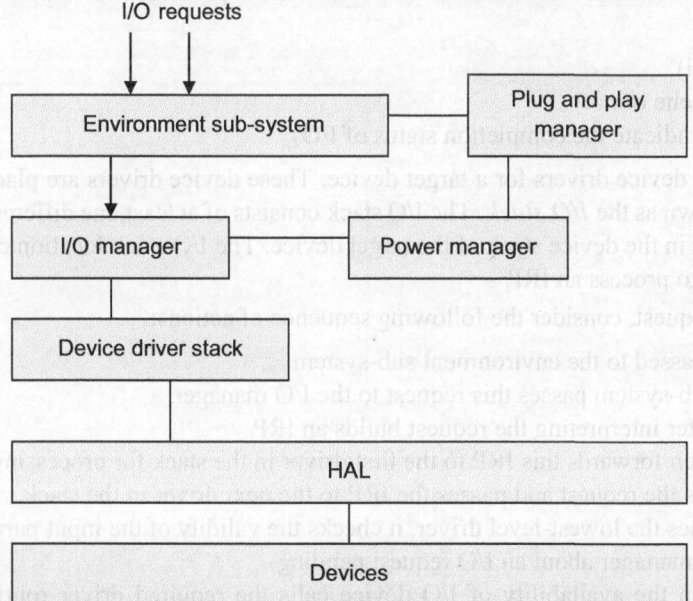

Fig. CS5.5 Input/Output management in Windows

track of device drivers, file systems, and even buffers used for I/O requests. There are a number of device drivers to cooperate with the I/O manager. This is known as *device driver stack*. Besides this, plug and play manager and power manager also help in I/O management. Plug and play manager recognizes the new devices when connected to the system and allocates or de-allocates the I/O to these newly connected devices. The power manager on the other hand, conserves energy as per the requirement of devices.

Device Driver Stack

Since an I/O request may involve a number of device drivers, the driver stack consists of a number of device drivers. Some of those are as follows:

Low-level driver   It interacts with HAL and controls a device.

High-level driver   It abstracts hardware details and passes the I/O requests to the low-level driver.

Intermediate driver   It is an intermediate driver that may filter or process I/O requests and export an interface for a specific device.

Windows has a standard driver model known as *Windows driver model* (WDM) defined by Microsoft. Windows driver model has three types of device drivers as follows:

Bus driver   It interfaces with a hardware bus and provides some generic functions for the devices on the bus.

Filter driver   It may add additional features to any device. It sorts I/O requests among several devices.

Function driver   It implements the main function of the device, that is it performs I/O processing and provides the device's interface.

In Windows, an I/O request is processed with an I/O request packet (IRP). An IRP consists of two parts: header block and I/O stack. Header block contains permanent information such the following:

- Mode (user or kernel)
- Flags (e.g., to use cache or not)
- I/O status block (to indicate the completion status of I/O)

There may be many device drivers for a target device. These device drivers are placed in a list for each device known as the *I/O stack*. The I/O stack consists of at least one different stack location for each driver in the device stack of the target device. The I/O stack location contains information necessary to process an IRP.

To process an I/O request, consider the following sequence of actions:

1. The I/O request is passed to the environment sub-system.
2. The environment sub-system passes this request to the I/O manager.
3. The I/O manager after interpreting the request builds an IRP.
4. The I/O manager then forwards this IRP to the first driver in the stack for processing.
5. The driver processes the request and passes the IRP to the next driver in the stack.
6. When the IRP reaches the lowest-level driver, it checks the validity of the input parameters and notifies the I/O manager about an I/O request pending.
7. The I/O manager on the availability of I/O device calls the required driver routine that handles the requested I/O operation.

There may be synchronous and asynchronous I/O requests. Windows supports both of them. The asynchronous mode is used when there is a need to enhance the performance of the application, as the application can continue processing after it initiates an asynchronous I/O request. However, there must be some mechanism by which the application that invoked the I/O request must know when the I/O request is complete. Windows provides multiple ways to signal this. A thread in the application may poll the device to check whether I/O has been performed. Another method is that the thread uses an event object and waits for this object. Another alternative method is to use a queue associated with a thread. This is known as *asynchronous procedure call (APC) queue*. In this method, when a thread makes an I/O request, it specifies a user mode procedure that is run when the I/O completes. On the Windows server, there is another method known as the *I/O completion port* for this purpose. The I/O completion signal is sent to this port only.

PART VI
Security and Protection

16   Security Issues

16.1   INTRODUCTION

Security is the most important and unavoidable parameter in the computer system in today's world. With increase in dependency on online systems today, there is an increase in the demand of the system's security. Hacking, of either stand-alone systems or online systems, has become the socio-technical problem of the world. In this chapter, the objectives of the security, required on any type of system, are discussed. Breaching the security objectives result in threats and attacks. Some of them have also been discussed. The security objectives can be fulfilled, only if we are able to devise some mechanisms to protect the systems. The protection mechanisms have been discussed in the next chapter.

16.2   SECURITY OBJECTIVES

A system is secure if its resources are used and accessed, as intended under all circumstances. Let us see what the expectations from a secure system are. The basic security concepts that need to be covered by system security are discussed in the following list:

- **Confidentiality**
  This concept refers to the protection against disclosure of information to any unauthorized entity.
- **Integrity**
  This concept refers to the protection against the altered message in transit or by other than the originator of the information.
- **Authentication**
  This concept deals with establishing the validity of a transmission, message, or originator. In other words, the information received by a receiver has been originated from a specific known source.
- **Authorization**
  This concept refers to the process, through which a requester is allowed to receive a service, or perform an operation.
- **Availability**

  This concept refers to the assurance that information and communications services are available for use, when needed.

Learning Objectives

After reading this chapter, you should be able to understand:

- Security objectives
- Threats to security objectives
- Role of intruders in security-breaching
- Standard security attacks
- Security levels
- Some security attacks that appear inside the system
- Some security attacks that appear from outside the system

16.3   SECURITY PROBLEM

The effects of security breaches could be extensive and can cause loss of information, corruption of information, misinformation, privacy violations, denial-of-service, and so on. The security breaches can be of two categories: malicious and accidental. *Malicious breaches* are the intentional misuse of the system resources, and *accidental breaches* are unintentional hardware, software, or human errors or any natural calamity.

Any security breach is a result of *vulnerability* in the system. Vulnerability is a weakness in the system that might be exploited to cause loss or harm. If a system does not provide password facility before accessing, it is considered as a vulnerability of the system. A *threat* to a computing system is a set of circumstances that has the potential to cause loss or harm, exploiting the vulnerability of the system. An *attack* is an attempt by an intruder to break the security. Both threat and attack are results of vulnerabilities in the system.

Some of these threats and their corresponding attacks are discussed in the subsequent sections.

16.3.1 Unauthorized Disclosure

It is a threat to the confidentiality of a system. An unauthorized user may disclose critical data, leading to loss or harm. The consequent attacks of this threat are:

- Sensitive data are exposed to an unauthorized entity. For example, passwords, credit card numbers, and so on.
- In communication, an unauthorized node receives the sensitive data that are supposed to be between two authorized parties. It is known as *interception*.
- An unauthorized entity may infer the information, by observing the traffic in a network, or from a database, and disclose the same. It is known as *inference*.

16.3.2 Deception

It is a threat to the integrity objective. An authorized entity receives some false/unauthorized data and believes those to be true/authorized. The consequent attacks of this threat are the following:

- An unauthorized entity may pose to be an authorized one and attempt to gain access to the system. This attack is known as *Masquerade*.
- A file or database may be altered or some data may be replaced with false data. This attack is known as *falsification*.
- A user may deny that he has sent or received data. This attack is known as *repudiation*.

16.3.3 Disruption

It is a threat to the availability objective. It interrupts or prevents the correct operation of the system. For instance, a system receives so much data that the communication system is not able to handle them, thereby, interrupting the operation on the system. This attack is known as *denial-of-service* (DoS).

16.4   INTRUDERS

The entity or a person, who tries to break the security objectives, is known as an intruder. According to the Anderson report published in 1980, there are three classes of an intruder:

- **Masquerader**

  It is an individual who does not have any authority to access a computer system, but gains the access control, to exploit a legitimate user's account. For an instance, a person somehow steals or breaks the password of a system and uses it.

- **Misfeasor**

  This type of intruder is an authorized user on the system, but misuses his/her privileges on it. For example, a person who is authorized to access a system may leak some secret information or password to someone else.

- **Clandestine User**

  This type of user somehow gains the supervisory control of the system by exploiting its vulnerabilities, and tries to elude the access control mechanisms implemented in the system, in order to gain administrative privileges to a computer resource.

There may be different behaviours of an intruder, based on the intention of intruding upon a system. Based on this behaviour, there may be two types of intruders:

- **Hackers**

  The intruders, who break into the system just for fun, or to pose a challenge, are known as hackers. Today, there is a big community of hackers who are motivated by these reasons. Hackers can also be hired Internet security experts, who find vulnerabilities in systems. These hackers are also known as *white hat hackers*.

- **Criminals**

  These are intruders, who work in organized groups to break the system for profits, and thereby, results in a business, but in an unethical way. These criminal hackers work systematically not just for fun or challenge, as hackers do, but with specific targets of gaining profits.

An intruder, once logged into a computer system, starts harming the system. These attacks are known as *insider attacks*. But there are a large number of attacks being faced externally by a system connected to the Internet. These attacks are known as *outsider attacks*. Another category of intruders is based on the type of damage they do. An intruder may silently observe the network traffic or retrieve the system's data, but does not modify anything. This type of intruder is known as *passive intruder*. The passive intruders do not harm at the moment, but exploit the retrieved information to harm in the future. An intruder, who modifies the data on the network or a system, is known as an *active intruder*.

A large variety of intrusion has been in practice through the use of malicious software by the attackers. The malicious software, also known as *malware*, is a program or set of programs that may infect the user's system in such a way, that this malicious program is hidden on the system and gets activated, according to some condition, or corrupts the files/data on the system, or the system is not available to use. In other words, the malicious software may harm the system in any way, and the consequences may be disastrous for the user. Some of the malicious software will be discussed later.

16.5 SOME STANDARD SECURITY ATTACKS

In this section, some standard attacks have been discussed that are in common use by the intruders. Intruders may use one or the other attack, or combination of some of the attacks, to attack on a computer system or a network system.

16.5.1 Denial-of-Service

This type of attack is attempted by an intruder to make a system's resource unavailable to its authorized and intended users. In general, DoS attacks are implemented, by either forcing the host computer to reset, or consuming all of its hardware or software resources, such that it can no longer provide its intended service. For instance, an intruder may flood a target machine with external communication requests, such that it responds slowly or even cannot respond to legitimate traffic. DoS mostly attacks websites or services, such as banks, credit card payment gateways, and so on. Some basic types of DoS attacks are:

- Consumption of computational resources, such as bandwidth, disk space, processor time, and so on.
- Disruption of configuration information like routing packet information.
- Disruption of state information like resetting of TCP sessions.
- Obstruction of the communication media.

16.5.2 Spoofing

In this type of attack, an intruder pretends to be a valid host in a communication by breaching the authentication, and then gains access for which they are not entitled. The following types of spoofing are in common use by intruders:

IP Spoofing

The attacker makes use of header of IP packets in this type of attack. Since the header contains the source and destination address, the attacker puts a forged source address in it, such that, to the receiver, it appears that the packet is from a different machine, hiding the true source. The receiver that receives this packet responds to the forged source address. IP spoofing can be used with DoS attacks as well.

Identity Spoofing

In this spoofing, an attacker gets passwords and login information, by using fictitious digital certificates or authorization prompts. Identity spoofing has effects, ranging from mild displeasure to extreme danger. A stolen identity may lead to accessing bank accounts and other personal information.

Web Spoofing

In this type of attack, the intruder first copies web pages of a website. A copied web page is then created and displayed on the web, when a victim user opens the same web page. The user opens the spoofed page, instead of the actual web page, and is led to believe that he/she is communicating with the real server.

Email Spoofing

In this technique, an email address is used, under false authentication or web spoofing, where domains are 'hijacked' or faked. It occurs when a person receives an email that appears to have originated from one source, but actually was sent from a fake source. It is an attempt to trick the user into releasing confidential information such as passwords, banking details, telephone numbers, and so on, to cause damage.

16.5.3 Session Hijacking

In this type, when two nodes in a communication network enter into a session, at the same time, the intruder enters into the communication; intercepts the traffic and carries on the session

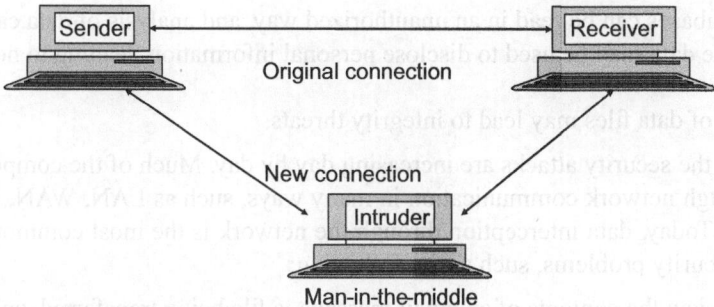

Fig. 16.1 Man-in-the-middle attack

in the name of any one of the two nodes. This is known as session hijacking as the session established between the two nodes has been hijacked by the intruder. For instance, the intruder may intercept the credit card details while online shopping.

16.5.4 Man-in-the-Middle Attack

In this type of attack, a malicious user observes the communication between the sender and receiver, and leaks any information being sent. The intruder intercepts the network traffic, collects the data, and then forwards it to the destination, which the user was originally intending to visit (see Fig. 16.1).

16.5.5 Replay Attack

In this attack, the attacker sends a data packet, which was earlier sent by some other user, in the hope of reproducing the effect. These attacks are like man-in-the-middle attacks that involve intercepting data packets and replaying them, that is, resending them to the receiving server.

16.6 SECURITY LEVELS

While considering the security of a computer system, there are various assets to be protected like hardware, software, data and communication lines, in case of a network system, and so on. In all these assets, there may be the possibility of a security threat. Hardware is most vulnerable to attack; it is prone to accidental or intentional damage or theft. It leads to the non-availability of the hardware, which is a major threat to the computer system.

Software also needs protection, as there may be several security problems, like the following:

- It can be deleted, leading to non-availability.
- It can be altered, such that it cannot be used, leading to non-availability.
- It can be modified in such a way, that it is working but behaving in a different manner, leading to threat to authenticity/integrity.
- The malicious software like viruses, Trojan horse, worms, and so on, attack the legal software, leading to some kind of threat to it.
- Unauthorized copying of software, resulting in software piracy.

The data on a computer system are also prone to attacks, as there may be several security problems, such as the following:

- The data files can be damaged, either accidentally or intentionally, leading to non-availability.

- The data files/databases can be read in an unauthorized way, and analysis of data can be done, such that the data may be used to disclose personal information, leading to non-confidentiality.
- The modification of data files may lead to integrity threats.

In network systems, the security attacks are increasing day by day. Much of the computer system data travel through network communication in many ways, such as LAN, WAN, Internet, wireless, and so on. Today, data interception through the network is the most common attack, leading to several security problems, such as the following:

- An intruder may view the contents of an email message, a file being transferred, and so on, leading to non-confidentiality.
- An intruder may analyze the network traffic in order to attack in future.
- An intruder may modify the data being transmitted, for example, replay attack, leading to non-integrity.
- When one intruder entity pretends to be another, like spoofing, it leads to non-authentication.
- DoS attacks lead to non-availability of the system.

It is evident from the discussions so far, that it is necessary to have security measures for the computer system. The security measures, in general known as protection mechanisms, will be discussed in the next chapter. But it is necessary here to understand at which levels security can be provided. The four security levels are:

- **Physical level**
  The computer systems must be protected physically, in any case. They must be protected from theft, accidental damage, intentional damage, and natural disasters like storm, rain, and so on.
- **User level**
  Only authorized persons should be allowed to access the computer systems.
- **OS level**
  The intruders attack on the system by finding out the vulnerabilities of the system at OS level. DOS attacks, stack overflow attacks, and so on are examples of OS-level security breaches. The system, thus, must be protected at the OS level.
- **Network level**
  As discussed, these days, a network system is highly prone to attacks, as we are more dependent on online systems. Any kind of information leakage, DoS attacks, modification of messages, masquerading, and so on, may occur in a network, thereby increasing the security need at this level as well.

This book aims to discuss security at the OS level. But the security and protection measures at the hardware level and user level must be maintained, so that appropriate protection measures can be designed at the OS level. For example, the hardware protection mechanisms, such as memory protection, dual mode, and so on, are needed to protect the system at the OS level.

16.7 INSIDE SYSTEM ATTACKS

This section discusses some of the inside system attacks that are in common use by the intruders.

16.7.1 Trap Door/Back Door

This is a code inserted in a program, in order to have a secret backdoor entry into it. Since the testing and debugging may take time, and due to this, the system programmers get irritated when they need to pass the authentication procedures again and again, to gain access to the program. This backdoor entry enables them to enter into the system, without passing through the normal security access checks, so that they can debug and test the programs. Originally the backdoors were used for debugging and testing purposes. However, the problem may start if the program is released with this backdoor code. The intruder may observe this backdoor as vulnerability in the program, and use it to have an illegitimate entry into the system. At the OS level, there cannot be any countermeasures, but backdoors can be avoided if there is proper code review before releasing the software.

16.7.2 Logic Bomb

It is a malicious code embedded in a legitimate program and is programmed to get activated, when some particular condition or some event occurs. The triggering of the logic bomb into computer systems or network may cause some kind of damage that the creator of logic bomb has desired for. The logic bomb is a predator of viruses and worms. In other words, the logic bombs are ancestors of viruses and worms used today by the intruders. The conditions or the events used for triggering the logic bombs may be a particular day of week, absence of a particular person's password entry, absence or presence of a file, and so on. Cleaning the hard disk, erasing or encrypting some files, and so on, are some of the havocs created by logic bombs.

16.7.3 Trojan Horse

The term Trojan horse has originated from Greek mythology about the Trojan War. In the software environment, the Trojan horse is a seemingly innocent program, but contains code that performs an unexpected and undesirable function. For instance, the intruder/hacker will create a game (Trojan horse) and place it on the Internet to attract users. Whenever the game program is executed, the Trojan horse code will also be executed. This may harm a user's system, without breaking into the computer system. Thus, Trojan horse codes are hidden inside useful programs and get activated as soon as the program containing them is executed. Trojans can also create backdoors, which can give unauthenticated users access to the system.

16.7.4 Login Spoofing

It is a technique used to steal login credentials through a fake screen presented to the user. Suppose, the user wishes to log in to a system. The attacker is active, and presents the user a screen that looks similar to the login screen of the system. The user, mistaking it as the original login screen, enters login ID and password on the fake screen. The intruder captures the entered information and attacks the system.

16.7.5 Buffer Overflow

Buffer is a temporary area in the main memory. Buffer overflow occurs, when the size of information written into the memory allocated to a variable, exceeds the size allocated to it at compile time. For instance, arrays used in 'C' language have no upper bound checks, that is, if the data stored in the buffer are larger than the size fixed for it, no message will be displayed for the overflow situation. Overflow results in overwriting of memory area. The memory area, being overwritten by the junk data, may result in chaos. For example, a program A is being executed. Its data variables are stored in the stack area of the memory. Suppose, the program A calls a function X. To start execution of the function X, the return address of the main program is stored in the stack. The data variables of X are also stored in the stack below the

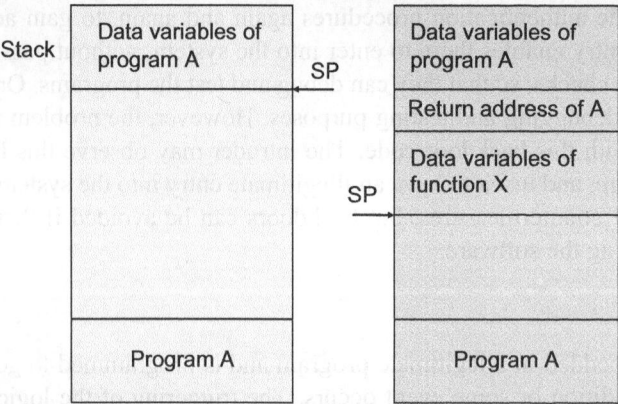

Fig. 16.2 Buffer overflow

data variables of the program A. If there is an array being used in the function X and data to be stored in this array crosses its boundary, the array will overflow and this overflown data will be overwritten in other parts of the stack (see Fig. 16.2). The possibility may be that the return address of the program A will get overwritten with some junk value. A will not be able to start, as its actual return address has been modified.

The intruders may use this buffer overflow method to attack the system by intentionally inputting some data that are too long to fit in the array of the program. Moreover, this long data will consist of the address of a module and the address will be overwritten in the return address of the program. This will lead to execution of the module, which may harm the system in a way the intruder wishes.

16.8 OUTSIDE SYSTEM ATTACKS

This section discusses some of the outside system attacks that are in common use by the intruders.

16.8.1 Viruses

A computer virus is a malicious software program that is loaded into someone's computer without his/her knowledge. Like a human virus, the computer viruses are of different types. Some of them can cause only mild effect, but some can be dangerous. The special thing about a virus is that it can replicate itself. Even a simple virus can be dangerous, because the multiple copies of the virus can quickly use all the available memory of the computer and bring the system to a halt. The more dangerous viruses are capable of transmitting themselves over the network. Some can even damage all the computer software, hardware, and the files.

A virus has, in general, three parts:

1. *Infection mechanism* or *infection vector*: The mechanism by which it replicates or spreads.
2. *Trigger*: It is an event or condition, on the occurrence of which, the virus starts damage.
3. *Payload*: The damage action a virus performs.

A virus has various phases in its life, from its initiation to execution. The virus, when hidden in a program but sitting idle, is in the *dormant phase*. It may be possible that a virus does not have any dormant phase. When a virus starts infecting other programs, it is known as the *propagation phase*. In this phase, a virus replicates itself to have multiple infected copies. When the trigger of a virus that is in the dormant phase activates, it is known as the *triggering phase*. When the virus starts its payload, it is known as the *execution phase*.

16.8.2 Types of Viruses

Some types of viruses in common use are as the following:

Appending Virus

It is a type of virus that adds its malicious code at the end of a host program. Its goal is not to destroy the host program, but to slightly modify it, by appending itself to hold the virus code, and then be able to run itself.

Polymorphic Virus

It is a type of virus that changes its binary pattern or its signature every time it replicates, and thereby, may infect a new file, making it undetectable by antivirus software. Polymorphic infections are thus difficult to be detected by antivirus detection programs, because one poly-morphic virus could have thousands of variants.

Macro Virus

There are many types of software like, Word, Excel, and programming languages, which pro-vide the functionality of a macro that groups several commands to be executed later with a single keystroke. The viruses can be attached within a macro, resulting in a macro virus. This macro virus may affect a chain of events executed by an application.

Companion Virus

It is a type of virus that does not infect the program, that is, does not inject its code into a file, but executes when the actual program is supposed to run. This virus is created with a file name that has the same name as of the actual program, but with different extension. For example, there is a program with the name *copy.exe*. The creator of the virus prepares the virus file with the name *copy.com*. When a user starts running the copy program, the virus file *copy.com* is first executed, and after its completion, the actual program *copy.exe* is executed. Since the actual program is running, the user is unaware that a virus file has been already executed on the system. This is how a companion virus works. The target of companion viruses are very commonly-used files, such as startup files in the system.

Memory Resident Virus

The types of viruses discussed till now execute and exit, that is, they are not in the memory after their execution, and run, only if the infected file is executed. But there are large numbers of viruses that stay resident in the memory, even after their execution, and perform mischievous actions. Such a virus must find a place in the memory to hide itself. This is because, on the execution of any system call, an interrupt is generated, and the corresponding interrupt handler from BIOS is executed (see Fig.16.3). The memory resident virus takes advantage of this concept. This type of virus captures IVT in the memory, copies the address of an interrupt to a temporary location, and replaces the actual interrupt address with its own address (see Fig. 16.4).

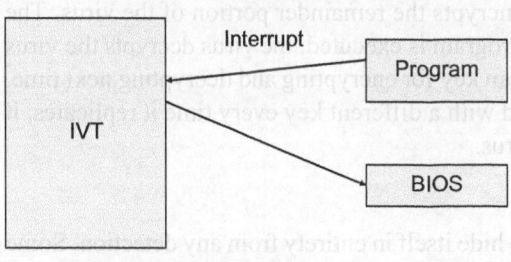

Fig. 16.3   IVT before virus attacks

It results in the execution of a virus, whenever a system call, corresponding to the replaced interrupt address, is executed. Thus, this virus hooks the execution of a code flow to itself.

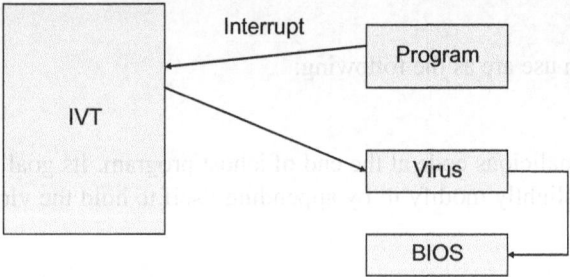

Fig. 16.4 IVT after virus attacks

Boot Sector Virus

This type of virus takes the advantage of the booting process: BIOS reads the boot sector from the disk, loads it in the memory, and executes to determine the partition-related information. The virus overwrites the boot sector program to load its own program in the memory. The boot sector virus first copies the actual boot sector on the disk and replaces its code with its own code. After the virus program has been loaded in the memory, it again puts the actual boot sector program in its place, so that the system can be booted. In this way, the virus has copied itself in the memory to infect other files, and the system has also booted, so that the user has no impression of any virus.

File/Executable Program Viruses

These viruses attach themselves to regular program files. The viruses may be attached at various locations in the file, by inserting their code, such that malicious part of the file inserted by the virus is executed, while accessing the file. The EXE files are usually the target of these viruses. But the file of the type COM, SYS, OBJ, and BAT can also be infected by these viruses. File viruses are typically memory-resident and wait in the memory, until the user runs another program.

A virus file, which overwrites an executable file with itself, is known as an executable virus. Whenever this executable file is executed or opened, the virus file gets activated, and it starts infecting other files. The executable viruses are so dangerous, that they can disable antivirus programs or may result in slowing down the system performance.

Encrypted Virus

This type of virus replicates itself with the help of encryption. A portion of virus generates a random encryption key, and using this key, it encrypts the remainder portion of the virus. The key is stored with the virus. When an infected program is executed, the virus decrypts the virus program, and is replicated with a different random key for encrypting and decrypting next time. Since the larger portion of the virus is encrypted with a different key every time it replicates, it is very difficult to observe the pattern of this virus.

Stealth Virus

This type of virus is designed such that it tries to hide itself in entirety from any detection. Some of the types of stealth virus, based on their techniques to hide themselves, are as the following:

Directory/Semi-stealth virus

The virus code is installed in the memory. The virus intercepts functions of a file and starts infecting the file, by modifying it. Due to the changes in the file, the size of this infected file

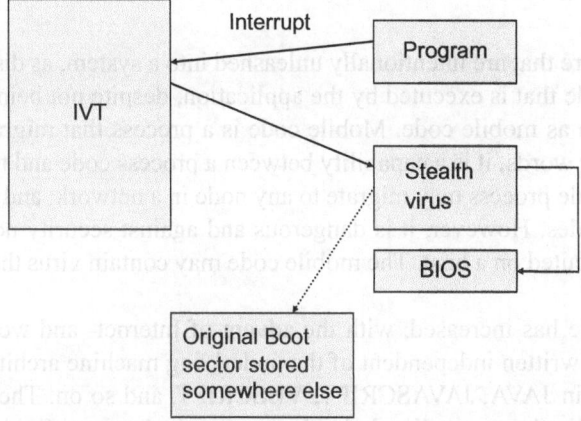

Fig. 16.5 Stealth virus

will change and must be reflected in the directory. But, the virus does not show the change in file size in the directory. In this way, the virus remains hidden in the system.

Read stealth virus

This type of stealth virus is based on the content simulation technique. It intercepts seek/read functions and simulates the content of a file. For example, boot sector virus discussed above is a type of read stealth virus. It reads the boot sector and stores it somewhere, such that it boots the system. It retains the actual boot sector, but infects it at the same time (see Fig. 16.5). In this way, the virus is hidden, as the system boots properly.

16.8.3 Worms

It is a special type of virus that has the property of replicating itself in seconds, on every machine it can gain access to, across network connections. Unlike a virus, a worm cannot attach itself to other programs. It takes advantage of the computer network to travel. A worm can create hundreds or thousands of copies of itself, creating a huge destructive effect. It first finds out the vulnerabilities in the system in order to gain an unauthorized access, and then spreads to the connecting machines, thereby, infecting these machines.

An example of a worm infection is to send a copy of the worm through email systems. The worm replicates and sends itself out to every address listed in each of the receiver's address book, and this replication continues down the line. Worms consume too much system memory and network bandwidth, causing web servers, network servers, and individual computers to stop working. They can even use remote login facility in the networks to spread themselves.

16.8.4 Bots

Bots are just like Internet worms that unknowingly take over a system connected on the Internet and use that system to spread infection. The difference between a bot and worm is that a bot is controlled from a central coordinator known as *botnet*, while worms are able to propagate and activate themselves. Using the bots, an attacker is able to control the host system remotely through a communication channel. The channel can be Internet Relay Chat (IRC), Peer-to-peer (P2P), or Hypertext Transfer Protocol (HTTP). Using these channels, the communication, between a control module and the bot on a remote system, is established. After that, the control module remotely issues commands to the bot remotely.

16.8.5 Mobile Code

There are various types of malware that are intentionally unleashed into a system, as discussed. However, there may be some code that is executed by the application, despite not being a part of it. This type of code is known as mobile code. Mobile code is a process that migrates and executes at remote hosts. In other words, it is a capability between a process code and the location where it executes. Mobile code process may migrate to any node in a network, and execute on any one of the destination nodes. However, it is dangerous and against security norms, to allow a foreign process to be executed on a host. The mobile code may contain virus that could infect the host on its execution.

Today, the risk of mobile code has increased, with the advent of Internet- and web-based programs, as applications can be written independent of the underlying machine architectures. The mobile code can be written in JAVA, JAVASCRIPT, VBSCRIPT, and so on. The mobile code can also be downloaded willingly or unwillingly by the user on the Internet. For instance, while downloading a web page, the associated applet programs are also downloaded and executed. With increase in usage of mobile code, the risk of welcoming the malicious code is also increasing.

There may be two types of mobile code, as discussed in the following list:

- **One-hop agents**
  This type of code is sent from a server to a client on demand and executed, thereby, having a weak mobility. After execution, the results of agent execution or agent itself are returned to the owner of the agent that sent it. Applet is an example of this type of mobile code.
- **Multi-hop agents**
  These types of agents are sent on the network without any client demand, and are free to move to any node on the network. They perform a series of tasks and return the result to their owner, but it is not necessary that the agents will also return. These agents also have the capability to communicate with other agents and coordinate among themselves. Mobile agents are examples of this type of mobile code.

Mobile code security has two aspects like the following:

- **Protection from malicious host**: The malicious host can harm the code as well as data associated with a crawling agent. So the mobile agent must be protected from the attack of malicious host. Denial of service, interception, and alteration of the agent are some of the main security attacks caused by a malicious host.
- **Protection of host from unauthorized agent**: An unauthorized entity can act as a mobile agent and can harm an agent-enabled host. So the hosts must be protected from such unauthorized agents. Denial-of-service and improper use of resources are two main security attacks caused by an unauthorized agent.

16.8.6 Rootkit

Rootkit is a set of programs that provides administrator access to a system. After gaining access to the root of a system, an intruder installs the rootkit, and thereby, gains access to all functions of the system. In other words, now the intruder has complete control of the system and may change, add, or delete the user and system files, processes, and so on, in order to stealthily alter its normal functionality. Thus, through the rootkit, an intruder is able to have a direct attack on a system, while hiding its intrusion and maintaining its privileged access. A rootkit does not spread on other systems, like viruses, but it can be installed by a virus or Trojan horse.

SUMMARY

Let us have a quick review of important concepts discussed in this chapter:

- The security breaches can be of two categories: Malicious and accidental. A *malicious breach* is the intentional misuse of system resources and an *accidental breach* is an unintentional hardware/software/human error or any natural calamity.
- Vulnerability is a weakness in the system that might be exploited to cause loss or harm.
- A *threat* to a computing system is a set of circumstances that has the potential to cause loss or harm, exploiting the vulnerabilities in the system.
- An *attack* is an attempt, by an intruder, to break the security.
- Both threat and attack are the result of vulnerabilities in the system.
- In communication, an unauthorized node receives the sensitive data that are supposed to be between two authorized parties. It is known as *Interception*.
- An unauthorized entity may infer the information from a database or by observing the network traffic, and disclose the same. It is known as *Inference*.
- An unauthorized entity may pose to be an authorized one and attempt to gain access to the system. This attack is known as *Masquerade*.
- A file or database may be altered or some data may be replaced with false data. This attack is known as *Falsification*.
- A user may deny that he has sent or received data. This attack is known as *Repudiation*.
- An intruder, called masquerader, is an individual who does not have any authority to access a computer system, but gains access control to exploit a legitimate user's account.
- An intruder, called misfeasor, is an authorized user on the system, but he/she misuses his/her privileges on it.
- An intruder, called clandestine, is a user who somehow gains the supervisory control of the system, by exploiting its vulnerabilities, and tries to elude the access control mechanisms implemented in the system, in order to gain administrative privileges to a computer resource.
- The intruders, who break the system just for fun, or to pose a challenge, are known as hackers.
- The intruders, known as criminals, work in organized groups and break the system with the motivations of profit, and thereby, results in a business, but in an unethical way.
- Insider attacks are attacks on a system which maybe from inside the system, while outsider attacks may be from outside the system.

- A passive intruder silently observes the network traffic or retrieves the system's data, but does not modify anything.
- An active intruder modifies the data on the network or a system.
- *Malware* is a program or set of programs that may infect the user's system in such a way, that malicious program is hidden on the system and this gets activated, according to some condition, or corrupts the files/data on the system, or system is not available to use.
- Denial-of-Service (DoS) attacks are implemented, by either forcing the host computer to reset, or consuming all of its hardware or software resources, such that it can no longer provide its intended service.
- When an intruder pretends to be a valid host in a communication, by breaching the authentication, and then gains access for which they are not entitled, it is known as spoofing.
- IP spoofing is carried out when an attacker sends a message to a computer with an IP address, indicating that the message is from a trusted and authenticated host.
- In identity spoofing, an attacker gets passwords and login information, by using fictitious digital certificates or authorization prompts.
- When an intruder displays a spoofed web page to mislead the user to believe that he/she is communicating with the real server, it is known as web spoofing.
- In email-spoofing, an email address is used under false authentication or web spoofing, where domains are 'hijacked' or faked.
- When the session established between the two nodes has been hijacked by the intruder, it is known as session hijacking.
- When a malicious user sits between the sender and receiver, intercepts the traffic coming from the computer, collects the data, and then forwards the same to the destination, which the user was originally intending to visit, it is known as man-in-the-middle-attack.
- In replay attacks, the attacker simply sends a data packet, which was previously sent by some other user, in the hope of reproducing the effect.
- Logic bomb is a malicious code embedded in a legitimate program, programmed to get activated when some particular condition, or some event, occurs.
- Trojan horse programs are hidden inside useful programs and get activated as soon as the program containing them is executed.
- Login spoofing is a technique used to steal a user's password through a fake screen, presented to the user.
- A computer virus is a malicious software program that is loaded into someone's computer, without his/her knowledge.

- A virus has three parts:
  Infection mechanism: mechanism by which it spreads
  Trigger: an event or condition, on the occurrence of which, it starts its action
  Payload: the damage action a virus performs
- A virus when hidden in a program, but sitting idle, is said to be in the *dormant phase*.
- When a virus starts infecting other programs, it is known as the *propagation phase*.
- When a triggering event happens on a virus that is in the dormant phase, it is known as the *triggering phase*.
- When the virus starts its payload, that is, damage action, it is known to be in the *execution phase*.

- Worm is a special type of virus that has the property of replicating itself in seconds, on every machine it can gain access to, across network connections, but cannot attach itself to other programs.
- Bots unknowingly takes over a system that is connected on the Internet, and uses that system to spread infection, but is controlled by botnet.
- Mobile code is a process that migrates and executes at remote hosts.
- There may be a virus attached with the mobile code that could infect the host on its execution.
- Rootkit is a set of programs that provides an intruder administrator access to a system.

MULTIPLE CHOICE QUESTIONS

1. ____ is a security measure which protects against the disclosure of information to unauthorized parties.
   (a) Confidentiality   (c) Authentication
   (b) Integrity   (d) Authorization

2. ____ is the process of determining that a requester is allowed to receive a service or perform an operation.
   (a) Confidentiality   (c) Authentication
   (b) Integrity   (d) Authorization

3. ____ is a measure intended to allow the receiver to determine whether the information it receives has not been altered in transit.
   (a) Confidentiality   (c) Authentication
   (b) Integrity   (d) Authorization

4. ____ is a measure, designed to establish the validity of a transmission, message, or originator.
   (a) Confidentiality   (c) Authentication
   (b) Integrity   (d) Authorization

5. Any security breach is a result of _____ in the system.
   (a) Threat   (c) Attack
   (b) Vulnerability   (d) none

6. A _____ to a computing system is a set of circumstances that has the potential to cause loss.
   (a) Threat   (c) Attack
   (b) Vulnerability   (d) none

7. ____ is an attempt by an intruder to break the security.
   (a) Threat   (c) Attack
   (b) Vulnerability   (d) none

8. ____ is an individual, who does not have any authority to access a computer system, but gains the access control to exploit a legitimate user's account.
   (a) Masquerader   (c) Clandestine user
   (b) Misfeasor   (d) None

9. ____ somehow gains the supervisory control of the system by exploiting its vulnerabilities.
   (a) Masquerader   (c) Clandestine user
   (b) Misfeasor   (d) None

10. ____ is an authorized user on the system, but he/she misuses his privileges on it.
    (a) Masquerader   (c) Clandestine user
    (b) Misfeasor   (d) None

11. ____ are Internet security experts hired to find vulnerabilities in systems.
    (a) Hackers   (c) Criminals
    (b) White hat hackers   (d) none

12. ____ are implemented, by either forcing the host computer to reset, or consuming all of its hardware or software resources, such that it can no longer provide its intended service.
    (a) Spoofing   (c) Man-in-middle-attack
    (b) DoS   (d) none

13. When an intruder pretends to be a valid host in a communication, by breaching the authentication, and then gains access for which they are not entitled, it is called _____.
    (a) Spoofing   (c) Man-in-middle-attack
    (b) DoS   (d) none

14. In ____ type of attack, a malicious user sits between the sender and receiver, and sniffs information being sent.
    (a) Spoofing   (c) Man-in-middle-attack
    (b) DoS   (d) none

15. Originally the ____ was used for debugging and testing purposes.
    (a) Logic bomb   (c) Trojan horse
    (b) Backdoor   (d) none

16. _____ is hidden inside useful programs, and gets activated, as soon as the program containing them is executed.
   (a) Logic bomb   (c) Trojan horse
   (b) Backdoor   (d) none

17. A _____ is a malicious code embedded in a legitimate program, programmed to get activated, when some particular condition or some event occurs.
   (a) Logic bomb   (c) Trojan horse
   (b) Backdoor   (d) none

18. _____ is a type of virus that changes its binary pattern or its signature, every time it replicates.
   (a) Macro   (c) Polymorphic
   (b) Companion   (d) Stealth

19. _____ is a type of virus that does not infect the program file, but executes when the actual program is supposed to run.
   (a) Macro   (c) Polymorphic
   (b) Companion   (d) Stealth

20. _____ virus is designed, such that it tries to hide itself in entirety from any detection.
   (a) Macro   (c) Polymorphic
   (b) Companion   (d) Stealth

21. _____ is a special type of virus that has the property of replicating itself in seconds on every machine it can gain access to, across network connections.
   (a) Encrypted virus   (c) Worm
   (b) Stealth virus   (d) none

REVIEW QUESTIONS

1. What are the security objectives to secure a computer system?

2. Differentiate between vulnerability, threat, and attack.

3. What is the difference between hackers and criminals?

4. What is malware?

5. How is a DoS attack implemented?

6. What is spoofing? Explain its various types.

7. What is session hijacking?

8. Differentiate between a logic bomb, Trojan horse, and a virus.

9. How does an attacker use buffer overflow to attack the system?

10. What is a memory resident virus? Explain its types.

11. How does a boot sector virus attack?

12. What is a stealth virus?

13. Differentiate between virus, bots, and worms.

BRAIN TEASERS

1. What kind of attacks are possible on the following systems:
   (a) Railway reservation system
   (b) A company having LAN system
   (c) A company having a LAN system, but is connected to the Internet as well..
   (d) A wireless system being used in warfare conditions
   (e) Mobile phone of a general user

2. Search engines also use mobile code in the form of web crawlers. The crawlers either visit the websites to download the web page, or deploy mobile agents for the same.

   What can be the security issues on these web crawlers or mobile agents?

3. Make a list of some common viruses that attack the wireless systems.

4. Make a list of some common viruses that attack the network systems.

5. Make a list of some common stealth viruses.

6. Make a list of some common viruses that take help of Trojan horses or vice versa.

17 Protection Mechanisms

17.1 INTRODUCTION

In Chapter 16, various security issues have been discussed. Various protection mechanisms are adopted in response to reduce or nullify the intruder attacks on the system. The protection mechanisms are driven by two principles. One is known as '*Need to know principle*,' which states that unless a user has a specific reason to access a piece of information, the permission to access is denied. It means that the information or part of it is not accessible to anyone. The second principle is '*Principle of least privilege*,' which states that a process or user must be able to access information or resources that are necessary for its legitimate purposes. All the protection mechanisms discussed in this chapter follow these two rules.

17.2 PROTECTION DOMAINS

There are various types of resources as discussed in Chapter 3. These resources are identified as objects. Thus, there are hardware, software, and virtual objects in a system. Each object needs a protection mechanism in a multi-programming environment. To have a protection mechanism, each object is distinguished and identified with its unique name and a finite set of operations. These operations are in fact the *rights* that can be exercised on an object. For example, a file can have read, write, and execute operations. A CD ROM can have only read operation. Some objects along with their corresponding operations have been listed in Table 17.1.

A process may not access all the resources all the time. A process should be authorized to access only those resources that it needs. Further, the resources may be restricted to access only required operations of a resource. For example, a process may be allowed to read a file but not for write operations. Therefore, there should be a mechanism that prohibits processes from accessing the resources for which they have no authorization. For this purpose, the concept of *domain* has been introduced. A domain is a set of object and right pairs (see Fig. 17.1). Each pair in the domain consists of object with its permitted operations that can be performed on it. In other words, a protection domain is a collection of access rights.

Learning Objectives

After reading this chapter, you should be able to understand:

- Protection domains
- Access control mechanisms
- Access control lists
- Capability lists
- Cryptography as a security tool
- Authentications and its methods
- Intrusion detection system
- Worm/bot/rootkit countermeasures
- Dealing with buffer overflow attacks
- Dealing with mobile code
- Security patches
- Secure file systems
- Trusted OSs

Table 17.1   File operations

Object	Operations
Program file	Create, read, write, execute, delete, open, close
Data file	Create, read, write, delete, open, close
Processor	Execute
Memory	Read and write
Semaphore	Wait and signal
Tape drive	Read, write, rewind
Cd/DVD ROM	Read

For example, in Fig. 17.1, there are two domains, Domain1 and Domain2. Domain1 consists of two resources *R1* and *R2*. In this domain, the access rights of *R1* and *R2* are read and write and execute, respectively. Similarly, Domain2 consists of *R3* and *R4* with their corresponding access rights.

It is not necessary that all domains will have separate resources. A resource may be present in multiple domains with same or different access rights. For example, in Fig. 17.2, it can be seen that read and write operations can be performed on *R1* in Domain1 while *R1* can be only read in Domain2.

Further, a resource can be shared by multiple domains. For example, a single printer may be shared by the domains as shown in Fig.17.3.

Using the domain structure, a process may specify a protection domain that specifies the resources that it wishes to access. In this way, a process is restricted to use only those resources and thereby, their corresponding operations that are mentioned in the protection domain. A process, however, may also switch the domains depending on its requirements. Thus, the relation between a domain and process may not be static but can be dynamic.

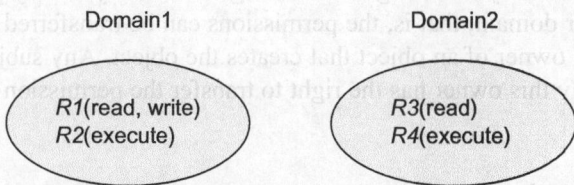

Domain1   Domain2

Fig. 17.1 Protection domains

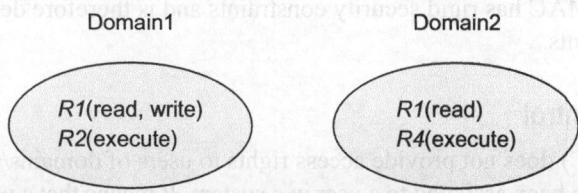

Domain1   Domain2

Fig. 17.2 Protection domains: a resource in multiple domains

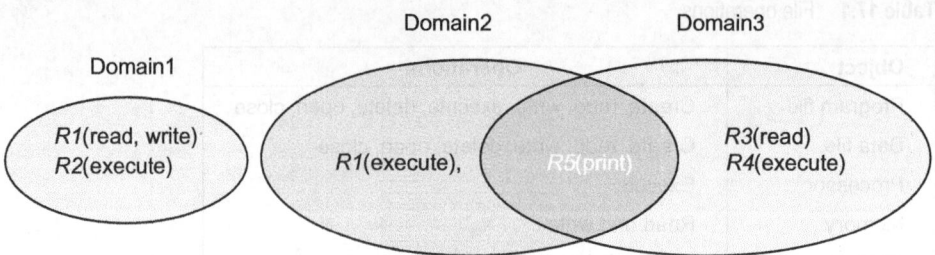

Fig. 17.3 Protection domains: shared resource in multiple domains

17.3 ACCESS CONTROL

Access control models can be formed using the protection domain discussed in Section 17.2. All these models will have the following elements:

- **Domain/Subject**
  As discussed earlier, the domain or sometimes called subject is the entity that exercises the access rights. Any user process gains control of an object only through the domain.

- **Object**
  Any resource for which an access control is necessary is an object. For example, files, memory, disk drives, and even domains may become the object.

- **Access rights**
  The permissions given to a subject to access objects are the access rights.

The access control policies are grouped into three following categories:

17.3.1 Discretionary Access Control

Discretionary access control (DAC) is for restricting access to objects based on the identity of subjects or domains corresponding to the objects with permitted access rights. Moreover, the control is discretionary such that the subject having an access right for an object may pass this permission to any other subject or domain, that is, the permissions can be transferred to other subjects. In this sense, there is an owner of an object that creates the object. Any subject may be the owner of an object and only this owner has the right to transfer the permission to other subjects.

17.3.2 Mandatory Access Control

Mandatory access control (MAC) is governed by a central policy to restrict the users to gain access to objects. Moreover, in contrast to DAC, this policy does not allow to further transfer the access rights to any subject. MAC has rigid security constraints and is therefore developed in response to military requirements.

17.3.3 Role-based Access Control

Role-based access control (RBAC) does not provide access rights to users of domains/subjects directly but to the 'roles' that have been assigned to a user in a system. It means that a user does not get the access rights on the basis of identity; rather, it is based on the role assigned to the user in an organization. In RBAC, the roles are first assigned to the users/subjects, and then all the permissions are assigned as in DAC.

There can be many relationships between role, user (subject), and access rights. Some of them are as follows:

- A user can be assigned multiple roles.
- Multiple users can be assigned the same role.
- A role can have multiple access rights.

17.4 ACCESS MATRIX

Another protection model that is used to store information about access rights within domains is access matrix. The rows of this matrix represent the domains, whereas columns represent the objects. The intersection of row and column, that is, the cell of matrix contains the access rights. With the help of access matrix, the system is now able to check the permissions of a resource in a domain and thereby, can control the processes.

Let us illustrate some examples for further understanding the concept of access matrix.

Example 17.1

The access matrix shown in the following table has three domains consisting of various access rights of four resources. In Domain1, File *A* can be read, whereas in Domain2, it can be read as well as written, and Printer*1* can be used. In Domain3, there are access rights of read, write, and execution for File *B*, and that of print for Printer*2* can be used.

Domain/Object	File *A*	File *B*	Printer*1*	Printer*2*
Domain1	Read			
Domain2	Read Write		Print	
Domain3		Read Write Execute		Print

Since a process may switch its domain, there should be permissions whether a switch from one domain to another is allowed or not. The access matrix may also provide provision for this purpose by realizing the domains as objects and incorporating domains among the objects in the matrix. The operation corresponding to domain switching is called *switch*. This provision in the access matrix will control the domain switching. A process will switch its domain from domain$_i$ to domain$_j$ if there is an entry *switch* in the access matrix.

Example 17.2

The access matrix in the following table illustrates that domains can also become objects to incorporate domain switching in the access matrix. A process is able to switch its domain from Domain1 to Domain3, from Domain2 to Domain1 and Domain3, and from Domain3 to Domain2 only. No other domain switching is allowed.

Domain/Object	File A	File B	Printer1	Printer2	Domain1	Domain2	Domain3
Domain1	Read						Switch
Domain2	Read Write		Print			Switch	Switch
Domain3		Read Write Execute		Print			Switch

The contents of a cell in the access matrix can be changed. However, these changes should also be controlled as an access matrix is a protected entity. There are three operations for this purpose: *copy, owner, and control.*

The copy operation is to copy an access right from one domain to another. However, this right is only valid for an object that has the permission. In other words, the access right is copied in the same column of the access matrix. The copy operation is denoted with an asterisk (*) appended after the access right.

Copy right has two variants. One of the variants is transfer operation. In this, the access right after copying to other domain is removed from the original domain. In this sense, this is a transfer of operation. Another variant is the limited propagation of copy operation. In this, the copy right is not allowed, that is, the copy privilege is not copied to the domain where the access right is copied. It means that the domain where the access right is being copied is without asterisk.

Example 17.3

The access matrix in the following table indicates that for object File *C*, copy operation is allowed. It means that a process executing in Domain2 can copy the read access right in other domains also.

Domain/Object	File A	File B	File C	Printer2
Domain1	Read			
Domain2	Read Write		Read*	
Domain3		Read Write Execute		Print

If the access right in Domain2 is copied to Domain3, then the access matrix will be given as follows:

Domain/Object	File A	File B	File C	Printer2
Domain1	Read			
Domain2	Read Write		Read*	
Domain3		Read Write Execute	Read	Print

If the transfer variant is chosen, then after the copy operation in Domain3, the access right from Domain2 will be removed and the access matrix will be as given as follows:

Domain/Object	File A	File B	File C	Printer2
Domain1	Read			
Domain2	Read Write			
Domain3		Read Write Execute	Read	Print

Suppose the propagation of copy right is not allowed. The access right in Domain3 is without asterisk as the copy privilege in Domain2 is not transferred.

Domain/Object	File A	File B	File C	Printer2
Domain1	Read			
Domain2	Read Write		Read*	
Domain3		Read Write Execute	Read	Print

Another right for access matrix is *owner*. The owner is necessary to provide privilege to a domain such that it is able to add or delete any access right for an object. The owner right is also specified in a domain in the access matrix. The process in that domain can add or delete any valid access right for the object where the owner right is specified. If the owner right is specified in access matrix(i,j), then a process in a domain$_i$ can add or delete any valid entry in the column j of the access matrix.

Example 17.4

The access matrix in the following table illustrates that Domain1 is the owner of File A and Domain3 is the owner of File C.

Domain/Object	File A	File B	File C	Printer2
Domain1	Owner Read			
Domain2	Read Write		Read*	
Domain3		Read Write Execute	Owner	Print

The processes in Domain1 and Domain3 can add or delete any access right for Files A and C, respectively, as shown in the following table in the modified access matrix. In the modified access matrix, the owner of File A has deleted the access right *write* in Domain2. Similarly, the owner of File C has added one access right *write* in Domain1.

Domain/Object	File A	File B	File C	Printer2
Domain1	Owner Read		Write	
Domain2	Read		Read*	
Domain3	Write	Read Write Execute	Owner	Print

There should be a provision to also modify the entries in a row of the access matrix. For this purpose, another right for access matrix is *control*. The *control* is necessary to provide privilege to a domain such that it is able to add or delete any access right for all the objects in a domain. The *control* right is also specified in a domain in the access matrix. The process in that domain can add or delete any valid access right for all the objects where the control right is specified. If the owner right is specified in access matrix(i,j), then a process in a domain$_i$ can add or delete any valid entry in the row i of the access matrix.

Example 17.5

The access matrix in the following table shows that Domain1 has been given the control privilege and therefore, it has added two new access operations, that is, write operation for File C and print operation for Printer2.

Domain/Object	File A	File B	File C	Printer2
Domain1	Read Control		Write	Print
Domain2	Read Write		Read*	
Domain3		Read Write Execute	Read	Print

Example 17.6

The access matrix in the following table illustrates that the control privilege is provided at Domain2 and Domain3.

Domain/ Object	File A	File B	Printer1	Printer2	Domain1	Domain2	Domain3
Domain1	Read						Switch
Domain2	Read Write		Print		Switch		Switch Control
Domain3		Read Write Execute		Print		Switch	

The Domain3 using its control operation has now deleted entries for File *B* in Domain3 row as shown in the following table:

Domain/Object	File A	File B	Printer1	Printer2	Domain1	Domain2	Domain3
Domain1	Read						Switch
Domain2	Read Write		Print		Switch		Switch Control
Domain3		Read		Print		Switch	

17.5 ACCESS CONTROL LISTS

It may be possible that an access matrix becomes large in size and sparse. In this case, finding a particular privilege of an object becomes difficult and time consuming. Moreover, the disk space used to store the access matrix is wasted as it also contains the empty entries. Therefore, it would be better to store only non-empty entries in the matrix. This approach will store column-wise entries for an object. Thus, storing only non-empty entries as access rights for objects is known as *access control lists* (ACL). Each column is then implemented as an ACL in the access matrix. The advantage of an ACL is that it reduces the space storage and increases the search efficiency as well. When an operation is to be performed on an object, its ACL is first searched to know the access right for the domain. If it is found in the ACL, only then the permission for the operation is granted.

There may be two types of privileges or access rights for an object: generic and object-specific. The *object-specific* access rights are defined in ACL, and the generic access rights are the rights that are by default all objects or an object category may exercise. Therefore, there must be another ACL for the generic access rights, which is called *generic ACL*. Generic ACL consists of all the access rights that all objects or an object category may have. While searching for the access rights for an object, first, the generic ACL is searched, and then the ACL for object-specific access rights is searched to increase the search efficiency.

Example 17.7

The access matrix shown in Example 17.5 can be reduced to ACL for various objects as follows:

Domain/Object	File A
Domain1	Read control
Domain2	Read write

Domain/Object	File B
Domain3	Read write execute

Domain/Object	File C
Domain1	Write
Domain2	Read*
Domain3	Read

Domain/Object	Printer2
Domain1	Print
Domain3	Print

17.6 CAPABILITY LISTS

In the ACL, column-wise non-empty entries of an access matrix are stored. Similarly, row-wise entries can also be stored. In this case, all the access rights for a domain are stored. These row-wise entries are known as *capability lists* or *C-lists*. Thus, a capability list for a domain is a list of objects with their allowed operations that the domain can have. Each row is then implemented as a capability in the access matrix. The space and efficiency advantages are also applicable in case of capability lists. When an operation is to be performed for a process in a particular domain, its capability list is first searched to know the objects that can be accessed in the domain. If the desired object is found, then the allowed access rights are observed in the C-list. After checking the required permissions, the permission for the operation is granted.

Example 17.8

The access matrix shown in Example 17.5 can be reduced to capability lists for various domains as follows:

Domain/Object	File A	File C	Printer2
Domain1	Read Control	Write	Print

Domain/Object	File A	File C
Domain2	Read Write	Read*

Domain/Object	File B	File C	Printer2
Domain3	Read Write Execute	Read	Print

Since a capability list is associated with a particular domain, it should be protected and should not be accessible by a user process executing in that domain. Therefore, the capability list is considered a protected object and maintained by the OS. The OS does not allow any direct access to it to avoid user tampering. Some methods are required for C-list protection. The idea is to distinguish a C-list from other objects. Therefore, a tag is associated with every object that will indicate whether the object is in C-list or not. For this purpose, a hardware or firmware support is required wherein each memory word has an extra tag bit to indicate the C-list. The tag bit is modified only by the processes running in kernel mode and cannot be used by any arithmetic or other ordinary instructions.

The next way of protection is to provide space in kernel memory only, that is, the C-lists are kept inside the kernel space. Since the C-list is inside the kernel space, no user process can modify it, thereby providing protection. The capabilities to a running process may be copied to it but not allowed to change as C-list within the process table is inside the kernel space.

The third method for protecting C-list is to keep the C-list in the user space only but cryptographically so that it cannot be modified by the user processes.

The C-list is implemented as a unique object identifier considering the C-list as an object. This identifier may be implemented as a pointer to the desired object where the object is stored. This is known as *pointer-based C-list*. For example, a file is opened by a user process with its allowed access rights as

$int \ fd \ fopen("/abc/text.c", \ O\_RDWR).$

The variable *fd* containing the index of a file descriptor in the process' file descriptor table is a capability.

Table 17.2 Token-based C-list

Object name	Access rights	Random bit pattern

Another method to implement the unique identifier for C-list is to use tokens. A token is a unique bit sequence as a name for an object as shown in Table 17.2. This is known as *token-based C-list*. The random bit pattern provides more protection as compared to the first method. According to this method, while creating the capability, a random bit pattern is created. After this, the bit pattern encodes it to an object name and stores it in the C-lists, along with its access rights. However, this method does not specify the location of the object in the memory. However, the object's initial address must be known when the C-list is first used.

As described for ACL, there may also be two types of privileges or access rights for an object in C-lists: generic and object-specific. The generic access rights are the rights that are by default all objects or an object category may exercise.

17.7 CRYPTOGRAPHY AS A SECURITY TOOL

Cryptography is a technique to hide the message using *encryption*. Encryption is a formal name for scrambling the data in a message. The unscrambled state of the data in message is called *clear text* or *plain text*, which is then transformed so that an outsider will not be able to see the message contents. The transformed data is called as *cipher text*. Thus, encryption is simply a process of encoding a message so that its meaning cannot be easily understood by unauthorized people. Since the intended receiver of the encrypted message needs to see the actual text message, the encrypted message is transformed back to plain text. This process is known as *decryption* (see Fig.17.4).

In a cryptosystem (shorthand for 'cryptographic system'), the encryption and decryption may be denoted as

$C = E(P)$
$P = D(C)$,
where C is Cipher text
E is encryption rule
P is Plain text
D is Decryption mechanism

17.7.1 Private Key Encryption

In this type of cryptosystem, a private or secret key is an encryption/decryption key, which is known only to the parties that exchange secret messages. In this method, a key is shared between the two communicating parties so that each one can encrypt and decrypt the messages (see Fig. 17.5).

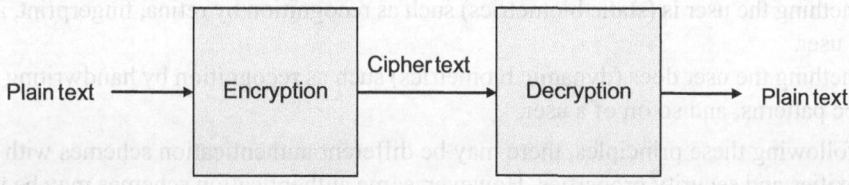

Fig. 17.4 Encryption and decryption

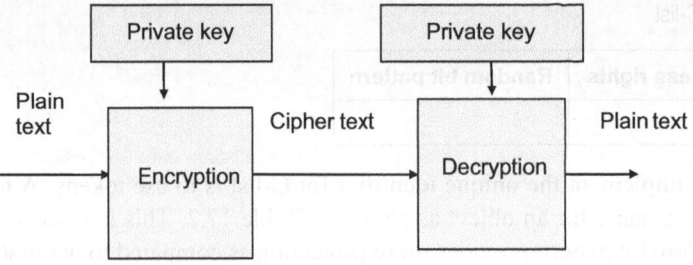

Fig. 17.5 Private key encryption

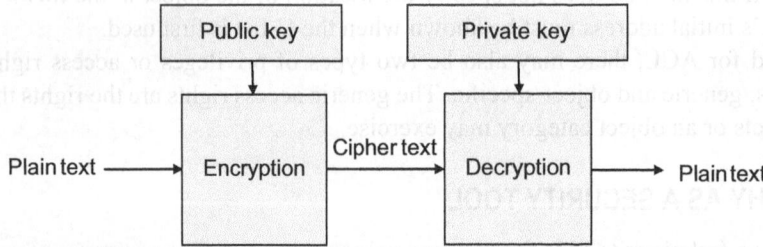

Fig. 17.6 Public key encryption

17.7.2 Public Key Encryption

In this type of cryptosystem, public and private keys are related in such a way that only the public key can be used to encrypt messages and only the corresponding private key is used to decrypt the encrypted message. It is virtually impossible to deduce the private key (see Fig. 17.6).

17.8 AUTHENTICATION

When a user logs into a computer, the OS needs to determine the identity of the user. This process is called *user authentication.*

The user authentication has two steps:

- **Identification**
  In this step, a unique identifier is specified to the user to authenticate.
- **Verification**
  In this step, the verification of a user is performed against the unique identifier, that is, it confirms the binding between the user and the identifier.

Most of the methods of authenticating the users when they attempt to log in are based on the following principles:

1. Something the user knows such as password, PIN, and so on.
2. Something the user has such as key, token, smartcard.
3. Something the user is (static biometrics) such as recognition by retina, fingerprint, and so on of a user.
4. Something the user does (dynamic biometrics) such as recognition by handwriting analysis, voice patterns, and so on of a user.

By following these principles, there may be different authentication schemes with different complexities and security properties. However, some authentication schemes may be weak and others may be strong. Some of the authentication schemes are discussed as follows:

17.8.1 Authentication Using Passwords

Passwords are widely used authentication mechanisms against unauthorized users. All systems, either standalone or online systems, opt for this type of authentication wherein a user provides a username and a password. Then the system compares that password to a previously stored password for that particular user ID, which is maintained in a system's password file.

The user ID determines whether the user is authenticated and authorized to gain access to a system. It determines the privileges given to the user. Some of the users have 'super user' status that enables them to perform functions that are especially protected by the OS. Some of the users have guest accounts that have limited privileges than others.

The password authentication mechanism, however, is prone to attacks. The hackers may be able to guess the passwords sometimes. One method of guessing is based on the information about the user. If the hacker is able to get some information about the user, then the password is breakable. Many users set their passwords as their spouse names, date of birth, and so on. Another way to guess the password is based on the brute force method, that is, trying all possible combinations of the password characters. In this case, the shorter passwords are more easily guessed as compared to longer passwords. Thus, the users should not use the obvious information as their passwords. Moreover, they should select passwords of more and more characters and mixture of alphabets (small and caps both), numerals, and special characters (if allowed).

Besides the guessing, the passwords may also be exposed accidentally if written somewhere to remember. They may also be transferred to some unauthorized users.

Encrypted Passwords

The password file being used in authentication process may not be safe as once an intruder manages to break into the system where the password file is stored, all the passwords are exposed. Thus, there is a requirement to keep these passwords secret in the system. One technique is to use encrypted passwords. As soon as the user enters his or her password, it is stored in an encrypted form. The encryption is done with the help of a simple but hard to deduce function. On the password, the function is applied and the *encrypted password* is obtained. These encoded passwords are only stored in the password file. Whenever the user logs into the system and enters the password, it is encoded, and this encoded password is compared with the already stored encoded password. The advantage of this encrypted password is that not even a super user is able to see the passwords in the password file. Therefore, the intruder, who is able to break into the system and get the password file, will not be able to see the original password.

Hashed Passwords

The encrypted passwords, however, can be attacked by the intruders. To reduce the possibility of the attacks, another method was devised that associates an n-bit random number with each password. This n-bit random number is known as a *salt value* as it helps in delaying the attacker to break the password. The password, along with the salt value, is fed to a hashing-based encryption algorithm that produces a fixed-length hash code. This encryption is thus based on cryptographic hash function. This hash function is an algorithm that takes an arbitrary block of data and returns a fixed-size bit string, that is, the cryptographic hash value. The advantage of this hash-encrypted password is that it is infeasible to modify a message without changing the hash code. Moreover, there cannot be two different messages with the same hash value.

The hash-encrypted password thus obtained (see Fig. 17.7) in the form of hashed code further slows down the attack of an intruder. Thus, corresponding to a user ID, the hashed code,

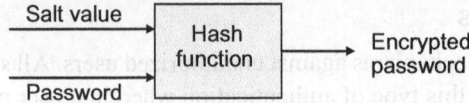

Fig. 17.7 Hash-encrypted password

along with its salt value, is stored in the password file, thereby forming a hashed-password file (see Table. 17.3).

Authentication using hash-encrypted password method is secure against a lot of security attacks. When a user tries to log into a system, the user provides a user ID and a password. The OS indexes into the password file with the User ID and retrieves the salt value and the hashed-encrypted password. The salt value is combined with the user-supplied password and then applied to hash-based encryption algorithm. The encrypted password thus obtained is compared against the already stored encrypted password corresponding to that user ID in the password file (see Fig. 17.8).

Table 17.3 Hashed-password file

User ID	Salt value	Encrypted password

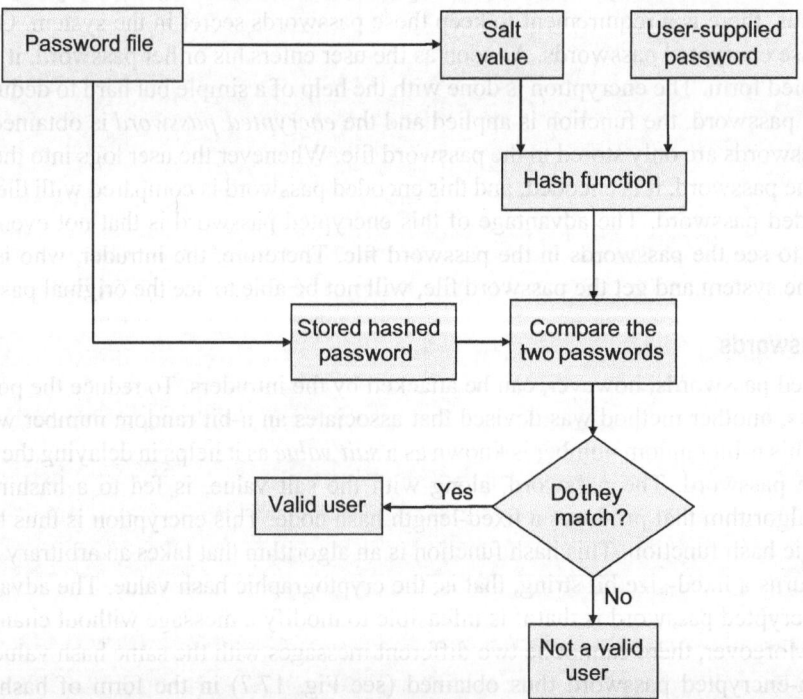

Fig. 17.8 Algorithmic flow for hash-encrypted password

One-time Passwords

To maintain the secrecy about the passwords, another method is to use a set of paired passwords. When a user logs into the system, the system randomly selects one part of a paired password and presents to the user. The user is then expected to enter the other part of that password. If the other part of the password matches with the stored one, then the login will be successful. The advantage is that every time a user wishes to log into the system, it will be challenged with a new password and the user has to respond with the correct another part of the password. In this way, the secret of a password is maintained by having paired passwords.

17.8.2 Token-based Authentication

The tokens are the objects that a user possesses for the purpose of user authentication. Two types of tokens that are widely used are

1. Smart card (already discussed in Chapter 1)
2. Memory card

Memory Card

A memory card is an electronic-flash data-storage device used for storing digital information. Memory cards are small, re-recordable, and able to retain data without power. However, these cards are not able to process data. The most common example of a memory card is a bank card with a magnetic stripe on its back. The magnetic stripe stores a security code to be read by the card reader. To identify an authentic user on a system, these cards are used with a password or a PIN. This combination of memory card, along with the password/PIN, provides significantly greater security.

17.8.3 Authentication Using Biometrics

Biometrics means 'life measurement'. Biometric measures and analyzes biological data. It refers to the technology that analyzes physiological characteristics to identify an individual. To authenticate a user's identity, a number of biometric traits are used, for example, face, fingerprints, retina, and so on. This authentication requires that the person to be identified be present physically at the time of identification procedures, thereby increasing the authenticity of the method. Moreover, there is no requirement of remembering the passwords as needed in other authentication methods. Thus, authentication using biometrics is a pattern recognition system, which is implemented by determining the authenticity of a specific physiological or behavioural characteristic possessed by the user. In this authentication, the samples of biometric traits are captured with the help of a sensing device such as camera, scanner, and so on and stored in a storage medium, which are then used for comparison purposes while authenticating a user.

17.9 INTRUSION DETECTION SYSTEM

Intrusion Detection System (IDS) is a security service that may be used along with other security suites such as a firewall and a good anti-virus. The idea of IDS is to have a system that monitors and analyzes system events such that there is no attempt to access the system in an unauthorized way. In other words, effective IDS can serve as a way to prevent intrusions.

There are two types of IDS:

17.9.1 Host-based Intrusion Detection System

In this type, a software is set-up on the system, which has to be monitored. This software makes use of log files in the form of sources of data. Host-based IDSs function as a specialized layer of security software to vulnerable or sensitive systems. They monitor as well as analyze a system's internals. Thus, the primary job of a host-based IDS is to detect intrusions, log suspicious events, and send alerts.

Host-based IDSs follow one of two general approaches to intrusion detection:

Anomaly Detection

This approach is based on the fact that intrusion may induce anomalies in the system. Therefore, in this detection, anomalous behaviour within a system is observed. Then statistical tests are applied to observed behaviour to determine whether it is genuine or not.

Signature Detection

In this approach, a set of rules or attack patterns is defined. The system input or network traffic is then examined with reference to these rules or behavioural patterns. Virus detection is an example as virus detection software examines the system input for known viruses only.

17.9.2 Network-based IDS

In this type of IDS, the network traffic of a network is observed and analysed for any unauthorised access on the network. This IDS scans network packets at the router or host level, analyses them and logs the suspicious packets in a separate file known as special log file. Thus, a network-based IDS is a system that monitors and analyses network traffic to detect any unauthorised access. The analysis is performed based on signatures. For example, the port signature is used wherein well-known ports are observed and analysed to detect an attack. Similarly, header signatures are used to detect an additional text with packet headers.

17.10 WORM/BOT/ROOTKIT COUNTER MEASURES

Worms can be detected by signature detection. The technique generates a certain signature for worms. Using only these signatures, worms' entry/exit is detected. This technique is very effective in detecting worms, but the only limitation is that it is slow. Therefore, it is only suitable for detecting slow-spreading worms but not effective for fast-spreading worms as no signature is available by the time the machines are already infected.

Another way to stop worms is network filtering. In this technique, the network packets that are used for worm spread are filtered-out. The source for these types of packets causing worm spread is blacklisted. This function can also be assigned to the existing firewall.

Since the botnet works in a coordinated manner, it is essential to detect and disable the botnet while they are being formed.

Once the rootkits are installed on the system, it is difficult to detect them even with the help of an anti-virus as they are in stealth mode and modify the scanning results to hide themselves. An alternative and effective method to check the presence of a rootkit on the system is to boot it from a trusted and clean OS source and scan the system. The rootkit at this time is not active and therefore, can be checked for its existence. The files will be found while scanning. Otherwise, the utilities/drivers may be compared with its clean copy. If they do not match, then the rootkits may be present. Chkrootkit and rkhunter are some of the tools that check for the presence of rootkits and also worms in a system.

17.11 DEALING WITH BUFFER OVERFLOW ATTACKS

As discussed in Chapter 16, buffer overflow may be used as a vulnerability by the intruders. There are some techniques through which this can be dealt. The techniques are as follows:

17.11.1 Writing Correct Code

Since the buffer overflow attack occurs due to a lack of poor programming practices, there is a lot of scope to deal with it. One way is to improve the way programming is done. The common problem of languages such as 'C' is that safe use of data structures and variables cannot be guaranteed as programmers may commit mistakes while programming. For instance, if there is no array-bound checking, then the attacker may exploit this vulnerability to attack the system. Therefore, the programmer must check the limits of the array; otherwise, the program is open to attacks. The programmer needs to check every read/write operation on the array being used in the program to ensure that that all are within range. This can be done with the help of automation tools, such as Compaq C Compiler, *gcc* patch developed by Jones & Kelly, Purify, and so on.

17.11.2 Safe Libraries

Another common problem in C language is that some library functions are not safe either and may invite attacks. For example, the library routine strcpy(), sprintf, and so on are not safe as they are not compiled with bound checking. In this case, it is better to replace these library functions with safer variants. This may include some new functions in place of old functions.

17.11.3 Use of Type-safe Programming Language

The other way is to choose modern programming language, for example, the code can be written in a type-safe language such as Java, that is, the type-safe operation can only be performed on a given variable. Such languages are safe from buffer overflow vulnerabilities as their compilers include additional code that takes care of bound checking.

17.11.4 Non-executable Buffers

Another defence against buffer overflow is to make the stack segment of the victim program's address space non-executable and preserve compatibility. To implement this feature, it requires support from the processor's memory management unit (MMU). To facilitate this, the MMU will tag virtual memory (VM) pages as non-executable. Since this type of protection is able to defend against many types of buffer overflow attacks, it is adopted in many OSs.

17.11.5 Address Space Randomization

The attacker predicts the approximate location of buffer and in turn uses this location to determine a suitable return address and thereby, transfers the control to the malicious code. If it is possible to manipulate the location of stack segment, then the buffer overflow attacks can be thwarted. Since the address range on modern processor is large, the stack memory region can be shifted randomly for every process so that the intruder is not able to predict the approximate location of the buffer. Similarly, the same approach can be used for standard library functions that are typically loaded at the same address by the same program. For the standard library routines, the security extension program randomises the order of loading standard libraries and their VM address locations.

17.12 DEALING WITH MOBILE CODE

As discussed in Chapter 16, mobile code may not be safe for the system. There are some techniques through which a malicious mobile code can be dealt. The techniques are discussed as follows:

17.12.1 Code Blocking Approach

This approach is based on blocking the code on the system. The blocking may be implemented by disabling the application (switching off Java in Java-enabled browsers), filtering (firewalls to filter out web pages containing applets), and so on.

17.12.2 Authentication Using Code Signing

In this approach, a list of trusted sources is maintained, which is based on digitally signed code assurance obtained from the source of code. When a mobile code is received, it is verified against the list that it has been signed by an authenticated source of code. The authentication ensures that the mobile code is trusted and has not been tampered. Digital signatures are created using public-key-based signature algorithms. This public key algorithm uses two parts: One is the public key known to all and the other is the private key known only to its user. However, these algorithms are inefficient to sign long documents. Therefore, another method is used wherein the hash of mobile code is signed and distributed along with the signed code. This method also checks the integrity as a single bit change in the code will change the hash code. At the host machine where the code has been received, the client computes the hash code and compares it with the copy sent with the signed code.

17.12.3 Safe Interpreters

Instead of using compiled executables, an interpreter is used that interprets the mobile code. Since the interpreter enforces the security policy, an instruction is executed only if it satisfies the security policy being enforced.

17.12.4 Code Inspection

The mobile code is intercepted, and inspection is done to check whether it is malicious or not; the code is checked against a known list of malicious codes. It may also validate digital certificates and hash values.

17.12.5 Sandboxing

Sandboxing is a technique that contains mobile code in such a way that it does not damage its executing environment. It is an idea to confine the mobile code to a limited range of virtual addresses. In fact, the range of virtual address is divided into equal-sized regions known as *sandboxes*. Each mobile code, such as applet, is allocated two sandboxes: one for code and another for data. Thus, sandboxing allows a foreign mobile code to execute but in a constrained manner. The mobile code in a sandbox can be controlled efficiently by allowing monitored access to the host machine resources. It means that the sandbox guarantees that a mobile code does not jump outside its code sandbox or reference data outside its data sandbox. In this way, no mobile code may try to modify its code while executing, thereby running in a constrained environment and cannot harm the system in any way.

The Sun's Java interpreter implements the sandbox idea and is found inside Internet browsers. There are three main components that secure the Java interpreter:

Class Loader

It is a special Java object that converts remote byte codes into data structures representing Java classes. The operations are classified by the class loader as safe and harmful. Only safe operations are allowed but harmful ones cause an exception and defer the decision to the security manager.

Verifier

It checks the mobile code before it is loaded to verify that the mobile code does not forge any pointers or access arbitrary memory locations.

Security Manager

The security manager consists of security policies that define the extents, rules, and restriction for execution of a mobile code. The security manager is invoked when a method is attempted to execute that is restricted by the security policy.

17.12.6 Proof-carrying Code

Since the mobile code to be executed on the host machine should not damage the host machine in any way and it does not use too many resources of host machine, the technique of proof-carrying code (PCC) is adopted by which the host establishes a set of safety rules that guarantees safe behaviour of mobile-code execution. The host uses a simple and fast-proof validator that checks the behaviour of the code such that the code is safe to execute.

17.13 SECURITY PATCHES

Intruders exploit system vulnerabilities to attack the system. Therefore, it is necessary to identify and close the vulnerabilities as soon as possible. The modifications done in response to the open vulnerabilities in the OS or any other critical software is known as a *security patch*. The security patches thus address the security flaws in the software, thereby providing security to a system. To reduce the chance of exploiting the software or OS vulnerabilities, the organization or software developers must discover the vulnerabilities, address them by notifying the concerned users, and provide the security patches as soon as possible.

17.14 SECURE FILE SYSTEMS

The files and other resources on the system can be protected using access control list as discussed earlier. However, these control policies may not protect the data stored when it is accessed by a different OS. Therefore, there is a need to protect the data irrespective of the mode of accessing the system. The idea is to protect the files in a file system using encryption. Thus, the file

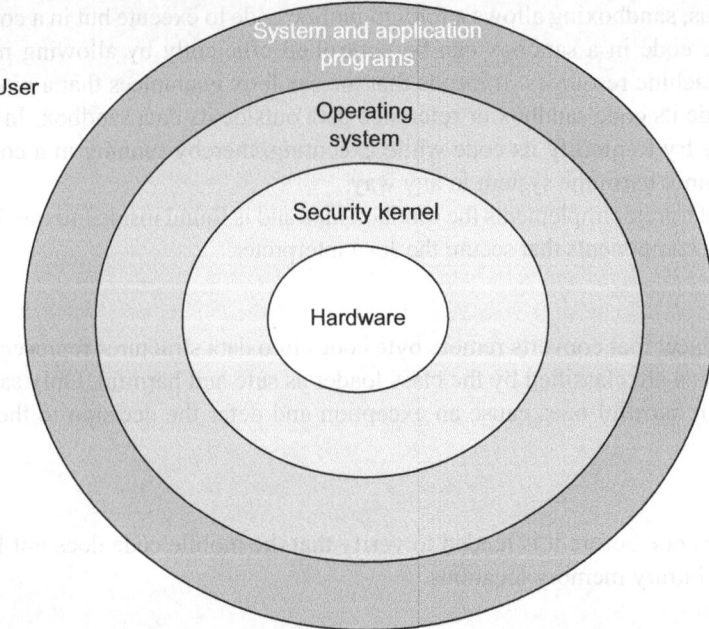

Fig. 17.9 Separate security kernel

systems that secure their files through access control as well as encryption are known as *secure file systems (SFS)* or encrypted *file systems (EFS)*. In Microsoft Windows, EFS was introduced in version 3.0 of NTFS. The EFS is implemented with a symmetric key known as *file encryption key (FEK)*. The large amounts of data can be encrypted and decrypted with the help of symmetric encryption algorithm. The FEK is then encrypted with a public key. The encrypted FEK thus obtained is stored in a data stream of encrypted file.

17.15 TRUSTED OPERATING SYSTEMS

A trusted system is the system that has formally stated security requirements and meets these requirements. In trusted systems, the objects such as processor, memory, I/O devices, and so on are surrounded by access control mechanism as discussed in the chapter, which incorporate technology to address both features and assurance. To design a trusted OS, a *security kernel* is designed such that it provides the security interfaces between the hardware, the OS, and other parts of the system, that is, security kernel is responsible for enforcing security mechanism for the entire OS. This will prevent any intruder to enter the system. The security kernel is designed on top of hardware. It monitors all OS hardware accesses and checks any illegal access, thereby performing all protection functions (see Fig. 17.9).

To enforce the security policy, there is a *trusted computing base* (TCB) acting as a shell (see Fig. 17.10) that protects the system. The TCB has access to most of the hardware (processor, memory, registers, and I/O devices) and OS functions (process creation, process switching, memory management, file management, and I/O management) that must be now a part of TCB. It seems that the TCB encompasses most of the OSs, but it is only a small sub-set and separate from the rest of the OS. The separate and small size of TCB also facilitates verification of its correctness and faster execution. It monitors the security sensitive information such as change

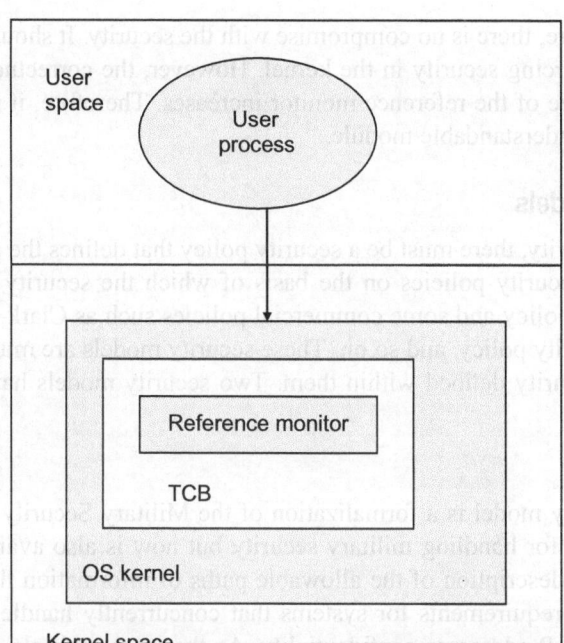

Fig. 17.10 Trusted computing base

of the process control block (PCB) fields when a process changes its state, memory references, and so on. In this way, all security-related codes are located in one place. To ensure the security effectiveness, the TCB must be run in a protected state, and that is why it is implemented in the kernel space.

Inside the TCB, there is a part known as *reference monitor*. The reference monitor is a part that controls accesses to objects, that is, all system calls accesses are now with security. It may consist of several modules consisting of access control for files, devices, memory, IPC, and so on. The reference monitor must be invoked whenever there is a request to access any object. When the request reaches the reference monitor, it decides whether to process after checking the authenticity of the request. The access control information is stored in a database. The security events are stored in an audit file (see Fig. 17.11). Thus, all the security checking is

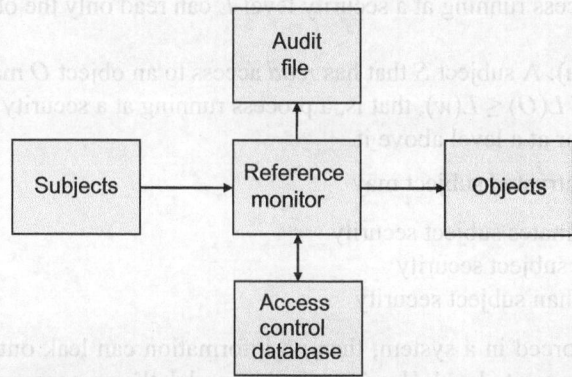

Fig. 17.11 Reference monitor

done only at one place and therefore, there is no compromise with the security. It should function correctly as it is the part enforcing security in the kernel. However, the correctness may decrease as the complexity and size of the reference monitor increases. Therefore, it must be designed as a small, simple, and understandable module.

17.15.1 Multi-level Security Models

Since the trusted OS enforces security, there must be a security policy that defines the security expected from the system. The security policies on the basis of which the security models have been developed are military policy and some commercial policies such as Clark–Wilson security policy, Chinese wall security policy, and so on. These security models are multi-level as there are multiple levels of security defined within them. Two security models have been discussed in this section.

Bell–La Padula Security Model

The Bell–La Padula (BLP) security model is a formalization of the Military Security Model. This model was initially designed for handling military security but now is also available to other organizations. It is a formal description of the allowable paths of information flow in a secure system. It defines security requirements for systems that concurrently handle data at different sensitivity levels. The BLP addresses confidentiality. As there are multiple security levels in this model, it is also called *multi-level security system*.

The classification at multiple levels: {U, C, S, TS}
where U = unclassified
C = confidential
S = secret
TS = top secret
The classifications are ordered as TS > S > C > U.

The BLP model is based on a subject–object paradigm. The system is described as a set of subjects S and objects O. Subjects are active elements of the system that execute actions. Objects are passive elements of the system that contain information. Subjects act on behalf of users who have a security level associated with them. The following are two properties to characterize the secure information of flow:

• **Simple security property (no read-up)**: A subject S may have *read* access to an object O only if $L(O) \leq L(S)$, that is, a process running at a security level L can read only the objects at its level or at a level below it.

• **The *-Property (no read-down)**: A subject S that has *read* access to an object O may have *write* access to an object w only if $L(O) \leq L(w)$, that is, a process running at a security level L can only write objects at its level or at a level above it.

*Star property means that an untrusted subject may

 i) *append* if object security dominates subject security
 ii) *write* if object security equals subject security
iii) *read* if object security is less than subject security

If these two properties are enforced in a system, then no information can leak out from a higher-security level to the lower-security level. However, in this model, the processes can read and write the objects but cannot directly communicate with each other.

Biba Model

Biba security model was developed to address a weakness in the BLP model. The BLP model addresses only confidentiality, but it does not ensure integrity. The Biba model addresses integrity, that is, deals with inappropriate modification of data and therefore, sometimes is known as *counterpart of BLP*. Two goals of maintaining the integrity are

1. To prevent unauthorized users from making modifications in data.
2. To maintain internal and external consistency of data.

The Biba model uses objects and subjects like the BLP model. The objects and subjects are classified according to integrity levels instead of security levels. The following are the security rules of this model:

- **Simple integrity property (no write-up)**: A subject at a given level of integrity can only write objects at its level or a lower level. A subject is permitted a write access only if the access class of the object dominates the access class of the subject.
- **The *- property (no read-down)**: A subject at a given level of integrity must not read an object at a lower-integrity level, that is, a subject is allowed a read access to an object only if the access class of the object dominates the access class of the subject.

SUMMARY

Let us have a quick review of important concepts discussed in this chapter:
- A domain is a set of objects and right pairs.
- The matrix containing the information of access rights of the resources within a domain is known as *access matrix*.
- Storing only non-empty entries as access rights for objects is known as *ACL*. Each column is then implemented as an ACL in the access matrix. The advantage of an ACL is that it reduces the space storage and increases the search efficiency as well.
- A capability list for a domain is a list of objects with their allowed operations that the domain can have.
- Passwords are widely used authentication mechanisms against unauthorized users.
- Authentication using hash-encrypted password method is secure against a lot of security attacks.

- Authentication using biometric system compares a registered biometric sample against a newly captured biometric sample.
- An IDS) is a security service that may be used along with other security suites such as a firewall and a good antivirus.
- A trusted system is the system that has formally stated security requirements and meets these requirements.
- To design a trusted OS, a *security kernel* is designed such that it provides the security interfaces between the hardware, the OS, and other parts of the system
- The security kernel is designed on the top of hardware. It monitors all OS hardware accesses and checks any illegal access, thereby performing all protection functions
- To enforce the security policy, there is a TCB acting as a shell that protects whatever in the system needs protection.

MULTIPLE CHOICE QUESTIONS

1. In _____, the subject having an access right for an object may pass this permission to any other subject or domain.
   - (a) DAC
   - (b) MAC
   - (c) RAC
   - (d) none

2. _____ does not provide access rights to users of domains/subjects directly.

   - (a) DAC
   - (b) MAC
   - (c) RAC
   - (d) none

3. _____ is governed by a central policy to restrict the users to gain access to objects.
   - (a) DAC
   - (b) MAC
   - (c) RAC
   - (d) none

4. Storing only non-empty entries as access rights for objects is known as
   - (a) access matrix
   - (b) ACL
   - (c) capability list
   - (d) none

5. _____ for a domain is a list of objects with their allowed operations that the domain can have.
   - (a) Access matrix
   - (b) ACL
   - (c) Capability list
   - (d) none

6. _____ are small, re-recordable, and able to retain data without power but are not able to process data.
   - (a) Passwords
   - (b) Memory cards
   - (c) Smart cards
   - (d) none

7. _____ has the processing power to serve many different applications.
   - (a) Password
   - (b) Memory card
   - (c) Smart card
   - (d) none

8. _____ is a technique that contains mobile code in such a way that it does not damage its executing environment.
   - (a) Code inspection
   - (c) Sandboxing

   - (b) Code signing
   - (d) none

9. The security kernel is designed on the top of ____.
   - (a) the OS
   - (b) user programs
   - (c) hardware
   - (d) none

10. In the design of a trusted OS, _____ must be invoked whenever there is a request to access any object.
    - (a) kernel
    - (b) security kernel
    - (c) shell
    - (d) reference monitor

11. In the _____ model, the processes can read and write the objects but can not communicate with each other directly.
    - (a) BLP
    - (b) Biba
    - (c) commercial security
    - (d) none

12. The _____ model addresses confidentiality.
    - (a) BLP
    - (b) Biba
    - (c) commercial security
    - (d) none

13. The _____ model addresses integrity.
    - (a) BLP
    - (b) Biba
    - (c) commercial security
    - (d) none

REVIEW QUESTIONS

1. Define protection domain.
2. What are the various policies of access control mechanisms?
3. What is an access matrix? What type of operation can be done on it?
4. Explain the variants of copy operation on access matrix.
5. Explain the *owner* access right on access matrix.
6. Explain the *control* access right on access matrix.
7. What is an ACL? What are its advantages?
8. What is a generic ACL?
9. What is a C-list? What are its advantages?
10. Why C-lists are kept inside the kernel space?
11. What is token-based C-list?
12. Explain how password authentication is prone to attacks.

13. What are encrypted passwords?
14. What are hashed passwords?
15. What are one-time passwords (OTPs)?
16. What is token-based authentication?
17. What is biometric-based authentication?
18. What is an IDS? Explain the various types of IDS.
19. What are the methods to counter-measure the worms?
20. How do you deal with mobile code?
21. How do you deal with buffer-overflow attack?
22. What is sandboxing?
23. What is a security kernel? How is it designed?
24. Explain and distinguish BLP and Biba security models.

BRAIN TEASERS

1. Access matrix, access list, and C-list are three types of protection. Which is the most efficient from implementation viewpoint?

2. Design a hashed password to protect an online web application.

3. There are mobile software agents that travel from node to node on the network. There can be two situations. One is that mobile agent code may not be authenticated. The other issue is that mobile agent may not be safe on the node on which it is executing. What kind of protection mechanisms can be there for these situations?

Case Study VI: Protection Mechanisms in UNIX/Solaris/ Linux/Windows

UNIX

In spite of the cryptic nature of UNIX, one of the foremost reasons for UNIX's popularity is the levels of security it ensures at various stages. One of the means to guarantee security is file access control. When a file is created, it has, associated with it, nine protection bits. The protection or permission bits specify who all can access the file and for what purpose. These protection bits specify read(r), write(w), and execute(x) permission for the owner of the file, other members of the group to which this file belongs, and all other users. This forms a hierarchy of owner, group, and all others, with the highest relevant set of permissions being used. For example consider a file *myfile*. If the permissions for the file *myfile* are, say, **rwx, rw, x**; they signify the following, respectively:

- The owner can read, write, as well as execute the file *myfile*.
- The members of the group can read and write the file but cannot execute it.
- All others can only execute *myfile*.

When applied to a directory, the read and write bits grant the right to

- list the files
- create, rename, or delete files in the directory.

The execute bit grants the right to search the directory for a particular component of a filename.

The read, write, and execute bits are also assigned weights (numerical value) that which provide an alternative means to change the permissions of a file. The weights assigned to the three permissions are shown in Table CS4.1.

Table CS6.1 Weights assigned to file permissions

Permission	Weight
Read	4
Write	2
Execute	1

When all the three permissions are available, the total weight is, thus $4 + 2 + 1 = 7$.

A level of security is increased in case of directories by using a *sticky bit*. This bit is used to guard the directories from intruders. When the sticky bit *sticks* to a particular directory, only the owner of this directory or its super user can delete files from this directory.

The UNIX system security has a login program that asks for login ID and a password from a user. It hashes the password and searches the password file to verify the login credentials entered by the user. The login program then uses *setid* command to provide a user ID and *setgid* to provide a group ID to the user who entered the system. When a file is opened by a process, the system first checks the protection bits in the file's inode against the user ID and group ID to verify whether the user is permitted access that file or not.

SOLARIS

In UNIX, there is an owner and a group corresponding to each file. A bit map of permissions is then assigned. However, this is not sufficient when different users want to have different permissions. Access control list (ACL) is the mechanism by which users with different permissions can be assigned to a file. Solaris introduced the ACL for protection in Version 2.5. The protected versions are known as *trusted Solaris*. Through Solaris ACLs, the administrator assigns a list of user IDs and groups to a file using *setfacl* command and ACL list is assigned. A file can be assigned to multiple users and groups. Access control lists may be permitted to directories as well. However, in Solaris, a sub-directory under directory does not inherit the ACL from its parent.

To perform privileged operations, some OSs require the users to be root users. However, this makes the application powerful. This is harmful if there is vulnerability in the application as it can be exploited by the hackers, thereby damaging data by escalating privileges. In Solaris 10, using the principle of least privilege, only appropriate privileges that are necessary to perform tasks are granted. Thus, by default, some privileges are already configured with applications. Thus, the applications are not granted unlimited system access, thereby reducing the chances of attack.

Instead of providing the full super-user privileges to the users, Solaris provides role-based access control. In this, it may define the role of users and appropriately assign the privileges. Each role of user defines the tasks and responsibilities that a user can perform. Solaris 10 has a pre-defined set of profiles that can be combined with roles. To have more security, the user assigned with a role needs to log in using the user ID and then can utilize the role he or she has been assigned.

The OSs that are configured to service external network connections after first booting may be prone to security attacks. Solaris 10 has an option of 'secure by default networking' during installation. The system while being installed is made secure from outside attacks.

Solaris 10 integrates an IP packet filtering firewall within the TCP/IP stack. The filtering may be on the basis of IP address, port, protocol, network interface, and so on. The specific Internet addresses that may attempt to gain access to the system may also be blocked. Solaris may restrict access to TCP services based on some criteria, such as domain name, host name, and IP address. This layer of protection is known as *TCP wrappers*.

Cryptographic framework in Solaris provides cryptographic operations at the application as well as kernel level. It helps to increase security with built-in cryptographic technology to have a quick encryption and decryption.

Solaris has a secure shell that protects against session eavesdropping, password theft, and session hijacking. The secure shell is able to encrypt all network traffic, have stronger authentication, and monitor the integrity of network sessions.

Solaris supports enhanced password management with the following features:

- Password length
- Account locking
- Defined password complexity levels

Since passwords used in networked environments can be intercepted, Solaris supports Kerberos. Kerberos provides stronger authentication methods based on industry-standard encryption algorithms.

Solaris has a number of features that check whether a system has been compromised and ensure data integrity. Besides this, Solaris has the following tools to validate:

Basic auditing and reporting tool (BART)   Using this tool, cryptographic hashes can be generated to validate data and files.

Fingerprint database   Solaris provides digital fingerprint database that may be used to check the integrity of files.

Solaris has an optional layer of secure label technology as a trusted extension to implement mandatory access control (MAC) security policies. The OS is able to support multi-level data access policies with labeled security policies. Furthermore, it does not necessitate modifying the existing applications. Through Solaris-trusted extensions, highly secured desktops, servers, firewalls, and so on are supported.

LINUX

Linux provides authentication to its users via username and password. Passwords are hashed using MD5 or data encryption standard (DES) algorithms. To avoid the brute-force attacks on passwords, Linux has the provision to load pluggable authentication modules that are capable of reconfiguring the system at run time to include enhanced authentication techniques. These authentication methods may include smart cards, Kerberos, and voice-authentication systems.

Conventionally, the access control policy is default access control (DAC) as discussed earlier. However, Linux supports the Linux security modules (LSMs) framework also, wherein customized access control policy can be designed through loadable kernel modules. Only the required modules to implement a customized access control policy are loaded. However, the LSM is only invoked if DAC policy has granted the access.

Linux also provides cryptographic API through which processes can encrypt information using various algorithms such as DES, AES, and MD5. The kernel uses this API to implement secure network protocols. It is also possible to create secure file systems using this API.

WINDOWS

Windows XP has several mechanisms that increase the security of stored data. One approach is that it runs in the background as a file system known as *guardian angel*. Guardian angel watches over the system files in root folder such as. dll,. exe,. sys, and so on. Whenever there is any update in these files, the file system restores the original version of the modified file.

Windows XP also offer encrypting file system (EFS) feature. However, this feature works only for disks that have been formatted with New Technology File System (NTFS). In EFS, a public key is used to encrypt a file and a private key decrypts it. The public and private keys used in EFS are handled in the background by Windows automatically. The encryption keys are stored on the disk only in the encrypted file's header. The EFS may use expanded DES, that is, DESX for encryption. The EFS is especially useful for mobile users. It may not be possible to access any of the files on the disk even if someone is able to gain access to the system somehow. This is because the files are encrypted. Since in Windows XP, the EFS is integrated with NTFS, the file encryption and decryption are transparent. It means when a user saves his file, it is encrypted and written to the disk.

Windows has the provision of personalized login facility. Through personalized login, security has a separate interface to the system now and no one can access or delete anyone's documents. Moreover, different profiles can be set with different security limits; for example, separate profile for children can be set so that some Internet sites can be filtered for them.

In Windows XP, there is *terminal services technology* feature, which runs unique user sessions due to which each user's data are isolated in a user session. It means that a user does not need to save another user's files before logging in. Users can log in with a password and open their session, thereby securing the session from one another.

For Internet security, there is a protection feature in Windows XP known as *Internet connection firewall (ICF)*. The ICF provides firewall security for the systems directly connected to the Internet. It protects the system from intruders through active packet filtering as soon as we start Windows XP. In this filtering, ports on the firewall are dynamically opened to access only the required services. This way, ports cannot be scanned by the intruders, thereby reducing the external attacks. The ICF is available for LAN, VPN, dial-up connections, and so on. The ICF does not allow any unsolicited traffic in by default. However, sometimes, if we need to host a website or for some other purpose, the system may require open holes in the firewall to allow traffic in some specific ports. The ICF facilitates this also and it is known as *port mapping*.

Windows XP professional supports the use of group policy objects (GPO). Through this feature, administrators can apply single security profile to multiple systems and authenticate users with smart card.

There are various security-related settings in Windows XP that can be implemented individually. Moreover, there are pre-defined security templates that can be used without modification or be customized as per needs.

Windows XP keeps the system safe from intruders by providing only guest-level privileges to anyone trying to access a system from the network. An intruder who is able to get the access to the system can only obtain the guest-level privileges and hence may not be able to harm the system much.

As an extension of the ICF, Windows XP professional has a location-aware group policy. This policy is useful for mobile users who work from home or other places. When a system is a member of domain and connected to the corporate network, the domain administrator enables a group policy that may prevent the use of the ICF. However, as soon as the system is brought to home or public Internet connection, the ICF is enabled. Since the ICF is a stateful packet filter, it blocks all the unsolicited connections over the public network. There is a data structure used by the ICF known as *flow table,* which is used to validate any incoming flow. The incoming flow is only allowed if it is originated within the protected network.

In Windows XP, to restrict the software on the system, there are software-restriction policies. Two types of software restriction policies are discussed as follows:

- If administrators are able to identify all the trusted software, they can lock down the system and do not allow any other software to be run on the system. In this case, the default is *disallowed.*
- In case the administrators are not able to identify the trusted software, they will react and identify undesirable software as it is encountered. The default in this case is *allowed.*

But the systems having Windows XP will now be more vulnerable to hackers' attacks as Microsoft has ended its technical support for Windows XP. The support ended on 8 April 2014.

In Windows 7, there is an application called *Windows biometric framework* (WBF), which aims to support biometric authentication devices. To provide a common interface for all biometric devices, there is a Windows biometric driver interface (WBDI). The WBDI consists of a variety of interfaces having the appropriate data structures and I/O controls for biometric devices.

PART VII

Advanced Operating Systems

18 Distributed Operating Systems

18.1 INTRODUCTION

Distributed systems make a convenient medium to share resources, speed up computation, and improve data availability and reliability. Distributed computing is provided by a distributed OS. This chapter discusses the characteristics of a distributed system, along with the differentiation between network and distributed OSs. However, the achievement of distributed computation is difficult. There are several issues in the distributed environment. There is no global clock or global state. The distributed system poses many challenges in terms of this constrained distributed environment. The issues discussed for the single-processor machine, such as mutual exclusion, deadlocks, process-scheduling, and so on, introduce numerous difficulties for implementation of distributed computation. All these are discussed in this chapter.

18.2 CHARACTERISTICS OF DISTRIBUTED SYSTEMS

Distributed systems are multi processor systems, but with the following differences:

- Distributed system works in a wide-area network, involving much more communication as compared to computation.
- Each node in a distributed system is a complete computer, having a full set of peripherals, including memory, communication hardware, possibly different OS and different file system, and so on.
- The users of a distributed system have an impression that they are working on a single machine.

Thus, a distributed system is a loosely-coupled architecture, wherein processors are inter-connected by a communication network. The processors and their respective resources for a specific processor in a distributed system are *remote*, while its own resources are considered as *local*. The distributed system is a network of workstations, wherein the system might have a single file system that facilitates all the files accessible from all the machines in the same way. A user, working on the distributed system, provides

Learning Objectives

After reading this chapter, you should be able to understand:

- Characteristics of a distributed system
- Differentiation between a network and a distributed OS
- Various issues in a distributed OS
- IPC methods in a distributed OS
- Concept of global clock and logical clock
- Lamport's logical clock algorithm for synchronization
- Global distributed system state
- Achieving global state through Chandy–Lamport algorithm
- Resolving mutual exclusion problem through:
- Centralized algorithm
- Ricart–Agarwala algorithm
- Token-ring algorithm
- Deadlock detection through centralized and distributed algorithms
- Deadlock prevention through wait-die and wound-wait algorithms
- Distributed process-scheduling algorithms
- Distributed shared memory

commands to it and gets the result. He/she is not aware whether the task has been divided into smaller tasks, and which task has been completed on which node of the system. In other words, a distributed system, as a whole, may look and act like it is a single-processor time-sharing system, and the user working on it has the perception that the work is being done on a single machine.

The major motivations/advantages behind the development of a distributed system are listed as the following:

- **Economy**

  Distributed systems, comprising micro-processors, have a better price performance ratio as compared to a single centralized system of the mainframe type. A number of cheap processors together, resulting in a distributed system, provide a highly cost-effective solution for a computation-intensive application.

- **Resource sharing**

  It is the main motive behind distributed systems. If we want to take advantage of hundreds of processors, all of them have to be on a single board, which may not be possible. But the multiple processors are realized as a single powerful machine in a network system, and the resulting machine is known as a distributed system. In this way, a number of users can share the resources of all the machines on the distributed system.

- **Computational speed-up**

  Besides resource sharing, distributed systems also provide computational speed-up, by partitioning a computation into sub-computations, which are distributed and run concurrently on various nodes on the system. It results in higher throughput and provides rapid response time in computing user tasks. Thus, a distributed system enhances the performance of a system.

- **Reliability**

  Since a distributed system may utilize an alternative path in the network, in case of any failure, it provides reliable services and resources. A distributed system also provides enhanced availability of resources through redundancy of resources and communication paths, thereby increasing the reliability of the system. For example, a distributed file system places files on separate machines and allows many users to access the same set of files reliably, providing the view of a single file system.

- **Communication**

  The users in a distributed system are able to exchange information at geographically-distant nodes, and may collaborate on a project with various communication facilities.

- **Incremental growth**

  The computational power of a distributed system is dynamic. It may be increased with the introduction of any new hardware or software resources. Thus, modular expandability is possible in the distributed system.

18.3 NETWORK OPERATING SYSTEMS

The distributed system discussed above will need an OS software layer that will coordinate all activities to be performed on the network system. The network OS is the earliest form of OS that coordinates the activities on a network system. Thus, a network OS may be considered as a loosely-coupled OS software on a loosely-coupled hardware that allows nodes and users of a distributed system to be independent of one another, but interacts in a limited degree. In a network, each node has its own local OS. A user sitting on a node may work as on the local

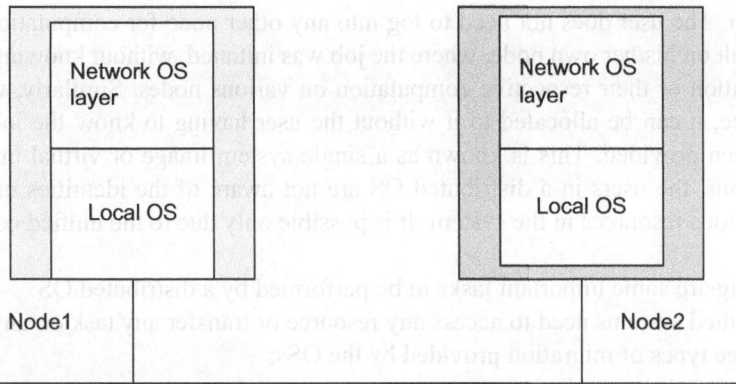

Fig. 18.1   Network operating system

machine through its local OS. However, on the network system, there may be some control operations that may be performed by the user, working on the machine. In other words, the user working on a node is also able to perform non-local functions. For example, the user may remotely log on to some other node. Similarly, the user may transfer the files to another node as well. For the functioning of these non-local operations, the OS software is required to coordinate the activities. The role of network OS starts here. The network OS may be considered as another layer of software on the OS on a local machine. This layer works between user computations and the kernel on the local machine. First, the processes of the user contact the network OS. If the operation to be performed on the node is local, the network OS passes the request to the local OS on the node. But if the operation to be performed is non-local, the network OS on that node contacts the network OS on the node, which needs to be contacted for the operation.

A network OS also targets the resource-sharing across multiple nodes of the network, where each node has its own local OS and a layer of network OS (see Fig. 18.1). Each node on the network is able to perform some control operations that are run locally as well as on some other node on the network. However, to work on a network system using network OS, the user must be aware of the network nodes and their access rights, to perform the control functions. For instance, if a user wants to log on to some other node on the network, that is, perform remote login, he/she must know the address of the node and must have permission to log into the system. Similarly, while transferring files, the user must be explicitly aware of where all the files are located and where they will be copied. Thus, in a network OS-based system, a user must know where a resource is located, in order to use it, leading to poor transparency of system resources and services.

18.4   DISTRIBUTED OPERATING SYSTEMS

Distributed OSs are tightly-coupled OS software on loosely-coupled hardware, that is, distributed system. These OSs, providing distributed computing facility, employ almost same communication methods and protocols, as in network OSs. But the communication is transparent to the users, such that they are unaware of the separate computers that are providing the service. A distributed OS has control of all the nodes in the system. When a user starts working on a node, the control functions like process creation, resource allocation, and so on, are performed on behalf of the distributed OS. With the facility of distributed OS, a complex user computation may be divided into sub-computations. Each sub-computation may be allocated different nodes for computation. The user does not need to log into any other node for computation. The user will get the result on his/her own node, where the job was initiated, without knowing the details of sub-computation or their respective computation on various nodes. Similarly, when a user needs a resource, it can be allocated to it without the user having to know the location from where it has been provided. This is known as a single-system image or virtual uni-processor to the users. Thus, the users in a distributed OS are not aware of the identities of nodes and locations of various resources in the system. It is possible only due to the unified control of the distributed OS.

The following are some important tasks to be performed by a distributed OS:

- Since distributed systems need to access any resource or transfer any task on any node, there are three types of migration provided by the OSs:

    i) Data migration: transferring the data from one site to another site
    ii) Computation migration: Transferring the computation on a particular node
    iii) Process migration: The process or its sub-processes may also need to be transferred to some other nodes, due to some reasons like load-balancing, computation speed, and so on.

- Distributed OS must provide the means for inter-process communication. Some methods are:
  Remote Procedure Call: A process, on one node, may invoke a function or procedure in a process executing on another node.
  Remote Method Invocation: This allows a Java process to invoke a method of an object on a remote machine.
  Common Object Request Broker Architecture (*CORBA*): It is a standardized language that supports different programming languages and different OSs for distributed communication.
  Distributed Component Object Model (*DCOM*): This is another standard developed by Microsoft, included in the Windows OS.
- Due to multiple processes, synchronization methods should be supported by the OS.
- There may be a deadlock, when processes distributed over several nodes in a network wait for resources not released by other processes. Therefore, deadlock should also be handled by the distributed OS.

18.5   ISSUES IN DISTRIBUTED OPERATING SYSTEMS

In a distributed system, the resources and computations are distributed across various nodes in the system. If there is an imbalance of these two on the nodes, it may affect the performance of the system. Therefore, to protect the features of the distributed system, and for the convenience of the users, the following design issues must be implemented:

18.5.1 Transparency

The most important feature of a distributed system is that it should have a single system or uni-processor image. The implementation of this feature comes in the form of transparency. The transparency is to hide the distribution and location details from the user. The transparency can be implemented in the following forms:

Location Transparency

In this type, the users are not aware of where the hardware or software components are located. The user will know only the name of the resource and the name should not be able to reveal its location in the system.

Migration Transparency

Along with the location transparency, the users must not be affected, if the location of resources is changed in the system. But the name of the resources must not be changed. This is known as migration transparency.

Replication Transparency

The OS may take the decision of making additional duplicate copies of the files and other resources, for the sake of fault tolerance in the system. But this replication of files and other resources is not visible to the user. The user may request for a file to the system and is not bothered from which server it has been retrieved. In this case, many servers may have replicated directory structure, containing the files. So on the request of a user for a file, the file can be retrieved from one or the other server. But the user is not aware of the location of the file being retrieved.

Concurrency Transparency

Since multiple users may be allowed to work on a distributed system, it may be possible that more than one user may try to access the same resource at the same time. In this case, the mutual exclusion must be provided, such that if one has gained the access to the resource, access must not be granted to the other. This facility must be provided by the distributed OS. But this should again be hidden from the user. The user must know the details about which resource is held currently by which user, how the mutual exclusion has been implemented on one resource, and so on. This is known as concurrency transparency.

Parallelism Transparency

Since the computation of a user task may be divided into multiple sub-computations, each of these sub-computations can be computed in parallel, on various nodes of the system. But all these details of division of the computation and their execution on various nodes are transparent to the user. The user will only submit his task, and be able to see the result on his machine, where he submitted the task.

18.5.2 Global Knowledge

Since in a distributed system, each node is a complete computer system, there is no global memory, and even no global clock. Moreover, there are unpredictable message delays. Therefore, it becomes difficult to have up-to-date information about the global state of a distributed computing system. Therefore, in the design of a distributed OS, the design of some efficient techniques to implement system-wide control in distributed systems is required. Moreover, in the absence of a global clock, it is difficult to order all the events that occur at different times at different nodes in the system.

18.5.3 Performance

In a distributed system, while designing, various performance parameters should be considered. Communication is typically quite slow in the distributed computing system, due to message communication among nodes. If we are distributing the computation over multiple nodes in the system, then the number of message communication also increases, thereby, causing slow communication. Therefore, the need is to minimize the number of messages. This depends on the grain size of computations. If there are multiple but small computations known as *fine-grained computations*, which have been distributed over the nodes and interact highly among themselves, then the distributed system will behave poorly. In contrast, if multiple but large computations, known as *coarse-grained computations*, are distributed over the nodes and their interaction rate is too low, then the distributed system will perform much better. Thus, coarse-grained based parallelism enhances the performance of a distributed computing system.

Another performance factor may be the *load-balancing* in the system. Since the computations are distributed on the nodes of the system, there may be the case that some nodes are heavily loaded, while some nodes may have only few computations. This imbalance of nodes may also cause poor performance of the system. Thus, load-balancing is required, such that all the nodes in the system are equally loaded. To improve the performance, migration techniques must be implemented. There are three types of migration provided by distributed OSs:

i) Data migration: transferring the data from one site to another site
ii) Computation migration: Transferring the computation on a particular node
iii) Process migration: The process or its sub-processes may also need to be transferred to some other nodes, due to some reasons like load-balancing, computation speed, and so on.

Thus, the distributed OS must be able to do process/computation migration as well as data migration, for the better performance of the system.

If the size of the distributed system increases, there may be some issues of increased delays and overheads. The number of users, and thus, the overheads may increase. But these issues should not degrade the performance of the system, that is, a distributed system must be scalable.

18.5.4 Reliability

Since the reliability is a major goal behind designing a distributed system, as compared to a centralized system, the distributed system must take care of reliability issues also. Reliability is achieved through two properties of data: availability and reliability. Availability means resources must be available, despite the failure of some components in the system, thereby, increasing the reliability of the system. The availability may be achieved through fault tolerance techniques. Fault tolerance is the demand of many systems, for example, real-time systems. It is implemented through redundancy, that is, software/hardware components and communication links are made redundant, having multiple copies. In case of failure of one component or communication link, another in the standby takes charge and the system continues to function. The consistency of data must be taken care of while designing fault tolerance techniques. If replicated data are to be modified, then the consistency must be maintained on all the copies of data.

18.5.5 Process Synchronization

Since there is no shared memory in the distributed systems, it is difficult to synchronize the processes executing at different nodes of the system. The distributed OS must be able to synchronize various processes when they try to access a shared resource concurrently, that is, mutual exclusion must be there while one process accesses the shared resource. Since in a distributed system, the processes may request and release resources locally or remotely, the sequence of their request and release may not be known in advance. This may lead to deadlocks in the system. The deadlocks must also be removed as soon as possible, otherwise, the system's performance may degrade.

18.6　COMMUNICATION IN DISTRIBUTED SYSTEMS

It was easy to have inter-process communication in a uni-processor environment, since it has shared memory. However, since, there is no shared memory in a distributed system; it becomes difficult to implement inter-process communication, as the processors are on different nodes in the system. So, there must be some other ways, through which processes can communicate. Message-passing model and remote procedure calls are the two communication methods implemented in distributed OSs.

18.6.1 Message-passing Model

The communication in a distributed system may be implemented through the use of *Transmission Control Protocol/Internet Protocol* (*TCP/IP*) or *Open Systems Interconnection* (*OSI*) connection-oriented protocols, but the overhead in these protocols becomes more, especially in a Local Area Network (LAN)-based system. Instead, a connection-less request/reply protocol, known as *client-server protocol*, is used. The client-server model adopts the simple message-passing mechanism for communication between processes. The main advantage is its simplicity, in which a client sends a request and receives a reply from its server machine. Another advantage is that due to its simplicity, that is, protocol stack being shorter (only physical layer, data link layer, and request/reply layer), it becomes efficient as well. Thus, the distributed OS uses two system calls, only for inter-process communication, that is, one for sending the message, and another for receiving the message. A client process requires some service and sends a message for the request to the appropriate server process. The server process receives the request, honours it, and sends the message back with the reply. The *send* primitive specifies a destination of the server process and the message contents. The *receive* primitive says from whom the message is desired, and a buffer is maintained, where the incoming message is stored. The client and server processes take the help of a message-passing module for send/receive primitives and the message content (see Fig. 18.2).

When the distributed message-passing system is used, there are several design issues related to it. These are as follows:

Blocking vs Non-blocking

When a client process sends a message to its destination, the sending process is blocked, and the process is not allowed to execute further, until the message has been completely sent or an acknowledgement has been received. Similarly, when the receive call from the server or receiving process is made, it does not return control, until a message has actually been received completely or placed in the message buffer. It means when the *send/receive* primitives are being called, the processes are blocked, and are not allowed to execute further. This is known as blocking or \ synchronous primitive. On the contrary, when the sending or receiving processes during *send/receive* primitives are not blocked, it is known as non-blocking or asynchronous primitives. The *send* primitive returns control to the process immediately

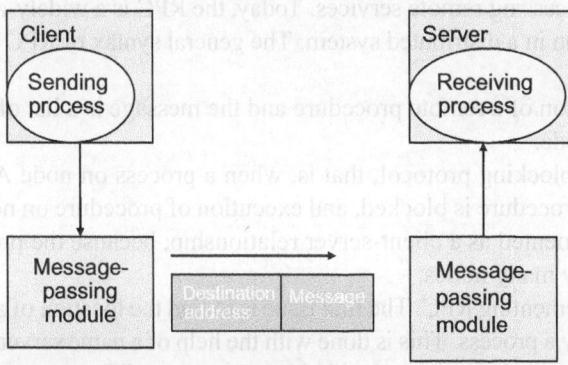

Fig. 18.2   Message-passing protocol

after the message has been queued for transmission, and thus, the sending process is able to compute in parallel to the message transmission. Similarly, the *receive* primitive does not block the receiving process. However, there must be provision for telling it that the message has been received. For this purpose, the receive process may periodically check for the arrival of the message or the OS must notify it upon the arrival of the message. Thus, the non-blocking or asynchronous primitives are advantageous, in the sense that *send/receive* processes have the flexibility to compute and communicate in the order they want.

Reliability vs Unreliability

When a client process sends a message, there is no guarantee that the message has been sent. The message may be lost even. Thus, there may be the requirement that in the distributed system, the reliable message must be sent. However, there may be a trade-off between reliable and unreliable communication. There may be different cases for providing reliability. The first case may be that the send primitive is unreliable. The second case may be that an acknowledgement must be sent to the sender. The receiving machine kernel sends the acknowledgement to the sending machine kernel. Similarly, when the reply message has been sent by the receiver process, it must be acknowledged again between two kernels. This case may be treated as a fully reliable solution. However, it may be improved in the way that there is no need to acknowledge the send message by the receiver process. Instead, when the receiver process sends the reply to the sender, the reply will itself act as an acknowledgement. The reply may be acknowledged again by the sender. But this acknowledgement may be ignored, depending on the request.

However, it may be the case that the requests made by the client are critical, and acknowl-edgements are necessary. In this case, another optimization may be done, such that when a request on the server machine arrives, a timer is started. If the server sends the reply before the timer expires, the reply functions as an acknowledgement. Otherwise, if the timer expires, a separate acknowledgement will be sent.

18.6.2 Remote Procedure Calls

Since the message-passing system in client server model makes use of send and receive primi-tives, these primitives are engaged in I/O operations. However, the idea in the distributed system is to make distributed computing look like it is done on a single machine. This is a programming language feature, designed for distributed computing, and it is intended to have the same semantics of a procedure call as in a programming language. This will allow programs on different machines to interact as various procedures are called and returned on a single machine. In other words, the simple procedure call is used for accessing remote services. Today, the RPC is a widely-accepted common method for communication in a distributed system. The general syntax of RPC is:

Call <proc_id> (<message>

where proc_id is the identification of a remote procedure and the message is a list of param-eters to be passed to the remote node.

The RPC is implemented as a blocking protocol, that is, when a process on node A calls a procedure on node B, the calling procedure is blocked, and execution of procedure on node B is started. Further, the RPC is implemented as a client-server relationship, because the procedure on a remote node may be called by many nodes.

There are two issues while implementing RPC. The first issue is to find the location of a remote procedure, which has been called by a process. This is done with the help of a name server. All the procedures, which may be invoked, must be registered with this name server. When a process calls a remote procedure, the name server is first contacted to get the location of the remote procedure.

Another issue is how to pass the parameters in a heterogeneous environment, where hardware and software architecture of the remote node may be different. In this case, the RPC must perform appropriate conversions of value parameters and must construct system-wide capabilities for reference parameters, which need to be passed along with the message to the remote node.

However, the client-server architecture viewed in the RPC mechanism may not be sufficient to implement the parameter conversion and get results over the network, as the RPC implementation must be syntactically and semantically similar to that of a conventional procedural call. For this purpose, we need to have some more components. Since the caller procedure on client node will not be able to call the remote procedure directly, we need some additional functionality for this purpose to implement RPC. There are two procedures for this purpose namely, *client stub* and *server stub*. Whenever a process on a node calls a remote procedure on another node on the network, the client process first calls the client stub with its parameters (see Fig. 18.3). The client stub, after preparing the message, calls the server stub. The RPC, with the help of client stub and server stub, is implemented in the following steps:

1. The client process calls the client stub with the parameters, through the normal procedure call. Obviously, according to the protocol, the client process is blocked until the procedure call is completed.
2. The client stub, after being called, collects the parameters, and converts them to a machine-independent format. Next, it prepares the message consisting of the converted parameters.
3. The client stub, after resolving the name of the remote procedure, that is, the address of the node where the remote procedure exists, traps to the kernel.
4. The client kernel sends the message to the remote kernel.
5. The remote kernel sends the message to the server stub.
6. The server stub receives the message sent by the kernel, unpacks the parameters, and converts them to a machine-specific format that is suitable to that node.
7. After conversion, the server stub calls the procedure with the converted parameters, that is, a local procedure call on the server, through the server process, is executed.
8. The server process, as a result of procedure call, returns the result to the server stub.
9. The server stub, after receiving the result, converts them into a machine-independent form.
10. The converted results are then put in the message form and then they trap to the remote kernel.
11. The remote kernel sends the message to the client kernel.
12. The client kernel sends the message to the client stub.
13. The client stub converts the result into the machine-specific format and returns to the client process.

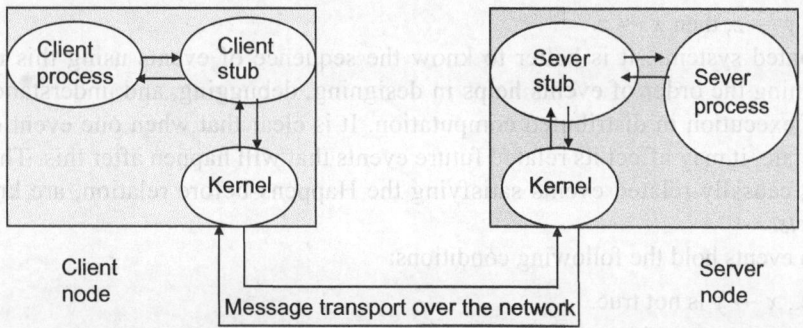

Fig. 18.3   Implementation of RPC

18.7   CLOCK SYNCHRONIZATION IN DISTRIBUTED SYSTEMS

A computer system contains a real-time clock, which may be accessed through an instruction meant for it. The user processes may access the clock to get the time of day, using a system call. The OS uses the clock to have a record at what instant of time an event happened in the system. Since in a distributed system, there are various nodes, there should be a global clock, which can be accessed from all the nodes of the system. But the concept of a global clock is not possible, due to communication components in the system. Due to unpredictable communication delays, the requests for time will be different for the processes on various nodes. There can be local clocks at each node of the system and all are synchronized to give the illusion of a global clock. However, this is also not achievable as all the local clocks may not show identical times. The reason is that the local clocks may work at different rates as all the crystals corresponding to the clocks may not run exactly at the same frequency; hence, they do not run synchronously. Thus, it is difficult to maintain the synchronization between different local clocks.

However, Lamport suggested that it is not necessary that absolute clock synchronization is required. If two processes on different nodes do not interact, it will not cause any problem, if the clocks of two nodes are not synchronized. Further, he added that it is not necessary to have the processes synchronized according to the real-time clock, but what is the order of events among the processes matters the most. Thus, there may be some cases when internal consistency of the clocks is required, but how close or equal they are to the real-time clock is not that important. In other words, it may be possible to ascertain the order in which two or more events occur. The order of events is not based on the real-time clock, but on the behaviour exhibited by the underlying computation. Since this concept does not have any relation to the real-time clock, this is known as *logical clock*.

18.7.1   Synchronizing Logical Clocks

To order the sequence of events among the processes, the logical clocks must be synchronized. For this purpose, Lamport defined a relation, known as *Happens-before* relation. This relation is basically for capturing the underlying dependencies between events. It may be denoted as $x \rightarrow y$. There may be following two situations for this relation:

- If x and y are events in the same process and x occurs before y.
- If x is the message-sending event by one process and y is the message-receiving event by another process, then x will always precede y.
- Happens-before relation is a transitive relation, that is,

  If $x \rightarrow y$, $y \rightarrow z$, then $x \rightarrow z$.

In distributed systems, it is better to know the sequence of events using this relation, and ascertaining the order of events helps in designing, debugging, and understanding the sequence of execution in distributed computation. It is clear that when one event changes the system state, it may affect its related future events that will happen after this. This influence among causally-related events satisfying the Happens-before relation, are known as *causal affects*.

If the two events hold the following conditions:

- $x \nrightarrow y$, i.e., $x \rightarrow y$ is not true.
- $y \nrightarrow x$, i.e., $y \rightarrow x$ is not true.
- There is no transitive Happens-before relationship between x and y.

Then these two events are known as concurrent, that is, it cannot be decided when one of the two events happened or which of the two happened first.

Lamport's Logical Clock Algorithm for Synchronization

To implement the logical clock, Lamport introduced the concept of time-stamp to be attached with each process in the system. The time-stamp may be a function that assigns a number $T_i(x)$ to any event x to process P_i. But these time-stamps have nothing to do with the actual real-time clock. Now, as per the time-stamp, the following conditions must be met:

- For any two events x and y in a process P_i, if $x \rightarrow y$, then,
  $$T(x) < T(y)$$
- If x is the message-sending event in process P_i and y is the message-receiving event in process P_j then
  $$T_i(x) < T_j(y)$$
- The time-stamp value T must always be increasing and never decreasing. Thus, for the implementation, the clock is incremented between any two successive events always with a positive integer d, that is,
  $$T_i(y) = T_i(x) + d, \text{ where } d > 0$$

Using all the conditions mentioned above, we can assign time-stamp to all events in the system, and thereby, provide a total ordering of all the events in the system.

Example 18.1

Consider there are two processes P1 and P2, running on different nodes of a distributed system. Each node has its own clock running at its own speed. This is why when the clock in process P1 has ticked 4 time units, the clock on process P2 has ticked 6 time units as shown in Fig. 18.4(a). The value of d in process P1 is 4 while it is 6 in P2.

It can also be seen that at time 8 in P1, it sends a message M to P2. In P2, it arrives at 18. The message M1 carries with it the time-stamp of P1, that is, 8. So it can be said that it took 10 ticks for the transmission delay. Further, a message M2 from process P2 is sent to P1. But M2 leaves at 30 and reaches at 24. This is undoubtedly impossible. The situation like this must be prevented in order to have synchronization between the processes. Lamport suggested the solution for this type of situation as:

When a message arrives from one node to another and the receiver's node clock shows a value prior to the time the message was sent, the receiver node must fast forward its clock to be one more than the sending time-stamp.

Thus, in Fig. 18.4(b), we can see that the M2 arrives now at 25, which is a possible value.

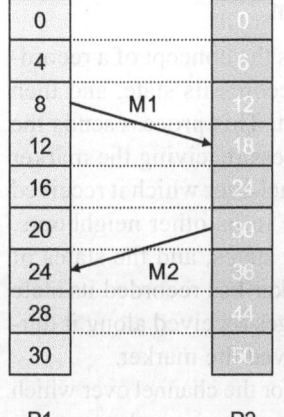

Fig. 18.4(a) Distributed clock scenario for Example 18.1

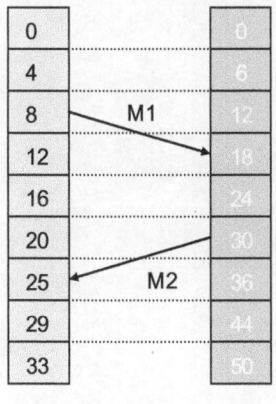

Fig. 18.4(b) Lamport's logical clock algorithm for synchronization in Example 18.1

18.8 GLOBAL STATE

An up-to-date state of the full system is required for a system's behaviour, debugging, fault recovery, synchronization, and so on. However, a distributed system does not have a global memory. Hence, the state of an entire system will not be available to the process, even if it wants to know. In the absence of a global clock and global memory, a coherent global state of the system is difficult to achieve. Chandy and Lamport worked in this direction and designed an algorithm known as *Chandy–Lamport Consistent State Recording algorithm*. This algorithm works on the following assumptions:

1. The channels being considered for communication are unidirectional.
2. All the channels are managed through FIFO.
3. All the channels have unbounded capacity to store messages.

Let us discuss the algorithm.

18.8.1 Chandy–Lamport Consistent State Recording Algorithm

To record a consistent global state, Chandy–Lamport algorithm uses the concept of a recording message, known as a *marker*. To begin with, a process first records its state, and then sends a marker to all its neighbouring processes, if not already sent. This process sends the marker before it sends any messages to other processes. Each process receiving the marker records its state, if not recorded earlier, records the state of the channel over which it received the message as an empty sequence, and sends the marker message to its other neighbours. This process continues, until all the processes have recorded their states, and the states of all the channels have been recorded. If a process receiving the marker has recorded its state earlier, it records the state of the channel, as the sequence of messages received along it during the last recorded state of the process and the time when it received the marker.

Let P_s be the process that initiates the state recording. C is denoted for the channel over which messages are communicated. There are the two rules of this algorithm. One is marker-sending rule and another is marker-receiving rule. The algorithms of both rules are shown in Fig. 18.5.

```
Marker sending  rule for a process Ps

    1.  Ps records its state.
    2.  for (i=1; i =n; ++i)
    3.  {
            If marker not sent to Ci
                Ps sends a marker on each outgoing Ci
        }

Marker receiving rule for a process Q

    1.  Process Q receives the marker message through a Ci.
    2.  If Q has not recorded its state earlier
            Call marker sending rule to record its state and
            to send the marker to each channel
        else
            Record the state of the channel as sequence of
            messages received after Q's state was recorded
            and before Q received the current marker.
```

Fig. 18.5 Chandy–Lamport consistent state recording algorithm

Example 18.2

Consider there are four processes, P_1, P_2, P_3, and P_4 at nodes N_1, N_2, N_3, and N_4, respectively. At time t = 0 (see Fig. 18.6 (a)), P_1 has sent message M_1 to P_4. M_1 presently exists in channel C_{14}, where C_{14} is the channel between N_1 and N_4. At t = 1, P_2 sends message M_2 to P_3. At t = 2, P_1 decides to record the state of the system. It records its own state and sends marker messages on its outgoing channels. Fig. 18.6 (b) shows the situation at t = 2^+. M_1 is still in channel C_{14} and M_2 is in C_{23}. The square along these channels indicates that the messages are still in channels. The triangle at N_1 indicates that the state of process P_1 has been recorded.

The process P_4 at N_4 receives the marker message along the channel C_{14}. At t = 3, P_4 records its own state and the state of C_{14} as empty. At t = 4, process P_2 sends message M_3 to P_3 and P_2 receives the marker along C_{12} at t = 5. P_2 now records its state and state of C_{12} as empty and sends the marker along C_{23}. The situation at t = 5^+ has been shown in Fig. 18.6(c).

At t = 6, the process P_3 receives the messages M_2 and M_3 and it sends the message M_4 to P_4. At t = 7, P_3 receives the marker and records its own state, and sends the marker along C_{34}. The situation at t = 7^+ has been shown in Fig. 18.6(d), where all the states of all the processes have been recorded.

At t = 8, P_4 receives the marker, but its state and others have already been recorded, it only records the state of the C_{34}, as M_4 is there in C_{34}. The recorded state of all the processes and channels are shown in Table 18.1.

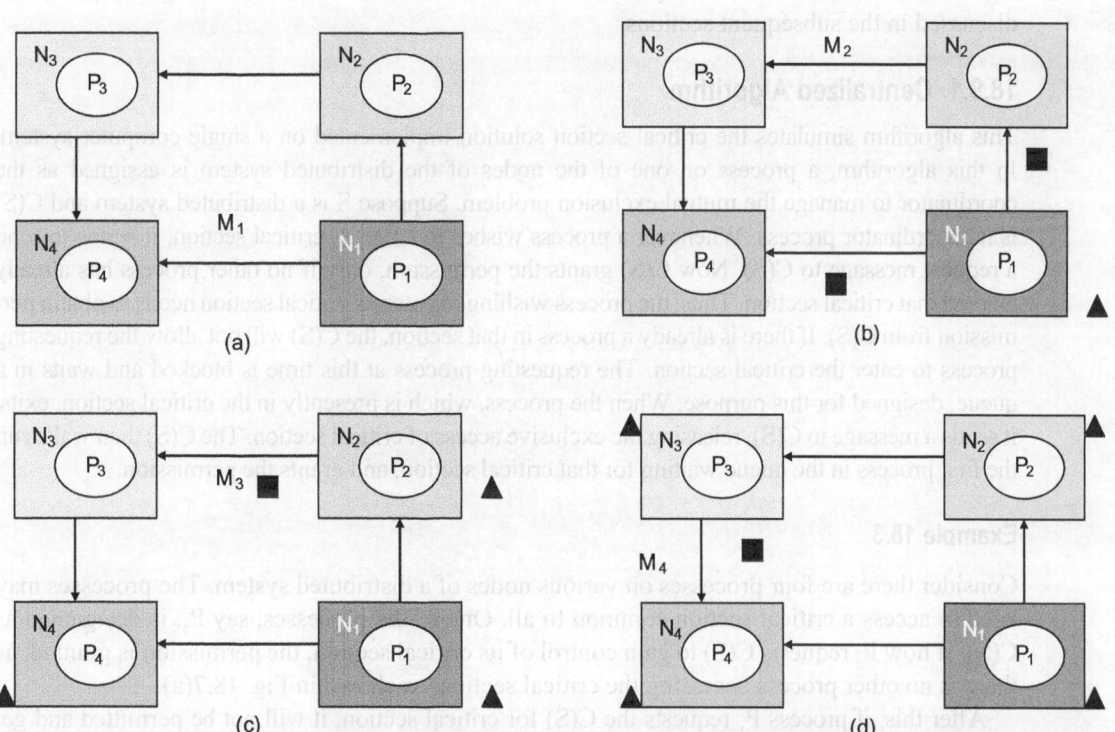

Fig. 18.6 Chandy–Lamport consistent state recording algorithm Example 18.2

Table 18.1   Chandy–Lamport consistent state recorded states Example 18.2

Entity	Recorded state
P_1	Message M_1 has been sent, no message has been received.
P_2	Messages M_2 and M_3 have been sent, no message has been received.
P_3	Messages M_2 and M_3 have been received and message M_4 has been sent.
P_4	No messages have been sent or received.
C_{12}	Empty
C_{14}	Empty
C_{23}	Empty
C_{34}	Contains message M_4.

18.9   MUTUAL EXCLUSION

In a distributed environment, the shared resources are distributed and there is no shared memory concept. Therefore, it becomes difficult to achieve mutual exclusion to share a resource. We achieved mutual exclusion between the processes on a single-computer system through the use of shared memory, semaphore, and so on. But all these solutions may not be valid in the distributed systems, due to lack of global state, global clock, and shared memory. Moreover, communication delay is also a factor affecting the message-passing system. Many algorithms help the distributed system to achieve mutual exclusion. These algorithms will be discussed in the subsequent sections.

18.9.1   Centralized Algorithm

This algorithm simulates the critical section solution implemented on a single-computer system. In this algorithm, a process on one of the nodes of the distributed system is assigned as the coordinator to manage the mutual exclusion problem. Suppose S is a distributed system and C(S) is its coordinator process. Whenever a process wishes to enter its critical section, it needs to send a request message to C(S). Now C(S) grants the permission, only if no other process has already entered that critical section. Thus, the process wishing to enter its critical section needs to obtain permission from C(S). If there is already a process in that section, the C(S) will not allow the requesting process to enter the critical section. The requesting process at this time is blocked and waits in a queue, designed for this purpose. When the process, which is presently in the critical section, exits, it sends a message to C(S), releasing the exclusive access of critical section. The C(S) then wakes up the first process in the queue waiting for that critical section, and grants the permission.

Example 18.3

Consider there are four processes on various nodes of a distributed system. The processes may need to access a critical section common to all. One of the processes, say P_3, is designated as C(S). If now P_2 requests C(S) to gain control of its critical section, the permission is granted, as there is no other process accessing the critical section, as shown in Fig. 18.7(a).

After this, if process P_1 requests the C(S) for critical section, it will not be permitted and get blocked. P_1 will wait in the queue, as shown in Fig. 18.7(b). If after some time, P_2 exits and leaves the critical section, it sends the release signal to C(S). C(S), in turn, takes off the first process in the queue, that is, P_1, and gives the permission to enter the critical section, as shown in Fig. 18.7(c).

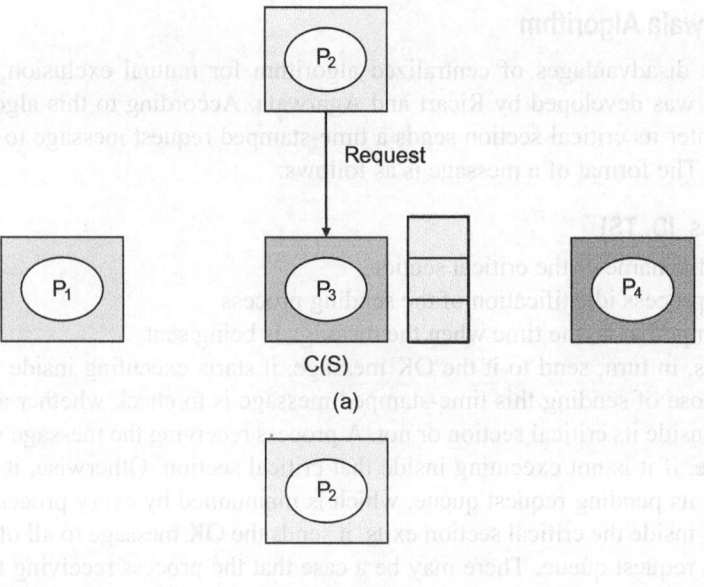

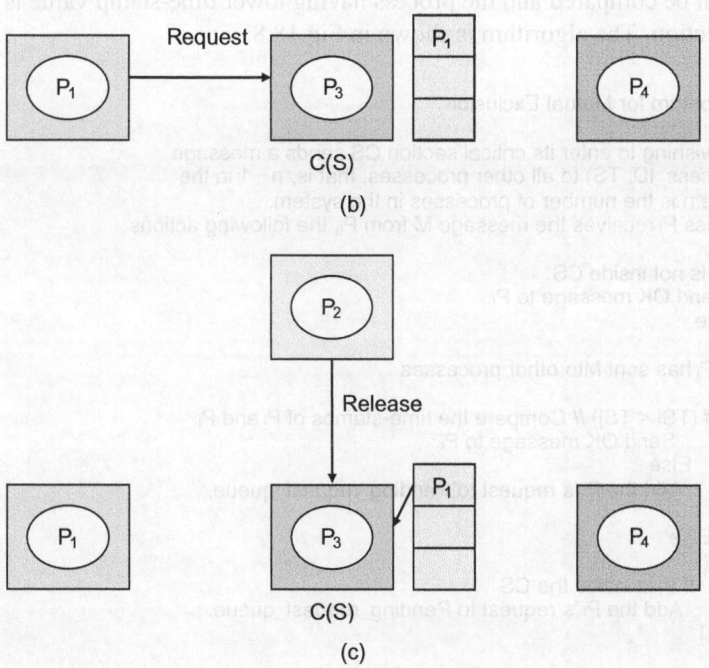

Fig. 18.7 Centralized algorithm for mutual exclusion Example 18.3

The centralized algorithm is able to control the mutual exclusion, as seen in the above example. Moreover, it is fair enough to maintain the sequence of requesting processes that wish to enter the critical section. However, the centralized algorithm has some disadvantages as well. If the process designated as the coordinator fails, then the whole system may crash in the absence of coordinated mutual exclusion. Moreover, the performance of the coordinator node may degrade as the load on it increases.

18.9.2 Ricart–Agarwala Algorithm

Keeping in view the disadvantages of centralized algorithm for mutual exclusion, a fully-distributed algorithm was developed by Ricart and Agarwala. According to this algorithm, a process wishing to enter its critical section sends a time-stamped request message to all other processes, and waits. The format of a message is as follows:

M (Name_CS, Process_ID, TS)

Where, Name_CS is the name of the critical section,

Process_ID is the process identification of the sending process

TS is the time-stamp, that is, the time when the message is being sent

If all the processes, in turn, send to it the OK message, it starts executing inside the critical section. The purpose of sending this time-stamped message is to check whether any other process is executing inside its critical section or not. A process receiving the message will send back the OK message, if it is not executing inside that critical section. Otherwise, it adds the requesting process to its pending request queue, which is maintained by every process. When the process executing inside the critical section exits, it sends the OK message to all of the processes in the pending request queue. There may be a case that the process receiving the time-stamped message has also sent a request to all other processes. In this case, the time stamps of both the processes can be compared and the process having lower time-stamp value is allowed to enter the critical section. The algorithm is shown in Fig.18.8.

Ricart-Agarwala Algorithm for Mutual Exclusion

1. A process P_i wishing to enter its critical section CS sends a message M(Name, Process_ID, TS) to all other processes, that is, n – 1 in the system; where n is the number of processes in the system.
2. When a process P_j receives the message M from P_i, the following actions may be taken:
   If P_i is not inside CS
     Send OK message to P_i.
   Else
     {
     If P_j has sent M to other processes
       {
       If (TSi < TSj) // Compare the time-stamps of P_i and P_j.
         Send OK message to P_i.
       Else
         Add the P_i 's request to Pending_request_queue.
       }
     Else
       {
        If P_j is inside the CS
         Add the P_i 's request to Pending_request_queue.
       }
     }

3. The process, if receives n – 1 OK messages from the processes, gets the permission to enter its CS, and starts executing inside it.
4. If the process P_j exits its CS
     {
     If items are there in Pending_request_queue
       Send OK message to all the processes inside the
                         Pending_request_queue
     }

Fig. 18.8 Ricart–Agarwala algorithm for mutual exclusion

Example 18.4

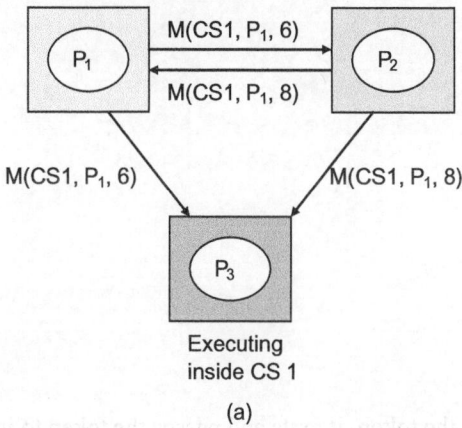

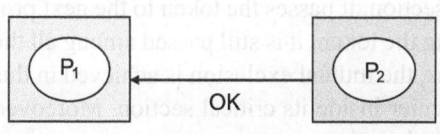

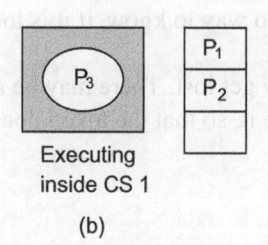

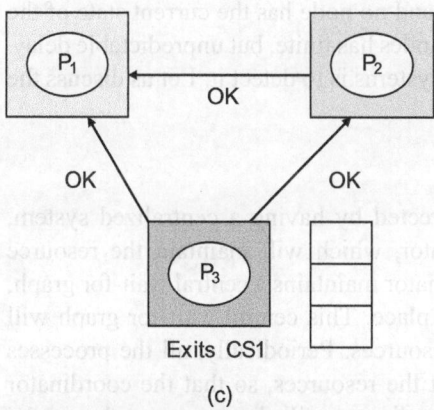

Fig. 18.9 Ricart–Agarwala algorithm for mutual exclusion Example 18.4

Consider there are three processes P_1, P_2, and P_3 as shown in Fig. 18.9(a). P_3 is executing inside the critical section CS1. P_1 sends a request message for CS1 to P_2 and P_3. P_2 also sends a request message to P_1 and P_3 for the same CS1. Implement Ricart–Agarwala algorithm for this scenario.

Solution

Both P_1 and P_2 do not get reply from P_3, as it is executing inside CS1. Since both of them have sent the request message to P_1, their time-stamps will be compared. As the time-stamp of P_1 (that is, 6) is less than the time-stamp of P_2 (that is, 8), P2 will send the OK message to P_1, as shown in Fig. 18.9(b). Since the process P_3 is busy inside CS1, it queues the incoming requests in its pending_request_queue.

As soon as P_3 exits CS1, it removes all the processes from its queue, and sends OK message to all the processes, as shown in Fig. 18.9(c). Since P_1 has received OK messages from all other processes, it starts executing inside CS1.

Ricart–Agarwala algorithm is fair enough as a distributed algorithm for mutual exclusion, but there may be multiple points of failures as compared to a single-point failure in a centralized algorithm. If any of the process fails and does not send OK message to a requesting process, the requesting process may interpret it as a denial of permission. Hence, the receiver process must always reply, either granting or denying the request. Otherwise, after sometime, the requester may time out. Another disadvantage is that, the permission sought from all the processes to enter inside its critical section, may slow down the performance of the system.

18.9.3 Token Ring Algorithm

This algorithm assumes a logical structure of all the processes in a ring, that is, all the processes are connected together in a ring sequence, and every process is aware of the next process in that sequence, as shown in Fig. 18.10. To initialize, a token is given to the first process in the ring. In the figure, the token is represented by a black square. This token serves the purpose of permission to gain the access inside the critical section. So the process, having the token, has the permission to enter inside its critical section, but only once, that is, the same token does not allow the

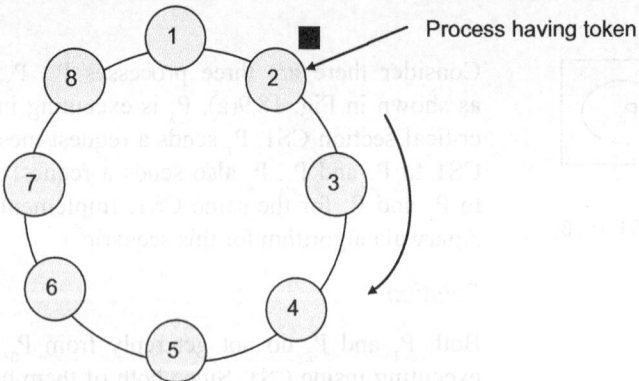

Process having token

Fig. 18.10 Token-ring algorithm for mutual exclusion

process to enter another critical section. After using the token, it exits and passes the token to its next process in the ring sequence. In this way, the token is circulated among every process, turn by turn. If a process does not wish to enter its critical section, it passes the token to the next process without using it. If no process is interested in using the token, it is still passed among all the processes. This is known as token ring algorithm. Thus, the mutual exclusion is achieved in this algorithm, as only one process having the token can enter inside its critical section. Moreover, each process gets its chance to execute inside the critical section.

However, there may be some shortcomings of this algorithm. They are:

- The token being circulated may get lost. But there is no way to know, if it is lost or still being used by some process.
- If a process receiving the token crashes, the token may get lost. There may be a provision that the process receiving the token must acknowledge it, so that the token does not get lost and is passed to the process next to the failed one.

18.10 DEADLOCK DETECTION

The deadlocks may appear in distributed systems also, even worse than in single-processor systems. In distributed systems, deadlocks are more difficult to prevent, avoid, or even detect, as the information on various processors are scattered, and no node has the current state of the system. Moreover, every communication between two nodes has finite, but unpredictable delay. The only method to handle the deadlock in distributed systems is to detect it. Let us discuss the deadlock detection in distributed systems.

18.10.1 Centralized Deadlock Detection

Like mutual exclusion, the deadlock may also be detected by having a centralized system, that is, a process is assigned as the central coordinator, which will maintain the resource allocation state of the entire system. The central coordinator maintains a central wait-for graph, combining wait-for graphs of all the processes at one place. This central wait-for graph will provide a complete view of the processes and their resources. Periodically, all the processes at various nodes send their updated information about the resources, so that the coordinator can update the central wait-for graph. The central coordinator will detect any cycles in the wait-for graph for deadlock detection in the system.

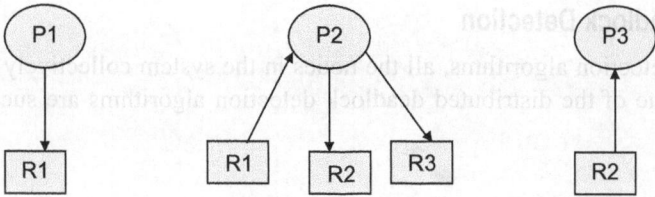

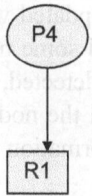

Fig. 18.11(a)   Distributed system RAG for Example 18.5

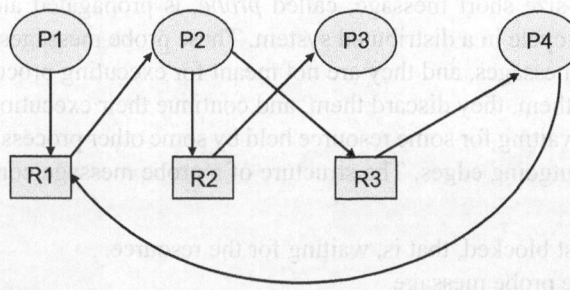

Fig. 18.11(b)   RAG for Example 18.5

Example 18.5

Consider the following scenario in a distributed system (see Fig. 18.11 (a)):

1. At node N1, P1 requests R1
2. At node N2, P2 holds R1 and requests R2 and R3.
3. At node 3, R2 is held by P3.
4. At node N4, P4 requests R1.

Discuss the centralized deadlock detection method for this scenario.

All processes at various nodes will send the status of resources to the central coordinator node, say N5. This coordinator node will combine the scenario of all the processes and prepare a combined RAG and wait-for graph, as shown in Fig. 18.11(b) and Fig. 18.11(c), respectively. It can be seen that there is a deadlock in the resultant wait-for graph (see Fig. 18.11 (c)).

There is one problem that may occur in central deadlock detection algorithm. It may be possible that the message sent by a process to the central coordinator, after receiving the resource, may not reach at the right time, due to communication delay. During this time, to resolve the deadlock, one of the processes may be killed or some other method will be adopted. Thus, a situation like this may lead to *false deadlock*. The solution to this may be to add the time-stamp with the message about the resource. Moreover, before taking any action to resolve the deadlock, the coordinator node must send a message to all the nodes asking to send any update.

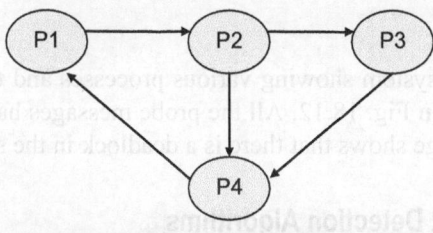

Fig. 18.11(c)   Wait-for graph for Example 18.5

18.10.2 Distributed Deadlock Detection

In distributed deadlock detection algorithms, all the nodes in the system collectively cooperate to detect a cycle. Some of the distributed deadlock detection algorithms are such as the following:

Path-pushing Algorithm

In this algorithm, a global wait-for graph is maintained for each node of the distributed system. At each node, whenever a deadlock computation is performed, its local wait-for graph is sent to all neighbouring nodes. After the neighbouring node receives the wait-for graph, it updates its wait-for graph, combining the information that was received. Then this updated wait-for-graph is sent to all its neighbouring nodes, and the procedure continues until some node has a sufficiently complete view of the global state, such that a deadlock can be detected, if there is one. However, this algorithm may not be correct as wait-for graphs, as all the nodes have been formed at different instants of time and therefore, the global state information may be inconsistent.

Edge-chasing Algorithm

In this algorithm, a special fixed-size short message, called *probe*, is propagated along the edges of wait-for graph to detect a cycle in a distributed system. These probe messages are not the same as the request and reply messages, and they are not meant for executing processes. If these executing processes receive them, they discard them, and continue their execution. Only those processes, which have been waiting for some resource held by some other process, propagate probe messages along their outgoing edges. The structure of a probe message consists of the following fields:

- The process number that has just blocked, that is, waiting for the resource.
- The process number sending the probe message.
- The process number to which the message is being sent.

According to the algorithm, any process that receives the probe message, first checks whether it itself is blocked or not. If it is blocked, it updates the probe message, keeping the first field of the message same, replacing the second field by its own number, and the third one by the process number for which it is waiting. The message is then sent to the process for which it is waiting. If this process is waiting for multiple processes, then the different messages are sent to all these processes. The algorithm is followed for all the resources, whether local or remote. If a message goes all the way around and reaches back to the original sender, it means a cycle exists. In other words, the deadlock has been detected.

Example 18.6

Consider the wait-for graph for a distributed system showing various processes and their dependencies, in the form of wait for resources in Fig. 18.12. All the probe messages have been shown in various nodes. The last probe message shows that there is a deadlock in the system.

18.10.3 Correctness Criteria for Deadlock Detection Algorithms

The deadlock detection algorithms discussed above must satisfy the following two conditions:

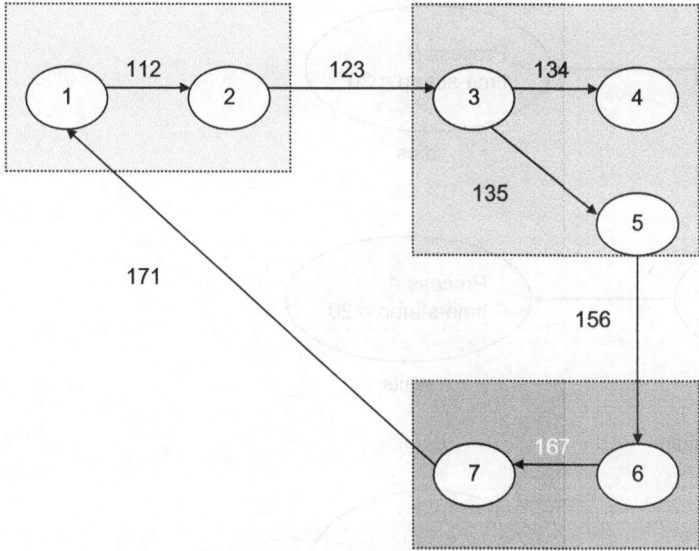

Fig. 18.12   Edge-chasing algorithm Example 18.6

1. The deadlock detection must be performed within a finite time. Once all wait-for graphs are generated, it should give its decision, based on the current situation, and should not wait for any other event to occur.
2. The algorithm should not detect any false deadlocks.

18.11   DEADLOCK PREVENTION

The deadlocks can be prevented, using all the methods that were explained in Chapter 8. The most suitable prevention method is to provide ordering of all the resources, that is., a unique number in increasing order, is provided to each resource in the system. The processes will require acquiring them, only in their increasing order. This scheme will not allow the cycles to exist and therefore, no deadlock will be present.

However, due to constraints of global time and state in distributed systems, some other algorithms to prevent the deadlocks are necessary. These algorithms are based on the concept of ranking provided to the processes. There may be various criteria for providing ranks. One of them is to use the time-stamp of the process. Each process in a distributed system is assigned a time-stamp, when it is created. The algorithms are as follows:

Wait-Die Algorithm

Let a process, say A, request for a resource, currently held by process B. The time-stamps of both processes are compared. If process A has time-stamp smaller than B, it is allowed to wait for the resource. On the other hand, if process B requests the resource currently held by A, the process B dies. The older process is allowed to wait for a younger process, but a younger process dies, if it tries to wait for an older process (see Fig. 18.13). The killed process is restarted after some time in the future. In this way, in this algorithm, the processes will always request in their increasing order of ranks, thereby, making cycles impossible.

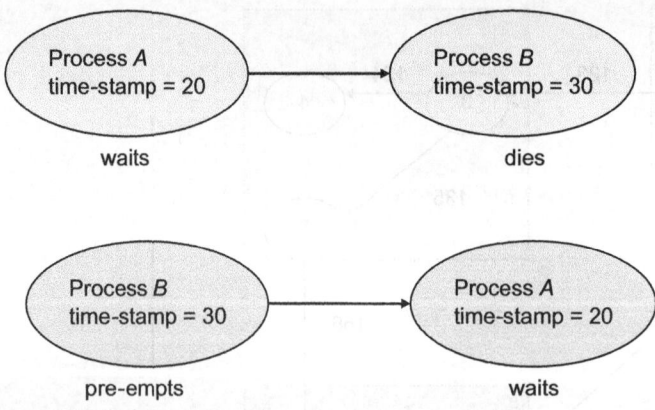

Fig. 18.13 Wait-die algorithm

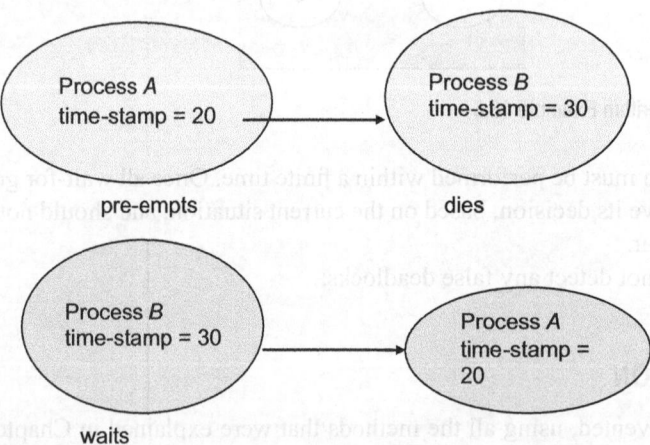

Fig. 18.14 Wound-wait algorithm

Wound-Wait Algorithm

Suppose process A requests for a resource, currently held by process B. The time-stamps of both processes are compared. If process A has time-stamp smaller than B, it pre-empts the process B and B's current transaction dies. On the other hand, if process B requests the resource currently held by A, it waits for the resource. In this algorithm, the older process pre-empts the younger process, but if the younger one requests, it is allowed to wait (see Fig. 18.14).

18.12 DISTRIBUTED PROCESS SCHEDULING

In a distributed system, various processors execute several processes. But to maximize the performance of the system, there must be a balanced distribution of the computational load. It may be possible that some computation-intensive processes are executing on only one processor, while other nodes either do not have any process or have some light processes; some processes on a node are executing very slowly, while on other nodes, the processes are being executed quickly. All this will cause unbalance in the system, leading to poor performance. The primary goal of process-scheduling in the distributed system is similar to that of a single-processor system, that is, processor utilization. Therefore, processors must be compared to understand the load distribution scenario and load-balancing may be performed, if required. Load-balancing is performed by transferring some processes from a heavily-loaded node to a lightly-loaded node. This is known as *process migration*. For characterizing the computational load at a node, various parameters, such as processor utilization at the node, the number of processes existing at the node, length of ready queue at the node, and so on, are considered.

Some issues faced while implementing distributed process scheduling are such as the following:

- **Process migration policy**
  The process migration policy decides if a process on one node should be migrated in a preemptive or non-pre-emptive manner. According to the pre-emptive policy, the executing process to be migrated is first suspended, and its code and current state are transferred from the current node to the node where it has to be migrated. Its execution is resumed at the new node. This policy needs extensive support from the kernel. In a non-pre-emptive policy, the process will be created on the new node only.

- **Transfer policy**
  This policy decides when the computational load must be transferred to another node. The simple policy for this may be to consider the load threshold on a node in the system. Whenever a process needs to be created or transferred to a node, the threshold load value of this node must be checked. If the load value exceeds the threshold value (overloaded node), then the process must be transferred to another node. In terms of threshold value, a node may be designated as a *sender node*, if the load value exceeds the threshold. Otherwise, it is called a *receiver node*. However, this policy may not be optimal, as it is considering only local information of a node. It would be better if global state information is taken into consideration to decide the transfer policy.

- **Selection policy**
  The selection policy selects a process that needs to be transferred. One of the methods is to select a newly-created process that has caused the node to exceed its threshold load value. The criterion for selecting a process among the existing processes is less overhead in transfer.

- **Location policy**
  The location policy decides where the selected process should be transferred. There may be two methods for finding out a suitable node for load-sharing. One method is that the node may poll another node to find out whether that node is suitable or not. Another method is to broadcast a query about whether any node is suitable for load-sharing. These two methods are sender-initiated, that is, the sender nodes are finding out receiver nodes. There can be receiver-initiated methods also. The receiver nodes may also announce that they have less or no computation to do.

- **Information policy**
  The information policy is to collect information about the states of all other nodes in the system by a node. The policy decides when to collect this information. The common methods are: *demand-driven and periodic*. In a demand-driven method, when a node becomes a sender or receiver, it becomes a suitable node to collect information about other nodes for load-sharing. In a periodic method, the node exchanges information periodically.

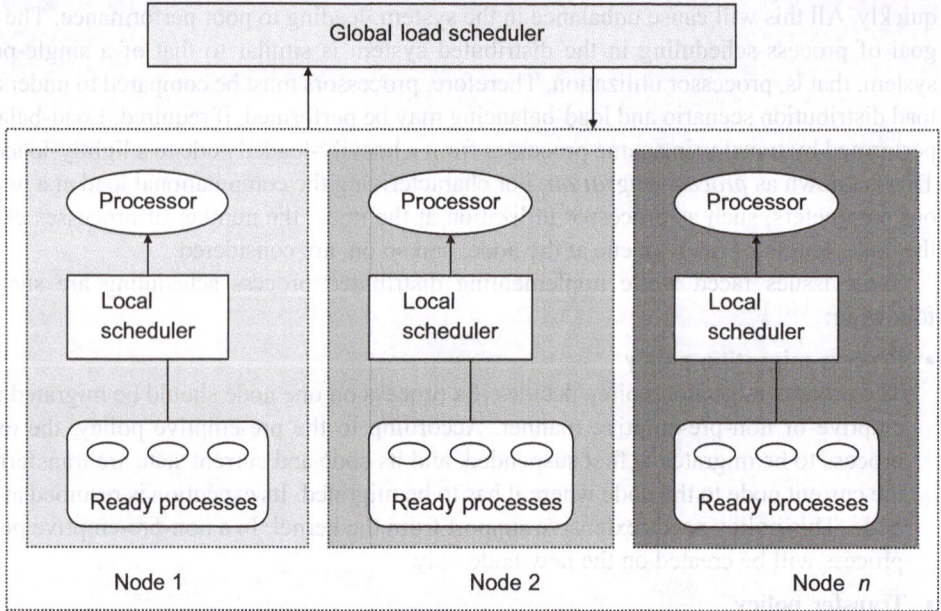

Fig. 18.15   Global load scheduler

The process-scheduling is performed at two levels. The first is scheduling the processes on various nodes in the system. Second is to schedule the processes on a node locally. On a local node, time slices are given to the process in order to achieve certain goals, such as response time, fairness, and so on. Thus, there are two types of schedulers: One is a local scheduler that schedules the processes on a node locally and another is global load scheduler that balances the load of various nodes in the system (see Fig.18.15). The global load scheduler decides the process migration, depending on the following factors:

- The number of processes on a processor
- Average waiting time of the processes in the ready queue of a node
- How many processors are available in the system
- Average response time of the processes on a node

Global load scheduler is of two types: static and dynamic. Static scheduler assigns the processes to processors only at their compile times while dynamic scheduler assigns the processors when the processes start execution. Static scheduler takes the decision only on information regarding processes such as expected execution time of processes, their I/O requirements, and so on. Moreover, it considers the static system characteristics such as processing power of processor, network configuration, and so on. On the other hand, dynamic scheduler takes its scheduling decisions, based on the current state of the system such as workload on a node, the queue length on a node, and so on.

Some of the scheduling algorithms adopted by global load scheduler are as follows:

18.12.1 Sender-initiated Algorithms

In this type of scheduling algorithms, the scheduling of a process is initiated by an overloaded node. The scheduling by a sender node may be done in various ways. The first method is *random*, that is, the sender node transfers the process to a random node. The drawback in this approach is that there may be many transfers if the randomly-selected node is not a receiver node. Another scheduling algorithm is based on the *threshold*. The threshold decides the criteria whether a node is receiver or not, based on their processor queue length. The sender node may poll a node, asking whether it is a receiver node or not. If the node is a receiver, then the process is transferred to the selected node. The threshold-based algorithm may be optimized if the processor queue lengths of the processors are available for comparison. Then, the processor having the *shortest* queue length is selected. Thus sender-initiated algorithms are categorized into three types: random-scheduling algorithm, threshold-based scheduling algorithm, and shortest queue length-based scheduling algorithm.

The sender-initiated algorithms are not effective at high system loads, causing instability in the system. The reason is that at high loads in the system, the probability of finding a receiver node is very low. The sender node continuously polls the nodes in search of a receiver node. Eventually, a time is reached where the cost of polling exceeds the benefit of load-sharing. Most of the processor cycles are wasted in unsuccessful polling, thereby, lowering the system's serving capacity. In turn, this causes the instability in the system.

18.12.2 Receiver-initiated Algorithms

Instead of the sender initiating the scheduling, an under-loaded receiver can also initiate the scheduling. Whenever a process finishes on this node, it checks its load value. If it is below the threshold, it randomly goes to the various highly-loaded nodes on the system, requesting for work. If it does not get any work, it finishes its work already in the queue, and starts probing the nodes again, after some time. The advantage of receiver-initiated algorithm is that all nodes will have balanced load, when the system is heavily loaded. Also, these algorithms do not cause instability in the system, because at high system loads, there is high probability of finding a sender node within a few polls. In turn, there will be very little wastage of processor cycles. However, these algorithms are expensive, as they make use of pre-emptive migration policy. This is because, a receiver node will migrate the processes only when a node has become the receiver. During this time, many sender nodes may receive a new process and start its execution. Therefore, when the receiver node starts migrating already-executing processes, there is cost involved in saving their states and resuming their executions on receiver node.

18.12.3 Symmetrically Initiated Algorithms

Symmetrically-initiated algorithms are designed to incorporate the benefits of both sender-, as well as receiver-initiated algorithms. In these algorithms, both sender and receiver nodes search for their respective nodes. At low system load, sender-initiated is more successful; while at high system loads, receiver nodes are able to find sender nodes. However, the drawbacks of both algorithms still exist. To reduce the drawbacks of both algorithms and make use of their advantages, a stable symmetrically-initiated algorithm is used. In this algorithm, the information gathered during polling by both types of nodes is utilized, and the nodes are classified as sender/over-loaded, receiver/under-loaded, and OK nodes. A data structure at each node is maintained to save the states of nodes. Thus, the data structure at each node has a sender list, a receiver list, and an OK list. The benefit of using these lists, with maintained states, is that the future sender-initiated polls are prevented and the component is deactivated at high system loads, thereby, having only a receiver-initiated component. Similarly, a receiver-initiated component is deactivated during low system loads. Moreover, within a moderate range, both sender- as well as receiver-initiated, components are activated.

18.13   DISTRIBUTED FILE SYSTEMS

In a distributed system, files can be stored and the computation can be done at any node. Thus, it may be the case that a node may require to access a file that is residing on some other remote node. The distributed file system implements remote accessing of files, but the user is unaware of the location of files distributed all over the system, giving the impression of a single-processor machine.

In a distributed system, some nodes are dedicated to store the files only. These nodes perform the storage and retrieval operation on the files, and are known as *file servers*. The other nodes used for computational purposes are known as *clients*. The client nodes request any remote file access from the file servers. To design a distributed system, the following goals should be fulfilled:

- **Access transparency**
  The clients are unaware that files are distributed over the network, and they can access them in the same way as on a single-processor file system.

- **Location transparency**
  There is a consistent name space, consisting of local as well as remote files. The name of a file to be specified by a client does not require the information about its location.

- **Concurrency transparency**
  All clients view the same state of the file system. If a file is being modified, then other processes in the network will observe the modification in a coherent manner.

- **Heterogeneity**
  There may be heterogeneous hardware and OS platforms in the network. But the file services must be provided across all the nodes, irrespective of their heterogeneity.

- **Replication transparency**
  To have the availability of certain files with file servers, the system may replicate these files. But the users are not aware of the replication of the files.

- **Migration transparency**
  The users are unaware of migration of the files from one node to another.

Now there are two services being used in a distributed system. The first is the mapping of logical file names, specified by the client node to physically-stored objects, such as files and directories. This is performed by a process known as *name server*. Whenever a process references a file name for the first time, the name server maps the file name to its stored object. The second service is to reduce the network communication delay in accessing the remote files. Since files are dispersed at various locations in a distributed system, every time a file is accessed, there will be a certain delay, due to network communication. Therefore, file caching is used to reduce this delay. Once the files are accessed from the file servers, they are cached at client node only. The subsequent accesses are now performed locally through the file cache. For this purpose, a process known as *cache manager* is used, which implements file caching. The caching may be used at file server nodes also. To reduce the disk I/O while accessing the remote files from file servers, the file cache stored in the main memory is used. Thus, cache managers may be present as client as well as servers. If multiple clients access the same file and store in their respective caches, and update it, the multiple copies of the same file become inconsistent. To avoid this problem, the cache manger coordinates the file access and caching, such that there is no inconsistency.

To discuss the files system in distributed systems, it is important to differentiate between the two terms: file service and file server. The primitives of the file system and their parameters, and what actions they perform, are described in the file service. But to implement this file service, there should be a process running on a machine that implements the file service. Thus, file server is that process. A system may have one or several file servers on different nodes of the system. But the client is unaware of the distribution of file servers and has an impression that he/she is working on a single-processor system.

A distributed file system has two components: file service and directory service. The details regarding the file service like file operations, file types, file attributes, and so on, are same as that of single-processor systems. In distributed systems, there are some files which can be created, but cannot be changed. These files are known as *immutable*. Immutable files are easy to cache and replicate across various file servers, as it is guaranteed that their contents will not change.

18.13.1 File-sharing Semantics

The manner, in which the results of file operations performed by the concurrent users are visible to one another, is known as file-sharing semantics. There are two methods of file sharing. One is sequential sharing, that is, the users access the shared file one after another. Second method is concurrent sharing, that is, multiple users share the file over the same period of time.

Let us suppose that a client modifies its cache copy of a file F, and at the same time another client accesses F from the file server. The second client will get the old copy of F. This is because sequential semantics are not valid in distributed file systems. It will be valid only if there is only one file server and when file caching is not used. However, this leads to poor performance of the system.

The following semantics may be used for a distributed file system:

- **Immutable file semantics**
  Whenever an immutable file is being shared, none of the sharing processes can modify it.

- **Session semantics**
  A session here means a group of clients processing a file. In a session, all the clients share a single mutable image of file F. Similarly, there may be another session where the image of the same file F is distinct. Thus, the idea of session semantics is that the write operation on F, performed by a client, can be observed by the clients of the same session, but it is not visible to the clients of other sessions. The session semantics, thus, support multiple images of mutable files. Each image represents one version of F. Whenever a client wishes to open the file, the distributed system decides which version of F to open.

- **Transaction semantics**
  According to this semantics, accessing a file or performing an operation on it are considered as atomic transactions. Whenever a client starts accessing a file or performing operations on it, a *begin transaction* primitive is executed first, to signal that all future operations will be done indivisibly. Once the operation is finished, *end transaction* primitive is executed, to signal the end of the atomic transaction. Thus, only a single version of the file is maintained, and only a single client can access it at a time. The advantage is that the file will always be in a consistent state.

18.14 DISTRIBUTED SHARED MEMORY

The only communication method in early distributed systems was message-passing. However, it was realized that a single-paged virtual address space can be created for a distributed system in exactly the same way as virtual memory can be implemented on single-processor systems. The pages here in the distributed shared memory are on different nodes. The data reside on disk or main memory of various nodes. Each node can own data, stored in the shared address space. Whenever there is reference to a data in shared address space, those need to be mapped to their actual physical location. For this purpose, there is a *mapping manager*, which may be implemented in the kernel, or as a run-time library routine. It may be possible that after mapping, it is found the data to be retrieved is local, that is, on the same node. In some cases, however, the data may be on a remote node. In this case, it will be considered as a page fault. This page fault then traps the OS. The OS then sends a message to the remote node to find the desired page. The page fault is thus serviced, and the desired page from the remote node is retrieved. But the user is unaware about all the mapping or dispersed pages on the network, and has the impression of using a single share memory. The transfer of pages from one node to other increases the network traffic, and due to this reason, there may be a delay while a user tries to access a shared memory data. It also incurs cost.

SUMMARY

Let us have a quick review of important concepts discussed in this chapter:

- A distributed system is a loosely-coupled architecture, wherein processors are inter-connected by a communication network.
- Network OSs are loosely-coupled OS software on a loosely-coupled hardware that allows nodes and users of a distributed system to be quite independent of one another, but interacts in a limited degree.
- Distributed OSs are tightly-coupled OS software on loosely-coupled hardware, that is, distributed system.
- Since in a distributed system, each node is a complete computer system, there is no global memory, and even no global clock.
- The distributed OS must be able to do process/computation migration as well as data migration for the better performance of the system.
- IPC in distributed systems is implemented through message-passing and remote-procedure-call.
- RPC is a programming language feature designed for distributed computing and is intended to have the same semantics of a procedure call as in a programming language.
- To provide mutual exclusion among processes in distributed system, the following algorithms are used:
  (a) *Centralized algorithm*: In this algorithm, a process, on one node of the distributed system, is assigned as coordinator to manage the mutual exclusion problem.

  (b) *Ricart–Agarwala algorithm*: It is a fully-distributed algorithm. According to this algorithm, a process, wishing to enter its critical section, sends a time-stamped request messages to all other processes, and waits.
  (c) *Token-ring algorithm*: This algorithm assumes the logical structure of all the processes as a sequential ring. Every process knows the next process in that sequence. Only the process, having the token, is permitted to enter inside its critical section, but only once.
- To provide deadlock detection in distributed system, the following algorithms are used:
  (a) *Centralized algorithm*: In this algorithm, a process is assigned as a central coordinator that will maintain the resource allocation state of the entire system.
  (b) Distributed algorithms: All the nodes in the system collectively cooperate to detect a cycle.
- To provide deadlock prevention in distributed system, the following algorithms are used:
  (a) *Wait-die algorithm*: The older process waits for a younger process, but a younger process is killed, if it tries to wait for an older process
  (b) *Wound-wait algorithm*: The older process pre-empts the younger one, but if the younger one requests, it is allowed to wait.
- To perform distributed process-scheduling, load-balancing is performed by transferring some processes from a heavily-loaded node to a lightly-loaded node. This is known as *process migration*.

- There are two types of schedulers. One is local scheduler that schedules the processes on one node locally. Another is global load scheduler that balances the load of various nodes in the system.
- Global load scheduler is of two types: static and dynamic. Static scheduler assigns the processes to processors at their compile time only, while dynamic scheduler assigns the processors when the processes start execution.
- In a distributed system, to have a distributed file system, some nodes are dedicated to store only files. These nodes perform the storage and retrieval operation on the files, and are known as *file servers*. The other nodes, used for computational purposes, are known as *clients*.

MULTIPLE CHOICE QUESTIONS

1. _____ are loosely-coupled OS software on a loosely-coupled hardware.
   (a) Distributed OS   (c) Real-time OS
   (b) Network OS   (d) none

2. _____ are tightly-coupled OS software on a loosely-coupled hardware.
   (a) Distributed OS   (c) Real-time OS
   (b) Network OS   (d) none

3. _____ is a programming language feature, designed for distributed computing, and is intended to have the same semantics of a procedure call as in a programming language.
   (a) RPC   (c) MPC
   (b) IPC   (d) none

4. The RPC is implemented as a _____ protocol.
   (a) blocking   (c) Internet
   (b) non-blocking   (d) none

5. Happens-before relation is a _____ relation.
   (a) transitive   (c) binary
   (b) non-transitive   (d) none

6. Which of the following is a mutual exclusion algorithm?
   (a) Path pushing   (c) Wait-die
   (b) Ricart–Agarwala   (d) none

7. Which of the following is a deadlock detection algorithm?
   (a) Path pushing   (c) Wait-die
   (b) Ricart–Agarwala   (d) none

8. Which of the following is a deadlock prevention algorithm?
   (a) Path pushing   (c) Wait-die
   (b) Ricart–Agarwala   (d) none

9. Which of the following is true for wait-die algorithm?
   (a) The older process waits for a younger process, but a younger process dies, if tries to wait for an older process.
   (b) The older process pre-empts the younger one, but if the younger one requests, it is allowed to wait.
   (c) The older process waits for the younger one, but if the younger one requests, it dies.
   (d) none

10. Which of the following is true for wound-wait algorithm?
    (a) The older process waits for a younger process, but a younger process dies, if tries to wait for an older process.
    (b) The older process pre-empts the younger one, but if the younger one requests, it is allowed to wait.
    (c) The older process waits for the younger one, but if the younger one requests, it dies.
    (d) None

11. _____ policy decides if a process on one node should be migrated pre-emptively or non-pre-emptively.
    (a) Transfer   (c) Selection
    (b) Migration   (d) Location

12. _____ policy decides when the computational load must be transferred to another node.
    (a) Transfer   (c) Selection
    (b) Migration   (d) Location

REVIEW QUESTIONS

1. What are the motivations behind developing a distributed system?
2. Differentiate between network OS and distributed OS?
3. What types of transparencies are required in designing a distributed OS?
4. Why does a distributed system not have a global clock and global system state?
5. What are the performance issues in designing a distributed OS?
6. How is message-passing protocol implemented in distributed OSs?
7. How is RPC implemented in distributed OSs?
8. Why is it difficult to maintain synchronization between different local clocks?
9. What is a logical clock?
10. Explain Happens-before relation algorithm for synchronizing the logical clocks?
11. Explain Chandy–Lamport Consistent State Recording algorithm.
12. Explain the implementation of the following algorithms for mutual exclusion. Discuss their advantages and disadvantages.

(a) Centralized algorithm

(b) Ricart–Agarwala algorithm

(c) Token-ring algorithm

13. Explain the implementation of the following algorithms for deadlock detection. Discuss their advantages and disadvantages.

(a) Centralized algorithm

(b) Path-pushing algorithm

(c) Edge-chasing algorithm

14. What is false deadlock?

15. Explain the implementation of wait-die and wound-wait algorithms for deadlock prevention.

16. What are the issues faced while performing distributed process-scheduling?

17. What is a global load scheduler?

18. Explain the types of global load scheduler.

BRAIN TEASERS

1. Why does Chandy–Lamport algorithm require channels to be FIFO?

2. In a fully-distributed mutual exclusion algorithm, if *n* is the number of processes in the system, how many messages have to be exchanged before a process can enter the critical section?

3. What is the effect of session semantics on file caching implementation?

4. File caching can be done at the file server's main memory. Since main memory is smaller as compared to the disk,

19. What is a sender and receiver node in distributed systems?

20. What are various criteria adopted by sender-initiated scheduling algorithm?

21. The sender-initiated algorithms are not effective at high system loads. Why?

22. The receiver-initiated algorithms are expensive. Why?

23. Explain Symmetrically-initiated Scheduling algorithms.

24. What are various goals while designing a distributed file system?

25. How is a distributed file system implemented?

26. Why could sequential file semantics not be implemented in a distributed file system?

27. What are various file-sharing semantics implemented in a distributed file system?

28. What is distributed shared memory?

some algorithm is needed to determine which files or part of files should be kept in cache. Design this algorithm that must solve the following problems:

(a) Does the cache manage the whole files or disk blocks?

(b) What is to be done when the cache fills up and something must be evicted?

5. 'Client caching may introduce inconsistency into the system.' Check the correctness of the statement.

19 Multi-processor Operating Systems

19.1 INTRODUCTION

Multi-processor systems are specialized OSs different from desktop OSs. The major feature of this OS is to exploit parallel computation in multi-processor systems. The types of multi-processor OSs have been discussed in this chapter along with the synchronization and scheduling issues faced in these systems. The memory sharing, process migration, and fault detection and recovery topics have also been discussed.

19.2 MULTI-PROCESSOR SYSTEMS

In the technological evolution of computer systems, there was a desire of parallel processing with the help of more than one processor. This has been realized through multi-processor systems. Multiprocessing systems contain more than one processor and share other resources. These types of systems are very useful for engineering and scientific applications by processing data in parallel on multiple processors. Another category of application suitable in multiprocessing environment is mission-critical and real-time systems. Since these systems are specially designed for defence systems, it is expected that they will continually work in warfare conditions. Therefore, in these types of systems, besides parallel computation, there is a high demand of fault tolerance and graceful degradation of services when any of the processor fails. Thus, multiprocessing systems are most suitable for these applications. These systems offer the advantage of increased throughput due to multiple processors, are economical to work on, and have increased reliability due to fault tolerance.

Unlike the distributed systems, the multi-processor systems are tightly coupled systems that share a common physical memory. All the processors operate under the control of a single OS. However, the users working on these systems have the perception of a single powerful system. The various processors, their coordination among themselves, and computation, all are transparent to the user.

Learning Objectives

After reading this chapter, you should be able to understand:

- Structure of multi-processor OSs
- Synchronization methods used by multi-processor OSs
- Scheduling methods used by multi-processor OSs
- Memory sharing
- Process migration methods
- Fault tolerance

19.2.1 Multi-processor System Architecture

There are three types of multi-processor architectures as the following:

Uniform Memory Access Architecture

In uniform memory access architecture (UMA), the main memory to be shared is placed at a central location such that all the processors are able to access the memory with the same speed, that is, it is equidistant in terms of access speed.

Non-uniform Memory Access Architecture

In non-uniform memory access architecture (NUMA), the memory is physically partitioned and the partitions are attached with different processors but all the processors share the same address space, thereby being able to access any memory partition directly. However, the access time to access memory partition attached with other processors is high as compared to the processor's own partition.

No Remote Memory Access Architecture

In no remote memory access architecture (NORMA), the memory is physically partitioned and the partitions are attached with different processors but no processor is able to access the partition directly. The way to access a memory partition is to send messages over the interconnected network to exchange information.

19.3 STRUCTURE OF MULTI-PROCESSOR OSs

It is obvious that for multiprocessing systems, a different OS is required to cater to the special requirements. These OSs are called multiprocessing OSs and have more challenges as compared to single-processor systems. Since in this environment there are multiple processors, all of them should be busy. The processes should be distributed on various processors for parallel computation. The process scheduling is another challenge as it is needed to schedule multiple processes on multiple processors. Moreover, the coordination of various processes should also be taken care of. Different inter-process communication and synchronization techniques are required. In multiprocessing systems, all processors share a memory; therefore, there is a need to check that all processors operate on consistent copies of data stored in shared memory. Thus, the multi-processor OSs are more complex as compared to single-processor OSs.

Since all the processors in multi-processor systems are under the control of a single OS, there is one design issue regarding the processor that should execute the OS code. Should this privilege be given to some selected processor or should all the processors share it. Based on this design issue, there are three structures for multi-processor OS, which are discussed as follows:

19.3.1 Separate Kernel Configuration

The simplest design of a multi-processor OS is to statically partition the resources in the system into different domains of control and assign these domains to various processors in the system. Each processor executes its own OS (see Fig. 19.1). Each processor has its own I/O devices and file system. Thus, there is very little interdependence among the processors. A process started on a process runs to completion on that processor only. However, there are some global OS data structures for interaction among processors, such as list of processes known to the system. These global data structures must be protected using some synchronization mechanisms such as semaphores.

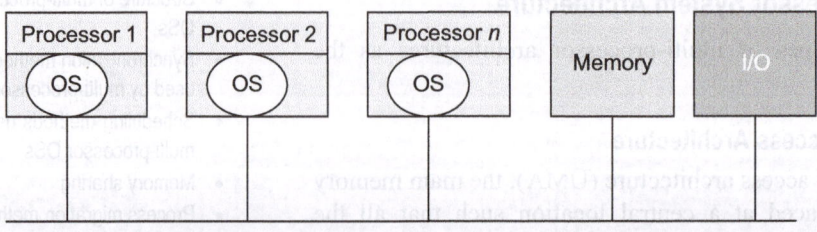

Fig. 19.1 Separate kernel configuration

Since the resources are distributed among the individual OSs, there is minimal contention over OS resources. Another benefit of this organization is its fault tolerance. If a single processor fails, there is no system failure as another processor may take over the charge. The fault tolerance becomes easy as there is little coupling between the processors. The disadvantage of this organization is that parallel execution of a single task is not possible, that is, a single task cannot be divided into sub-tasks and distributed among several processors, thereby losing the advantage of computational speed-up. Moreover, there may be the case that some processor is sitting idle in the absence of a task while other processors are heavily loaded. Similarly, the resources cannot be utilized properly due to static partition of resources among processors.

19.3.2 Master–Slave Configuration

This configuration assigns one processor as master and other processors in the system as slaves. The master processor runs the OS and processes while slave processors run the processes only (see Fig. 19.2). The master processor is connected to all I/O resources in the system. Any interrupt generated is directed to the master only. It performs interrupt handling, resource allocation and I/O management and also decides which process to be executed on which slave processor, that is, the process scheduling is also performed by the master processor. Since in this configuration, there is a single data structure that keeps track of ready processes, the parallel processing is possible as a task can be broken down into sub-tasks and assigned to various processors. All the processors may have fairly distributed load, and it cannot be the case that one processor is heavily loaded and another is idle.

In this configuration, the limitation is that the slave process can execute only processor-bound processes efficiently. Since the system calls are handled by the master processor only, in case of I/O-bound processes, the slave requires frequent services of master processor only. Thus, it affects the computation capability of the system. Another drawback is from the fault-tolerance viewpoint, that is, if the master processor fails, the system fails. Since all the OS functionalities required on the slave processors are handled by a single OS on the master processor, it becomes a bottleneck sometimes as the slave processors generate interrupt and wait for the master to handle them. Thus, the slave processors may saturate the master processor whose most of the time is spent in handling the system calls. The situation worsens if the number of processors is increased.

19.3.3 Symmetric Configuration

In master–slave configuration, there was an asymmetry as the master processor has the central control and other processors are treated as slaves. In the symmetric configuration, symmetry is

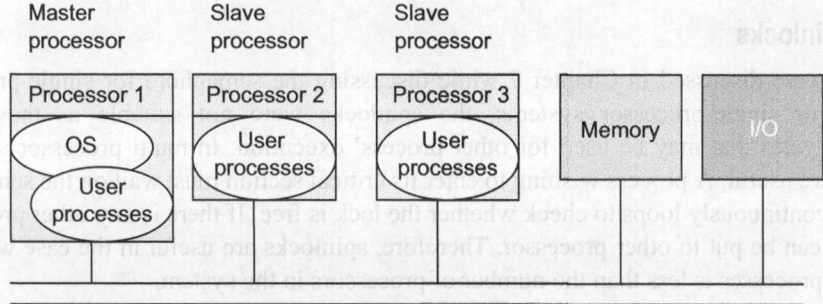

Fig. 19.2   Master-Slave multi-processor configuration

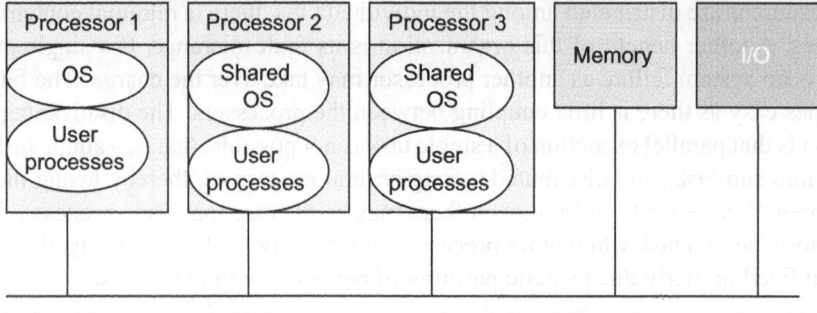

Fig. 19.3 Symmetric multi-processor configuration

established by same treatment to all the processors. All the processors are able to execute the OS in this configuration. However, there is only one copy of OS shared among all the processors (see Fig. 19.3). Any processor can access any device and can handle any interrupts generated on it. Thus, the system calls generated on a processor are serviced on the same processor only. Thus, the overheads, delays, and unreliability caused in these two structures are eliminated here. A processor when receives an interrupt can start executing the kernel. This configuration is very flexible and parallel execution of a single process is possible. It makes efficient use of resources and in case of failure, degrades gracefully.

Any processor can execute the OS but there is only a single copy of it. It may be the case that multiple processors start executing the OS concurrently. In this case, the shared data structures of the kernel must be protected and their access needs to be controlled to maintain integrity. Thus, mutual exclusion must be enforced such that only one processor is allowed to execute the OS at one time. However, this arrangement may produce a long queue of processors waiting for the OS code that has been made a critical section. It prevents the concurrency of the processes then. The solution to this is that many parts of the OS are independent of each other such as scheduler, file system call, page fault handler (PFH), and so on. Therefore, the OS is divided into independent critical section such that the data structures inside them are accessible to only one process but more than one critical sections can be accessed by more than one processor as they are independent.

19.4 PROCESS SYNCHRONIZATION

Most of the process synchronization methods adopted for single-processor systems do not work in multi-processor systems. Therefore, other methods to synchronize are required. These are discussed as follows:

19.4.1 Spinlocks

Spinlocks were discussed in Chapter 7 while discussing the semaphore for single-processor systems. For single-processor systems, the spinlocks were not suitable as they waste processor cycles that may be used for other process' execution. In multi-processor systems, spinlocks are useful. A process wishing to enter its critical section must wait on the semaphore or lock. It continuously loops to check whether the lock is free. If there is any other process to execute, it can be put to other processor. Therefore, spinlocks are useful in the case when the number of processes is less than the number of processors in the system.

As discussed in Chapter 7, to reduce the time wasted in continuous looping in spinlocks, the process is blocked. However, this solution incurs the cost of context switching as the process state needs to be switched from running to blocked, blocked to ready, and then ready to running. Therefore, when the waiting is of very short time comparable to context-switch time, then there is no need to block the waiting process and spinlocks are useful. Another factor for using the spinlocks in multi-processor systems is response time. If the busy waiting time is short, it is better to be in busy waiting because the process gets the lock as soon as it is released by the process holding it, thereby minimizing the response time of the process in the system.

19.4.2 Queued Locks

Another lock that may be used is queued lock, which is the same as conventional lock described as the solution of spinlock in Chapter 7. The idea is to block a process that requests the lock to access a shared item but does not get the access. In this case, the process does not perform busy waiting and relinquishes the processor. A global queue is maintained where all waiting processes reside. When the process holding the lock releases it, the process in the queue is *woken up*.

19.4.3 Special Hardware for Process Synchronization

Spinlocks may put traffic on the memory bus and the network. Similarly, queued locks may not provide the desired response time to the user. Therefore, a special hardware is designed for avoiding all these problems and achieving mutual exclusion. An example of this is *system link and interface controller* (SLIC) chip. A SLIC chip contains 64-bit registers and the registers of various processors are connected over the specially designed SLIC bus. Each bit in the register represents a spinlock. Therefore, each SLIC chip supports 64 locks. When a processor wishes to set a lock, it attempts to set the corresponding bit in the SLIC register. If it is already set, then it means that a process is already in the critical section. The advantage here is that a processor spins on a local lock, thereby avoiding memory and network traffic.

19.5 PROCESSOR SCHEDULING

Since in multi-processor environment, parallel processing is possible, there may be several tasks. These tasks must be assigned to various processors in the system to maximize the performance of the system. However, these tasks may be of a single program or from different programs. Furthermore, they need to cooperate and communicate among themselves via shared memory or message passing. Therefore, the processor scheduling is a difficult task in multi-processor systems. The task of scheduler here is complex as it has to decide which task of a program will execute on which processor. Thus, scheduling is two dimensional: One, to decide which process to schedule and the other where to schedule.

Many multi-processor scheduling algorithms maintain a global run queue where they store their processes or threads. The global run queue contains processes or threads that are ready to execute. Each processor may also use its own ready queue known as per-process run queue. However, it is suitable to only those algorithms when processes are attached with a specific processor only.

There are various factors to be considered while scheduling the processes in multi-processor systems. The most important factor to be considered is the parallelism, that is, to run processes simultaneously to get advantage of multi-processor architecture.

Another factor is cache corruption. If the processes come from different programs and are executed by a processor successively, there are chances that a big portion of data needed by one process is stored in the cache of that processor. If another process is to be executed on that processor, that data must be purged from the cache so that new data of the current process is brought into the cache. However, this will cause high miss ratio while a process tries to access the cache. This high miss ratio is known as *cache corruption* that leads to bad performance of the system. In this case, the working set data of a process needs to be loaded in the cache.

The context switch as described for single-processor systems also becomes a bottleneck for the performance of multi-processor systems. While scheduling, the context-switch time must also be considered so that this overhead is reduced, thereby having minimal time wastage.

The processor-scheduling algorithm in multi-processor systems is generally divided into the following categories:

19.5.1 Job-blind Scheduling Algorithms

The job-blind scheduling algorithms schedule processes on any processor without considering any parallel computation of processes or any other preferences. The FCFS, SPN, SRN, round-robin scheduling algorithms as discussed in Chapter 6 for single-processor systems are all examples of job-blind scheduling type as no process parallelism or other factors are considered.

19.5.2 Job-aware Scheduling Algorithms

The job-aware scheduling algorithms consider various factors while scheduling the processes or threads. Largely, three factors are considered: parallelism, cache corruption, context-switch time.

Let us discuss some job-aware scheduling algorithms.

Time-sharing Scheduling

Since one of the objectives of scheduling is to maximize parallelism in multi-processor system, this type of scheduling considers the independent processes of a program to be executed in parallel. In this algorithm, a global data structure for ready processes is maintained wherein the processes are stored with their priorities. As soon as a processor finishes its current work or becomes idle, the process with highest priority is selected from this global data structure and assigned to that processor.

Since all the processes are unrelated, the scheduling in this way shares the time of processors. Moreover, it balances the load in the system as no processor is idle while there is some ready process in the global data structure.

Table 19.1 Processes with their priority

Priority	Processes
4	P3, P5
3	P0, P5
2	P2, P4
1	P1
0	P6

Example 19.1

See Table 19.1 wherein the processes according to their priorities have been shown. Processes P3 and P5 are of the highest priority. As soon as a processor becomes available, it first selects these processes to execute.

Affinity-based Scheduling

For this purpose, another scheduling algorithm is used known as *affinity-based scheduling*. In this type of scheduling, a process is scheduled to be on the same processor where it last executed. In other words, if a process has shown affinity to a processor, it is scheduled to be executed on the same processor. This scheduling will increase the hit ratio to access the cache as the working set data of the process is already in the cache. However, this will restrict the load balancing in the system as the scheduler will not be able to schedule the process on some other idle processor creating an imbalance in the system.

Space-sharing Scheduling

This type of scheduling is for the related processes. Or the case may be that a process creates its multiple threads. A program consisting of related processes or a process consisting of related threads is the same thing. Scheduling multiple processes or threads at the same time across multiple processors is known as *space sharing*. When a group of related processes or threads is created, the scheduler looks for available processors. If the number of processors available is equal or more than the number of processes, then the processes are scheduled on different processors. Otherwise, no process is started until enough number of processors is available. Each process executes

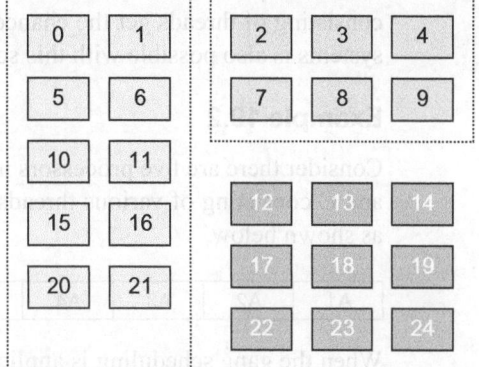

Fig. 19.4   Space sharing

on the same processor till its termination. If a process blocks on an I/O, it continues to hold the processor. According to this scheduling, at an instant of time when there is need to schedule related processes on the processors, a static partition can be done such that a group of related processes is assigned to one partition of the processors (see Fig. 19.4). The number and size of partitions, however, may change with time as the number of processes appear and get executed. In Fig. 19.4, there are two partitions. One partition is of 10-processor partition and second is of 6-processor partition. The remaining processors are not part of any partition and are therefore unassigned.

The advantage of space-sharing algorithms is that there is no context-switch time as there is no multi-programming on the processors. However, there is disadvantage of time wasted when a process or thread blocks and the processor sit idle.

Gang Scheduling

This scheduling takes the benefits of both time sharing as well as space sharing. This is helpful especially in scheduling the processes of same program or the multiple threads of a process. These processes or threads need to communicate with each other. When we consider only time sharing or space sharing, it may be possible that these threads are not able to synchronize their communication. When one sends some message, the other thread has not even started or received the message. To overcome this problem, gang scheduling is used. In this algorithm, a group or gang of threads from the same process is scheduled as a unit, that is, all the threads in the gang are scheduled at the same time and start to run on the processors. A global run queue is maintained wherein all the threads are stored. The threads of the same process are stored contiguously. The scheduler maintains a window whose size is equal to the number of processors in the system. The scheduler schedules a gang of threads on the window in round-robin fashion, that is, on the processors in first time quantum. All the processors in the window are scheduled synchronously. All threads in a window start executing in parallel on different processors in the window. After expiry of the time quantum, another gang in the global run queue is scheduled in the window. All the processors in the window are re-scheduled with a new thread. If sufficient number of threads of a process are not there to fit in the window, then the threads of another process may also be scheduled in the same window.

Since all the threads of a process start simultaneously, the communication between the threads is possible now. Since the algorithm takes the round robin approach, all the gangs consisting of threads get the chance for execution. The parallel computing of multiprocessing systems is also possible with this scheduling.

Example 19.2

Consider there are five processors in a multiprocessing system. There are three processes A, B, and C consisting of various threads. The window size here is five and the global run queue is as shown below.

A1	A2	A3	A4	A5	B1	B2	B3	C1	C2

When the gang scheduling is applied, the gangs of processes A, B, and C are made and scheduled accordingly in round robin fashion shown as follows:

A1	A2	A3	A4	A5

First time quantum

B1	B2	B3	C1	C2

Second time quantum

A1	A2	A3	A4	A5

Third time quantum

B1	B2	B3	C1	C2

Fourth time quantum

Smallest Number of Threads First Scheduling

This algorithm adopts the criterion of scheduling a process that has the smallest number of threads in the system. In this way, a program gets the priority based on its number of threads. The larger the number of threads in the process, the least is its priority.

19.6 MEMORY SHARING

Since the processors in a multi-processor system share a common memory, there may be the problem of *memory or cache coherence*. A memory is considered to be coherent if the data item read from the memory is always updated. However, this may not always be the case in multi-processor systems since each processor accesses data from the shared memory and may store its copy in its local memory or cache. If this data item is modified, then each copy of this data item in the shared memory or in the cache or local memory of other processors must be updated or the data item on other processors' local memory or cache must be removed. Thus, the memory or cache coherence is complicated here as each processor has its private cache.

For NUMA multi-processors, a home node is assigned. Each physical memory address is associated with this home node. The home node is responsible to store the data item with that main-memory address. If a processor wishes to modify the copy of data item in its cache, then it gains exclusive permission from the home node. Similarly, a recent copy of the data item if it is not in a processor's cache is requested through home node. If a processor faces a cache miss, it contacts the home node. If the data item is clean, that is, no other processor has modified it, then the home node forwards this copy of data item to the requester processor's cache. Otherwise, it forwards the request to the processor that has recently modified it. The processor that has recently modified the data item sends the modified copy of data item to the requester processor and home node. In this way, memory coherence is maintained because for every new read and write, every processor first contacts the home node.

19.7 PROCESS MIGRATION

Process migration can also be done in multi-processor systems as discussed in distributed systems. The node from which the process is to be migrated is called *sender node*. The node where the process is migrated is known as *receiver* or *remote node*. The process migration can be done for various reasons. In case of failure of a processor, the processes being executed on it are migrated on some other processors. Thus, process migration helps in fault tolerance. In case there is a processor that has no load or very less load, some processes from heavily loaded processor may be migrated to it. Thus, process migration helps in load balancing. This will in turn increase the throughput of the system and reduce the response time of a process. While migrating a process from one node to another, its *residual dependency*, that is, process dependency on its former node, must be checked. The residual dependency decides the strategy for process migration as discussed further.

The simple strategy to migrate a process is to transfer all its state information and pages to the receiver node. This is known as *eager migration strategy*. This enables the process to be executed efficiently on the receiving node as it performed on the sender node. However, transferring all pages related to the process may delay the process to be started on the receiver node and requires more bandwidth. Moreover, in case the process on the receiver node does not access most of its address space, the delay and required bandwidth become overhead in this strategy.

To reduce the drawbacks of eager migration strategy, another strategy to migrate is to transfer only *dirty pages*, that is, modified pages. This strategy is known as *dirty eager migration strategy*. In this strategy, it is assumed that there is a common secondary storage that may be accessed by any node in the system. Any clean page required by the receiver node is then accessed from the secondary storage. This strategy reduces the initial time required for transferring the process information and eliminates residual dependency.

If the residual dependency is high, then the receiving node where the process is being migrated must communicate with the sending node while executing the migrated process. However, this IPC between the two nodes will increase the network traffic and the performance of the system is degraded due to high latencies. In case there is high residual dependency of a process, the *lazy migration strategy* is adopted. According to this, the process is migrated with minimum required pages. At the receiving node, the migrated process can be started early without migrating all the required pages from the sender node. Only the process state information is migrated. The process pages are migrated only when the migrated process gets started on the receiver node and references the process pages that are still on the sender node. However, for each access to a page that is on the sender node, a memory reference must be initiated. However, due to these memory accesses, it may degrade the performance of an application on the system.

19.8 FAULT TOLERANCE

A multi-processor system has the inherent benefit of reliability and fault tolerance due to the multiplicity of processors. However, the OS designed for multi-processor systems must also support reliability and fault-tolerance features. There are several issues for the OS to take care. It needs to detect a failure, restructure the system, and recover it with low overhead. The following issues and their solution are discussed:

19.8.1 Fault Detection

The multi-processor OS must detect the failure quickly and also take measures to isolate it. If the failure is not isolated to the failed component, then it may harm others. For an instance, if a component fails, then it may corrupt the shared memory and, consequently, other processors may also fail. There are several ways to detect a failure. Various error-detecting codes may be used for this purpose but the cost of logic hardware for the generation and detection of error-detecting codes may sometimes be very high. Therefore, it would be better if we duplicate the component itself. The operations are executed on both original and duplicated component and compared to detect any discrepancy. Another way to detect fault is protocol monitoring. There is a sequence and timing of the communication between the two components. If one component is waiting for another component that has failed, then the component will wait forever. Thus, we can check the violation in sequence and timing of the protocol through protocol monitoring.

19.8.2 Fault Recovery

When a fault has occurred, it is important to recover it. For recovery, the system should be able to reconstruct a consistent state of all the affected processes due to failure such that the system can resume working. The common technique used for recovery in both hardware and software is redundancy. We can have redundant stand-by copies of hardware as well as software. In case of failure of the original component, the stand-by component takes charge and the system continues working.

SUMMARY

Let us have a quick review of important concepts discussed in this chapter:

- Multiprocessing systems offer the advantage of increased throughput due to multiple processors, are economical to work on, and have increased reliability due to fault tolerance.
- There are three structures for multi-processor OSs: separate kernel configuration, master-slave configuration, and symmetric configuration.
- There are various factors to be considered while scheduling the processes in multi-processor systems:
  (a) to run processes simultaneously
  (b) cache corruption
  (c) context-switch time
- There are two types of scheduling algorithms:
  (a) Job-blind scheduling algorithms that schedule processes on any processor without considering any parallel computation of processes or any other preferences.
  (b) The job-aware scheduling algorithms that consider various factors while scheduling the processes or threads.

- Some job-aware scheduling algorithms are as follows:
  (a) Time-sharing scheduling
  This type of scheduling considers the independent processes of a program to be executed in parallel.
  (b) Affinity-based scheduling
  If a process has shown affinity to a processor, then it is scheduled to be executed on the same processor.
  (c) Space sharing
  Scheduling multiple processes or threads at the same time across multiple processors is known as *space sharing*.
  (d) Gang scheduling
  A group or gang of threads from the same process is scheduled as a unit, that is, all the threads in the gang are scheduled at the same time and start to run on the processors.
  (e) Smallest number of threads first scheduling
  Schedules a process that has the smallest number of threads in the system.
- While migrating a process from one node to another, its residual dependency must be checked beforehand.

MULTIPLE CHOICE QUESTIONS

1. In _____ type, the main memory to be shared is placed at a central location such that all the processors are able to access the memory with the same speed.
   - (a) NORMA
   - (b) UMA
   - (c) NUMA
   - (d) none

2. In _____ type, the memory is physically partitioned and the partitions are attached with different processors but all the processors share the same address space.
   - (a) NORMA
   - (b) UMA
   - (c) NUMA
   - (d) none

3. In _____ type, the memory is physically partitioned and the partitions are attached with different processors but no processor is able to access the partition directly.
   - (a) NORMA
   - (b) UMA
   - (c) NUMA
   - (d) None

4. _____ algorithms schedule processes on any processor without considering any parallel computation of processes or their any other preferences.
   - (a) Job scheduling
   - (b) Job-aware scheduling
   - (c) Job-blind scheduling
   - (d) None

5. _____ algorithms consider various factors while scheduling the processes or threads. Largely, three factors are considered: parallelism, cache corruption, and context-switch time.

6. In _____ type of scheduling, a process is scheduled to be on the same processor where it last executed.
   - (a) time-sharing
   - (b) space sharing
   - (c) affinity-based
   - (d) none

7. _____ type of scheduling considers the independent processes of a program to be executed in parallel.
   - (a) times-haring
   - (b) space sharing
   - (c) affinity-based
   - (d) none

8. Scheduling multiple processes or threads at the same time across multiple processors is known as _____ scheduling.
   - (a) times-haring
   - (b) space sharing
   - (c) affinity-based
   - (d) none

9. Process migration helps in _____ in multi-processor systems.
   - (a) load balancing
   - (b) increase the throughput
   - (c) a and b
   - (d) none

10. In case there is high residual dependency of a process, the _____ migration strategy is adopted.
    - (a) dirty eager
    - (b) lazy
    - (c) eager
    - (d) none

Options also listed:
   - (a) Job scheduling
   - (b) Job-aware scheduling
   - (c) Job-blind scheduling
   - (d) None

REVIEW QUESTIONS

1. Explain three types of multi-processor system architectures.
2. Explain various structures for multi-processor OSs.
3. Explain the role of spinlocks in achieving synchronization in multi-processor systems.
4. What are the advantages of SLIC chip?
5. What are the various scheduling criteria considered in multi-processor scheduling?
6. What is cache corruption?
7. What is residual dependency?
8. What is the difference between job-blind and job-aware scheduling algorithms?
9. What is affinity-based scheduling?
10. What is gang scheduling?
11. What are the various process-migration strategies used in multi-processor systems?

BRAIN TEASERS

1. In a system, the processes have longer critical sections. Which type of synchronization mechanism between them is suitable?

2. In multi-processor systems, when multiple processes wait for the spinlock to be released, indefinite postponement may occur. How do the OSs resolve this?

20 Real-time Operating Systems

20.1 INTRODUCTION

Real-time systems are the most critical systems for which special software and hardware need to be designed. These systems are deadline-driven. Real-time OSs (RTOSs) adopted for these systems demand unique features that must be met in order to have deadlines in the system. All the features required in RTOSs have been explained in this chapter. The other important issues in this type of systems are scheduling and synchronization. The scheduling algorithms and synchronization-related issues have been discussed in detail.

20.2 REAL-TIME SYSTEMS

A real-time system is one whose logical correctness depends on both the correctness of the outputs and their timeliness. The timeliness factor makes these systems different from other systems. Real-time systems are the systems in which data need to be processed at a regular and timely rate. The tasks in the system must meet their defined deadlines for a specified time interval, otherwise the purpose of the system is lost or the system performance is degraded. In one sense, the general-purpose systems may also be considered as real-time. For example, we are able to echo a character on the screen typed on the keyboard within a specified time. But it does not mean that a general-purpose system is a real-time system. The real-time systems are not general in nature, but are designed for a specific application and are embedded. Another point of difference is that consequences of the failure are more drastic in real-time systems as compared to general-purpose systems. The real-time systems are largely useful in defence applications, which are mission specific; that is, if there is no timely response, there might be loss of equipment, and / or even life. Therefore in these systems, deadlines should be met to prevent failures; else, the purpose of the system is lost. For example, there is an electric motor being controlled through a computer system. If the motor running at a speed crosses a threshold speed, it will burn. The system controls the motor in such a way that if it crosses the threshold, it will lower the speed of the motor. Now, say, the motor is crossing the threshold speed, and the system does not respond in that time period, the motor will end up burning.

Learning Objectives

After reading this chapter, you should be able to understand:

- Characteristics of a real-time system
- Structure of a real-time system
- Characteristics of a real-time OS
- Rate-monotonic scheduling algorithm
- Earliest deadline first scheduling algorithm
- Priority inversion problems that occur during mutual exclusion implementation
- Priority inheritance protocol
- Priority ceiling protocol

This is an example of a real-time system, which, in case of failure, results in loss of equipment. Similarly, there are many defence applications like guided missile systems, air traffic control systems, and so on, which, in case of failure, result in loss of equipment/life.

However, real-time systems are affecting every walk of our lives without us even knowing it. Today real-time systems are meant not only for applications such as nuclear reactors or aircrafts but also are playing a huge role in airline reservation systems, consumer electronics (music systems, air-conditioners, microwaves, etc.), card verifiers in security systems, control systems, industry automation, and so on.

20.2.1 Characteristics of a Real-time System

As discussed earlier, real-time systems are deadline driven. The timing constraints are in the form of period and deadline. The period is the amount of time between iterations of a regularly repeated task. Such repeated tasks are called *periodic tasks*. The deadline is a constraint of the maximum time limit within which the operation must be complete.

Real-time systems can be characterized as *hard real-time systems* and *soft real-time systems*. The systems that have hard deadlines and must be met for certain are called hard-real-time systems. All defence applications are of this type. Hard real-time systems are those in which one or more activities must never miss a deadline or timing constraint, or else, the system will fail. A failed system implies that the purpose of designing the system is lost. The failure includes the damage to the equipment or injury, or even death to users of the system. For example, let us consider a system that has to open a valve within 30 milliseconds, when the humidity exceeds a particular threshold. If the action is not carried out within the deadline, a catastrophe may occur. Thus, hard real-time systems are those in which disastrous or serious consequences may happen if deadlines are missed. These systems must have deterministic guarantees to meet deadlines. There is another type known as soft real-time systems, in which a missed deadline may be acceptable. For example, in a video conferencing system, if some audio or video data are somehow delayed for a fraction of time, and there is no harm, then it may be acceptable. Thus, digital audio, multimedia systems, virtual reality, and so on, are all examples of soft real-time systems. However, missing deadlines does not mean that they are not real-time systems. The delay of soft real-time systems must be bounded and predictable, and should not be infinite. The hard and soft real-time systems can be depicted in a real-time system spectrum as shown in Fig. 20.1.

Real-time systems are *deterministic* in the sense that deadlines and other assertions involving time are exact or fixed values. The terms 'aggregate' or 'average' are not meant for these systems. A real-time system is *predictable*. Its timing behaviour is always within the acceptable range. The behaviour is specified on a system-wide basis such that all tasks will meet deadlines. To become a predictable system, the period, deadline, and worst case execution time of each task need to be known.

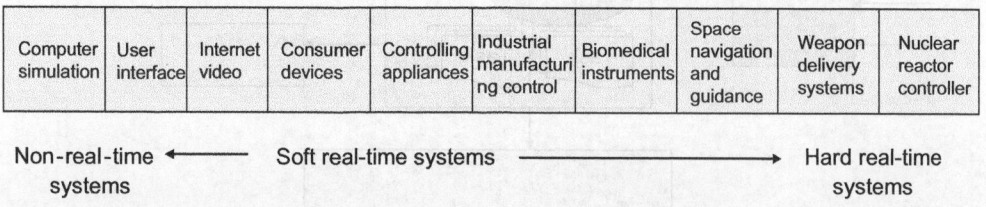

Computer simulation	User interface	Internet video	Consumer devices	Controlling appliances	Industrial manufacturing control	Biomedical instruments	Space navigation and guidance	Weapon delivery systems	Nuclear reactor controller

Non-real-time systems ← Soft real-time systems ────────→ Hard real-time systems

Fig. 20.1   Real-time system spectrum

Real-time systems are such that they have to handle inherent physical *concurrency* that is part of the external world to which they are connected. Multiple input sensors are there that can generate simultaneous inputs, which, due to timeliness constraints, must be handled concurrently.

Another characteristic connected to real-time systems is *fault tolerance*. Fault tolerance is concerned with the recognition and handling of failures. While handling failures, the graceful degradation of the system is essential. We need to adopt several methods in order to accomplish the fault tolerance of the system. The main idea behind the fault tolerance in a real-time system is that even in worst conditions, the system must continue to work. For example, the systems used in defence applications being used in warfare conditions must continuously work despite failures that may have occurred in the system.

20.2.2 Structure of a Real-time System

In general, a real-time system consists of two parts: controlling system (computer) and a controlled system (environment). The controlling system interacts with its environment, based on information available about the environment. The real-time computer controls a device or process through sensors that provide inputs at periodic intervals, and the computer must respond by sending signals to the actuators. There may also be irregular events, which must receive a response as well. But in any case, periodic or aperiodic, there will be a time limit within which the response should be delivered. Thus, a real-time system consists of the following components (see Fig. 20.2):

Computing Hardware

It includes the processor, memory, and communication networks.

Sensors and Actuators

The sensors are used to determine the state of the physical world relevant to the software. They sense the status of the system. Actuators are used to actuate the system according to the current status of the system. The output of the whole real-time system is fed to the actuators and displays.

Real-time Software

The software is the embedded part of the real-time system that interacts with sensors and actuators. It also interacts directly with the computing hardware. It consists of the tasks and real-time OS.

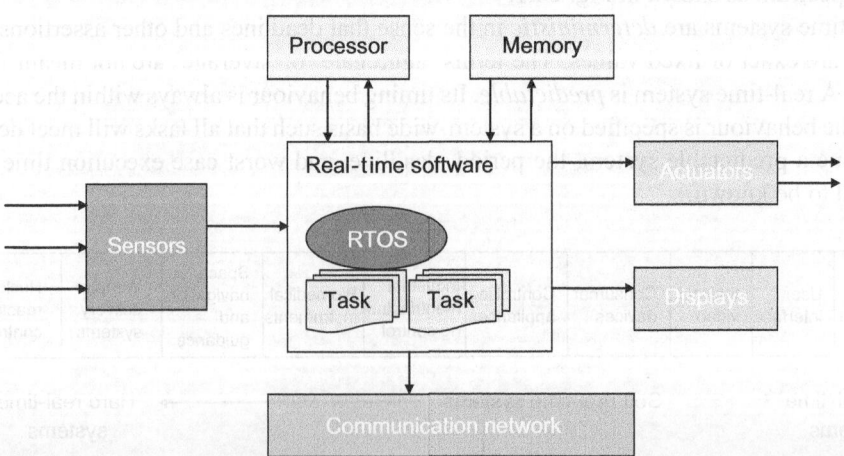

Fig. 20.2 Structure of a real-time system

20.3 REAL-TIME OS

Real-time operating systems (RTOSs) are there to meet the special needs of a real-time system. To support multiple tasks in a real-time system, the RTOS must be multi-tasking. Being deadline driven in nature, the tasks in a real-time system have priorities depending on its design. To execute a higher-priority task, the scheduler in the RTOS must be able to pre-empt a low-priority task. Thus, to meet the deadline requirements of real-time systems, the kernel must be pre-emptive. The RTOS must have sufficient priority levels to support priority-based scheduling. The priority assigned to the tasks depends on how quickly a task has to respond to the event. Based on the facilities provided by the RTOSs, there can be three broad levels of priority:

Interrupt level At this level, the tasks that require very fast response, are considered.

Clock level At this level, the tasks that require repetitive processing and accurate timing, are considered.

Base level At this level, the tasks that are of low priority and have no deadlines, are considered.

Apart from providing other facilities, the major characteristic of RTOS is to provide timely response to applications. The major challenge for an RTOS is to schedule the real-time tasks. In a real-time system design, all deadline requirements are gathered and analysed. The RTOS schedules all tasks according to the deadline information and ensures that all deadlines are met. Since the behaviour of a real-time system is predictable, RTOS should also have predictable behaviour under all system load scenarios. Further, it is important to have inter-process communication (IPC) that has predictable delays and is controllable. The RTOS must have the algorithms to control this IPC.

Since a real-time system responds to external events in the environment, it is event driven in nature. The real-time system waits for an event to occur in real time. When the event occurs, the system must respond to it quickly. The latencies associated with the event processing, however, may delay the processing. There are two types of such latencies: the interrupt latency, that is, the time elapsed between the last instruction executed on the current interrupted task and start of the interrupt handler; and the other is dispatch latency, that is, the time to switch from the last instruction in the interrupt handler to the next task that is scheduled to execute. The RTOS must be selected in a way such that these latencies are minimal.

Another feature of a real-time system is to have fault tolerance. Since a real-time system must work continuously in every condition, in case of any hardware or software failure, the system should not stop working. To achieve this target, fault tolerance is provided by means of redundancy, both in hardware and software. For example, if one processor fails, another processor in standby will take over and the system will continue to work. The RTOS must use some special techniques such that the system can tolerance the faults and continue its operations. Obviously, with the fault tolerant feature, there is degradation in the performance of the system. But the OS should take care that this degradation is graceful, that is, no critical functioning should be stopped or delayed. This is known as *fail-soft operation*. It is the ability of a system to maintain stability, so as to preserve as much capability of the system as possible.

Based on the earlier characteristics, an RTOS is different as compared to other OSs. An RTOS must have the capability to respond quickly to external interrupts. The context switch time must be very low. Commercial RTOSs are characterized by deterministic response times, ranging from milliseconds to microseconds. The size of RTOSs is also an issue for providing quick responses to external events. Therefore, an RTOS does not come with all modules. RTOSs come with their minimal functionalities, and if there is any need, other modules can be loaded. In general, an RTOS occupies 10 KB to 100 KB size, as compared to other OSs consuming several megabytes. The RTOS with minimum functionality must include task management, including task scheduling, task synchronization, memory management (excluding virtual memory management), and timers.

The RTOS is neither loaded from the disk nor is already available, as we see in case of desktop OSs. Since the real-time system is embedded in most applications, the RTOS with the software and board-support package (BSP) is bundled into a single executable file that is burnt onto a boot-ROM or flash memory. Board-support package is the component that is used to provide board/hardware-specific details to the OS. Through BSP, RTOS will interact with the hardware present on the board. It is highly specific, both to the board and the RTOS. The BSP start-up code is the first to be executed while starting the system in order to initialize the processor and memory. It sets up the clock and various components, such as cache.

20.4 REAL-TIME SCHEDULING

The following are the scheduling criteria in a real-time system:

- The timing constraints of the system must be met.
- In case of simultaneous access of shared resources and devices, the processes must be prevented.
- The cost of context switches, while pre-empting, must be reduced.

The scheduling in real-time systems may be performed in the following ways: pre-emptively, non-pre-emptively, statically, and dynamically. The RTOS should allocate and schedule tasks on processors in order to ensure that deadlines are met. Some basic terms related to scheduling are as follows:

Periodic, Aperiodic, and Sporadic Tasks

In real-time systems, many tasks are repetitive. For example, sensor data need to be collected at regular intervals of time. These tasks are known as periodic tasks. In contrast, there are some tasks that occur occasionally. These tasks are, in fact, actions in response to some event. Consider for example, the closing of a valve when the level of liquid in a tank reaches a threshold. These are known as aperiodic tasks. These tasks are, in general, used to indicate alarm conditions. Sporadic tasks are also real-time tasks, which are activated irregularly like aperiodic tasks, but with some known bounded rate, which means that a minimum inter-arrival period is known for these tasks.

Release Time

Release time of a task is the time instant at which the task becomes available for execution. The task can be scheduled and executed at or after its release time.

Absolute Deadline

The absolute deadline of a task is the instant of time by which it must complete its execution.

Relative Deadline

It is the maximum allowable response time of a task. The absolute deadline of a task is, in fact, the sum of its relative deadline and release times.

Offline Scheduling

Since the period of arrival of periodic tasks is known in advance, an offline schedule can be prepared of the operation. This may provide the information about when the periodic tasks will run, including the slots for aperiodic and sporadic tasks.

Online Scheduling

In online scheduling, the tasks are scheduled as they arrive in the system.

Static Scheduling

The static scheduling algorithm has complete knowledge of the following:

    i) Task set and its constraints
    ii) Deadlines
    iii) Computation times
    iv) Release times

For example, in a simple process control application, static scheduling is appropriate.

Dynamic Scheduling

In dynamic scheduling, there is complete knowledge of tasks set, but new arrivals are not known. Therefore, the schedule changes over the time. For example, dynamic scheduling is appropriate in all defence applications.

Schedulability Analysis

It is an analysis to know whether a schedule of tasks is feasible or not. A set of tasks is schedulable only if all the tasks in the task set meet their timing constraints. For this, we can have an offline scheduling that produces a schedule. The tasks are then scheduled and dispatched at run time, using static or dynamic scheduling.

    The short-term scheduler in RTOS must ensure that all hard real-time tasks are completed by their deadline, and that as many as possible soft real-time tasks are also completed by their deadline. In real-time systems, pre-emptive priority-based schedulers are used in order to accommodate the high-priority real-time tasks.

20.4.1 Rate Monotonic Scheduling Algorithm

Rate monotonic(RM) scheduling algorithm is one of the most widely used real-time scheduling algorithms executed on a uni-processor environment. It is a static priority-based pre-emptive scheduling algorithm. The base for scheduling in this algorithm is to take the task that has the shortest period, that is, the task that has the highest frequency rate of arrival. The task with the shortest period will always pre-empt the executing task. If we plot the priority of the tasks as a function of their frequency rate of arrival in the system, there is a monotonically increasing graph (see Fig. 20.3). Thus, the priority of a task is inversely proportional to its period. The following are the assumptions during the execution of this scheduling algorithm:

- There is no such region in any task that is non-pre-emptable.
- The cost incurred in pre-emption is negligible.
- All tasks are independent, that is, there is no precedence constraint among them.
- All tasks in the task set are periodic.
- The relative deadline of a task is equal to only its period.

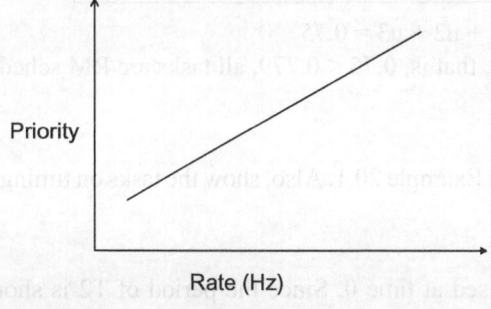

Fig. 20.3 Priority of tasks vs frequency of arrival

The schedulability test for this algorithm is based on the total utilization of the processor.

The utilization in our case is e/p, where e is the execution time and p is the period of the task. Thus, to meet all the deadlines in the system, the following must be satisfied:

$$e_1/p_1 + e_2/p_2 + \ldots + e_n/p_n \leq 1$$

where, n is the number of tasks to be scheduled in the system.

The equation indicates that the sum of the processor utilizations of the individual tasks cannot exceed a bound. The bound value 1 is for a perfect scheduling. However, the bound may also be lower. The worst case processor utilization for scheduling processes may be given as the following:

$$e_1/p_1 + e_2/p_2 + \ldots + e_n/p_n \leq n(2^{1/n} - 1)$$

If the number of tasks in a system tends towards infinity, the earlier equation will be ln $2 = 0.693$. It means this scheduling algorithm is able to schedule all tasks in general, if the processor utilization is 69.3%.

Example 20.1

Consider a real-time system in which there are three tasks. Their period and execution time are as follows:

Task	Execution time, e	Period, p
T1	35	100
T2	10	50
T3	30	150

Check whether the tasks are RM schedulable.

Solution

The upper bound schedulability in this case is equal to
$3 * (2^{1/3} - 1) = 0.779$
Now calculate the utilization for each task as follows:

Task	Execution time, e	Period, p	Utilization, (e/p)
T1	35	100	0.35
T2	10	50	0.2
T3	30	150	0.2

The total utilization of processor $U = u1 + u2 + u3 = 0.75$
Since the U is less than the upper bound, that is, $0.75 < 0.779$, all tasks are RM schedulable.

Example 20.2

Explain the RM scheduling of the tasks in Example 20.1. Also, show the tasks on timing diagram.

Solution

We assume that all three tasks are released at time 0. Since the period of T2 is shortest, it is allowed to execute first. After that, T1 starts executing as its period is smaller as compared to T3. T1 finishes at 45 and finally T3 starts executing. But when T3 has just completed 5 time units, T2 reappears as its next period starts. So it starts executing and completes its execution till 60 time units. After that, T3 resumes and completes its execution at 85. At this time, there is no task to be executed and therefore the processor is idle till 100. At this point, T1 reappears as its next period starts, and so on. All the tasks complete their execution within their deadlines as shown in the following diagram.

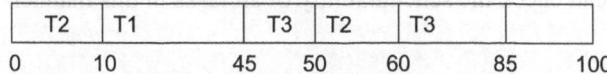

| T2 | T1 | | T3 | T2 | T3 | |

0   10   45   50   60   85   100

RM schedulability condition discussed here is a sufficient but not necessary condition. This is because there may be task sets with a utilization greater than $n(2^{1/n} - 1)$ that are schedulable by this algorithm. The next example demonstrates this fact.

Example 20.3

Consider a real-time system in which there are three tasks with their period and execution time as follows:

Task	Execution time, e	Period, p
T1	20	100
T2	30	145
T3	68	150

Check whether the tasks are RM schedulable?

Solution

The upper bound schedulability in this case is equal to
$3 * (2^{1/3} - 1) = 0.779$
Now calculate the utilization for each task as follows:

Task	Execution time, e	Period, p	Utilization, (e/p)
T1	20	100	0.2
T2	30	145	0.206
T3	68	150	0.454

The total utilization of processor U = u1 + u2 + u3 = 0.86

Since U is greater than the upper bound, that is, $0.779 < 0.86$, all tasks are not RM schedulable. However, if we see the execution of the tasks on the timing diagram, all tasks are schedulable, as they complete their execution within their deadlines as shown in the following diagram.

| T1 | T2 | T3 | | T1 | T3 | | |

0   20   50   100   120   138   145

For the condition for schedulability, we need to find a time t such that the tasks complete their execution, and, if possible, the iteration of a task, if started, must be completed within that time t. Suppose, in a system of three tasks, task T1 is schedulable, if $e_1 \leq P_1$. Now for T2, we need to see how many iterations (t/P_1) of T1 have been released over [0, t]. All these iterations must be completed within [0, t] and e2 must be available to execute T2. Thus,

$$t = (t/P_1 * e_1) + e_2$$

We must find this t such that $t \in [0, P2]$.
Similarly for T3, we must have

$$t = (t/P_1 * e_1) + (t/P_2 * e_2) + e_3$$

such that $t \in [0, P3]$. Thus, we can check the schedulability of all tasks in this manner.

Example 20.4

The schedulability of the tasks in Example 20.3 can be checked as in follows:

T1: $e_1 \leq 100$ (true)

T2: $e_1 + e_2 \leq 100$ (true)

  or

$2e_1 + e_2 \leq 145$ (true)

T3: $e_1 + e_2 + e_3 \leq 100$ (false)

  or

$2e_1 + e_2 + e_3 \leq 145$ (true)

  or

$3e_1 + 2e_2 + e_3 \leq 100$ (false)

20.4.2 Earliest Deadline First Scheduling Algorithm

Earlier deadline first (EDF), also known as *least time to go*, is a uni-processor priority-driven scheduling algorithm, in which the tasks need not be periodic. The scheduling criterion here is based on the absolute deadline of the tasks. The task whose absolute deadline is earlier, is scheduled first, that is, the earlier the deadline, the higher the priority of the task. It is a dynamic priority scheduling algorithm, as the deadlines are computed at run-time. The task priorities are not fixed as well, and may change, depending on the closeness of their absolute deadlines. When a process is able to run, it must declare its deadline requirements. Priorities at this time may need to be changed in order to adjust the deadline of new runnable tasks. The following are the assumptions while executing this scheduling algorithm:

- There is no such region in any task that is non-pre-emptable.
- The cost incurred in pre-emption is negligible.
- All tasks are independent, that is, there is no precedence constraint among them.

Example 20.5

Consider the following set of tasks in a real-time system:

Tasks	Release time	Execution time	Absolute deadline
T1	0	4	40
T2	2	7	15
T3	5	10	20

Perform EDF scheduling on this task set.

Solution

T1 is the first task to arrive, so it starts executing. After 2 time units, T2 arrives, whose deadline is shorter than T1. Therefore, it pre-empts T1 and T2 starts executing. After 5 time units, T3 arrives but T2 continues, as absolute deadline of T3 is more than T2. Therefore T2 continues and completes its execution. After this, now there are T1 and T3 tasks that need the processor. Since T3 has a less absolute deadline, it starts executing and completes execution. Finally, T1 resumes and completes its execution. The tasks on the timing diagram are as follows:

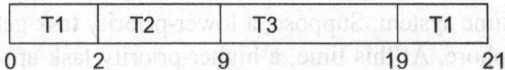

20.4.3 Precedence Constraints

In the scheduling methods discussed earlier, it has been assumed that the processes are independent, and have no precedence constraints. However, the processes of a real-time system depend on one another. Therefore, precedence constraints must be taken into account while scheduling and determining deadlines. For this purpose, a process precedence graph (PPG) is typically used. The nodes of this graph represent processes with their execution times. The execution time is written inside the node and the process number is outside the node. The edges between the nodes show the precedence constraints. For example, the PPG in Fig. 20.4 shows that P2 can be initiated only after P1 and P4 can be initiated, only after P2 and P3 complete.

It is assumed that each process is CPU-bound and is executed in a non-pre-emptable manner. The deadline of a task Pi can be calculated as follows:

$$D_i = D_{application} - \sum_{k \in descendent(i)} X_k$$

where, $D_{application}$ is the deadline of the application under consideration and $k \in descendent(i)$ is the set of descendants of P_i in PPG, that is, a set of tasks which lie on some path between P_i and exit node of PPG. Thus, deadline of a task is such that all tasks, which directly or indirectly depend on it, can also finish by the overall deadline of the application. Let us suppose that deadline of an application is 40 s, the deadlines of the tasks are shown in Table 20.1.

Table 20.1 Deadlines of tasks

Process	Finishing deadline
P1	23
P2	31
P3	31
P4	35
P5	35
P6	40

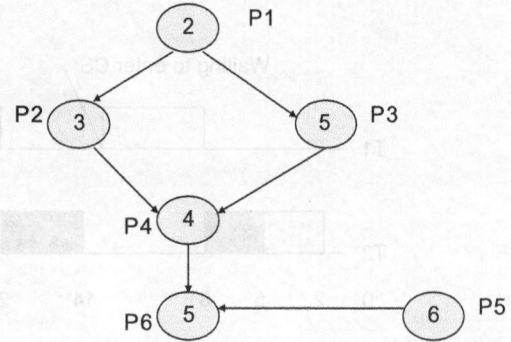

Fig. 20.4 PPG of a system

Deadline scheduling policy needs to incorporate several other constraints as well. One important constraint while calculating deadlines is I/O time in a task. If I/O of one task is overlapped with execution of some independent tasks, the deadline of its predecessors in PPG can be relaxed by the amount of I/O overlap. In the example PPG shown earlier, P2 and P3 are independent tasks. If execution of P2 includes one second of I/O time, the deadline of P1 is 24, instead of 23.

20.5 MUTUAL EXCLUSION

The mutual exclusion in real-time tasks is implemented through binary semaphores and monitors. But with the use of binary semaphore, a problem arises. In this section, the idea is to discuss this problem and solutions to overcome it. The problem is that a low-priority task may block a higher-priority task in the real-time system. Suppose, a lower-priority task gets access to its critical section through the semaphore. At this time, a higher-priority task appears and wishes to access the critical section. But being a higher-priority task, it will not be allowed to execute until the lower-priority task finishes, and is blocked. This problem is known as *priority inversion*. The priority inversion may result in some unpleasant side effects on the system. In 1997, NASA's Rover Robot (Path finder) on Mars project failed due to such a priority inversion problem.

Example 20.6

Consider two tasks T1 and T2 in a real-time system. T1 has the higher priority and T2 the lower priority. T1 and T2 share a critical section CS. Suppose, T2 is released at time 0 and starts execution. At time 5, it needs to access the CS and enters it, as there is no other task that wishes to enter the CS. At time 8, T1 appears and being the higher priority task, it pre-empts T2 and starts execution. At time 14, T1 needs to access the CS and tries to gain access, but it cannot get access as the CS is already locked by T2. So T1 is blocked and T2 resumes its execution in the CS. The problem of priority inversion has occurred here at this point such that the higher priority task has been pre-empted by the lower-priority task. T2 releases the CS at 20 and T1 gains access and continues its execution.

T1 is blocked for the time period that is required to execute inside critical section by T2. Thus, the time period for blocking of T1 can be determined. Therefore, this type of priority inversion is called *bounded priority inversion* (Fig. 20.5).

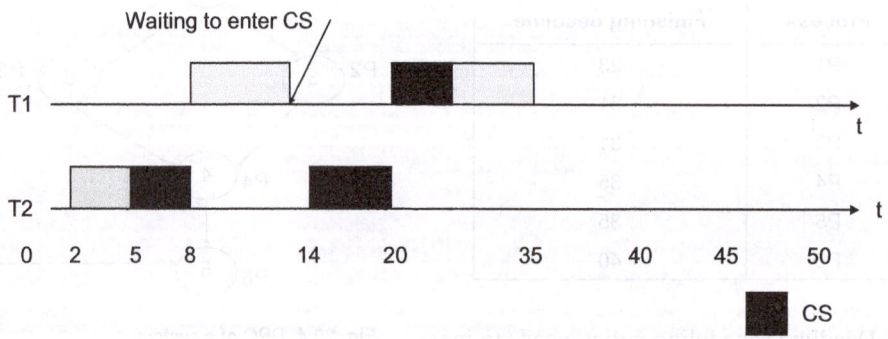

Fig. 20.5 Bounded-priority inversion

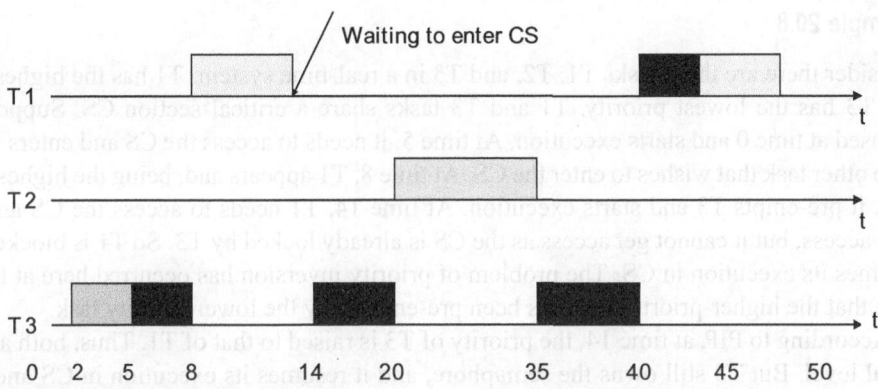

Fig. 20.6 Unbounded priority inversion

Example 20.7

Consider there are three tasks T1, T2, and T3 in a real-time system. T1 has the highest priority and T3 has the lowest priority. T1 and T3 share a critical section CS. Suppose, T3 is released at time 0 and starts execution. At time 5, it needs to access the CS and enters it as there is no other task that wishes to enter the CS. At time 8, T1 appears, and being the highest-priority task, it pre-empts T3 and starts execution. At time 14, T1 needs to access the CS and tries to gain access, but it cannot get access as the CS is already locked by T3. So T1 is blocked and T3 resumes its execution in the CS. The problem of priority inversion has occurred here at this point, such that higher-priority task has been pre-empted by the lower-priority task. At time 20, T2 appears and starts execution, pre-empting T3. At time 35, T2 finishes its execution. This is another case of the priority inversion problem, such that T2, being the lower-priority task as compared to T1, gets the execution. At time 35, T3 resumes and releases the CS at time 40. At only this time, T1 is able to access the CS. It executes inside the CS, releases it at time 45, and completes its execution at time 50.

In this example, we can see that T1 execution is being further delayed for an intermediate task, that is, T2. It may be possible that some other intermediate tasks may appear and get the same execution as that of T2. In this case, the blocked period of T1 is unbounded, that is, it cannot be determined. Therefore, this type of priority inversion problem is known as *unbounded priority inversion*, as shown in Fig. 20.6.

There are two protocols for solving priority inversion problem:

1. Priority inheritance protocol (PIP)
2. Priority ceiling protocol (PCP)

Let us discuss these protocols.

20.6 PRIORITY INHERITANCE PROTOCOL

When the priority inversion problem occurs, the higher-priority task is blocked by the lower-priority task. Therefore, in this protocol, a provision is made such that when a higher-priority task attempts to lock a semaphore owned by a lower-priority task, the priority of the owning task is raised to the priority of the blocked task. When the owning task releases the lock, its original priority is restored. This temporary increase in the priority eliminates the effect of unbounded priority inversion.

Example 20.8

Consider there are three tasks T1, T2, and T3 in a real-time system. T1 has the highest priority and T3 has the lowest priority. T1 and T3 tasks share a critical section CS. Suppose, T3 is released at time 0 and starts execution. At time 5, it needs to access the CS and enters it as there is no other task that wishes to enter the CS. At time 8, T1 appears and, being the highest-priority task, it pre-empts T3 and starts execution. At time 14, T1 needs to access the CS and tries to gain access, but it cannot get access as the CS is already locked by T3. So T1 is blocked and T3 resumes its execution in CS. The problem of priority inversion has occurred here at this point, such that the higher-priority task has been pre-empted by the lower-priority task.

According to PIP, at time 14, the priority of T3 is raised to that of T1. Thus, both are now at equal level. But T3 still owns the semaphore, and it resumes its execution in CS and releases it at time 25. At time 20, T2 appears but does not get the execution, as its priority is lower as compared to both T1 and T3. At time 25, T1 gets the access into the CS and completes its execution till time 35. Only after this, T2 gets the execution. Thus, unbounded priority inversion has been converted into bounded one. This has been shown in Fig. 20.7.

There are some problems in the implementation of this solution. The first problem is that the PIP may lead to deadlocks. Consider two tasks T1 and T2, using two critical sections CS1 and CS2. At time t1, T2 starts execution and locks CS2. At t2, T1 appears, and being the highest-priority task, pre-empts T2. At t3, T1 locks CS1. After this, it tries to access CS2 but cannot, and is blocked. Now, according to the PIP, T2 inherits the priority of T1 and starts executing. After some time, it tries to access CS1 but cannot and is blocked. In this case, both tasks are waiting for each other to release the desired locks. Thus, a deadlock situation arises.

Another problem in PIP is chained blocking. Although PIP helps in bounded blocking duration, it can be substantial if the highest-priority task is chain-blocked. Consider task T3 of lowest-priority, executing inside CS, locking CS1. After some time T2, being of higher-priority than T3, appears and pre-empts it. It executes by locking CS2. After this, T1 being the highest-priority task, appears and pre-empts T2. It wishes to execute CS1 and CS2 sequentially. But it cannot as it is blocked for the duration of two critical sections. This results in chained blocking.

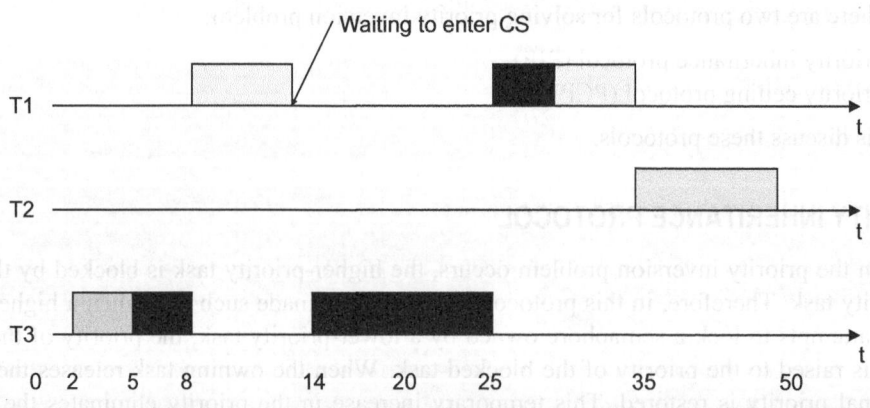

Fig. 20.7 Priority inheritance protocol

20.7 PRIORITY CEILING PROTOCOL

The idea behind PCP is to prevent deadlocks and chained blocking. PCP assigns to each sema-phore, a priority ceiling, which is equal to the highest-priority task that may use this semaphore. According to this protocol, it allows a task to start a new critical section only if the task's priority is higher than all priority ceilings of all the semaphores locked by other tasks.

Example 20.9

Consider three tasks T1, T2, and T3 in a real-time system. T1 is the highest-priority and T3 is the lowest-priority task. There are three critical sections guarded by three semaphores S1, S2, and S3. The sequencing of tasks is as follows:

T1 = {...., P(S1), ..., V(S1)....}

T2 = {....,P(S2),..., P(S3), ..., V(S3),..., V(S2)...}

T3 = {..., P(S3),..., P(S2),..., V(S2),..., V(S3)...}

Since T2 and T3 access S2 and S3, the priority ceiling of S2 and S3 equals to T2.

At time t0, T3 is initiated, begins execution, and locks S3. At t1, T2 is initiated and thereby pre-empts T3. At time t2, task T2 tries to enter its critical section by executing P(S2). Since T2's priority is not higher than priority ceiling of locked semaphore S3, T2 is blocked. T3 inherits the priority of T2 and executes. At time t3, task T1 is initiated and pre-empts T3. It tries to lock S1. Since priority of T1 is higher than priority ceiling of S3, T1 is able to lock S1. After some time, at t4, T1 has unlocked S1 and completes its execution. At this time, T3 resumes its execution, since T2 has been blocked by T3. T3 continues its execution and locks S2. At t5, task T3 releases S2. At t6, T3 releases S3 and resumes its original priority. After this, T2 is signalled and T2 resumes its execution by pre-empting T3. T2 locks S2 and then locks S3, executes, and unlocks S3, and then S2. At t7, T2 completes its execution and T3 resumes. At t8, T3 completes its execution. The PCP has been shown in Fig. 20.8.

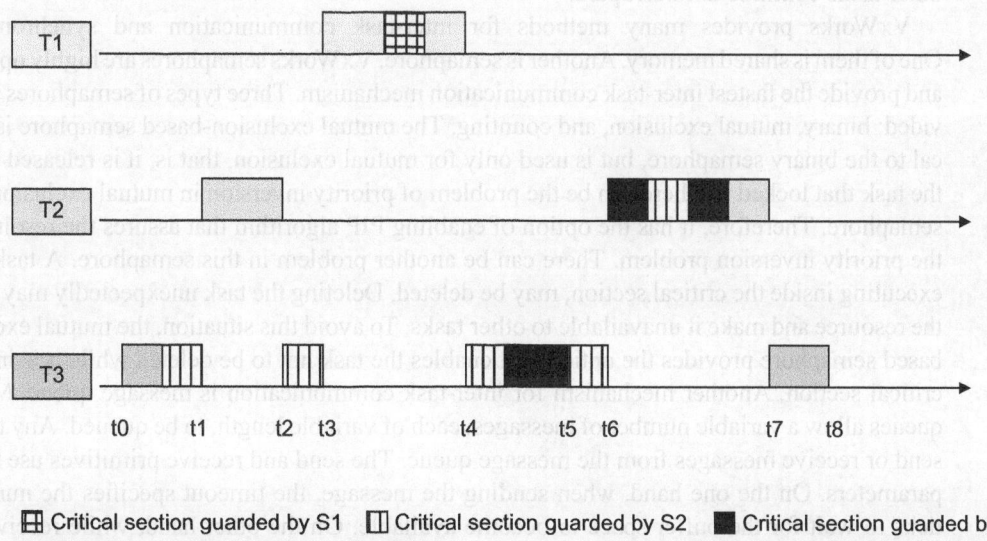

⊞ Critical section guarded by S1   ⊞ Critical section guarded by S2   ■ Critical section guarded by S3

Fig. 20.8 Priority ceiling protocol

20.8 CASE STUDIES

20.8.1 VxWorks

VxWorks is a high-performance RTOS designed by WindRiver Systems. It is supported on almost all popular architectures such as x86, PowerPC, ARM, MIPS, and so on. VxWorks is a flexible OS that may be configured as a minimal kernel having some minimal kernel functionalities, which may be extended by adding some custom components. It has a highly scalable hard real-time kernel, *wind*, which provides the basic multi-tasking environment. The kernel maintains the current state of each task in the system through the TCB. There are four task states. A newly created task enters the system through *suspended* state. After activation, the task enters the *ready* state. The state of the task, when it waits for a resource, is known as *Pend*. The task may also enter the state *delayed* if it waits for a fixed time.

Priority-based pre-emptive scheduling algorithm is the default algorithm to allocate ready tasks to the processor. But there is also a provision with which round robin scheduling can be selected in case there is requirement of the same. In general, round robin scheduling is used for tasks having the same priority. The kernel has 256 priority levels, numbered from 0 to 255. Priority number 0 is considered as the highest and 255 as the lowest. As a task is created in the system, its priority is assigned, based on the design of the system.

The wind scheduler can be explicitly enabled and disabled as per the requirement of a task. A pre-emption lock is used for this purpose. When the scheduler is disabled by a task, no priority-based pre-emption can take place while the task is running. But after some time, if that task blocks, the scheduler selects the next higher priority task to execute. When the blocked task unblocks and begins execution again, the scheduler is disabled again. The pre-emption locks can be used for mutual exclusion, but for the duration of pre-emption locking, that is, disabling the scheduler must be for a short duration.

There is an exception handling package that takes care of exceptions produced in the system due to errors in program code or data. The default exception handler suspends the task that caused the exception and saves the state of the task when exception occurs. The kernel and other tasks continue uninterrupted.

VxWorks provides many methods for inter-task communication and synchronization. One of them is shared memory. Another is semaphore. VxWorks semaphores are highly optimized and provide the fastest inter-task communication mechanism. Three types of semaphores are provided: binary, mutual exclusion, and counting. The mutual exclusion-based semaphore is identical to the binary semaphore, but is used only for mutual exclusion, that is, it is released only by the task that locked it. There can be the problem of priority inversion in mutual exclusion-based semaphore. Therefore, it has the option of enabling PIP algorithm that assures the resolution of the priority inversion problem. There can be another problem in this semaphore. A task, while executing inside the critical section, may be deleted. Deleting the task unexpectedly may corrupt the resource and make it unavailable to other tasks. To avoid this situation, the mutual exclusion-based semaphore provides the option that enables the task not to be deleted while it is inside its critical section. Another mechanism for inter-task communication is message queue. Message queues allow a variable number of messages, each of variable length, to be queued. Any task can send or receive messages from the message queue. The send and receive primitives use timeout parameters. On the one hand, when sending the message, the timeout specifies the number of ticks to wait for the buffer space to become available. On the other hand, while receiving the message, the timeout specifies the number of ticks to wait for the message to become available. There may be some urgent messages. These messages may be added at the head of the queue.

In VxWorks, across the network, inter-task communication is provided through sockets. When a socket is created, the Internet communication protocol (ICP) needs to be specified. VxWorks supports TCP and UDP. VxWorks also supports signal facility, which is more appropriate for error and exception handling as compared to other IPC methods.

Since interrupt handling is a major issue in real-time systems, as the system is informed of external events only through these interrupts, ISRs in VxWorks run in a special context outside of any task's context. Thus, interrupt handling incurs no context switch. VxWorks has a mechanism of watchdog timer. It allows any C function to be connected to a specified time delay. It is maintained as part of system clock ISR.

To have an overview of VxWorks kernel, some important system calls are listed in Table 20.2.

Table 20.2 System calls in VxWorks

S. No.	System call	Description
1	kernelTimeSlice()	Time slice used in controlling round-robin scheduling
2	taskPrioritySet()	Changes the priority of a task
3	taskLock()	Disables scheduler
4	taskUnlock()	Enables scheduler
5	taskSpawn()	Creates a new task
6	taskInit()	Initializes a new task
7	taskActivate()	Activates an initialized task
8	taskPriorityGet()	Returns the priority of a task
9	taskTcb()	Returns the pointer to TCB of task
10	taskSuspend()	Suspends a task
11	taskResume()	Resumes a task
12	semBCreate()	Allocates and initializes a binary semaphore
13	semMCreate()	Allocates and initializes a mutual-exclusion semaphore
14	semCCreate()	Allocates and initializes a counting semaphore
15	msgQCreate()	Allocates and initializes a message queue
16	msgQSend()	Sends a message to a message queue
17	msgQReceive()	Receives a message from a message queue
18	wdCreate()	Allocates and initializes a watchdog timer

20.8.2 QNX

QNX is one of the first commercially successful microkernel-based OSs that has been adopted in medical instruments, cars, nuclear monitoring systems, military communications, and mobile phones. It is supported on almost all popular architectures such as x86, PowerPC, ARM, MIPS, and so on. QNX is a multi-tasking priority-driven real-time OS that provides fast context switching. The microkernel contains only scheduler, IPC, interrupt handling, and timers. The other modules run in the user mode, including a special process called *proc* that performs process creation and memory management functions in conjunction with the microkernel. The priorities assigned to the processes range from 0 to 31. Priority number 0 is considered as the lowest and 31 as the highest priority. The default priority for a new process is inherited from its parent.

QNX provides three types of scheduling, depending on the needs of various applications: FIFO, round robin, and adaptive scheduling. When processes have the same priority, FIFO, and round robin are used. In adaptive scheduling, if a process consumes its time slice, its priority is reduced by 1. This is known as *priority decay*. It is used in environments where potentially computation-intensive background processes are sharing the processor with interactive processes. Adaptive scheduling is used in order to give sufficient processor time to these processes.

QNX uses the message passing method as the fundamental means of implementing IPC. Message passing is used not only to communicate between processes, but also to synchronize them. Three primitives are used for message passing: send, receive, and reply. Suppose process A sends a message to process B, issuing a request. Process B issues a receive message. After completing the processing associated with the message it received from process A, process B issues the reply message. The synchronization between A and B also happens in the sense that as process A issues a send request, it is unable to resume execution, that is, it is blocked. This is known as send-blocked state. Similarly, we have reply-blocked and receive-blocked states.

Another IPC mechanism in QNX is the proxy. Proxy is a non-blocking message that is suitable only for event notification, and the sending process does not wish to interact with the receiving process. In the proxy, the sending process does not expect any reply or acknowledgement from the receiver process. A proxy may be used in the following situations:

- A process wishes to notify another process about the occurrence of an event. But it cannot afford to send a message for this purpose.
- A process wishes to send data to another process, but does not expect any reply or acknowledgement.
- An interrupt handler wishes to inform a process that some data are available for processing.

A proxy can be triggered more than once. It sends a message each time it is triggered. A proxy process can queue up to 65535 messages for delivery.

QNX also supports the signals as a traditional method of asynchronous communication and semaphores for the synchronization. Sometimes, it is necessary to block a signal temporarily without any change in the method of its delivery when it is delivered. QNX provides a set of functions that helps in blocking of signals.

The IPC across the network in QNX is implemented through virtual circuits. The virtual circuits enable a QNX application to communicate with another process on another node in the network, just as if it were another process on the same node. These are paths to transmit messages, proxies, and signals across the network.

QNX has the provision that interrupts are fully enabled almost all the time, making interrupt latency insignificant. However, some critical sections of code need to disable the interrupts temporarily. The maximum disable time defines the worst case interrupt latency. This worst case interrupt latency in QNX is very small. Similarly, scheduling latency is also kept very small in QNX. However, the scheduling latency is larger than interrupt latency.

QNX maintains a system timer for time management. A process can also create timers with the time interval as absolute or relative. The absolute time interval is the time relative to zero hours, zero minutes, zero seconds, 1 January 1970. The relative time interval is the time relative to the current clock value.

To have an overview of VxWorks kernel, some important system calls are listed in Table 20.3.

Table 20.3 System calls in QNX

S. No.	System call	Description
1	Send()	Sends message to a process
2	Receive()	Receives message from a process
3	Reply()	Reply is sent to the sending process
4	Qnx_proxy_attach()	Creates a proxy message
5	Trigger()	Causes the proxy to deliver its predefined message
6	Qnx_vc_attach()	Sets up the virtual circuit between two processes
7	Sem_wait()	The process waits on the semaphore
8	Sem_post()	The process releases the semaphore
9	Getprio()	Determines the priority of a process
10	Setprio()	Sets the priority of a process
11	Getscheduler()	Determines the scheduling method for a process
12	Setscheduler()	Sets the scheduling method for a process
13	Spawn()	Creates a new process
14	Timer_create()	Creates timer
15	Timer_delete()	Removes timer

SUMMARY

RTOSs have been discussed in details keeping in view the nature of real-time systems. The features of an RTOS such as deadlines, predictability, fault tolerance and so on, have been discussed in the chapter. Two important scheduling algorithms used, that is, rate monotonic scheduling and earliest deadline first scheduling algorithms have been discussed. While implementing the mutual exclusion in the real-time systems the problem of priority inversion occurs. The priority inversion problem has been discussed in detail, along with their solution in the form of two protocols: priority inheritance protocol and priority ceiling protocol.

Let us have a quick review of important concepts discussed in this chapter:

- A real-time system is one whose logical correctness depends on both the correctness of the outputs and their timeliness.

- The tasks in the real-time system must meet their defined deadlines for a specified time interval, otherwise the purpose of the system is lost or the system performance is degraded.

- The real-time systems are not general in nature, but are designed for a specific application and are embedded.

- Hard-real-time systems are those in which one or more activities must never miss a deadline or timing constraint, otherwise the system fails.

- Soft-real-time systems are those where missing some deadline is acceptable.

- Real-time systems are *deterministic* in the sense that deadlines and other assertions, involving time, are exact or fixed values.

- The systems, which have hard deadlines and must be met, are called hard-real-time systems.

- The systems, in which missing some deadline is acceptable, are called soft-real-time systems.
- Real-time operating systems (RTOS) must be multi-tasking, pre-emptive, and deadline-driven in nature.
- The RTOS must have sufficient priority levels to support priority-based scheduling.
- RTOS must have minimum interrupt latency, dispatch latency, and context switch time.
- In real-time systems, the repetitive tasks, which occur at regular period of interval, are called periodic tasks.
- The tasks that occur occasionally are known as aperiodic.
- Release time of a task is the time instant at which the task becomes available for execution.
- Absolute deadline of a task is the instant of time by which it must complete its execution.
- Relative deadline is the maximum allowable response time of a task.
- The short term scheduler in RTOS must ensure that all hard real-time tasks are completed by their deadline, and that as many as possible soft-real-time tasks are also completed by their deadlines.
- Rate monotonic (RM) scheduling algorithm schedules the task which has the highest frequency rate of arrival.
- In RM scheduling, the worst case processor utilization for scheduling processes may be as the following:
$$e_1/p_1 + e_2/p_2 + \ldots + e_n/p_n \leq n(2^{1/n} - 1)$$
where, e is the execution time, p is the period of the task, and n is the number of tasks to be scheduled in the system.
- Earliest deadline first (EDF) scheduling algorithm schedules the task whose absolute deadline is earlier, that is, the earlier the deadline, the higher the priority of the task.
- Implementing mutual exclusion through semaphores in real-time systems cause a problem known as priority-inversion, wherein a lower-priority task is able to block the higher-priority task.
- There are two solutions to the priority inversion: priority inheritance protocol and priority ceiling protocol.
- In PIP, a provision is made such that when a higher-priority task attempts to lock a semaphore owned by a lower-priority task, the priority of the owning task is raised to the priority of the blocked task.
- PIP suffers from two problems: deadlock and chained blocking.
- PCP assigns a priority ceiling to each semaphore, which is equal to the highest priority task that may use this semaphore.

MULTIPLE CHOICE QUESTIONS

1. _____ is a constraint of the maximum time limit at which the operation must be complete.
   (a) Period
   (b) Deadline
   (c) Iteration
   (d) None

2. Which of the following is the characteristic of a real-time system?
   (a) Multi-tasking
   (b) Deadline-driven
   (c) Priority-driven
   (d) All of the above

3. The interrupt latency and dispatch latency in real-time system must be
   (a) Maximum
   (b) Minimum
   (c) No effect
   (d) None

4. The context switch time in a real-time system must be
   (a) Maximum
   (b) Minimum
   (c) No effect
   (d) None

5. _____ are also real-time tasks, which are activated irregularly like aperiodic tasks, but with some known bounded rate.
   (a) Periodic
   (b) Aperiodic
   (c) Sporadic
   (d) None

6. In a simple process-control application, _____ scheduling is appropriate.
   (a) Static
   (b) Dynamic
   (c) Online
   (d) Offline

7. In _____ scheduling, there is complete knowledge of tasks set, but new arrivals are not known.
   (a) Static
   (b) Dynamic
   (c) Online
   (d) Offline

8. In _____ scheduling, the tasks are scheduled as they arrive in the system.
   (a) Static
   (b) Dynamic
   (c) Online
   (d) Offline

9. RM is _____ scheduling algorithm.
   (a) Static
   (b) Dynamic
   (c) Online
   (d) Offline

10. EDF is ____ scheduling algorithm.
    (a) Static   (c) Online
    (b) Dynamic   (d) Offline

11. In RM, the priority of a task is inversely proportional to its ____.
    (a) Period   (c) Iteration
    (b) Deadline   (d) None

REVIEW QUESTIONS

1. List out the characteristics of a real-time system?

2. Which kind of applications are applicable for a real-time system?

3. Explain the structure of a real-time system.

4. What is an RTOS? Explain its characteristics.

5. Differentiate between periodic, aperiodic, and sporadic tasks.

6. Differentiate between
    (a) Absolute and relative deadlines.
    (b) Static and dynamic scheduling
    (c) Online and offline scheduling

    (d) Hard- and soft-real-time system

7. Explain RM scheduling algorithm.

8. What is the necessary and sufficient condition for schedulability in RM scheduling?

9. Explain EDF scheduling algorithm.

10. What is priority inversion?

11. Explain PIP. What are the problems in its implementation?

12. Explain PCP. How does it remove the problems of PIP.

13. Explain the major features of VxWorks.

14. Explain the major features of QNX.

BRAIN-TEASERS

1. Why is it important to minimize the context switch time in real-time scheduling?

2. Can we adopt non-pre-emptive scheduling in real-time systems?

3. Can there be a case that higher-priority tasks cause starvation on lower -priority tasks in real-time systems? What is the remedy for it?

4. Consider a real-time system, in which there are three tasks, with their period and execution times as the following:

Task	Execution time e	Period p
T1	25	70
T2	20	50
T3	10	100

Check whether the tasks are RM schedulable. If yes, explain the RM scheduling of the tasks and show the tasks on timing diagram also.

5. Consider the following set of tasks in a real-time system:

Tasks	Release time	Execution time	Absolute deadline
T1	0	5	30
T2	3	9	20
T3	4	8	30
T4	5	10	20

Perform EDF scheduling on this task set.

6. Linux has a real-time version known as RTLinux. Survey the features of this RTOS on the basis of the following points:
    (a) Type of RTOS (Hard or Soft)
    (b) Structure (layered/microkernel)
    (c) Scheduling type
    (d) Synchronization type

21 Mobile Operating Systems

21.1 INTRODUCTION

We are living in a world of mobile devices such as smartphones, laptops, and tablets. These mobile devices are different as compared to general desktop systems. These are designed and run in very restricted environment/resources. Therefore, the OSs, for these devices cannot be the same as those for desktop systems. The mobile OSs have been designed for each category of mobile devices. This chapter explores the types and characteristics of mobile devices and then discusses the mobile OSs. Since mobile OSs pose many new challenges such as power management, as power is a critical issue in mobile devices, all such issues have been discussed in detail. Finally, the most popular mobile OS today, that is, Android has been discussed in detail.

21.2 INTRODUCTION TO MOBILE DEVICES

Mobile devices are multifunctional devices serving both consumer and business use. In consumer electronics market, these devices have a wide range of products today. Furthermore, these devices have emerged as an extension to the conventional computer as most of the activities we do on a computer are possible now on these mobile devices. While we work conveniently on these mobile devices irrespective of place or time, the same can be synchronized with our work on the PC itself. For example, we use smartphones and tablets for e-mail, instant messaging, web browsing, chatting, working on official documents, and lots more. In general, a mobile device consists of the following hardware:

- Microprocessor
- Memory (volatile and non-volatile)
- Radiofrequency communication capability
- Input-output units such as keypad, LCD screen
- Power source, i.e., battery

Let us discuss some mobile devices as follows:

21.2.1 Personal Digital Assistant

Personal digital assistants (PDAs) are electronic organizers that are also able to share information with our computer. A typical PDA manages well our daily-life activities such as contact list and task planner. These are also known as hand-held or palm-top devices. Today, PDAs with the advancement of technology are equipped with more advanced features. For example, they are able to connect to the Internet,

Learning Objectives

After reading this chapter, you should be able to get acquainted with:

- Types of mobile devices
- Characteristics of mobile devices
- Characteristics of mobile OSs
- Design issues of mobile OSs
- Design features of Android OS

support multimedia software applications, and so on. Thus, a typical PDA functions as a cellular phone, web browser, personal information organizer, and so on.

21.2.2 Smartphones

The conventional cellular phone was not equipped with all modern features and it was in use as a phone only. With the advancement of technology, the concept of smartphones emerged with integration of the PDA features on the mobile phone. Later on, new features kept on adding in smartphones. Some features are ability to access digital media, digital cameras, pocket video games, GPS navigation, high resolution touch screens, Internet access, and so on.

21.2.3 Tablet PC

Tablet PC is a mobile computer with all its components placed in a single unit. Tablets do not use the conventional input device such as mouse or keyboard. Primarily, these devices are operated with touch screens and are equipped with camera, microphone, buttons to control basic features like volume, ports to communicate, and so on. The size of tablets is in general larger than a PDA or smartphone. For a longer battery life, they use ARM processor.

21.3 CHARACTERISTICS OF MOBILE DEVICES

Mobile devices are different as compared to other computing devices. These devices require very limited hardware configuration as these are portable. Some of their characteristics are as follows:

Limited Processing Power

The processing speed is in accordance with the power of battery. The processors used are of low processing power normally in the range of 50 MHz to 100 MHz. If high-power processors are used, then they need high-power batteries and high-power batteries cannot be adopted in mobile devices due to limitation of space.

Small Screen Size

The mobile devices have a very limited screen area due to limited space available on the device.

Limited Keypad

The input keys on the keypad available are also designed to utilize the space available. All the keys present on normal keyboard are not available on the mobile devices.

Limited Memory

There are two types of memories in mobile devices as well: read only memory (ROM) and random access memory (RAM). ROM is for the OS and pre-installed programs and RAM is for user data. Due to processing power and space limitations, RAM is of low capacity. Mobile devices use flash memory as non-volatile memory instead of hard disk.

Limited Battery Capacity

The mobile devices are based on secondary batteries connected to them. These batteries are of low power as they cannot be of high power due to space limitations.

The battery power cannot be increased beyond a limit as it demands more space in the mobile device. Consequently, the processing speed is limited due to limited power of battery.

Therefore, power management for the mobile devices is a big challenge. In case of any power loss, the data safety must also be provided. Some mobile devices demand that the device shoul always be on. For example, mobile phone is always on and therefore must be functional forever. Thus, mobile phone functionality is always at the highest priority and therefore mobile devices have

- constrained physical characteristics;
- less battery life; and
- limited computing and communication capabilities.

21.4 MOBILE OS

Since the mobile devices are different as compared to conventional desktop systems, they need different OSs too. These are known as *mobile OSs*. Depending on the capabilities of the mobile devices and what they support, mobile OSs may also differ. For example, the mobile OS for a PDA is different from that of a smartphone. Since in mobile devices some tasks are real-time driven , that is, must be handled within the deadline, a mobile OS utilizes a real-time operating for embedded systems including drivers for peripheral devices, communication software, and libraries shared between applications. The application software is placed on top of these mobile OSs. The mobile OS is designed keeping in view the physical and other limitations of the mobile devices. Moreover, the features of mobile devices and their types keep on changing. Therefore, an efficient OS is needed to support all these existing and upcoming new features. Let us discuss some design issues for a mobile OS.

21.4.1 Power Management

Since a mobile device gets operating power through a battery only, it is important that limited battery power be utilized efficiently. It is helpful in lower heat dissipation also, which consequently reduces the effect on environment. However, due to advancement of technology, the modern mobile devices consume more battery power as compared to earlier generations. For example, smartphones are being used for phone calls, accessing Internet, making video recording, writing e-mails, and much more of what the user does on the desktop. Therefore, power management has never been an important issue to give users more battery life. On the traditional desktop computers, power management is handled within the BIOS only. However, the BIOS-based power management is dependent on static hardware configurations and needs to be ported on specific platforms that are being supported. Moreover, it was difficult to update the firmware once the BIOS is shipped in a product. This results in minimal support for power management.

To have better power-management features, BIOS must take the cooperation of OS. In this direction, an application programming interface (API) known as *advanced power management (APM)* was developed by Intel and Microsoft. An APM has the APIs that allow the OS to make policy decisions and make calls into the BIOS to initiate power-management controls. However, later on, it was realized that APM has added complexity and only BIOS controls power management. Microsoft support for APM in Windows Vista was therefore dropped. Another abstract interface between the OS and the hardware to move the power-management controls into OS was designed by HP, Intel, Microsoft, Phoenix, and Toshiba. This interface is known as *advanced configuration and power interface (ACPI)*. The idea is to gather power-management information from users, applications, and the hardware together into the OS that will enable better power management due to the following reasons:

- Power management function is not restricted to the hardware and BIOS level but is available on every machine on which the OS is installed.
- The BIOS does not retain much information as the OS manages it.
- The hardware vendors do not provide any power-saving mechanisms. Integrating power management in the OS itself will help in reducing the conflicts between hardware and firmware, thereby increasing the reliability.

Thus, ACPI was developed to have an OS-directed device configuration and power management (OSPM). Thus, the goal to have an OSPM through ACPI stresses on the concept that systems should conserve energy in an optimized way. Although ACPI has been designed for every class of computers, this specification is much suitable for mobile devices where optimization of power has become a necessary requirement. This is the reason that mobile OSs must support ACPI.

System Power Management

The OS must collect the information from devices so that the device that is not being used can be turned off. The OS may collect the information from application and user settings so that the system as a whole may be put into a low-power state. For system-power management, the following power states may be implemented:

Working

In this state, the device is in running state. If devices and processor are not in use, they are put into low-power state. However, these devices can be turned on depending on the type and its use of the device.

Sleeping

When the device is not in use or the user has pressed power button, the OS must put the device in the sleeping state. The nature of a sleeping state may differ on how an event can change the state to working and how much time it takes.

Device Power Management

To manage the power of all the devices, the OS may use standard methods specified in ACPI to send commands to the devices. The standard methods specify the following:

- The operations that can be used to manage power of devices
- The power states the devices may put into

The OS tracks the information about the state of all the devices on the bus. After having the current device requirements on that bus, it puts the bus in a particular power state accordingly. If all the devices do not require power presently, the OS sends a command to bus control chip to remove power from the bus.

Processor Power Management

The power can also be saved if the processor power is managed. When the OS enters in its idle state, it first determines how much time will be spent in idle loop with the help of ACPI power-management timer. After determining the idle time, the OS puts the processor in low-power state, thereby saving the power.

21.4.2 Battery Management

The OS collects the information about the state of the batteries in the mobile device and, through the user interface, notifies/warns the user about the low-power state of the device. In case of battery discharge, the OS must perform an emergency shutdown. However, in this shutdown, the damage to the mobile device integrity must be minimized.

21.4.3 Thermal Management

As the mobile devices operate with batteries, heat dissipation is also an issue. Therefore, thermal management is also mentioned in the ACPI where OS may reduce the power consumption of devices at the cost of performance to reduce the temperature of the mobile device.

21.4.4 Memory Management

The mobile OS should consume very less space in the memory, that is, it should have a small footprint of about 100KB along with plug-in modules if any. However, to avoid RAM space, the kernel code, application, and libraries should be directly executed in ROM area instead of copying into the RAM area. This is known as *execute-in-place mechanism*. However, this increases the ROM space and the access in ROM is slower as compared to RAM. Thus, to reduce the memory space, the kernel and libraries should be customized to utilize the memory space. The microkernel structure of mobile OS may also help in reducing the memory.

The OS should be able to manage memory automatically. For example, when memory is low at one instant of time, it must make space for the application or process by killing a process that is inactive for a long time.

The application running on the mobile devices must free the unused objects in it and, thereby, memory used by them. If unused objects are not freed, the memory footprint grows and the performance degrades. The OS must handle all allocation and de-allocation of memory properly to avoid the memory leakage. Memory leakage is a state when there is possibility that applications may not return the memory after being allocated and occupy unnecessary memory. There may be two cases: a running application continuously being allocated new memory and an application after being closed still occupying the memory.

Memory leakage is a serious issue in mobile devices as it can affect the performance of a mobile device. There may be several reasons for memory leakage in mobile devices. The OS with the help of some utility must be able to monitor the memory leaks. For example, a data structure named *live bytes* can show memory currently being used by active applications. If this data structure continues to grow as the user uses application, there is a memory leakage.

The OS may have a provision that allows multiple processes to run where the same code chunk is used for each of the processes. This reduces RAM usage.

21.4.5 Shortening Boot-up Time

The boot-up time in mobile devices must be managed to be short such that initializing time for the devices is short. Some of the following solutions will help in reducing the boot-up time:

- Small footprint as discussed in memory management helps in shortening the boot-up time.
- If initialization of device drivers can be deferred for some time, the boot-up time is reduced.
- The structure of OS should be microkernel.

21.4.6 Scheduling

Since the mobile devices may need real-time response, the OS should have pre-emptive scheduling mechanism. These devices are required to meet specific time deadlines for the tasks to occur. However, pre-emptive task scheduling requires interrupting the low-priority tasks when high-priority tasks appear. However, pre-emption may take long time. When an external interrupt arrives, the interrupt handler executes in the corresponding device driver in the kernel and sends the data to the corresponding user process. Finally, the process is pre-empted. This increases interrupt latency and, thereby, reduces system responsiveness. Similarly, the scheduling and dispatching may take a long time. Thus, interrupt latency and dispatch latency must be minimized in mobile OSs. For mobile device, the desired interrupt latency is in several microseconds.

The reason for increased interrupt latency is that in an interrupt processing, there is a substantial amount of work. Some part of this work is done in the context of interrupt and the rest is passed to the kernel context for further processing. The interrupt handler runs in *interrupt context*. In interrupt context, some or all interrupts are disabled during this time, thereby increasing the latency. Therefore, it is desirable to minimize the work done in the interrupt context and pushing the rest in kernel context. Therefore, in interrupt processing, there are two parts: *top-half* and *bottom-half*. Device data to a device-specific buffer are saved in the top-half that exits after scheduling its bottom half. During the execution of the bottom-half, all interrupts are enabled. Therefore, the bottom-half is the part of the ISR that must be executed at a safer time and can be executed with a delay. This provision enables the top-half to start servicing another interrupt while the bottom half is still working.

One solution to reducing the interrupt latency is to use deferrable functions. The deferrable functions are the mechanisms through which we delay the execution of functions that are not time critical (e.g., awaken the process, start servicing another I/O request, etc.) in interrupt handlers. Taking the example of a network interface, when a new packet arrives, there is an interrupt. The interrupt handler, which is in the top-half, retrieves the data and pushes it up in the hierarchy of protocol layer. However, the actual processing of the packet in bottom half may be done with a delay.

In Linux kernel, many deferrable functions have been used. Some of them are tasklets, Softirqs, taskqueue, and work queue. Here, we discuss tasklets. Tasklets are the implementation of the bottom-half adopted in Linux kernel used by the device drivers in kernel to schedule a function some time in future. Tasklets are thus special functions that may be scheduled in interrupt context to run at a system-determined safe time. An interrupt handler in interrupt context is secure that a tasklet will not start executing until the interrupt handler has finished. However, during the execution of a tasklet, another interrupt can be serviced. The tasklets may either be enabled or disabled. For example, if a device driver is handling an exceptional situation and requires that a tasklet not execute during this handling, then the tasklets may be disabled.

The scheduler on its invocation incurs overhead and provides different execution time depending on the input such as number of processes in the system. It would be a kernel scheduling design point that if we are able to design a scheduler that is not dependent on its input but provides a constant time of execution. Therefore, the scheduler must be a completely fair scheduler that schedules the processes within a constant amount of time irrespective of the number of the processes in the system.

All these functions required in the kernel are related to the real-time performance of the mobile devices. The real-time performance can be gained with the 2-CPU solution. This solution consists of two processors. On one processor, the normal OS runs for the application and, on other real-time OS, runs for the real-time tasks.

Thermal management in mobile devices may be combined with a scheduler. Through temperature sampling, hot processes may be identified in the system based on past power dissipation history. The idea is to provide reduced time quantum to a process due to which temperature rises above a certain threshold. Furthermore, the processes that are likely to generate more heat will be penalized more in terms of their reduced quantum time. For this purpose, the scheduler needs to be executed in two modes. In the normal mode, the scheduler runs as usual and the process that gets scheduled is allocated a fixed time quantum. In the second mode, the scheduler allocates varying time quanta based on the heat dissipation by the processes.

21.4.7 File System

On mobile devices, there may be inconsistencies in the file system due to the following reasons:

- The power supply of battery may stop suddenly in a very short time
- The user may remove the battery
- The battery is dead

This is the reason that flash file systems are used in mobile devices. The mobile devices use flash memory as a persistent memory that may be recorded and erased. Flash memory devices offer a fast-read access. There are two types of flash memories: NAND-based and NOR-based. NOR-based flash memories provide low-density, fast-read, and slow-write operations. On the other hand, NAND-based flash memories provide low-cost, high-density, fast-write, and slow-read operations. Flash memory device is divided into one or more sections of memory known as *partitions*. This multi-partition architecture has the advantage that system processor may read from one partition while writing or erasing in another partition. The partitions are further divided into blocks. When the blocks are of same size, it is known as *symmetrically blocked architecture*; otherwise, it is *asymmetrically blocked architecture*. Flash memory devices allow programming values from '1' to '0' as the initial value is '1'. However, we cannot program from value '0' to '1'. It means that when any data is to be edited, it must be written to a new location in flash memory and the old data is invalidated. Consequently, the invalidated data is reclaimed as a background process.

The data recorded in flash memory must be in a structured way such that it is easy to organize, search, and retrieve the desired data. However, there must be flash file systems designed to cater to the needs of flash memory as traditional file systems cannot be applied for the same. Therefore, OSs must support these file systems. The log-based file systems are suitable for flash memory devices.

A flash file system is required for the following reasons:

- The traditional file systems have been designed with the aim to reduce the seek time on disk but there is no such seek time on the flash memory.
- Repeated over-writing of a single block tends to wear out the flash memory device, which means that each block on the flash memory has a limited number of erase–write cycles. Therefore, the files systems are required that are designed to spread out writes and erases evenly on the flash memory to maintain a wear level of each block.
- Editing to a data is done by writing it to a new location in the memory and the old data is invalidated. However, this invalid data must be cleaned up at regular intervals. This cleaning up of invalid data is known as *reclaim* or *garbage collection*. After completion of reclaim process, the old block is erased to make it available as a new spare block. The reclaim process is in general a low-priority background process. However, if there is a situation when the file system does not have free space on the memory, it will call a state of emergency and convert the reclaim process into a high-priority foreground process.
- Many flash devices are with multi-partition each of which is capable of performing read and write operations independent of each other.

- More than one flash memory devices may be stacked together to have a larger memory configuration required for an application such that stacked flash memories appear as a contiguous memory. In this case, the flash file system must be able to map the contiguous memory.
- Flash memory devices can be used to store both code and data. In general, when we want to execute the code, it is first stored into RAM and then executed. However, in flash devices, code can be directly executed from it without copying the code into RAM. The flash file system must support writing code to flash in a contiguous and sequential address space. The file system may also support code compression to reduce the amount of space allocated for code on a flash device.
- On the flash devices, there may be power loss during program and erase as well. If there is power loss during read operation, the read operation does not happen. However, the file system must be able to recover during write and erase operation if power loss happens. During write operation, it needs to return to a last good state of the file system. The data and file-system data structures must not be corrupted. Similarly, during erase operations, there must be a recovery mechanism so that the erase is completed. Furthermore, there may be power loss while recovering from the first power loss. This is known as *double power loss*. The file system must be able to recover from single as well as double power loss.
- There may be bad blocks that are unusable. These bad blocks may be shipped with the device and blocks may become bad during the operation. The flash file system must be able to recognize and account for both types of bad blocks. Moreover, the incomplete operation in the second type of bad blocks must be completed in some other good blocks. The file system should also track the number of bad blocks such that they do not exceed the maximum number.

Since the flash file system is used in most of the mobile devices, the performance of the device must not be compromised. The response time is one measure of performance on these devices. The flash file system must be optimized to ensure acceptable performance. The devices such as smartphones may contain a variety of files from system files to large multimedia files. The file system should support all these file types and operations on them. The factors that may affect the performance are read–write speed, reclaim, initialization time, file operations such as create, open–close, and delete. The file system should adopt

- the memory management techniques that minimize the fragmentation problem,
- caching techniques, and
- intelligent reclaim techniques.

21.4.8 Security

Since mobile devices incorporate all the features of a computer system, the challenges in these devices are also becoming same as of traditional OSs. One of the major issues is security. These devices can also be infected with worms, Trojan horses, or other viruses. They in turn may compromise user's security and privacy. Due to advancements in mobile-network technologies, malicious contents can easily be spread out. This may cause mobile OS to compromise, thereby enabling malicious applications to access other devices, intercept messages, or gain location information. This is another instance that these security breaches may compromise the user's privacy.

The attacker may have the following goals on mobile devices:

- Since the mobile devices today are the rich source of personal information, the attackers target the confidentiality and integrity of stored information. This enables the attacker to read

SMS and MMS, read and forward e-mails, access the personal organizer and calendar, and so on. Furthermore, if the user is able to tap into a mobile phone's basic hardware features, additional data from the surroundings can be collected. For example, by utilizing the voice recording hardware or camera, the attacker can misuse the device as a listening device or take photos or videos. Furthermore, the user's privacy can be compromised by exploiting the location information using GPS.

- Since the mobile devices are equipped with high-frequency processor and high-capacity memory, the attackers also exploit the raw computing power along with the broadband network access. The high-speed Internet links are also used to deploy the botnets.
- The attacker sometimes aims at performing harmful malicious actions on the mobile devices. The actions may result in loss of data, draining the device battery, generating network congestion, disabling the device completely, and so on.

Thus, the mobile devices, especially smartphones are prone to attacks any time. The mobile OS therefore must provide the security mechanisms to address the security issues.

21.5 ANDROID OS

Android is a software stack including mobile OS that has been primarily designed for touch-screen-based mobile devices. It was originally developed by Android Inc. and was later sold to Google in 2005. Android consists of the following components (see Fig. 21.1):

1. **Linux kernel**: It is as an underlying OS interface. It acts as an abstraction hardware layer for Android. The Linux kernel provides memory management, networking, and other basic OS facilities.
2. **Native libraries**: These are hardware-specific shared libraries developed in C/C++ language and are pre-installed on the device by vendor.
3. **Android runtime**: It includes Dalvik Virtual Machine (DVM) code (that runs the Java programmed applications) and core Java libraries.
4. **Application framework**: It consists of classes used in writing Android-based applications.
5. **Android applications**: It is the highest level layer that provides the end-user applications including the applications shipped with Android and the applications that can be downloaded by the user. These applications run on DVM just like Java Virtual Machine (JVM). DVM is tailor-made according to the requirements of mobile devices. Moreover, it runs on a relatively smaller RAM and slower processor.

Our concern here is to discuss only the OS part of Android. Android OS is a low-cost, customizable, and light-weight OS that not only has become the world's best environment for smartphones but also has been integrated in microwaves, digital cameras, refrigerators, smart watches, media players, robots, set-top box, and so on. The first version of Android appeared in 2008 and has gone through several versions till now (see Table 21.1).

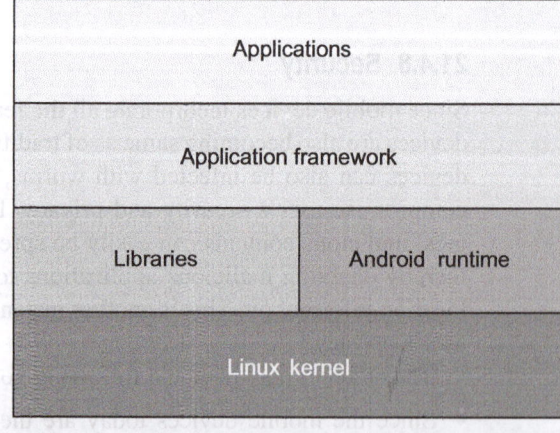

Fig. 21.1 Android architecture

Table 21.1   Android versions

S. No.	Android version
1	Android 1.0
2	Android 1.1
3	Android 1.5 Cupcake
4	Android 1.6 Donut
5	Android 2.0 Éclair
6	Android 2.0.1 Éclair
7	Android 2.1 Éclair
8	Android 2.2–2.2.3 Froyo
9	Android 2.3–2.3.2 Gingerbread
10	Android 2.3.3–2.3.7 Gingerbread
11	Android 3.0 Honeycomb
12	Android 3.1 Honeycomb
13	Android 3.2 Honeycomb
14	Android 4.0–4.0.2 Ice Cream Sandwich
15	Android 4.0.3–4.0.4 Ice Cream Sandwich
16	Android 4.1 Jelly Bean
17	Android 4.2 Jelly Bean
18	Android 4.3 Jelly Bean
19	Android 4.4 KitKat

The main hardware platform on which Android runs is the ARM architecture. It is based on Linux kernel version 3.x. However, Android Linux kernel has been modified to include some enhancements in the form of additional drivers supported in Android platform. Some of these enhancements are the following:

- Binder: It provides the IPC facilities in the system.
- Power-management driver: It facilitates the power-management issues.
- Low-memory killer: It frees up memory by killing off the inactive processes.
- Logger: It is an extended kernel-logging facility.
- Android alarm: It provides timers used to wake the sleeping devices.

Let us discuss various issues related to Android OS.

21.5.1 Power Management

The Android power management has been designed on top of Linux power management that uses APM and ACPI. However, Linux power management is not directly suitable for mobile devices. Therefore, some modifications have been done to cater to the needs of mobile devices in Android power management that adopts a more aggressive policy to manage and save power. The philosophy in power management is that a processor should not consume any power if applications or services in fact require no power. The Android power management has been designed as a wrapper to Linux power management implementing a light-weight

ACPI driver. Android uses the concept of *wakelocks* and timeout mechanism to switch the state of system power to decrease the power consumption. Through the wakelocks, Android is able to dynamically power down while the system is still running. Any application or service requests processor resources with wakelocks through Android application framework. By default, Android puts the system into a sleep or suspend mode as soon as possible. If there is no active wakelock, that is, no application is running, then processor will be turned off. The running application needs to gain the wakelock with a timeout so that within that time period the application is active. Furthermore, there is a concept of partial wakelocks. The types of wakelocks available are as follows:

- **partial wakelock**
  In this case, the processor is running but the screen and keyboard are turned off.
- **screen dim wakelock**
  In this case, the screen is on but the keyboard back light is turned off and the screen back light is made dim.
- **screen bright wakelock**
  In this case, the screen is on with full brightness but the keyboard back light is turned off.
- **full wakelock**
  In this case, the full device including screen and keyboard with backlight is on.

A finite state machine of the power management in Android can be designed (see Fig. 21.2) that works as follows:

- When a user application is active (E1) or touch screen/keyboard is pressed (E2), it acquires full wakelock and the machine is in the state AWAKE.
- If timeout occurs for an activity or the power key of the device is pressed (E3), the machine is in the NOTIFICATION state. Moreover, if there are any partial wakelocks (E4), the machine will be in this state only.
- When all partial wakelocks are released (E5), the machine will be in the SLEEP state.
- When the resources are awake, the machine will transit to AWAKE (E6).

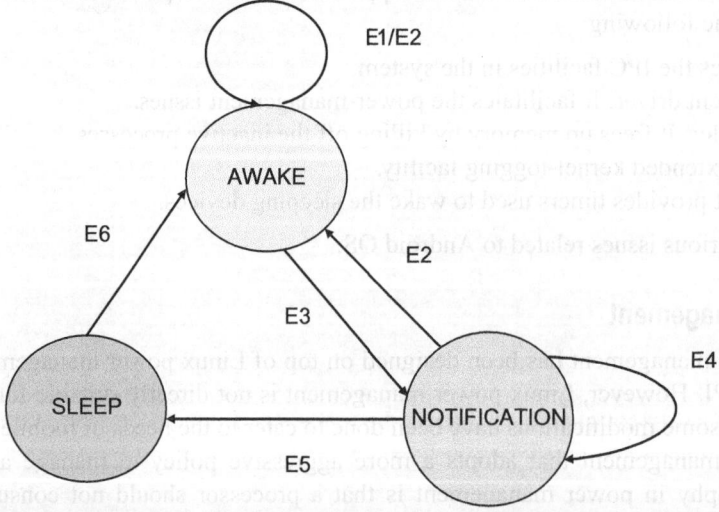

Fig. 21.2 Android power management

21.5.2 Memory Management

The inactive applications are suspended in memory automatically in Android. However, the suspended application is still considered open but not consuming any resources, battery life, processing power, and so on. If we close the application, it needs to be re-opened from scratch consuming the time in closing and re-opening the application again and again. Thus, the suspended applications in the background increase the responsiveness of the applications. This management reduces the memory requirements also utilizing the other resources.

In case of low memory, the system needs to accommodate the processes. Android selects the victim applications and starts killing them according to the priority provided to them. The process with lowest priority is killed first. In Android, there are various types of processes maintained and given priority as follows:

- **Foreground/Active processes**
  These are the processes that interact with the user and are responsible to maintain responsiveness to the user. Only few processes at a given time exist in the system but are of the highest priority and will be killed only if there is no other low-priority process to be killed.
- **Visible processes**
  These are not the foreground processes, that is, the user is not interacting but these processes host the activities that are visible to the user. Visible processes are also important and, therefore, get the next to the foreground processes in priority.
- **Service processes**
  These are the processes that are not responsible directly to the user but support services that have been started by the user and should continue without a visible interface, for example, playing a song in the background, downloading data on the network, and so on.
- **Background processes**
  These are the processes that are neither interacting with the user nor visible and do not support any service. There are a number of background processes in the system that get the lower priority as compared to all other processes.
- **Empty processes**
  These are the processes that do not have any active application component but are used for caching purposes.

The empty processes are first victims selected for killing and then the background processes. In general, the victim applications may be inactive applications that have not been active for a long time. However, the user is unaware of this memory management and is performed automatically.

The priority assigned to a process depends on the components currently active in it. If a process has more than one component, then the process will have the highest priority as of the component. For example, if a process has two components: visible and background, then the process is assigned the priority as of visible process.

For utilizing the small capacity of RAM, Android uses some new ways of allocating memory to the kernel. The two methods are anonymous/Android shared memory (ASHMEM) and physical memory (PMEM) described as follows:

ASHMEM: It is a shared-memory block that can be shared across multiple processes.

PMEM: It provides physically contiguous memory blocks to drivers and libraries.

21.5.3 Scheduling

Every application runs as a single process. The pre-emptive priority-based scheduling is performed by Linux. It uses $O(1)$ scheduling algorithm according to which every scheduling is guaranteed to execute within a certain constant time irrespective of the number of tasks in the system. The Linux kernel 2.6.8.1 has the scheduler that consists of two data structures: run queues and priority arrays. These two data structures help in achieving $O(1)$ time. The time for finding a process to execute does not depend on the number of processes but on the number of priorities and number of priorities is fixed. This is the reason that scheduling has constant execution time. The run queue is a list of runnable processes on a given processor. It also contains the processor-scheduling information. The run queue maintains two priority arrays: active and expired array of processes. Each priority array references all processes with the given priority. The active array contains the processes associated with the run queue with remaining time slices. When a process on the active array uses all of its time slices, its time slice is re-calculated and is moved to the expired array. When each process has its time slice as zero, the pointers for the active and expired arrays are swapped, thereby making the expired priority list the active one. There are three classes of scheduling:

1. First-in-first-out (FIFO) for real-time tasks
2. Round robin for real-time tasks
3. Time-sharing for all non-real-time tasks

There are 140 priority levels and a separate run queue is maintained at each priority level. Priority levels 0 to 99 are fixed for real-time processes with static priority and priorities 100 to 139 are for normal processes with dynamic priority. The priorities of normal processes are adjusted based on time run and priority class. The priority class for instance may be that I/O-bound processes get higher priority and CPU-bound processes get lower priority. Each process here is having an initial priority known as nice value.

21.5.4 Inter-process Communication

Android supports all traditional IPC mechanisms provided by the Linux kernel: mechanisms such as pipes, shared memory, message queues, and signals that are not used by OS libraries and platform APIs to perform IPC. Therefore, as discussed in the Android architecture, binder is the component that facilitates the IPC in Android OS. Its implementation runs under Linux and extends the existing IPC mechanisms. Binders provide a low overhead RPC utility for synchronous communication among processes.

Binders can be used in two ways: direct and indirect. In direct use of binder, a client is able to communicate with a server. When a successful connection is established between a client and a server, the client receives a proxy object to the server. The binder uses this object for object mapping and referencing to know which object belongs to what process. In this way, the binder sends notifications to the clients to inform about the presence of server or service. Furthermore, the binder wakes up sleeping client or server if they are sleeping during any request, acknowledgement, or notifications.

In indirect use of a binder, it becomes a security token. As a security token, it will not allow certain services to certain clients.

21.5.5 File Management

There are three parts of file system in Android:

1. System partition: It contains the entire Android OS including the pre-installed applications, system libraries, and so on.

2. SD card: This is the area where files can be written and read.
3. User data partition: This is the area used to store user data, both pre-installed and down-loaded.

21.5.6 Security

Since Android has rich application-development framework, it is prone to security issues, such as applications stealing private data and malicious disruption of an application or even the OS by another application. Therefore, to handle the security issues, Android provides a permission-based security model. This model isolates the applications in a sandbox environment. This environment restricts each application to execute in its own environment and does not allow an application to affect or modify other applications. Android utilizes Linux standard access-control mechanisms for this purpose. Each application is assigned a unique ID. One application can access files of other applications as per the permissions granted to an application. However, it will be useful from the application viewpoint to access some critical resources such as network services and camera. In this case, the Android provides flexibility in the form of shared user ID and permissions. With shared user ID, applications can share data and components of other applications. However, for shared user ID, the two applications must sign a digital certificate with the same private key. Furthermore, Android provides four types of permissions described as follows:

- **Normal permissions**: These are isolated application-level permissions. Since these permissions do not affect any user's privacy or application, there is no security risk.
- **Dangerous permissions**: These permissions give access to private data and some critical systems. Since these permissions have a high security risk, permissions must be confirmed.
- **Signature permissions**: These permissions are granted when two applications need to share data and other components by signing same digital certificate. This is refinement of shared user ID. Care must be taken when giving these permissions.
- **Signature-or-system permissions**: Signature permissions when extended by allowing to access Android system applications become signature-or-system permissions. Care must be taken when giving these permissions.

SUMMARY

Mobile OS characteristics to cater to the needs of mobile devices have been explained in the chapter. The mobile OSs have very different design issues as compared to general OSs. The major issues such as power management, battery management, thermal management, and flash file system have been discussed in detail. After this, the Android OS has been discussed in the light of issues of mobile OSs.

Let us have a quick review of important concepts discussed in this chapter:

- The mobile devices are different as compared to other computing devices. These devices require very limited hardware configuration as these are portable.
- Since the mobile devices are different as compared to conventional desktop systems, they need different OSs known as *mobile OSs*.

- Since a mobile device gets operating power through a battery only, it is important that limited battery power be utilized efficiently.
- ACPI was developed to have an OSPM. The goal to have an OSPM through ACPI stresses on the concept that systems should conserve energy in an optimized way.
- The OS must collect the information from devices so that the device that is not being used can be turned off.
- The OS tracks the information about the state of all devices on the bus. Based on the current device requirements on that bus, it puts the bus in a power state accordingly.
- When the OS enters its idle state, it first determines how much time will be spent in idle loop with the help of ACPI power-management timer. After determining the idle time, the OS puts the processor in low-power state,

thereby saving the power.

- The OS collects the information about the state of the batteries in the mobile device and, through the user interface, notifies the user about any warning about the low-power state of the device.
- The mobile OS should consume very less space in memory, that is, it should have a small footprint.
- Memory leakage is a serious issue in mobile devices as it can affect the performance of a mobile device.
- The boot-up time in mobile devices must be managed to be short.
- Since mobile devices may need real-time response, the OSs should have pre-emptive scheduling mechanism.

- Interrupt dispatch latency must be minimized in mobile OSs.
- One solution in reducing the interrupt latency is to use deferrable functions. The deferrable functions are the mechanisms through which we delay the execution of functions that are not time-critical in interrupt handlers.
- Mobile devices use flash memory as a persistent memory that may be recorded and erased.
- Flash file systems are designed to cater the needs of flash memory as traditional file systems cannot be applied for the same.
- Mobile devices can also be infected with worms, Trojan horses, or other viruses.

MULTIPLE CHOICE QUESTIONS

1. _____ has the APIs that allow the OS to make policy decisions and make calls into the BIOS to initiate power-management controls.
   (a) CPM   (c) ACPI
   (b) APM   (d) None

2. An abstract interface between the OS and the hardware to move the power-management controls into OS designed by HP, Intel, Microsoft, Phoenix, and Toshiba is known as ____.
   (a) CPM   (c) ACPI
   (b) APM   (d) none

3. To avoid RAM space, the kernel code, application, and libraries should be directly executed in ROM area instead of copying into the RAM area. This is known as ____.
   (a) direct execution   (c) execute-in-place
   (b) ROM execution   (d) none

4. The _____ saves device data to a device-specific buffer, schedules its bottom half, and exits.
   (a) top-half   (c) Context-half
   (b) bottom-half   (d) none

5. _____ is the part of the ISR that must be executed at a

safer time and can be executed with a delay.
   (a) top-half   (c) context-half
   (b) bottom-half   (d) none

6. The ____ functions are the mechanisms through which we delay the execution of functions that are not time critical.
   (a) non-critical   (c) deferrable
   (b) delay function   (d) none

7. ____ are special functions in Linux kernel that may be scheduled in interrupt context to run at a system-determined safe time.
   (a) tasklets   (c) workqueue
   (b) taskqueue   (d) none

8. ___ based flash memories provide low-density, fast-read, and slow-write operations.
   (a) NAND-   (c) XOR-
   (b) NOR-   (d) AND-

9. ____ based flash memories provides low-cost, high-density, fast-write, and slow-read operations.
   (a) NAND-   (c) XOR-
   (b) NOR-   (d) AND-

REVIEW QUESTIONS

1. What are the characteristics of a mobile device?

2. What is a mobile OS? How is it different from traditional desktop OS?

3. Define the following: APM, ACPI, and OSPM.

4. Explain the power states for system power management.

5. What is thermal management in mobile devices?

6. What is execute-in-place mechanism?

7. In the context of interrupt processing, explain the following: interrupt context, top-half, bottom-half.

8. What is a deferrable function?

9. What is a tasklet?

10. What is 2-CPU solution?

11. Why is a flash file system required?

12. What is double power loss?

13. How does Android perform power management?

14. Explain the types of processes and their priorities in Android.

15. Explain the following: ASHMEM and PMEM

16. What is O(1) scheduling?

17. What is the mechanism used for IPC in Android and how does it work?

BRAIN TEASERS

1. What is the reason that the boot-up time in mobile devices must be managed to be short?

2. Explain some programming tricks that may help in reducing the memory leakage.

3. Study the log-structured file systems in relation to flash file systems.

4. Study some more mobile OSs and investigate how various issues (as discussed for Android) have been resolved in them.

22 Multimedia Operating Systems

22.1 INTRODUCTION

To make a user file attractive, multimedia has opened up many new ways with a long host of features such as graphics, video clips, audio, sound effects, animation, and so on. Multimedia systems demand large bandwidth to transmit files high processing power. The general OS may not be able to cope with these high requirements. Therefore, OSs that support multimedia features must be designed. In this chapter, all issues regarding multimedia OSs have been discussed.

22.2 MULTIMEDIA

Today, multimedia contents in applications today are increasing continuously. Multimedia is the field that integrates text, graphics, images, videos, animation, audio, and any other media and represents, stores, transmits, and processes every type of information digitally. Multimedia applications largely consist of audio, video, and animation, in addition to traditional media. Movies, video clips, songs, webcasts of events, and so on, are all examples of multimedia applications. Thus, multimedia data are stored in the file system like any other data but captured by distinct devices. For example, digital video can be created using cameras or recorded from broadcasts. Compared to regular files, multimedia files have two unique characteristics. First, multimedia files are accessed at a specific rate. For example, to view a video, a series of images are displayed in rapid succession. In general, a video is displayed at 25 or 30 frames per second. The higher the rate at which these are displayed, the finer the video appears to the user. The same is the case with audio files. These are also known as *continuous media data*. The second unique feature of multimedia files is the need of real-time delivery when delivered on the network. In the sense of real-time delivery, multimedia files are of two types: live streaming and on-demand streaming. In live streaming, multimedia contents are delivered as the event occurs, for example, the lecture delivery of a person through video-conferencing. On the other hand, in on-demand streaming, the delivery of contents is from stored systems, for example, on-demand movies from the cable television operator. In on-demand streaming, the event is not actually taking place when it is being delivered. In multimedia, the files are considerably large in size. To resolve the issue and reduce the files to acceptable sizes, the files need to be compressed.

Learning Objectives

After reading this chapter, you should be able to understand:

- Multimedia system
- Multimedia OSs
- Process and disk scheduling in multimedia OS
- Memory management in multimedia OSs
- File management in multimedia OSs

A multimedia system should have the following desirable features:

- It should run on a system having very high processing power.
- The file system should support multimedia files.
- The system should support efficient and high I/O.
- The system should support high capacity storage.
- The system should have network support.

22.3 MULTIMEDIA OSs

Since multimedia applications require soft-real-time response and consist of continuous media data, a general OS cannot fulfil specific rate and timing requirements. Therefore, multimedia OSs are designed to support multimedia applications. The requirements of specific data rate and timing requirements of continuous media in multimedia OSs are known as quality of service (QoS) guarantees. The following are some features that must be supported by these specialized OSs:

- There may be multiple scheduling requirements. Besides the traditional scheduling, there may be requirement of both hard-real-time and soft-real-time scheduling. Thus, the scheduler must guarantee hard and soft deadlines through tasks with certain priorities. Each real-time task has a timing constraint and resource requirements.
- In multimedia applications, frames have a deadline and the system cannot afford to drop any frame or have any delay.
- In multimedia applications, audio and video files that are different as compared to general text files having an internal structure. Moreover, these files are captured as well as played back by different devices.
- A file in a multimedia application may consist of sub-files, for example, a digital movie file may consist of video file, audio files, text files, and so on. Thus, the file system must keep track of multiple sub-files per file and these multiple sub-files must be synchronized with each other. The audio and video files cannot be out of synchronization, or else the viewer will not be able to enjoy the movie.
- There should be low latency and high responsiveness. There must be some acceptable ranges within which the delay or other parameter is confined. For example, end-to-end delay for audio streams should be below 150 ms for most multimedia applications.
- Since multimedia streams tend to be periodic and consistent, schedulability consideration is much easier.
- To cope with the high bandwidth requirement, compression and lower resolution may be used.

22.4 PROCESS SCHEDULING

The multimedia scheduling algorithm must allocate resources used by different tasks so that all deadlines are met. For example, while running a movie, all frames must be displayed at the right times. Since multimedia systems have the requirement of traditional scheduling and soft- as well as hard-real-time scheduling, they adopt multiple scheduling algorithms.

One scheduling algorithm adopted in multimedia systems is the *proportional share scheduling*. In this scheduling, resource requirements are specified by the relative share of the resource. The resource is allocated on the basis of share of the competing requests (fair-share scheduling, as discussed in Chapter 6). Another criterion is to have a combination of more than one scheduling algorithms that support any type of scheduling (real-time and non- real-time) requirement in a hierarchy. For example, round robin or proportional share scheduling is combined with real-time scheduling algorithms such as EDF or RM. In any case, the real-time tasks need to be prioritized.

There may be a situation in multimedia systems when the total load is difficult to predict and execution times of individual applications vary considerably. For this issue, the scheduler must have the feedback controller that may dynamically adjust processor utilization.

22.5 FILE SYSTEM

The access speed of storage devices has not been much improved as compared to the exponentially increased performance of processors and networks. Since multimedia files are too large in size, it is difficult for general file systems to handle multimedia data. Moreover, the real-time playback and retrieval of multimedia data require intense bandwidth on the storage device. Thus, general file systems are not designed to meet the real-time performance requirement of the audio and video data retrieval. To cope with this issue, the following are required:

- The physical bandwidth of the disk must be exploited effectively.
- The disk fragmentation must be avoided by tailoring the file system layout, meta data structure, file organization, file allocation, and so on.
- The time to locate the data blocks on disk must be minimized.

The following file systems are used for multimedia systems:

22.5.1 Partitioned File Systems

This file system consists of multiple sub-file systems. Each sub-file system targets handling of a specific data type. It also has one integration layer that provides transparent access to the data handled by different sub-file systems.

22.5.2 Integrated File Systems

These systems multiplies all available resources in the system among all multimedia data.

22.6 FILE ALLOCATION

Since multimedia files demand very high storage space, general file allocation may not be suitable. The following methods are being used for allocating files in multimedia OSs:

22.6.1 Scattered Allocation

In this method, blocks are allocated at arbitrary locations on the disk. The random placement is beneficial for mixed-media workloads in multimedia systems.

22.6.2 Contiguous Allocation

The data blocks in this method are allocated successively on the disk. It is better when compared to scattered allocation, but this causes external fragmentation. This allocation works well in case a video server is preloaded with movies that will not change afterwards.

22.6.3 Locally Contiguous Allocation

In this method, a file is divided into fragments. All blocks of a fragment are then stored contiguously. However, fragments can be scattered. This method causes less external fragmentation as compared to contiguous allocation.

22.6.4 Constrained Allocation

This method puts the constraint of distance measured in tracks for a finite sequence of block allocation, that is, the allocation is for finite blocks measured in finite number of tracks.

22.6.5 Distributed Allocation

This is applicable to systems where multiple storage devices exist. These multiple storage devices, say disks, can be used to store multimedia data. One simple method is to use one full file on only a single disk. For instance, one full movie is stored on a single disk *A*. Another movie is stored on disk *B*. One disk may also contain more than one full movie. But the drawback of this method is that if one disk fails, one or more full movies are lost. Moreover, the load on the disks is not distributed.

Data striping may be implemented to have a large logical sector by accessing many physical sectors from multiple disks. One method is to stripe each movie on multiple disks. Here the assumption is that all frames are of same size, so that a fixed number of bytes from a movie are written to disk *A* and the same number of bytes are written to disk *B*, and so on. One drawback in this method is that all movies start on the first disk only, thereby increasing the load on this disk. To balance the load among disks, *staggered striping* may be used, wherein the starting disk is staggered every time. Another way to balance the load is to use *random striping*, wherein each file may be randomly allocated.

The assumption of all frames with same size cannot be implemented every time. For example, in MPEG-2 movies, different frames are of varying sizes. So the idea is to stripe by frame. In *frame striping*, the first frame of a movie is stored on disk *A*. The second frame goes to disk *B* and so on. This striping will not help in increasing the accessing speed but will help in spreading the load among disks in a better way. Another method may be *block striping*. In this method, fixed-size units are written on the disks as blocks. Each block may contain one or more frames.

22.7 DISK SCHEDULING

General disk scheduling algorithms target to optimize the seek time. But multimedia OSs, along with the seek time, must target the QoS guarantees also. The following are some disk scheduling processes for multimedia OSs:

22.7.1 EDF Scheduling

Since multimedia data need to be delivered in real-time consideration, sorting the disk requests based on deadlines is a good idea. The EDF discussed in real-time scheduling may be adopted here. This will help in processing disk requests in deadline order and minimize the chance of missing deadlines. In this scheduling, a block request with nearest deadline is served first. However, it has been observed that pure EDF may cause low throughput and high seek times.

22.7.2 SCAN-EDF

EDF can be combined with other scheduling algorithms in order to increase the throughput and lower the seek time. SCAN algorithm, when merged with EDF, gives the desired result. The requests are first ordered as per EDF, and SCAN is applied when multiple requests have same deadline.

22.7.3 Group Sweeping Strategy

In this scheduling, the requests of continuous media are first split into multiple groups or fragments. Within a group, SCAN algorithm is applied. Among the groups, round robin scheduling is used. For example, if each group has one request, the scheduling is just like round robin. This method may be modified by providing a constant time to each fragment. This time is an upper limit for play out duration of each fragment, representing as the length of one round. These algorithms are known as *work-ahead-augmenting* algorithms.

22.8 MEMORY MANAGEMENT

The memory for multimedia data can be managed cost effectively in the following manner:

22.8.1 Batching

When several clients request the same multimedia data, for example, batching can be done in case of a movie. In this case, the video transmission will start only when there is a batch of clients who want to watch the same movie.

22.8.2 Buffering/Bridging

It uses cache for repeated disk requests. The general caching techniques may not be applicable to multimedia data. This is because, in general, we keep the data in cache which is to be frequently used in future. But in case of multimedia data, a block is unlikely to be used a second time. For example, while playing a movie, the same block will not be used if the movie starts and is played sequentially. But in some different manner, we can use caching. The idea is to use the predictable nature of multimedia data. The system may know in advance that if there is more than one user who wants the same data. For example, it may know if there is more than one user who wishes to watch the same movie on demand. But it may not be possible that all start watching the movie at the same time. There may be some time gap in between the instants the users start watching the same movie. Caching can be used if the time gap is known. Let one user start watching the movie at time t and the second user starts at *t+4*. In this case, the blocks played for the first movie till *t+4* can be cached, and then played back for the second user. This is known as *block caching*.

22.8.3 Stream Merging

The memory space can be saved for caching also. As explained for block caching, there may be some time delay in between the instants in which the users start watching the same movie. Instead of caching technique, the video clips of the first user can be displayed at some slower rate so that both users can catch up with each other after some time and the same movie can be shown to both of them without any extra cost of memory. This is known as *stream merging* or *adaptive piggybacking*. Another method to implement stream merging is to have *content insertion* wherein some additional video clips, say advertisements are inserted in between the movie played to the second user, so that both users' viewing can be synchronized.

22.8.4 Prefetching

To support continuous playback of time-dependent multimedia data, the data are fetched in advance from the disk to memory. Prefetching is the mechanism by which data are preloaded from slow and high-latency storage devices such as disk, to faster storage like memory. It results in reduced response time of a data read request and further increases the storage I/O bandwidth. In multimedia systems, it is easy to predict that the data to be retrieved are sequential. In this case, the data are prefetched.

SUMMARY

Multimedia systems are different in nature and demand resources in high capacity. Therefore, multimedia OSs are designed in order to cope with the specialized requirements of multimedia data.

Let us have a quick review of important concepts discussed in this chapter:

- Multimedia applications largely consist of audio, video and animation in addition to traditional media. Movies, video clips, songs, webcasts of events, and so on, are all examples of multimedia applications.
- Multimedia files are accessed at a specific rate.
- The multimedia files are of two types: live streaming and on-demand streaming. In live streaming, the multimedia contents are delivered as the event is occurring. In on-demand streaming, the delivery of contents is from some stored systems.
- The requirements of specific data rate and timing requirements of continuous media in multimedia OSs are known as quality of service guarantees.
- Since multimedia systems have the requirement of traditional scheduling and soft as well as hard real-time scheduling, they adopt multiple scheduling algorithms.
- Since multimedia files are too large in size, it is difficult to handle multimedia data by the general file systems.

MULTIPLE CHOICE QUESTIONS

1. Multimedia files are accessed at a specific rate. Therefore, multimedia data are also known as
   - (a) continuous media data
   - (b) real-time data
   - (c) specific data
   - (d) none

2. Multimedia systems should have _____ processing power.
   - (a) very low
   - (b) very high
   - (c) medium
   - (d) none

3. There should be _____ latency and _____ responsiveness in multimedia OSs.
   - (a) high, low
   - (b) low, high
   - (c) low, low
   - (d) high, high

4. Since multimedia streams tend to be periodic and consistent, schedulability consideration is _____.
   - (a) impossible
   - (b) difficult
   - (c) much easier
   - (d) none

5. Multimedia OSs must have _____ process scheduling algorithm.
   - (a) single
   - (b) two
   - (c) three
   - (d) multiple

REVIEW QUESTIONS

1. Differentiate between:
   - (a) continuous media and real-time data
   - (b) live streaming and on-demand streaming

2. What are the desired features of multimedia OSs?

3. The general file systems are not able to cope with multimedia files. Discuss the guidelines of how multimedia file systems must be designed, considering the nature of multimedia files.

4. Explain the distributed file allocation method.

5. Explain the GSS disk scheduling method.

6. What is stream merging?

PART VIII

Shell Programming

23. Shell Programming and UNIX Shells

23 Shell Programming and UNIX Shells

23.1 INTRODUCTION

This chapter gives an overview of the UNIX shells and how to perform shell-programming exercises. The shell programming is as simple as we do in any high-level language. The only difference is the syntax of the commands used in the shell. Therefore, the prerequisite for this chapter is that the reader should be well aware of any high-level language constructs. This chapter introduces various UNIX shells and the related programming constructs with the help of programming examples.

23.2 ROLE OF SHELL

UNIX or Linux shell is a command line interpreter that handles users' interactions with the computer system. It is a command-programming language that acts as an intermediate between the user and the kernel. Its features include control-flow primitives, parameter passing, variables, and string substitution. A shell allows you to easily create a new program with all the privileges of any other UNIX program.

There are various types of a shell that have come into the market since its inception. These shells share many similarities but each shell also has its own set of recognized commands, syntax, and functions that are important for advanced users.

23.3 TYPES OF SHELLS

There exist various types of shells in UNIX and UNIX-like systems. In this section, some important ones are discussed.

sh: It was developed by Stephen Bourne, of AT&T Bell Laboratories and is also known as *Bourne shell* after his name. The binary program of the Bourne shell is located at/bin/sh on most UNIX systems and provides a user interface to a huge number of UNIX utilities. It is good for I/O control but not well-suited for interactive users. Its default command prompt is denoted as $ sign.

ash: *Almquist shell*, also known as *A shell* or *ash*, is a high-speed, POSIX-compatible UNIX shell designed to replace the Bourne shell in later BSD distributions. Its initial versions did not support command history feature. Its recent versions support UNIX text-editing programs, such as emacs and vi modes.

Learning Objectives

After reading this chapter, you should be able to understand:

- Shell and its types
- File- and directory-related commands in UNIX
- Filters and related commands
- Input/Output redirection and related commands
- Communication-related commands in UNIX
- Shell meta-characters
- Vi editor and its various commands
- Shell scripts
- Shell programming constructs
- Shell script examples

bash: Standing for *Bourne shell*, bash is a UNIX shell written for the GNU Project. It was created in 1987 by Brian Fox. Bash is the default shell on most Linux systems as well as on Mac OS X and can be run on most UNIX-like OSs.

dash: *Debian Almquist shell* (dash) is a POSIX-compliant UNIX shell, much smaller and faster than bash. The advantage of this shell is that it takes less disk space and the drawback is that it has fewer features. This shell was included in Linux by Herbert Xu in early 1997. As compared to bash, this shell depends on fewer libraries. It is believed to be more reliable in case of upgrade problems or disk failures.

fish: The name of this shell is an acronym for *friendly interactive shell*. This shell provides the user with numerous powerful features in a way that are easy to discover, remember, and use.

ksh: Standing for *Korn shell*, this shell is a UNIX variant that was developed by David Korn of AT&T Bell Laboratories in the early 1980s. It is backwards compatible with the Bourne shell and includes many features of the C shell as well, like a command history. Its differentiating feature from other shells is its ability to be used as a programming language.

 # csh: The C shell (csh) is a UNIX shell developed by Bill Joy for the BSD UNIX system. As the name suggests, syntax of this shell is modeled after the C programming language. This shell is upward compatible with Bourne shell, adding many new features to it such as aliases and command history.

 # tcsh: TENEX C (tcsh) shell is a UNIX shell based on and compatible with the C shell (csh). It is essentially the C shell with (programmable) filename completion, command-line editing, and a few other features.

 # es: This shell works like a fully functional programming language as a UNIX shell. It was majorly developed in the early 1990s. Unlike other modern shells, es does not have job control. Patches to provide job control have been offered, but the currently available ones have memory-leak problems.

 # scsh: *Scheme shell* (scsh) is a POSIX application programming interface (API) limited to 32-bit platforms. It is layered on top of the Scheme programming language (a programming language used to write OSs, optimizing compilers, text editors, graphics packages, etc.) in a manner to make the most of the scheme's capability for scripting.

23.4 FILE AND DIRECTORY-RELATED COMMANDS

UNIX is a very powerful OS and its strength lies in its huge set of commands. Table 23.1 shows the list of various file- and directory-related commands.

Table 23.1 File- and directory-related commands

S. No.	Syntax of command	Options (if any)	Description
1.	$ touch file-name		This command creates a file of size zero bytes. We can create several empty files quickly.
2.	$ cat>filename	$ cat>filename	To store something in a file after pressing enter and escape key via ctrl + d.
		$ cat filename	To display content of a file.

(Contd)

(Table 23.1 Contd)

		$ cat filename f2 name> f3 name	To concatenate contents of two files and store them in a third file.
		$ cat fname >>fname	To append to a file without overwriting its contents.
3	$ cp file1 file2		This command copies the content of one file to other.
4	$ rm	$ rm file1	Removes given file.
		$ rm –i file1	Removes file interactively; you are asked before deleting file.
		$ rm-r dir1	Recursively removes all contents of dir1 and dir1 itself.
5	$ mv file1 file2		Renames file file1 to file2.
6	$ ls	$ ls	Gives directory listing or lists contents of current or specified directory.
		$ ls-a	Displays hidden files in addition to its regular contents.
		$ ls b*	Interprets presence or absence of any number or characters.
		$ ls[char]*	This indicates first character of filename to be listed, must be any one of the letters given in square brackets.
		$ ls-l	Used for long listing.
7	$ ln file1 file2		Establishes one more link to a file file1 in the form of file2. Default link to a directory is 2 and to a file is 1.
8	$ umask		Sets permission of all files or directories at the time of creation, unmask value is subtracted from default value, which for file is 606 and directory is 777.
			Internal weightage
			Read-4
			Write-2
			Execute-1

(Contd)

(*Table 23.1 Contd*)

9	$ chmod [per-mission] f1		For setting permissions other than at the time of creation.
10	$ lf		Used to differentiate various types of files. It puts a * after all executable files and '/' after all sub-directories present in current directory.
11	$ pwd		Prints the absolute pathname of present working directory.
12	$ logname user1		Prints login name of user user1.
13	$ uname		To find the name of UNIX system.
14	$ tty		To find out name of the terminal.
15	$ who		Lists all the users on systems with terminal names, data, and login names.
16	$ who am i		Lists the details of the current user.
17	$ pwd		Gives the details of the directory in which the user is currently working.
18	$ mkdir	$ mkdir –p directory/f1	This command is used to create a file f1 by creating all the parent directories specified in the path.
19	$ wc filename		Counts the number of lines, words, and characters in specified files or file.
		$mkdir –m [permissions] newdir	Creates the directory newdir with the specified permissions.
20	$ rmdir	$ rmdir dir1	Removes directory dir1.
		$ rmdir –p dir1/dir2/f1	Removes the file recursively, that is, if on removing file f1, dir2 gets empty it removes dir2, and so on
21	$ cd newdir		It is used for changing over to a new directory.

23.5 FILTERS

When a program takes its input from standard input, performs some operation on that input, and writes the result to the standard output, it is referred to as a *filter*. Table 23.2 shows some of the most commonly used filters.

Table 23.2   Filter-related commands

S. No.	Syntax of command	Options (if any)	Description
1.	$ wc filename	-	Counts the no. of lines, words, and characters in specified files or file.
		-l	Allows user to obtain number of lines.
		-w	Allows user to obtain number of words.
		-c	Allows user to obtain number of characters.
2.	$ sort filename		For sorting the contents of file.
		(i) (ii) (iii) (iv)	where '-' stands for standard input, i.e., keyboard
		-o	Instead of displaying sorted output on screen, we can store it in a file.
		-u	Allows output in unique lines.
		–m	Combines contents of the file with input from keyboard and then does sorting.
		-	where '-' stands for standard input, i.e., keyboard
3.	$ grep 'string' filename		Stands for 'globally search a regular expression and print it'
			Returns number of matches without quoting text
			(iv) Suppresses error message
			Returns lines that do not match the text
		-i	Makes it case sensitive
		-n	Returns line number and text itself
		–c	Returns number of matches without quoting text
		-s	Suppresses error message
		-v	Returns lines that do not match the text
4.	$ cut –f x,y filename	(i) –d	It cuts and picks up given number of characters or fields from the file (i) It cuts and picks up ' allow us to set the delimiter'
5.	$ head filename		Displays first 10 lines in a file
6.	$ tail –x filename		Displays last 10 lines in a file

Table 23.3   Characters used in I/O redirection and piping

Character	Action
>	Redirect standard output from regular monitor to the specified destination
>&	Redirect standard output and standard error
<	Redirect standard input from keyboard to the specified file or pipe
|	Redirect standard output to another command (pipe)
>>	Append standard output in the existing file
>>&	Append standard output and standard error in the existing file

23.6 INPUT/OUPUT REDIRECTION COMMANDS

This section provides a description of I/O-related commands. Numerous UNIX commands take their input from *standard input stream* and write both the output and error to *standard output stream*. By default, standard input is connected to the terminal keyboard and standard output and error to the terminal screen. However, both standard input and standard output can be changed temporarily. This technique is known as *I/O redirection* and *piping*. The form of a command with standard input and output redirection is as follows:

% command -[options] [arguments] input file > output file

Characters that help the user to perform I/O redirection and piping are shown in Table 23.3.

23.7 COMMUNICATION IN UNIX

Anyone on a shared UNIX system may communicate with other users who are logged in at the same time. There are several UNIX utilities that are useful for users computing in a networked and distributed environment. The various commands for communication in UNIX are shown in Table 23.4.

23.8 SHELL META-CHARACTERS

Certain characters in a shell have been assigned special meanings. These characters are called shell meta-characters. These characters are classified on the basis of the tasks they do as shown in Table 23.5.

Table 23.4   Communication-related commands

S. No.	Syntax	Description
1	$ write user	The write command is a basic communication-related command used by the user sitting on his machine to write something on someone else's machine, provided communication is permitted.
2	#/etc/wall	The command can only be used by the superuser. 'wall' enables the superuser to 'write to all'.
3	$ news	Whenever we log in, if any fresh news has come in, it is displayed on our terminal. To see/read the particular news, this command is used.
4	$ mail	To send the mail to user.

Table 23.5 Shell meta-characters

S. No.	Type	Meta-characters
1	Filename substitution	? * [...] [!...]
2	I/O redirection	> < >> << m> m>&n
3	Process execution	; () & && ||
4	Quoting meta-characters	\ " " ' '
5	Positional meta-characters	$1.....$9
6	Special meta-characters	$0 $* $@ $# $! $$ $-

23.9 Vi EDITOR

Standing for visual editor, it is a screen editor that is available on almost all UNIX systems. It, however, differs from traditional editors as it has no menus but instead uses combinations of keystrokes to accomplish command. The commands given in this editor are case sensitive and have two modes of execution, each of which is briefly defined as follows:

Command Mode

- The mode users are in when they start (default mode) and in which all keystrokes are interpreted as commands.
- This mode enables the user to perform administrative tasks such as saving files, executing commands, moving the cursor, cutting (yanking) and pasting lines or words, and finding and replacing.
- Most commands do not appear on the screen as the user types them.

Insert (or Text) Mode

- The mode in which text is created, edited, and/or replaced.
- Everything that is typed in this mode is interpreted as input.

23.9.1 Starting the Vi Editor

Vi editor can be started in many ways as can be seen in Table 23.6.

23.9.2 Navigating within a File

To navigate within a file without affecting the text, the user must be in command mode. Some of the navigation-related commands that can be used to move around one character at a time are shown in Table 23.7.

Table 23.6 Vi editor start commands

Command	Description
vi filename	Creates a new file if it already does not exist, otherwise opens existing file.
vi –R filename	Opens an existing file in read only mode.
View filename	Opens an existing file in read only mode.

Table 23.7   File-navigation commands

Command	Description
K	Moves the cursor up one line
J	Moves the cursor down one line
H	Moves the cursor to the left one character position
L	Moves the cursor to the right one character position
$	Positions cursor at end of line
W	Positions cursor to the next word
B	Positions cursor to previous word
(	Positions cursor to beginning of current sentence
)	Positions cursor to beginning of next sentence
E	Move to the end of Blank delimited word
{	Move a paragraph back
}	Move a paragraph forward
[[	Move a section back
]]	Move a section forward
n|	Move to the column n in the current line
1G	Move to the first line of the file
G	Move to the last line of the file
nG	Move to nth line of the file
:n	Move to nth line of the file
Fc	Move forward to c
Fc	Move back to c
H	Move to top of screen
nH	Moves to nth line from the top of the screen
M	Move to middle of screen
L	Move to bottom of screen
nL	Move to nth line from the bottom of the screen
:x	Colon followed by a number would position the cursor on line number represented by x

23.9.3 Editing Files

To edit a file, the user must be in insert mode. There are various ways to enter insert mode from the command mode as shown in Table 23.8.

Table 23.8   File editing commands

Command	Description
I	Inserts text before current cursor location
I	Inserts text at beginning of current line
A	Inserts text after current cursor location
A	Inserts text at end of current line
O	Creates a new line for text entry below cursor location
O	Creates a new line for text entry above cursor location

Table 23.9 Characters for deletion operations in a file

Command	Description
X	Deletes the character under the cursor location
X	Deletes the character before the cursor location
Dw	Deletes from the current cursor location to the next word
d^	Deletes from current cursor position to the beginning of the line
d$	Deletes from current cursor position to the end of the line
D	Deletes from the cursor position to the end of the current line
Dd	Deletes the line the cursor is on

23.9.4 Deleting Characters

The important commands that are used to delete characters and lines in an opened file are shown in Table 23.9.

Most commands in vi can be prefaced by the number of times we want the action to occur. For example, 2x deletes two characters under the cursor location and 2dd deletes two lines the cursor is on.

23.9.5 Copy and Paste Commands

The copy and paste commands are shown in Table 23.10.

23.9.6 Quitting Vi Editor

Vi editor allows us to quit both with or without saving the work done. To exit, the user must be in command mode (press Esc to enter the command mode). The user can exit the editor in various ways from the command mode (see Table 23.11).

Table 23.10 Copy and paste commands

Command	Description
Yy	Copies the current line
Yw	Copies the current word from the character the lowercase w cursor is on until the end of the word
P	Puts the copied text after the cursor
P	Puts the yanked text before the cursor

Table 23.11 Quit from Vi editor commands

Command	Description
ZZ	Write (if there were changes), then quit
:wq	Write, then quit
:q	Quit (will only work if file has not been changed)
:q!	Quit without saving changes to file

23.10 SHELL SCRIPTS

Shell script is a short program or a sequence of instructions/commands given to UNIX kernel. A typical shell script integrates the power of commands with the versatility of programming language. In addition, no separate compiler is required to execute a shell program. The shell itself interprets the commands in the shell program and executes them. Shell scripting can be used to perform a variety of jobs such as the following:

- Make the work environment tailor-made
- Automate repetitive tasks
- Automate daily tasks

23.10.1 Shell Variables and Keywords

Like any other programming language, shell variables store and manipulate information within a shell program. Any number of variables can be created and destroyed as per the requirement of the program.

A valid shell variable is one that follows one or more of the following rules:

- It is a combination of alphabets, digits, and underscore ('_') with the first character being either an alphabet or an underscore.
- No commas or blanks are allowed within a variable name.
- Variable names are case-sensitive.

Shell variables are of two types:

UNIX-defined/System-defined Variable

These are standard variables to which shells provide the values. These variables are mostly used by the system itself.

However, just like an ordinary variable, these variables can be customized according to the user preferences. Table 23.12 shows some of the most common system variables used in UNIX and UNIX-like systems:

User-defined Variables

These variables are defined by the user and are used broadly by shell programmers. They can also be made to have a constant or fixed value using the keyword 'read only'.

Table 23.12   Variables used in UNIX

Variable	Meaning
IFS	Defines the internal field separator (IFS), which is a space, tab, or a newline
LOGNAME	Stores the login name of the user
PATH	Defines the path the shell must search to execute any command or file
SHELL	Defines the name of the default working shell
TERM	Defines the name of the terminal on which the user is working
HOME	Stores the default working directory of the user
MAIL	Defines the path of the file where the mail of the user is stored

Table 23.13   List of keywords in UNIX

S. No.	Keyword	Its task
1	Echo	To display the output
2	Read	To read input
3	Set	Assign values to positional parameters
4	Unset	
5	Shift	Shifts the value of positional parameters
6	If	Begins the decision control structure block
7	Else	Contains the instruction(s) to be executed when the exit status of control command is one
8	Fi	Ends the decision control structure block
9	While	Begins the loop control structure block
10	Do	Contains the instructions that are executed till the exit status of control command remains true
11	Done	Ends the decision control structure block
12	Break	Passes the control to the first statement after the loop
13	Umask	Contains the value that decides which three permissions should be denied to a file

Shell keywords or 'reserved words' are special variables whose meaning is already explained to the shell; hence, they cannot be used as ordinary variable names. Table 23.13 shows the list of keywords available in Bourne shell.

Example of a shell script

```
# FIRST INTERACTIVE SHELL SCRIPT
# filename : f1
```

echo What is your name \?
read name
echo Hell $name

In this example, *echo* displays the contents on the screen. *read* is used to store the value in the variable (name here).

23.11 PROGRAMMING CONSTRUCTS IN SHELL

Like a regular programming language, shell scripts also make use of control instructions to specify the order in which the various instructions in the program are executed. There are three types of control instructions in a shell. They are as follows:

Decision Control Instructions

These constructs help in selecting between the two given options (selection among multiple options can be done using nesting of these constructs).

Loop Control Instructions

These constructs help in performing a given task for a specified number of times.

Case Control Instructions

These instructions help in selecting from the *n* given options.

The following are the constructs that help in performing one or more of these tasks:

1. **if-then-else**

The syntax of the if-then-else construct is

if (expr) simple-command

or

if (expr) then
commandlist-1
[else
commandlist-2]
endif

The expression expr is evaluated. If it is found true, then the commandlist-1 is executed. else the commandlist-2 is executed. The portion of the construct enclosed in '[' and ']' is optional

Example

```
if [ $counter -lt 10 ]
then
number=0$counter
else
number=$counter
fi
```

2. **while loop**

The syntax of while loop construct is

while (expr)
commandlist
end

The commandlist will be executed until the expr evaluates to false.

Example

```
while sleep 60
do
if who | grep -s $1
then
echo "$1 is logged in now"
fi
done
```

3. **for loop**

```
for x [in list]
do
...
done
```

The loop executes once for each value in list. *List* is a string that is made up of words where each word is separated from the other using the characters specified in the IFS variable. Since IFS is a system variable, it is generally set to space, tab, and newline (the whitespace characters).

The part [in list] is optional. If [in list] is omitted, it is substituted by positional parameters. The value of *x* is accessed by $x.

Example

```
for file in *.cpp
do
echo -n "$file "
wc -l $file | awk '{printf "\t"$1"\n"}'
done
```

4. case statement
```
case value in
pattern1) commands1 ;;
pattern2) commands2 ;;
.
.
.
*) commands for default ;;
esac
```
– Patterns can contain file-generation meta-characters/wildcards
– Multiple patterns can be specified on the same line by separating them with the | symbol.

Example

```
case $m in
[jJ]an* ) m=1 ;;
[fF]eb* ) m=2 ;;
[mM]ar* ) m=3 ;;
[aA]pr* ) m=4 ;;
[mM]ay* ) m=5 ;;
[jJ]un* ) m=6 ;;
[jJ]ul* ) m=7 ;;
[aA]ug* ) m=8 ;;
[sS]ep* ) m=9 ;;
[oO]ct* ) m=10 ;;
[nN]ov* ) m=11 ;;
[dD]ec* ) m=12 ;;
[1-9] | 0[1-9] | 1[0-2] ) ;; # numeric month
*)
esac
```

5. until loop
```
until condition
do
commands
done
```

Example

```
until who | grep -i $1
do
sleep 90
done
if [ $? ]
then
echo "$1 is logged in now"
fi
```

23.12 SHELL SCRIPT EXAMPLES

Example 1

This shell script displays the date, time, username, and current directory.
```
# Display today's date and the list of all the users who are currently logged in
echo "the date today is:"
date
echo
echo "the various users logged in now are: \n"
who
```

Example 2

This script determines whether the number entered through the keyboard is even or odd.
```
echo "enter the number"
read a
result = 'expr $a % 2'
if [ result –eq 0]
echo "it is an even number"
else
echo "it is an odd number"
fi
```

Example 3

This script displays a pattern for n lines.
```
# Print a pattern of asterisks(*) for the number of lines being entered by the user.
Echo "Enter the number of lines for which you want the pattern"
Read n
a=0
while [ "$a" –lt n ] # this is loop1
do
b="$a"
while [ "$b" -ge 0 ] # this is loop2
do echo -n "* "
b=`expr $b - 1`
```

```
done
echo
a=`expr $a + 1`
done
```

Example 4

This script demonstrates the use of *for loop*.
```
# Prints the list of fruits according to the choice made.
fruitlist="Apple Pear Tomato Peach Grape"
for fruit in $fruitlist
do
if [ "$fruit" = "Tomato" ] || [ "$fruit" = "Peach" ]
then
echo "I like ${fruit}es"
else
echo "I like ${fruit}s"
fi
done
```

Example 5

This script counts and reports the number of entries present in each sub-directory mentioned in the path that is supplied at the command-line argument.
```
# To count the number of entries present in each sub-directory.
pathname = $1
oldifs = "$IFS"
IFS =/
flag=no
set $pathname
for dir in S*
do
if [! –d $dir]
then
echo $ dir is not a directory
flag = yes
break
else
num = 'ls | wc –l'
echo $dir has $num entries
fi
done
if [flag = yes]
then
echo Abrupt end of for loop
fi
IFS = $olfifs
```

Example 6

This script counts the number of lines supplied at the standard input.
Prints the no. of lines in a given file where filename is supplied at command line.

```
if [ $# -eq 0]
then
echo "No filename available"
else
exec< $1
flag = 1
fi
numlines = 0
while read line
do
numlines = '$expr $ numlines + 1'
set --$line
done
echo "Number of lines = $numlines"
if [ "$flag" = 1]
then
exec<$terminal
fi
```

Example 7

This script prints prime numbers from 1 to a given value.
#This script finds prime numbers.

```
echo Enter range
read range
echo 2
j = 3
while test $j -le -$range
do
i= 2
x= 'expr $j -1'
while test $i -le $x
do
if [ expr '$j % $i ' -ne 0]
then
i= 'expr $i +1'
else
break
fi
done
if [$i -eq $j]
```

```
then
echo $j
fi
j= 'expr $j +1'
done
```

Example 8

This script determines whether the file has read, write, and execute permissions associated with it.

```
# Prints the permissions associated with a file.
echo "Enter any filename \c"
read filename
if [ -z "$filename"]
then
[ !-z "$filename"]
then
if [ -r "$filename" –a -w "$filename" –a -x "$filename"]
then
echo the user has read write and execute permissions to the desired file
else
echo Permissions denied
fi
else
echo Improper filename
fi
```

SUMMARY

This chapter discussed the basics of UNIX shell programming. Shell programming includes the knowledge of shell, the various commands that can be run on it, and its programming constructs. The reader using these constructs can write shell programs and thus do programming exercises.

Let us have a quick review of the important concepts discussed in this chapter:

- UNIX or Linux shell is a command-line interpreter that handles users' interactions with the computer system.
- UNIX shell is a command programming language that acts as an intermediate between the user and the kernel.
- When a program takes its input from standard input, performs some operation on that input, and writes the result to the standard output, it is referred to as a *filter*.

- Certain characters in shell have been assigned special meanings. These characters are called shell meta-characters.
- The Vi editor is a screen editor used on almost all UNIX systems. It has no menus but instead uses combinations of keystrokes to execute commands.
- Shell script is a short program or a sequence of instructions/commands given to UNIX kernel.
- Like a regular programming language, shell scripts also make use of control instructions to specify the order in which the various instructions in the program are executed.
- There are three types of control instructions in a shell: decision control instructions, loop control instructions, and case control instructions.

REVIEW QUESTIONS

1. Explain various types of shells in UNIX.

2. Give the syntax and meaning of the following command:
   (a) touch
   (b) cat
   (c) cp
   (d) rm
   (e) who
   (f) grep
   (g) cut
   (h) head
   (i) tail

3. What is I/O redirection?

4. Explain various communication-related commands in UNIX.

5. What are shell meta-characters?

6. What is Vi editor? Explain various commands to use it.

7. What is a shell script?

SHELL PROGRAMMING EXERCISES

1. Write a shell script to read marks of 10 students in a particular subject (say chemistry) and calculate the average result of that class in that particular subject.

2. Write a script to print the Fibonacci series upto the number entered by the user.

3. Write a script to list the details of all the C++ (*.cpp) files in the current directory.

4. Write a shell script that displays only those lines that contain the word of in the file supplied as argument to this script.

5. Write a shell script to read temperature value and convert it from degrees to Celsius.

6. Write a menu-driven script that has the following options:
   - Circle
   - Triangle
   - Rectangle

   The program calculates the area of the geometric figures that the user selects. Make use of case statement.

Bibliography

Part I Introduction

Corbato, F.J., Saltzer, J.H., and Clingen, C.T.: "MULTICS—The First Seven Years," Proc. AFIPS Spring Joint Computer Conf., AFIPS, pp. 571–583, 1972.

Corbato, F.J., and Vyssotsky, V.A.: "Introduction and Overview of the MULTICS System," Proc. AFIPS Fall Joint Computer Conf., AFIPS, pp. 185–196, 1965.

Engler, D.R., Kaashoek, M.F., and O'Toole, J. Jr.: "Exokernel: An Operating System Architecture for Application-Level Resource Management," Proc. 15th Symp. on Operating Systems Principles, ACM, pp. 251–266, 1995.

Kaashoek, M.F., Engler, D.R., Ganger, G.R., Briceno, H., Hunt, R., Mazieres, D., Pinckney, T., Grimm, R., Jannotti, J., and Mackenzie, K.: "Application Performance and Flexibility on Exokernel Systems," *Proc. 16th Symp. on Operating Systems Principles*, ACM, pp. 52–65, 1997.

Ng, S.W.: "Advances in Disk Technology: Performance Issues," *Computer*, vol. 31, pp. 75–81, May 1998.

Stallings, W.: *Operating Systems, 4th Ed.*, Upper Saddle River, NJ: Prentice Hall, 2001.

Tanenbaum, A.S., and Van Steen, M.R.: *Distributed Systems*, Upper Saddle River, NJ: Prentice Hall, 2002.

Goyeneche, J., and Souse, E. "Loadable Kernel Modules." IEEE Software, January/February 1999.

McDougall, R., and Mauro, J. Solaris Internals: Solaris 10 and Open Solaris Kernel Architecture. Palo Alto, CA: Sun Microsystems Press, 2007.

Milenkovic, M., *Operating Systems : Concepts and Design,* New York: McGraw Hill, 1992.

Ritchie, D. "UNIX Time-Sharing System. A Retrospective." The Bell System Technical Journal, July-August, 1978.

Ritchie, D. "The Evolution of the UNIX Time-Sharing System." AT & T Bell Labs Technical Journal, October 1984.

Part II Process Management

Anderson, T.E., Bershad, B.N., Lazowska, E.D., and Levy, H.M., "Scheduler Activations: Effective Kernel Support for the User-level Management of Parallelism," ACM Trans. on Computer Systems, vol. 10, pp. 53–79, Feb, 1992.

Andrews, G.R., and Schneider, F.B.: "Concepts and Notations for Concurrent Programming," Computing Surveys, vol. 15, pp. 3–43, March 1983.

Arora, A.S., Blumofe, R.D., and Plaxton, C.G.: "Thread Scheduling for Multiprogrammed Multiprocessors," Proc. Tenth Symp. on Parallel Algorithms and Architectures, ACM, pp. 119–129, 1998.

Blumofe, R.D., and Leiserson, C.E.:"Scheduling Multithreaded Computations by Work Stealing," Proc. 35th Annual Symp. on Foundations of Computer Science, IEEE, pp. 356–368, Nov. 1994.

Bricker, A., Gien, M., Guillemont, M., Lipkis, J., Orr, D., and Rozier, M.: "A New Look at Microkernel-Based UNIX Operating Systems: Lessons in Performance and Compatibility," Proc. EurOpen Spring '91 Conf., EurOpen, pp. 13–32, 1991.

Buchanan, M., and Chien, A.: "Coordinated Thread Scheduling for Workstation Clusters Under Windows NT." The USENIX Windows NT Workshop, USENIX, pp. 47–??, 1997.

Carr, R.W., and Hennessy, J.L.: "WSClock—A Simple and Effective Algorithm for Virtual Memory Management," Proc. Eighth Symp. on Operating Systems Principles, ACM, pp. 87–95, 1981.

Chandra, A., Adler, M., Goyal, P., and Shenoy, P.: s10 "Surplus Fair Scheduling: A Proportional-Share CPU Scheduling Algorithm for Symmetric Multiprocessors," Proc. Fourth Symp. on Operating Systems Design and Implementation, USENIX, pp. 45–58, 2000.

Corbalan, J., Martorell, X., and Labarta, J.: "Performance-Driven Processor Allocation," Proc. Fourth Symp. on Operating Systems Design and Implementation, USENIX, pp. 59–71, 2000.

Courtois, P.J., Hevmans, F., and Parnas, D.L.: "Concurrent Control with Readers and Writers," Commun. of the ACM, vol. 10, pp. 667–668, Oct. 197.

Duda, K.J., and Cheriton, D.R.: "Borrowed-Virtual-Time (BVT) Scheduling: Supporting Latency-Sensitive Threads in a General-Purpose Scheduler," Proc. 17th Symp. on Operating Systems Principles, ACM, pp. 261–276, 1999.

Havender, J.W.: "Avoiding Deadlock in Multitasking Systems." IBM Systems Journal, vol. 7, pp. 74–84, 1968.

Hoare, C.A.R.: "Monitors, An Operating System Structuring Concept," Commun. of the ACM, vol. 17, pp. 549–557, Oct. 1974; Erratum in Commun. of the ACM, vol. 18. p. 95, Feb. 1975.

Isloor, S.S., and Marsland, T.A.: "The Deadlock Problem: An Overview," Computer, vol. 13, pp. 58–78, Sept. 1980.

Newton, G.: "Deadlock Prevention, Detection, and Resolution: An Annotated Bibliography," *Operating Systems Review*, vol. 13, pp. 33–44, April 1979.

Peterson, G.L.: "Myths about the Mutual Exclusion Problem," *Information Processing Letters*, vol. 12, pp. 115–116, June 1981.

Petrou, D., Milford, J., and Gibson, G.: "Implementing Lottery Scheduling," *Proc. USENIX Annual Tech. Conf.*, USENIX, pp. 1–14, 1999.

Philbin, J., Edler, J., Anshus, O.J., Douglas, C.C., and Li, K.: "Thread Scheduling for Cache Locality," *Proc. Seventh Int'l Conf. on Architectural Support for Programming Languages and Operating Systems*, ACM, pp. 60–71, 1996.

Tai, K.C., and Carver, R.H.: "VP: A New Operation for Semaphores," *Operating Systems Review*, vol. 30, pp. 5–11, July 1996.

Walker, W., and Cragon, H.G.: "Interrupt Processing in Concurrent Processors," *Computer*, vol. 28, pp. 36–46, June 1995.

Zobel, D.: "The Deadlock Problem: A Classifying Bibliography," *Operating Systems Review*, vol. 17, pp. 6–16, Oct. 1983.

Abramson, T. "Detecting Potential Deadlocks". Dr. Dobb's Journal, January, 2006

Anderson, T.; Laxowska, E; and Levy H. "The Performance Implications of Thread Management Alternatives for Shared-Memory Multiprocessors." IEEE Transaction on Computers, December 1989.

Anderson, T.; Bershad, B; Laxowska, E; and Levy H. " Thread Management Alternatives for Shared-Memory Multiprocessors." In [TUCK04].

Andres,G., and Schneider, F. "Concepts and Notations for Concurrence Programming," Computer Surveys, March 1983.

Axford, T. Concurrent Programming: Fundamental Techniques for Real-Time and Parallel Software Design. New York: Wiley, 1988.

Barkely, R., and Lee, T. "A Lazy Buddy System Bounded by Two Coalescing Delays per Class." Proceedings of the 12th ACM Symposium on Operating Systems Principles, December 1989.

Birrell, A. An Introduction to Programming with Threads. SRC Research Re-available at http://www.research.compaq.com/SRC.

Buhr, P., and Fortier, M. "Monitor Classification." ACM Computing Surveys, March,1995

Carr, S; Mayo, J.;and Shene, C. "Race Conditions: A Case Study." The journal of Computing in Small Colleges, October,2001.

Corbett, J. "Evaluating Deadlock Detection Methods for Concurrent Software," IEEE Transactions on Software Engineering, March 1996. Datta, A., and Ghosh, S. "Deadlock Detection in Distributed Systems." Proceedings, Phoenix Conference on Computers and Communications, March 1990.

Datta, A.; Javagal, R.; and Ghosh, S. "An Algorithm for Resource Deadlock Detection in Distributed Systems," Computer System Science and Engineering, October 1992.

Denning, P. The Locality Principle" Communications of the ACM July 2005.

Dimitoglou, G. "Deadlocks and Methods for Their Detection, Prevention and Recovery in Modern Operating Systems." Operating Systems Review, July, 1998.

Downey, A. The Little Book of Semaphores. www.greenteapress.com/semaphores.

Gray, J. Inter process Communications in UNIX: The Nooks and Crannies. Upper Saddle River, NJ: Prentice Hall, 1997.

Haldar, S., and Subramanian, D. "Fairness in Processor Scheduling in Time Sharing Systems" Operating Systems Review, January, 1991.

Hartig, H., et al. "The Performance of a u-Kernel-Based System." Proceedings Sixteenth ACM Symposium on Operating Systems Principles, December 1997.

Henry, G. "The Fair Share Scheduler." AT & T Bell Laboratories Technical Journal, October 1984.

Hoare, C. "Monitors: An Operating System Structuring Concept." Communications of the ACM October, 1974.

Howard, J. "Mixed Solutions for the Deadlock Problem." Communications of the ACM July, 1973.

Johnston, B.; Javagal, R.; Datta, A.; and Ghosh, S. "A Distributed Algorithm for Resource Deadlock Detection." Proceedings, Tenth Annual Phoenix Conference on Computers and Communications, March 1991.

Kang, S., and Lee, J. "Analysis and Solution on Non-Preemptive Policies for Scheduling Readers and Writers." Operating Systems Review, July 1998.

Kay, J., and Lauder, P. "A Fair Share Scheduler." Communications of the ACM, January 1988. Kent, S. "On the Trail of Intrusions into Information Systems." IEEE Spectrum, December 2000.

Kleiman, S. "Interrupts as Threads." Operating System Review, April, 1995.

Kleiman, S.; Shah, D.; and Smallders, B. Programming with Threads. Upper Saddle River, NJ: Prentice Hall 1996.

Lamport, L. "A New Solution to Dijkstra's Concurrent Programming Problem." Communications of the ACM, August 1974.

Lamport, L. "The Mutual Exclusion Problem." Journal of the ACM, April 1986.

Lamport, L. "The Mutual Exclusion Problem Has Been Solved." Communications of the ACM January 1991.

Levine, G. "Defining Deadlock with Fungible Resources." Operating Systems Review, July 2003.

Lewis, B, and Berg, D. Threads Primer, Upper Saddle River, NJ: Prentice Hall, 1996.

Liedtke, J. "On u-Kernel Construction." Proceedings of the Fifteenth ACM Symposium on Operating Systems Principles, December 1995. Liedtke, J. "Toward Real Microkernels." Communications of the ACM, September 1996.

Liedtke, J. "Microkernels Must and Can Be Small." Proceedings, Fifth International Workshop on Object Orientation in Operating Systems, October 1996.

Liu, C., and Layland, J. "Scheduling Algorithms for Multiprogramming in a Hard Real-time Environment." Journal of the ACM February 1973.

Part III   Memory Management

Denning, P.J.: "Thrashing: Its Causes and Prevention," Proc. AFIPS National Computer Conf., AFIPS, pp. 915–922, 1968b.

Denning, P.J.: "Virtual Memory," Computing Surveys, vol. 2, pp. 153–189, Sept. 1970.

Jacob, B., and Mudge, T. "Virtual Memory: Issues of Implementation." Computer, June 1998.

Jacob, B., and Mudge, T. "Virtual memory in Contemporary Microprocessors." IEEE Micro, August 1998.

Johnson, T., and Davis, T. "Space Efficient Parallel Buddy memory Management." Proceedings Third International Conference on Computers and Information, May 1992.

Khalidii, Y.; Talluri, M.; Williams, D.; and Nelson, M. "Virtual Memory Support for Multiple Page Sizes." Proceedings, Fourth Workshop on Workstation Operating Systems, October, 1993.

"Microsoft Windows Timeline", www. Technicalminded.com/widows-timeline.htm.

Peterson, J.L., T.A. Normann, "Buddy Systems", Communications of the ACM, 20(6), pp. 421–431.

Aho, A.V., P.J. Denning, J.D. Ullman, "Principles of optimal page replacement", Journal of ACM, 18(1), pp. 80–93, 1971.

Jeff Bonwick. The slab allocator: An object-caching kernel memory allocator. Usenix proceedings, 1994. Electronic document, available on www.usenix.org/publications/library/proceedings/bos94/full_papers/bonwick.ps.

Gorman, M., Understanding the Linux Virtual Memory Manager, Upper Saddle River, NJ: Prentice Hall, 2004.

Part IV   File Management

Rosenblum, M., and Ousterhout, J.K.: "The Design and Implementation of a Log- Structured File System," Proc. 13th Symp. on Oper. Sys. Prin., ACM, pp. 1–15. 1991.

Roselli, D., and Lorch, J.R.: "A Comparison of File System Workloads," Proc. USENIX Annual Tech. Conf., USENIX, pp. 41–54, 2000.

Rubini, A., "The Virtual File System in Linux", Linux Journal, May 1997 p4.

Part V Input-Output Management

Chen, P.M., Lee, E.K., Gibson, G.A., Katz, R.H., and Patterson, D.A.: "RAID: High Performance Reliable Storage," Comp. Surv., vol. 26, pp. 145–185, June 1994.

Chen, S., and Towsley, D.: "A Performance Evaluation of RAID Architectures," IEEE Trans. On Computers, vol. 45, pp. 1116–1130, Oct. 1996.

Geist, R., and Daniel, S.: "A Continuum of Disk Scheduling Algorithms," ACM Trans. on Computer Systems, vol. 5, pp. 77–92, Feb. 1987.

Patterson, D.A., Gibson, G., and Katz, R.: "A Case for Redundant Arrays of Inexpensive Disks (RAID)," *Proc. ACM SIGMOD Int'l Conf. on Management of Data*, ACM, pp. 109–166, 1988.

Reddy, A.L.N., and Wyllie, J.C.: "Disk Scheduling in a Multimedia I/O System," *Proc. ACM Multimedia Conf.*, ACM, pp. 225–233, 1992.

Rompogiannakis, Y., Nerjes, G., Muth, P., Paterakis, M., Triantafillou, P., and Weikum, G.: "Disk Scheduling for Mixed-Media Workloads in a Multimedia Server," *Proc. Sixth Int'l Conf. on Multimedia*, ACM, pp. 297–302, 1998.

Worthington, B.L., Ganger, G.R., and Patt, Y.N.: *'Scheduling Algorithms for Modem Disk Drives*," Proc. 1994 Conf. on Measurement and Modeling of Computer Systems, pp. 241–251, 1994.

Chen, P.; Lee, E; Gibson, G,; Katz, R.; and Patterson, D. "RAID: High-Performance, Reliable Secondary Storage." ACM Computing Surveys, June 1994.

Chen,S., and Towsley, D. "A Performance Evaluation of RAID Architectures." IEEE transactions on Computers, October 1996.

Eischen, C. "RAID 6 Covers More Bases," Network World, April 9, 2007.

Iyer, S., and Druschel, P. "Anticipatory Scheduling: A Disk Scheduling Framework to Overcome Deceptive Idleness in Synchronous I/O." Proceedings, 18th ACM Symposium on Operating Systems Principles, October, 2001.

Pai, V; Druschel, P; and Zwaenepoel, W. "IO-Lite: A Unified I/O Buffering and Caching System." ACM Transactions on Computer Systems, February 2000.

Seltzer, M.; Chen, P; and Ousterhout, J. "Disk Scheduling Revisited." Proceedings, USENIX Winter Technical Conference, January 1990.

Jonathan Corbet, Alessandro Rubini, and Greg Kroah-Hartman. *Linux Device Drivers.*O'Reilly, 3rd edition, 2005.

Sreekrishnan Venkateswaran. *Essential Linux Device Drivers*. Prentice Hall, 2008.

Part VI Security and Protection

Klein, D.V.: "Foiling the Cracker: A Survey of, and Improvements to, Password Security," *Proc.UNIX Security Workshop II*, USENIX, Summer 1990.

Milojicic, D.: "Security and Privacy," *IEEE Concurrency*, vol. 8, pp. 70–79, April-June 2000.

Morris, R., and Thompson, K.: "Password Security: A Case History," *Commun. of the ACM*, vol. 22, pp. 594–597, Nov. 1979.

Pankanti, S., Bolle, R.M., and Jain, A.: "Biometrics: The Future of Identification," *Computer*, vol. 33, pp. 46–49, Feb. 2000.

Aycock, J. Computer Viruses and Malware, New York: Springer, 2006.

Chen, S., and Tang, T. "Slowing Down Internet Worms," Proceedings of the 24th International Conference on Distributed Computing Systems, 2004.

Chess, D. "The Future of Viruses on the Internet." Proceedings, Virus Bulletin International Conference, October, 1997.

Chinchani, R., and Berg, E. "A Fast Static Analysis Approach to Detect Exploit Code Inside Network Flows." Recent Advances in Intrusion Detection, 8th International Symposium,2005.

Kephart, J.; Sorkin, G.; Chess, D.; and White, S. "Fighting Computer Viruses." Scientific American, November 1997.

Levine, J; Grizzard, J; and Owen, H. "Detecting and Categorizing Kernel-Level Rootkits to Aid Future Detection." IEEE Security and Privacy, May-June 2005.

I hee, K., and Chapin, S., "Buffer Overflow and Format String Overflow Vulnerabilities." Software – Practice and Experience, Volume 22, 2003.

McHaugh, J: Christie, A; and Allen, J. "The Role of Intrusion Detection Systems." IEEE Software, September/October 2000.

Morris, R., and Thompson, K. "Password Security: A Case History." Communications of the ACM November 1979.

Sandhu, R. and Samarati, P. "Access Control: Principles and Practice." IEEE Communications, September 1994.

Sandhu, R. et al. "Role-Based Access Control Models." Computer, September 1994. Scarfone, K., and Mell P. Guide to Intrusion Detection and Prevention Systems. NIST Special Publication SP 800–94, February 2007.

Stallings, W., and Brown L. Computer Security: Principles and Practice. Upper Saddle River, NJ: Printice Hall, 2008.

Wagner, D., and Goldberg, I. "Proofs of Security for the UNIX Password Hashing Algorithm." Proceedings, ASIACRYPT'00, 2000.

Zou, C., et al. "The Monitoring and Early Detection of Internet Worms." IEEE/ACM Transactions on Networking, October, 2005.

Parts I – VI

Crowley, C. Operating Systems: A Design-oriented approach, Tata McGraw Hill, 1998.

Dhamdhere, D.M. Operating Systems: A Concept based approach, Tata McGraw Hill, 2002.

Silberschatz A., P.B. Galvin, G. Gagne, Operating system concepts, John Wiley & Sons, Inc., 2002.

Godbole, A.S. Operating Systems, Tata McGraw Hill, 2005.

Bach, M.J. The Design of UNIX Operating System, PHI, 1986.

Deitel H.M., P.J. Deitel, D.R. Choffnes, Operating Systems, Pearson Education, 2008.

Tanenbaum, A.S. Modern Operating Systems, Pearson Education, 2002.

Stallings, W. Operating Systems: Internals and Design Principles, Pearson Education, 2009.

Bovet, D.P. and Marco Cesati. Understanding the Linux Kernel. O'Reilly, 3rd Ed, 2005.

Greg Kroah-Hartman, Linux Kernel in a Nutshell. O'Reilly, 2007.

Remy Card, Eric Dumas, Franc Mevel, The Linux Kernel Book, Wiley, 1998.

Bovet, D., Cesati, M., Understanding the Linux Kernel, Sebastopol, CA: O'Reily, 2006.

Love, R., Linux Kernel Development, Indianpolis, IN: Novell Press, 2005.

Part VII   Advanced Operating Systems

Bal, H.E., R. Van Renesse, A.S. Tanenbaum, "Implementing distributed algorithms using remote procedure calls", Proceedings of the National Computer Conference, AFIPS, 1987, pp. 499–505.

Bershad, B.N., T.E. Anderson, E.D. Lazowska, H.M. Levy, "Lightweight Remote Procedure Call", Proceedings of the 12th ACM Symposium on Operating system Principles, Special issue of Operating system Review, vol. 23, no. 5, Dec. 1989, pp. 1102–113.

Rozier, M., J.M. Legatheaus, "The Chorus Distributed Operating system: Some Design Issues", Proceedings of the NATO Advanced Study Institute on Distributed Operating Systems: Theory and Practice, Springer –Verlag, New York, 1986, pp. 261–289.

Sinha, P.K., M. Maekawa, K. Shimizu, X. Jia, H. Ashihara, N. Utsunomiya, K.S. Park, H. Nakano, "The GALAXY Distributed Operating system", IEEE Computer, vol. 24, no. 8, 1991, pp. 34–41.

Tanenbaum, A.S., R. Van Renesse, H. Van Staveren, G. J. Sharp, S.J. Mullender, J. Janesen, G. van Rossum, " Experience with the Amoeba Distributed Operating System", Communications of the ACM, vol. 33, no. 12, 1990, pp. 46–63.

Chandy, K.M., L. Lamport, "Distributed Snapshots- Determining Global states of Distributed Systems", ACM Transactions on Computer Systems, vol. 3, no. 1, 1985, pp. 272–314.

Lai, T.H., T.H. Yang, "On Distributed Snapshots", Information Processing Letters, vol. 25, 1987, pp. 153–158.

Lamport, L., "Time, Clocks, and the orderings of events in a Distributed system", Communications of the ACM, vol. 21, no. 7, 1978, pp. 558–565.

Bracha, G., S. Toueg, "Distributed Deadlock Detection", Distributed Computing, vol. 2, 1987.

Chow, T.C.K., and Abraham, J.A.: "Load Balancing in Distributed Systems," IEEE Trans. On Software Engineering, vol. SE-8, pp. 401–412, July 1982.

Howard, J.H., Kazar, M.J., Menees, S.G., Nichols, D.A., Satyanarayanan, M., Sidebotham, R.N., and West, M.J.: "Scale and Performance in a Distributed File System," ACM Trans. on Computer Systems, vol. 6. pp. 55–81, Feb. 1988.

Artsy, Y., ed. Special Issue on Process Migration. Newsletter of the IEEE Computer Society Technical Committee on Operation Systems, Winter 1989.

Artsy, Y., "Designing a Process Migration Facility: The Charlotte Experience." Computer September 1989.

Barbosa, V. "Strategies for the Prevention of Communication Deadlock in Distributed Parallel Programs." IEEE Transactions on Software Engineering, November,1990.

Douglas, F., and ousterhout, J. "Transparent Process Migration: Design Alternatives and the Sprite Implementation.' Software Practice and Experience, August 1991.

Eager, D.; Lazowska, E.; and Zahnorjan, J. "Adaptive Load Sharing in Homogeneous Distributed Systems." IEEE Transactions on Software Engineering, May 1986.

Eskicioglu, M. "Design Issues of Process Migration Facilities in Distributed Systems." Newsletter of the IEEE Computer Society Technical Committee on Operating Systems and Application Environments, Summer 1990.

Lamport, L. "Time, Clocks and the Ordering of Events in a Distributed System." Communications of the ACM, July 1978.

Raynal, M., and Helary, J. Synchronization and Control of Distributed Systems and Programs. New York: Wiley, 1990.

Singh, H. Progressing to Distributed Multiprocessing. Upper Saddle River, NJ: Prentice Hall, 1999.

Sinha, P. Distributed Operating Systems. Piscataway, NJ: IEEE Press, 1997.

Smith, J. "A Survey of Process Migration Mechanisms." Operating Systems Review, July 1988.

Tanenbaum, A., and Renesse, R. "Distributed Operating Systems." Computing Surveys, December 1985.

Tray, B., and Ananda, A. "A Survey of Remote Procedure Calls." Operating Systems Review, July 1990.

Mukesh Singhal, N.G. Shivaratri, Advanced Concepts in Operating Systems, Tata McGraw Hill, 2004.

Hwang, K., F. Briggs, Multiprocessor Systems Architecture, McGraw-Hill, New York, 1984.

Lazowska, E., M.Squillante, "Using Processor-Cache Affinity in shared-memory Multiprocessor Scheduling", Tech. Report, Dept. of computer science, University of WA, 1989.

M.Squillante, "Issues in Shared-Multiprocessor Scheduling: A performance evaluation", Ph.D. dissertation, Dept. of Computer Science & Engg., Univ of Washington, WA, 1990.

Li, K.: "Shared Virtual Memory on Loosely Coupled Multiprocessors." Ph.D. Thesis. Yale Univ., 1986.

Chapin, S., and Maccabe, A., eds. "Multiprocessor Operating Systems: Harnessing the Power." Special issue of IEEE Concurrency, April-June 1997.

Rashid, R. et al. "Machine-Independent Virtual Memory Management for Paged Uniprocessor and Multiprocessor Architectures." IEEE Transactions on Computers, August 1988.

Tucker, A., and Gupta, A. "Process Control and Scheduling Issues for multiprogrammed Shared-Memory Multiprocessors." Proceedings, 12th ACM Symposium on Operating System Principles, December 1989.

Mukesh Singhal, N.G. Shivaratri, Advanced Concepts in Operating Systems, Tata McGraw Hill, 2004.

Axford, T. Concurrent Programming: Fundamental Techniques for Real-Time and Parallel Software Design. New York: Wiley, 1988.

Hong, J.; Tan, X.; and Towsley, D. "A Performance Analysis of Minimum Laxity and Earliest Deadline Scheduling in a Real-Time System." IEEE Transactions on Computers, December 1989.

Liu, J. Real Time Systems. Upper Saddle River, NJ: Prentice Hall, 2000.

Morgan, K. "The RTOS Difference." Byte, August 1992.

Ramamritham, K., and Stankovic, J. "Scheduling Algorithms and Operating Systems Support for Real-Time Systems." Proceedings of the IEEE, January 1994.

Sha, L; Rajkumar, R.; and Lehoczky, j, "Priority Inheritance Protocols: An Approach to Real-Time Synchronization." IEEE Transactions on Computers, September 1990.

Sha,L.; Klein, M; and Goodenough, J. "Rate Monotonic Analysis for Real-Time Systems." In [TILB91].

Sha, L.; Rajkumar, R; and Sathaye, S. "Generalized Rate-Monotonic Scheduling Theory: A Framework for Developing Real-Time Systems." Proceedings of the IEEE January 1994.

Stankovic, J., et al. "Strategic Directions in Real-Time and Embedded Systems." ACM Computing Surveys, December 1996.

Takada, H. "Real-time Operating System for Embedded Systems." In Imai, M. and Yoshida, N. (eds). Asia South-Pacific Design Automation Conference, 2001.

TimeSys Corp. "Priority Inversion: Why You Care and What to Do about It? TimeSys White Paper, 2002. http://www.techonline.com/community/ed_resource/tech_paper/21779.

Warren, C. "Rate Monotonic Scheduling." IEEE Micro, June 1991.

VxWorks Application Programmer's guide 6.2, Wind River Systems Inc. 2005.

Paul Kohout, "Hardware Support for Real-time operating systems", Master's Thesis, Master of Science, 2002.

Jim Collier, An Overview Tutorial of the VxWorks **Real-Time Operating System**, 2004.

R. Dick, G. Lakshminarayana, A. Raghunathan, and N. Jha. "Power Analysis of Embedded Operating Systems." In *Proceedings of the 37th Design Automation Conference*, Los Angeles, CA, June 2000.

Y. Li, M. Potkonjak, and W. Wolf. "Real-Time Operating Systems for Embedded Computing." In *Proceedings of the 1997 International Conference on Computer Design (ICCD '97)*, Austin, TX, October 1997.

David E. Simon, *An Embedded Software Primer*, Pearson Education, 2001.

Sriram V. Iyer, Pankaj Gupta, *Embedded Realtime Systems Programming*, Tata McGraw Hill, 2006.

Phillip. A. Laplante, *Real-time Systems: Design and Analysis*, PHI, 2002.

Stuart Bennett, *Real-Time Computer Control*, Pearson Education, 2003.

Jane W.S. Liu, Real-time systems, Pearson Education, 2004.

C.M. Krishna, Kang G. Shin, Real-Time Systems, McGraw Hill International Editions, 1997.

Flash File systems, Intel White paper, 2006.

Kaushik Velusamy, Shriram K.V., "Adapting Linux as Mobile operating system", Journal of Computer Science, 9(6): 740–748, 2013.

P. Dharanya Devi, S. Poonguzhali, T. Sathiya, G.Yamini, P. Sujatha and V. Narasimhulu, "Survey on Multimedia Operating systems", International journal of computer science and emerging technologies (IJCSET), Vol. 1, Issue 2, 2010.

Deepali Kayande, Urmila Shrawankar, "Priority Based Pre-emptive Task Scheduling for Android Operating System", International Journal of Computer Science and Telecommunications,Volume 2, Issue 7, October 2011.

MA Wei-feng, WANG lia-hai, "Analysis of the Linux 2.6 kernel scheduler", International Conference on Computer Design and Appliations (ICCDA), 2010.

XU Long, et. al, "An Improved Algorithm to Optimize the Access Time of Data Broadcast in Mobile Computing Environments", Second International Workshop on Education Technology and Computer Science, 2010.

Sangchul Lee, Jae Wook Jeon, "Evaluating Performance of Android Platform Using Native C for Embedded Systems", International Conference on Control, Automation and Systems, 2010.

Nasr addin Al-maweri, et.al, "Runtime CPU Scheduler Customization Framework for a flexible mobile operating system", Student Conference on Research and Development (SCOReD), 2009.

Li Lo, et.al, "A Modified Interactive Oriented Scheduler for GUI-based Embedded Systems", 8th IEEE International Conference on Computer and Information Technology, 2009.

C.S. Wong, et. al, "Fairness and Interactive Performance of O (1) and CFS Linux Kernel Schedulers", International Symposium on Information Technology, 2008. ITSim, 2008.

Wang Chi, Zhou Huaibei, "A Modified O (1) Scheduling Algorithm for Real-Time Tasks", International Conference on Wireless Communications, Networking and Mobile Computing, 2006. WiCOM, 2009.

Yan ZHAO, et. al, "Research on the Priority-based Soft Real-time Task Scheduling in TinyOS", International Conference on Information Technology and Computer Science, 2009.

"Android.com", Available: http://www.android.com

"Android SDK| Android Developers", http://developer.android.com/sdk/index.html.

Advanced Configuration and Power Interface Specification, Hewlett-Packard Corporation, Intel Corporation, Microsoft Corporation, Phoenix Technologies Ltd., Toshiba Corporation, Revision 4.0a, April 5, 2010.

Greg Kroah-Hartman. "Android and the Linux kernel community" http://www.kroah.com/log/linux/android-kernel-problems.html.

"Linux developer explains Android kernel code removal". http://news.zdnet.com/2100–9595_22–389733.html.

"What is Android". Android Developers. http://developer.android.com/guide/basics/what-isandroid.html.

Open Handset Alliance. "Industry Leaders Announce Open Platform for Mobile Devices" http://www.openhandsetalliance.com/press_110507.html.

Bort, Dave. "Android is now available as open source". Android Open Source Project. http://source.android.com/posts/opensource.

Honan, Matthew. «Apple unveils iPhone». Macworld. http://www.macworld.com/article/54769/2007/01/iphone.html.

Android architecture. http://www.slideshare.net/deepakshare/android-arch-presentation.

An overview of iPhone OS architecture. http://thecoffeedesk.com/news/index.php/2009/05/17/iphone-architecture/.

Bornstein. Dalvik vm internals, 2008 google i/o session, 01 2008. http://sites.google.com/site/io/dalvik-vm-internals.

Brady, Anatomy & physiology of an android, 2008 google i/o, 2008. URL http://sites.google.com/site/io/anatomy--physiology-of-an-android.

Winandy Davi, Sadeghi. Privilege escalation attacks on android, 2010. http://www.ei.rub.de/media/trust/veroeffentlichungen/2010/11/13/DDSW2010_Privilege_Escalation_Attacks_on_Android.pdf.

Enck, Understanding android security. *IEEE S*, JanuaryFebruary:50pp, 2009.

Freyo, Android get signature by uid, 2010. URL http://www.xinotes.org/notes/note/1204/.

Google. Android documentation - fundamentals, 2011. http://developer.android.com/guide/topics/fundamentals.html.

Google. Android security, 2011. URL http://developer.android.com/guide/topics/security/security.html.

David A Rusling. *The Linux Kernel*. 1999.

Chin Felt Greenwood Wagner. Analyzing inter-application communication in android, 06 2001. www.cs.berkeley.edu/~afelt/intentsecurity-mobisys.pdf.

Android memory usage, 2011. URL http://elinux.org/Android_Memory_Usage.

Goyal, P., Guo, X., and Vin, H.M.: "A Hierarchical CPU Scheduler for Multimedia Operating Systems," Proc. Second Symp. on Operating Systems Design and Implementation, USENIX, pp. 107–121, 1996.

Mercer, C.W.: "Operating System Support for Multimedia Applications," *Proc. Second Int'l Conf.on Multimedia*, ACM, pp. 492–493, 1994.

Nieh, J., and Lam, M.S.: "The Design, Implementation and Evaluation of SMART a Scheduler for Multimedia Applications," *Proc. 16th Symp. on Operating Systems Principles*, ACM, pp. 184–197, 1997.

Reddy, A.L.N., and Wyllie, J.C: "I/O Issues in a Multimedia System," *Computer*, vol. 27, pp. 69–74, March 1994.

Part VIII   Shell Programming

Kernighan, B.W., and Pike, R.: *The UNIX Programming Environment*, Upper Saddle River, NJ: Prentice Hall, 1984.

Newham, C., and Rosenblatt, B.: *Learning the Bash Shell*, Sebastopol, CA: O'Reilly & Associates, 1998.

Robbing A.: *UNIX in a Nutshell: A Desktop Quick Reference for SVR4 and Solaris 7*, Sebastopol, CA: O'Reilly & Associates, 1999.

B.A. Forouzan, R.F. Gilbery, *UNIX and Shell Programming*, Cengage Learning, 2012.

Yashavant Kanetkar, UNIX Shell programming, BPB Publications, 1996.

B.M. Harwani, UNIX and Shell Programming, Oxford University Press, India, 2013.

Index

Related Titles

WEB TECHNOLOGIES [9780198066224]

Uttam K. Roy, *Department of Information Technology, Jadavpur University, Kolkata*

This textbook is specially designed for undergraduate and postgraduate students of computer science, information technology, and computer applications (BE/BTech/BCA/MCA). It provides a comprehensive coverage of the complete range of topics taught in this course. The text is supported by numerous illustrations, examples, program codes, and screenshots.

Key Features

- Demonstrates where and how to use web technologies effectively
- Provides relevant software installation and configuration information wherever necessary
- Covers advanced concepts such as MVC and struts and emerging topics such as XQuery

SOFTWARE ENGINEERING [9780195694840]

Deepak Jain, *HCL Technologies Ltd, Noida*

The book provides a focused and to-the-point approach to the presentation of the concepts of software engineering, which both the students and teachers will find instructive and easy to understand. Provision of pertinent case studies facilitates understanding of the practical nature of software engineering.

Key Features

- Lays emphasis on automated processes for development and testing of software
- Discusses various software development process models of latest industrial practices including a section on Capability Maturity Model (CMM)
- Provides exhaustive coverage of software project cost estimation models like Cost Constructive Model (COCOMO) and Delphi model
- Incorporates several case studies to bring out the practical implications of software engineering
- Contains sample question papers and interview questions for cracking university examinations and job interviews

THEORY OF COMPUTATION [9780198084587]

Vivek Kulkarni, *Principal Architect, Persistent Systems Ltd, Pune*

This book is designed to serve as a textbook for undergraduate students of computer science and engineering, computer applications, and information technology. It seeks to provide a comprehensive coverage of all the essential concepts of the subject.

Key Features

- Provides comprehensive coverage of fundamental concepts of the theory of computation and formal languages
- Includes algorithms and program codes in C for implementation and description of the key concepts
- Describes different computational models such as Turing model, Post machine model, and Markov model in detail
- Contains appendices on implementation of concepts learnt in C and five model test papers

PROGRAMMING IN C# [9780198097402]

Harsh Bhasin, *Visiting Faculty, Delhi Technological University, Delhi*

This is a textbook designed for undergraduate and postgraduate students of computer science, information technology, and computer applications. It helps the students to understand the fundamentals and applications of C# programming using .NET Framework. The book will also serve as a useful reference for researchers and practising programmers who intend to pursue a career in C# programming.

Key Features

- Entails dedicated chapters on basic and advanced window forms and controls, common dialogs, data connectivity, networking, deployment, and introduction to WPF and WCF
- Includes projects on IP addresses, greedy algorithm, student management system, notepad, and genetic algorithms
- Provides numerous screenshots to help students assimilate the concepts learned.

Other Related Titles

- 9780198070887 Pal: Systems Programming
- 9780198066774 Trivedi: Computer Networks
- 9780195696561 Datta: Software Engineering
- 9780198071068 Nagpal: Formal Languages and Automata Theory